1 MONTH OF
FREE
READING

at

www.ForgottenBooks.com

By purchasing this book you are eligible for one month membership to ForgottenBooks.com, giving you unlimited access to our entire collection of over 1,000,000 titles via our web site and mobile apps.

To claim your free month visit:

www.forgottenbooks.com/free165587

ISBN 978-1-5285-8957-4
PIBN 10165587

This book is a reproduction of an important historical work. Forgotten Books uses
state-of-the-art technology to digitally reconstruct the work, preserving the original format
whilst repairing imperfections present in the aged copy. In rare cases, an imperfection in
the original, such as a blemish or missing page, may be replicated in our edition. We do,
however, repair the vast majority of imperfections successfully; any imperfections that
remain are intentionally left to preserve the state of such historical works.

REPORTS OF CASES

DETERMINED IN THE

APPELLATE COURTS

OF ILLINOIS

WITH A DIRECTORY OF THE JUDICIARY OF THE STATE
CORRECTED TO MARCH 31, 1914, AND ABSTRACTS OF
CASES AS DESIGNATED BY THE COURTS
UNDER ACT APPROVED JUNE 27, 1913,
IN EFFECT JULY 1, 1913.

VOL. CLXXXIV
A. D. 1914.

LAST FILING DATE OF REPORTED CASES:

FIRST DISTRICT, JANUARY 26, 1914.
THIRD DISTRICT, OCTOBER 16, 1913.

EDITED BY
THE PUBLISHERS' EDITORIAL STAFF

.

CHICAGO
CALLAGHAN & COMPANY
1914

DIRECTORY OF THE JUDICIARY DEPARTMENT OF THE STATE OF ILLINOIS.

CORRECTED TO MARCH 31, 1914.

The judiciary department of the State of Illinois is composed of (1) the Supreme Court; (2) Appellate Courts; (8) Circuit Courts; (4) Courts of Cook County; (5) City Courts; (6) Municipal Court of Chicago; (7) County and Probate Courts.

(1) THE SUPREME COURT.

The Supreme Court consists of seven justices, elected for a term of nine years, one from each of the seven districts into which the State is divided.

Formerly the State was divided into three grand divisions, Southern, Central and Northern, in which the terms were held, with one clerk for each of the three grand divisions elected for a term of six years, the court sitting at Mount Vernon, Springfield and Ottawa.

In 1897 these divisions were consolidated into one, comprising the entire State, and provision made that all terms of the court be held in the city of Springfield, on the first Tuesday in October, December, February, April and June of each year.

REPORTER.
SAMUEL P. IRWIN..........................Bloomington.

JUSTICES.
First District—ALONZO K. VICKERS..............East St. Louis.
Second District—WILLIAM M. FARMER..........Vandalia.
Third District—FRANK K. DUNN................Charleston.
Fourth District—GEORGE A. COOKE..............Aledo.
Fifth District—CHARLES C. CRAIG................Galesburg.
Sixth District—JAMES H. CARTWRIGHT..........Oregon.
Seventh District—ORRIN N. CARTER.............Chicago.

The Chief Justice is chosen by the court, annually, at the June term. The rule of the court is to select as successor to the presiding justice the justice next in order of seniority who has not served as Chief Justice within six years last past. Mr. Justice Cooke is the present Chief Justice.

CLERK.
J. McCAN DAVIS, Springfield.

LIBRARIAN.
RALPH H. WILKIN, Springfield.

(2) APPELLATE COURTS.

These Courts are held by the Judges of the Circuit Courts assigned by the Supreme Court for a term of three years. One clerk is elected in each district.

REPORTERS.

Reported by the publishers' editorial staff.

FIRST DISTRICT.

Composed of the county of Cook.

Court sits at Chicago on the first Tuesdays of March and October.

CLERK—Alfred R. Porter, Ashland Block, Chicago.

WM. H. McSURELY, Justice, Ashland Block, Chicago.

FRANK BAKER, Justice, Ashland Block, Chicago.

EDWARD O. BROWN, Justice, Ashland Block, Chicago.

BRANCH B.*

THOMAS C. CLARK, Presiding Justice, Ashland Block, Chicago.

ALBERT C. BARNES, Justice, Ashland Block, Chicago.

FREDERICK A. SMITH, Justice, Ashland Block, Chicago.

BRANCH C.**

WARREN W. DUNCAN, Presiding Justice, Marion.

JAMES S. BAUME, Justice, Galena.

EMERY C. GRAVES, Justice, Geneseo.

BRANCH D.**

MARTIN M. GRIDLEY, Presiding Justice, Ashland Block, Chicago.

JOSEPH H. FITCH, Justice, Ashland Block, Chicago.

KICKHAM SCANLAN, Justice, Ashland Block, Chicago.

SECOND DISTRICT.

Composed of the counties of Boone, Bureau, Carroll, DeKalb, Du-Page, Grundy, Henderson, Henry, Iroquois, Jo Daviess, Kane, Kankakee, Kendall, Knox, Lake, La Salle, Lee, Livingston. Marshall, McHenry, Mercer, Ogle, Peoria, Putnam, Rock Island, Stark, Stephenson, Warren, Whiteside, Will, Winnebago and Woodford.

Court sits at Ottawa, La Salle county, on the first Tuesdays in April and October.

CLERK—Christopher C. Duffy, Ottawa.

DORRANCE DIBELL, Presiding Justice, Joliet.

DUANE J. CARNES, Justice, Sycamore.

CHARLES WHITNEY, Justice, Waukegan.

THIRD DISTRICT.

Composed of the counties of Adams, Brown, Calhoun, Cass, Champaign, Christian, Clark, Coles, Cumberland, DeWitt, Douglas, Edgar, Ford, Fulton, Greene, Hancock, Jersey, Logan, Macon, Macoupin, Mason, McDonough, McLean, Menard, Montgomery, Morgan, Moultrie, Piatt, Pike, Sangamon, Schuyler, Scott, Shelby, Tazewell and Vermilion.

Court sits at Springfield, Sangamon county, on the first Tuesdays in April and October.

CLERK—W. C. Hippard, Springfield.

GEORGE W. THOMPSON, Presiding Justice, Galesburg.

EDGAR ELDREDGE, Justice, Ottawa.

† WILLIAM B. SCHOLFIELD, Justice, Marshall.

---

* This court is a branch of the Appellate Court of the first district, and is held by three judges of the Circuit Court, designated and assigned by the Supreme Court under the provisions of the act of the General Assembly, approved June 2, 1897. Hurd's Statutes, 1897, 503, Laws of 1897, 186, J. & A. ¶ 2981.

** Established under act of June 6, 1911, J. & A. ¶ 2989.

† Succeeded Justice Solon Philbrick, of Champaign, who died April 13, 1914.

FOURTH DISTRICT.

Composed of the counties of Alexander, Bond, Clay, Clinton, Crawford, Edwards, Effingham, Fayette, Franklin, Gallatin, Hamilton, Hardin, Jackson, Jasper, Jefferson, Johnson, Lawrence, Madison, Marion, Massac, Monroe, Perry, Pope, Pulaski, Randolph, Richland, Saline, St. Clair, Union, Wabash, Washington, Wayne, White and Williamson.

Court sits at Mount Vernon, Jefferson county, on the fourth Tuesdays in March and October.

CLERK—Albert C. Millspaugh, Mount Vernon.

JAMES C. McBRIDE, Presiding Justice, Taylorville.
HARRY HIGBEE, Justice, Pittsfield.
THOMAS M. HARRIS, Justice, Lincoln.

———

(3) CIRCUIT COURTS.

Exclusive of Cook county, the State of Illinois is divided into seventeen judicial circuits, as follows:*

FIRST CIRCUIT.

The counties of Alexander, Pulaski, Massac, Pope, Johnson, Union, Jackson, Williamson and Saline.

Judges: A. W. LEWIS, Harrisburg.
WARREN W. DUNCAN, Marion.
WILLIAM N. BUTLER, Cairo.

SECOND CIRCUIT.

The counties of Hardin, Gallatin, White, Hamilton, Franklin, Wabash, Edwards, Wayne, Jefferson, Richland, Lawrence and Crawford.

Judges: ENOCH E. NEWLIN, Robinson.
WILLIAM H. GREEN, Mt. Vernon.
JACOB R. CREIGHTON, Fairfield.

THIRD CIRCUIT.

The counties of Randolph, Monroe, St. Clair, Madison, Bond, Washington and Perry.

Judges: LOUIS BERNREUTER, Nashville.
GEORGE A. CROW, East St. Louis.
WILLIAM E. HADLEY, Collinsville.

FOURTH CIRCUIT.

The counties of Clinton, Marion, Clay, Fayette, Effingham, Jasper, Montgomery, Shelby and Christian.

Judges: ALBERT M. ROSE, Louisville.
JAMES C. McBRIDE, Taylorville.
THOMAS M. JETT, Hillsboro.

FIFTH CIRCUIT.

The counties of Vermilion, Edgar, Clark, Cumberland and Coles.

Judges: WILLIAM B. SCHOLFIELD, Marshall.
E. R. E. KIMBROUGH, Danville.
MORTON W. THOMPSON, Danville.

* Laws, 1897, 188, J. & A. ¶ 3070.

SIXTH CIRCUIT.

The counties of Champaign, Douglas, Moultrie, Macon, DeWitt and Piatt.

Judges: WILLIAM G. COCHRAN, Sullivan.
        * SOLON PHILBRICK, Champaign.
        WILLIAM C. JOHNS, Decatur.

SEVENTH CIRCUIT.

The counties of Sangamon, Macoupin, Morgan, Scott, Greene and Jersey.

Judges: JAMES A. CREIGHTON, Springfield.
        ROBERT B. SHIRLEY, Carlinville.

EIGHTH CIRCUIT.

The counties of Adams, Schuyler, Mason, Cass, Brown, Pike, Calhoun and Menard.

Judges: HARRY HIGBEE, Pittsfield.
        ALBERT AKERS, Quincy.
        GUY R. WILLIAMS, Havana.

NINTH CIRCUIT.

The counties of Knox, Warren, Henderson, Hancock, McDonough and Fulton.

Judges: GEORGE W. THOMPSON, Galesburg.
        HARRY M. WAGGONER, Macomb.
        ROBERT J. GRIER, Monmouth.

TENTH CIRCUIT.

The counties of Peoria, Marshall, Putnam, Stark and Tazewell.

Judges: JOHN M. NIEHAUS, Peoria.
        THEODORE N. GREEN, Pekin.
        NICHOLAS E. WORTHINGTON, Peoria.

ELEVENTH CIRCUIT.

The counties of McLean, Livingston, Logan, Ford and Woodford.

Judges: COLOSTIN D. MYERS, Bloomington.
        GEORGE W. PATTON, Pontiac.
        THOMAS M. HARRIS, Lincoln.

TWELFTH CIRCUIT.

The counties of Will, Kankakee and Iroquois.

Judges: DORRANCE DIBELL, Joliet.
        CHARLES B. CAMPBELL, Kankakee.
        FRANK L. HOOPER, Watseka.

THIRTEENTH CIRCUIT.

The counties of Bureau, La Salle and Grundy.

Judges: SAMUEL C. STOUGH, Morris.
        JOE A. DAVIS, Princeton.
        EDGAR ELDREDGE, Ottawa.

* Died April 13, 1914.

FOURTEENTH CIRCUIT.

The counties of Rock Island, Mercer, Whiteside and Henry.
Judges: ROBERT W. OLMSTED, Rock Island.
FRANK D. RAMSAY, Morrison.
EMERY C. GRAVES, Geneseo.

FIFTEENTH CIRCUIT.

The counties of Jo Daviess, Stephenson, Carroll, Ogle and Lee.
Judges: RICHARD S. FARRAND, Dixon.
JAMES S. BAUME, Galena.
OSCAR E. HEARD, Freeport.

SIXTEENTH CIRCUIT.

The counties of Kane, Du Page, De Kalb and Kendall.
Judges: CLINTON F. IRWIN, Elgin.
DUANE J. CARNES, Sycamore.
MAZZINI SLUSSER, Downers Grove.

SEVENTEENTH CIRCUIT.

The counties of Winnebago, Boone, McHenry and Lake.
Judges: ARTHUR H. FROST, Rockford.
CHARLES H. DONNELLY, Woodstock.
CHARLES WHITNEY, Waukegan.

(4) COURTS OF COOK COUNTY.

The State Constitution recognizes Cook county as one judicial circuit, and establishes the Circuit, Criminal and Superior Courts of said county. The Criminal Court has the jurisdiction of a Circuit Court in criminal and quasi-criminal cases only, and the judges of the Circuit and Superior Courts are judges, ex officio, of the Criminal Court.

CRIMINAL COURT.

CLERK—Frank J. Walsh, Criminal Court Building, Chicago.

CIRCUIT COURT.

CLERK—JOHN W. RAINEY, County Building, Chicago.

JUDGES.

EDWARD O. BROWN,
RICHARD S. TUTHILL,
JESSE A. BALDWIN,
FRANK BAKER,
KICKHAM SCANLAN,
THOMAS G. WINDES,
MERRITT W. PINCKNEY,

JOHN GIBBONS,
ADELOR J. PETIT,
LOCKWOOD HONORE,
GEORGE KERSTEN,
JOHN P. McGOORTY,
FREDERICK A. SMITH,
CHARLES M. WALKER.

SUPERIOR COURT.

CLERK—RICHARD J. McGRATH, County Building, Chicago.

JUDGES.

WILLIAM H. McSURELY,	MARCUS A. KAVANAGH,
JOHN M. O'CONNOR,	JOSEPH H. FITCH,
THEODORE BRENTANO,	HENRY V. FREEMAN,
RICHARD E. BURKE,	ALBERT C. BARNES,
THOMAS C. CLARK,	HUGO PAM,
WILLIAM FENIMORE COOPER,	M. L. McKINLEY,
WILLIAM E. DEVER,	CLARENCE N. GOODWIN,
MARTIN M. GRIDLEY,	CHARLES M. FOELL,
CHARLES A. McDONALD,	DENIS E. SULLIVAN.

(5) CITY COURTS.

City Courts existing prior to the Constitution of 1870 were continued until abolished by the qualified voters of the city. These courts may now be established under Sec. 21 of Chap. 37, R. S., J. & A. ¶ 3309, and when so established have jurisdiction as defined by Sec. 1 of an act entitled "An Act in relation to courts of record in cities," approved May 10, 1901, J. & A. ¶ 3289.

THE CITY COURT OF ALTON.
JAMES E. DUNNEGAN, Judge.   ALLAN G. MACDONALD, Clerk.

THE CITY COURT OF AURORA.
EDWARD M. MANGAN, Judge.   J. W. GREENAWAY, Clerk.

THE CITY COURT OF BEARDSTOWN.
J. J. COOKE, Judge.   JOHN LISTMANN, Clerk.

THE CITY COURT OF CANTON.
H. C. MORAN, Judge.   ERNEST HIPSLEY, Clerk.

THE CITY COURT OF CENTRALIA.
ALBERT D. RODENBERG, Judge.   GUY C. LIVESAY, Clerk.

THE CITY COURT OF CHARLESTON.
CHARLES A. SHUEY, Judge.   ARTHUR C. SHRIVER, Clerk.

THE CITY COURT OF CHICAGO HEIGHTS.
CHARLES H. BOWLES, Judge.   EDWARD H. KIRGIS, Clerk.

THE CITY COURT OF DE KALB.
JOHN A. DOWDALL, Judge.   JOHN C. KILLIAN, Clerk.

THE CITY COURT OF DU QUOIN.
BENJAMIN W. POPE, Judge.   HARRY BARRETT, Clerk.

THE CITY COURT OF EAST ST. LOUIS.
ROBERT H. FLANNIGAN,
W. M. VANDEVENTER,   Judges.   WILLIAM J. VEACH, Clerk.

THE CITY COURT OF ELGIN.
EDWARD M. MANGAN, Judge.   CHARLES S. MOTE, Clerk.

THE CITY COURT OF GRANITE CITY.
M. R. SULLIVAN, Judge.   JACK MELLON, Clerk.

THE CITY COURT OF HARRISBURG.

WM. H. PARISH, JR., Judge.   HOMER WADE, Clerk.

THE CITY COURT OF HERRIN.

ROBERT T. COOK, Judge.   DAVID BAKER, Clerk.

THE CITY COURT OF KEWANEE.

H. STERLING POMEROY, Judge.   CHARLES L. ROWLEY, Clerk.

THE CITY COURT OF LITCHFIELD.

DAN W. MADDOX, Judge.   LAURETTA SALZMAN, Clerk.

THE CITY COURT OF MACOMB.

DEAN FRANKLIN, Judge.   WM. H. WILSON, Clerk.

THE CITY COURT OF MARION.

WM. W. CLEMENS, Judge.   HARRY HOLLAND, Clerk.

THE CITY COURT OF MATTOON.

JOHN McNUTT, Judge.   THOMAS M. LYTLE, Clerk.

THE CITY COURT OF PANA.

J. H. FORNOFF, Judge.   G. W. MARSLAND, Clerk.

THE CITY COURT OF STERLING.

CARL E. SHELDON, Judge.   EARL L. HESS, Clerk.

THE CITY COURT OF SPRING VALLEY.

WILLIAM HAWTHORNE, Judge.   WILLIAM H. BURNELL, Clerk.

THE CITY COURT OF ZION CITY.

V. V. BARNES, Judge.   O. L. SPRECHER, Clerk.

(6) MUNICIPAL COURT OF CHICAGO.

Established by Act of May 18, 1905 (L. 1905, p. 158), J. & A.
¶¶ 3313 et seq.

FRANK P. DANISCH, Clerk.

CHIEF JUSTICE,
HARRY OLSON.

ASSOCIATE JUDGES.

HARRY M. FISHER	HUGH J. KEARNS	JOHN J. ROONEY
EDWARD T. WADE	JOSEPH S. LaBUY	HENRY C. BEITLER
JOHN K. PRINDIVILLE	JOHN R. NEWCOMER	JOSEPH E. RYAN
JOSEPH P. RAFFERTY	JOHN R. CAVERLY	FREDERICK L. FAKE, JR.
JOHN COURTNEY	CHAS. A. WILLIAMS	CHARLES N. GOODNOW
JOHN J. SULLIVAN	JACOB H. HOPKINS	OSCAR M. TORRISON
JOHN A. MAHONEY	HARRY P. DOLAN	HOSEA W. WELLS
WILLIAM N. GEMMILL	JOSEPH SABATH	SHERIDAN E. FRY
FRANK H. GRAHAM	JAMES C. MARTIN	HUGH R. STEWART
DAVID SULLIVAN	THOMAS F. SCULLY	JOSEPH Z. UHLIR

(7) COUNTY AND PROBATE COURTS.

In the counties of Cook, Kane, LaSalle, Madison, Peoria, Rock Island, Sangamon, St. Clair, Vermilion and Will, each having a population of over 70,000, probate courts are established, distinct from the county courts. In the other counties the county courts have jurisdiction in all matters of probate. (Laws 1881, 72.), J. & A. ¶ 3259.

JUDGES.	COUNTIES.	COUNTY SEATS.
LYMAN McCARL	Adams	Quincy.
WILLIAM S. DEWEY	Alexander	Cairo.
WM. H. DAWDY	Bond	Greenville.
WM. C. DE WOLF	Boone	Belvidere.
WILLARD Y. BAKER	Brown	Mt. Sterling.
JAMES R. PRICHARD	Bureau	Princeton.
CHARLES E. COOKE	Calhoun	Hardin.
JOHN D. TURNBAUGH	Carroll	Mt. Carroll.
CHARLES Æ. MARTIN	Cass	Virginia.
WILLIAM G. SPURGIN	Champaign	Urbana.
CHARLES A. PRATER	Christian	Taylorville.
HERSHEL R. SNAVELY	Clark	Marshall.
ALSIE N. TOLLIVER	Clay	Louisville.
JAMES ALLEN	Clinton	Carlyle.
JOHN P. HARRAH	Coles	Charleston.
JOHN E. OWENS	Cook	Chicago.
DANIEL H. GREGG, Pro. J.	Cook	Chicago.
JOHN C. MAXWELL	Crawford	Robinson.
STEPHEN B. RARIDEN	Cumberland	Toledo.
WILLIAM L. POND	DeKalb	Sycamore.
FRED C. HILL	DeWitt	Clinton.
W. J. DOLSON	Douglas	Tuscola.
CHARLES D. CLARK	DuPage	Wheaton.
DANIEL V. DAYTON	Edgar	Paris.
PETER C. WALTERS	Edwards	Albion.
BARNEY OVERBECK	Effingham	Effingham.
JOHN H. WEBB	Fayette	Vandalia.
M. L. McQUISTON	Ford	Paxton.
THOMAS J. LAYMAN	Franklin	Benton.
HOBART S. BOYD	Fulton	Lewistown.
HARMON P. BOZARTH	Gallatin	Shawneetown.
THOMAS HENSHAW	Greene	Carrollton.
GEORGE BEDFORD	Grundy	Morris.
ISAAC H. WEBB	Hamilton	McLeansboro.
J. ARTHUR BAIRD	Hancock	Carthage.
ELIHU N. HALL	Hardin	Elizabethtown.
RUFUS F. ROBINSON	Henderson	Oquawka.
LEONARD E. TELLEEN	Henry	Cambridge.
JOHN H. GILLAN	Iroquois	Watseka.
WILLARD F. ELLIS	Jackson	Murphysboro.
H. M. KASSERMAN	Jasper	Newton.
ANDREW D. WEBB	Jefferson	Mt. Vernon.
HARRY W. POGUE	Jersey	Jerseyville.
JOHN C. BOEVERS	Jo Daviess	Galena.
J. F. HIGHT	Johnson	Vienna.
FRANK G. PLAIN	Kane	Geneva.
JOHN H. WILLIAMS, Pro. J.	Kane	Geneva.
ARTHUR W. DESELM	Kankakee	Kankakee.
CLARENCE S. WILLIAMS	Kendall	Galesburg.
R. C. RICE	Knox	Yorkville.
PERRY L. PERSONS	Lake	Waukegan.
WILLIAM H. HINEBAUGH	La Salle	Ottawa.

JUDGES.	COUNTIES.	COUNTY SEATS.
ALBERT T. LARDIN, Pro. J.	La Salle	Ottawa.
JASPER A. BENSON	Lawrence	Lawrenceville.
ROBERT H. SCOTT	Lee	Dixon.
PHILLIP A. GIBBONS	Livingston	Pontiac.
CHARLES J. GEHLBACH	Logan	Lincoln.
ORPHEUS W. SMITH	Macon	Decatur.
TRUMAN A. SNELL	Macoupin	Carlinville.
JOHN E. HILLSKOTTER	Madison	Edwardsville.
JOSEPH P. STREUBER, Pro. J.	Madison	Edwardsville.
CHAS. E. JENNINGS	Marion	Salem.
DANIEL H. GREGG	Marshall	Lacon.
JAMES A. McCOMAS	Mason	Havana.
WILLIAM F. SMITH	Massac	Metropolis.
CONRAD G. GUMBART	McDonough	Macomb.
DAVID T. SMILEY	McHenry	Woodstock.
HOMER W. HALL	McLean	Bloomington.
G. E. NELSON	Menard	Petersburg.
HENRY E. BURGESS	Mercer	Aledo.
FRANK DURFEE	Monroe	Waterloo.
JOHN L. DRYER	Montgomery	Hillsboro.
EDWARD P. BROCKHOUSE	Morgan	Jacksonville.
ISAAC HUDSON	Moultrie	Sullivan.
FRAN E. REED	Ogle	Oregon.
CLYDE E. STONE	Peoria	Peoria.
WALTER A. CLINCH, Pro. J.	Peoria	Peoria.
MARION C. COOK	Perry	Pinckneyville.
ELIM J. HAWBAKER	Platt	Monticello.
PAUL F. GROTE	Pike	Pittsfield.
WILLIAM A. WHITESIDE	Pope	Golconda.
WM. A. WALL	Pulaski	Mound City.
WILLIAM H. WESTCOTT	Putnam	Hennepin.
WM. M. SCHUWERK	Randolph	Chester.
STEPHEN C. LEWIS	Richland	Olney.
ROBT. W. OLMSTED	Rock Island	Rock Island.
BENJ. S. BELL, Pro. J.	Rock Island	Rock Island.
KENNETH C. RONALDS	Saline	Harrisburg.
JOHN B. WEAVER	Sangamon	Springfield.
C. H. JENKINS, Pro. J.	Sangamon	Springfield.
JOHN C. WORK	Schuyler	Rushville.
F. C. FUNK	Scott	Winchester.
J. K. P. GRIDER	Shelby	Shelbyville.
FRANK THOMAS	Stark	Toulon.
JOHN B. HAY	St. Clair	Belleville.
FRANK PERRIN, Pro. J.	St. Clair	Belleville.
ANTHONY J. CLARITY	Stephenson	Freeport.
JAMES M. RAHN	Tazewell	Pekin.
MONROE C. CRAWFORD	Union	Jonesboro.
LAWRENCE T. ALLEN	Vermilion	Danville.
CLINTON ABERNATHY, Pro. J.	Vermilion	Danville.
MILBURN J. WHITE	Wabash	Mt. Carmel.
L. E. MURPHY	Warren	Monmouth.
W. P. GREEN	Washington	Nashville.
VIRGIL W. MILLS	Wayne	Fairfield.
JULIUS C. KERN	White	Carmi.
WM. A. BLODGETT	Whiteside	Morrison.
GEORGE J. COWING	Will	Joliet.
JOHN B. FITHIAN, Pro. J.	Will	Joliet.
W. F. SLATER	Williamson	Marion.
LOUIS M. RECKHOW	Winnebago	Rockford.
ARTHUR C. FORT	Woodford	Eureka.

CASES IN THIS VOLUME IN WHICH CERTIORARI HAS BEEN DENIED.

The following table shows the Appellate Court cases reported in this volume in which certiorari has been applied for and denied, thus making the opinion of the Supreme Court final. (See Practice Act, sec. 121, J. & A. ¶ 8658.)

(xiii)

TABLE OF CASES REPORTED.

A.

B.

(xiv)

C.

D.

E.

F.

G.

H.

I.

J.

K.

N.

O.

P.

R.

S.

T.

U.

V.

W.

CASES

DETERMINED IN THE

FIRST DISTRICT

OF THE

APPELLATE COURTS OF ILLINOIS

DURING THE YEAR 1913.

Arabella Louisa Dunbar, Appellee, v. Royal League, Appellant.

Gen. No. 17,893.

1. CORPORATIONS, § 326*—*how powers are determined.* The powers of a corporation organized under a general statute must be determined from its charter alone.

2. INSURANCE, § 815*—*when affianced wife is not a dependent.* Where the charter of a fraternal benefit society declares the objects of the corporation to be to benefit the widows, orphans and dependents of deceased members thereof and to establish a fund to pay benefits to the family or dependents of a member, an affianced wife is not a dependent.

3. INSURANCE, § 810*—*what beneficiaries included within term "devisee."* The term "devisee" in the Incorporation Act of 1872, J. & A. ¶ 2449, is capable of including anybody so long as he or she is designated in the benefit certificate of a fraternal beneficial society if the charter is broad enough to include such person, and where sufficiently broad an affianced wife of a member is eligible as a beneficiary.

4. INSURANCE, § 747*—*when amendment to charter gives no right to designate affiancee beneficiary.* Where the charter of a fraternal benefit society declares it to be the object of the corporation to benefit the widows, orphans and dependents of deceased members,

---

*See Illinois Notes Digest, Vols. XI to XV, same topic and section number.

(1)

and is subsequently amended so as to include husbands as eligible beneficiaries, there is no such alteration of its charter as to give it the right to authorize members to designate an affianced wife as a beneficiary.

5. INSURANCE, § 758*—*when insured not bound by own construction of charter.* Where the charter of a fraternal benefit society declares its purpose to be to benefit widows, orphans and dependents of deceased members, a construction and interpretation of the charter by the society as giving the right to authorize members to designate an affianced wife as a beneficiary is the basis of an *ultra vires* act and is not binding on the society.

6. INSURANCE, § 758*—*when not estopped to deny eligibility of beneficiary.* A fraternal benefit society construing and interpreting its charter, which declares its purpose to be to benefit widows, orphans and dependents of deceased members, as giving the right to authorize members to designate an affianced wife as a beneficiary, is not estopped to deny the eligibility of an affianced wife as a beneficiary.

7. INSURANCE, § 815*—*when charter limits power to designate beneficiary.* Where a fraternal benefit society is incorporated under the Incorporation Act of 1872, J. & A. ¶¶ 2418 *et seq.*, and its charter limits the beneficiaries of deceased members to their widows, orphans and dependents, which is narrower than the limits of the statute, the powers must be determined from the charter; it has no power to enact a by-law providing for benefits to an affianced wife and an affianced wife is not eligible as a beneficiary.

Appeal from the Circuit Court of Cook county; the Hon. WILLIAM B. SCHOLFIELD, Judge, presiding. Heard in the Branch Appellate Court at the October term, 1911. Reversed and remanded. Opinion filed December 2, 1913.

MANN & MILLER and ARTHUR J. DONOVAN, for appellant.

JAMES R. WARD, for appellee.

MR. PRESIDING JUSTICE F. A. SMITH delivered the opinion of the court.

The main question presented by the record is whether or not an affianced wife is an eligible beneficiary under appellant's charter. This question is presented by the pleadings and orders of court thereon.

The declaration alleged that appellant was an incorporated fraternal beneficiary society under the laws of Illinois, and that on April 25, 1896, it issued a benefit certificate to Alfred Gustav Henriques, one of its members, wherein it promised to pay out of its widows' and orphans' benefit fund, upon the death of the said member, four thousand dollars to appellee by name and style of Arabella Louisa Dunbar, affianced wife of said Alfred Gustav Henriques, in accordance with and under the provisions of the laws governing said fund; that at the date of the said certificate appellee was and remained to the time of the death of the member his affianced wife; that the member died February 3, 1904, in good standing in the order and that appellee made and delivered satisfactory proofs of death to appellant whereby said four thousand dollars became due and payable to appellee, but appellant failed and refused to pay it. The common counts were also pleaded and a copy of the benefit certificate was attached.

A general issue and a first additional plea and replications thereto were filed, and afterwards withdrawn so that they are not now before the court. Appellant filed a second additional plea, which is the only plea now in question, and, therefore, all references to appellant's plea hereafter made will refer to said second additional plea. This plea alleges, so far as here material, that appellant is a corporation not for pecuniary profit, organized and existing under an act of the State of Illinois entitled, "An Act Concerning Corporations," approved April 18, 1872, and in force July 1, 1872, (J. & A. ¶¶ 2418 *et seq.*), as a fraternal beneficiary society, and that it received in the year 1883, in accordance with the law, a charter or articles of association under which it has operated and conducted its business as such fraternal insurance society and continues to operate and conduct its business; that in said charter, in setting forth the business for which appellant is formed, it is recited as follows:

"2nd. The object for which it is formed is   *   *   * to benefit the widows, orphans and dependents of deceased members thereof.   *   *   *

. To establish a widows' and orphans' benefit fund out of which shall be paid, on the death of a member, while in good standing in the order, to his family or those dependent upon him, as he may have directed, a sum not exceeding four thousand dollars, as may be provided in the constitution and laws of the order."

That in 1901, the first paragraph above quoted was amended so as to read, "The object for which it is formed is   *   *   * to benefit the widows, orphans, husbands and dependents of deceased members thereof."

The plea further alleges that Henriques was admitted to membership on April 18, 1896, and the benefit certificate referred to in the declaration was issued to him on April 25, 1896, on certain conditions therein set forth, and in which it was provided that these conditions being expressly consented to and complied with appellant thereby promised and bound itself to pay out of its widows' and orphans' benefit fund to appellee, Arabella Louisa Dunbar, named and described therein as the affianced wife of Henriques, a sum not exceeding four thousand dollars; that at the time of the issuing and delivering to said Henriques of said certificate, appellee was not nor was she at the time of the death of said Henriques a member of his family nor did she come within the designation of widow or orphan nor was she dependent upon said Henriques within the meaning of the law and that she was not and is not eligible to take said fund or any part thereof.

To this plea appellee filed three replications. The first admits the charter provision to establish a fund to be paid to a member's family or those dependent upon him and sets up the adoption of a constitution and law by appellant alleged to be declaratory of the objects of the order, wherein it was provided that a benefit certificate may be made payable to an affianced wife, among others, in which class of beneficiary no proof of dependency shall be required, that said charter, constitution and law were in full force and effect before and at the time said certificate was issued and so remained up to the member's death; that said certificate was issued in pursuance of and in accordance with said charter, constitution and law, and by reason thereof the designation of appellee as the affianced wife of the member was a designation of a person dependent upon him within the terms and requirements of said constitution and law and objects stated in the articles of association of appellant, therefore she is eligible.

The second replication alleges that after the designation of appellee by the member as beneficiary and affianced wife, the member paid all dues and assessments required to be paid and continued in good standing in the order until his death, and that the members of the order, after the issuing of said certificate, paid into the widows' and orphans' benefit fund of said order dues and assessments therefor down to and prior to the commencement of this suit an amount exceeding four thousand dollars, which sum was payable to appellee and was then and there held in trust for the use and benefit of appellee in accordance with the constitution and law of appellant aforesaid.

The third replication alleges *precludi non* because before and at the time of the issuing of said certificate, appellee was and continued to be up to the member's death the affianced wife of and dependent upon said member, and concludes to the country.

General and special demurrers were filed to each of these replications which were overruled, and, upon appellant's election to stand by its demurrers, the judgment was entered from which this appeal was prayed.

The main question above stated is thus presented by the plea, replications and the demurrers thereto. We think it is a settled principle of law of this State that where a corporation is organized under a general stat-

ute, the powers of such corporation must be deter-
mined from its charter alone. *Rockhold v. Canton
Masonic Mut. Ben. Soc.*, 129 Ill. 440; *Norwegian Old
People's Home Soc. v. Wilson*, 176 Ill. 94; *Grimme v.
Grimme*, 198 Ill. 265; *Murphy v. Nowak*, 223 Ill. 301.

In the *Rockhold* case, *supra*, the Supreme Court said
at page 455: " 'The particular business and objects'
of the corporation, as declared in the certificate of the
promoters filed in the office of the Secretary of State,
are 'to give financial aid and benefit to the widows,
orphans and heirs or devisees of deceased members,'
and the certificate of incorporation is a license only for
'the particular business and objects' enumerated in
the certificate of the promoters."

So far as here material, the charter of appellant
declared the objects of the corporation to be to benefit
the widows, orphans and dependents of deceased members thereof, and to establish a widows' and orphans'
benefit fund out of which should be paid, on the death
of a member, to his family or those dependent upon
him, as he may have directed, a sum not exceeding
four thousand dollars. By the amendment in 1901,
husbands were added to the list.

There is no question in this case that appellee does
not come within the classification of widow, orphan
or member of the family of the member, and it is contended by appellant that it is equally clear that she
does not come within the classification of dependents.
We think this contention is sound. A dependent, as
the term is used in connection with fraternal societies,
has a well-defined meaning in the law of this State.
In *Alexander v. Parker*, 144 Ill. 355, the Court said:

"Where the statute and charter of an association
provide for the payment of benefit funds to persons
dependent upon the members, the word, 'dependent,'
means 'some person or persons dependent for support
in some way upon the deceased.' (*Ballou v. Gile*, 50
Wis. 614; Bacon on Ben. Soc. and Life Ins., Sec.
261.) Dependence for favor, or for affection, or for

companionship, or as servants, or retainers, is excluded. A dependent, as the term is used in reference to these benevolent associations, is one who is sustained by another, or relied for support upon the aid of another."

To the same effect are *Royal League v. Shields*, 251 Ill. 250, and *Murphy v. Nowak, supra*. In *Alexander v. Parker, supra*, the society was incorporated under the statutes of Massachusetts, which provided that for the purposes of assisting the widows, orphans or other persons dependent upon deceased members such societies may provide for payments by the member of fixed sums to be held until his death and then paid to the persons entitled thereto. The charter declared the objects of the corporation to be "for the purpose of * * * aid to its members and their dependents * * * assisting the widows and orphans of deceased members, establishing a fund for the relief of sick and distressed members, and one for a widows' and orphans' benefit fund," etc. The member designated his affianced wife and, upon his death, a bill of interpleader was filed by the society, making the affianced wife and the member's children parties defendant. The trial court found that the affianced wife was entitled to the fund, and the Appellate Court affirmed the decree. The Supreme Court, however, reversed the judgment.

It seems to us, therefore, that appellee does not come within any of the classes of beneficiaries authorized by the charter of appellant, and if the charter expressed the limit of appellant's corporate power, it had no authority to pay a benefit to the beneficiary named in the certificate in question out of its benefit fund, under the authorities above cited. To these may be added *Palmer v. Welch*, 132 Ill. 141; *Steele v. Fraternal Tribunes*, 215 Ill. 190; *Sowersby v. Royal League*, 159 Ill. App. 626.

The amendment in 1901 of appellant's charter set forth in the plea was intended to and did affect only the first paragraph of the objects of the association stated in its original charter. It did not modify or affect the remaining four paragraphs. The purpose of the amendment was to enlarge the classes eligible to membership in the order and did not in any wise affect the charter or constitution of appellant relating to beneficiaries and the payment of benefits from the widows' and orphans' benefit fund. Therefore the objects of appellant association stated in its original charter relating to beneficiaries which might be designated by a member, and the payment of benefits to the beneficiaries continued in force and effect after the amendment of 1901, the same as before that amendment. This, however, affords no basis for the argument advanced by appellee that appellant so interpreted its charter and constitution as to give it the right to authorize members to designate an affianced wife as a beneficiary. Furthermore, appellant is not bound by its construction and interpretation of its charter where that construction is the basis of an *ultra vires* act.

In *Norwegian Old People's Home Soc. v. Wilson, supra,* the society was organized under the same statute as was appellant. The member had a certificate payable to his daughter. In 1896 he surrendered it and procured another certificate payable to his brother and the Old People's Home. On his death, his daughter filed a bill to recover all of the fund. The brother and the Home filed a cross-bill claiming the fund. In holding that the fund belonged to the daughter and brother and that the Home was ineligible, the Supreme Court declared that "the whole question as to who may be made beneficiaries must be settled, in the first place, by reference to the certificate of incorporation" of the association; and that the Home was incompetent to take under the terms of the certificate of incorporation, for it could not in any way be held to be a member of the deceased's immediate family. The Court further said: "It is no answer to say that the statute of the State under which the association was organized was broad enough to permit such society to take. The incorporators of the association chose to restrict the objects of its benevolence to the immediate family of the member, and the courts must construe the contract as they find it," citing the *Rockhold* case, *supra*.

The Court proceeds to say further on in its opinion:

"The Policemen's Benevolent Association is an Illinois corporation, which has voluntarily chosen to restrict its benevolences to the immediate families of its members, and we must apply the restrictions found in the statement of the object of the association as specified in the certificate of incorporation, and not the statute itself in its broadest scope. It is obvious that there is nothing illegal or against public policy in the action of the association in narrowing the scope of its beneficial action."

To the same effect is *Murphy v. Nowak, supra*.

In so far as the eligibility of an affianced wife is concerned, the statute of 1893, relating to fraternal beneficiary societies (Hurd's Revised Statutes of 1912 J. & A. ¶¶ 6646 *et seq.*, added nothing to nor detracted anything from that which was already provided in the statute of 1872 (J. & A. ¶ 2449). An affianced wife was eligible under the latter statute as a devisee. *Stake v. Stake*, 228 Ill. 630. And there is no reason why a member may not have the policy made payable to the proposed beneficiary directly, in lieu of doing the same thing by a will. *Bloomington Mut. Ben. Ass'n v. Blue* 120 Ill. 121. The term "devisee" in the statute of 1872 (J. & A. ¶ 2449) is capable of including anybody so long as he or she is designated in the certificate, if the charter is broad enough to include such person. The only effect of the Act of 1893, in regard to beneficiaries, was to restrict the scope of fraternal societies in regard to the persons who might be beneficiaries, and to exclude all others. Those classes of beneficiaries enumerated in the statute were unaffected and retained the same rights as before.

The authorities above cited dispose of appellee's contention that appellant is bound by its construction of its charter in issuing certificates payable as its constitution provides. This contention is not sound when such construction would establish a contract which appellant had no power to make. They also dispose of appellee's contention that appellant is estopped to deny the eligibility or dependency of appellee under its charter.

The broad contention between the parties may be stated as follows: Appellee contends that the statute in its fullest scope and not the charter fixes the limits of appellant's corporate power, and that, therefore, since an affianced wife is within the classes permitted by the statute, she is eligible, while appellant contends that the charter fixes the limits of such corporate power even though it is narrower than the statute, and since an affianced wife as such does not come within the classes permitted by the charter, appellee is ineligible. Under the authorities above cited and many others, the contention of appellee is not the law in our opinion. If, as we think, the charter fixes the limit of the corporate power of appellant, it follows that appellant had no power to enact the by-law set up in the first replication to the second additional plea, providing for payment of benefits to an affianced wife, and thus broaden its charter powers. It was powerless to provide by the by-law or otherwise for a beneficiary belonging to a class which did not come within its charter.

These considerations and the authorities cited apply to the subject-matter of all the replications and compel us to hold that the replications are bad in substance, and do not answer the plea. It is therefore unnecessary for us to discuss the formal and specific defects of the replications.

The trial court erred in overruling the demurrers to the replications and in entering judgment. The judgment is reversed and the cause is remanded.

Reversed and remanded.

William Brand, Administrator, Defendant in Error, v. W. Irving Osborne et al., Plaintiffs in Error.

Gen. No. 18,625.　(Not to be reported in full.)

Error to the Circuit Court of Cook county; the Hon. SAMUEL C. STOUGH, Judge, presiding. Heard in the Branch Appellate Court at the October term, 1912. Reversed. Opinion filed December 2, 1913. Rehearing denied December 16, 1913.

Statement of the Case.

Action by William Brand, as administrator of the estate of Charles Brand, deceased, against W. Irving Osborne, D. B. Hanna and George G. Moore as receivers of the Chicago & Milwaukee Electric Railroad Company, a corporation, to recover damages for alleged wrongful death of plaintiff's decedent. From a judgment for plaintiff for two thousand dollars defendants bring error.

BULL & JOHNSON, for plaintiffs in error.

GEORGE W. WOODBURY and RICHARD J. FINN, for defendant in error.

MR. PRESIDING JUSTICE F. A. SMITH delivered the opinion of the court.

Abstract of the Decision.

1. RAILROADS, § 667*—*duty on approaching grade crossing.* A traveler approaching a railroad crossing at grade over a highway has the duty to approach cautiously and to endeavor to ascertain if there is present danger in crossing.

2. RAILROADS, § 667*—*when negligent not to look or listen at crossing.* While failure to look and listen will not as a matter of law under all circumstances bar a recovery, yet as a question of fact, if there is no evidence that a traveler looked or listened, and if there is no excuse for failing to do so and no obstructions to prevent seeing an approaching train before entering upon a dangerous crossing, it will be *held* as a question of fact that the traveler did not exercise ordinary care, when, if he had looked or listened, he could not have failed to have seen or heard the train.

*See Illinois Notes Digest, Vols. XI to XV, same topic and section number.

3. RAILROADS, § 667*—*when evidence shows failure to look or listen.* A person familiar with the situation and use of electric tracks in a city was killed by a car at a crossing at night. The view of the track for from three hundred to four hundred feet was unobstructed by anything except a few trees from which the leaves had fallen, and when within fifty or sixty feet of the track a clear view could be had for over a thousand feet. The car was brightly lighted and had a powerful electric searchlight burning that could have been seen for a mile. *Held*, the deceased did not look or listen and was contributorily negligent.

CLARK, J., dissenting.

4. RAILROADS, § 651*—*effect of contributory negligence.* A person crossing a railroad crossing not exercising due care and caution is negligent, and if such negligence contributes to his death by being struck by a train there can be no recovery.

Robert White et al., Appellants, v. Annie Rezek and Harry A. Rezek, Appellees.

Gen. No. 18,643.   (Not to be reported in full.)

Appeal from the Municipal Court of Chicago; the Hon. WILLIAM N. GEMMILL, Judge, presiding. Heard in the Branch Appellate Court at the October term, 1912. Affirmed. Opinion filed December 2, 1913.

Statement of the Case.

Action by Robert White, Roy B. Tabor and J. P. Strickland, copartners trading as White & Tabor, against Annie Rezek and Harry A. Rezek to recover commissions for negotiating a sale of real estate. From a judgment for defendants, plaintiffs appeal.

GANN, PEAKS & TOWNLEY, for appellants.

LEWIS F. JACOBSON, for appellees.

MR. PRESIDING JUSTICE F. A. SMITH delivered the opinion of the court.

Abstract of the Decision.

1. BROKERS, § 50*—*terms of sale must be accepted before offer is withdrawn.* Where a broker representing the seller of land conducts negotiations with both the purchaser and the seller and there is no unconditional acceptance of all the terms of the sale before the offer of sale is withdrawn, the broker is not entitled to commissions.

2. BROKERS, § 40*—*when willingness of purchaser to accept terms offered is not shown.* Parties to a contract of sale were bargaining upon the understanding that a written and binding contract would have to be drawn up and signed by the parties, stating the terms of the contract in full, before the broker could claim commissions. There was a dispute as to who should pay a special assessment and the broker offered to pay the amount and deduct it from his commissions, but neither party acceded to the proposition. The broker prepared a contract that both parties refused to sign. *Held,* there was no meeting of the minds between the parties and the broker was not entitled to commissions.

CLARK, J., dissenting.

Robert Halpin, Appellee, v. The National Safe Deposit Company, Appellant.

Gen. No. 18,815.   (Not to be reported in full.)

Appeal from the Superior Court of Cook county; the Hon. CLARENCE N. GOODWIN, Judge, presiding. Heard in the Branch Appellate Court at the October term, 1912. Affirmed. Opinion filed December 2, 1913. *Certiorari* denied by Supreme Court (making opinion final.)

Statement of the Case.

Action by Robert Halpin against the National Safe Deposit Company to recover damages for personal injuries sustained by plaintiff while in the employ of defendant and in attempting to oil the bearing of a shaft of an overhead coal conveyor in the basement of defendant's buildings. From a judgment in favor of plaintiff for ten thousand dollars defendant appeals.

*See Illinois Notes Digest, Vols. XI to XV, same topic and section number.

FRANK M. COX and R. J. FELLINGHAM, for appellant; EDWARD E. BROWN, of counsel.

ASHCRAFT & ASHCRAFT, for appellee; E. M. ASHCRAFT, of counsel.

MR. PRESIDING JUSTICE F. A. SMITH delivered the opinion of the court.

Abstract of the Decision.

1. MASTER AND SERVANT, § 685*—*when evidence sustains verdict for injuries resulting from revolving shaft containing an unprotected set screw.* In an action for personal injuries resulting from the clothes of plaintiff being caught by a set screw in a revolving shaft while plaintiff was attempting to oil the bearings, a verdict for plaintiff *held* sustained by the evidence.

2. MASTER AND SERVANT, § 193*—*duty to warn inexperienced servant of dangerous machinery.* Where an inexperienced person employed to oil machinery is put to work by his superior, failure to warn him of a set screw projecting from a safety collar which was covered by dust and could not be seen when the machinery was in motion, *held* to render the master liable for injuries resulting therefrom.

3. MASTER AND SERVANT, § 663*—*what may be considered in determining questions of assumed risk and contributory negligence.* In an action by a servant for injuries sustained by him while engaged in his duties in oiling machinery, the situation of the machinery, its unprotected condition, the light maintained about the machinery, its operation, surrounded with coal dust to such an extent that it was difficult to see the machinery in operation, the safety collar, the projecting set screw, together with the age of plaintiff, his lack of knowledge and want of experience, *held* to be facts of controlling importance in weighing the questions of assumed risk and contributory negligence.

4. MASTER AND SERVANT, § 706*—*when assumed risk and contributory negligence are questions of law.* Questions of assumed risk and contributory negligence are ordinarily questions of fact. They only become questions of law where, from the facts admitted or conclusively proved, there is no reasonable chance that reasonable minds would reach a different conclusion.

5. MASTER AND SERVANT, § 833*—*when admission of models of appliances harmless.* Admission in evidence of the model of the safety collar and projecting cap screw which caused the injury to the plaintiff, *held* not reversible error.

*See Illinois Notes Digest, Vols. XI to XV, same topic and section number.

6. MASTER AND SERVANT, § 833*—*when permitting proof that defendant removed appliance subsequent to accident harmless.* Permitting plaintiff to prove that the defendant removed the projecting set screw after the accident to the plaintiff, *held* not reversible error.

7. MASTER AND SERVANT, § 833*—*when questions asked by court concerning appliances, not reversible error.* Action of trial court in asking a witness whether or not it was necessary that a set screw by which plaintiff was injured extend beyond the periphery of the safety collar in order to firmly attach the collar to the shaft, *held* not reversible error.

8. MASTER AND SERVANT, § 833*—*when permitting witness to answer questions as to appliances harmless.* Permitting a witness to answer a question whether there were other safety collars in the building like the one which caused the injury, *held* not reversible error where the purpose of the question was to show the witness' knowledge as to the use of safety collars.

Mr. JUSTICE CLARK took no part in the consideration of this case.

The Order of Columbian Knights, v. Elmer Matzel et al.

On Appeal of Amanda Schmidt, Appellant, v. Elmer Matzel, Appellee.

Gen. No. 18,856.

New York Life Insurance Company, v. Amanda Z. Schmidt et al.

On Appeal of Amanda Schmidt, Appellant, v. Emma Matzel, Appellee.

Gen. No. 18,857.   (Not to be reported in full.)

Appeal from the Circuit Court of Cook county; the Hon. CHARLES M. WALKER, Judge, presiding. Heard in this court at the October term, 1912. Reversed and remanded. Opinion filed December 2, 1913. Rehearing denied December 16, 1913.

Statement of the Case.

Consolidated causes consisting of two bills of interpleader, one filed by The Order of Columbian

Knights against Elmer Matzel and Amanda Schmidt and one filed by New York Life Insurance Company against Amanda Schmidt and Emma Matzel. Both bills were filed by the respective complainants to determine the conflicting claims of the respective defendants to sums paid into court and admitted to be due as insurance on the life of John Schmidt, husband of Amanda Schmidt. Issues were made up by the answers of the conflicting claimants and the complainants to the bills filed dismissed out of the case. From a decree finding Elmer Matzel and Emma Matzel entitled respectively to the sums admitted to be due by the separate interpleaders, Amanda Schmidt appeals.

POPHAM, WOLFNER, RITTENHOUSE & BEILMAN, for appellant; RUDOLPH WOLFNER, of counsel.

ROBERT F. KOLB and TATGE & KOEPKE, for appellees.

MR. PRESIDING JUSTICE F. A. SMITH delivered the opinion of the court.

Abstract of the Decision.

1. INSURANCE, § 822*—*when beneficiary has a vested right entitled to protection in equity.* A beneficiary acquires a vested right in insurance which equity will protect if such beneficiary assists in paying the assessments or premiums under an agreement by which the proceeds of the insurance are to be paid to the beneficiary.

2. INSURANCE, § 825*—*when member not entitled to change designation of beneficiary.* Where a certificate is taken out for the benefit of a person named therein and delivered to such person in consideration of an agreement by the beneficiary which has been fully performed, the member is not entitled to a change of beneficiary without the beneficiary's consent.

3. INSURANCE, § 825*—*by-laws of mutual benefit association as affecting right to change beneficiary.* Provision in by-laws of a mutual benefit association that a change of beneficiary may be made at any time, without the consent of any existing beneficiary, has no application to a case where the beneficiary has acquired rights in and under the certificate for a valuable consideration.

*See Illinois Notes Digest, Vols. XI to XV, same topic and section number.

4. INSURANCE, § 503*—*when vested rights of beneficiary protected in equity.* The principle that vested rights may be acquired in mutual benefit insurance which courts of equity will enforce applies likewise to life insurance policies.

5. INSURANCE, § 822*—*assignability of benefit certificate.* While a benefit certificate is not assignable at law, all beneficial interest therein may be transferred in equity; and equitable rights may be acquired in a benefit certificate which will be enforced in equity.

6. WITNESSES, § 155*—*when wife is competent concerning transactions regarding certificate of insurance.* As against the claim of another to the proceeds of insurance as beneficiary, the wife of the member originally designated in the benefit certificate is incompetent to testify to any admissions or conversations of her husband relative to transactions concerning the certificate; but she is competent to testify to transactions relating to the certificate, such as the delivery of the certificate to her by her husband, the keeping of the certificate, the payment of dues and assessments by her with her own money, and the disappearance of the certificate while she was absent from home.

Walter Carlson, by Alfred Carlson, Appellee, v. John B. Johnson, Appellant.

Gen. No. 18,003.   (Not to be reported in full.)

Appeal from the Superior Court of Cook county; the Hon. JOHN McNUTT, Judge, presiding. Heard in the Branch Appellate Court at the October term, 1911. Affirmed. Opinion filed December 2, 1913.

Statement of the Case.

Action by Walter Carlson, a minor, by Alfred Carlson his next friend, against John B. Johnson to recover for the loss of sight of one eye while plaintiff was on a public sidewalk and alleged to have been caused by a nail or other object falling or thrown from the roof of defendant's building while such building was being repaired by his servants and agents. From a judgment in favor of plaintiff for four thousand two hundred and fifty dollars, defendant appeals.

*See Illinois Notes Digest, Vols. XI to XV, same topic and section number.

CHYTRAUS, HEALY & FROST, NELS J. JOHNSON and EDWIN WHITE MOORE, for appellant.

GOLDZIER, RODGERS & FROEHLICH, for appellee.

MR. JUSTICE BARNES delivered the opinion of the court.

Abstract of the Decision.

1. **MASTER AND SERVANT, § 863*—**_what evidence inadmissible under the general issue._ In an action against the owner of a building for personal injuries resulting from objects falling from the roof to the public sidewalk, evidence offered by defendant to show that the building was in the exclusive possession and control of an independent contractor and that defendant was not therefore liable, _held_ not admissible under the general issue.

2. **PLEADING, § 476*—**_when defective statement of cause of action cured by verdict._ In an action against the owner of a building in the course of being repaired for injuries sustained by falling objects, declaration failing to aver that men on the roof were defendant's servants, _held_ a defective statement of a cause of action cured by verdict.

3. **APPEAL AND ERROR, § 785*—**_when bill of exceptions construed against party preparing same._ A bill of exceptions is a pleading of the party alleging the exception, and when liable to the charge of uncertainty or omission it ought, like any other pleading, to be construed most strongly against the party preparing it.

4. **APPEAL AND ERROR, § 785*—**_when bill of exception uncertain as to grounds for trial court's ruling._ Language of bill of exceptions _held_ not to support appellant's contention as to the grounds upon which trial court refused his motion for leave to file a special plea.

*See Illinois Notes Digest, Vols. XI to XV, same topic and section number.

Pauline Tischler, Defendant in Error, v. Erie Railroad Company, Plaintiff in Error.

Gen. No. 18,654.   (Not to be reported in full.)

Error to the Municipal Court of Chicago; the Hon. CHARLES E. JENNINGS, Judge, presiding. Heard in the Branch Appellate Court at the October term, 1912. Reversed and remanded. Opinion filed December 2, 1913.

Statement of the Case.

Action by Pauline Tischler against the Erie Railroad Company, a corporation, to recover for the loss of certain articles alleged to have been accepted and checked by defendant at Ellis Island for shipment therefrom to Rockford, Illinois. The affidavit of merits denied that the goods were lost, that there was a total damage, that they were of the value alleged, and claimed that they did not constitute personal baggage and were not knowingly accepted and checked as such. From a judgment for plaintiff for three hundred and twenty-five dollars, defendant brings error.

W. O. JOHNSON and BULL & JOHNSON, for plaintiffs in error; ARTHUR S. LYTTON, of counsel.

C. S. EVERETT, for defendant in error.

MR. JUSTICE BARNES delivered the opinion of the court.

Abstract of the Decision.

1. EVIDENCE, § 396*—*when knowledge of market value is insufficient.* Testimony to the value of articles by one who did not know the market value of them, is incompetent.

2. CARRIERS, § 565*—*when evidence of market value of lost baggage is necessary.* Where in an action against a carrier for loss of personal baggage it is apparent that the articles had a market value, a verdict for the plaintiff cannot be sustained where there is no competent evidence of the market value.

3. CARRIERS, § 544*—*when goods received as baggage.* Where an immigrant receives a baggage check for a basket trunk and a bundle from the railroad company selling her a ticket and they are sent through to the point of destination, in the absence of proof to the contrary it cannot be questioned that the check came from an authorized agent and that the goods were received as baggage.

4. CARRIERS, § 541*—*when responsible in accepting articles as baggage.* A railroad company accepting from an immigrant as baggage a bundle done up in a waterproof sack of heavy goods and tied with heavy ropes is responsible for the articles as if they were personal baggage.

Charles S. Rieman, Plaintiff in Error, v. Edward W. Morrison, Defendant in Error.

Gen. No. 18,767.

1. ESTOPPEL, § 7*—*when plaintiff cannot deny nature of cause of action.* Though replications formally traverse the allegations in several pleas that the several supposed causes of action are one and the same, yet when plaintiff's affidavit of claim states that "said cause is a suit upon contract for the payment of money" and all of the counts, except the common counts and the count of *quantum meruit,* expressly declare upon such contract, the cause of action will be regarded as founded thereon and plaintiff will not be heard to assert to the contrary.

2. PLEADING, § 124*—*what qualities replication should contain.* A replication to a plea lacking the quality of certainty and failing to put in issue material and issuable matters set up in the plea is bad.

3. CONTRACTS, § 362*—*when plea met by improper replication will bar action.* Where in an action on a contract for compensation in aiding in the recovery of stolen property a replication to one of several pleas is uncertain, evasive and unresponsive in denying what the plea does not aver and in not putting in issue material and issuable matters, if the untraversed allegations of the plea are a complete answer to the declaration then the action is barred and the sufficiency of other replications will not be considered.

4. CONTRACTS, § 357*—*when construction of is aided by pleadings.* When untraversed allegations of the plea are a complete answer to the declaration, the contract sued on will be construed in the light of the untraversed averments of the plea.

*See Illinois Notes Digest, Vols. XI to XV, same topic and section number

5. CONTRACTS, § 148*—*when against public policy.* Where in an action on a contract for compensation in aiding in the return of stolen property the untraversed allegations in a plea disclose that plaintiff represented to defendant that he knew the property was stolen, and knew the whereabouts and names of those who had it and that they were wrongfully withholding it; that plaintiff concealed the names and whereabouts of the holders; that he led defendant to believe the property was stolen from him and that plaintiff could secure its return; that part of the consideration was that plaintiff possessed secret beneficial information relating to the larceny and was to receive compensation for its use, and that plaintiff was entitled to claim such compensation for the information alone if any of the property was recovered through it, in the light of the statutes relating to the recovery and return of stolen property and of lost property, J. & A. ¶¶ 3892, 5509, the contract is illegal and against public policy.

6. PLEADING. § 209*—*when demurrer not carried back.* A demurrer to a replication will not be carried back to the plea where no motion is made to carry it back.

Error to the Municipal Court of Chicago; the Hon. JAMES C. MARTIN, Judge, presiding. Heard in the Branch Appellate Court at the October term, 1912. Affirmed. Opinion filed December 2, 1913. Rehearing denied December 16, 1913.

FYFFE, ADCOCK & RYNER and DANIEL W. SCANLAN, for plaintiff in error.

JAMES R. WARD, for defendant in error.

MR. JUSTICE BARNES delivered the opinion of the court.

This was an action in *assumpsit* brought by plaintiff in error against defendant in error. The declaration contained the common counts, a count of *quantum meruit* and special counts declaring upon a contract in writing which, as set out in *haec verba* in some of them, reads as follows:

"This agreement, made and entered into this 12th day of June, 1909, by and between Edward W. Morrison and C. S. Rieman, both of Chicago, Illinois, Witnesseth:

That whereas said Morrison believes from infor-

mation furnished him by said Rieman that certain
money or moneys, real or personal property, rightfully belonging to him under the law, have been wrongfully withheld from him by others, and whereas said
Morrison believes said Rieman is in position to secure
the return to him of said money or moneys, property,
real or personal, wrongfully withheld from said Morrison by others, now, therefore,

In consideration of the premises and of the services
rendered and to be rendered by said Rieman to said
Morrison in his efforts to recover the money, or
moneys, real or personal property, said Morrison
hereby agrees to and with said Rieman that said Rieman shall have and retain as his compensation for
his efforts (or for information furnished by him on
which any recovery may be made as aforesaid by said
Morrison) and for his services in recovering or assisting to recover money or moneys or real or personal
property for said Morrison as aforesaid, one-half (½)
of the cash so recovered through the efforts, services
or information furnished by said Rieman, also cash to
the amount of one-half (½) of the value of whatever
property, real or personal, may be recovered for said
Morrison as aforesaid; said valuation to be determined
by three appraisers, one to be chosen by each of the
parties hereto and the third by the two so selected,
whose findings shall be final as a basis for discharging
the provisions of this contract.

Said Morrison hereby gives and grants to said Rieman full authority to represent him in securing the
return of the money or moneys, real or personal property, and to receive same in said Morrison's name and
behalf, and authorizes said Rieman to secure legal
services to assist, if necessary, in the recoveries to be
attempted as aforesaid, or to invoke the aid of the
authorities, if necessary, to that end. Said Morrison
further authorizes said Rieman to employ attorneys
and fully represent said Morrison in any litigation
that may be necessary to make the recoveries as aforesaid, and to represent him in all other matters in the
same connection.

In Witness Whereof the parties hereto have hereunto set their hands and seals the day and year first above written.

(Signed) EDWARD W. MORRISON,
C. S. RIEMAN.

To the replications to the special pleas there were filed several special demurrers, and one in the nature of a general demurrer, referred to as "demurrer 14," which was sustained. Plaintiff electing to stand by his replications, judgment *nil capiat* was entered, the court finding that the contract sued on was void. Exceptions were taken to the sustaining of said demurrer and to the finding.

While the replications formally traverse the allegation in several pleas that the several supposed causes of action are one and the same, yet plaintiff's affidavit of claim states that "said cause is a suit upon contract for the payment of money," dated June 12, 1909, and all of the counts, except the common counts and the count of *quantum meruit*, expressly declare upon such contract. In the face of this solemn admission of record, the cause of action cannot be regarded otherwise than one founded upon such contract, and plaintiff cannot be heard to assert the contrary.

The eighth special plea avers, among other things, that the plaintiff represented to defendant that he "knew of the whereabouts of divers moneys and personal property and effects, the subjects of larceny, the property of, and rightfully belonging to the defendant, and that the said moneys and property belonging to the defendant aforesaid, had been unlawfully and feloniously stolen and carried away from the dwelling house of the defendant under circumstances amounting to the commission of the crime of larceny thereof, and that said moneys and property were wrongfully withheld from the defendant by divers persons who the plaintiff then and there claimed were known to him, and whose names and the whereabouts of said accused

persons the plaintiff then and there unlawfully concealed from the defendant and from the magistrates
then and there in the County of Cook and State of
Illinois, contrary to the statute in such case made and
provided; and further represented to the defendant
that by reason of his knowledge, he, the plaintiff, was
in a position to secure the return to the defendant of
his said moneys and property so wrongfully withheld
from him; and the defendant avers that the plaintiff
not then and there standing in the relation of husband
or wife, parent or child, brother or sister to the offenders or either of them, and with the intention of pro-
moting and controlling litigation between the defendant and divers persons respecting the moneys and
property aforesaid, and with the intention of obtaining from the defendant as a compensation for information to be furnished by the plaintiff and used and acted
upon, on which recovery may be made of the moneys
and personal property of and to the defendant, or in
assisting to recover said moneys and property to the
defendant, thereby then and there obtained the supposed writing without any good and lawful consideration therefor, contrary to the statutes in such case
made and provided, and for the purposes and upon the
assurances aforesaid. Wherefore the defendant says
that by reason of the premises, and the statutes in such
case made and provided, the supposed writing was and
is contrary to the common law and the statutes of this
State and against the public policy of this State, and
is null and void, and this the defendant is ready to
verify, Wherefore, etc.''

The replications to this plea not only lack the quality
of certainty which is said to be more requisite in a
replication than in a declaration (1 Chitty on Pleading, 647), but they fail to put in issue material and
issuable matters set up in said plea.

The only replication which purports to answer the
several averments is uncertain, evasive and unrespon-

sive in several particulars. It denies what the plea does not aver—the unlawful concealment of the property, but not the unlawful concealment of the names and whereabouts of the accused persons. It denies that plaintiff represented that he was in a position to return the stolen property but not the representations that he knew its whereabouts, who withheld it and that it was wrongfully withheld. It denies the intentions or motives ascribed to plaintiff in obtaining the writing, but not the fact that he did obtain it "upon the assurances aforesaid," which manifestly relate to said representations.

If the untraversed allegations, which stand admitted and confessed by the plaintiff on this record, constitute a complete answer to the declaration, then no consideration need be given to the sufficiency of the other replications to which the demurrer was also sustained; for "When a defendant succeeds on one plea which is a complete answer to a declaration, he is entitled to judgment in his favor in bar of the action." *People v. Bug River Drainage Dist.*, 189 Ill. 55; *Ward v. Stout*, 32 Ill. 399.

The first question presented, therefore, is whether the untraversed allegations present a complete answer to the declaration, and in considering it the contract must be regarded as the sole cause of action, and construed in the light of the untraversed averments in the plea. As said by Lord Campbell in *Sprye v. Porter*, 7 Ellis & Blackburn (Q. B.) 57; "There can be no doubt that the defendant is at liberty to allege that the written agreement declared upon was merely colorable, and to disclose, as a defence, the real nature of the transaction."

Viewing the transaction, therefore, as disclosed by the untraversed averments in the plea, we find: (1) that as an inducement to defendant's entering into the contract, plaintiff represented to him that he knew that the property was stolen from him, that he knew the whereabouts and names of those who had it, and that they were wrongfully withholding it, if not criminally withholding it, for the contract contemplated the possibilty of 'invoking the aid of the authorities,' if necessary; (2) that he then and there concealed from the defendant their names and whereabouts; (3) that from the information furnished defendant was led to believe that the property was stolen from him and that plaintiff was in position to secure its return; (4) that part of the consideration was the fact that plaintiff possessed secret information, relating to the larceny, unknown to the defendant, which might lead to recovery of the stolen property, and that he was to receive compensation for its use; (5) that he was entitled to claim such compensation for the information alone if any of such property was recovered through it.

We cannot escape the conclusion that the parties so withholding the property were known by plaintiff to be amenable to criminal prosecution, and that knowing their names and whereabouts, plaintiff was bartering for the return of the stolen property for his personal benefit, at least, without divulging the identity of those criminally implicated unless compelled to do so in order to realize the compensation agreed upon.

Can such a contract be upheld? The real test of its validity is its tendency. "If the performance of the obligations imposed by the contract has an evil tendency or furnishes a temptation to use improper means, the contract is illegal and *contra bonos mores.*" *Critchfield v. Bermudez Paving Co.*, 174 Ill. 466.

That such a contract has an evil tendency admits of no discussion. That public policy and good morals imposed upon plaintiff the obligation to impart the information he possessed as to a larceny and the identity of the guilty parties is clear. No one can hesitate to say that such a man voluntarily aids criminals to escape their just deserts, and, morally speaking, is almost if not quite as guilty as the principal offenders.

Story's Conflict of Laws, sec. 253. Presented in the most favorable light plaintiff appears in the position of withholding such information unless compensated for it. From his affidavit of claim it appears that the value of the stolen property recovered was at least $165,000. His claim is for one-half thereof. That defendant might voluntarily reward one for information leading to the return of his property, or contract for proper services connected with it, will not be seriously questioned. But to enforce a contract in favor of one seeking and requiring compensation for such information, while concealing and perhaps aiding criminals, would encourage either secret bartering with thieves or their confederates for return of the stolen property, or arrangements facilitating its marketing, or the compounding of felonies, or the suppression of information that would lead to the punishment of the guilty, or all of these.

The provisions of our Criminal Code (Chapter 38, Revised Statutes, J. & A. ¶¶ 3430 *et seq.*) clearly indicate that such a contract is against public policy. Our statutes prescribe punishment not only for the thief but the guilty receivers of stolen property and accessories after the fact. They make him guilty as a receiver of stolen property who, for his own gain, aids in concealing stolen goods knowing them to have been so obtained. (Section 239, ch. 38, Hurd's R. S., J. & A. ¶ 3892.) They make him guilty as an accessory after the fact who, not standing in the relation of husband or wife, parent or child, brother or sister to the offender, conceals, maintains or assists any principal felon or an accessory before the fact, knowing him to be such (section 276, J. & A. ¶ 3969.) So stringent is the law in its manifest policy to prevent any person from receiving a benefit from stolen property, and thereby to discourage larceny, that it requires all property obtained by larceny shall be restored to the owner (section 243, J. & A. ¶ 3892), and that police regulation shall be exercised over the business of pawnbrokers, into whose possession such property is likely to come, and, to protect the owner's title thereto, gives him the right to maintain an action against any person in possession thereof (section 243). Our statutes impose upon even the finders of lost property the duty to inform the owner thereof and to make restitution of the same without compensation (except when voluntarily given), and to take action calculated to restore the property to unknown owners (section 27, ch. 50, J. & A. ¶ 5509).

While it may be said that there is nothing in the contract or admitted averments of the plea clearly indicating that plaintiff stood in a criminal relation to the subject-matter of the contract, yet, the admitted facts place him in an unenviable light. They at least raise a suspicion that the information he sought to barter was not innocently acquired. They are clearly consistent with his being a medium through whom criminals sought to realize a profit from their crimes. Whatever his true position, both public policy and good morals required him to impart such information without first seeking to be rewarded for it. Public interest demanded the arrest and prosecution of those who he must have known were violators of the law.

While most of the authorities cited upon this subject relate to the receiving of compensation by officers or those in a fiduciary relation for that which it was their duty to do without compensation, yet the principle is none the less applicable to the case at bar. The contract in question was not merely one for services. It contemplated that the compensation bargained for might be for the information alone provided it led to the recovery of any of the property, and it is a fair implication that the information would not have been available but for the agreement to compensate plaintiff for it. The tendency of the contract to encourage suppression of such information alone is enough to vitiate it. It is not necessary to its invalidity that it appear that the party seeking to enforce it was in complicity with the guilty parties. If the nature of it is such that it tends to aid those in such relation so as to secure them immunity from arrest and punishment, or to promote their criminal enterprise, it is illegal and unenforcible. It is the plain duty of any honest citizen voluntarily to divulge such information, either to the authorities or to the injured party. But to acquire it and then seek to capitalize it for personal profit is not only repugnant to good morals but tends to protect guilty parties and encourage crime. A contract resting upon such a consideration, or with such pernicious tendencies, will not be enforced.

It is contended that the demurrer should have been carried back to said plea. It is enough to say that we do not think the plea was obnoxious to a general demurrer. Besides no motion was made to carry it back. *People v. Central Union Tel. Co.,* 192 Ill. 307.

We are of the opinion that the demurrer was properly sustained and that the court properly found the contract is void.

Affirmed.

Maude L. Robinson, Appellee, v. Elsie Waddell et al., on appeal of Jacob Glos, Appellants.

Gen. No. 18,855.   (Not to be reported in full.)

Appeal from the Circuit Court of Cook county; the Hon. ADELOR J. PETIT. Judge, presiding. Heard in the Branch Appellate Court at the October term, 1912. Affirmed. Opinion filed December 2, 1913. Rehearing denied December 16, 1913.

Statement of the Case.

Bill in equity by Maude L. Robinson against Elsie Waddell, Jacob Glos and others to foreclose a trust deed to secure the payment of a promissory note. From a decree of foreclosure, Jacob Glos appeals.

JOHN R. O'CONNOR, for appellants.

WILLIAM GIBSON and EDWARD J. PHILLIPS, for appellee.

MR. JUSTICE BARNES delivered the opinion of the court.

Abstract of the Decision.

1. LIMITATION OF ACTIONS, § 94*—*when indorsement of part payment on note is new promise.* An indorsement of payment on a promissory note not in the handwriting of the debtor but in that of the then holder, is not, standing alone, such evidence of part payment as will support the implication of a new promise and toll the statute of limitations (J. & A. ¶ 7211); but it will be considered in connection with corroborative evidence tending to show actual payment at the time of the indorsement.

2. LIMITATION OF ACTIONS, § 94*—*when indorsement of part payment with other evidence shows new promise.* An indorsement of part payment on a promissory note by the then holder, made shortly after the maturity of the note and nine years before the statute of limitations (J. & A. ¶ 7211) would run, in connection with such holder's evidence that at the time of the indorsement he as owner of the note received from its maker, who was indebted to him for nothing else, the sum indorsed or a certificate from which he obtained that amount, is presumptive evidence of payment on the note.

E. P. Stacy & Sons, Appellee, v. Oregon Short Line Railroad Company, Appellant.

Gen. No. 18,000.   (Not to be reported in full.)

Appeal from the Municipal Court of Chicago; the Hon. FREEMAN K. BLAKE, Judge, presiding. Heard in the Branch Appellate Court at the October term, 1911. Affirmed. Opinion filed December 2, 1913. *Certiorari* denied by Supreme Court (making opinion final.)

Statement of the Case.

Action by E. P. Stacy & Sons, a corporation, against Oregon Short Line Railroad Company to recover damages for negligence in the transshipment of a number of carloads of peaches from Brigham City, Utah to various points in other States, the defendant being the initial carrier. From a judgment in favor of plaintiff for $10,080.75, defendant appeals.

DAVIS & RANKIN, for appellant; EDMUND P. KELLY, of counsel.

CHARLES A. BUTLER, for appellee.

MR. JUSTICE CLARK delivered the opinion of the court.

Abstract of the Decision.

1. CARRIERS, § 139*—*when evidence sufficient to sustain verdict for negligence in shipment.* In an action for negligence of the transportation of peaches, evidence *held* sufficient to show that plaintiff was the legal holder of the bills of lading and a verdict for plaintiff *held* not to be against the manifest weight of the evidence.

2. MUNICIPAL COURT OF CHICAGO, § 28*—*when objection to statement of claim not preserved for review.* In an action against a carrier for negligence in the shipment of peaches, objection that plaintiff did not set out in its statement of claim that it was the lawful holder and owner of the bills of lading cannot be raised for the first time on appeal.

*See Illinois Notes Digest, Vols. XI to XV, same topic and section number.

George John Spoeri, Appellee, v. Modern Brotherhood of America, Appellant.

Gen. No. 18,775.   (Not to be reported in full.)

Appeal from the Superior Court of Cook county; the Hon.
JOSEPH H. FITCH, Judge, presiding. Heard in the Branch Appel-
late Court at the October term, 1912. Affirmed. Opinion filed
December 2, 1913. Rehearing denied December 16, 1913.

Statement of the Case.

Action by George John Spoeri against Modern
Brotherhood of America, a corporation, to recover
upon a benefit certificate issued by defendant to George
H. Spoeri, in favor of plaintiff as beneficiary. From
a judgment in favor of plaintiff for $1,081.39, defend-
ant appeals.

CHURCH, SHEPARD & DAY, for appellant; WILLIAM T.
CHURCH, of counsel.

MORTON L. ROBERTS and SAMUEL B. KING, for appellee.

MR. JUSTICE CLARK delivered the opinion of the
court.

Abstract of the Decision.

1. INSURANCE, § 752*—*when statements in application for reinstatement are representations and not warranties.* A member's
statements as to his health in an application for reinstatement,
which states "I * * * do declare and warrant on my honor,
that I am of sound condition, good health and temperate habits,
etc.," and which further states "It is further expressly agreed and
understood that my said reinstatement shall be null and void if the
above warranties and representations or any of them shall be un-
true," *held* to be representations and not warranties, and an instruction to the jury to that effect held justified.

2. INSURANCE, § 877*—*proof necessary to avail of false representations in application.* To avail of false representations in an
application for reinstatement, a benefit association has the burden
of proving that the insured knew the statements to be false.

*See Illinois Notes Digest, Vols. XI to XV, same topic and section number.

Tillie Eckersberg, Appellee, v. Paul Dunklau, Appellant.

Gen. No. 18,799.   (Not to be reported in full.)

Appeal from the Circuit Court of Cook county; the Hon. DUANE J. CARNES, Judge, presiding. Heard in the Branch Appellate Court at the October term, 1912. Affirmed. Opinion filed December 2, 1913.

Statement of the Case.

Action by Tillie Eckersberg against Paul Dunklau for damages for an assault made upon plaintiff by defendant. From a judgment in favor of plaintiff for five hundred dollars, defendant appeals.

ARNOLD TRIPP, for appellant.

CHESTER FIREBAUGH and HENRY W. HUTTMANN, for appellee.

MR. JUSTICE CLARK delivered the opinion of the court.

Abstract of the Decision.

1. ASSAULT AND BATTERY, § 14*—*when evidence sufficient to sustain verdict for assault*. In trespass to recover damages for an alleged assault, a verdict for plaintiff on conflicting evidence *held* sustained by the evidence.

2. APPEAL AND ERROR, § 1561*—*when refusal of requested instructions harmless*. Refusal of requested instructions not error when so much of the instruction as was proper was covered by other instructions given.

*See Illinois Notes Digest, Vols. XI to XV, same topic and section number.

Filippo Ganguzza, Plaintiff in Error, v. Marshall E. Sampsell, Receiver, Defendant in Error.

Gen. No. 18,806.   (Not to be reported in full.)

Error to the Superior Court of Cook County; the Hon. HOMER ABBOTT, Judge, presiding. Heard in the Branch Appellate Court at the October term, 1912. Affirmed. Opinion filed December 2, 1913. Rehearing denied December 16, 1913.

Statement of the Case.

Action by Filippo Ganguzza against Marshall E. Sampsell, sole surviving receiver of the Chicago Union Traction Company, to recover damages for personal injuries sustained from the sudden starting of a street car. From a judgment for defendant, plaintiff brings error.

HARRY W. STANDIDGE, for plaintiff in error.

JOSEPH D. RYAN and WILLIAM H. SYMMES, for defendant in error; JOHN R. GUILLIAMS and FRANK L. KRIETE, of counsel.

MR. JUSTICE CLARK delivered the opinion of the court

Abstract of the Decision.

1. APPEAL AND ERROR, § 1017*—*when bill of exceptions must contain all the evidence.* Error in giving an instruction claimed not to have been supported by the evidence will not be considered where the bill of exceptions does not give all the evidence, or a complete synopsis thereof in narrative form.

2. INSTRUCTIONS, § 151*—*when embodied in instruction given.* Plaintiff's instruction as to effect of the number of witnesses on either side may be refused where it is fully covered by defendant's instruction.

3. TRIAL, § 128*—*when testimony is not misread to jury.* A charge that counsel misstated to the jury the testimony of a witness

in a street railroad accident case by adding the words "at Ohio
street" to an answer is not sustained, where counsel insisted he was
reading from his own notes, there was no showing he was reading
from a stenographic report of the evidence, and as a fair inference
the street was referred to in the question and the jury were instructed not to decide the case upon statements of counsel outside
of the evidence.

Edwin S. Popper and Emil L. Popper, Appellees, v. Frederick W. Spelz, Appellant.

Gen. No. 18,817.   (Not to be reported in full.)

Appeal from the County Court of Cook county; the Hon. VIRGIL
W. MILLS, Judge, presiding. Heard in the Branch Appellate Court
at the October term, 1912. Reversed. Opinion filed December 2,
1913. Rehearing denied December 16, 1913.

Statement of the Case.

Action by Edwin S. Popper and Emil L. Popper,
partners, trading as Leo Popper & Sons, against Frederick W. Spelz upon an alleged guaranty of payment
of an order made by a corporation which the corporation had given the plaintiffs, the defendant being an
officer of the corporation. From a judgment for plaintiffs for $221.58, defendant appeals.

EDWIN L. WAUGH, for appellant.

WILLIAM J. STAPLETON, for appellees.

MR. JUSTICE CLARK delivered the opinion of the
court.

Abstract of the Decision.

1. GUARANTY, § 3*—*when letters "O. K." are not.* The letters
"O. K." written by an officer on an order given by the corporation

*See Illinois Notes Digest, Vols. XI to XV, same topic and section number.

do not of themselves constitute a contract of guaranty, and will be understood generally as meaning that the order had the approval of the officer whose name appears.

2. GUARANTY, § 3*—*when officer of corporation not liable.* An officer of a corporation refused to sign a form guarantying payment of the corporation's order but marked the order with the letters "O· K.," and his clerk without authority wrote the seller in his name, the seller that the "O· K.." would have to suffice as a guaranty. The alleged guarantor testified the clerk had no authority to write such letter, that it was not written in accordance with the directions given and that he marked the order as an approval. *Held,* a guaranty was not established and a verdict should have been directed.

3. GUARANTY, § 12*—*scope of liability.* The liability of a guarantor is limited to the express terms of his undertaking and cannot be extended by implication.

Edward J. Welch, Appellee, v. Helen M. Newbold, Appellant.

Gen. No. 18,818. (Not to be reported in full.)

Appeal from the Municipal Court of Chicago; the Hon. JACOB H. HOPKINS, Judge, presiding. Heard in the Branch Appellate Court at the October term, 1912. Affirmed. Opinion filed December 2, 1913. Rehearing denied December 16, 1913.

Statement of the Case.

Action by Edward J. Welch against Helen M. Newbold upon an account stated made up of items of disbursements by plaintiff as attorney and business agent for defendant and including charges for professional services based upon a monthly compensation fixed by a written contract. From a judgment for plaintiff for $6,135.41, defendant appeals.

JOSEPH B. FLEMING, for appellant.

HENRY R. RATHBONE, for appellee.

MR. JUSTICE CLARK delivered the opinion of the court.

Abstract of the Decision.

1. MUNICIPAL COURT OF CHICAGO, § 29*—*when refusal to require more specific statement of claim is not reviewed.* The discretion vested in a trial judge in not requiring a more specific statement of claim was not abused where interrogatories and answers, as permitted under the practice of the Municipal Court of Chicago, were filed by the defendant.

2. EVIDENCE, § 164*—*when letter is not self-serving.* Where an attorney writes to his client a letter in the nature of a demand for payment of his fees and disbursements and the client replies promising payment, his letter is not a self-serving declaration and both letters are admissible in evidence.

3. LIMITATION OF ACTIONS, § 117*—*when evidence is sufficient to show promise.* Where in an action upon an account stated the plaintiff testifies he presented the account and was promised payment in part at a certain time and the balance later and is corroborated by another witness, which testimony is denied by the defendant, there is sufficient proof of the admission of the debt and a promise to pay so that the statute of limitations does not apply.

4. INSTRUCTIONS, § 28*—*when oral instruction proper.* Written instructions may be refused in the Municipal Court of Chicago, where the court determines to charge the jury orally.

Frank L. Tuttle, Appellee, v. Helen M. Newbold, Appellant.

Gen. No. 18,825.   (Not to be reported in full.)

Appeal from the Municipal Court of Chicago; the Hon. JACOB H. HOPKINS, Judge, presiding. Heard in the Branch Appellate Court at the October term, 1912. Affirmed. Opinion filed December 2, 1913.

Statement of the Case.

Action by Frank L. Tuttle against Helen M. Newbold to recover on a claim for services and disbursements alleged to have been performed and made by one Welch. Plaintiff sues as assignee of said claim. From a judgment in favor of plaintiff for $1,409.79, defendant appeals.

JOSEPH B. FLEMING, for appellant.

HENRY R. RATHBONE, for appellee.

MR. JUSTICE CLARK delivered the opinion of the court.

Abstract of the Decision.

1. ACCOUNT, ACTION ON, § 1*—*when verdict sustained by the evidence.* In an action to recover on an account for services and disbursements assigned to plaintiff, a verdict for plaintiff *held* not manifestly against the weight of the evidence.

2. EVIDENCE, § 164*—*when letter is not self-serving.* Where an attorney writes to his client letters in the nature of demands for payment of his fees and disbursements, and the client replies promising payment, the attorney's letters are not inadmissible, in an action to recover for his services, as self-serving declarations and the client's letters are admissible as admissions. Following Welch v. Newbold, Gen. No. 18,818, ante. p. 36.

Peter Larsen, Appellee, v. Ward Corby Company, Appellant.

Gen. No. 18,826.

1. EVIDENCE, § 105*—*when efforts to suppress testimony admissible.* All efforts to suppress material testimony made by a party or his authorized agent is admissible to show an implied admission that he has no right to recover if the case was tried on the evidence in the case as it exists, and that it is not sufficient to entitle him to recover unless he is aided by suppressing evidence or the fabrication of more evidence.

2. APPEAL AND ERROR, § 1777*—*when exclusion of evidence of subornation of witness reversible error.* In an action for per-

sonal injuries resulting from a collision, refusal of court to permit a witness for the defendant, who was in the employ of the defendant at the time of the collision, to answer a question with reference to a conversation had between himself and the plaintiff and an attorney for the plaintiff, *held* reversible error, where on behalf of the defendant it was stated that the purpose of the question was to show that plaintiff and his attorney made a proposition to the witness "to stay away from the trial, offering to make it right if he would not appear and testify on behalf of the defendant."

Appeal from the Superior Court of Cook county; the Hon. CHARLES M. FOELL, Judge, presiding. Heard in the Branch Appellate Court at the October term, 1912. Reversed and remanded. Opinion filed December 2, 1913.

HERBERT S. DUNCOMBE and LOUIS J. BEHAN, for appellant.

HIRAM BLAISDELL and FRANK D. BURGESS, for appellee; HARRY F. BREWER, of counsel.

MR. JUSTICE CLARK delivered the opinion of the court.

The appellee, as plaintiff, brought suit against the appellant, as defendant, for damages for personal injuries alleged to have been sustained through the negligence of the defendant, resulting in a collision between a bicycle upon which plaintiff was riding and a wagon of the defendant.

We have reached the conclusion that the judgment must be reversed and the cause remanded. Inasmuch as there may be a new trial we refrain from discussing the evidence in the case.

A man who at the time of the trial was not employed by the defendant, but who was in the employ of the defendant and the driver of the team at the time of the collision, was a witness for the defendant. During his examination he was asked with reference to a conversation had between himself and the plaintiff and an attorney for the plaintiff. The court refused to allow the question to be answered. On behalf of the defendant it was stated that the purpose of the question was to show that the plaintiff and his attorney at that time made a proposition to the witness "to stay away from the trial, offering to make it right if he would not appear and testify on behalf of the defendant company." On behalf of the plaintiff it is urged that the offer was not specific enough, and, second, that even if there was error in the refusal to admit the testimony it was harmless error.

The rule as stated in *Chicago City Ry. Co. v. Mc-Mahon,* 103 Ill. 485, is that all efforts to suppress material testimony made by a party or his authorized agent, are proper to be shown "because it is in the nature of and implies an admission that he has no right to recover if the case was tried on the evidence in the case as it exists—that it is not sufficient to recover unless aided by suppressing evidence, or the fabrication of more evidence." The doctrine of this case was approved in *United States Brewing Co. v. Ruddy,* 203 Ill. 306, and it has been followed in various cases in the Appellate Courts of the State.

We are not persuaded that it was the duty of the trial court to direct a verdict for the defendant.

For the error pointed out the judgment will be reversed and the cause remanded.

Reversed and remanded.

————

In re Estate of Oscar Schroeder, Deceased.

On Appeal of Catherine L. Fox et al., Appellants, v. Henry Ehlers et al., Executors, Appellees.

Gen. No. 18,858.   (Not to be reported in full.)

Appeal from the Circuit Court of Cook county; the Hon. H. STERLING POMEROY, Judge, presiding. Heard in the Branch Appellate Court at the October term, 1912. Reversed and remanded. Opinion filed December 2, 1913.

Statement of the Case.

Appeal to the Circuit Court in the matter of the estate of Oscar Schroeder, deceased, in which Catherine L. Fox and Sophia Lord are appellants and Henry Ehlers and others as executors are appellees to review an order of the Probate Court approving the final account of the executors and ordering their discharge upon the filing of receipts of distributees. From an order of the Circuit Court dismissing the appeal for want of jurisdiction to review the order, Catherine L. Fox and Sophia Lord, appellants below, appeal.

DAVID STEWART and BENNER & WELD, for appellants; E. K. SMITH, of counsel.

CHARLES P. ABBEY, for appellees.

MR. JUSTICE CLARK delivered the opinion of the court.

Abstract of the Decision.

1. APPEAL AND ERROR, § 632*—*limitation for perfecting an appeal where a previous order was vacated and re-entered with amendments.* Where an order of the Probate Court is entered vacating a previous order and re-entering the same with amendments, the time for perfecting an appeal to the Circuit Court begins to run from the date of the second order.

2. APPEAL AND ERROR, § 1105*—*when appeal from order should not be dismissed for abuse of discretion in entering the order.* Such appeal should not be dismissed upon the allegation that the court abused its discretion in entering the second order.

*See Illinois Notes Digest, Vols. XI to XV, same topic and section number.

Bessie Apthorp, Appellee, v. Paul O. Domke, Appellant.

Gen. No. 18,859.   (Not to be reported in full.)

Appeal from the Circuit Court of Cook county; the Hon. RICHARD
S. TUTHILL, Judge, presiding.   Heard in the Branch Appellate
Court at the October term, 1912.   Affirmed.   Opinion filed December
2, 1913.

Statement of the Case.

Action by Bessie Apthorp against Paul O. Domke
to recover damages for personal injuries sustained by
plaintiff alleged to have been caused by the negligence
of defendant's servant in driving a horse and wagon
so as to strike down and run over plaintiff at a street
intersection.   From a judgment in favor of plaintiff
for four hundred and twenty-seven dollars, defendant
appeals.

WILLIAM DANIEL JOHNSON, for appellant.

No appearance for appellee.

MR. JUSTICE CLARK delivered the opinion of the
court

Abstract of the Decision.

1. NEGLIGENCE, § 138*—*when plaintiff need not prove ownership
of instrument causing the injury.*   In an action for personal injuries resulting from the negligent driving of a horse and wagon,
burden is not upon plaintiff to prove defendant's ownership of the
horse and wagon where the only plea filed by defendant was the
general issue.

2. APPEAL AND ERROR, § 1561*—*when refusal of requested instructions not error.*   Refusal of requested instructions which were
covered by other instructions given, *held* not error.

*See Illinois Notes Digest, Vols. XI to XV, same topic and section number.

Henry Carraher, next friend of Kathryn Carraher, Plaintiff in Error, v. Chicago Telephone Company, Defendant in Error.

Gen. No. 18,532.

MASTER AND SERVANT, § 703*—*when evidence insufficient to show negligence of telephone company in maintaining safe switchboard for operator.* In an action for injuries sustained by a telephone operator, alleged to have been caused by the negligence of the telephone company in permitting a powerful current of electricity to pass through the wires and in maintaining wires and attachments not insulated, plaintiff's evidence *held* insufficient to prove the allegations of negligence.

Error to the Circuit Court of Cook county; the Hon. THOMAS G. WINDES, Judge, presiding. Heard in the Branch Appellate Court at the October term, 1912. Affirmed. Opinion filed December 4, 1913, *nunc pro tunc* as of December 2, 1913.

THEODORE G. CASE, for plaintiff in error; MUNSON T. CASE, of counsel.

HOLT, WHEELER & SIDLEY, for defendant in error.

MR. PRESIDING JUSTICE McSURELY delivered the opinion of the court.

Kathryn Carraher, hereinafter called plaintiff, by next friend brought suit against the Chicago Telephone Company, hereinafter called defendant, to recover damages for personal injuries alleged to have been received by her while working as a switchboard operator for the defendant. At the conclusion of the introduction of testimony on behalf of the plaintiff, upon motion of the defendant, the court instructed the jury to find the defendant not guilty. The jury so found and judgment was entered on the verdict. Plaintiff contends that the court should not have given this peremptory instruction and urges that the judgment should be reversed.

In her original declaration plaintiff alleges the duty of the defendant to allow "only a small current of electricity, sufficient to carry telephonic messages" to pass through its wires, and that it was negligent in permitting " a larger and stronger current of electricity to suddenly be transmitted through its lines." Subsequently two additional counts were filed, in the first of which it was alleged that the defendant negligently maintained its wires and attachments, not insulated, and that they were allowed to cross and come in contact with other wires charged with powerful currents of electricity, and that this condition so continued and remained for several days, and that on February 11, 1902, a powerful and destructive current of electricity passed from said other wires and attachments into the telephone wires, attachments and switchboard of the defendant, whereby they became charged with a large and destructive current of electricity, dangerous and destructive to life and health. No attempt was made to prove the averments of the second additional count; hence it is unnecessary to advert further to it.

The evidence as to the occurrence itself is that of a fellow-switchboard operator, who, while working at her own board, heard the plaintiff say that she had gotten a shock, and saw the plaintiff with the telephone cord, hereinafter described, in her hand, and that she "was dazed" and was assisted into another room. There was evidence that shortly afterwards she appeared nervous, which condition seemed to advance until about a year after that time, when her friends and relatives were led to believe from her conduct and condition that she was unsound mentally. The evidence also showed that she was suffering with some form of dementia at the time of the trial, which was nearly nine years after the date of the occurrence.

We have arrived at the conclusion that the ruling of the trial court was proper for the reason that plaintiff produced no legal evidence tending to prove the allegations of either the original declaration or the first additional count. As we have noted above, the original declaration averred the duty of defendant to pass through its wires a small current of electricity, sufficient only to carry telephonic messages, the breach alleged being the passing through its lines of a larger and stronger current of electricity than this.

It appears from the evidence that at the time of the occurrence in question the so-called "talking current" was about twenty-four volts. As the words indicate, this is the current of electricity used for the transmission of messages. The so-called "ringing current" has a voltage of seventy-five or eighty when one bell is rung, and less voltage when a number are rung at the same time. This obviously refers to the current used in ringing the telephone bell for the purpose of attracting the attention of a subscriber. There is nothing whatever in the record evidencing any duty upon the defendant to pass through its lines only a "talking current," and from the very nature of the case no such evidence could be produced. It is impossible to conceive of a usable telephone system without some device for calling subscribers to the instrument, and that this "ringing current" necessitates a larger voltage is conceded. Even if the plaintiff received an electrical shock as is claimed, this standing alone could not support the charge of negligence now under consideration, especially in view of the evidence of plaintiff's witness that the resisting powers of the particular individual concerned is the important factor determining the amount of shock received, and that the plaintiff might have been in exactly the same condition of injury as she appeared to be in after the occurrence, as the result of receiving a current of even as low as ten volts.

Neither is there any evidence that the wires and attachments belonging to defendant were not insulated or that they were allowed to cross and come in contact with other wires and attachments from which passed a powerful and destructive current of electricity into the wires, attachments and switchboard of the defendant, as alleged in the first additional count.

There was evidence tending to show some defect in the device called the "cord" and "plug" used in operating the switchboard. It would unduly extend this opinion to attempt any technical detailed description of this device. Any one who has seen even a small telephone switchboard will recognize the device as the black rubber plug, about the thickness of a lead pencil, which is inserted by the operator into a small hole or opening in the face of the switchboard when a telephone connection is desired. This rubber plug is attached to the end of a cord which runs down through a hole in a horizontal shelf, where a counterweight and pulley tend to draw the plug down when not in use, leaving it sticking up from the face of the shelf. This cord contains a wire or wires through which, when used, a current of electricity passes. The fellow-operator of the plaintiff testified that for two or three days before the occurrence in question one of the plugs had a white paper cap sticking on it, which was understood as notice that the particular plug or cord was out of order; that a repair man worked with tools for a time on this cord and then told the plaintiff that it was in repair and that she could use it; that shortly thereafter the witness heard plaintiff say, "Oh, I got a shock," and that witness turned and saw that plaintiff had this particular cord in her hand.

To conclude that this evidence either directly or inferentially tends to prove the allegations of the additional count is to indulge merely in speculation. To reach such a conclusion we should be compelled to presume that the cord was not repaired by the repair man, although the evidence tends to show the contrary; also that the alleged defect was absence of insulation; and upon this we must presume that there was a contact with other wires and attachments charged with powerful and destructive currents of electricity, and further that the result was the transmission of such a current to the wire in the cord held by plaintiff. Such indulgence in presumptions upon presumptions the law will not permit.

It is also important to note that plaintiff's expert mechanical witness testified that even if there existed any defect in the cord or plug causing a shock to the operator, it would be only a shock from the normal "ringing current" and that she might receive this shock with no defect in the apparatus if she should improperly handle it. In this connection we again recall Dr. Kiernan's statement that the comparative difference in voltage between the talking current and ringing current had no causal relation to the alleged injuries.

We deem it unnecessary to consider other points presented and discussed by both counsel, including what is urged in support of the claim that this is a *res ipsa loquitur* case. We have given consideration to these points, and are not led thereby to any different conclusion from that which we have indicated.

Plaintiff by her declaration alleged specific and particular acts of negligence, and upon the trial was bound to produce legal evidence tending to support at least one of such charges. In this, as we view the matter, she has failed, and the action of the trial court in instructing the jury as was done was proper, and therefore, for the reasons indicated, the judgment will be affirmed.

Affirmed.

Caroline E. Knipping, Appellee, v. Chicago Telephone Company, Appellant.

Gen. No. 18,452. (Not to be reported in full.)

Appeal from the Superior Court of Cook county; the Hon.
CLARENCE N. GOODWIN, Judge, presiding. Heard in the Branch Appellate Court at the March term, 1912. Affirmed. Opinion filed
December 4, 1913, *nunc pro tunc* as of December 2, 1913. Rehearing denied December 24, 1913.

Statement of the Case.

Action by Caroline E. Knipping against the Chicago
Telephone Company to recover damages for personal
injuries sustained by plaintiff alleged to have been
caused by a shock received by plaintiff while answering a telephone call. From a judgment in favor of
plaintiff for two thousand dollars defendant appeals.

HOLT, WHEELER, CUTTING & SIDLEY, for appellant.

THEODORE G. CASE, for appellee; MUNSON T. CASE,
of counsel.

MR. PRESIDING JUSTICE McSURELY delivered the
opinion of the court.

Abstract of the Decision.

1. NEGLIGENCE, § 204*—*when plaintiff's evidence tends to support
declaration.* In an action against a telephone company to recover
damages for a shock sustained by plaintiff while answering a telephone call, plaintiff's evidence *held* sufficient to warrant court in
denying a motion to direct a verdict for defendant.
2. NEGLIGENCE, § 185*—*what evidence sufficient to prove personal
injuries.* Evidence of a condition of good health prior to an accident and illness and poor health immediately succeeding it, is
sufficient evidence from which the jury might legitimately conclude
that the latter condition was caused by the accident.
3. TRIAL, § 187*—*rule regarding direction of verdict.* Correct
rule applicable to a motion to direct a verdict is that admitting

the evidence in favor of the plaintiff to be true, does it, together with all legitimate conclusions which may be drawn therefrom, fairly tend to establish plaintiff's cause of action as laid in the declaration? If it does, then the court commits no error in refusing the motion and in permitting the facts to be passed upon by the jury.

4. TRIAL, § 186*—*questions considered on motion to direct a verdict.* On motion to direct a verdict, it is not for the court to consider whether the evidence is weak or strong, or whether or not discredit has been cast upon it by cross-examination. All such matters are for the jury to weigh and pass upon.

5. APPEAL AND ERROR, § 606*—*what necessary to preserve ruling on motion to direct a verdict.* Ruling of court denying a motion to direct a verdict for defendant is preserved by exception taken to the ruling, without the necessity of any further motion, not even the motion for a new trial.

6. APPEAL AND ERROR, § 607*—*when special findings of jury not reviewable.* Special findings of jury are conclusive when not asked to be set aside on motion for a new trial.

W. W. Wilcox Company, Defendant in Error, v. J. E. Ingram, Plaintiff in Error.

Gen. No. 18,557.   (Not to be reported in full.)

Error to the Municipal Court of Chicago; the Hon. CHARLES E. JENNINGS, Judge, presiding. Heard in the Branch Appellate Court at the October term, 1912. Affirmed. Opinion filed December 4, 1913, *nunc pro tunc* as of December 2, 1913. Rehearing denied December 16, 1913.

Statement of the Case.

Action by W. W. Wilcox Company, a corporation, against J. E. Ingram on a claim for goods sold and delivered, work and materials furnished, money received by defendant for use of plaintiff, interest on divers sums of money and money due on account stated. From a judgment in favor of plaintiff for $368.19, defendant brings error.

*See Illinois Notes Digest, Vols. XI to XV, same topic and section number.

Mangold et al. v. King, 184 Ill. App. 50.

SIMON T. SUTTON and H. J. ROSENBERG, for plaintiff in error; JAMES D. POWER, of counsel.

E. C. FERGUSON, for defendant in error.

MR. PRESIDING JUSTICE MCSURELY delivered the opinion of the court.

Abstract of the Decision.

MUNICIPAL COURT OF CHICAGO, § 26*—*when stenographic report improperly filed nunc pro tunc.* Where a stenographic report is presented to and signed by the trial judge within apt time, an order of court entered nearly eight months thereafter permitting it to be filed *nunc pro tunc* as of the day it was presented to and signed by the trial judge is void and of no effect, and the stenographic report may on motion be stricken from the record.

Louis A. Mangold and William F. Coughenor, trading as Louis A. Mangold & Co., Plaintiffs in Error, v. H. E. King, Defendant in Error.

Gen. No. 18,650.

1. ATTACHMENT, § 246*—*when verdict may be directed for defendant upon the attachment issue.* In attachment proceeding evidence that defendant withdrew his bank balance and tried to collect other moneys from those who held it subsequent to the dismissal of a prior attachment suit, is not sufficient evidence of itself, to give rise to any legitimate inference of fraud, concealment, etc., and direction of a verdict for defendant *held* proper.

2. MUNICIPAL COURT OF CHICAGO, § 30*—*when refusal of requested instructions not error.* Refusal of requested instructions which so far as they were material and correct were covered by the oral charge of the court, *held* not error.

3. MUNICIPAL COURT OF CHICAGO, § 26*—*when document is sufficient as a statement of facts or stenographic report.* A document purporting to be a correct statement by the judge of "matters pertaining to proceedings at the trial" which "do not otherwise so fully appear of record," including a transcript of all the evidence, the rulings of the court upon the admissibility of evidence the instruc-

Mangold et al. v. King, 184 Ill. App. 50.

tions of the court, the objections made and a statement of the court's rulings upon these matters and upon the motion for a new trial and in entering judgment, *held* sufficient compliance with Municipal Court Act, § 23, J. & A. ¶ 3336, requiring a statement of facts or a stenographic report.

4. MUNICIPAL COURT OF CHICAGO, § 26*—*when certificate of trial judge to statement of facts conclusive.* A judge's certificate to a document purporting to be a statement of facts showing on its face that it was presented to the judge who tried the case for signing and filing at the proper time, and that it was in fact signed by him as of the date it was presented, cannot be contradicted by another certificate made by another judge that it was presented to him for signing and filing on the same day.

5. MUNICIPAL COURT OF CHICAGO, § 26*—*when presumed that certificate of statement of facts was signed in apt time.* Where nothing affirmatively appears to the contrary it will be presumed that the trial court signed the certificate to the statement of facts in apt time.

Error to the Municipal Court of Chicago; the Hon. JACOB H. HOPKINS, Judge, presiding. Heard in the Branch Appellate Court at the October term, 1912. Affirmed. Opinion filed December 4, 1913. Rehearing denied December 16, 1913.

LEWIS EDWARD DICKINSON, for plaintiffs in error.

ALDEN, LATHAM & YOUNG, for defendant in error; CHARLES MARTIN, of counsel.

MR. JUSTICE FITCH delivered the opinion of the court.

This writ of error is brought to review the proceedings and judgment of the Municipal Court in a fourth class case, wherein the plaintiffs, Louis A. Mangold & Co., sued the defendant, H. E. King, in attachment, to recover commissions alleged to have been earned by the plaintiffs in and about the sale of the leasehold and fixtures of a hotel in Chicago owned by defendant. The case was tried before a jury. At the close of the plaintiffs' evidence, the court peremptorily instructed the jury to find for the defendant on the attachment issue, which was done. After defendant had then put in his evidence, a verdict was returned in his favor on the *assumpsit* issue.

*See Illinois Notes Digest, Vols. XI to XV, same topic and section number.

A motion was heretofore made to strike the statement of facts, or stenographic report, from the record, and this motion was reserved to the hearing. The record shows that the judgment was entered on May 18, 1912. On June 13, 1912, an order was entered extending the time in which to file a statement of facts to July 17, 1912. On July 17, 1912, there was filed in the office of the clerk of the Municipal Court a document called (by the clerk) a "statement of facts." This document begins with a statement that "By authority of the statutes * * * I, Jacob H. Hopkins, one of the judges of said court," by whom the case was tried, "do cause to be prepared, signed by me and filed herein, at the instance of plaintiffs, a statement pursuant to such statutes, containing and setting forth, to-wit: the matters and things in the manner and form following, pertaining to proceedings at the trial thereof, and such other proceedings in the case as plaintiffs have desired to be included." Then follows a brief recital of the contents of the affidavit for attachment, the attachment bond, the answer of the garnishee and the affidavit of merits. Following these recitals is what seems to be a stenographic report of the evidence heard at the trial, with the objections made to the evidence as it was introduced, and a digest of the contents of the exhibits offered in evidence; all of which concludes with the statement that "the above and foregoing was and is all of the evidence, offered, introduced and considered upon the trial of said cause." Then follow the instructions given by the court, a statement that each of said instructions was objected to by plaintiffs' counsel and that he requested other instructions to be given, which are set out at length, and that the court refused to give the instructions so requested. Then follows a statement that the jury returned a verdict for the defendant on April 22, 1912; that the plaintiffs entered a motion for a new trial; that said motion was heard and denied on May 18, 1912; and that judgment for costs was thereupon entered against the plaintiffs. Then follows a copy of the writ of error from this court, after which is the following conclusion:

"Whereupon plaintiffs upon to wit, July 17th, A. D. 1912, tendered in open court the above and foregoing statement, which was examined by the court and approved as hereinafter set forth.

Forasmuch as the matters and things hereinabove recited and contained do not otherwise so fully appear of record, the above and foregoing correct statement is signed and ordered filed pursuant to the statutes of said state in such cases made and provided, this 9/21/12 as of July 17th A. D. 1912.

JACOB H. HOPKINS, (SEAL.)

Judge of the Municipal Court of said City of Chicago.

Presented for signing and filing, July 17th, A. D. 1912.

FREEMAN K. BLAKE,

Judge of the Municipal Court of said City of Chicago and Acting Chief Justice."

On the next page of the document appears an affidavit by the plaintiffs' attorney, subscribed and sworn to July 16, 1912, to the effect that he made diligent inquiry as to the whereabouts of Judge Hopkins, and was informed and believes that said judge left Chicago on his vacation June 24, 1912, to go to Portland, Oregon, and has not been heard from since; that the affiant is unable to present "said statement of facts, etc.," to Judge Hopkins because of the absence of said judge from the State of Illinois and, therefore, presents the same to acting Chief Justice Blake. A notice of such application accompanies the affidavit. At the bottom of this additional page, Judge Blake certified that "the above and foregoing statement, affidavit and notice were duly presented in open court for signing and filing this July 17, A. D. 1912."

It is urged that the document above described is neither "a correct statement of the facts appearing upon the trial and of all questions of law involved in such case, and the decisions of the court upon such questions of law," nor "a correct stenographic report of the proceedings at the trial," within the meaning of the sixth paragraph of section 23 of the Municipal Court Act. (J. & A. ¶ 3336.) There is much force in the contention. But we do not think the document should be stricken from the record merely because it cannot be technically classified. Taking all its statements together, it purports to be a correct statement by the judge of "matters pertaining to proceedings at the trial" which "do not otherwise so fully appear of record," including a transcript of all the evidence, the rulings of the court upon the admissability of evidence, the instructions of the court, the other instructions requested, the objections made and a statement of the court's rulings upon these matters and upon the motion for a new trial and in entering judgment. Section 23 of the Municipal Court Act (J. & A. ¶ 3336), permits the party who prepares either a statement of facts or a stenographic report for the judge's signature, to omit therefrom, with the approval of the judge, all such proceedings, "other than the evidence and rulings of the court with respect thereto and the charge of the court, as the judge may deem unnecessary for the presentation to the Supreme Court or the Appellate Court of the merits of the case." The document here presented contains "the evidence and rulings of the court with respect thereto, and the charge of the court;" and we must therefore presume that if anything was omitted, it was omitted with the approval of the trial judge and because he deemed the omissions, if any, were "unnecessary for the presentation" to this court "of the merits of the case." The document is therefore, whatever it may be called, within the spirit of the statute, even if it is not strictly within the letter of the law.

It is also urged that the document in question shows upon its face that it was not presented to Judge Hopkins within the time allowed by the court, but that it was presented to Judge Blake during the temporary absence of Judge Hopkins from the State of Illinois. In *Jaggle v. Nagle* (No. 18610 of this court, opinion filed November 20, 1913), 183 Ill. App. 237, we held that section 23 of the Municipal Court Act requires the "application" mentioned in that section (to sign and place on file either a correct statement of the facts or a correct stenographic report) to be made to the judge "by whom the judgment was entered," whose duty it is, under that section, to grant such an application. It was also suggested in the opinion filed in that case (but without deciding the point) that if it appeared that the judge by whom the judgment was entered was unable, "by reason of death, sickness or other disability," to sign and place on file such a statement of facts or stenographic report, then possibly section 81 of the Practice Act (J. & A. ¶ 8618), taken in connection with section 19 of the Municipal Court Act (J. & A. ¶ 3331), might be applicable. If it be assumed that by reason of the temporary absence from the State of Judge Hopkins an application might have been made on the theory suggested, to some other judge of the Municipal Court, and that such other judge, if in his opinion he was able to do so, might have had the authority to sign and place on file the statement tendered, that was not done in this case. Judge Blake did not assume to "sign" it, in the sense of certifying to its correctness. He merely marked it *"presented* for signing and filing," etc. It does not appear, by the certificate of Judge Blake or any other judge that Judge Hopkins was, in fact, under any disability at that time. True, the plaintiffs' attorney made an affidavit that he had been unable to find Judge Hopkins and was informed and believed that he had temporarily left the State; but Judge Blake does not certify that such was the case, nor that he acted upon the information contained in the affidavit. Judge Hopkins himself certifies that the document was "tendered" on July 17, "in open court." Judge Hopkins does not say in his certificate that it was so "tendered" *to him*, nor does Judge Blake say in his certificate, to whom it was "presented." If the certificate of Judge Hopkins stood alone, it would apparently show that the statement of facts was presented to him for signing and filing at the proper time, and was, in fact, signed later by him as of the date it was so presented. If this was the fact, then the additional statement by Judge Blake that it was "presented for signing and filing" on the same day, apparently *to him*, makes no difference whatever. In any event, the certificate of the judge by whom the judgment was entered, who is the only judge authorized by the Municipal Court Act to make such a certificate, cannot be contradicted by another certificate made by a judge who did not try the case nor enter the judgment. *David v. Bradley*, 79 Ill. 316; *Parker v. Village of LaGrange*, 167 Ill. 623. All the cases in this State, so far as we are advised, in which a similar document has been stricken from the record of the Appellate Court because it was not signed and filed within the time limited, are cases in which it affirmatively appeared, or was conceded, that the document was never, in fact, presented to the judge for his signature within the time fixed. Where such fact is not conceded and does not affirmatively appear, it will be presumed, from the fact that the trial judge signed the document, that he would not have signed it unless it had been presented to him in apt time. *Underwood v. Hossack*, 40 Ill. 98; *Village of Hyde Park v. Dunham*, 85 Ill. 569, 571; *Olds v. North Chicago St. R. Co.*, 165 Ill. 472, 474. This presumption cannot, in our opinion, be overcome by the certificate of another judge. The motion to strike will, therefore, be denied.

Upon the merits of the case, the errors assigned may be summarized as follows: (1) the court erred in directing a verdict upon the attachment issue; (2) the verdict is contrary to the evidence; (3) the court erred in refusing to give the instructions offered by plaintiffs.

The record filed in this court does not contain a copy of the affidavit for attachment. The "statement" certifies that it contains "the usual attachment allegations." Waiving any question as to this method of presenting an alleged error, we find no evidence in the record fairly tending to prove any ground for attachment. It is true that there is some evidence to the effect that the defendant withdrew his bank balance of about fifty dollars and tried to collect other money from those who held it subsequent to the dismissal of a prior attachment suit; but such evidence of itself, does not give rise to any legitimate inference of fraud, or concealment, or an attempt to hinder, delay or defraud creditors. (We infer from the argument of counsel that these grounds are intended by the terms "usual attachment allegations".) The court properly directed a verdict upon the attachment issue.

There was a sharp conflict in the evidence between the plaintiffs' witnesses and those of the defendant as to whether the price at which the property was sold was fixed at a gross sum, including commissions, or was fixed at a net price, without commissions. Upon that issue of fact, we think the jury were fully and fairly instructed, and we cannot say from the record before us that the verdict was manifestly contrary to the preponderance of the evidence. As to the instructions offered and refused by the court, we find, upon examination, that so far as they were pertinent, material or correct, they were covered by the oral charge of the court.

Finding no substantial error in the record, the judgment of the Municipal Court will be affirmed.

Affirmed.

Otto Geiersbach, Defendant in Error, v. John A. Fippinger et al., Plaintiffs in Error.

Gen. No. 18,235.   (Not to be reported in full.)

Error to the Superior Court of Cook county; the Hon. CHARLES A. McDONALD, Judge, presiding. Heard in the Branch Appellate Court at the October term, 1912. Reversed and remanded with directions. Opinion filed December 4, 1913.

Statement of the Case.

Petition by writ of mandamus by Otto Geiersbach against John A. Fippinger and others, as members of the board of trustees and the board of local improvements of the village of Bellwood, to compel the respondents to take steps to put into collection a special assessment and to issue proper vouchers for paving work done by petitioner. From a judgment awarding the writ, respondents bring error.

GEORGE E. BRANNAN, for plaintiffs in error.

JOHN A. BROWN and CHARLES W. HADLEY, for defendant in error.

MR. JUSTICE GRIDLEY delivered the opinion of the court.

Abstract of the Decision.

1. MANDAMUS, § 82*—*when proper to compel collection of special assessment.* A writ of mandamus may be resorted to, to compel a village to proceed to enforce the collection of a special assessment if it has failed to discharge its duty in that respect.

2. MANDAMUS, § 143*—*sufficiency of petition.* Allegations of petition for mandamus *held* to sufficiently show, at least as against a general demurrer, such a state of facts as to entitle petitioner to a writ commanding a village to take necessary steps to put into collection a special assesment.

*See Illinois Notes Digest, Vols. XI to XV. same topic and section number.

3. MANDAMUS, § 173*—*form of judgment.* Judgment that a writ of mandamus "do issue herein," etc., *held* not defective for not specifying what respondents are to do where the prayer of the petition is clear and specific.

4. MANDAMUS, § 172*—*what relief warranted by petition.* Allegations of a petition for mandamus to compel a village to put into collection a special assessment for paving work done, *held* not to warrant court in directing respondents to issue vouchers to petitioner.

5. MUNICIPAL CORPORATIONS, § 377*—*when village estopped to assert informality of contract for improvement.* Village authorities accepting work done by contractor in laying sidewalks in accordance with an ordinance, and under the superintendence of agents for the village, are estopped from setting up the irregular manner in which the contract was entered into as a defense to a petition for mandamus to compel the village to put into collection a special assessment.

The People of the State of Illinois for use of State Board of Health, Defendant in Error, v. Frank Klimek, Plaintiff in Error.

Gen. No. 18,477.   (Not to be reported in full.)

Error to the Municipal Court of Chicago; the Hon. JOHN D. TURNBAUGH, Judge, presiding. Heard in the Branch Appellate Court at the October term, 1912. Affirmed. Opinion filed December 4, 1913.

Statement of the Case.

Action by the People of the State of Illinois for the use of the State Board of Health against Frank Klimek to recover the sum of two hundred dollars as a penalty for a second offense of practicing medicine without a license. From a judgment against defendant for two hundred dollars, defendant brings error.

BRADY & LEVY, for plaintiff in error; JOSIAH BURNHAM, of counsel.

---

*See Illinois Notes Digest, Vols. XI to XV, same topic and section number.

CHARLES ALLING, JR., for defendant in error.

MR. JUSTICE GRIDLEY delivered the opinion of the court.

Abstract of the Decision.

1. PENALTIES, § 5*—*when suit for penalty is a civil proceeding.* Where an offense is created by statute and a penalty is fixed for its commission which is to be recovered in an action of debt and not by prosecution, the action is civil and the rules of criminal pleading and procedure do not apply to it.

2. PHYSICIANS AND SURGEONS, § 8*—*nature of proceeding to recover statutory penalty for practicing without a license.* A proceeding under the Act of 1899, relating to the practice of medicine, J. & A. ¶ 7390, to recover a penalty for the offense of practicing medicine without a license, is not a criminal proceeding requiring the offense to be proved beyond a reasonable doubt.

3. PHYSICIANS AND SURGEONS, § 8*—*burden of proof.* In action to recover a penalty for offense of practicing medicine without a license, the burden is upon defendant to prove that he had such a license.

4. APPEAL AND ERROR, § 479*—*when objections to instructions not available.* Objections to instructions not specifically called to the attention of the trial court, not preserved for review.

Oscar D. Olson, Executor, Plaintiff in Error, v. Pennsylvania Company, Defendant in Error.

Gen. No. 18,517.   (Not to be reported in full.)

Error to the Municipal Court of Chicago; the Hon. HUGH R. STEWART, Judge, presiding. Heard in the Branch Appellate Court at the October term, 1912. Affirmed. Opinion filed December 4, 1913.

Statement of the Case.

Action by Oscar D. Olson, executor of the will of George B. Gibson, deceased, against Pennsylvania Company, a corporation, to recover a certain sum de-

---

*See Illinois Notes Digest, Vols. XI to XV, same topic and section number.

ceased had on deposit in the "Employees' Saving Fund of the Pennsylvania Lines west of Pittsburg." The defense was that said sum was not a part of the estate of the deceased and that it was paid to the mother of the deceased, who was rightfully entitled thereto. From a judgment in favor of defendant, plaintiff brings error.

DAVID G. EINSTEIN, for plaintiff in error.

LOESCH, SCOFIELD & LOESCH, for defendant in error.

MR. JUSTICE GRIDLEY delivered the opinion of the court.

Abstract of the Decision.

1. MUNICIPAL COURT OF CHICAGO, § 26*—*presumption in the absence of a correct statement of facts.* In the absence of a correct statement of the facts appearing upon the trial, it must be presumed that there was sufficient evidence to warrant the finding and judgment.

2. MUNICIPAL COURT OF CHICAGO, § 26*—*when statement of facts insufficient.* A statement of facts reciting that the cause was heard on a stipulation of facts is insufficient where such stipulation is not appended to or in anyway made a part of the statement of facts.

8. APPEAL AND ERROR, § 761*—*when stipulation of facts is not a part of the record.* A stipulation of facts appearing in the transcript of the record as having been filed in the cause is not a part of the record so that it may be considered on review.

N. Mazzarella, Plaintiff in Error, v. Olives Kamberos, Defendant in Error.

Gen. No. 18,534.   (Not to be reported in full.)

Error to the Municipal Court of Chicago; the Hon. JOHN R. NEWCOMER, Judge, presiding. Heard in the Branch Appellate Court at the October term, 1912. Affirmed. Opinion filed December 4, 1913,

*See Illinois Notes Digest, Vols. XI to XV, same topic and section number.

Statement of the Case.

Action by N. Mazzarella against Olives Kamberos to recover fifty dollars claimed to be due to plaintiff for goods sold and delivered to defendant. Defendant filed a statement of set-off or counterclaim for seventy dollars which he claimed to be due to him from plaintiff in a transaction unconnected with plaintiff's cause of action. From a judgment in favor of defendant for twenty dollars, entered on a finding against plaintiff on defendant's claim of set-off, plaintiff brings error.

CAIROLI GIGLIOTTI, for plaintiff in error.

No appearance for defendant in error.

MR. JUSTICE GRIDLEY delivered the opinion of the court.

Abstract of the Decision.

1. MUNICIPAL COURT OF CHICAGO, § 26*—*presumption in the absence of statement of facts, etc.* In the absence of a statement of facts, stenographic report or bill of exceptions, presumed that there was sufficient evidence to warrant the finding and judgment.

2. MUNICIPAL COURT OF CHICAGO, § 26*—*what transcript of record must disclose.* Error of court in denying plaintiff's motions to strike defendant's statement of set-off from the files cannot be considered where the transcript of the record does not disclose that such motion and ruling were made.

3. SET-OFF AND RECOUPMENT, § 38*—*burden of proof.* Burden of proof is upon defendant to establish the existence and validity of his claim of set-off by a preponderance of the evidence.

*See Illinois Notes Digest, Vols. XI to XV, same topic and section number.

**Helen Iles, Plaintiff in Error, v. Inter Ocean News-
paper Company, Defendant in Error.**

Gen. No. 18,310.   (Not to be reported in full.)

Error to the Superior Court of Cook county; the Hon. PAUL MC-
WILLIAMS, Judge, presiding. Heard in this court at the March term,
1912. Reversed and remanded. Opinion filed December 22, 1913.

Statement of the Case.

Action by Helen Iles against the Inter Ocean Newspaper Company to recover damages for an alleged
libel concerning plaintiff published in the newspaper
of the defendant. From a judgment of not guilty,
plaintiff brings error.

CHARLES C. SPENCER, for plaintiff in error.

JAMES J. BARBOUR, for defendant in error.

MR. PRESIDING JUSTICE BAKER delivered the opinion
of the court.

Abstract of the Decision.

1. LIBEL AND SLANDER, § 140*—*requisites of pleadings in justification*. In an action for libel, a plea or notice justifying the words
as true must aver the truth of the very charge.

2. ·LIBEL AND SLANDER, § 123*—*matters provable under the issues.*
In an action for libel where defendant pleads only the general
issue and gives notice of special matters, testimony offered by defendant as to the acts, conduct and language of plaintiff not mentioned in the notice of special matters is not admissible.

3. LIBEL AND SLANDER, § 143*—*when evidence of character of
plaintiff admissible*. In an action for libel, evidence of general bad
reputation of plaintiff is admissible under the general issue in
mitigation of damages, but it is a general rule that the character of
a party cannot be impeached by proof of special acts.

4. LIBEL AND SLANDER, § 174*—*when admission of evidence of
conduct of plaintiff is error*. Permitting a witness for defendant
to testify to disgraceful acts and conduct on the part of plaintiff

*See Illinois Notes Digest, Vols. XI to XV, same topic and section number.

occurring more than two years after the publication of the alleged libel, *held* error.

5. LIBEL AND SLANDER, § 123*—*when matters occurring after the publication inadmissible.* Evidence of facts occurring more than two years after the publication of the alleged libel does not tend to show the truth of the publication nor is it admissible in mitigation of damages.

6. LIBEL AND SLANDER, § 146*—*when proof of the truth of the publication insufficient.* In an action for libel, where the principal charge in the publication was that plaintiff was a boy disguised as a girl, proof that plaintiff was masculine in her behavior and guilty of acts indicating an undue affection for women, *held* not to amount to proof of the truth of the publication.

7. LIBEL AND SLANDER, § 160*—*questions for court.* The purport of the publication is a question of law for the court.

8. WITNESSES, § 210*—*form of questions on cross-examination.* It is the province of counsel on cross-examination to ask questions, not to state facts. A question so framed that the answer "No sir" would deny only a part of a question is improper.

9. WITNESSES, § 210*—*what questions on cross-examinations are improper.* In an action for libel, question asked of plaintiff on cross-examination concerning whether plaintiff's mother had been married eight times, *held* improper.

John F. Devine, Administrator, Appellant, v. Northwestern Elevated Railroad Company, Appellee.

Gen. No. 18,328.   (Not to be reported in full.)

Appeal from the Superior Court of Cook county; the Hon. JOHN McNUTT, Judge, presiding. Heard in this court at the March term, 1912. Affirmed. Opinion filed December 22, 1913.

Statement of the Case.

Action by John F. Devine, administrator of Josephine Welter, deceased, against Northwestern Elevated Railroad Company, a corporation, to recover damages for the death of deceased alleged to have been caused by being struck by one of defendant's

Devine v. Northwestern Elevated R. Co., 184 Ill. App. 64.

cars at a street crossing. From a judgment in favor of defendant, plaintiff brings error.

O'Donnell, Dillon & Toolen, for appellant.

Addison L. Gardner for appellee.

Mr. Presiding Justice Baker delivered the opinion of the court.

Abstract of the Decision.

1. Trial, § 268*—*right to special findings.* In any case in which the jury renders a general verdict they must, on the request of a party, be required to find specially upon any material question or questions of fact.

2. Negligence, § 247*—*right to special finding with reference to question of due care of plaintiff.* In an action for damages for negligently causing death, defendant is entitled both to an instruction to find for defendant if deceased was guilty of negligence contributing to the accident and also to a special finding whether deceased was in the exercise of proper care and caution at the time of the accident.

3. Negligence, § 250*—*when failure of instruction to define care required of plaintiff, not reversible error.* Failure of instructions on question of due care of plaintiff to define "due and proper care and caution" and "ordinary care," *held* not reversible error where it is doubtful whether any attempted definition of the words used would have made their meaning clearer.

4. Negligence, § 250*—*when omission in instruction not reversible error.* Omission of an instruction to state that the failure by the deceased to exercise due and proper care which would prevent a recovery for plaintiff is limited to cases where such failure caused or contributed to the injury and death of deceased, *held* not reversible error.

5. Negligence, § 247*—*when error in excluding questions asked on cross-examination not reversible error.* Error in sustaining objections to questions asked on cross-examination concerning defendant's negligence, *held* not reversible error in view of a special finding of jury that deceased was not in the exercise of due care at the time of the accident.

*See Illinois Notes Digest, Vols. XI to XV, same topic and section number.

Anna Hoffman, Defendant in Error, v. Wellington T. Stewart et al., trading as Col. W. A. Thompson Co., Inc., Plaintiffs in Error.

Gen. No. 18,332.

1. PARTNERSHIP, § 269*—*persons liable as partners on contracts made prior to formation of partnership.* Persons advancing money under an agreement to join with another in a theatrical business previously conducted by the latter, the parties having in contemplation the organization of a corporation which was never in fact organized, *held* liable as partners on a prior contract for the services of one of the players.

2. PARTNERSHIP, § 269*—*rule as to liability of incoming partner on prior contracts.* Though, as a rule, a person who enters into a partnership with another does not become liable to the creditors of his partner for anything done before he became a partner, there are exceptions to the rule. One is that where a contract made by a person or firm remains executory until a partnership is created or a new partner is admitted into the firm, and such contract, while it remains executory, is adopted by the incoming partner, who acquires all the benefit as if he had been a partner in the original transaction, a promise may be implied to assume the liability of the partner or firm on such contract.

Error to the Municipal Court of Chicago; the Hon. JOSEPH Z. UHLIR, Judge, presiding. Heard in this court at the March term, 1912. Affirmed. Opinion filed December 22, 1913.

Statement by the Court. The plaintiff, Anna Hoffman, recovered in the Municipal Court a judgment against Thompson, Stewart and Marhoefer for one hundred and three dollars for services as prima donna at the Angelus Theatre rendered from September 2 to October 1, 1911, at forty-five dollars a week, less a credit of eighty-seven dollars, to reverse which Stewart and Marhoefer prosecute this writ of error.

July 18, 1911, plaintiff and defendant Thompson entered into a contract in writing, wherein it was agreed that plaintiff should render services to Thompson as prima donna for a period of not less than ten months, commencing September 2, 1911; that Thompson should pay her therefor forty-five dollars per week and that the contract would be terminated by giving two weeks' notice. Thompson did business under the name of the Thompson Opera Company and had a lease of the theatre, contracts with players for the season beginning September 2, advertising matter, programs for the first performance, etc. About August 25 he decided to change the name of his theatrical business from the Thompson Opera Company to the Col. W. A. Thompson Company, incorporated, and caused an application for a license to form a corporation under that name to be prepared and forwarded to the Secretary of State. He found, as the day fixed for the opening approached, that he could not open unless he secured a considerable sum of money, and said to Stewart that he wanted to get some one to join him in the venture. Through Stewart he met Marhoefer, and the three entered into a written contract dated September 1, which recited that Thompson had a lease of the Angelus Theatre and was the owner of the Thompson Opera Company, and provided that Thompson should be president and general manager of the company at a salary of fifty dollars per week, and Stewart treasurer at a salary of twenty dollars per week; that the funds received from the business should be deposited in a bank and drawn out on checks signed by Thompson and countersigned by Stewart; that it was understood that Thompson had invested "in this proposition" sixteen hundred dollars, Stewart fifteen hundred dollars, and Thompson and Stewart represented to Marhoefer that on the "investment" by him of fifteen hundred dollars that said sum, together with the sums invested by them, would pay the debts "incurred in this enterprise" up to the date of said agreement; that it was further agreed that the fifteen hundred dollars "hereby invested" by Marhoefer should be a first lien on the property of the Thompson Opera Company and the leasehold of said theatre; that Thompson should re-

ceive three thousand dollars of the capital stock of
the Thompson Opera Company, Stewart fifteen hundred dollars and Marhoefer fifteen hundred dollars,
and that the remaining four thousand dollars of the
capital stock of said company should be treasury
stock.   Stewart and Marhoefer each paid fifteen hundred dollars, which was deposited in a bank to the
credit of the Col. W. A. Thompson Co., incorporated,
and drawn out on checks signed in the name of that
company by W. A. Thompson, President, and countersigned W. T. Stewart, Treasurer.   September 12th,
Stewart and Marhoefer advanced seventeen hundred
and fifty dollars more and the following writing was
executed:

"CHICAGO, Sept. 12, 191—.

For and in consideration of Seventeen hundred fifty
Dollars advanced by E. H. Marhoefer & Dr. W. Stewart, in addition to what was previously advanced that
the said Marhoefer and the said Stewart are to receive ($2,000) two Thousand Dollars each of the cap-
ital stock of the Thompson Opera Co. and Col. Wm.
Thompson to receive Two Thousand Dollars in said
Co. balance of stock to remain in treasury, said Col.
Thompson to be paid a salary of one hundred dollars
per week after the said Marhoefer and the said Stewart have been repaid all moneys advanced.

W. A. THOMPSON,
EDWARD H. MARHOEFER,
W. T. STEWART."

FRED C. HARBOUR and P. H. BISHOP, for plaintiffs
in error.

G. M. PETERS, for defendant in error.

MR. PRESIDING JUSTICE BAKER delivered the opinion
of the court.

From the evidence the trial court might properly
find that the transactions between Thompson of the
one part and Stewart and Marhoefer of the other part

was not the lending of money by the latter to the former, but was the purchase by each of an interest in the theatrical business conducted by Thompson under the name of the Thompson Opera Company, and that the parties had in contemplation the organization of a corporation, of which a specified amount of the capital stock should be issued to each of said parties and the remainder should be treasury stock. No corporation was ever organized and the parties to the contract from the time it was made must be held to have been partners.

It is true that a person who enters into partnership with another does not thereby become liable to the creditors of his partner for anything done before he became a partner, yet there are exceptions to the rule. One is that where a contract made by a person or firm remains executory until a partnership is created or a new partner is admitted into the firm, and such contract, while it remains executory, is adopted by the incoming partner, who acquires all the benefit as if he had been a partner in the original transaction, a promise may be implied to assume the liability of the partner or firm on such contract. *Frazer v. Howe,* 106 Ill. 583; *Lucas v. Coulter,* 104 Ind. 81; *Watt v. Kirby,* 15 Ill. 200; *Hellsby v. Mears,* 5 B. & C. 504, 11 E. C. L. 539; *Ex parte Peele,* 6 Ves. Jr., 602-604.

In this case Stewart and Marhoefer knew that Thompson had made contracts with plaintiff and other players and knew that she and they were playing at the Angelus Theatre for the benefit of themselves and Thompson, and we think that the court might properly find that they became liable with Thompson to pay her for her services.

We think the record is free from error, and the judgment is affirmed.

Affirmed.

Joseph Haber, Appellee, v. W. A. Jones Foundry &
Machine Company, Appellant.

Gen. No. 18,350.   (Not to be reported in full.)

Appeal from the Superior Court of Cook county; the Hon. FARLIN
Q. BALL, Judge, presiding. Heard in this court at the March term,
1912. Affirmed. Opinion filed December 22, 1913.

Statement of the Case.

Action by Joseph Haber against W. A. Jones Foundry & Machine Company to recover damages for the
partial loss of plaintiff's thumb caused by being
caught in an unprotected speed gear of an iron pulley
lathe which plaintiff was operating for defendant at
the time of the injury. From a judgment in favor of
plaintiff for one thousand dollars, defendant appeals.

WINSTON, PAYNE, STRAWN & SHAW, for appellant;
EDWARD W. EVERETT, J. SIDNEY CONDIT and RUPERT
DONOVAN, of counsel.

GALLAGHER & MESSNER, for appellee.

MR. PRESIDING JUSTICE BAKER delivered the opinion
of the court.

Abstract of the Decision.

1. MASTER AND SERVANT, § 688*—*when verdict for injuries to
servant sustained by the evidence.* In an action by a servant
for injuries resulting from the defective condition of the coupling
appliances of an iron pulley lathe, a verdict for plaintiff *held* not
so clearly against the weight of the evidence that trial court erred
in denying defendant's motion for a new trial.

2. MASTER AND SERVANT, § 399*—*when servant assumes risk after
promise to repair.* Servant does not assume the risk because he
was injured more than four hours after defendant promised to
repair a defective machine. Whether plaintiff continued in employment longer than a reasonable time is a question of fact for
the jury.

The People of the State of Illinois ex rel., Maclay Hoyne, State's Attorney, Appellee, v. Michael Hennessey et al., Appellants.

Gen. No. 20,056.

1. QUO WARRANTO, § 1*—*nature of remedy.* The office of an information in the nature of a quo warranto is not to tender any issue of fact, but simply to call upon the defendant, in general terms, to show by what warrant the office or privilege is held and exercised.

2. QUO WARRANTO, § 45*—*sufficiency of plea.* The respondent, by his plea, must either disclaim or justify. If he seeks to justify he must do so fully and specifically; must show upon the face of his plea such facts as, if true, will vest in him the legal title to the office.

3. QUO WARRANTO, § 54*—*burden of proof.* The burden of proving his title rests on the respondent, and if he fails to establish his title by proof, the State is entitled to judgment against him.

4. QUO WARRANTO, § 56*—*when People entitled to judgment.* In a quo warranto proceeding where respondents attempt to justify by a plea which is traversed by a replication, failure of respondents to offer evidence in support of their plea entitles the People to a judgment against them.

Appeal from the Circuit Court of Cook county; the Hon. JOHN P. McGOORTY, Judge, presiding. Heard in this court at the October term, 1913. Affirmed. Opinion filed December 22, 1913. Rehearing denied January 5, 1914.

GEORGE E. BRANNAN, for appellants.

SAMUEL K. MARKMAN, for appellee.

MR. PRESIDING JUSTICE BAKER delivered the opinion of the court.

October 15, 1912, Wayman, State's Attorney of Cook county, filed in the Circuit Court a petition for leave to file an information in the nature of a quo warranto in the name of the People of the State of Illinois, at the relation of Draper, Welch and Pelsma, trustees of the village of Franklin Park, against Hen-

---

*See Illinois Notes Digest, Vols. XI to XV, same topic and section number.

nessey, Craig and Eiler, requiring them to show by what warrant they claimed to hold and execute respectively the office of trustee of the said village. The court granted leave to file the information and it was filed the same day. The information states that the State's Attorney for the People of the State of Illinois and in their name and by their authority, at the relation of Draper, Welch and Pelsma, gives the court to understand, etc., that Hennessey, Craig and Eiler hold and execute, without any warrant, right or lawful authority, the respective offices of village trustee of the village of Franklin Park, and prays that they may be required to answer to the People of the State of Illinois by what warrant they claim to hold and execute said offices, etc. The information was signed by the State's Attorney and bears also the name of the present attorney for appellee as "of counsel." January 15, 1913, the respondents filed what is called in the abstract a "plea of justification," to which was filed January 30 a replication in the name of the People of the State of Illinois. Neither the plea of justification nor the replication follow the form of common law pleading, but we will treat the "plea of justification" as a plea disregarding the technical distinction between a plea and answer, as was done in *People ex rel. Burgess v. Percells,* 8 Ill. (3 Gil.) 59. February 6 the respondents obtained leave to rejoin in five days and the cause was set for trial March 3. No rejoinder was filed nor was any further action taken in the case until March 25, when Hoyne, then State's Attorney, entered his appearance in lieu of Wayman, whose term had expired. On the same day a stipulation was filed signed by an assistant State's Attorney and by the attorney of the respondents, that the cause be continued to April 16, but no order continuing the cause was made by the court. March 25 the respondents moved that the cause be continued and the court postponed the trial until March 31. On that day the respondents again moved to continue the cause and the court denied their motion. Then followed various motions by respondents, including a motion to dismiss, another for leave to withdraw the answer and demur, all of which were denied. The respondents offered no evidence and the court gave judgment ousting the respondents from the office of trustee. The judgment order contains a finding that the relators were at the time of the filing of the information and still were village trustees of the village of Franklin Park, but there was no order or judgment that the relators be installed in or restored to their respective offices as trustee. From the judgment the respondents appealed to the Supreme Court and the cause was by that court transferred to this court.

No evidence was offered tending to show that the proceeding was different from what it purported to be, that is, one begun in good faith by a public officer in the name and on behalf of the People. We find no cause to reverse the judgment because the court refused to further postpone the trial of the cause under the circumstances shown by the record, nor because of the finding in the judgment order that the relators were trustees of the village of Franklin Park, nor because the court refused to dismiss the cause on the ground that the relators were represented by Mr. Markman, whose name appears on the information as of counsel for the petitioner.

The office of an information in the nature of a quo warranto is not to tender any issue of fact, but simply to call upon the defendant, in general terms, to show by what warrant the office or privilege claimed is held and exercised. The respondent by his plea must either disclaim or justify. If he seeks to justify he must do so fully and specifically; must show upon the face of his plea such facts as, if true, will vest in him the legal title to the office. The burden of proving his title rests on the respondent, and if he fails to establish his title by proof, the State is entitled to a judgment against him. In this case the respondents by their plea attempted to justify. The replication traversed the plea, the respondents offered no evidence in support of their plea and the People were entitled to a judgment against them. This conclusion makes it unnecessary to consider many of the questions argued in the briefs.

The judgment of the Circuit Court is affirmed.

Affirmed.

Frank Pinter, Defendant in Error, v. Bunte Brothers, Plaintiff in Error.

Gen. No. 18,204.   (Not to be reported in full.)

Error to the Municipal Court of Chicago; the Hon. HOSEA W. WELLS, Judge, presiding. Heard in this court at the March term, 1912. Affirmed. Opinion filed December 22, 1913.

Statement of the Case.

Action by Frank Pinter, by Frank Majcan his next friend, against Bunte Brothers, a corporation, to recover for personal injuries sustained by plaintiff while employed in a candy factory of defendant by having his thumb caught between the conveyor and sprocket wheel of a starch machine. To reverse a judgment in favor of plaintiff for one thousand dollars, defendant sues out a writ of error.

JOHN CLARK BAKER, for plaintiff in error.

GEORGE H. MEYER, for defendant in error.

MR. JUSTICE BROWN delivered the opinion of the court.

Fieldstack v. Chicago City Ry. Co., 184 Ill. App. 75.

Abstract of the Decision.

1. MASTER AND SERVANT, § 739*—*when question of assumed risk properly left to the jury.* In an action by an inexperienced servant for injuries, the question whether the plaintiff in the absence of warning and explanation understood and appreciated the danger which resulted in his injury, *held* properly left to the jury where there was no contention that the danger was not obvious, but there was a dispute and a conflict in the evidence as to what opportunities of observation and what experience plaintiff had concerning the operation of a similar machine the plaintiff used.

2. MASTER AND SERVANT, § 739*—*rule as to when assumption of risk becomes a question of law.* On question when the assumption of risk by plaintiff is for the court as a matter of law and not a question of fact to be left to the jury, rule expressed in *Grace & Hyde Co. v. Sanborn*, 124 Ill. App. 472, quoted as stating the rule of law in this State.

3. MASTER AND SERVANT, § 695*—*when verdict sustained by the evidence.* In an action by a servant for injuries sustained because of the failure of defendant to warn plaintiff of the dangers of operating a machine, a verdict for plaintiff *held* sustained by the evidence.

4. MASTER AND SERVANT, § 802*—*instructions as to warning of servants of dangers.* Instructions as to duty of employer to instruct servants of immature age as to the dangers of the employment and as to the care required to be exercised by such servant, *held* proper in connection with other instructions on the subjects of contributory negligence and assumption of risks.

5. MASTER AND SERVANT, § 1491*—*when exclusion of evidence offered not reversible error.* In an action by a servant for personal injuries, exclusion of evidence offered by the defendant to the effect that plaintiff, though an orphan, had friends rather than was destitute of them, *held* not reversible error.

Blondon Fieldstack, Plaintiff in Error, v. Chicago City Railway Company, Defendant in Error.

Gen. No. 18,284.   (Not to be reported in full.)

Error to the Superior Court of Cook county; the Hon. CHARLES A. McDONALD, Judge, presiding. Heard in this court at the March term, 1912. Affirmed. Opinion filed December 22, 1913.

*See Illinois Notes Digest, Vols. XI to XV, same topic and section number.

Statement of the Case.

Action by Blondon Fieldstack against Chicago City Railway Company to recover damages for injuries sustained by plaintiff while alighting from one of defendant's street cars at a street intersection and alleged to have been caused by the slanting and slippery condition of the street leading down to the street car track. To reverse a judgment of *nil capiat* and for costs against the plaintiff, plaintiff prosecutes this writ of error.

RICHARD J. FINN, for plaintiff in error.

JOHN E. KEHOE and WATSON J. FERRY, for defendant in error; LEONARD A. BUSBY, of counsel

MR. JUSTICE BROWN delivered the opinion of the court.

Abstract of the Decision.

1. CARRIERS, § 493*—*when instructions not misleading.* In an action for injuries sustained by plaintiff while alighting from a street car, instructions proper on the subject of due care on the part of plaintiff *held* not objectionable as misleading because they were drawn on the theory that the negligence charged is the negligence of the defendant in the operation of its car.

2. CARRIERS, § 482*—*when instruction not reversibly erroneous or misleading.* Instruction which begins, "It is not every accident that makes a railway company liable for damages to the person injured by its cars," *held* not reversibly erroneous or misleading because it speaks of a person "injured by its cars" when plaintiff was "injured by the car" although the negligence charged was not in its operation.

3. CARRIERS, § 493*—*when instruction on care required of plaintiff not erroneous.* Instruction requiring the plaintiff to exercise prudence and vigilance for his own safety, *held* not misleading and reversibly erroneous because it contains the word "vigilance."

4. CARRIERS, § 493*—*when instruction on care required of plaintiff not erroneous.* Instruction not directing a verdict but stating an abstract proposition of law defining "ordinary care" and referring the definition "to the situation and position" a person "is

about to take," in which he "finds himself," *held* not erroneous as not confining the plaintiff's duty to exercise care to the time and place of the accident.

5. INSTRUCTIONS, § 48*—*when instruction on weight of testimony not erroneous.* Instruction relating to the weight of testimony containing the expression "it is the duty of the jury to receive the testimony of such witness," *held* not objectionable because the word "receive" means "admit as true."

6. INSTRUCTIONS, § 82*—*when not improper as mentioning the name of a witness.* Fact that plaintiff's name is introduced in an instruction as to the weight of the testimony, *held* not objectionable where plaintiff's name is not mentioned as a witness.

N. M. Ingham, Defendant in Error, v. Merchants Lithographing Company, Plaintiff in Error.

Gen. No. 18,309.   (Not to be reported in full.)

Error to the Municipal Court of Chicago; the Hon. THOMAS F. SCULLY, Judge, presiding. Heard in this court at the March term, 1912. Affirmed. Opinion filed December 22, 1913.

Statement of the Case.

Action by N. M. Ingham, trading as N. M. Ingham & Company, against Merchants Lithographing Company for the price of certain paper sold by plaintiff to defendant. To reverse a judgment in favor of plaintiff for $306.13, defendant prosecutes a writ of error.

HELMER, MOULTON & WHITMAN, for plaintiff in error.

LOUIS J. PIERSON, for defendant in error.

MR. JUSTICE BROWN delivered the opinion of the court.

*See Illinois Notes Digest, Vols. XI to XV, same topic and section number.

Abstract of the Decision.

1. SALES, § 401*—*when evidence insufficient to show a warranty.* In an action for the price of paper sold and delivered to defendant in which the defendant claims a set-off for breach of warranty, a finding against the defendant on the question whether there was any warranty of the character of the paper and a failure of such warranty, *held* sustained by the evidence.

2. SALES, § 282*—*when evidence insufficient to prove an implied warranty.* A finding that there is no implied warranty of the adequacy of paper sold for the use designed will not be disturbed where there is nothing to show that the seller or her salesman was better qualified to judge of the particular fitness of the paper than was the buyer, and moreover there were questions of fact whether the seller knew for what purpose the paper was bought, and even whether it was sufficiently proved that it was not reasonably fit for that purpose.

Francis Peabody, Defendant in Error, v. Daniel Lynch and John Dionne, Plaintiffs in Error.

Gen. No. 18,316.

1. DAMAGES, § 49*—*measure of, for injury to automobile.* In an action for damage done to an automobile, the reasonable cost of repair is the proper measure of damages, and such cost of repair would be what an automobile repair man would, in accordance with the market and usual rates, charge for the work and materials necessary.

2. DAMAGES, § 172*—*when evidence of actual cost of repairs admissible.* In an action for damage to an automobile, evidence of what was actually paid for repairs is only admissible as showing what the reasonable cost of repairs would be.

3. EVIDENCE, § 373*—*when opinion of repair man as to cost of repairs admissible.* Automobile repair man who supervised the repairs may testify as to what would be the reasonable cost of repairs of automobile.

Error to the Municipal Court of Chicago; the Hon. HENRY C. BEITLER, Judge, presiding. Heard in this court at the March term, 1912. Affirmed. Opinion filed December 22, 1913.

---

*See Illinois Notes Digest, Vols. XI to XV, same topic and section number.

MAYER, MEYER, AUSTRIAN & PLATT, for plaintiffs in error.

ROBERT J. FOLONIE, for defendant in error.

MR. JUSTICE BROWN delivered the opinion of the court.

The defendant in error, the plaintiff below, secured a judgment against the plaintiffs in error, the defendants below, for $225.75 for damage done to his automobile through the negligence of said defendants. This writ of error is brought to reverse this judgment. The only point argued is that thus summed up in the brief of the plaintiffs in error:

"We respectfully submit that the testimony of Mr. Politz should have been excluded; that it was admittedly incompetent except as expert testimony; that no expert evidence was admissible on the question of the cost of repairs, there being better evidence available; that he was not properly qualified and could not properly have testified as an expert even if expert evidence had been admissible. Excluding his testimony, we submit that there is no evidence of damage and can be no recovery, at least none beyond nominal damages."

We do not think these objections are well taken.

For the purposes of our review it is established that the injury to plaintiff's automobile was caused by plaintiff's negligence. The reasonable cost of repair of that injury was the proper measure of damages. That reasonable cost of repair was what an automobile repair man would, in accordance with the market and usual rates, charge for the work and material necessary. This was what Politz testified to. We think he was eminently qualified from his proved experience to be a judge of it. In addition he supervised the repairs. What was actually paid would only be admissible in such a case as this as showing what the reasonable cost would be. *Travis v. Pierson*, 43 Ill. App. 579.

The judgment is affirmed.

Affirmed.

Wyllys K. Smith, Defendant in Error, v. The Baltimore & Ohio Chicago Terminal Railroad Company, Plaintiff in Error.

Gen. No. 18,326.

1. RAILROADS, § 874*—*when evidence insufficient to negligence in maintaining defective gate at farm crossing.* In an action against a railroad company to recover the value of a bull killed on the defendant's right of way, alleged to have been caused by failure of defendant to maintain a sufficient gate at a farm crossing in compliance with the Act of 1874, J. & A. ¶ 8811, the evidence *held* insufficient to sustain a judgment for plaintiff, where it appeared that the bull escaped to railroad track by lifting the hinge end of the gate so as to sever its connection with post, the evidence also showing that the gate with its fastenings was standard in make.

2. RAILROADS, § 292*—*sufficiency of fence.* Act of 1874, J. & A. ¶ 8811, requiring railroads to erect and maintain a suitable and sufficient fence, does not require such a fence as will withstand breachy cattle, nor does it require gates at farm crossings to be fastened so that it would be impossible for stock to open them.

Error to the Municipal Court of Chicago; the Hon. J. J. COOKE, Judge, presiding. Heard in this court at the March term, 1912. Reversed and judgment here. Opinion filed December 22, 1913.

JESSE B. BARTON, for plaintiff in error.

WILSON & MAY, for defendant in error.

MR. JUSTICE BROWN delivered the opinion of the court.

The defendant in error in this case (plaintiff below) recovered a judgment for four hundred and fifty dollars against the plaintiff in error (the defendant below) in the Municipal Court of Chicago on January 30, 1912. The amount of the judgment was made up of three hundred and fifty dollars, which was the conceded value of a bull belonging to the plaintiff, and one hundred dollars attorney's fees allowed for the prosecution of the case. This case was tried by the court without a jury.

The bull belonged to the plaintiff. It escaped from a farm adjoining the defendant's right of way and railroad two miles north of the Chicago Heights station in Cook county. It went upon the tracks of the defendant and was killed by a train which struck and ran over it.

The action was brought under the "Act in relation to fencing and operating railroads," approved March 31, 1874. (J. & A. ¶ 8811.) This act is as follows:

"Every railroad corporation shall within six months after any part of its line is open for use erect and thereafter maintain fences on both sides of its road or so much thereof as is open for use, suitable and sufficient to prevent cattle, horses, sheep, hogs or other stock from getting on such railroad, except at the crossings of public roads and highways, and within such portion of cities and incorporated towns and villages as are or may be hereafter laid out and platted into lots and blocks, with gates or bars at the farm crossings of such railroads, which farm crossings shall be constructed by such corporation when and where the same may become necessary, for the use of the proprietors of the lands adjoining such railroad; and shall also construct, where the same has not already been done, and thereafter maintain at all road crossings now existing or hereafter established, cattle guards suitable and sufficient to prevent cattle, horses, sheep, hogs and other stock from getting on such railroads; and when such fences or cattle guards are not kept in good repair such railroad corporations shall be liable for all damages which may be done by the agents, engines or cars of such corporation to such cattle, horses, sheep, hogs, or other stock thereon, and reasonable attorney's fees in any court wherein suit is brought for such damages or to which the same may be appealed, but where such fences and guards have been duly made and kept in good repair such railroad corporation shall not be liable for any such damages unless negligently or wilfully done."

The statement of claim by the plaintiff alleged that the Railroad Company failed to maintain on the side of its right of way "a fence suitable and sufficient to prevent cattle from getting on said railroad" and failed "to maintain gates or bars at a certain farm crossing of such railroad" * * * "suitable and sufficient to prevent cattle from getting on such railroad," by reason of which failures the bull was run over.

The Railroad Company answered that it did erect and maintain on the side of its right of way adjoining the farm in which the bull was pastured "a good, suitable and sufficient fence as required by the laws of the State of Illinois," and that "said fence and gate were in good repair at the time the bull in question got upon the right of way of said railroad company."

The counsel for defendant in error says that the question before us is purely one of fact. We think it one of mixed law and fact. The Company is made by the law liable for killing of the bull in question if it did not *keep*, in good repair, such a fence along its right of way as is provided for by the statute, and the bull got to the track in consequence. "Such a fence" is thus described: A fence (with gates or bars at the farm crossings) "suitable and sufficient to prevent cattle, horses, sheep, hogs or other stock from getting on such railroad." Of course if the bull reached the track notwithstanding the Railroad Company had performed its duty in this matter, because some human agency had taken a gate from its hinges and thrown it on the ground during the night in which the bull was killed and before the Company had notice of that situation, the Company is not liable. *Illinois Cent. R. Co. v. Swearingen*, 47 Ill. 206; *Chicago & A. R. Co. v. Umphenour*, 69 Ill. 198; *Indianapolis & St. L. R. Co. v. Hall*, 88 Ill. 368; *Chicago & A. R. Co. v. Saunders*, 85 Ill. 288.

The defendant in this case maintains that the evidence that this was not the fact in the case at bar was not sufficient. The bull was found dead on the track on the early morning of October 28, 1910, and a gate in the fence about one hundred feet away was hanging by the latch end to the fence post, but was twisted, with the hinge end off the hinges and down on the ground. There was space enough for the bull to walk through between the fence post at the hinge end and the end of the unhinged and overthrown gate. The man who found him said: "I examined the gate and from the marks and scratches it looked to me as if the bull had got his horns caught in the gate and had thrown the gate from its hinges and then walked out on the tracks and was killed by some train or engine."

From the evidence it looked the same way to the court below, and looks so to us, and we may consider this therefore a decision of fact by the court below, approved by us. But this leaves still a question of mixed law and fact to be decided, namely,—Was the fence including the gate "suitable and sufficient to prevent cattle, horses, sheep, hogs or other stock from getting on the railroad?" If "suitable and sufficient" were to be taken according to the strict letter, it might be properly said, as the counsel for the defendant in error does say in his argument, *res ipsa loquitur*. The fence did not actually prevent the bull from getting on the railroad; therefore in this strict literal sense it was not "sufficient" to do so. Used in that sense "sufficient" means "equal to the end desired." But to its use in the statute in question and in its predecessors the Supreme Court of Illinois has applied the "rule of reason," and given to it in connection with its accompanying word "suitable" in the act much the same meaning as this latter word, namely, "fit," "satisfactory." Thus Judge Caton says in *Illinois Cent. R. Co. v. Dickerson*, 27 Ill. 55, speaking in a case where a fence was up at nightfall and there was a gap in it in the morning through which gap cattle had passed to the tracks during the night: "When up, the proof does not show that the fence at this point was not good and sufficient. It cannot be the duty of the railroad company to keep a patrol all night the whole length of their road to see that the fence is not broken down by breachy cattle, by evil men, or by a whirlwind. If the company use all reasonable diligence to keep up the fence, that is all the law requires, and it is not guilty of negligence in that particular.''

This language at least implies that ''sufficient'' in the statute did not mean sufficient to withstand ''breachy'' cattle.

The same general doctrine is that applied in *Illinois Cent. R. Co. v. Swearingen,* 47 Ill. 206; *Indianapolis & St. L. R. Co. v. Hall,* 88 Ill. 368, and *Chicago & A. R. Co. v. Umphenour,* 69 Ill. 198; although in this last case the Court indicates that the mere fact that animals had not broken bounds during a considerable time was not proof that the fence was ''sufficient,'' which was to be determined by the character of the fence.

Judge Higbee in the Appellate Court of the Third District, says of a gate which was lifted by a horse so that a hook was released and the gate opened:

''The company was not required to fasten the gate so that it was impossible for stock to open it under any and all circumstances. It had a right to use the fastenings commonly adopted in the country by persons reasonably prudent and careful, and regarded by them as safe, for the purpose. It is not likely that many gates could be found in city or country, fastened with latch or hook, that it would be impossible to open by the nose or teeth of a horse if dexterously applied for that purpose. To hold that the company must provide against such contingencies, would be to adopt a standard of diligence that would make it an insurer of the sufficiency of its fences under all circumstances. This the law does not require.'' *Chicago & A. Ry. Co. v. Buck,* 14 Ill. App. 394.

This language is as applicable to the horns of a bull as to ''the nose or teeth of a horse,'' and while not authoritative to us commends itself to our sense of reason and justice. To the same effect is the language of the Appellate Court of the Second District in *Chicago, B. & Q. R. Co. v. Evans,* 45 Ill. App. 79.

In the case at bar the gate and its fastenings were thus described in the evidence. There was no serious dispute about them. The gate was made of four boards and was about sixteen feet long and four feet high. It was "standard" as to hinges and fastenings, as the carpenter for the Railroad, who built it, testified. It had been considered proper for its purpose for four years before, and had performed that purpose of keeping cattle confined satisfactorily. The bull which came through seems to have been restrained by it for a year or more, certainly all the summer before. On its hinge end it was attached to a cedar post six feet high by two hinges, each made thus: An iron bolt driven into the post was turned up to make an upright of about two inches and around that upright a loop of strap iron about two inches wide attached to the gate made the connection and allowed the gate to swing when opened at the other end. It is a little difficult to follow with exactness the descriptions and measurements given in the testimony, simple as the construction evidently was. But it is quite plain that the gate and the hinges were of a common type known in farm gates. There is no reason to doubt the Railroad carpenter's assertion that the gate was "standard." It remained the same at the time of the trial as it was before the escape of the bull. The gate could not have been thrown down from the hinge end unless it had been lifted a matter of at least two inches. It is a matter of common knowledge that while cattle do not as a rule lift latches and raise gates off their hinges, there is here and there a "breachy" animal who exercises apparently almost human ingenuity in doing it. It is not for such cattle that the railroad company has to provide. It seems to us evident from the testimony in this case that the bull here in question was for the nonce at any rate a "breachy" animal. He could in all probability have

lifted the gate four inches as well as two, if disposed
to throw it down and intelligent enough (as he seems
to have been) to know how. There was no evidence,
we think, of a failure of the Railroad Company to
perform its statutory duty, and therefore none to justify the finding and judgment of the trial judge.

The judgment of the Municipal Court of Chicago is
reversed, and a judgment of *nil capiat* will be entered here.

Reversed and judgment here.

Max Gittelson et al., Plaintiffs in Error, v. Fannie Reichman and Samuel Reichman, Defendants in Error.

Gen. No. 18,329.   (Not to be reported in full.)

Error to the Municipal Court of Chicago; the Hon. WILLIAM N.
GEMMILL, Judge, presiding. Heard in this court at the March term,
1912. Reversed and remanded. Opinion filed December 22, 1913.

Statement of the Case.

Action by Max Gittelson, J. Bloom, I. Breskin and
S. Goldberg against Fannie Reichman and Samuel
Reichman for brokery commissions on a sale or exchange of real estate. To reverse a judgment of *nil
capiat* and for costs against the plaintiffs, the plaintiffs prosecute a writ of error.

HARRY M. FISHER, for plaintiffs in error.

ALBERT MARTIN, for defendants in error.

MR. JUSTICE BROWN delivered the opinion of the
court.

Abstract of the Decision.

JUDGMENT, § 405*—*when decree in equity no bar to action for brokers' commissions.* In an action to recover commissions for the sale or exchange of real estate wherein the plaintiffs have established a *prima facie* case, a decree in a cause in equity to which the plaintiffs were not parties, nor by which they were bound because in privity with or represented by the actual parties, *held* not admissible to bar plaintiffs' right to recover where there is no evidence connecting the plaintiffs with the decree so as to make it binding on them.

Alfred A. Hallgren, Appellee, v. John E. Cowles et al., Appellants.

Gen. No. 18,843.   (Not to be reported in full.)

Appeal from the Circuit Court of Cook county; the Hon. KICKHAM SCANLAN, Judge, presiding. Heard in this court at the March term, 1912. Affirmed. Opinion filed December 22, 1913. Rehearing denied January 5, 1914.

Statement of the Case.

Petition for a mechanic's lien filed by Alfred A. Hallgren against John E. Cowles and George M. Groves, owners of an apartment building, constructed for them by the complainant. Other defendants to the petition were the trustee in a trust deed conveying the property and the unknown owners of notes secured thereby. The cause was referred to a master who, after taking the proofs reported, recommended a lien for four thousand three hundred dollars with costs. From a decree entered in accordance with the recommendations of the master, defendants, who were owners of the premises, appeal.

BITHER, GOFF & FRANCIS, for appellants.

HENRY M. HAGEN, for appellee.

MR. JUSTICE MCSURELY delivered the opinion of the court.

Abstract of the Decision.

1. MECHANICS' LIENS, § 49*—*when contractor not accountable for delay in completion of building.* In a proceeding to enforce a mechanic's lien contractor *held* not liable for any damage caused by delay in completing the work, where the evidence shows that the work was stopped by the city authorities on account of the building plans, and that the owner by ordering frequent changes caused much delay, and the decorating was postponed at owner's request so that the tenants might select their own decorations.

2. MECHANICS' LIENS, § 212*—*when abstract of record must set out provisions of contract.* On appeal from a decree enforcing a mechanics' lien, an objection that no architect's certificate for final payment was ever issued, as required by the contract before final payment would become due, cannot be entertained where such provision in the contract does not appear in the abstract of record.

3. BUILDING AND CONSTRUCTION CONTRACTS, § 44*—*when owner is entitled to no substantial damages for delay.* Where a contract requires an apartment building to be completed on August 1, but building is not completed until September 22, *held*, to be no substantial loss in the rental value of the building by reason of the delay, where the evidence shows that the ordinary renting seasons commence on May 1 and October 1, and that it is customary in renting flats in August or September to give concessions in the matter of rent to October 1st.

4. APPEAL AND ERROR, § 1214*—*when errors affecting parties not appealing, not considered.* A decree enforcing a mechanic's lien will not be reversed for the reason that no default was entered against the defendants described in the bill as unknown holders and owners of notes secured by a trust deed conveying the premises, or for failure of the trial court to fix the rights of such parties in the decree, where such party defendants are not parties to the appeal.

*See Illinois Notes Digest, Vols. XI to XV, same topic and section number.

Annie Dunne, Appellee, v. Frank Bernardy, Appellant.

Gen. No. 18,346.   (Not to be reported in full.)

Appeal from the Circuit Court of Cook county; the Hon. SAMUEL
C. STOUGH, Judge, presiding. Heard in this court at the March
term, 1912. Affirmed. Opinion filed December 22, 1913.

Statement of the Case.

Action by Annie Dunne against Frank Bernardy
to recover damages resulting from defendant spitting
tobacco juice on plaintiff's face and clothes during an
altercation between defendant and plaintiff's husband,
in which plaintiff attempted to be peacemaker. From
a judgment in favor of plaintiff for one hundred and
fifty dollars defendant appeals.

FRANK F. ARING, for appellant.

JOHN D. CASEY and ELMER & COHEN, for appellee.

MR. JUSTICE McSURELY delivered the opinion of the
court.

Abstract of the Decision.

1. ASSAULT AND BATTERY, § 14*—*sufficiency of the evidence.* In
an action against defendant for spitting tobacco juice on the face
and clothes of plaintiff, a verdict for plaintiff on conflicting evidence sustained.

2. APPEAL AND ERROR, § 1514*—*when inflammatory remarks of
counsel not reversible error.* Inflammatory remark of plaintiff's
counsel in his speech to the jury though highly improper and
would justify a reversal if it was not manifest that their intemper-
ance worked a disadvantage to the plaintiff rather than to the
defendant, *held* not reversible error, it appearing from the amount
of *ad damnum* in plaintiff's declaration, five thousand dollars, and
the amount of the verdict, one hundred and fifty dollars, that the
jury was not influenced to the prejudice of the defendant.

*See Illinois Notes Digest, Vols. XI to XV, same topic and section number.

CASES

DETERMINED IN THE

THIRD DISTRICT

OF THE

APPELLATE COURTS OF ILLINOIS

DURING THE YEAR 1913.

R. M. Owen & Company, Appellant, v. Walter E. Johnson et al., Appellees.

1. CORPORATIONS, § 755*—*when service upon a sales agent of nonresident corporation is sufficient.* In an action against a nonresident corporation engaged in the selling of motor cars in this State, service upon a sales agent appointed by a general agent and recognized by the corporation as such agent, *held* sufficient under R. S. c. 110, § 8, J. & A. ¶ 8545.

2. APPEAL AND ERROR, § 1332*—*conclusiveness of default judgment.* On appeal from a decree dismissing a bill to set aside a default judgment and to enjoin its collection, it cannot be urged that there was no legal liability or consideration upon which to base the judgment, where the question was to some extent inquired into when the default was taken and on one of the issues made by the bill and answer the master found the amount of the judgment was due and the court approved the master's finding.

Appeal from the Circuit Court of McLean county; the Hon. COLOSTIN D. MYERS, Judge, presiding. Heard in this court at the October term, 1912. Affirmed. Opinion filed April 18, 1913. Rehearing denied October 15, 1913. *Certiorari* denied by Supreme Court (making opinion final).

JOHN STAPLETON and CHARLES L. CAPEN, for appellant.

A. M. HESTER and WELTY, STERLING & WHITMORE, for appellees.

---

*See Illinois Notes Digest, Vols. XI to XV, same topic and section number.

MR. JUSTICE CREIGHTON delivered the opinion of the court.

A brief history of the proceedings had in relation to the litigation in question is, that in the early summer of 1908 the appellees, Walter E. Johnston and William Hurt, partners under the firm name and style of Johnston & Hurt, entered into a contract with O. C. Owen, who represented himself to be the general agent of R. M. Owen & Co., a nonresident corporation, for the sale of Reo motor cars, as sole agents for McLean county, Illinois. The condition upon which they were appointed sole agents was, that each of them should buy a car, and they were to receive as compensation twenty per cent. of the list price of the cars sold by them, including their own cars. Johnston & Hurt bought and paid for and received their two cars as per agreement, and commenced a canvass of the county for the sale of cars, and succeeded in closing sales for two or three of such cars.

Shortly after Johnston & Hurt began work under their contract, and after they had closed deals for two or three cars, one W. G. Bell, who had been instructing them under the direction of O. C. Owen, opened up selling Reo cars on his own account in McLean county, and received from O. C. Owen, who was agent for appellant in Illinois, and sold and delivered such cars to citizens of McLean county.

On October 28, 1908, said Johnston & Hurt commenced suit in the McLean Circuit Court against the appellant to recover commissions upon sales of cars made by them individually and by said Bell, and service of summons was had and the following return made thereon: "Executed this writ the 28th day of October, 1908, by reading and delivering a true copy of the same to W. G. Bell, local agent for the within named defendant, R. M. Owen & Co., incorporated, the president, vice-president, treasurer, secretary, superintendent or other officer not found in my county."

The cause was continued until the April term, 1909,

and, defendant failing to plead, default was entered and judgment rendered in the sum of $1,747.05, and costs of suit, on the 2d day of July, 1909. At the November term, 1910, of the said court, appellants entered a limited appearance and filed a motion to vacate the said judgment, on the ground that W. G. Bell was not an agent for appellant at the time of the service upon him and never had been such agent. No question is raised as to the correctness of the demand against them. Again, at the February term, 1911, of the said court, a like motion was made, under a limited appearance, and on the same grounds, and no question was there raised as to the correctness of the demand in this motion. Each of the said motions were denied and exceptions taken as to the denial of the latter motion, and an appeal prayed from the said order of the court,

On April 28, 1911, the bill in chancery before us for consideration was filed by appellants in the McLean Circuit Court, reciting, among other things, the suit by appellees Johnston & Hurt against appellant, the service upon said Bell, who, as they claim was not an agent, the rendition of the judgment against them and that they had no information of the suit until December, 1910; that they do not owe this debt or any part thereof, and pray to have the judgment set aside, vacated and that they be granted a new trial in said cause, and that appellees be restrained and enjoined from proceeding further with a cause pending in Lansing, Michigan, or any other place, or from taking out execution or any other writ on said judgment, and with prayer for general relief.

To this bill answers were filed on behalf of all appellees, averring that appellants were justly indebted to them for commissions under the contract for the sale of automobiles in McLean county, in the sum of the said judgment referred to in the complainant's bill; and that W. G. Bell was the agent of the appellants and was at work for them in McLean county at the time of the service of the summons; that before the filing of this bill said judgment was assigned by Johnston & Hurt to George H. Marshall, of St. Johns, Michigan, and that he is, and has been since the said assignment, the legal owner of said judgment. Appellees further deny that they are now, or have at any time, been seeking by suit or otherwise, to collect said judgment off of and from the appellants since the date of the said assignment.

Issue being joined, the cause was referred to the master in chancery to take and report the proof, together with his conclusions of both law and fact.

The master reported that he took the testimony of all witnesses presented by the respective parties, attached same to his report, and found that the court had jurisdiction of the subject-matter and that W. G. Bell, the person upon whom service was had in the common law action, was the agent of the appellant; that the amount of the judgment rendered in the common law proceeding was correct.

Objections to the report of the master were duly filed by the appellant, and were overruled, and exceptions entered by appellant to the report of the master were, by the court, overruled and the report approved; and a decree was rendered dismissing the bill for want of equity and dissolving the preliminary injunction; and decreeing further, that the judgment theretofore rendered be of full force and binding effect, and that appellees and their assigns, be entitled to proceed to the collection of the same by process of law and that appellant pay the costs of the proceeding. Exceptions were duly taken and this appeal perfected, thus bringing the record before us for review.

The first question to be considered in determining this cause is the relation that W. G. Bell sustained to the appellant herein at the time of the service of summons in the common law proceeding, here sought to be set aside and the collection of the judgment entered therein enjoined.

There seems to be no question but that W. G. Bell was appointed, September 23, 1908, as the agent for the sale of automobiles, by O. C. Owen, whom it is contended was in charge of the Chicago office of appellant, with power and authority to appoint local agents, define their territory, fix their compensation and supervise their work, and that he, said O. C. Owen, as the agent of appellant, acted under the advice and directions of appellant and its officers, and, from time to time, reported his acts and doings to them, and continued to hold himself out as the general agent of appellant.

If this contention is sustained by the evidence in this case, then the appointment of Mr. Bell, by said O. C. Owen, would constitute Mr. Bell an agent of appellant at the time the said service was had.

The evidence and exhibits in this record are voluminous, and we will not undertake to refer specifically to all or any considerable portion thereof. The record shows that in the spring or early summer of 1908, the said Mr. Bell was working with said O. C. Owen at Chicago, as sales agent and demonstrator of the Reo car, the exclusive sale of which, east of the Rocky mountains, was under the management and control of appellant. The first correspondence between the appellees and appellant relate to the purchase of two cars and the securing of the agency for McLean county, and the following letter was received in reply thereto:

"DEAR SIR:—

You state you intend to visit Chicago in the near future with a view to examining one of our machines at that place. Kindly call upon Mr. O. C. Owen, who looks after the trade in central and northern Illinois, for us, and who will be glad to go into the matter in detail with you and make you a proposition on the purchase of the car in which you are interested. If, as you intimate, you are in a position to dispose of some machines in your territory, you can, no doubt, arrange with Mr. Owen to purchase them on terms that will be very satisfactory and assure you of good profit on the sales made. Our representatives will be glad to work with you in every way.

Yours very truly,

R. M. OWEN & Co.

By H. M. LEE.''

Among other correspondence between O. C. Owen and appellant, we quote the following:

''R. M. OWEN & Co.,

Lansing, Mich.

GENTLEMEN:—

We wish to call your attention to the fact R. R. Lash, of Henry, Ill., is selling cars in Lostant township, in LaSalle county. This township belongs to O. T. Watson, of Morris. I realize it is all the same to me who sells the cars, but do not want to have hard feelings between my agents, and I want you to take it up with Mr. Lash at once and tell him to work his own territory.

O. C. OWEN.''

To this we find in the record the following reply:

''We have just looked up Lash's contract. It reads Putnam, Tonica and Lostant, in LaSalle county. You will see from this he has a perfect right to sell in these towns.

Yours very truly,

R. M. OWEN & Co.''

The following letter also appears in this record:

Nov. 13, 1908.

O. C. OWEN,

Chicago, Ill.

''DEAR SIR:—

Our records do not show that Hatcher at the present time has, or ever did have, a deposit with us. It may be the books of the New York office, in connection with the Chicago branch, show a balance of $50. Would suggest your writing New York on this subject.

Yours very truly,

R. M. OWEN & Co.''

In addition to this, the form of the letter head used by O. C. Owen in his correspondence with appellees had the name of R. M. Owen & Co., imprinted thereon, and many had the words: "O. C. Owen, Manager," also printed on them.

As specifically relating to the agency of W. G. Bell, we quote from a letter upon the letter head of R. M. Owen & Co., dated July 16, 1908, written by O. C. Owen, to appellees, where it is said: "If you think you can work this territory without Mr. Bell we will put Mr. Bell in the territory further south."

In a letter bearing date September 23, 1908, to R. M. Owen & Co., signed O. C. Owen, it is said: "Kindly mark up McLean county to Mr. W. G. Bell, who is going to take care of that county for me the coming year."

In a letter addressed to appellant, signed by O. C. Owen, dated October 5, 1908, it is said: "We are enclosing you names and addresses, together with location of the territory, of all the agents that we have closed up to date;" and in the list appears the following: "W. G. Bell, McLean county."

In a letter signed by appellant, addressed to O. C. Owen, dated December 20, 1908, it is said: "The package he mentions we sent him on the strength of advice received from Bell that he had been appointed as agent in his territory."

The following letter also appears of record:

Dec. 31, 1908.

"MR. OTTO C. OWEN,
    Chicago, Ill.
"DEAR SIR:—
We made a deal at St. Louis that requires a little assistance, and I would like to have you write me at once if you could let Bell go down for three or four days when the sample machines get there, which will be about next Tuesday, and help them demonstrate and teach their men so they can operate the cars. If

I remember correctly Bell is located at Bloomington, and it will not cost us much to have him go down, etc.

R. M. Owen & Co.''

The following extract from a letter from R. M. Owen & Co. to O. C. Owen appears in the record: "We are having printed 60,000 catalogues and will be careful how many we supply the agents with on their first order." In a letter from O. C. Owen to appellant, we find the following: "I wish to say that I consider these agents yours as much as mine." And in another letter from O. C. Owen to appellant we find this language: "Just as soon as I return from Decatur I will let you know the result of my visit, which I hope will be satisfactory to us both."

The following appears in a letter from O. C. Owen to appellant: "In regard to sending a man to Mt. Sterling, will be very glad to do so. We have the man now working for us whom you spoke about. Hope the letter to Danville will wake up our agent."

In a letter of May 13, 1908, O. C. Owen wrote to appellant asking appellant's advice as to the employment of a certain man to be sales agent in certain territory, to which appellant, in a letter dated May 14, gave advice as to the employment of the salesman and the method or manner of building up trade in the territory.

Under the date of June 16, 1908, O. C. Owen addressed a letter to appellant, in which he said: "I have got to have some cars or you will not have an agent in Illinois. I have closed up with C. B. Johnston & Co., of Arrowsmith, for McLean county."

In a letter from appellant to O. C. Owen, dated August 15, 1908, the following appears: "We have had nothing but complaints from our agents, and when it comes from one of the family it does not help matters." In a letter from appellant to O. C. Owen, of October 10, 1908, we find the following: "We received a list of agents you have closed to date. We will send them supplies of such literature as we have."

A letter bearing date December 11, 1908, from appellant to O. C. Owen, contains the following language: "I have always figured the Chicago end as being a part of R. M. Owen & Co."

This record discloses that appellant kept a list of all subagents, their post office address and distributed literature to them, in some instances, and in other instances through the Chicago agency; that the agency in Chicago kept an office in which, it is insisted by appellees, appellant's name was painted on the front; that in many letters not herein referred to the same language, or similar language, pertaining to the business, was used as in these we quote from. In many of the letters written to the appellee the letter heads used by O. C. Owen contained the name of R. M. Owen & Co., with the words, "O· C. Owen, Manager." In all payments for cars, as disclosed by this record, the checks were made payable directly to appellant and with appellant's name indorsed on the back by "O. C. Owen, Mgr." All orders for cars were taken on blanks of R. M. Owen & Co., and many of the orders contained the name of W. G. Bell, as salesman.

Under all of the circumstances appearing from this record, would it not be reasonably inferred by persons dealing with O. C. Owen or W. G. Bell, that he or they were acting as the agent or agents of appellant?

Section 8 of chapter 110, R. S. (J. & A. ¶ 8545), entitled "Practice," provides that any "incorporated company may be served with process by leaving a copy thereof with its president" or certain other enumerated officers, "or any agent found in the county."

In Meacham on Agency, par. 728, we find the following rule announced: "If the sub-agent be one whom the agent was expressly or impliedly authorized to appoint, he is to be deemed to be the agent of the principal, and notice to such sub-agent would be notice to the principal as in the case of other agents."

In the case of *Board of Trade of City of Chicago v. Hammond Elevator Co.*, 198 U. S. 424, which was one where service was obtained upon an alleged agent, in discussing the subject of agency, the Court said: "The question turns upon the character of the agent, whether he is such that the law will imply the power and impute the authority to him, and if he be that kind of an agent, the implication will be made, notwithstanding a denial of authority on the part of the officers of the corporation."

In *Italian-Swiss Agric. Colony v. Pease,* 194 Ill. 98, in discussing the same subject, our Supreme Court said: "If a corporation knowingly and voluntarily permits a person to hold himself out to the world as its agent, said corporation will be bound as principal to those dealing with such person to act upon the faith that such agency exists; and this is true irrespective of whether or not an agency in fact exists."

In the case of *Cadillac Auto. Co. v. Boynton,* 142 Ill. App. 381, the Court reviewed the above authorities and announced the same doctrine.

In *Crowley, Cook & Co. v. Sumner,* 97 Ill. App. 301, the Court used the following language: "The language of the statute (section 8) is broad, and considering the fact that the commercial, manufacturing and transportation business of the country is to-day mainly carried on by corporations that act through agents, it should be liberally construed to affect what was clearly the intention of the legislature to secure. Corporations doing business over wide areas of territory, are practically beyond the jurisdiction of local courts in such territory where the business is done, unless they can be reached by service upon their representatives there found. That a representative for limited purposes may be an agent for purposes of service under the statute, is plainly seen from the fact that not only a general agent may be served, but also any agent may be served."

When it is considered that O. C. Owen advertised himself as general agent or manager for appellant, entered into contracts for the sale of automobiles as such general agent, upon blanks furnished by appellant, used forms furnished by appellant for sale orders containing appellant's name, received checks made payable to appellant and indorsed appellant's name on the back thereof as manager to the extent of thousands of dollars, consulted and corresponded with appellant as to the appointment of agents, covering a wide territory, can it be reasonably said that he was not acting in the capacity of a representative of appellant?

Mr. Bell was a salesman appointed by O. C. Owen, evidently with the knowledge and consent of the appellant, but certainly with their acquiescence and approval, because the proof shows that the appellant was notified by O. C. Owen of his appointment on the 23d day of September, 1908. The proof also shows that he sold seven or eight cars in McLean county alone and took the orders therefor on blank forms furnished by appellant and on which his name appeared as salesman, and when cars were delivered he took checks payable to the appellant and they were presented to the banks and paid, and evidently deposited to the credit of appellant, as their name was indorsed thereon by O. C. Owen, their manager.

In addition to this, this record shows that on one occasion Mr. Bell made orders upon the appellant for repairs for one of the machines sold by him, and his order was filled and he was recognized as an agent, and such recognition appears in one of the letters referred to and quoted from herein. On another occasion appellant desired that Mr. Bell be sent to St. Louis for a few days to help in making some demonstrations of cars. His name had been furnished to appellant in the list of agents, and that fact is referred to in one of the letters in the record.

Hence we conclude that Mr. Bell was the recognized agent of the appellant in and for the county of McLean at the date service was had upon him, and for

R. M. Owen & Co. v. Johnson, 184 Ill. App. 90.

some time before and after that date. There is a controversy as to whether the appellant had any knowledge of the commencement of the suit until after judgment had been taken. Both R. M. Owen and O. C. Owen deny any such knowledge, while appellees insist that they had knowledge both through Mr. Bell, their agent, and one of the appellees. Be that as it may, we fail to see how that could affect their legal standing and rights in this case. If they were notified in the manner required by our statute, they were in court for all of the purposes of the suit.

It is further contended that there was no legal liability or consideration upon which to base a judgment in the common law suit.

That question was inquired into to some extent when default and judgment was taken in that case. But, aside from that, it was one of the issues made by the bill and answer in the cause now in hearing. Proof was taken, and the master found that the amount of the judgment rendered in the common law case was due to the appellees from appellant, and the court approved the master's finding.

We have gone sufficiently into the accounts of appellant and appellees, and we concur in the finding of the master and the decree of the chancellor.

For the reason given, the decree of the Circuit Court is affirmed.

Affirmed.

S. W. Love, Trustee, and A. J. Wagner, Executor, Defendants in Error, v. Metropolitan Church Association and Nicholas H. Larry, Plaintiffs in Error.

1. RELIGIOUS SOCIETIES, § 22*—*power to acquire real estate.* An incorporated church association has power to purchase real estate for its corporate purposes and to borrow money and mortgage such property to secure the loan.

2. RELIGIOUS SOCIETIES, § 25*—*when church association estopped to question authority of its officers to mortgage.* Where the president and secretary of the board of trustees of an incorporated church association give a mortgage on real estate purchased by them for a church site to secure notes given for the purchase money, the association is estopped to question the authority of such officers to give the mortgage, where it has received the benefits, and the acts of the association in taking possession and control of the property warrant the conclusion that the acts of such officers have been ratified.

3. CORPORATIONS, § 346*—*ratification of acts of officers.* Very slight circumstances are sufficient to establish a ratification by a corporation of the acts of its officers where the benefits have all inured to its advantage.

Error to the Circuit Court of Champaign county; the Hon. SOLON PHILBRICK, Judge, presiding. Heard in this court at the October term, 1912. Affirmed. Opinion filed April 18, 1913. Rehearing denied October 15, 1913. *Certiorari* granted by Supreme Court.

F. WM. KRAFT, for plaintiffs in error.

SCHAEFER & DOLAN, for defendants in error.

MR. JUSTICE CREIGHTON delivered the opinion of the court.

This was a bill filed by the defendants in error in the Champaign County Circuit Court, to foreclose a mortgage against the plaintiffs in error, in favor of the defendants in error.

The plaintiffs in error filed answer to the bill, in which it was averred that the plaintiff in error, Metropolitan Church Association, is an incorporated company, organized and incorporated under the laws of the State of Illinois, not for pecuniary profit; that it was governed by a board of three trustees; that there had never been passed by the said plaintiff in error or its board of trustees any by-law, resolution or any authority whatever, to authorize the president and secretary to execute the trust deed and note described in complainant's bill; that the board of trustees of the said plaintiff in error had not, at any time, ratified the action of its president and secretary in executing said instruments. The answer admitted being indebted on December 31, 1909, to the defendant in error in the sum of $2,000, and admitted to having received of the defendant in error the $2,000 mentioned in complainant's bill.

Replication was filed to the answer, and the cause was referred to the master in chancery to take and report the proofs.

Upon the incoming of the report of the master, exceptions were filed thereto, and the cause submitted to the court. A decree was entered in favor of the defendants in error in the sum of $2,370.05, and foreclosure awarded. From this decree this record is brought before us for review by a writ of error.

The undisputed facts, as appear from this record, are, that the debt for which the note and trust deed here involved were given for money borrowed from a former conservator of the defendant in error's intestate, by the president and secretary of the board of trustees of the plaintiff in error, for the purpose of making a payment upon the purchase price of the property described in the trust deed here involved, which was purchased by the said president and secretary of such board of trustees of plaintiff in error for a church site. Immediately after the completion of the loan in question, a deed to the site was delivered to the said president and secretary of the plaintiff in error, and the plaintiff in error, the Metropolitan Church Association, took possession and have held and used such property for church purposes from that time on.

The note and trust deed were signed as follows:

> "METROPOLITAN CHURCH ASSOCIATION.
> DUKE M. FARSON, Pres.
> E. L. HARVEY, Secy."

and the same was attested by the corporate seal.

It is contended by the plaintiff in error that the president and secretary of its board of directors or trustees had no power or authority to bind the corporation; that they acted without the direction or approval of the plaintiff in error.

The plaintiff in error, the Metropolitan Church Association, had power, under our statute, to purchase real estate for its corporate purposes, and to borrow money and mortgage such property to secure such loan, so that the question of its being an act *ultra vires,* so far as the corporation is concerned, need not be considered. It had the power and it remains to be seen whether or not it exercised the power in any of the methods recognized by law.

The subject of the power of such corporations and their agents to act for them in cases of the character of the one at bar is fully discussed by our Supreme Court in *Alton Mfg. Co. v. Garrett Biblical Institute,* 243 Ill. 298, from which we quote:

"Might exercise this authority in a number of ways: (1) They might appoint one of their number as agent of the corporation for that purpose and expressly or impliedly clothe him with authority to borrow money and give notes; (2) where no actual authority has been conferred upon the agent of the corporation to borrow money and give notes but where the agent has done so, and with full knowledge of all the facts the corporation has approved and ratified the acts of the agent, it will be liable to the same extent as if actual authority had been given to perform the acts; (3) where no authority had been given or existed in the agent to borrow money but where the corporation received the use and benefit of the money it will be liable; (4) by holding an agent out to the public as possessing authority to exercise the powers assumed by the agent and to do the acts performed by him, in which case the corporation would be bound to the extent of the agent's apparent authority."

It appears from the record in this case that immediately upon the purchase of the property in question, the congregation, for which the president and secretary (two of the trustees) acted, moved in and took possession and exercised all of the acts of control over said property. It would be marvelous to say, without any notice or knowledge of the action of the two trustees or any one else, that the whole congregation, of one accord, would from thenceforth assemble there weekly for religious services and be ignorant of the act of the officers in securing the property.

The proof further shows that the treasurer of the plaintiff in error, who was the third member of the board of trustees, paid two instalments of interest upon the note secured by the trust deed in question, and sent the third instalment of interest, in form of a check, to Mr. Webber, who had previously acted as conservator of defendants in error's intestate at the time of the making of the loan, but who had resigned at the date of the receipt of the check for the third instalment of interest. This check was signed: "Metropolitan Church Assn., by Mrs. Harvey, Treas." and was returned to her with directions to send it to the defendant in error. These facts present the action of the congregation covering a period of more than eighteen months after the property had been bought, possession taken, loan made and mortgage executed.

Very slight circumstances are sufficient to establish a ratification by the plaintiff in error of the acts of its officers where the benefits all inured to the advantage of the plaintiff in error.

In *National Home B. & L. Ass'n v. Home Sav. Bank,* 181 Ill. 35, the Court uses the following language:

"It (meaning *ultra vires*) has been applied indis-criminately to different states of fact in such a way as to cause considerable confusion. When used as applica-ble to some conditions, it has been frequently said that a corporation is estopped to make such a defense where it has received the benefit of the contract. For example, the term has been applied to acts of directors or officers which are outside and beyond the scope of their author-ity, and therefore are invasions of the rights of stock-holders, but which are within the powers of the corpor-ation. In such case the act may become binding by ratification, consent and acquiesence, or by the cor-poration receiving the benefit of the contract."

The facts in this case warrant us in concluding that the action of the trustees, or officers, was ratified, con-sented to and acquiesced in; and, beyond question, the plaintiff in error received the benefit of the loan to se-cure which the note and trust deed were given, and still hold and retain such benefit. In equity the plaintiff in error will not be permitted to accept the benefits of the agent's contract, and, at the same time, repu-diate that part of the agent's acts by which it secured title to the property.

Believing that exact justice has been done in this case, the decree will be, and is, affirmed.

Affirmed.

MR. JUSTICE PHILBRICK took no part.   ·

James A. Elward, Appellee, v. Illinois Central Railroad Company, Appellant.

1. DAMAGES, § 207*—*when instruction misleading.* In an action for personal injuries, an instruction relating to assessment of damages which closes with a statement to the effect that it is not necessary for any witness to express an opinion as to the amount of damages claimed in the declaration, *held* misleading and erroneous.

2. DAMAGES, § 42*—*when expert evidence as to effect of injury improper.* In an action for personal injuries, opinions of medical experts as to the effect of injury on plaintiff's life, *held* improper under the circumstances of the case.

3. DAMAGES, § 42*—*consequential damages.* Consequences which are contingent, speculative or merely possible are not proper to be considered in ascertaining damages. To entitle plaintiff to recover present damages for apprehended future consequences there must be such a degree of probability of their occurring as amounts to a reasonable certainty.

4. EVIDENCE, § 444*—*when opinion of medical expert incompetent.* Expert evidence which is a result of personal examination made during the trial, based in part upon subjective symptoms, is incompetent.

Appeal from the Circuit Court of DeWitt county; the Hon. WILLIAM G. COCHRAN, Judge, presiding. Heard in this court at the April term, 1912. Reversed and remanded. Opinion filed April 18, 1913. Rehearing denied October 16, 1913.

LEMON & LEMON, for appellant; JOHN G. DRENNAN, of counsel.

HERRICK & HERRICK and EDWARD J. SWEENEY, for appellee.

MR. JUSTICE CREIGHTON delivered the opinion of the court.

This suit was begun by appellee against the appellant Company in the Circuit Court of DeWitt county, to recover damages for injuries alleged to have been sustained by appellee by reason of the breaking in two of a freight train on appellant's road, while the train was running down grade, and when the rear part of the train caught up with and ran into the front portion thereof, appellee, who was in the caboose, was thrown from his seat and injured.

This cause was before us once heretofore (*Elward v. Illinois Cent. R. Co.*, 161 Ill. App. 630), where it was found error had intervened, as disclosed by the opinion filed in that cause, and the judgment was reversed and the cause remanded for another trial. Upon the second trial in the Circuit Court the jury found the issues for the appellee and rendered a judgment for twelve thousand dollars, and the court entered judgment on the verdict for that sum, after overruling motions for new trial and in arrest of the judgment, and the cause is brought before us again by a further appeal.

A careful examination of the record presented for our inspection upon this appeal discloses the fact that on the trial of the cause the question of the extent and permanent character of the injury to appellee was the only matter for the jury, the liability of the appellant having been practically admitted.

The account of the accident and the various movements of the patient and his subsequent treatment were given at great length and with minute detail, and are, largely, unimportant to the determination of the cause. It is important, however, to learn the extent of the injury and it was important to have that presented to the jury according to the rules of practice in this State.

In addition to the evidence presented in this case bearing directly upon the accident and the circumstances surrounding it, we have before us the statements of twelve medical experts, about one-half of whom had treated the appellee at different times for the injury received in this accident, and the other half had personally examined appellee during the trial with a view to testifying in the case.

The chief controversy among the medical experts, as appears from the record, was whether the spinal cord or bony structure of the spinal column of appellee had been injured, and whether he still was suffering from the same. Upon this vital question the experts disagreed, the greater number, in our judgment, concluding that there was no injury to the vertebrae or spinal cord, while the remaining experts contended that there was a curvature of the spine and an injury to the spinal cord and that this created the condition in which appellee was found to be.

The expert evidence that was the result of a personal examination made during the trial was based, in part, upon subjective symptoms, and, therefore, was not competent evidence. *Elward v. Illinois Cent. R. Co.*, 161 Ill. App. 630; *Lauth v. Chicago Union Traction Co.*, 244 Ill. 244.

A portion of these medical experts gave their opinion, over the objection of appellant, as to the effect of this injury upon appellee's life, which we regard as being improper under the circumstances developed in this case. In the case of *Lauth v. Chicago Union Traction Co., supra*, at page 252 of the opinion, the Supreme Court said: "Consequences which are contingent, speculative or merely possible, are not proper to be considered in ascertaining the damages. It is not enough that the injuries received may have developed into a more serious condition than those which are visible at the time of the injury, nor, even that they are likely to develop. To entitle plaintiff to recover present damages for apprehended future consequences, there must be such a degree of probability of their occurring, as amounts to a reasonable certainty." See also *Chicago City Ry. Co. v. Henry*, 62 Ill. 142.

The following instruction is objected to by appellant as being erroneous and misleading:

"The court instructs the jury, that if you find for

the plaintiff, you will be required to determine the
amount of his damages. In determining the amount
of damages the plaintiff is entitled to recover in this
case, if any, the jury have a right to, and they should
take into consideration all the facts and circumstances
as proven by the evidence before them, the nature and
extent of plaintiff's physical injuries, if any, so far
as the same are shown by the evidence to be the direct
result of the injury; his suffering in mind and body,
if any, resulting from such physical injuries, and such
future suffering and loss of health, if any, as the jury
may believe from the evidence before them in this case,
he has sustained or will sustain by reason of such injuries; his loss of time and inability to work, if any,
on account of such injuries; the necessary expense
of medical care and attendance, if any is shown by
the evidence on account of such injuries, if any, and
you may find for him such sum as in the judgment
of the jury under the evidence and instructions of the
court in this case, will be a fair compensation for the
injuries he has sustained or will sustain, if any, so far
as such damages and injury, if any, are claimed and
alleged in the amended declaration or additional
counts and proven; and it is not necessary for any
witness to express an opinion as to the amount of such
damages.''

The declaration alleges, among other things, that
the appellee was damaged by reason of the injury
complained of because he could not follow his usual
employment and thereby earn a salary, and also was
damaged in consequence of being compelled to lay out
large sums of money for medical care and attendance
in an effort to be cured of his injury. These two items
constitute a material part of the damages sought to
be recovered in this suit, and for the Court, in the closing part of the above quoted instruction, to announce
as a proposition of law, that ''it is not necessary for
any witness to express an opinion as to the amount

of such damages,'' is clearly misleading and erroneous.

It was incumbent upon the appellee to prove by evidence the amount of damages he had sustained by reason of these two items.

The evidence was very conflicting and close upon the question of whether there was or was not an injury to the spinal cord or bony structure of the spinal column; and the evidence as to the extent of the injury leaves the matter in serious doubt as to the permanent character of the injury complained of.

If, as contended by the medical experts above referred to, the spinal column was not injured, and from the whole evidence we are inclined to entertain that view, then, in that case, the damages as fixed by the judgment are excessive.

The conduct of counsel for appellee, in the closing argument of the cause, is justly complained of. Courts cannot indorse the action of attorneys which are calculated to inflame the minds of the jury, in cases so closely contested as to the extent of the injury and the amount of the damages, as in this case. And while we do not mention this as ground of reversible error, it certainly added to the cause of complaint.

For the reasons above indicated we are compelled to reverse the judgment of the trial court, and the judgment is reversed and the cause will be remanded.

Reversed and remanded.

W. P. Potter, Plaintiff in Error, v. S. A. Gibson et al., Defendants in Error.

(Not to be reported in full.)

Error to the Circuit Court of Sangamon county; the Hon. JAMES A. CREIGHTON, Judge, presiding. Heard in this court at the October term, 1912. Affirmed. Opinion filed April 18, 1913. Rehearing denied October 15, 1913.

Statement of the Case.

Action by W. P. Potter against S. A. Gibson, A. C. Gibson, G. A. Gibson, J. Francis Miller, Illinois National Bank and H. M. Merriam, to recover the sum of four thousand dollars alleged to have been paid by plaintiff for stock in a certain corporation upon the misrepresentations of defendants as to the solvency and financial condition of such corporation. Plaintiff dismissed the action as against the Gibsons. From a judgment entered in favor of other defendants on a directed verdict, plaintiff brings error.

J. E. WINTERBOTHAM and E. A. PERRY, for plaintiff in error.

McANULTY & ALLEN, for defendants in error, H. M. Merriam and Illinois National Bank.

MR. JUSTICE PHILBRICK delivered the opinion of the court.

Abstract of the Decision.

FRAUD, § 35*—*when statements as to financial condition of corporation not actionable.* In an action on the case to recover money paid for stock in a corporation, alleged to have been induced by the misrepresentations concerning the financial condition of the company made by defendants to whom plaintiff had been referred by the seller, a direction of a verdict for defendants *held* not error

*See Illinois Notes Digest, Vols. XI to XV, same topic and section number

where some of the statements and representations were mere expressions of opinion and others were made after the plaintiff had raised money to make the investment so that plaintiff could not have relied thereon.

Nellie M. Pressley, Administratrix, Appellee v. Kinloch-Bloomington Telephone Company and Bloomington & Normal Railway and Light Company, Appellants.

1. ELECTRICITY, § 27*—*when verdict against telephone company not sustained by the evidence.* In an action against an electric light company and a telephone company for the death of plaintiff's intestate, alleged to have been caused by an electric light current while acting as a city electric light trimmer, a verdict in favor of the plaintiff against the telephone company *held* manifestly against the weight of the evidence in that the evidence failed to show that the telephone wire which fell on the electric light wire and made the current belonged to the defendant telephone company.

2. APPEAL AND ERROR, § 1793*—*joint judgment.* Where a joint judgment against two defendants is erroneous as to one defendant, it will be reversed as to both.

Appeal from the Circuit Court of McLean county; the Hon. COLOSTIN D. MYERS, Judge, presiding. Heard in this court at the October term, 1912. Reversed and remanded. Opinion filed October 16, 1913. Rehearing denied November 5, 1913.

LILLARD & WILLIAMS, for appellant Kinloch-Bloomington Telephone Co.

SIGMUND LIVINGSTON and WILLIAM R. BACH, for appellant Bloomington & Normal Railway and Light Co.

JACOB P. LINDLEY, JOHN E. POLLOCK and EDWARD BARRY, for appellee.

MR. JUSTICE CREIGHTON delivered the opinion of the court.

This was an action on the case brought by appellee,

*See Illinois Notes Digest, Vols. XI to XV, same topic and section .number.

Vol. CLXXXIV 8

as administratrix of the estate of John W. Pressley, deceased, to recover for the death of her intestate, caused by an electric current received by him while acting as an electric light trimmer for the city of Bloomington. Both the appellant companies were made defendants.

This cause has been in this court on two different appeals (*Pressley v. Kinloch-Bloomington Tel. Co.*, 158 Ill. App. 220, and 164 Ill. App. 167), where the facts relative to the cause of action are fully stated, and the cause was reversed and remanded each time. No change occurred in the pleadings since the last appeal.

In the judgment of the court, on the last appeal the cause was reversed and remanded because of the fact that the evidence contained in that record failed to show the appellant Telephone Company was the owner of the wire which broke, fell and caused the injury to appellee's intestate by reason of the cross-circuit thereby caused; and as the suit was a joint one and the judgment appealed from was a joint judgment, it was held that if it was necessary to reverse the judgment as to one of the appellants it was necessary as to both.

Upon the retrial of the cause in the Circuit Court the evidence upon the former hearing, as to the ownership of the wire which it is alleged caused the injury, was read from the notes of the reporter, except that two of appellee's witnesses, and one new witness, were called and testified.

On the last hearing a verdict and judgment was entered in the sum of four thousand five hundred dollars against both appellants and in favor of the appellee, and thereupon this appeal was perfected.

This court, in the last opinion herein filed, used the following language, with reference to the wire which caused the injury to appellee's intestate: "The Mc-Lean County Telephone Company owned other pairs of wires upon this pole and number 5 was one of these wires. There is evidence in the record that that wire extended to and was connected with a cable which entered the telephone exchange of the McLean County Telephone Company which was located a block or more from the telephone exchange of the Kinloch-Bloomington Telephone Company; this wire was upon the top cross-arm of that pole. The Kinloch-Bloomington Telephone Company owned wires upon the second cross-arm and these wires extended to and were connected with a cable which entered the telephone exchange of the defendant telephone company.

There being no proof in this record that the defendant telephone company owned, controlled, operated or was in any manner responsible for the condition of the telephone wire complained of, the verdict of the jury as to that company is clearly and manifestly against the evidence, and as to it must be reversed."

After a careful study of all the evidence in this record, including the new evidence of the witnesses heard to testify orally, we cannot but conclude the evidence here preserved fails to show the appellant Kinloch-Bloomington Telephone Company was the owner of the wire which fell and injured appellee's intestate.

Mr. Hamilton, after testifying as to a state of facts relative to the ownership of the wire which fell, on cross-examination gave evidence as to the wires of the McLean County Telephone Company having been removed from the point where the wire in controversy fell, and said his statements were "as reported to the director's meeting," and that he "did not know personally."

Mr. Gulliford, construction chief of the McLean County Telephone Company, who was heard to again testify, stated, as to the condition of certain wires, that the said company had no wires in this alley.

But, as against this evidence, there was the positive and direct testimony of several witnesses who identified the particular wire which fell, and gave evidence as to the location of this wire upon the cross-arm on

the pole, and testified directly that the wire was that
of the McLean County Telephone Company. The wire
which fell was identified as being wire number 5 on
the top cross-arm on the pole. The witness, Mr. Far-
well, testified that wires number 3, 4, 5, 6, 7 and 8 on
the top cross-arm of that pole were the wires of the
McLean County Telephone Company, and that the
wire which fell was wire No. 5.

Mr. Ross testified that the six wires on the top cross-
arm on the pole were bridled into the cable of the
McLean County Telephone Company, and that the
wire which fell was wire number 5, and that it did not
belong to the appellant Telephone Company.

Mr. Philbrook, a city employe in the fire alarm department, testified that he had had sixteen years' experience as an electrician and telephone man; that he
helped build the first lines of the McLean County Telephone Company and that they had wires on the pole
in this alley and that he examined them in the month
of the accident here involved and that the wires of
the McLean County Telephone Company were on the
top cross-arm of the pole in question.

Many other facts and circumstances are shown by
this record which fully convince us that the wire which
fell and made the connection of the current on to the
city light plant wire was not that of the appellant Telephone Company.

The appellants having been sued jointly, and the
judgment here appealed from having been a joint judgment against both appellants, the judgment must be
affirmed as to both or reversed as to both. There
being no sufficient evidence showing the appellant Telephone Company was the owner of the wire which is
alleged to have caused the injury, the judgment as to it
is erroneous and must be reversed, and therefore must
be reversed as to both appellants.

For the reason indicated the judgment is reversed
and the cause is remanded.

Reversed and remanded.

Jesse Havron, Appellee, v. Shoal Creek Coal Company, Appellant.

1. MINES AND MINERALS, § 91*—*when mine examiner cannot recover for injuries resulting from failure to close cross-cuts.* In an action by an assistant mine examiner to recover for injuries resulting from an explosion of accumulated gases while engaged in examining a mine, alleged to have been caused by wilful failure of mine owner to comply with section 14 of Miners' Act, J. & A. ¶ 7488, requiring certain cross-cuts to be closed, *held* that trial court erred in refusing to direct a verdict for defendant for the reason that the declaration was based solely on a statute which the evidence shows was inapplicable to plaintiff in his employment, and even under allegations of neglect of a common law duty to plaintiff *held* that plaintiff would not be entitled to recover under evidence showing that plaintiff was inexcusably careless in making an examination of the mine with an open lamp.

2. MINES AND MINERALS, § 82*—*persons entitled to protection under the provisions of the Miners' Act.* Person employed as mine examiner under section 21 of Miners' Act, J. & A. ¶ 7495, does not come within the class entitled to protection under the provisions of section 14 of the Miners' Act, J. & A. ¶ 7488.

3. MINES AND MINERALS, § 82*—*"operative miners" within meaning of constitution.* Mine examiner is not an "operative miner" within the meaning of the constitutional provision, requiring "the legislature to pass such laws as may be necessary for the protection of operative miners."

Appeal from the Circuit Court of Montgomery county; the Hon. ALBERT M. ROSE, Judge, presiding. Heard in this court at the October term, 1912. Reversed. Opinion filed October 16, 1913. *Certiorari* denied by Supreme Court (making opinion final).

W. B. McBRIDE, for appellant; MILLER & McDAVID and MASTIN & SHERLOCK, of counsel.

LANE & COOPER and HILL & BULLINGTON, for appellee.

MR. JUSTICE CREIGHTON delivered the opinion of the court.

This was an action on the case filed in the Montgomery Circuit Court by the appellee against the appellant Company, to recover for damages alleged to

have been caused by the wilful failure of the appellant
to comply with the provisions of paragraph "f" of
section 14 of chapter 93, Hurd's R. S. 1911 (J. & A.
¶ 7488), entitled "Mines and Miners."

The cause was heard by the court and a jury, and
a verdict was returned against appellant in the sum of
fifteen hundred dollars and, after overruling motions
for new trial and in arrest of the judgment,
the court entered judgment in the amount of the verdict against appellant, whereupon the record was
brought before us by appeal on the part of appellant.

The declaration charges, in substance, that appellant owned and was operating a certain coal mine at
Panama, in said county, and that in the operation and
construction thereof there were, among others, the
third and fourth west entries which were inlet and outlet air courses; that the ends of the said entries were
known as the face; that between the third and fourth
entries were two cross-cuts open, the westward one
being about sixty feet west of the first one, allowing
the full current of air between the inlet and outlet air
courses to circulate through it, and thus preventing the
air from circulating through the first cross-cut nearest the said face of said inlet and outlet air courses;
that appellant wilfully failed and neglected to close
the cross-cut farthest from the face in said entries, as
provided by said paragraph "f" of said chapter 93
J. & A. ¶ 7488 of the statute; that appellee was employed in said mine as assistant mine examiner, and
while traveling through said mine to examine it, as requested by appellant to do at a point about thirty
feet east of the cross-cut nearest the said face of said
entry, suddenly, and without warning, certain gaseous
substances which had at that time accumulated therein,
by reason of the said eastward cross-cut being and remaining open, ignited and exploded, whereby appellee
received the injuries complained of.

The general issue was pleaded.

The real contention of the appellant is that the appellee while engaged as assistant mine examiner, did not come within the class contemplated by the provision of the Mines and Miners' Act.

The paramount question in this case is, did the appellee, at the time of the injury complained of, come within the class designated by the constitution as "operative miners?"

The provision of the constitution upon which the Mines and Miners' Act is based, J. & A., Vol. I p. 187, is, in part, as follows: "It shall be the duty of the legislature to pass such laws as may be necessary for the protection of operative miners, by providing ventilation and constructing safety escapement shafts, or such other appliances as may secure safety in all coal mines."

The paragraph of the statute here involved ("f" of section 14 of chapter 93, J. & A. ¶ 7488), reads as follows: "All cross-cuts connecting inlet and outlet air courses, except the last one nearest the face, shall be closed with substantial stoppings, to be made as nearly air-tight as possible. In the making of the air-tight partition or stoppings, no loose material or refuse shall be used."

It is contended by appellant that the appellee, at the time of the accident complained of, was not a miner engaged in digging coal, but that he was at the time an employe, having been assigned to the duty of assistant examiner of mines, and, therefore, does not come within the class described as "operative miners," and construes the statute as applying only to those engaged in digging coal.

The statute makes it the duty of all persons or corporations operating coal mines to employ a mine examiner, and the duties of such mine examiner are fixed by statute (section 21, chapter 93, entitled "Mines and Miners," J. & A. ¶ 7495) and are as follows:

(1) "To examine the underground workings of the

mine within twelve hours preceding every day upon which the mines are to be operated."

(2) "When in the performance of his duties to carry with him a safety lamp in proper order and condition and a rod or bar for sounding the roof."

(3) "To see that the air current is traveling in its proper course and in proper quantity; and to measure with an anemometer the amount of air passing in the last cross-cut or break-through of each pair of entries, or in the last room of each division of long wall mines, and at all other points where he may deem it necessary; and to note the results of such measurements in the mine examiner's book kept for that purpose."

(4) "To inspect all places where men are required in the performance of their duties to pass or work, and to observe whether there are any recent falls or dangerous roof or accumulations of gas or dangerous obstructions in rooms or roadways; and to examine especially the edges and accessible parts of recent falls and old gobs and air currents."

(5) "As evidence of his examination of said rooms and roadways, to inscribe in some suitable place on the walls of each, not on the face of the coal, which chalk, the month and day of the month of his visit."

(6) "When working places are discovered in which there are recent falls or dangerous roof or dangerous obstructions to place a conspicuous mark or sign thereat as notice to all men to keep out; and in case of accumulation of gas, to place at least two conspicuous obstructions across the roadway not less than twenty feet apart, one of which shall be outside the last open cross-cut."

(7) "Upon completing his examination, to make a daily record of the same in a book kept for that purpose, for the information of the company, the inspector and all other persons interested; and this record shall be made each morning before the miners are permitted to enter the mine."

(8) "To take into his possession the entrance checks of all men whose working places have been shown by his examination and record to be dangerous, and to give such entrance checks to the mine manager before the men are permitted to enter the mine in the morning."

A careful study of this section and all of its provisions discloses the fact that it is there made the duty of the mine examiner to examine the workings of the mine within twelve hours preceding every working day in the mine; to carry a safety lamp properly equipped; to see that the air current is traveling properly; to measure the amount of air passing in the last cross-cut or break-through; to inspect all places where men are required, in the performance of their duties, to pass or work; to observe whether there are any recent falls, dangerous roof or accumulation of gas; to place conspicuous marks or signs in places where there are recent falls or dangerous roof, and in case of an accumulation of gas, to place conspicuous obstructions across the roadway, one of which shall be outside the last open cross-cut, and to make a daily record of all of the above in a book kept for that purpose, for the information of the company, the inspector and all other persons interested, and that this record shall be made each morning before the miners are permitted to enter the mine.

This examination of the section convinces us that it was passed by the legislature as being in compliance with the requirement of the provision of the Constitution above quoted, namely, "to pass such laws as may be necessary for the protection of operative miners." It is evident this employe of the appellant was employed for the purpose of examining the mine as required by said section 21, J. & A. ¶ 7495, in order that the operative miners might know, before they entered the mine, that it was safe. He is the agency designated by the legislature to see that the mine is safe for the operative miners. This law was not passed for the protection of the man who was required to make the examinations, but for the protection of those whom the Constitution made it the duty of the legislature to protect by statute. The very purpose of his employment was that he should go into the mine in advance of the miners and ascertain whether or not it was safe from the dangers from which it was the legislative duty to protect them.

It is a matter of universal knowledge that employment in a coal mine is a dangerous occupation, and when appellee accepted employment as an examiner he knew it was a dangerous position to fill, or he would not be required. He knew all of the requirements of the law as to the duties to be performed by him, and when he accepted such employment he assumed all of the dangers incident to such employment. He was not an operative miner, but was the means selected by the legislature in the passage of the law, under the constitutional rquirement, for the protection of the operative miners.

The declaration herein is grounded alone upon the failure of the appellant to comply with a statutory requirement which was only applicable to operative miners. No common law duty of the appellant is counted upon, and no allegation is made as to the duty of the appellant to use reasonable care to give to the appellee a safe place in which to perform his labor, and to allege a failure of such duty.

But even if there had been such allegation of neglect of a common law duty of appellant towards appellee, the evidence would not be such as to warrant a judgment in his favor. The evidence clearly discloses that appellee, at the time of the accident, was making his examination of the mine with an open lamp. He was at the time in the mine looking for any accumulation of gas, lack of air, loose roof or any other dangers that might lurk there. He knew he was likely to encounter, as he did, an accumulation of gas at any time, and for him to proceed to make an examination with an open lamp was inexcusable carelessness. The section of the Mines and Miners' Act here involved was not enacted for his protection.

Counsel for the appellant, at the close of the evidence, asked the court to give a peremptory instruction to the jury, directing them to find the issues for the appellant, defendant below, but this was refused and this action of the court is here assigned as for error.

Under the view we are compelled to take of this case, we think it was error for the court to have refused to give the peremptory instruction, for the reason the declaration was based solely on a statute which the evidence shows was not applicable to the appellee in his employment.

For the reason above stated, the judgment of the trial court is reversed.

Reversed.

D. H. Harts, Appellee, v. Chicago and Alton Railroad Company, Appellant.

1. RAILROADS, § 941*—*when instruction as to origin of fire erroneous.* In an action against a railroad company for damages by fire alleged to have been caused by sparks and cinders being thrown upon plaintiff's building by defendant's locomotive, an instruction on question of the origin of the fire, which in effect states that plaintiff is entitled to a verdict if it furnished more evidence on that point than defendant, *held* inaccurate and misleading.

2. RAILROADS, § 943*—*when verdict for damages resulting from railroad fire excessive.* In an action for damages resulting from loss of plaintiff's mill and machinery therein resulting from emitting of sparks and cinders of defendant's locomotive, a verdict and judgment for plaintiff for $16,000 *held* excessive, where the evidence shows that plaintiff purchased the mill and machinery and lot for $15,000 and the machinery was out of date and the business of conducting the mill had run down and was unprofitable.

---

*See Illinois Notes Digest, Vols. XI to XV, same topic and section number.

3. RAILROADS, § 919—*burden of proving origin of fire.* In an action against a railroad for loss of a building by fire alleged to have been caused by sparks from defendant's locomotive, it is incumbent upon the plaintiff to furnish evidence sufficient to establish to the satisfaction of a reasonable mind the fact that the engine did throw sparks and cinders that started the fire.

4. JURY, § 80*—*questions which may be propounded to jurors.* In an action against a railroad company for loss of a building by fire caused by sparks from defendant's locomotive, *held* error for trial court to refuse to permit defendant on examination of jurors to ask the jurors if they were acquainted with the officers of, had stock in, or were agents of, or had any connection with certain insurance companies which were beneficiaries in the suit.

Appeal from the Circuit Court of Logan county; the Hon. THOMAS M. HARRIS, Judge, presiding. Heard in this court at the April term, 1912. Reversed and remanded. Opinion filed October 16, 1913. Rehearing denied and modified opinion refiled November 6, 1913.

BLINN & COVEY, for appellant; SILAS H. STRAWN, of counsel.

DAVID H. HARTS, JR., BATES, HARDING, EDGERTON & BATES and BARGER & HICKS, for appellee.

MR. JUSTICE CREIGHTON delivered the opinion of the court.

This was an action on the case brought by the appellee against appellant Company, to recover for damages alleged to have been caused by reason of a locomotive engine of appellant throwing sparks and cinders to, upon and into the building of the appellee whereby the building of appellee was destroyed by fire and the machinery therein greatly damaged.

The plea of the general issue was filed and the cause was heard by the court and a jury and a verdict returned assessing the damages of the appellee at the sum of $16,000. After overruling motions for new trial and in arrest of the judgment, the court entered judgment in the sum of the verdict, and thereupon this appeal was perfected.

The building belonging to the appellee which was

destroyed by fire was a mill, located on a lot adjoining the right of way of the appellant's railroad, in Lincoln, Illinois. The fire occurred in the afternoon of the 15th day of August, 1910, destroying the mill building and damaging the machinery.

The question of how the mill was set afire was a very closely contested question of fact. There was no direct testimony bearing upon this question. Two witnesses for appellee testified to a heavily loaded coal train passing along the track of appellant's railroad, going north, just a short time prior to the discovery of the fire. One of them, a Miss Gwynn, testified that the train passed shortly before the fire, going north, and that she saw sparks and cinders coming from the engine. She was unable to tell whether it was daylight or dusk at the time, and stated that it did not rain that evening, while many others stated it did rain. Miss Gwynn was in the company of a Mr. Hoblit, who testified to the same state of facts. Mr. Hoblit's testimony, while very definite as to the fact of the train passing along on that evening, going north, was very uncertain as to other matters about which he was questioned, and his admission that he was not engaged in any business of any kind and that he had but recently served a term in the penitentiary did not serve to strengthen his statements.

On the part of the appellant it was shown by the records of the train dispatcher's office that the last engine passed through Lincoln more than an hour before the fire was discovered. Moreover, the evidence shows conclusively that a wreck had occurred at Williamsville, sixteen miles south of Lincoln, at 3.25 on the same afternoon, and that no trains were able to pass through that point going north until about eight o'clock that night, some two hours after the fire had been discovered. The train crews which passed through Lincoln that afternoon testified that the locomotive engines on their respective trains were equipped with the latest approved and most efficient spark arresters, and that the said engines were in the hands of skilful employes at the time.

There is much other evidence tending to support the respective positions of the parties hereto, but the foregoing chiefly is relied upon by them upon the question of the origin of the fire, and shows how closely contested this particular point was on the hearing. In this condition of the proof, the jury should have been carefully and accurately instructed on this point.

At the request of the appellee the court gave to the jury the following instruction:

"The court instructs the jury that while it devolves upon the plaintiff to show by a preponderance of the evidence that the fire in question was caused or set out by fire, sparks or cinders thrown or escaping from a locomotive engine of the defendant company, while passing along its, defendant company's railroad and that the property of the plaintiff was burned or destroyed or damaged without fault on his part, yet it is not necessary for the plaintiff, in order to make such proof to sustain the declaration to show that such sparks, cinders or fire were seen thrown or were seen to escape from the defendant's engine and alight or set fire by some person or persons; it is sufficient on that point if, from all the circumstances detailed by the witnesses and all other evidence introduced on the trial, that the greater weight on that point is on the side of the plaintiff then you are at liberty to say that the plaintiff has established that fact by a preponderance of the evidence."

This instruction is inaccurate and misleading, and might easily have been understood by the jury to have advised them that very slight circumstances tending to show that appellant's engine emitted sparks and cinders on the occasion in question would be sufficient to warrant a verdict in favor of the appellee.

It was incumbent upon the appellee to furnish evidence sufficient to establish to the satisfaction of a reasonable mind the fact that the engine did throw sparks and cinders that did, in fact, start the conflagration. This duty was imposed by law upon the appellee, and it cannot be said that because the appellee furnished more evidence on that point than the appellant, that he is thereby entitled to a verdict, and yet that is what this instruction said to the jury. If the appellant had not introduced any evidence the appellee would not have been relieved from proving his case by evidence,—not to create a suspicion, not more evidence than an opponent who did not furnish any evidence,—but evidence sufficient to establish, as a fact, the origin of the fire.

In addition to the proof being so closely contested upon the question of whether appellant's engine threw sparks and cinders and thereby set fire to the mill, the evidence is uncertain and unsatisfactory as to the amount of the damages sustained by the appellee.

The proof shows the mill building which was destroyed had been built for about fifty years, and that the machinery in the mill had been there for some twenty-five years; that the appellee had purchased the mill, including the machinery and the lot upon which the mill was built, for $15,000; that very little had been expended for improvements; that after the fire appellee found that machinery to the value of $1,300 or $1,400 had been saved; that the business conducted in the mill had run down and was not profitable; that much of the machinery in the mill was out of date and was not in use and that the mill was not operated as a regular mill, but for grinding feed. The lot upon which the mill stood is still the property of the appellee.

From a full and careful examination of all evidence in this record upon the point of the damages, we feel that the amount of the judgment herein, $16,000, is excessive, in the light of the price paid for the whole property, the value of the machinery saved, the use to which the mill building was put and the fact that the appellee still has the lot upon which the mill stood. There is much evidence in the record upon this point, but a careful reading of it has failed to overcome the view here expressed, that the judgment is excessive.

It is insisted by appellant that the trial court erred in refusing to permit it, on the examination of the jurors for the purpose of ascertaining whether or not they were acceptable, to ask the jurors if they were acquainted with the officers of, had stock in, or were agents of or had any connection with the Hartford Fire Insurance Company, the Hanover Fire Insurance Company or the Springfield Fire & Marine Insurance Company.

These insurance companies, while not mentioned as plaintiffs in the declaration, were, in fact, beneficiaries in the suit to the extent of $10,000; and being thus interested it became important, in determining as to the qualifications of the jurors, to learn of their connection with, relation to, or prejudice in favor of such companies.

The interest of these several insurance companies seems to have been well understood by counsel, and for the purpose of guarding against any prejudicial influence against appellant these questions were properly propounded to the jurors, and it was error to deny to appellant the right of inquiry.

For the reasons above set forth, the judgment is reversed and the cause is remanded.

Reversed and remanded.

William E. Wilson, Appellee, v. Polly Ann Phares, Administratrix, Appellant.

1. EXECUTORS AND ADMINISTRATORS, § 269*—*when receipt for advancement not evidence of settlement for labor and services performed for deceased.* In a proceeding to have certain notes, executed by deceased, to her son, allowed as claims against the estate of deceased, the son's receipt for an advancement which stated that interest thereon would not be charged, *held* not evidence that the parties understood the remission of interest to be in settlement for

labor and services performed by the son, so as to show that a note executed by deceased therefor two and one-half years thereafter was without consideration.

2. EXECUTORS AND ADMINISTRATORS, § 270*—*when evidence insufficient to show consideration for promissory note executed by deceased.* Judgment of Circuit Court, on appeal from Probate Court, allowing notes given by deceased to claimant as claims against the estate, affirmed on condition of remittitur of a portion of the amount of one of the notes, there being no evidence to show the sufficiency of the consideration therefor and it appearing that the note representing such portion was clearly a gift without consideration.

Appeal from the Circuit Court of DeWitt county; the Hon. WILLIAM G. COCHRAN, Judge, presiding. Heard in this court at the October term, 1912. Affirmed if remittitur filed; otherwise reversed and remanded. Opinion filed October 16, 1913.

INGHAM & INGHAM and JOHN FULLER, for appellant.

EDWARD J. SWEENEY and HERRICK & HERRICK, for appellee.

MR. JUSTICE CREIGHTON delivered the opinion of the court.

This was a claim filed on the 7th day of August, 1911, by the appellee in the Probate Court of DeWitt county against the estate of appellant's intestate, in the aggregate sum of $9,960.27, where a judgment was rendered for the sum of $10,472.54, and by appeal of the administratrix the cause was heard in the Circuit Court of that county, by the court and a jury, and a verdict was returned for appellee in the sum of $10,472.54. Upon the coming in of the verdict appellee remitted $3,369.66, whereupon judgment was entered in favor of appellee in the sum of $7,102.88. From this judgment the cause has been brought to this court by the further appeal of said administratrix.

The following may be stated as the substantial facts in the case relative to the claim.

At the death of appellee's mother, which occurred in May, 1911, appellee held three promissory notes, bearing dates and for the amounts as follows: One note for the sum of $1,000 dated May 1, 1902, due one year after date, and not providing for interest; one note for the sum of $2,000 bearing no date but being due July 5, 1904, and not providing for interest; and one note for $4,100 dated July 15, 1904, providing for interest at the rate of six per cent. from date and due in one year. All of these notes were signed by Elizabeth Wilson, appellant's intestate, the mother of both appellee and appellant.

The appellee was called by appellant as a witness, and his statement, in effect, was that the consideration for the first note of $1,000 was for insurance money arising from the collection of an insurance policy upon his father's life by his mother, and by his consent used by the mother, and the interest, which, together with the interest amounted to the sum of the face of the note at the date thereof; that the consideration for the second, or $2,000 note, was part payment for ten years' labor for his mother by appellee, after he attained his legal majority on the farm, at $20 per month; that the consideration for the third note was the $400 balance due him for labor on the farm of his mother and interest thereon; and that the remainder of the note was, in the language of appellee, for "standing by my mother for thirty-one years."

The further evidence appears in the record that an advancement was made by the mother to appellee, which was shown by the following instrument, to-wit: "STATE OF ILLINOIS.

DeWITT COUNTY.

To Elizabeth Wilson and her children:

This certifies that I, William E. Wilson, son of Elizabeth Wilson, do hereby acknowledge in writing the receipt of Thirty-seven Hundred dollars ($3700.00) from my mother Elizabeth Wilson as an advancement on my interest in the estate of Elizabeth Wilson, my mother, at her death. That I received the same as an advancement as one of her children but that there is to be no interest to be charged up to me on the said

Thirty-seven hundred dollars ($3700.00) what would be the interest of the said $3700.00 is to be set off by the labor and services that I performed for my mother Elizabeth Wilson, after I had attained the age of twenty-one years. And I hereby consent that my interest in the estate of my mother Elizabeth Wilson shall be charged with said sum of $3700.00 at the death of my mother. It is further stipulated that my mother and my sisters and brother were consulted and informed as to the terms of this acknowledgment of my advancement before it was reduced to writing.

Dated this 3rd day of January A. D. 1902.

WILLIAM E. WILSON (SEAL).''

The consideration as to the first or $1,000 note is conceded to be sufficient, and this should be allowed together with interest at five per cent. per annum from the maturity thereof.

The consideration for the second or $2,000 note has, in our opinion, been established by proof of labor and services rendered by appellee to his mother during her lifetime and after his arriving at his legal majority, and interest should be computed on the amount of this note from maturity.

The consideration for the third or $4,100 note consists of three items: First, the $400 being the balance due appellee for labor for ten years on the farm of appellant's intestate after the $2,000 note had been given; second, the sum of $1,416, composing the consideration for this note, is for the interest agreed by appellant's intestate to be paid to appellee upon the amount due to him for labor on the farm of his mother, as aforesaid. These two items are supported by proof as being a valuable consideration for the part of the note represented and are legal and just claims against this estate, and, taken together, with interest at the rate of six per cent. being the rate fixed in this note, from the maturity of the note until said 16th day of July, 1912, amounts to the total sum of $2,689.50.

As to the remainder of said note, amounting to the

sum of $2,284, the sufficiency of the consideration is not shown by the evidence. It was clearly a gift, without consideration, and cannot be allowed as a claim against the estate of the deceased. This is clearly established by the evidence of appellee.

It is insisted by appellant that the receipt for the advancement of $3,700 to appellee is evidence of a settlement for the labor performed by appellee for the deceased.

When it is considered that the advancement was made January 3, 1902, and two and one-half years thereafter the note representing a part of the value of the labor performed by appellee on the deceased's farm was executed, it would seem there could not be any reason for the contention of appellant upon this point. The mother seems to have been, from all of the transactions, competent to transact any ordinary business, and to accept the theory of appellant that she regarded this advancement as a settlement of the labor question between herself and her son would be to hold that she was incompetent and did not understand the ordinary methods of transacting business. In the face of the proof in this record we would not be warranted in concluding that the advancement was considered by either of the parties thereto as a settlement for the labor performed by appellee for appellant's intestate.

We are, therefore, of the opinion a judgment in favor of appellee and against the estate of appellant's intestate should be allowed in the sum of $6,952.68. The judgment appealed from was for $7,102.88, being for the sum of $150.20 more than the proof shows should have been allowed.

If the appellee shall within fifteen days remit from the judgment all of the said judgment in excess of the sum of $6,952.68, it will be affirmed for that sum, otherwise the judgment will be reversed and the cause remanded.

Affirmed if remittitur filed; otherwise reversed and remanded.

O. P. Stufflebeam and Phillip Cadle, Appellants, v. Charles A. Allen and W. B. Redden, Appellees.

1. ARBITRATION AND AWARD, § 81*—*when findings of trial court setting aside an award sustained by the evidence.* On bill to set aside an award in an accounting between partners, findings of trial court as to the award being erroneous and as to the different amounts due the various partners, *held* sustained by the evidence.

2. ARBITRATION AND AWARD, § 76*—*when whole award will not be set aside.* On bill to set aside an award, it is not the duty of the court to set aside the whole award when any item in the award is a result of fraud, there being no allegations of fraud applicable to or affecting the whole award.

3. ARBITRATION AND AWARD, § 74*—*sufficiency of decree setting aside an award in part.* A decree setting aside an award in part, under a prayer for general relief should make all proper corrections of the award and should direct the enforcement of the award as amended by it, and provide for the payment of the various sums to whom they are due and make its decree final as to all matters involved.

4. ARBITRATION AND AWARD, § 81*—*when allowance of salary to partner on bill to set aside award not error.* On bill to set aside an award made in an accounting between partners, an allowance to a partner of a certain sum as salary during the partnership, *held* not error, there being no allegation in the bill as to fraud, irregularity or illegality on the question of the salary item, and no error is assigned upon the record as to such item.

Appeal from the Circuit Court of Vermilion county; the Hon. WILLIAM B. SCHOLFIELD, Judge, presiding. Heard in this court at the October term, 1912. Remanded with directions. Opinion filed October 16, 1913. *Certiorari* denied by Supreme Court (making opinion final).

ACTON & ACTON, THOMAS A. GRAHAM and H. M. STEELY, for appellants.

JOSEPH B. MANN and LAWRENCE T. ALLEN, for appellee Charles A. Allen.

AUGUSTUS A. PARTLOW, for appellee W. B. Redden.

*See Illinois Notes Digest, Vols. XI to XV, same topic and section number.

MR. JUSTICE CREIGHTON delivered the opinion of the court.

This is an appeal from a decree entered in the Circuit Court of Vermilion county, and the facts leading up to the institution of the suit are substantially as follows:

In the year 1893, O. P. Stufflebeam, Phillip Cadle, Charles A. Allen, W. B. Redden, with other parties, engaged as partners in operating a canning factory at Rossville, Illinois, and later they engaged in operating an electric light plant, the canning factory having been destroyed by fire, and this partnership continued to do business up until the year 1904, as such partners.

On the 22d day of September, 1907, Charles A. Allen filed a bill in the Circuit Court of Vermilion county for an accounting of the partnership business and for a dissolution of the partnership. Answers were filed by all the defendants. The cause was continued from term to term until the January term, 1910, when the cause was referred to the master in chancery to take and report the proofs, together with findings. Pending the taking of the proofs before the master, the several parties to the suit entered into an agreement to arbitrate all matters in dispute, claims or controversies whatsoever involved in the settlement of the said partnership, and selected three arbitrators and provided for administering the oath to the witnesses, hearing the evidence and for a full and final adjustment of the matter, and for a written finding and report to the court. Such evidence as the master had taken was submitted, and the evidence of the witnesses was heard by the arbitrators. Charles A. Allen testified, in his own behalf, to the effect that the firm was indebted to him for money furnished or advanced by him, and that he held at one time a note for the sum of $5,000 given by the firm, as evidence of the same, but that he had lost or mislaid the same, and he produced a receipt from the

State treasurer, showing that he did have such a note and had deposited it with said treasurer as collateral security for a loan. Mr. Stufflebeam and Mr. Cadle each swore they had never signed any such note. The arbitrators allowed Mr. Allen, for principal and interest, the sum of $10,219.65.

After the award was made and filed by the arbitrators objections were made to the allowance of the above claim, and the bill in chancery here involved was filed by Mr. Stufflebeam and Mr. Cadle, praying for a decree to set aside the award and to enjoin the allowance of Mr. Allen's claim based upon the said note with the interest aforesaid, and averring that the evidence given by Mr. Allen in support of the validity of the claim was false, and that the claim had been allowed by the arbitrators because of the fraud and perjury of Mr. Allen, and further averring they could furnish positive proof that the claim was not a just claim. The said partners were all parties and the defendants were served with summons, came into court and filed answers. The answer of Mr. Allen denied that his testimony before the arbitrators was false and his answer was otherwise formal. The answer of Mr. Redden was a formal one. Replications were filed to the answers and the cause was, at the January term, 1912, referred to the master in chancery to take and report the evidence and his conclusions of law and fact.

At the August term, 1912, of the said court, the master made his report. Objections were filed by appellants to the findings of the master and were overruled, and the same were filed as exceptions to his report before the chancellor. The court sustained the exceptions so far as the findings related to the allowance of the said $5,000 note and interest, and all other exceptions were overruled.

The court found that the account of the partners, and the amounts advanced by each of them, to be as follows:

Charles A. Allen.................$15,809.63
W. B. Redden.................... 24,151.18
O. P. Stufflebeam............... 16,985.11
Phillip Cadle................... 17,533.46

Making a total of............$74,479.38
contributed by all four of the partners, of which each
should have contributed an equal one-fourth part, or
the sum of $18,619.84 each, and that on the basis of these
amounts as contributed there was due to W. B. Redden
from Phillip Cadle the sum of $1,086.38; that there was
due from O. P. Stufflebeam to W. B. Redden the sum
of $1,634.73, making a total due to W. B. Redden from
Cadle and Stufflebeam the sum of $2,721.11; that there
was due from Charles A. Allen to W. B. Redden the
sum of $2,810.22; and it was ordered, adjudged and
decreed that Charles A. Allen be enjoined from collecting or attempting to collect from Cadle and Stufflebeam the sum found due by the arbitrators; that W. B.
Redden be enjoined from collecting from said Cadle, on
account of said award, any more than the sum of
$1,086.38; that said Redden be enjoined from collect-
ing from said Stufflebeam, on account of said award,
any more than the sum of $1,634.73; and that Charles
A. Allen pay to the said W. B. Redden the sum of
$2,810.22, and that the costs of the suit be taxed to said
Charles A. Allen and that execution issue therefor.

Thereupon this appeal was perfected, thus bringing
the record before us for review.

It is contended by appellants that it was the duty of
the court when any item in the award was the result
of fraud to set the whole award aside.

We cannot agree with this contention, as in this case
there was no fraud charged except as to the allowance
of the claim for the note and interest allowed to Mr.
Allen, amounting to the sum of $10,219.65, and that item
was eliminated by the court. Had the allegations of
fraud applied to or affected the whole award and had

the court found such to be true, then the rule would have been different.

It is further contended by appellant that the allowance to W. B. Redden of the sum of $3,900 as salary during the partnership was in violation of law. The fact that no allegation appears in the bill as to fraud, irregularity or illegality on the question of this salary item is sufficient to justify us in saying the court made no error in this regard. No error is assigned upon this record as to this item.

We think the evidence in this case fully sustains the findings of the trial court. We find, however, that while the trial court found that the award was erroneous and restrained Charles A. Allen from collecting the proceeds of the $5,000 note, and found that different sums were due the various partners than those contained in the award, the decree did not attempt to cancel the award or provide for the payment of the various sums found to be due to the parties to whom it was found owing.

The decree, under the prayer for general relief, should have made all of the proper corrections of the award, and having jurisdiction of the subject-matter should have directed the enforcement of the award as amended by it, and provided for the payment of the various sums to whom they were due and made its decree final as to all matters involved.

The cause will be remanded to the trial court with directions to enter a decree in accordance herewith.

Remanded with directions.

Louis Oswald, Defendant in Error, v. Marcus D. Hexter, Plaintiff in Error.

1. MORTGAGES, § 32*—*when evidence sufficient to show deed was intended as a mortgage.* On bill filed to have certain deeds and assignments, absolute in form, declared to be in the nature of a mortgage and for an accounting, findings of trial court that certain transfers were intended as security in the nature of a mortgage and that others were gifts in the nature of family settlements, *held* sustained by the evidence.

2. FRAUDS, STATUTE OF, § 48*—*when parol agreement sufficient to show absolute deed a mortgage.* To prove that an absolute deed is in the nature of a mortgage, a parol agreement is sufficient when it is established to the satisfaction of the court to take the case out of the statute of frauds.

Error to the Circuit Court of Greene county; the Hon. JAMES A. CREIGHTON, Judge, presiding. Heard in this court at the April term, 1913. Affirmed. Opinion filed October 16, 1913. *Certiorari* denied by Supreme Court (making opinion final).

FRANK A. WHITESIDES and ALBERT SALZENSTEIN, for plaintiff in error.

J. M. RIGGS and THOMAS HENSHAW, for defendant in error.

MR. JUSTICE CREIGHTON delivered the opinion of the court.

This was a bill in chancery filed in the Circuit Court of Green county by the defendant in error against Marcus D. Hexter, Lena Hexter, Herman Oswald and others. The bill alleges that the defendant in error was on November 28, 1904, indebted in the sum of $9,000; that he was the owner at the time of 40 acres of land, a residence, a business building in Whitehall, eight thirty-fifths interest in 56.40 acres and ten two-hundred tenths interest in 23.78 acres of land situated in St. Clair county, Illinois, and a real estate mortgage for $2,140, all of the value of $20,000 over and above any incumbrances; that Marcus D. Hexter and

Herman Oswald and Lena Hexter were desirous of
obtaining the title to the defendant in error's property,
thereby getting said property out of his name and control, and to convert the same to their use and benefit;
that the defendant in error did not, at said time or for
months thereafter, know of the design and purpose of
the plaintiff in error to strip and deprive him of the
fee title of his property; that while the defendant in
error was worried and anxious as to the condition of
his wife, who was sick with an incurable disease, the said
Marcus D. Hexter, Lena Hexter and Herman Oswald
falsely represented to him that his creditors were intending to bring suits against him, and that his property would be sacrificed and wasted by judgment, execution and sale; that Marcus D. Hexter, with the
knowledge and approval of Lena Hexter and Herman
Oswald, proposed to the defendant in error that he
would pay the indebtedness of the defendant in error,
if the defendant in error would secure him by assigning
and conveying all of the said property to said Marcus
Hexter, Lena Hexter and Herman Oswald, such deeds
and assignments to stand as a mortgage to secure the
said Hexter for the amount paid out by him on said indebtedness, and save the remainder of the property for
the defendant in error; that after the debts had been
paid the remainder of the property would be returned
to the defendant in error; that in pursuance of the said
agreement, and for the purpose aforesaid, he did assign and convey the said property to them; that
after the conveyances and assignments aforesaid the
said plaintiff in error received from the sale of the said
property and collection of the said debts, the sum of
$13,608, which said sum is largely in excess of the
amount paid out under the agreement; that the representations made by the said Marcus D. Hexter, Lena
Hexter and Herman Oswald to the defendant in error
that his creditors were intending to bring suit were
not true and were known by the plaintiff in error to be

false when made, but were used as a means to get the
property of the defendant in error in their names, and
that said plaintiff in error now claims that both the
conveyances and the assignments were absolute and
not in the nature of a mortgage, and refuse to account
to the defendant in error for the proceeds of the sale
of said property and the collection of said debts, and
also refuse to reconvey the unsold real estate or re-
assign said property to the defendant in error.

The bill prayed for an accounting and a return of the
unsold property. A joint answer was filed by said Marcus D. Hexter, Lena Hexter and Herman Oswald, and
admits that the defendant in error was indebted in the
sum of $9,000; that he owned the property described in
the bill, but deny that they made any false representations to the defendant in error to induce him to convey the property to them, but aver that the residence
in Whitehall was deeded to Lena Hexter as a gift, and
that the business property in said city was deeded to
Herman Oswald as a gift, both of said gifts being in
the nature of a family settlement; that the remainder
of the property was deeded and assigned to Marcus
D. Hexter and Herman Oswald in consideration that
they would pay certain debts of the defendant in error,
and that the deeds were not understood to be mortgages, but were absolute conveyances, without any
agreement or understanding that any part was to be
returned.

Upon a hearing the court found that on the 28th day
of November, 1904, Marcus D. Hexter assumed and
agreed to pay the indebtedness of the defendant in
error, and that in order to secure the said Hexter in
paying said debts the defendant in error and his wife
conveyed to Marcus D. Hexter and Herman Oswald
the forty acres of land in Greene county, subject, however, to a joint and several life estate in the grantors;
that said deed, though absolute in form, was in the nature of a mortgage to secure said Hexter for such sums
of money as he should pay in the discharge of the

debts of the defendant in error; that at the same time the defendant in error assigned and transferred his interest in certain real estate in St. Clair county to Marcus D. Hexter and Herman Oswald, and that said assignment and transfer was in the nature of a mortgage, to further secure the said Hexter for the discharge of the indebtedness of defendant in error. The court further found that the deeds of conveyance made by the defendant in error to the business property at Whitehall to Herman Oswald, and the residence property to Lena Hexter, were gifts in the nature of a family settlement, both of said conveyances, however, being subject to a life estate reserved to the grantors, but the court further held that the defendant in error's life estate in the property conveyed to Lena Hexter was not involved in this cause, and the bill was dismissed as to Lena Hexter without prejudice.

The decree further found that Marcus D. Hexter and Herman Oswald should be required to account to the defendant in error for all moneys received by them, or either of them, arising from the sale of the lots or lands in St. Clair county, and also for all moneys received by them, or either of them, on the mortgage for $2,140, executed by Peter Kinser; that they be required to render an accounting showing what moneys they, or either of them, paid out on the indebtedness of the defendant in error, to whom paid, when paid and all sums paid out by them for taxes or insurance on the said mortgaged property; that Lena Hexter is a daughter and Herman Oswald a son of the defendant in error; that on account of the family relationship the defendant in error placed trust and confidence in said Marcus D. Hexter and Herman Oswald, and conveyed the Greene county land and assigned and transferred his interest in the St. Clair county property and in the Kinser mortgage to them, and that said conveyances and assignments were made to secure the said Hexter as aforesaid, and are in the nature of mortgages; that the defendant in error should be allowed

to redeem the forty acres of land in Greene county
and the unsold equities in the St. Clair county real estate, upon the payment to Hexter and Oswald of whatever sum shall be found, upon an accounting, to be due
to them; it was further decreed that upon an accounting said Marcus D. Hexter and Herman Oswald shall
be charged with all moneys received by them, or either
of them, from the proceeds of all of said property and
for the amount received from the Kinser note and
mortgage.

From this decree this writ of error was sued out,
and all of the findings of the decree are questioned by
the respective parties assigning upon the record, errors and cross-errors.   .

The principal issue presented for determination in
this case is one of fact, i. e., whether the transfers of
the property mentioned in the defendant in error's bill
were intended to convey to the grantees therein the
absolute title to the property.

We think the evidence is abundant to show that the
agreement entered into by these parties was not intended to convey the property absolutely, but was to
indemnify said Hexter against loss in the payment
of certain debts of the defendant in error, as to all of
the property, except the business and residence property in Whitehall, conveyed to Herman Oswald and
Lena Hexter, respectively.

While there is a conflict in the testimony, and many
circumstances tending to show that as to these two
pieces of property they were also intended to be security for the payment of the debts of the defendant
in error, yet, we are not able to say that the allegations
of the bill of the defendant in error have been supported by a preponderance of the evidence upon this
question. The chancellor saw the witnesses and heard
their evidence and was in a superior position to judge
of the worth and credibility of their various statements. The chancellor found these two pieces of property were conveyed to the two children of the defend-

ant in error and were in the nature of a family settlement and to equalize these two children with another child to whom gifts had before then been made. We are inclined to the opinion that this finding was supported by the evidence.

The conveyances of the other property, being in the nature of a mortgage, could not pass absolute title to the plaintiffs in error, although, in form deeds, they were in fact intended to be mortgages.

Section 12 of chapter 95, R. S. (J. & A. ¶ 7587) provides: "Every deed conveying real estate, which shall appear to have been intended only as a security in the nature of a mortgage, though it be an absolute conveyance in terms, shall be considered as a mortgage."

" 'If confidence is reposed, it must be faithfully acted upon and preserved from any intermixture of imposition. If influence is acquired, it must be kept free from the taint of selfish interest and cunning and overreaching bargains.' (1 Story's Eq. Jur. sec. 308.) Where a person is entrusted as a confidential agent with a conduct of business where he professes not to act for himself, but for others who have placed their confidence in him, he is disabled in equity, even though he may be a volunteer, from dealing in the matter of his agency on his own account. 'The agency being established, he will be compelled to transfer the benefit of his contract, although he may swear he purchased on his own account.' (*Dennis v. McCagg*, 32 Ill. 429.) The rule applies not only to persons standing in a direct fiduciary relation towards others, but also to those who occupy any position out of which a similar duty ought, in equity and good morals, to arise." *Conant v. Riseborough*, 139 Ill. 383.

It is contended by the plaintiff in error that the mere refusal of a trustee to execute an express trust does not constitute such fraud as takes the case out of the statutes of frauds.

A parol agreement is sufficient, in this character of

case, when established to the satisfaction of the court, to take the case out of the effect of the statute of frauds. *Reigard v. McNeil*, 38 Ill. 401.

A careful review of all of the evidence preserved in this record leads us to believe that the decree of the Circuit Court should be sustained. It is sound in principle and seems to be an equitable adjustment of the rights of the parties.

The decree is, therefore, affirmed.

Affirmed.

Mary E. Lee, Administratrix, Defendant in Error, v. Toledo, St. Louis and Western Railroad Company, Plaintiff in Error.

1. DEATH, § 48*—*admissibility of evidence.* In an action by widow to recover for the death of her husband, permitting plaintiff to prove that she had no means of support other than that furnished by her deceased husband, *held* error. The limit of inquiry along this line is as to the earning capacity of the deceased and his contribution to the support of his family.

2. DEATH, § 73*—*when instruction not based on evidence erroneous.* In an action against a railroad company to recover damages for the death of a fireman, an instruction permitting recovery for negligence of the engineer *held* improper where there was no proof upon which to base the conclusion that engineer acted improperly in the operation of the engine or that his conduct in anyway contributed to the death of plaintiff's intestate.

3. DEATH, § 73*—*when instruction asking jury to consider all the evidence improper.* In an action for death, an instruction given for plaintiff *held* objectionable in asking the jury to consider, in determining as to the measure of damages, all the evidence, there being improper evidence admitted on the part of the plaintiff.

4. DEATH, § 73*—*when requested instruction improperly refused.* In an action against a railroad company for death of a fireman occasioned by derailment, a requested instruction for defendant that, "If, from the evidence in this case, you are unable to say, under

*See Illinois Notes Digest, Vols. XI to XV, same topic and section number.

your oaths as jurors, what caused the derailment of the engine, then the court instructs you to find the defendant not guilty," *held* improperly refused.

5. Death, § 73*—*when refusal of requested instruction is error.* In an action for death, refusal of a requested instruction on question of proof of the cause of the injury and defendant's negligence, *held* error.

6. Trial, § 233*—*when error to permit jury to take pleadings to the jury room.* In an action for death, *held* error to permit certain counts of the declaration to be taken by the jury to the jury room without some explanation or instruction where there is no proof to support the theory of such counts. As a general rule, where any of the pleadings are permitted to go to the jury the whole of the pleadings should go.

Error to the Circuit Court of Coles county; the Hon. William B. Scholfield, Judge, presiding. Heard in this court at the April term, 1913. Reversed and remanded. Opinion filed October 16, 1913.

A. J. Fryer and C. E. Pope, for plaintiff in error; Charles A. Schmettau, of counsel.

S. S. Anderson and H. A. Neal, for defendant in error.

Mr. Justice Creighton delivered the opinion of the court.

This is a writ of error sued out by the plaintiff in error to bring into review a judgment entered in the Circuit Court of Coles county, in the sum of seven thousand five hundred dollars in favor of the defendant in error and against the plaintiff in error, in a suit wherein the defendant in error brought the action to recover for the death of her husband, and which suit was prosecuted under the Employer's Liability Act of the United States.

The declaration contains four counts. The first count alleges, in substance, that Robert E. Lee, plaintiff's intestate, was the husband of the defendant in error; that he was employed as a fireman on the engine pulling a train belonging to the plaintiff in error working on a division of the road which extends from

*See Illinois Notes Digest, Vols. XI to XV, same topic and section number.

Vol. CLXXXIV 10

Charleston, Illinois, to Frankfort, Indiana; that while he was so employed it became the duty of the plaintiff in error to provide him with a reasonably safe place in which to work; that the plaintiff in error neglected its duty in this respect and failed to furnish the deceased a safe place in which to work, but furnished to the deceased an unsafe track upon which the train was run and upon which he was working, to wit, a track with insufficient rails, decayed cross-ties, the nails being insecurely spiked, by reason of which the track spread and the engine of the plaintiff in error, upon which the deceased was working, turned over and fell upon the deceased and killed him; that the deceased was a married man, having a wife and two children, and was earning one hundred dollars per month at the time of his death.

The second count was practically the same as the first, except that it averred that the engine used in propelling the train upon which deceased was working was of the weight of fifty tons, and that said engine by reason of its great weight, when attached to a light train, was wholly unfit for such service and endangered the life of the deceased; that the deceased had taken the examination and was admitted to the roll of eligible engineers and, when so employed, to a salary of one hundred and fifty dollars per month.

The third count charges that it was the duty of the plaintiff in error to furnish a safe place for defendant in error's intestate to work and a safe engine upon which to work, but that the plaintiff in error utterly failed so to do; that the plaintiff in error furnished a defective engine upon which the deceased was required to ride and work as such fireman; "that the springs supporting the boiler and frame of said engine were broken and the springs over the front driving wheels were rendered ineffective and useless by having placed beside them, upon the driving box of said engine, beside said front driving wheels, beneath the frame of said engine, solid blocks of iron, to-wit: of the thickness of three and one-half inches, removing the weight of the wheels off the pony trucks, and causing them to leave the rails of the said railroad upon which said engine the plaintiff's intestate was required to ride as such fireman, in the transaction of the business of the defendant in the carrying of passengers between the State of Illinois and Indiana; that by reason of such defective engine, broken springs, etc., the engine was thrown from the track and overturned, and the plaintiff's intestate, by reason of the overturning of the said engine, was scalded and burned, thereby causing his death."

The fourth count, in addition to the allegations mentioned in the first count as to the defective track, ties, rails, etc., averred that the plaintiff in error had in its employ and service at the time of the injury one C. S. Bennett, who, as such servant of the plaintiff in error, by the direction of the plaintiff in error, alone had charge of the said engine as locomotive engineer; that it was then and there the duty of the said Bennett, so in charge and having sole management of said engine and sole control of the speed of the said engine, to operate the said engine at a reasonable rate of speed, yet said Bennett carelessly and negligently ran said engine on the said track at a dangerous and reckless rate of speed at, to wit, fifty miles per hour, and caused the said engine to leave the said track, overturn and crush, scald and cause the death of the defendant in error's intestate.

Each count pleads the Federal Employer's Liability Act.

To the declaration a plea of the general issue was filed.

Upon the trial of the cause numerous objections were offered on behalf of the plaintiff in error to the evidence introduced by the defendant in error, but we do not deem it proper to discuss the weight of the evidence in the cause, for the reason the judgment must be reversed upon other grounds.

It is urged by the plaintiff in error that upon the trial of the cause the defendant in error was permitted to prove that she had no means of support other than that furnished by her said deceased husband. The objection to this evidence should have been sustained. The limit of inquiry along this line is as to the earning capacity of the deceased and his contributions to the support of his family.

In no instance can the inquiry lead to the financial ability of the widow or next of kin. This doctrine was announced in *Chicago & N. W. R. Co. v. Moranda*, 93 Ill. 302, in the following language: "It is error to admit proof that the plaintiff and her children had no other means of support save that arising from his daily earnings."

In the case of *Brennen v. Chicago & Carterville Coal Co.*, 241 Ill. 610, the same rule is announced, as follows: "While it is erroneous to admit evidence of the resources of the widow or next of kin or their financial condition, it is not error to allow questions concerning the earnings of the deceased and whether the wife and children were supported by him." See also *Jones & Adams Co. v. George*, 227 Ill. 64 and *Illinois Cent. R. Co. v. Atwell*, 198 Ill. 200.

Objection is urged by plaintiff in error to the action of the court in permitting the declaration to be taken by the jury to the jury room and withholding from the jury the pleas of the plaintiff in error.

As a general rule, where any of the pleadings are permitted to go to the jury, the whole of the pleadings should go. In this particular case it was error to permit the third and fourth counts of the declaration to go to the jury without some explanation or instruction, for the reason there is no proof to support the theory of such third count and the portion of the fourth count which alleged the accident occurred because of the high rate of speed and reckless operation of the engine.

Objection is made to the third instruction given on behalf of the defendant in error, and it is as follows:

"You are instructed that if you believe from the evidence that Robert E. Lee, plaintiff's intestate, was an employe of the defendant and that the defendant was a common carrier by railroad engaged in commerce between the State of Illinois and the State of Indiana, and that while in the employ of the defendant, said Robert E. Lee was injured, scalded and burned by reason of the engine of the defendant getting off the track and overturning, as in plaintiff's declaration alleged, and that from such injuries said Robert E. Lee died, as alleged in plaintiff's declaration, and that such injuries were caused in whole or in part from the negligence of C. S. Bennett, an engineer in the employ of the defendant, or by reason of the defect in the track or roadbed of the defendant due to the negligence of the defendant, as alleged in the declaration or any count thereof, then you should find the defendant guilty and assess the plaintiff's damages at such sum as you believe from the evidence she is entitled to, not exceeding the amount claimed in the declaration."

This instruction is subject to the objection that there is no proof in the record upon which to base a conclusion that the engineer, Bennett, acted improperly in the operation of the engine, or that his conduct was in any manner improper or contributed to the injury to defendant in error's intestate.

The form of instruction six, given at the request of the defendant in error, is, to say the least, questionable; and instruction number seven, also given at the request of the defendant in error, is subject to objection because reference is made, and the jury are asked to consider, in determining as to the measure of damages, all of the evidence which, of course, included the improper evidence admitted on the part of the defendant in error.

Other instructions are subject to the same objections, and to others which we do not deem it necessary to particularly name and point out.

Instruction number eleven, asked by the plaintiff in error, and by the court refused, is as follows:

"If, from the evidence in this case, you are unable to say, under your oaths as jurors, what caused the derailment of the engine, then the court instructs you to find the defendant not guilty."

This instruction states a correct principle of law and should have been given.

Objection is made by the plaintiff in error as to the action of the court in refusing to give instruction fifteen asked in its behalf, which is as follows:

"The Court instructs the jury that under the law it is not enough for a plaintiff, in order to recover damages, to merely prove that an injury or death resulted from defects or insufficiency in defendant's cars, engines, appliances, machinery, roadbed, works, boats, wharves, or other equipment; but before a recovery can be legally had under the law applicable in this case, it must appear from a preponderance of the evidence that the defect or insufficiency in the cars, engines, appliances, machinery, track, roadbed, works, boats, wharves or other equipment was due to the negligence of the officers, agents or employes of the defendant, and if you believe from the evidence in this case that the engine, appliances, machinery, track, roadbed or other equipment of the defendant was not due to any negligence on the part of the defendant's officers, agents or employes, then the court instructs you that the defendant in this case would not be liable under the first, second or third count of the declaration."

We are inclined to the opinion instruction fifteen should have been given, and that it was error to have refused it.

For the reasons given the judgment will be reversed and the cause remanded.

Reversed and remanded.

The People of the State of Illinois ex rel., A. C. Moffett et al., Appellees, v. William R. Turnbull, Mayor, et al., Appellants.

1. MUNICIPAL CORPORATIONS, § 1173*—*when duty of city council to pass appropriation and tax levy ordinance to maintain free library.* Under section 1 of Act of 1872, J. & A. ¶ 7074, authorizing cities, incorporated towns and townships to establish and maintain free public libraries and reading rooms, where a city council passes an ordinance providing for the establishment and maintenance of such a library and by resolution accepts a donation for the erection thereof, *held* that the council by adopting such ordinance and resolution elected to come under the provisions of the statute and could not, on its own motion, refuse to pass appropriation and tax levy ordinances to maintain the library.

2. MANDAMUS, § 148*—*when petition to compel city officials to pass appropriation ordinance and make levy for city library sufficient.* Petition filed by members of a city library board for the issuance of a writ of mandamus to compel the mayor and city council to pass an appropriation ordinance, and to levy, in the tax levy ordinance, the sum of one and two-tenths mills on the dollar of the taxable property of the city, *held* to state facts showing a clear right to demand the issuance of the writ.

3. STATUTES, § 225*—*word "may" construed.* The word "may" in a statute will be construed to mean "shall" whenever the rights of the public or of third persons depend upon the exercise of the power or the performance of a duty to which it refers, and such is its meaning in all cases where the public rights or interests are concerned. The term "public" does not necessarily mean all the inhabitants of a State, but may properly be applied either to the inhabitants of a State, a county or a community.

4. STATUTES, § 225*—*when word "may" means "shall."* The word "may" in section 1 of the Act of 1872, J & A. ¶ 7074, wherein it says "The city council * * * shall have power to establish and maintain a public library * * * and may levy a tax, etc.," *held* to mean "shall."

Appeal from the Circuit Court of Morgan county; the Hon. OWEN P. THOMPSON, Judge, presiding. Heard in this court at the April term, 1913. Affirmed. Opinion filed October 16, 1913.

*See Illinois Notes Digest, Vols. XI to XV, same topic and section number.

C. F. WEMPLE and BELLATTI, BARNES & BELLATTI, for appellants.

ROBERT TILTON and KIRBY, WILSON & BALDWIN, for appellees.

MR. JUSTICE CREIGHTON delivered the opinion of the court.

This was a petition filed by the members of the Library Board of the city of Waverly asking for the issuance of a writ of mandamus against the mayor and city council of said city, to compel them to pass an ordinance appropriating a sum of money for the purpose of maintaining a free public library and also to compel them to levy, in the tax levy ordinance, the sum of one and two-tenths mills on the dollar of the taxable property of said city, for said library, for the fiscal year beginning the third Tuesday of April, 1912.

A demurrer was filed to the petition, and upon the overruling of said demurrer the appellants elected to abide by same. Thereupon the court entered judgment directing the writ to issue, commanding the said mayor and city council to pass the ordinance appropriating a sum of money for said free library, and to levy, in the annual tax levy ordinance, the said sum for the maintenance of the said library.

This is an appeal perfected by a portion of the defendants below, bringing the proceedings before us for review.

The question presented for our consideration upon this record is, whether or not the petition herein filed contains allegations sufficient to authorize the issuance of the peremptory writ of mandamus.

The allegations of the petition, in substance, are: that on the 9th day of May, 1911, the city council of the city of Waverly passed an ordinance providing that a free public library should be established under the provisions of an act of the General Assembly, entitled, "An Act to authorize cities, incorporated towns and townships to establish and maintain free public libraries and reading rooms," approved and in force March 7, 1872, as amended by Acts approved June 17, 1889, May 25, 1889 and June 14, 1909 (J. & A. ¶ 7079), and such ordinance provided: "a library shall be established and maintained by taxation to be appropriated and levied, in the sum of one and two-tenths mills on the dollar on all the taxable property in the city in accordance with the provisions of the said act, for the free use of the inhabitants of the City of Waverly, the said library to be under the supervision and management of a board of directors to be appointed according to the provisions of the statute," etc.; that after the passage of the said ordinance, the mayor of the city appointed said board of directors, consisting of nine persons, and said appointees were duly confirmed by the city council, and that the said board of directors adopted rules governing their own actions and the management of said library; that on the 23d day of February, 1912, the said city council adopted a resolution accepting a donation from Andrew Carnegie in the sum of $4,500 for the erection of a free public library building, "on condition that said city shall pledge itself, by resolution of the council, to support a free public library, at a cost of not less than $450 a year and to provide a suitable site for said building," and providing, after resolving to furnish said site, "that an annual levy shall hereafter be made upon the taxable property of said city, sufficient in amount to comply with above requirements," that the said Andrew Carnegie deposited said sum of $4,500 in a certain trust company to pay for the erection of said building; that a site was conveyed to said library board, for the building; that a contract was entered into by the library board for the erection of the building on the said site, which said contract is now in force and effect, and the contractor has purchased materials and is proceeding with the erection and construction of the said building, which will be completed and ready for occupancy on or about September 1, 1912; that on the

6th day of June, 1911, the said city council passed an ordinance appropriating money for the purposes of said library, and on the 6th day of September, 1911, the annual levy ordinance was passed, in which said ordinance there was levied the sum of $450 for the library fund; that on the 7th day of May, 1912, the city council of said city passed an ordinance, by a vote of four to two, repealing the ordinance of May 9, 1911, establishing such library, which said ordinance was not approved or signed by the mayor, but was published on May 31, 1912; that in passing the appropriation ordinance for the year 1912, the said city council omitted to make any appropriation of any sum for maintaining the library; that the resolution of February 23, 1912, above set forth, is still in full force and effect and that said library board has not been dissolved by any legal steps or proceedings; that said city council has refused to make the appropriation for the purpose of maintaining the library, and has declared its purpose of not making such appropriation and has also declared it will not levy the said sum of $450 in the tax levy ordinance for the present fiscal year; that unless said appropriation is made no tax can be legally levied in the annual tax levy ordinance for the purpose of maintaining said library; that in view of their appointment under the ordinance of May 9, 1911, the library board procured, by public subscriptions, the sum of about $1,200, to procure the lot upon which to erect the library building and to care for a few minor expenses; that the lot has been purchased and the library building is in course of construction and about $1,000 worth of material is now on the grounds. The prayer of the petition is that the individual officers of the city be compelled, by writ of mandamus, to pass an ordinance appropriating a sum of money for the purposes of the library, to publish said ordinance, and to thereafter levy, in the annual tax levy ordinance, said sum of money for the purpose of maintaining said free public library, for the fiscal year beginning the third Tuesday of April, 1912, etc.

Attached to the petition and made parts thereof are the various ordinances, resolution and contract for the building of the library building.

The statute which the city council referred to in the ordinance of May 9, 1911, in section 1 thereof (J. & A. ¶ 7079), provides: "The city council * * * shall have power to establish and maintain a public library and reading room for the use and benefit of the inhabitants of such city, and may levy a tax of not exceeding one and two-tenths mills on the dollar annually on all the taxable property in the city."

Under the view we take of this case, the city council, when the question arose before them, had authority to provide by resolution or ordinance that they would or would not provide for the establishment and maintenance of a free public library and reading room. When the said council adopted the ordinance of May 9, 1911, they, by such adoption, declared they would establish and maintain a free public library.

In our view the latter part of the above quoted section providing "and may levy a tax," etc., is to be construed to mean that if the city council elects to provide for the establishment and maintenance of a free library, then they "shall levy" a tax. The word "may" as used in the section is a grant of power to do so, if the first clause of the section is accepted by the city council. They may or may not determine to establish and maintain a free public library, but if they elect to adopt an ordinance providing that they will establish and maintain a free public library, then the power is granted to them to extend a tax for that purpose, and shall be exercised by them.

The word "may" in a statute will be construed to mean "shall," whenever the rights of the public or of third persons depend upon the exercise of the power or the performance of a duty to which it refers, and such is its meaning in all cases where the public rights or interests are concerned. *Brokaw v. Commissioners of Highways*, 130 Ill. 490. Also see *Binder v. Langhorst*, 234 Ill. 587.

The term "public" does not necessarily mean all of the inhabitants of a State, but may properly be applied either to the inhabitants of a State, a county or a community. *Byrne v. Chicago General Ry. Co.* 169 Ill. 75, at page 84.

In the action to be taken by the city council in this cause, the rights of all of the inhabitants (the public) of that community were involved.

By the adoption of the ordinance of May 9, 1911, the city council had elected to establish and maintain a free public library. By the resolution of February 23, 1912, it had accepted the gift of $4,500 for the erection of the library building from the donor. By the various acts of the council the inhabitants of the city had been induced to subscribe the sum of $1,200, in order to secure a site for the building and had met, by way of taxation, the levy made by the council for the maintenance of the library for the year 1911. The library was to be for the free use of the inhabitants (the public) of the city.

In our view, by the adoption of the ordinance of May 9, 1911, and the resolution of February 23, 1912, the city council had elected to come under the provisions of the statute relating to libraries, and to permit them to refuse of their own motion, to maintain by appropriation and tax levy ordinances the library which they had agreed to maintain, would be to allow the city council to abuse the power vested in them.

As was held by our Supreme Court in *Young v. Carey*, 184 Ill. 613: The duty of the board is clearly implied. This is within that class of cases in which courts may control discretionary powers to sustain a right or prevent an injury.

We think the petition in the case at bar sets up a state of facts showing a clear right to demand the issuance of the writ of mandamus; and the judgment appealed from is hereby affirmed.

Affirmed.

Lizzie Rostetter, Appellee, v. American Insurance Company, Appellant.

1. INSURANCE, § 120*—*when policy construed in favor of insured.* Where clauses in an insurance policy are susceptible of two constructions, in conflict, the one most favorable to the insured will be adopted by the courts.

2. INSURANCE. § 219*—*when provision in policy against foreclosure proceedings without consent of insurer inoperative.* A provision in a policy of fire insurance that the policy shall be null and void if foreclosure proceedings are commenced without the consent of the insurance company, *held* to be inoperative as between insurer and the mortgagee where a mortgage clause is attached to the policy making the loss payable to the mortgagee, the mortgage containing a clause giving mortgagee the right to foreclose in case of default in the payment of interest, which the insurer must have known when attaching the mortgage clause to the policy, and to require mortgagee to obtain the consent of the insurer would in effect destroy the purpose of the mortgage clause.

3. INSURANCE, § 456*—*denial of liability as waiving proof of loss.* Insurance company refusing to pay a loss on the ground of its nonliability in any event cannot insist, in defense of an action for the insurance, that the preliminary proof of loss was not made or was insufficient.

4. INSURANCE, § 674*—*propositions of law.* Propositions of law concerning the effect of a mortgage clause attached to a fire insurance policy containing a clause against foreclosure proceedings with the consent of the insurer, and as to what constitutes a ·waiver of preliminary proof of loss, *held* to be properly held as law by the trial court.

Appeal from the Circuit Court of McLean county; the Hon. COLOSTIN D. MYERS, Judge, presiding. Heard in this court at the April term, 1913. Affirmed. Opinion filed October 16, 1913. Rehearing denied November 12, 1913.

LIVINGSTON & BACH, for appellant.

S. P. ROBINSON, for appellee.

MR. JUSTICE CREIGHTON delivered the opinion of the court.

This was a suit commenced in the Circuit Court of

*See Illinois Notes Digest, Vols. XI to XV, same topic and section number.

McLean county by the appellee to recover upon a fire insurance policy issued January 9, 1911, by the appellant to George H. Jones, insuring his one story frame building against loss by fire, etc., with the following clause attached thereto: "Loss, if any, on building insured under this policy, is hereby made payable to Lizzie Rostetter, mortgagee, as her interest may appear at the time of the loss, subject, however, to all the conditions and stipulations of this policy No. 09791, of the" appellant Company, and is dated January 17, 1911.

The policy also contained, among others, a provision as follows: " or, if foreclosure proceedings be commenced without the consent of this company endorsed hereon, then in each and every one of the above cases, this policy shall be null and void."

Still another provision of the policy provided that "no officer, agent, or other representative of this company shall have power to waive any provision or condition of this policy."

On January 17, 1911, the said George H. Jones was indebted to the appellee in the sum of four hundred dollars and gave a promissory note therefor and a mortgage upon the premises covered by the insurance policy, to secure the same, and the said mortgage contained a clause which provided: "if default be made in the payment of the interest when due, the whole debt may be declared due and foreclosure proceedings instituted."

Mr. Jones failed to pay the first instalment of interest, and a foreclosure proceeding was instituted and a decree taken upon the same and the said premises advertised for sale by the master in chancery for the 8th day of July, 1911. Two days before the time so advertised for sale of the premises the building was entirely destroyed by fire, the loss being total. On the next morning after the fire a Mr. Falkingham, agent of the appellant, learned of the fire and went to the home of

Mr. Jones and told him he would report the loss to the Company. About one week after the fire a Mr. Hubbel, an agent and adjuster for appellant, appeared at Towanda, the home of Mr. Jones, and sent for him to come to the hotel. After considerable talk about the fire and loss, Mr. Jones asked the adjuster if he was going to adjust and pay his loss and Mr. Hubbel replied that he was not, and after some further conversation the adjuster departed. Upon the witness stand Mr. Hubbel explained that the reason for not adjusting the loss was the foreclosure proceeding, which he believed, under the clause above quoted, relieved the Company from liability.

Appellee afterwards, and before the beginning of the suit herein, notified appellant on two different occasions of her rights in the matter, and demanded payment. Appellant declined to pay.

This suit was begun in the Circuit Court of McLean county, and the declaration contained two counts, being in the usual form in such proceedings, and avers a total loss and the granting of the mortgage clause in her favor, etc. A plea of the general issue was filed by appellant and a stipulation was entered into by the respective parties provided that all proper defenses might be made under said plea, to the same extent as if special pleas had been filed. The jury was waived and the cause submitted to the court, and a judgment was entered in favor of appellee in the sum of five hundred and thirty-two dollars and costs of suit. This appeal was prayed and perfected, bringing the record to this court for review.

W. A. Freese, an insurance agent of appellant, knew of the default in the payment of the interest and that foreclosure proceedings had been commenced. During that period he had the policy in his possession and knew it contained a mortgage clause in favor of appellee, but he failed to communicate such facts to the home office of appellant.

No written proof of loss was filed with appellant by anyone.

The application for the insurance, which was signed by Mr. Jones, provided for the insertion of a mortgage clause when the policy issued.

The following propositions of law were submitted on behalf of appellee and held to be the law applicable to this cause:

1. The court holds that the foreclosure of the mortgage upon the premises covered by the insurance policy sued upon in this case did not invalidate said policy.

2. The court holds that the defendant, by adding the mortgage clause to the policy of insurance, rendered the condition in the policy, against foreclosure of mortgages, inoperative.

3. The court holds that as between the mortgagee and the defendant the condition of the policy of insurance, providing that the policy should be void, in the event suit was commenced to foreclose a mortgage, was inoperative, and the suit by the plaintiff to foreclose a mortgage, on the premises covered by the insurance policy did not render the policy void.

4. The court holds that the right of the plaintiff to foreclose her mortgage was incident to her security given by the defendant, by adding the mortgage clause to the policy, and the policy was not affected by the plaintiff's suit to foreclose her mortgage.

5. The court holds that the defendant Company, by its agent, Falkingham, waived the condition of the policy requiring sworn proof of loss.

6. The court holds that the defendant Company, by its adjuster, Hubbel, waived the condition in the policy requiring sworn proof of loss.

7. The court holds that the sworn proof of loss required by the policy was waived by the agent, Falkingham, telling Jones he would report the loss to the Company and attend to that matter for him.

8. The court holds that the plaintiff is entitled to

recover the face of the policy, with interest at five per cent. per annum, from the commencement of suit.

There is no material controversy in this case as to the facts. The chief objection relied upon by appellant, as ground for the reversal of the judgment, is that the court held the above propositions to be the law applicable to the cause.

When an insurance company refuses to pay a loss on the ground of its nonliability in any event, it cannot insist, in defense of an action, that the preliminary proof was not made or was insufficient. *Williamsburg City Fire Ins. Co. v. Cary*, 83 Ill. 453; *Grange Mill Co. v. Western Assur. Co.*, 118 Ill. 396; *Continental Ins. Co. v. Ruckman*, 127 Ill. 364.

In the case at bar, within a week after the loss, the adjuster who came on that occasion with instructions from the Company to investigate the loss was informed of the loss and of the foreclosure proceedings. He at once determined that the Company was not liable and announced to Mr. Jones that the Company would not pay, and the appellant has maintained and does now maintain that it is not liable on account of the commencement of the foreclosure proceeding. We must, therefore, conclude that the question of the proof of loss did not in any manner control the appellant's action in refusing to pay. When an insurance company denies liability it is estopped from making any formal objection to the proof of loss.

The question of the effect of the foreclosure proceedings as raised by the propositions of law held by the court, set out in the first, second, third and fourth propositions, is vital to the decision of this case.

The rule, as announced in the case of *Lancashire Ins. Co. v. Boardman*, 58 Kan. 339, is: "These provisions appear in an entirely different light when construing the policy with the mortgage clause attached, in an action brought by the mortgagee. The commencement by the mortgagee of proceedings to foreclose a mortgage is not prohibited by the express terms of the mortgage clause, nor by any fair implication contained therein. If prohibited at all, it must be by reason of the provisions of the policy quoted. Construing both the original policy and the mortgage clause together, in the light of the plain purpose to insure the interest of the mortgagee, the commencement of foreclosure proceedings cannot be held in violation of any stipulation forbidding the mortgagee.''

The appellant must have known, when attaching the mortgage clause to the policy in question, that it might become necessary for the mortgagee, in order to protect her interests under the mortgage, to commence forclosure proceedings. *German Ins. Co. of Freeport v. Churchill,* 26 Ill. App. 206.

In *Getman v. Guardian Fire Ins. Co.,* 46 Ill. App. 489, the following language is used: ''The contract created by the policy and the added clause, was one between the insurer, the insured and the beneficiary. Their relations to each other were within the contemplation of each contracting party, and neither one should be permitted to avoid a duty imposed by the contract because of the interposition of a legal result which, from the nature of the objects to be secured by the contract, must have been within the knowledge of all as one likely to follow.''

Where clauses in an insurance policy are susceptible of two constructions, on conflict, the one most favorable to the insured will be adopted by the courts. In this case there is a conflict between the rights of appellee and appellant as to whether or not appellant's consent must be had before appellee could legally proceed to foreclose her mortgage lien. The object and purpose of appellee in obtaining the mortgage clause to be inserted in the policy in question was to add additional security to the note and mortgage mentioned, and that fact was well understood by appellant at the time the clause was inserted. It must have been equally well understood by appellant that there might be a default in the payment of the mortgage and that a foreclosure proceeding would necessarily follow. To say that appellant's consent was necessary before a foreclosure proceeding could be instituted is in effect to destroy the very object and purpose of the insertion of the mortgage clause.

Applying the rule as hereinabove announced, we cannot agree with the contention of appellant that the propositions of law as held by the court, which we think control this case, were erroneously held.

Therefore, the judgment is affirmed.

Affirmed.

Servian J. Kauffman, Appellee, v. David G. Sanner, Appellant.

(Not to be reported in full.)

Appeal from the County Court of Shelby county; the Hon. J. K. P. GRIDER, Judge, presiding. Heard in this court at the April term, 1913. Affirmed. Opinion filed October 16, 1913.

Statement of the Case.

Action by Servian J. Kauffman against David G. Sanner to recover a balance claimed to be due to plaintiff on a contract for tiling land of defendant. From a judgment in favor of plaintiff for $117.92, defendant appeals.

STEIDLEY & CROCKETT, for appellant.

MARION WATSON, for appellee.

MR. JUSTICE CREIGHTON delivered the opinion of the court.

Abstract of the Decision.

1. CONTRACTS, § 401*—*when judgment for plaintiff will be sustained on appeal.* In an action to recover a balance claimed to be due on a tiling contract, a verdict in favor of plaintiff *held* sustained by the evidence and errors in instructions *held* not prejudicial error.

2. APPEAL AND ERROR, § 1420*—*when irregularity during trial not cause for reversal.* Courts will not reverse a cause merely because of some irregularity during the trial, if from all the facts and circumstances in the record it appears that equal and exact justice has been done.

Alva J. Hendricks, Appellee, v. William F. Roley, Appellant.

(Not to be reported in full.)

Appeal from the Circuit Court of Shelby county; the Hon. JAMES C. MCBRIDE, Judge, presiding. Heard in this court at the April term, 1913. Affirmed. Opinion filed October 16, 1913. Rehearing denied and modified opinion refiled November 6, 1913.

Statement of the Case.

Action by Alva J. Hendricks against William F. Roley to recover $500 designated as liquidated damages due, and the value of certain personal property turned over to defendant under a written contract between plaintiff and defendant for the exchange of real and personal property. From a judgment in favor of plaintiff for $940, defendant appeals.

U. G. WARD and WILLIAM H. CRAIG, for appellant.

RICHARDSON & WHITAKER, for appellee.

MR. JUSTICE CREIGHTON delivered the opinion of the court.

*See Illinois Notes Digest, Vols. XI to XV, same topic and section number.

Hendricks v. Roley, 184 Ill. App. 164.

Abstract of the Decision.

1. **Exchange of property, § 1***—*when party receiving part of property not entitled to its retention for failure of other party to comply with contract.* Where a party to a contract for the exchange of real estate and personal property receives from the other party personal property as part payment of the purchase price, he cannot retain the same for failure of such other party to further comply with the contract, where he himself fails to comply with the terms of the contract in furnishing sufficient abstracts of title, in failing to make and deliver a sufficient deed and in being unable to deliver immediate possession.

2. **Exchange of property, § 1***—*when party in default under contract to give immediate possession.* Where a party in a contract for the exchange of lands reserves all growing crops and agrees to give immediate possession, he fails to comply with his contract to give immediate possession where his tenant is in possession under an unexpired lease. In such case the provision reserving the growing crops does not annul the other provision for immediate possession.

3. **Exchange of property, § 1***—*when party to contract not in default for failure to give possession.* Under a contract for the exchange of land and personal property, one party cannot claim that the other failed to give him possession of the land where the evidence shows that personal property had been delivered to him as part of the purchase price and the other party had asked leave to permit his stock to remain in the pasture.

4. **Exchange of property, § 1***—*when agreement is to convey subject to incumbrance.* Where a party to a contract for the exchange of lands agrees to convey his "land incumbered to the extent of $8,000, plus interest from Jan. 10, 1910, on the $8,000," the agreement when construed in connection with the evidence, *held* to mean that the conveyance was to be subject to the incumbrance.

5. **Trover and conversion, § 45***—*when verdict not excessive.* In an action to recover liquidated damages and the value of personal property delivered to defendant as part of purchase price, *held*, that defendant was liable for the value of the property retained and converted to his use, and a verdict in favor of plaintiff for $940 sustained as not excessive.

6. **Crops, § 3***—*effect of provision in contract reserving right to growing crops.* A clause in a contract for the exchange of lands, reserving to one party the right to growing crops and also providing to give to the other party immediate possession, gives to the former the right to ingress and egress to look after, harvest and remove such crops and to the latter the right to immediate possession of all other portions of the farm.

---

*See Illinois Notes Digest, Vols. XI to XV, same topic and section number.

7. CONTRACTS, § 172*—*construction of antagonistic clauses.* When two clauses in a contract are antagonistic in part only, they should be enforced in such parts as are not in conflict.

Howard Thornley, Appellant, v. John Shey, Appellee.

1. NUISANCE, § 20*—*when bill to enjoin continuance of a smoke nuisance sufficient on demurrer.* Bill by owner of a farm to enjoin defendant from using soft coal in his kilns for burning brick and tile so as to cause large volumes of dense black smoke, vapor, gases and offensive odors contaminating the air over, in and around complainant's residence, orchard, garden and grape arbor, *held* sufficient on demurrer.

2. NUISANCE, § 21*—*when bill to enjoin a continuing nuisance sufficient to give court of equity jurisdiction.* Where a bill for an injunction alleges that the acts complained of constitute a continuing nuisance and cannot be adequately compensated or established in an action at law and that an injunction is the only remedy to avoid a multiplicity of suits and irreparable damages to the complainant and his property, *held* that a court of equity has jurisdiction without a prior determination of the question by a court of law.

3. INJUNCTION, § 183*—*when bill need not be verified.* Bill for an injunction, which prays for an injunction upon the final hearing and not for a temporary injunction, need not be verified in order to give it a standing in court.

4. INJUNCTION, § 216*—*laches.* Bill to enjoin a continuance of a nuisance, *held* not subject to demurrer on the ground of laches where it appears that complainant was active and persistent in his effort to rid himself thereof almost from the beginning and, having failed by the usual and ordinary means, appealed to the court to secure his legal rights.

Appeal from the Circuit Court of Cass county; the Hon. ALBERT AKERS, Judge, presiding. Heard in this court at the April term, 1913. Reversed and remanded with directions. Opinion filed October 16, 1913.

*See Illinois Notes Digest, Vols. XI to XV, same topic and section number.

NEIGER & GORDLEY, for appellant.

HARDIN W. MASTERS, CHARLES A. GRIDLEY and THOMAS D. MASTERS, for appellee.

MR. JUSTICE CREIGHTON delivered the opinion of the court.

This was a bill in chancery filed by the appellant to restrain an alleged nuisance said to have been maintained by the appellee. A general demurrer together with special causes for demurrer were filed to the bill, and were, by the court, sustained, and the bill dismissed at the cost of appellant for want of equity.

An appeal has been perfected by the appellant, thus bringing the record of the proceedings before us for review.

The bill, in substance, charges that appellant is the owner of a farm of about two hundred and six acres, situated in Cass county, Illinois, and that he resides thereon with his family; that said farm is improved with a residence, barn and outbuildings, and is bounded on the south by a public highway, and along the said highway is appellant's residence, orchard, vegetable garden and grape arbor; that at the time of the purchase of the said farm by appellant, and for a long space of time prior thereto, the appellee was engaged in the business of manufacturing brick and had his plant located on the south of appellant's residence, across the public highway, a distance of about two hundred and twenty feet, and that at that time the only fuel used by the appellee for burning the brick was wood, and that said business as then conducted managed and used caused no offense whatever to appellant or injury to his property, premises or the health of himself and his family; that in the year 1909 the said appellee removed the brick kilns formerly used in the said business of manufacturing brick and erected in place thereof two large kilns for the purpose of burning brick and tile, and connected therewith three large smokestacks of the height of twenty feet, and commenced to operate the said plant in the spring of 1910 and continued to operate the same from thenceforth almost day and night, using soft coal in large quantities for fuel in burning the said brick and tile; that because of the use of soft coal, as aforesaid, large volumes of dense black smoke, vapor, gases and offensive odors contaminated the air over, in and around appellant's residence, orchard, garden and grape arbor so as to render the air unhealthy and render the premises unfit for habitation; that said smoke, soot, gas, vapor and offensive odors greatly damaged the fruit in his orchard, the grapes, vegetables and trees of the appellant, and at times the smoke was so dense and the air so charged with smoke, soot, and gases that the residence of appellant was required to be kept closed in order to make it possible to remain therein, insomuch so that the said plant became a nuisance; that during the said time the family of appellant were prevented from using their porches or lawns because of the smoke, soot, gas and noxious odors sent forth by the appellee from the said brick and tile plant, by reason of the use of said soft coal; that appellant repeatedly requested appellee to desist from the use of said soft coal in his said plant, but that appellee failed and refused to so desist and abate the said nuisance. The prayer of the bill is that appellee might be enjoined from using his said brick and tile plant and kilns so as to cause dense black smoke, noxious gases and offensive odors to be emitted from the smokestacks of said plant and to pass out and be carried into, upon and around appellant's said dwelling, garden, orchard and grape arbors, to the damage of his home and premises, etc.

Appellee filed demurrers, general and special, to the said bill, raising the following objections to the sufficiency thereof:

That appellant had been guilty of laches.

That there was no equity in the face of the bill.

That appellant had an adequate remedy at law.

That the bill fails to disclose any foundation upon which a court of equity could act.

The first objection urged to the sufficiency of the bill is that appellant was guilty of laches. From the allegations of the bill we cannot believe appellant's action in the premises could be regarded as laches. The bill states that in the spring of 1910 the appellee began to operate the said kilns by the use of soft coal, which put forth large quantities of smoke, soot, gases and noxious odors, and that the same covered his premises, entered his home, destroyed his crops and made it impossible for him to use his porches or lawns, and rendered his residence almost uninhabitable; that many times during the interval between that date and the filing of the bill herein, appellant requested and demanded of appellee that he desist from the use of soft coal as a fuel in his kilns, and that on all occasions appellee refused so to do and continued and threatened to continue in the use of soft coal, knowing its effect upon the property and comfort and health of appellant and his family.

If these allegations are true, and so far as the question raised by the demurrer is concerned they must be taken as true, instead of being guilty of laches the appellant seems to have been active and persistent in his efforts to rid himself of what he terms a nuisance, almost from the beginning, and having failed by the usual and ordinary means resorted to by men he appealed to the court to secure what he thought to be his legal rights.

It is next urged as ground of objection to the bill that the facts stated therein show appellant had an adequate remedy at law.

The allegations of the bill upon this feature of the case are that the acts of the appellee therein complained of constitute a continuing nuisance and cannot be adequately compensated or established in an action at law, and that injunction is the only remedy to avoid a multiplicity of suits and irreparable damage to appellant and his property.

Under this state of fact, a court of equity has jurisdiction, without a prior determination of the question by a court at law. *Oehler v. Levy*, 234 Ill. 595.

It is also insisted by appellee that inasmuch as the bill was not verified the court could not grant the relief prayed therein. This bill does not pray for temporary injunction, but does pray for an injunction upon the final hearing of the cause. Appellant was not required to verify his bill in order to give it standing in court. In support of this view innumerable authorities can be cited, but we deem it sufficient to quote from *Shobe v. Luff*, 66 Ill. App. 414, where it is said: "Of course, it is well known to the members of the bar that an injunction may be decreed on the hearing of a case when that is the proper relief, whether the bill is verified by affidavit or not."

We are of the opinion the bill is a good bill and requires answer.

The decree is, for the reason given above, reversed and the cause is remanded with directions to the chancellor to overrule the demurrer and require appellee to answer the bill.

Reversed and remanded with directions.

Marcella M. Rives by Lillie C. Rives, Appellee, v. The Hanover Fire Insurance Company, Appellant.

1. INSURANCE, § 621*—*parol evidence.* Parol evidence cannot be received in a court of law to vary or change the terms of a written contract for insurance, though a different rule may prevail in equity.

2. INSURANCE, § 571*—*when declaration in action on fire policy demurrable.* In an action at law to recover fire insurance where

the declaration sets out the policy showing that the same was issued to plaintiff's father, with an indorsement thereon, "It is agreed and understood that the interest of insured is a life estate only," there being no mention of plaintiff's name in the policy, *held* that the declaration is demurrable for the reason that parol evidence would be inadmissible to show that plaintiff's interest as owner of the fee was understood to be included in insurance.

Appeal from the Circuit Court of Greene county; the Hon. Owen P. Thompson, Judge, presiding. Heard in this court at the April term, 1913. Reversed and remanded with directions. Opinion filed October 16, 1913.

Barger & Hicks, for appellant; C. O. Carlson, of counsel.

Rainey & Jones, for appellee.

Mr. Justice Creighton delivered the opinion of the court.

This is an action of *assumpsit* brought by the appellee, by next friend, against the appellant Company, in the Circuit Court of Greene county, to recover upon an insurance policy.

The declaration, in substance, is as follows: that on the 16th day of September, 1908, James W. Rives, then being the owner of a life estate in the real estate mentioned in the policy, and desiring to insure the buildings thereon against loss or damage by fire for a period of three years from said date, to the end that he and the plaintiff, who was and is his infant child and was seized with an estate in fee simple in said real estate, subject to said life estate, should be reimbursed in case of loss or damage to the buildings thereon by fire, to the extent of their respective interests in said buildings, obtained from the appellant Company its policy of insurance upon the two story dwelling house situated on said real estate; and that the appellant thereby promised, in the terms of the said policy and the conditions thereto annexed, a copy of which policy and conditions are attached to the declaration;

that the policy is in the standard form used by the appellant at that time and contains a provision that the entire policy, unless otherwise provided by agreement indorsed thereon or added thereto, should be void if the interest of the insured be other than unconditional and sole ownership; that said James W. Rives informed the defendant, appellant, of the title of said James W. Rives and the appellee, and that the appellant at such time well knew that the interest of said James W. Rives and the appellee were the same as herein averred and as represented to appellant by said James W. Rives; that in order said policy might not be rendered void on account of its provisions hereinbefore set forth, and in order that said James W. Rives and the appellee might obtain the benefits of said insurance in case of loss or damage by fire, and in order to comply with the provisions requiring an agreement to be indorsed or added to said policy that the interest of the insured was other than unconditional and sole ownership, and to the end that said policy should not be void the following agreement was indorsed and added to said policy by the appellant, to wit: "It is agreed and understood that the interest of insured is a life estate only;" that at the time of making the policy and from thence to the time of the happening of the loss and damage hereinafter mentioned, the appellee had an interest in said policy to the amount of $1,600, by the appellant insured on said dwelling and additions; that said James W. Rives died on March 9, 1909, and that afterwards, on August 17, 1911, the said farm dwelling and additions were consumed and destroyed by fire, whereby the plaintiff then and there sustained loss and damage to the said property to the amount of $1,600, which said loss was not occasioned by any means excepted by the policy; that notice of loss was given the appellant and that appellant denied any liability, etc.

The policy of insurance is set out in *haec verba* and made a part of the declaration, and, so far as is here necessary to be considered, is as follows: "This policy is made and accepted subject to the foregoing stipulations and conditions, together with such other provisions, agreements or conditions as may be endorsed hereon or added hereto, and no officer, agent, or other representative of this company shall have power to waive any provision or condition of this policy except as by the terms of this policy may be the subject of agreement endorsed hereon or added hereto, and as to such provisions and conditions, no officer, agent, or other representative shall have such power or be deemed or held to have waived such provisions or conditions unless such waiver, if any, shall be written upon or attached hereto, nor shall any privilege or other permission affecting the insurance under this policy exist or be claimed by the insured, unless so written or attached."

A general demurrer was filed by appellant to the declaration. The court overruled the demurrer and appellant excepted to such ruling and elected to stand by its demurrer, and judgment was rendered in favor of appellee and against appellant in the sum of $1,600 and costs of suit. Exception was taken to this action of the court, and this appeal was thereupon perfected.

The chief question presented for our determination in this case is, whether or not parol evidence can be received to change or vary the terms of a written contract, in this, a court of law?

It is contended by appellant that the declaration, when taken as true, does not set out facts sufficient to show that there was an agreement by which the appellee, the owner of the fee title to the lands, was intended to be included in the policy. It contends that all averments relating to that subject are and were conclusions of the pleader.

Whether this be true or not, in our opinion does not enter into the legal question involved for our consideration. The only legal question here presented is, whether or not parol evidence can be received in a court of law to vary or change the terms of a written contract?

We do not think it can.   In the case of *Mercantile Ins. Co. v. Jaynes,* 87 Ill. 199, it is said a court of law will not receive parol evidence to contradict or enlarge the terms of a written contract, but that the written instrument must be considered as furnishing the true agreement between the parties, and as furnishing better evidence than any which can be supplied by parol.   But, in equity, such evidence is admissible to show the real intention of the parties.   The same doctrine is announced in *Commercial Mutual Acc. Co. v. Bates,* 176 Ill. 194, in the following language: "Where a written application is required to be signed by the assured, and is so signed, and a policy of insurance is issued upon the application, as was the case here, the application and the policy constitute a written contract by and between the assured and the insurance company, and where a controversy arises in regard to what the contract is between the parties, that controversy must be determined by the application and the policy.   *   *   *   A contract of that character cannot rest partly in writing and partly in parol. It cannot be varied, explained or added to by parol evidence.   'Parol evidence of what passed at the time of making a policy is not admissible to restrain the effect of the same.' "

A different rule may, and undoubtedly does, prevail in courts of equity, but not, in our State, in courts at law.

In the policy under consideration there is no reference to the appellee or his interest in the property. Neither are there words or language used in the policy that could be construed to mean that he, or anyone for him, had ever claimed an interest in the policy or had the property insured for his benefit.

For the reasons given above, the judgment herein is reversed, and the cause is remanded with directions to the trial court to sustain the demurrer filed to the declaration.

Reversed and remanded with directions.

Springfield Light, Heat and Power Company, Appellee, v. Philadelphia Casualty Company, Appellant.

1. INDEMNITY, § 23*—*sufficiency of declaration in action on indemnity policy.* In an action on an employer's indemnity policy, declaration alleging that plaintiff, the employer, sustained loss by being required to pay a judgment recovered against him in an action for the death of an employe, and that the death of such employe was caused by a certain coal bunker, then being installed in plaintiff's plant, falling upon him, *held* sufficient on general demurrer.

2. INDEMNITY, § 23*—*when special pleas in action on indemnity policy demurrable.* In an action on an employer's indemnity policy to recover loss sustained by plaintiff on account of being compelled to pay for the death of an employe, a demurrer to defendant's special pleas setting up that such employe was killed by the falling of coal bunkers then being installed in plaintiff's plant, which bunkers were not repairs or renewals of bunkers theretofore existing in said plant, *held* properly sustained.

THOMPSON, J., dissenting.

3. INDEMNITY. § 8*—*indemnity policy construed.* Where the employment specified in an indemnity policy is "manual classification of work operating and maintenance of electric plant and distributing system, including ordinary repairs and renewals, etc.," the words "ordinary repairs and renewals" may be construed to allow employer to attach labor saving machinery to his plant to assist in getting coal to its furnaces.

4. INDEMNITY, § 24*—*admissibility of evidence.* In an action on an employer's indemnity policy, evidence offered by defendant tending to the kind and character of coal bunkers being installed in plaintiff's plant at the time of the accident to an employe, *held* properly refused.

5. INDEMNITY, § 26*—*computation of interest.* In an action on a policy of indemnity against loss under the Employer's Liability Act, a judgment entered against the indemnity company allowing interest to be computed on the time intervening between the time verdict was returned and the judgment was entered against the employer in an action against him for the death of his employe, *held* error, but not reversible error, and the judgment was affirmed on condition of remittitur as to such amount.

6. INTEREST, § 33*—*when attaches to judgments.* Under R. S. c. 74, § 3, relating to interest, J. & A. ¶ 6692, interest cannot attach until the judgment is rendered.

*See Illinois Notes Digest, Vols. XI to XV, same topic and section number.

Appeal from the Circuit Court of Sangamon county; the Hon. JAMES A. CREIGHTON, Judge, presiding. Heard in this court at the April term, 1913. Affirmed after remittitur filed, otherwise reversed and remanded. Opinion filed October 16, 1913. *Certiorari* denied by Supreme Court (making opinion final).

GRAHAM & GRAHAM, for appellant.

WILSON, WARREN & CHILD, for appellee.

MR. JUSTICE CREIGHTON delivered the opinion of the court.

The appellee Company, which employed at the time a large force of men in the management and operation of its plant located in the city of Springfield, applied to the appellant Company and obtained a policy of indemnity against loss by reason of accident or death of certain men employed in said plant, by reason of the Employer's Liability Act.

Subsequently suit was brought by the appellee to recover for alleged loss sustained under the said policy.

The declaration averred, in substance, that at the time of the issuance of the policy one George Whitehead, an employe, was in the class and one of the persons included in said indemnity policy, and that on the 9th day of December, 1909, while the said George Whitehead was so employed and while appellee was so operating said plant, a certain coal bunker, then being placed in the said plant and to become a part of the heating apparatus of said plant, fell over and against the said George Whitehead and instantly killed him; that notice was duly served upon the appellant Company of the accident and death of said deceased; that the administratrix of the estate of the said George Whitehead, deceased, commenced suit against appellee and recovered a judgment against appellee in the sum of $6,000 and costs of suit; that appellant was notified of the commencement of the said suit and appeared and defended it in the name of appellee; that in consequence of said judgment appellee was required to pay to the administratrix of the estate of the said George Whitehead, deceased, the sum of $6,533, in satisfaction of said judgment, by reason whereof appellant became liable to pay to the appellee the said sum of money under and by virtue of said policy of indemnity so issued as aforesaid.

General demurrer was filed to the declaration, and same was, by the court, overruled.

Thereupon appellant filed a plea of the general issue and two special pleas.

The substance of the two special pleas was, to wit: That the deceased, George Whitehead, was killed by the falling of one of the coal bunkers which plaintiff was then installing on its plant, and that said bunkers were not repairs or renewals of the bunkers theretofore existing in said plant but were a new addition to said plant.

Demurrer was interposed to the said two special pleas, and same were sustained by the court, to which action by the court appellant excepted.

The cause was tried by the court and a jury, and a verdict was returned in favor of the appellee in the sum of $6,122. After overruling a motion for new trial, the court entered judgment in the sum of the verdict. Exception was taken by appellant, and this appeal perfected.

Appellant assigns as for error the action of the court in overruling the demurrer to the declaration.

We are inclined to the view the declaration was sufficient, and that the action of the court in overruling the demurrer was correct.

It is next complained that the court erred in sustaining the demurrers interposed to the two special pleas.

The question raised by these pleas is, whether the employment of the deceased at the time he met with his death was of the character and kind specified in said policy. The following clauses of the application and policy are relied upon by appellant:

"Manual classification of work operating and maintenance of electric plant and distributing system, including ordinary repairs and renewals, extension of lines in territory covered by present ordinance, and the making of service connections;" also, "The place or places where work is to be carried on, the kind of work at each such places, the number of employes and the estimated pay roll including over time and all allowances at each such place, are stated in schedule on opposite page. The operations carried on are those usual to the trade or kind described therein."

The record in this case shows that the deceased, at the time of his injury and death, was what was called a "coal passer," his duties being to assist in getting the coal from the window, where it was unloaded from cars, to the furnaces, and he was so employed at that time.

We do not think it can be said to be a strained construction of the language above quoted, to say that the words "ordinary repairs and renewals" may be construed to allow appellee to attach labor saving machinery to the plant to assist in getting coal to its furnaces.

Even the language of the plea averring that appellee was in the act of making extensive additions to its plant, when describing the additions, the pleader says they were sheet iron coal bunkers, a coal bunker being a device used to assist the coal shovelers in keeping the furnaces provided with coal. This was really an improved method of handling the coal. It cannot be said it was an addition to the business. It was only a different method or mode of getting the coal to the furnaces.

Can it be said that a bunker, when used as the one in question, was "unusual to the trade" or business engaged in by appellee? If it was usual, or if it was a repair or an improvement upon the method of handling coal used in said furnaces, it could not reasonably be said it was an addition to the plant, and not being an addition, the appellant could not be relieved from liability by reason thereof.

We think the demurrers to the said pleas were properly sustained.

The further objection is urged by appellant, that the court excluded evidence offered in its behalf, tending to show the kind and character of the bunkers that were, at the time of the accident, being installed, to wit: that they were seven feet high, ten feet long and four feet wide, each weighing twelve hundred pounds.

Under our view of this case the evidence offered was not important to the decision of the issues involved, and was, therefore, properly refused.

It is further contended that the amount of the judgment was not warranted by the evidence introduced. After a careful examination of the evidence contained in this record, we find that the case of Cornelia Whitehead, administratrix of the estate of George Whitehead, deceased, v. Appellee, was tried in the Circuit Court of Sangamon county on the 7th day of May, 1910, and a verdict was then and there returned in favor of the plaintiff; that on July 19, 1910, the motion for new trial in said cause was overruled and judgment then and there entered in favor of the plaintiff and against the defendant, appellee here. In computing the amount of expense, costs and interest in the case at bar, the court permitted interest to be computed on the time intervening between May 7, 1910, and the rendition of the judgment.

We do not understand that interest can attach until judgment has been rendered. Section 3 of chapter 74, R. S. (J. & A. ¶ 6692) provides: "Judgments recovered before any court or magistrate shall draw interest at the rate of five per centum per annum from the date of the same until satisfied." It was therefore error to include in the judgment the interest from May 7, 1910, to July 19, 1910, which amount is estimated to be $49.99. But this error is not necessarily reversible.

If the appellee shall remit the said amount from its judgment, the judgment will be affirmed in the sum of the remainder, otherwise the judgment will be reversed and the cause remanded.

Affirmed after remittitur filed; otherwise reversed and remanded.

MR. JUSTICE THOMPSON dissents on the ground that the demurrer should have been overruled to the second plea.

John Wilson, Appellee, v. Danville Collieries Coal Company, Appellant.

1. MINES AND MINERALS, § 108*—*duty to timber-man.* The fact that the mine manager, who was a licensed mine examiner, informed a timber-man of the dangerous places in the mine and directed him to make them safe does not relieve the operator of mine from complying with the statute in making an examination of the roof of the mine, marking dangerous places and making entry thereof in a book.

2. DAMAGES, § 120*—*when not excessive for personal injuries.* A verdict for four thousand five hundred dollars for injury to a timber-man in a mine, *held* not excessive where he was confined to his house for six weeks and was severely injured about the hips, abdomen and kidneys, and unable to perform manual labor.

3. MINES AND MINERALS, § 176*—*when evidence sufficient to show failure to make inspection caused the injury.* In an action by a timber-man employed in a mine for injuries resulting from a fall of rock from roof of the mine, on account of failure of mine operator to comply with statute in inspecting the mine, evidence *held* sufficient to show that the rock which caused the injury was loose at the time inspection should have been made, and might have been discovered by a careful examination.

Appeal from the Circuit Court of Vermilion county; the Hon. WILLIAM B. SCHOLFIELD, Judge, presiding. Heard in this court at the April term, 1913. Affirmed. Opinion filed October 16, 1913. Rehearing denied November 5, 1913. *Certiorari* granted by Supreme Court.

CHARLES TROUP, for appellant; MASTIN & SHERLOCK, of counsel.

CLARK & HUTTON and J. ED THOMAS, for appellee.

MR. JUSTICE CREIGHTON delivered the opinion of the court.

This cause was before this court at the October term, 1911 (171 Ill. App. 65.) The opinion there filed contains a full statement of the pleadings and the facts, as they appeared in that record. The facts presented here for our consideration do not differ materially from the facts stated in the former opinion, and the pleadings are identical.

This cause was again tried before the court and a jury, and verdict was rendered in favor of appellee in the sum of four thousand five hundred dollars. Motions for new trial and in arrest of the judgment were filed and overruled, and thereupon judgment was entered in the sum of the verdict. Exceptions were duly taken to the action of the court, and this appeal was prayed, granted and perfected, bringing the record before us.

Many of the errors assigned upon this record are formal, and it will not be necessary to give special attention to them in order to determine the rights of the parties hereto.

It is insisted by appellant that the fact that the mine manager, who was also a licensed mine examiner, informed appellee of the dangerous places and directed him to make them safe, obviated the legal necessity of the mine inspector's personal examination, marking such places as dangerous places, and recording same in a book to be kept for that purpose at the entry to the mine.

This same question was presented to this court on the former appeal, and in the opinion then filed, it was said: "It is insisted by defendant that plaintiff was at all times in the mine by and under the direction of the mine manager, who was also a licensed mine examiner, no separate examiner having been employed. No record of the condition of this mine was made or entered in the book required to be kept at the top of the mine on the 20th or 21st days of April, and there was no means of plaintiff deriving any information from this book on either of those days. Although plaintiff was employed as a timber man and it was his duty to make all dangerous places safe, and although he was working at the time of the injury under the direction of the mine manager and was not permitted to enter the mine except under the direction of the mine manager, it was, nevertheless, the duty of the defendant to comply with the other provisions of the statute which required it to make an examination of the roof of this mine and to mark thereon by a conspicuous mark all dangerous and unsafe conditions and to make entry thereof in the book at the top of the mine for the purpose of giving plaintiff and others who were working in the mine, information concerning such conditions."

The proposition of law here involved is thus clearly announced, and disposes of the question so far as this court is concerned.

It is further urged by appellant, as a ground for the reversal of the judgment, that such judgment is excessive in amount.

In the former opinion rendered in this case, it was said: "The jury was warranted on the record in this case in finding that the defendant wilfully failed to comply with the provisions of the statute in that regard. Plaintiff was very severely injured and is unable to perform any manual labor and can only move around or get about by the use of crutches. He was confined to his house for six weeks or more, and was severely injured in and about the hips, abdomen and kidneys. The judgment rendered in this case is not excessive."

The judgment from which this appeal is taken is for a smaller sum by five hundred dollars than the former judgment, and the condition of the appellee is substantially the same as then.

It is contended that the proof is not sufficient to show that the rock which caused the injury to appellee was loose and dangerous when he entered the mine.

The circumstances connected with this case lead us to conclude that the overhanging rock was loose at the time the inspection should have been made, and might have been discovered by a careful examination. Otherwise, it would not have been likely to have fallen in such a short time after appellee entered the mine. There was evidence and circumstances tending to prove the overhanging rock was loose and dangerous when appellee entered the mine. There being facts and circumstances in proof tending to establish this fact, and it being a question of fact for the determination of the jury, we must conclude the jury were justified in their finding upon this question.

Under the view we here take as to the duty of the appellant to cause an examination of its mine to be made, and to mark the dangerous places, and record such dangerous places in the book to be kept at the top of the mine where the employes could inspect the same before allowing them to enter the mine, the instructions complained of are not subject to the objections urged against them.

Finding no reversible error in this record, the judgment must be, and is, affirmed.

Affirmed.

Mike Polonious, Appellee, v. The National Bank of Benld, Appellant.

(Not to be reported in full.)

Appeal from the Circuit Court of Macoupin county; the Hon. JAMES A. CREIGHTON, Judge, presiding. Heard in this court at the April term, 1913. Reversed with finding of fact. Opinion filed October 16, 1913. Rehearing denied November 5, 1913.

Statement of the Case.

Action by Mike Polonious, a miner, who sues by his next friend, against The National Bank of Benld to recover damages sustained by plaintiff alleged to have resulted from the fall of a radiator which defendant left standing on the sidewalk outside of its building. From a judgment in favor of plaintiff for three thousand dollars defendant appeals.

EDWARD C. KNOTTS and PEEBLES & PEEBLES, for appellant.

RINAKER & RINAKER, for appellee.

MR. JUSTICE CREIGHTON delivered the opinion of the court.

Abstract of the Decision.

NEGLIGENCE, § 19*—*when owner not liable for injury to child resulting from leaving a radiator on sidewalk.* In an action by a minor, fourteen years of age, to recover for personal injuries resulting from the fall of a radiator left standing on a sidewalk by defendant outside of its building, a verdict for plaintiff *held* not sustained by evidence sufficient to show that plaintiff was of such tender years as to render him incapable of knowing or realizing the danger arising from his act in pushing the radiator so that it fell upon him.

*See Illinois Notes Digest, Vols. XI to XV, same topic and section number.

James Burbridge, Appellant, v. John A. Howard et al., Appellees.

(Not to be reported in full.)

Appeal from the Circuit Court of Macon county; the Hon. WILLIAM C. JOHNS, Judge, presiding. Heard in this court at the April term, 1913. Reversed and remanded. Opinion filed October 16, 1913.

Statement of the Case.

Action by James Burbridge against John A. Howard and others to recover on an attachment bond. From a judgment in favor of the defendants entered upon a directed verdict, plaintiff appeals.

WILLIAMS & WILLIAMS and BUCKINGHAM & McDAVID, for appellant.

BALDWIN & CAREY, WHITLEY & FITZGERALD and J. L. McLAUGHLIN, for appellees.

MR. JUSTICE CREIGHTON delivered the opinion of the court.

Abstract of the Decision.

1. ATTACHMENT, § 351*—*when action lies on attachment bond.* Action lies on an attachment bond to recover at least nominal damages, where the attachment suit was dismissed at the plaintiff's cost, the bond providing that if attachment plaintiffs shall prosecute their suit with effect or in case of failure therein to pay costs and such damages as shall be awarded against them in any suit thereafter brought for wrongfully suing out the attachment, then the bond shall be null and void.

2. PLEADING, § 230*—*statute permitting amendments construed.* Practice Act, ch. 110, § 39, J. & A. ¶ 8576, permitting amendments to be made on such terms as may be just and reasonable, does not permit the trial court in its discretion to deprive a party of a substantial right through defects or omissions in pleadings.

*See Illinois Notes Digest, Vols. XI to XV, same topic and section number.

3. PLEADING, § 232*—*discretion as to allowance of amendments.* Though the power to grant leave to amend pleadings is within the discretion of the court, such discretion must in all cases be reasonably exercised.

4. APPEAL AND ERROR, § 1362*—*when refusal to permit amendment of declaration reversible error.* In an action on an attachment bond, refusal of court to permit plaintiff to amend his declaration at the time of trial, *held* reversible error.

Mike Metas, Appellee, v. Peter Sanichas, Appellant.
(Not to be reported in full.)

Appeal from the Circuit Court of Vermilion county; the Hon. WILLIAM B. SCHOLFIELD, Judge, presiding. Heard in this court at the April term, 1913. Reversed with finding of fact. Opinion filed October 16, 1913.

Statement of the Case.

Action by Mike Metas against Peter Sanichas to recover damages alleged to have been occasioned by the defendant compromising, without authority, a certain suit instituted by plaintiff against a third party. From a judgment in favor of plaintiff, defendant appeals.

CLARK & HUTTON, for appellant.

OLIVER D. MANN, for appellee.

MR. JUSTICE CREIGHTON delivered the opinion of the court.

Abstract of the Decision.

COMPROMISE AND SETTLEMENT, § 4*—*authority to compromise suit.* In an action to recover damages resulting from defendant

---

*See Illinois Notes Digest, Vols. XI to XV, same topic and section number.

compromising, without authority, a suit instituted by plaintiff against a third party and receipting for the money in the name of plaintiff, a verdict in favor of plaintiff *held* to be manifestly against the weight of the evidence, the defendant's evidence showing that defendant was authorized to take care of the case and to apply the amount collected on an account due him from plaintiff.

David F. Turney, Appellee, v. John W. Coventry, Appellant.

(Not to be reported in full.)

Appeal from the Circuit Court of Shelby county; the Hon. JAMES C. McBRIDE, Judge, presiding. Heard in this court at the April term, 1913. Reversed with finding of fact. Opinion filed October 16, 1913.

Statement of the Case.

Action by David F. Turney against John W. Coventry to recover for coal furnished to defendant from plaintiff's coal mine. From a judgment in favor of plaintiff for $113.26, defendant appeals.

TOM HEADEN and RICHARDSON & WHITAKER, for appellant.

STEIDLEY & CROCKETT, for appellee.

MR. JUSTICE CREIGHTON delivered the opinion of the court.

Abstract of the Decision.

1. PRINCIPAL AND AGENT, § 179*—*rights of third persons under a contract with an agent of an undisclosed principal.* Where a third person who has entered into a contract with an agent in ig.

---

188   APPELLATE COURTS OF ILLINOIS.

Taylor v. Peoria, B. and C. Trac. Co., 184 Ill. App. 188.

norance of the fact that he was not the real principal as he assumed to be is sued upon the contract by the real principal, he may avail himself, as against such principal, of every defense which existed in his favor against the agent at the time the principal first interposed and demanded performance of the contract to himself, and the rule is the same though a credit is sought to be made upon an old account with the agent.

2. PRINCIPAL AND AGENT, § 179*—*when undisclosed principal not entitled to benefit of contract with agents.* Where a third person contracted with former owners of a coal mine for coal to apply on an account owing to him from such owners, such owners being apparently in charge of the mine at the time and such third person having no knowledge that such former owners had leased the mine to another, *held* in an action by the lessee against such third person for the coal furnished that a judgment in favor of plaintiff was not sustained by the evidence, the evidence clearly showing that defendant had no notice of plaintiff's interest in the mine, and that the former owners were apparently in charge thereof in the same capacity as they were previous to the lease.

Ada Nieukirk Taylor, Appellee, v. Peoria, Bloomington and Champaign Traction Company et al., Appellants.

1. DAMAGES, § 203*—*when instruction calling special attention to disfigurement of plaintiff erroneous.* In an action for personal injuries, an instruction given for plaintiff calling special attention to the disfigurement of plaintiff in consequence as a basis for estimating damages, *held* erroneous.

2. DAMAGES, § 115*—*when verdict for personal injuries excessive.* Verdict for four thousand dollars for personal injuries sustained by plaintiff by being thrown from her seat due to collision while a passenger in a street car, *held* excessive, it not appearing that the injury was dangerous or serious.

Appeal from the Circuit Court of Tazewell county; the Hon. THEODORE N. GREEN, Judge, presiding. Heard in this court at the April term, 1913. Reversed and remanded. Opinion filed October 16, 1913.

Prettyman, Velde & Prettyman, for appellants; George W. Burton, of counsel.

Jesse Black, Jr., and James P. St. Cerny, for appellee.

Mr. Justice Creighton delivered the opinion of the court.

This was an action of trespass on the case brought by the appellee against the appellants to recover damages because of personal injury complained of. The declaration contained two counts which were substantially the same, and avers that the Peoria Railway Company and the Peoria, Bloomington & Champaign Traction Company, appellants herein, were using the same track from Peoria and thence across the bridge over the Illinois river, and thence eastward for about one-fourth of a mile across Farm creek bridge, to a switch where a junction was formed, where the cars of the Railway Company turn to the right, up Washington street, while the cars of the Traction Company keep to the left; that on the 4th day of September, 1911, at the city of Peoria the appellee boarded the car of the Railway Company for the purpose of being conveyed to East Peoria; that when the car she was riding on reached the said junction a certain passenger car of the Traction Company approached the said junction on its way to Peoria; that the appellants then and there so negligently, carelessly and recklessly drove and managed their said cars that the car of the said Traction Company ran into the car of the Railway Company on which appellee was riding as a passenger, and because of said collision between the said cars, appellee was thrown from her seat with great force and violence and was cut, bruised, wounded and disfigured.

Each of the appellants filed the plea of the general issue.

The cause was tried by the court and a jury and a

verdict was rendered against both appellants jointly, in the sum of four thousand dollars. After overruling motion for a new trial, the court entered judgment upon the verdict. Each of the appellants joined in perfecting this appeal.

It is assigned as ground of error that instruction number 12, given on behalf of the appellee, was erroneous and should not have been given. Said instruction is as follows:

"You are further instructed that in determining the amount of damages the plaintiff is entitled to recover, if any, the jury have a right to, and should take into consideration all the facts and circumstances in evidence before them, the nature and extent of the plaintiff's physical injuries, if any, concerning which there is any evidence in the case, her suffering in body and mind, if any, resulting from such injuries, her physical disfigurement, if any is shown, resulting from such injuries, and also her prospective suffering and loss of health, if any, as the jury may believe from the evidence before them in this case the plaintiff has sustained or will sustain by reason of such injuries, and it will be proper for the jury to consider the effect of the injuries, if any, in the future upon the plaintiff and her ability to attend to her affairs generally in pursuing her ordinary occupation, if the evidence shows that it will be affected in the future, and all damages, if any, present and future, which from the evidence can be treated as the necessary and direct result of the injuries complained of."

We are inclined to the opinion that this instruction is erroneous. It called special attention to the disfigurement of the appellee in consequence of the injury as a basis for estimating her damages. Instructions of this character have frequently been condemned. *Chicago City Ry. Co. v. Schaefer,* 121 Ill. App. 334.

In *Lake Street El. R. Co. v. Gormley,* 108 Ill. App. 59, it was said: "The marring of personal appearance and humiliation resulting from contemplation of bodily disfigurement are not elements entering into the computation of pecuniary damages for personal injuries.''

It is also insisted by appellant that the damages are excessive, and that, therefore, the judgment should be reversed. The injury complained of does not appear to be dangerous or serious. We are of the opinion the judgment, under all of the circumstances, is very excessive, but as the judgment is to be reversed for other reasons, we do not desire to discuss the evidence bearing upon the permanent character and extent of the injury.

For the reasons herein set forth, the judgment is reversed and the cause remanded.

Reversed and remanded.

Arthur G. Haines, Appellant, v. State Board of Agriculture, Appellee.

1. MUNICIPAL CORPORATIONS, § 948*—*liability for acts of officers and employes.* Quasi corporations, such as counties, towns, school districts, hospitals and other institutions of like character, cannot be held responsible in damages for the negligence of their officers or employes, unless by statutory enactment.

2. AGRICULTURE, § 3*—*when State Board of Agriculture not liable for personal injuries sustained by guest at State fair.* In an action against the State Board of Agriculture to recover for injuries sustained by plaintiff on account of the collapse of certain bleachers at the State fair conducted by defendant, a general demurrer to the declaration *held* properly sustained, the defendant not being liable for the negligence of its officers and employes.

3. AGRICULTURE, § 3*—*liability of State Board of Agriculture for negligence of officers and employes.* State Board of Agriculture is one branch or arm of the State government, and though the statute creating it provides it may sue and be sued, it is not liable for the negligence of its officers and employes.

Appeal from the Circuit Court of Sangamon county; the Hon. JAMES A. CREIGHTON, Judge, presiding. Heard in this court at the April term, 1913. Affirmed. Opinion filed October 16, 1913.

*See Illinois Notes Digest, Vols. XI to XV, same topic and section numbers

SMITH & FRIEDMEYER, for appellant.

SIDNEY S. BREESE and SEDDON & HOLLAND, for appellee.

MR. JUSTICE CREIGHTON delivered the opinion of the court.

This was an action on the case brought by the appellant against the appellee, in the Circuit Court of Sangamon county, to recover for a personal injury alleged to have been sustained by the appellant through the collapse of certain bleachers at the State fair held in Springfield, in the year 1911, and which bleachers were alleged to have been negligently constructed.

The declaration alleges that the Illinois State Board of Agriculture is an association authorized by the laws of the State of Illinois to act in a corporate capacity for the purpose of holding an annual State fair at Springfield, and authorized to hold and acquire property and make improvements thereon, and arrange for exhibits at such State fair, and which was carried on by annual appropriations made by the legislature of the State, in addition to profits derived from the holding of said fair by way of admission fees and the sale of concessions; that the said Board of Agriculture held a State fair at Springfield from September 28 to October 7, 1911, and charged and collected admission fees of fifty cents for each person admitted, and was then and there, in its corporate capacity, in possession and control of the State fair grounds, and erected certain seats, commonly called bleachers, along and near the race tracks located upon said land, for the use and accommodation of the public; that the plaintiff, on the 4th day of October, 1911, attended the said fair, so held, as a visitor and paid an admission fee of fifty cents; that certain races were scheduled to take place on said tracks, and persons desirous of seeing the races were invited to take seats on said bleachers; that the plaintiff got upon said bleachers, together with a large number of other people, to watch the said races, not knowing the said bleachers were unsafe, and while in the exercise of reasonable care for his own safety, the section upon which he was seated suddenly fell to the ground and injured the back and spine of the plaintiff, etc.

A general demurrer was filed to the declaration, and was, by the court, sustained. Plaintiff elected to stand by the declaration, whereupon judgment was entered in favor of the defendant and against the plaintiff for the costs of the proceeding. Thereupon this appeal was prayed, granted and perfected, bringing the record before us for review.

Section 1 of the act of the legislature creating the Agricultural Department is, in part, as follows: There is hereby created and established a department in the State, to be known and styled the "Department of Agriculture," the object of which shall be to promote agriculture, horticulture, manufacturing and domestic arts. The business of such department shall be conducted by a board, to be styled the "State Board of Agriculture."

The second section of the act provides that said State Board of Agriculture shall have the sole control of the affairs of the Department of Agriculture of the State fairs, etc., and may make such by-laws and rules for the management of the department as shall be deemed necessary.

Section 4 of the act provides that whatever money shall from time to time be appropriated to the Department of Agriculture shall be paid to the State Board of Agriculture, and may be expended by them as in the opinion of said board will best advance the interests of agriculture, horticulture, manufactures and domestic arts in this State.

Section 8 provides for annual reports to the Governor of the transactions of the Department of Agriculture.

From the statute above referred to we may reason-

ably conclude that the Department of Agriculture was
created and has been continued as a department of the
government of the State, possessing certain powers
granted by the legislature and owing certain duties,
defined by the legislature, to the public at large, and
particularly those branches of industry specified as
agriculture, horticulture, manufacturing and domestic
arts. These four branches are to receive special consideration, and any moneys remaining after the necessary expenses of administering the affairs of the department have been met must be devoted to the advancement of those four industries. Thus it will be
seen there was no profit contemplated by the legislature
of the State, to the State or to the officers of the department.

But it is contended by the appellant that the act
creating the Department of Agriculture provides in
terms that it may sue and be sued in any court of competent jurisdiction, and that hereby it places the department in the class of corporations organized for
profit.

We conclude the legislature meant to grant the usual
and ordinary power to transact the necessary business
incidental to the administration of the department.
It, in the course of administering the affairs of the
department, has power to contract debts, and when
contracted to enforce them in courts of competent
jurisdiction, and if it failed to meet its obligations, it
might be sued and recovery had, but this does not
necessarily imply that it shall be held liable for the
negligence of its officers and employes.

A county or a town may contract debts and may be
sued in any court of competent jurisdiction, and yet
the authorities are abundant holding that they are not
liable for personal injuries by reason of the negligence
of their employes.

The true rule controlling the question at issue in
this case is clearly stated in the case of *Kinnare v.
City of Chicago*, 171 Ill. 332, as follows: "It therefore

appears the appellee board is a corporation or *quasi* corporation created, *nolens volens,* by the general law of the State to aid in the administration of the State government, and charged, as such, with duties purely governmental in character. It owns no property, has no private corporate interests, and derives no special benefits from its corporate acts. It is simply an agency of the State, having existence for the sole purpose of performing certain duties, deemed necessary to the maintenance of an 'efficient system of free schools' within the particular locality of its jurisdiction. The State acts in its sovereign capacity, and does not submit its action to the judgment of courts and is not liable for the torts or negligence of its agents, and a corporation created by the State as a mere agency for the more efficient exercise of governmental functions is likewise exempted from the obligation to respond in damages, as master, for negligent acts of its servants to the same extent as is the State itself, unless such liability is expressly provided by the statute creating such agency.''

In discussing this same subject, the same rule was clearly announced in the case of *Elmore v. Drainage Commissioners,* 135 Ill. 269, in the following language: ''In regard to public involuntary *quasi* corporations the rule is otherwise, and there is no such implied liability imposed upon them. These latter—such as counties, townships, school districts, road districts, and other similar *quasi* corporations—exist under general laws of the State, which apportion its territory into local subdivisions, for the purposes of civil and governmental administration, and impose upon the people residing in said several subdivisions, precise and limited public duties, and clothe them with restricted corporate functions, co-extensive with the duties devolving upon them. In such organizations the duties, and their correlative powers, are assumed *in invitum,* and there is no responsibility to respond in damages, in a civil action, for neglect in the performance of duties, unless such action is given by statute.''

The doctrine announced in the above authorities is in perfect accord with the earlier decisions of our Supreme Court, with one exception, which is fully explained in later decisions. See also 15 Am. & Eng. Encyc. of Law, p. 1164, and 2 Dillon on Mun. Corp. p. 1193.

From the above cited authorities it is apparent that *quasi* corporations, such as counties, towns, school districts, hospitals and other such institutions of like character, cannot be held responsible in damages for the negligence of their officers or employes, unless by statutory enactment. They have long been held as involuntary organizations and as agencies of the State for the performance of duties for which they are organized.

In our view, the same principle of law will apply to the appellee, Department of Agriculture. It is not a corporation for profit or special benefit to any particular individuals. The Board of Agriculture, in theory of law, has no individual interest in the appropriations or profits of the department. They are simply the agents of the State, charged with the responsibility of administering the affairs of the Department of Agriculture.

While it is true they receive appropriations made for the benefit of the said department, and it is equally true that there is a sum of money arising from the admission fees and concessions at the annual State fair, yet these various sums are accounted for, and are used for the sole and only purpose of defraying the expenses of the Agricultural Department and advancing the interests of agriculture, horticulture, manufacturing and domestic arts. Every dollar received must be accounted for and reported to the Governor of the State.

This department, therefore, is one branch or arm of the State government. It was brought into existence by the legislature of the State, it is supported by the provisions of the laws of the State, its servants and agents are but representing a department of the State in the discharge of their duties under the statute, and the State has power to abolish this department, while the Board of Agriculture has no power to either create or destroy. They can only serve the public in the way pointed out by statute.

Appellant has submitted a long list of authorities from sister States, which are not in accord with the view here announced, neither are they in accord with the holdings of our Supreme Court.

For the reasons above given the judgment appealed from is affirmed.

Affirmed.

John Maxon, Appellee, v. George W. Farley, Appellant.

(Not to be reported in full.)

Appeal from the County Court of Logan county; the Hon. CHARLES J. GEHLBACH, Judge, presiding. Heard in this court at the April term, 1913. Reversed and remanded with directions. Opinion filed October 16, 1913. Rehearing denied November 12, 1913.

Statement of the Case.

Action commenced by John Maxon against George W. Farley before a justice of the peace, where a trial was had and judgment rendered against the defendant for $82.85 and costs of suit. Defendant then perfected an appeal to the County Court. From an order of the County Court dismissing the appeal, defendant appeals.

GEORGE H. COX and BEACH & TRAPP, for appellant.

MCCORMICK & MURPHY, for appellee.

MR. JUSTICE CREIGHTON delivered the opinion of the court.

Abstract of the Decision.

1. JUSTICES OF THE PEACE, § 203*—*sufficiency of transcript to give court jurisdiction on appeal.* In order to give a court to which an appeal is perfected jurisdiction of the subject-matter, the transcript from the justice must be in substantial compliance with the statute.

2. JUSTICES OF THE PEACE, § 203*—*when transcript on appeal from justice insufficient.* Transcript does not comply with R. S. c. 79, § 15, J. & A. ¶ 6976, so as to give County Court jurisdiction of subject-matter of an appeal from a justice, where there is no certificate or pretended certificate of the justice attached to or accompanying the transcript.

3. JUSTICES OF THE PEACE, § 209*—*jurisdiction to dismiss appeal.* On appeal from a justice of the peace where no certificate of the justice is attached to or accompanying the transcript, the court to which such appeal is taken has no jurisdiction to dismiss the appeal for failure of appellant to comply with a rule to pay the docket fee, and for want of prosecution.

4. JUSTICES OF THE PEACE, § 162*—*jurisdiction on appeal when insufficient transcript filed.* Where insufficient transcript is filed on appeal from a justice of the peace, the court to which the appeal is taken has no jurisdiction of the subject-matter, and is without power to make any order affecting the rights of the parties as to the merits of the cause. In such case the court would have power to order a perfect transcript to be filed and enter any other order necessary to the preparation of the case for trial, but its power is limited to preliminary orders.

5. JUSTICES OF THE PEACE, § 202*—*when appearance of appellant insufficient to confer jurisdiction on appeal in absence of sufficient transcript.* Fact that appellant appeared in court and entered a motion to set aside an order of the court, *held* not to give the court jurisdiction of the subject-matter, where no sufficient transcript is on file.

*See Illinois Notes Digest, Vols. XI to XV, same topic and section number.

Kate Brown Wyzard, Administratrix, Appellee, v. Vivian Collieries Company, Appellant.

(Not to be reported in full.)

Appeal from the Circuit Court of Macoupin county; the Hon. JAMES A. CREIGHTON, Judge, presiding. Heard in this court at the April term, 1913. Reversed with finding of fact. Opinion filed October 16, 1913.

Statement of the Case.

Action by Kate Brown Wyzard, administratrix of the estate of George Brown, deceased, against Vivian Collieries Company to recover for the death of deceased by being run over by a motor car and a train of coal cars while he was working in defendant's mine as a trapper and switchman. From a judgment in favor of plaintiff for two thousand five hundred dollars, defendant appeals.

C. C. TERRY and RINAKER & RINAKER, for appellant.

JESSE PEEBLES and HILL & BULLINGTON, for appellee.

MR. JUSTICE CREIGHTON delivered the opinion of the court.

Abstract of the Decision.

1. MINES AND MINERALS, § 74*—*proximate cause.* In order to recover for the death of an employe in a mine alleged to have been caused by the wilful failure of defendant to comply with the Miners' Act, the plaintiff must prove by a preponderance of the evidence that such failure was the proximate cause of the accident.

2. MINES AND MINERALS, § 185*—*when error to refuse to direct verdict for defendant in action for death of a switchman.* In an action to recover for the death of plaintiff's intestate while deceased

was employed as a trapper and a switchman in defendant's mine, the declaration alleging that death resulted from large quantities of gob on either side of the track, where deceased met with the accident, which created a dangerous condition and that defendant was guilty of negligence in failing to have said dangerous condition examined and marked, as the statute requires, *held* that court's refusal to exclude all of plaintiff's evidence and to direct a verdict for defendant was error, there being no evidence to prove that the place was made dangerous by the accumulation of gob or that the absence of gob at such place would have prevented the accident, nor any evidence in the record to show that deceased could not have secured his safety by stepping off the track.

R. C. Cox et al., Trustees, Appellants, v. K. A. Flagg, Appellee.

(Not to be reported in full.)

Appeal from the Circuit Court of Sangamon county; the Hon. JAMES A. CREIGHTON, Judge, presiding. Heard in this court at the April term, 1913. Affirmed. Opinion filed October 16, 1913.

Statement of the Case.

Action by R. C. Cox and others, trustees of the American Lodge, I. O. O. F., 920, against K. A. Flagg, to recover thirty dollars claimed to be due to plaintiff from defendant for rents collected by plaintiff from subtenants of defendant. From a judgment in favor of plaintiff for ten dollars, plaintiff appeals.

ROBERT H. PATTON, for appellants.

M. U. WOODRUFF, for appellee.

MR. JUSTICE CREIGHTON delivered the opinion of the court.

Abstract of the Decision.

SET-OFF AND RECOUPMENT, § 6*—*when officer of a lodge entitled to set-off for amount paid for rent of building.* Where an officer of a lodge leased a building and paid the rent as it became due, sometimes out of money belonging to the lodge and at other times out of his own money, in which case he had presented bills therefor which were approved and allowed, and such arrangement continued for some time without objection by the lodge, and later such officer leased the building from the owner in his own name, notifying the lodge that it could use the building as it always had and that he was to receive the same rent as formerly, *held* in an action against him by the lodge for certain money collected from subtenants that he was entitled to a set-off for the amount he had paid for rent from his own money, it appearing that he had acted in good faith in paying the rent and fully expected to be reimbursed as he previously had and that there was an implied obligation on the part of the lodge to give him credit for such amount for the reason that the lodge had received the use of the building and the services of the officer in like capacity for years without objection.

Joseph E. Helfrich, Appellee, v. John F. Scott, Appellant.

(Not to be reported in full.)

Appeal from the Circuit Court of Hancock county; the Hon. HARRY M. WAGGONER, Judge, presiding. Heard in this court at the April term, 1913. Affirmed. Opinion filed October 16, 1913.

Statement of the Case.

Action by Joseph E. Helfrich against John F. Scott to recover upon a promissory note given by defendant to plaintiff. From a judgment in favor of plaintiff for $217.82, defendant appeals.

HARTZELL, CAVANAGH & BABCOCK, for appellant.

GEORGE V. HELFRICH, for appellee.

*See Illinois Notes Digest, Vols. XI to XV, same topic and section number.

MR. JUSTICE CREIGHTON delivered the opinion of the court.

Abstract of the Decision.

GAMING, § 18*—*when note given to take up check lost at gambling not given for gambling debt.* In an action on a promissory note, a plea setting up that the note was given for a gambling debt *held* no defense, it appearing that the note was given to plaintiff by defendant after plaintiff had been requested to take up a check lost by defendant at gambling with a third person, and the amount of the note included the face value of check and a meat bill owing to plaintiff by defendant.

L. A. Clingan, Appellee, v. Cleveland, Cincinnati, Chicago and St. Louis Railway Company, Appellant.

1. CARRIERS, § 30*—*Carmack amendment to Interstate Commerce Act as affecting liability of carriers in interstate shipments.* Under the Carmack Amendment to Interstate Commerce Act it became the duty of interstate carriers to fix, publish and file with the Interstate Commerce Commission all rates for interstate shipment, and it would seem that it was the manifest intention of congress to take possession of the subject of liability of a carrier under contracts of interstate shipments and to supersede all State regulations in reference to that subject.

2. CARRIERS, § 158*—*contract limiting liability as affected by the Carmack Amendment to Interstate Commerce Act.* Under the provisions of the Carmack Amendment of the Interstate Commerce Act the limited liability contract agreeing to a valuation of the property in transportation is valid, and the shipper is conclusively presumed to know the terms of the bill of lading and the published rate filed with the Interstate Commerce Commission.

3. CARRIERS, § 239*—*when limitation of liability in contract for interstate shipment of live stock governs.* In an action against a railroad company to recover for the loss of a race horse shipped over defendant's road from a point in another State to a point in this State under a contract of shipment limiting defendant's liability to one hundred dollars, *held* that a judgment in favor of

plaintiff for one thousand two hundred dollars could not be sustained for such amount, and judgment was affirmed in the sum of one hundred dollars on condition of remittitur.

4. CARRIERS, § 241*—*when indorsement on receipted freight bill extends time for filing claim for loss.* Where a contract for shipment of live stock provides that notice of loss shall be filed with railroad's claim agent within five days after removal of stock from the car, and was signed by the shipper's agent, who could neither read nor write, and the shipper had no knowledge of such limitation until after he had received the property and paid the freight bill, *held* that an indorsement by the company's agent on the receipted freight bill delivered to shipper, granting four months within which to file claim extended the time within which to file claim.

5. CARRIERS, § 31*—*when extension of time for filing claim for loss not a violation of Interstate Commerce rules.* The power of a railroad company to extend the time of presenting claim for loss by making an indorsement on a receipted freight bill delivered to shipper, *held* not a violation of the Interstate Commerce Commission rules and regulations.

Appeal from the Circuit Court of Vermilion county; the Hon. WILLIAM B. SCHOLFIELD, Judge, presiding. Heard in this court at the April term, 1913. Affirmed if remittitur filed; otherwise reversed and remanded. Opinion filed October 16, 1913.

GEORGE B. GILLESPIE, for appellant; R. J. CAREY and REARICK & MEEKS, of counsel.

CLARK & HUTTON and WILLIAM L. CUNDIFF, for appellee.

MR. JUSTICE CREIGHTON delivered the opinion of the court.

This was an action brought by the appellee against the appellant in the Circuit Court of Vermilion county, to recover for loss of a race horse shipped over appellant's road from Indianapolis, Indiana, to Danville, Illinois.

This cause was before this court at a former term, where a full statement of the cause will be found (*Clingan v. Cleveland C., C. & St. L. Ry. Co.,* 163 Ill. App. 568.)

*See Illinois Notes Digest, Vols. XI to XV, same topic and section number.

204   APPELLATE COURTS OF ILLINOIS.

Clingan v. Cleveland, C., C. and St. L. Ry. Co., 184 Ill. App. 202.

The facts disclosed by this record are, in all substantial respects, the same as those stated in said former opinion, save and except the pleadings in this case
are made to conform to the view of the court as announced in the opinion filed on the former appeal.

A trial was had before the court and a jury and
verdict and judgment in the sum of one thousand two
hundred dollars and costs were rendered, and the
record is again before us for review by an appeal perfected by the appellant Company.

Since the rendition of the former opinion by this
court, the Federal Courts have passed upon and construed what is known as the Carmack Amendment to
the Interstate Commerce Act. *Chicago & A. Ry. Co.
v. Kirby*, 225 U. S. 155; *Chicago, St. P., M. & O. Ry. Co.
v. Latta*, 226 U. S. 519.

Under the said act it became the duty of interstate
carriers to fix, publish and file with the Interstate Commerce Commission all rates for interstate shipments,
and it would seem from the authorities above cited
that it was the manifest intent of Congress to take possession of the subject of liability of a carrier under
contracts of interstate shipment, and to supersede all
State regulations in reference to that subject; that
under the provisions of the Federal law the limited
liability contract agreeing to a valuation of the property in transportation is valid and that the shipper is
conclusively presumed to know the terms of the bill
of lading and the published rate filed with the Interstate Commerce Commission.

The contract in question, entered into between the
appellee and appellant, provided for the shipment of
one race horse from Indianapolis, Indiana, to Danville,
Illinois, and limits the liability of appellant to one
hundred dollars. It would seem, therefore, that recovery cannot be had, under this contract, for more
than the liability stated therein.

A further objection is made to the judgment of the

lower court that the terms of the contract provided that notice of loss should be filed with the claim agent of appellant at Cincinnati, Ohio, by the shipper within five days after the stock was removed from the car. This section of the contract reads as follows: "That no claim for damages which may accrue to the said shipper under this contract, shall be allowed or paid by the said carrier or sued for in any court by the shipper, unless a claim shall be made in writing, verified by an affidavit of the said shipper or his agent, and delivered to the freight claim agent of the said carrier at his office in the city of Cincinnati, Ohio, within five days from the time said stock is removed from said car or cars, and that if any loss or damage occur upon the line of a connecting carrier, then such carrier shall not be liable unless a claim shall be made in like manner and delivered in like time to some officer or agent of the carrier on whose line or lines the injury occurred."

It further appeared from the evidence in this case that the contract of shipment was made and the bill of lading was signed by the mark of an agent of the appellee who could neither read or write, and that the appellee did not sign the contract, and had no knowledge of the provision as to the time of filing claim for loss or damage, until after he had received his property at Danville and paid the freight bill. The agent of the appellant who received the payment of the freight bill indorsed, at the foot of the receipt given to appellee, the following: "Claim for loss, damage or delay must be made in writing to the carrier at the point of delivery or at the point of origin, within four months after delivery of the property; or in case of failure to make delivery, then within four months after reasonable time for delivery has elapsed. Unless claims are so made the carrier shall not be liable."

We are inclined to the opinion that the extension granted to appellee to file his claim for damage under the limitation attached to the bottom of the receipted freight bill and signed by appellant's agent, granting four months time in which to so file, was binding upon appellant. This power to extend the time of presenting a claim for damage is not a violation of the Interstate Commerce Commission rules and regulations, and, therefore, we conclude that appellant is bound by said extension.

From the record we find the freight receipt was signed September 13, 1909, and that a demand was filed with the agent of the appellant at Danville, Illinois, for damages to his horse, on the 20th day of September, 1909, and that this suit was begun long before the expiration of the four months period. We think the demand was sufficient and that appellee has a right of recovery under the contract, in the sum of one hundred dollars. The circumstances under which the property was injured and the evidence as to the value of the property was abundant to warrant the court in rendering judgment for a much larger sum, aside from the liability limitation clause in the contract.

The judgment will be affirmed in the sum of one hundred dollars at the cost of appellee on condition the appellee will remit his judgment to that sum within ten days, otherwise the judgment will be reversed and the cause remanded.

Affirmed if remittitur filed; otherwise reversed and remanded.

Clarence Swango, Appellee, v. Cleveland, Cincinnati, Chicago and St. Louis Railway Company, Appellant.

(Not to be reported in full.)

Appeal from the Circuit Court of Edgar county; the Hon. E. R. E. KIMBROUGH, Judge, presiding. Heard in this court at the April term, 1913. Reversed with finding of fact. Opinion filed October 16, 1913.

Statement of the Case.

Action by Clarence Swango against the Cleveland, Cincinnati, Chicago and St. Louis Railway Company to recover damages for the injury to plaintiff's horses which had escaped through a gate at a farm crossing upon defendant's right of way and were struck by defendant's locomotive and train. From a judgment in favor of plaintiff for six hundred and ninety dollars, defendant appeals.

GEORGE B. GILLESPIE, for appellant; R. J. CAREY, SHEPHERD & TROGDON and GILLESPIE & FITZGERALD, of counsel.

F. E. SHOPP, for appellee; F. C. VAN SELLAR, of counsel.

MR. JUSTICE CREIGHTON delivered the opinion of the court.

Abstract of the Decision.

RAILROADS, § 874*—*when evidence insufficient to show a defective gate at farm crossing.* In an action against a railroad company for damages occasioned by the killing of plaintiff's stock alleged to have escaped upon defendant's right of way by reason of a defective gate constructed by defendant at a farm crossing, evidence *held* insufficient to sustain a verdict for plaintiff, it appearing that the gate was open when the stock escaped, that the gate was of the

*See Illinois Notes Digest, Vols. XI to XV, same topic and section number.

usual pattern of sliding gates, made of good material and of sufficient height, and that the only objection to the gate was that it was lower at the "hinge" end than the other so that it could easily slide back and might be opened on account of wind or by horses rubbing against it, there being no evidence to show that the gate was thus opened but there was evidence to show that it had not been thus opened for a period of five years.

Fannie Coulter, Administratrix, Appellee, v. Illinois Central Railroad Company, Appellant.

1. RAILROADS, § 641*—*when liable for death of street car conductor resulting from backing trains at crossing.* In an action against a railroad company to recover damages for the death of a street car conductor at a railroad crossing caused by a street car being struck by an approaching train of cars being switched by defendant while the conductor had gone upon the railroad tracks to flag the crossing, the declaration alleging that defendant was negligent in backing a string of cars without lights on the hindmost car, in not providing such car with sufficient brakes in the care of a brakeman and in backing such train at a dangerous rate of speed, *held* that a verdict in favor of plaintiff would be sustained upon remittitur.

2. RAILROADS, § 752*—*when due care on part of street car conductor in leaving street car to flag railroad crossing question for jury.* In an action against a railroad company for the death of a street car conductor caused by a street car being struck by an approaching train of cars being switched by defendant at a railroad crossing, when street car conductor had gone upon the tracks to flag the crossing, *held* that the question of due care upon the part of the conductor was a question for the jury.

3. DEATH, § 71*—*when due care on the part of deceased becomes a question of law.* In an action for death, the question of due care on the part of the deceased becomes a question of law only where there is no conflict in the evidence, and the evidence is such that the minds of all reasonable men must arrive at but one conclusion.

4. RAILROADS, § 651*—*when failure of street car conductor to discover approaching train at railroad crossing not negligence*

per se. Failure of street car conductor to discover the approach of a string of railroad cars at a railroad crossing when he goes upon the railroad tracks to flag the crossing in compliance with the rules of the street car company and a city ordinance, *held* not contributory negligence *per se.*

5. DEATH, § 67*—*when recovery for death excessive.* Verdict for ten thousand dollars for death of a street railway conductor *held* excessive, and judgment affirmed on condition of remittitur of three thousand dollars.

Appeal from the Circuit Court of Macon county; the Hon. WILLIAM C. JOHNS, Judge, presiding. Heard in this court at the October term, 1911. Affirmed on remittitur; otherwise reversed and remanded. Opinion filed October 16, 1913. *Certiorari* granted by Supreme Court.

HUGH CREA and HUGH W. HOUSUM, for appellant; JOHN G. DRENNAN, of counsel.

WHITLEY & FITZGERALD and J. L. McLAUGHLIN, for appellee.

MR. PRESIDING JUSTICE PHILBRICK delivered the opinion of the court.

Plaintiff's intestate was in the employ of the Decatur Railway and Light Company as a conductor. The defendant owned and operated a line of railway into and through the city of Decatur, with five tracks running north and south across Wood street, and one track extending south from Wood street, these tracks are designated as number one, two, three, four, five and six, numbering from the west. The width of the right of way of defendant at Wood street is two hundred feet. Commencing in Wood street was a spur leading north, off from the west side of track number two, to the Decatur Gas Light and Railway Company's gas plant. Track number six, or the east track, was the northbound main, track number five was the southbound main, the other tracks, two, three and four, which crossed Wood street were used for switching and other purposes. Broadway street intersected Wood street in a northeasterly direction at a point a short distance east of where the tracks of the defendant Company crossed Wood street.

On the evening of November 4, 1910, at about eight o'clock, plaintiff's intestate had charge of a street car running west on Wood street. This car arrived at the crossing of the defendant Company, was stopped a short distance east of track number six. There was an electric arc lamp at the intersection of Wood street, Broadway and the defendant's tracks; this lamp was suspended above the streets, but the evidence is conflicting as to whether it was burning at the time of this accident. There were no buildings located on the west side of Broadway; there was nothing to obstruct the view of defendant's tracks south of Wood street from a point about eighty-five feet east of the east rail of track number six. There was a switch connecting track number three with track number five crossing track number four.

On approaching this railroad crossing when the street car stopped, the deceased conductor alighted and went ahead of the car upon the tracks of the defendant Company for the purpose of ascertaining whether it was safe for the car to proceed; he went as far as track number three, and while either between tracks three and four or between the rails of track four, the record does not disclose just where, he hallooed and motioned to the motorman upon the street car to cross the tracks, indicating that the way was clear. The motorman proceeded with the car in accordance with the directions given him by plaintiff's intestate who was in the meantime standing either between tracks three and four or between the rails of track number four, awaiting the coming of the street car; as the street car approached track number four, the motorman discovered a string of cars on track number three being pushed across Wood street it was then too late to stop the street car and avoid a collision, and the motorman threw on all his power in the hope of crossing ahead of the approaching cars. The string of cars hit the street car about the third window from its front end; the street car contained five passengers, the impact threw it from the track and pushed it north from twenty-five to thirty feet, it fell upon its side, caught plaintiff's intestate under it and injured him so that he died in a short time; the passengers in the car were not injured. The string of cars, the front one of which hit the street car, consisted of sixteen coal cars being pushed by an engine on track number five. This cut of cars extended from track number five, on which the engine was, across track number four, to and upon track number three, the car that hit the street car was on track number three.

On the east side of Broadway, at the corner of Broadway and Wood street, was a saloon, the next room south of that was a barber shop, next to that was a cigar factory. The south line of Wood street and the east line of the right of way of the defendant Company intersected at the corner of Broadway and Wood streets.

On the west side of the Illinois Central tracks, on the north side of Wood street, about one hundred feet from the place of the accident, was located a gas house where a gas light was burning, and about twenty feet north of Wood street just west of track number one was a retort house where a 16-candle power electric light was burning.

The engine which was pushing the string of sixteen cars had a headlight both upon the front and rear of the engine; this headlight could be seen from Wood street over the tops of the string of cars, there being no cars in the string except coal cars. There was no man and no light upon the front car which hit the street car.

Track number two was located twenty feet west of track number three. From the west rail of track number three to the line of the right of way on the east side is about one hundred and thirty feet; after the street car reached the right of way on the east it would travel one hundred and thirty feet before reaching track number three. Track number one is twenty feet west of track number two, it is eighty-four feet from the east line of the right of way to the east rail of track number six.

It was about thirty feet from the south rail of the street car track crossing the railroad to the south line of the sidewalk on the south side of Wood street. There was a cut of four or five cars standing on track number four south of Wood street. The string of sixteen cars which were attached to the engine on track number five crossed track four with its foremost car on track number three, was in charge of a switching crew composed of a fireman, engineer and three brakemen. One of the men in charge of this string of cars was located near the sidewalk on the south side of Wood street; he had a lantern and was directing the movement of these cars by signals which were communicated from him by another of the crew located about half way between Wood street and the engine, and then to another member of the crew located near the engine and by him to the engineer. On account of the cars on track number four south of Wood street the brakeman nearest Wood street could not see the street car after it stopped east of the tracks, until it passed track four. There is no evidence in the record that plaintiff's intestate proceeded farther west than track number three in his attempt to ascertain whether the tracks were clear. He did not cross all of the tracks, but while on track four or between tracks three and four, signaled the motorman to cross, he remained standing at this point and awaited the approach of the car. The night was dark, misty and foggy.

The declaration contains various counts charging that the defendant negligently backed the string of cars over and across Wood street without having and maintaining a light on the front end of the car; also without having a man stationed on that car; that no bell of the weight required by the statute was rung or whistle blown on approaching this crossing; that an ordinance of the city of Decatur required that a headlight should be carried upon the front car; that the train was backed at a high and dangerous rate of speed; that the string of cars so being backed upon the tracks of the defendant was not then provided with a sufficient brake attached to the rear or hindmost car in care of a trusted and skilful brakeman; that the brakes were not operated from the locomotive by power applied there.

Plaintiff recovered a judgment for ten thousand dollars.

Defendant insists upon a reversal of the judgment, and insists that plaintiff was not in the exercise of due care for his own safety; that the failure to observe the approach of the cars from the south was such an act of contributory negligence as will defeat a recovery; that the street car company by which plaintiff's intestate was employed had a rule which required him to observe in flagging this crossing; that he failed to comply with this rule; that in permitting the car to proceed at the time it did he violated an ordinance of the city of Decatur, and that this was negligence *per se;* that the court erred in the admission and rejection of evidence; that the court erred in the giving and refusing of instructions; and that the judgment is excessive.

The question of due care is one of fact which must ordinarily be determined by the jury from all the evidence and circumstances in the case; the court submitted to the jury all the evidence tending to prove or disprove the question of due care and the jury had before it all of the circumstances leading up to and the surrounding condition which brought about this accident, the manner in which plaintiff's intestate went upon the tracks for the purpose of flagging the crossing and all the detail of his actions from the time he left the street car standing on the east side of the tracks up to and including the time when the car was hit by the string of cars on defendant's road, pushed by defendant and until plaintiff's intestate was taken from the track, as well as all the conditions surrounding the backing of the string of cars by defendant, and upon this question of due care the jury has found against the contention of the defendant; but it is insisted by the defendant that there is no material conflict in his evidence and that where such is the case it becomes a question of law for the court and not one of fact for the jury. This rule of law is applicable only where there is no conflict in the evidence, and the evidence is such that the minds of all reasonable men must arrive at but one conclusion; and from a review of the evidence, we are not able to say that the minds of all reasonable men must arrive at the same conclusions from these facts, nor are we able to say that the jury was not warranted in arriving at the conclusion which it did upon this question.

Appellant further contends that it was an absolute requirement on the part of plaintiff's intestate that he discover the approach of these cars before permitting the street car to pass, and that the failure so to do constituted contributory negligence, this was also a question of fact for the jury. The defendant bases its contention upon a rule of the street car company for which plaintiff's intestate was working, and also an ordinance of the city of Decatur, both of which required him to so ascertain; while it will be conceded a failure to have obeyed this rule would be such negligence as would create a liability against the company for which plaintiff's intestate was working in favor of passengers carried by it, but so far as the rule related to the defendant Company and his duty in flagging this crossing, he was only required to use ordinary care, and he must be considered as any other traveler of the public highway, and the fact that he had in his charge the lives and persons of passengers upon the car of the company for which he worked created no greater obligation for his own protection so far as this defendant is concerned.

The rule of the street car company which it is contended plaintiff's intestate violated is as follows:

"Steam railway crossings. Except at crossings provided with interlocking towers and at such track crossings as may be by bulletin excluded before steam railway tracks motormen must bring car to a full stop not nearer than 25 feet from the steam track. The motorman must not proceed with his car until the conductor has gone ahead on to the steam railway tracks and looked both ways and given him the signal to start. Before starting the motorman will look back and see that no one is getting on or off the car. After the car has crossed the railroad tracks the conductor will get on the rear platform of the car and give the motorman the signal to go ahead. If the motorman does not receive the signal to go ahead he will immediately bring his car to a full stop after passing the railroad tracks. All steam railroad crossings must be flagged."

The ordinance of the city of Decatur which it is insisted was violated is as follows:

"At all railway crossings where watchmen are not located or other sufficient and proper signals operated to designate the approach of trains or cars, all cars used by said company shall stop at least 10 feet before passing over the railway crossing, and the person or persons in charge of said car shall go upon said railway crossing and ascertain that no train or car is approaching and that there is no visible danger in running said car over said railway crossing."

We have been cited to no authority in this State determining this question of want of due care raised by reason of the failure of deceased to ascertain that no car was approaching, but we find upon examination of the various authorities submitted from other States, and which seem to be of equal weight, that the authorities are in conflict, part of them holding that a violation of a rule of this character is such negligence as will defeat a recovery, others holding that the duty imposed upon plaintiff's intestate by this rule created no additional duty to the defendant railroad company. The Court of Appeals of the State of Texas, in *Texas Traction Co. v. Bogue*, 139 S. W. 1042, and the same court in the case of *Clark v. St. Joseph Terminal Ry. Co.*, 148 S. W. 473, sustained the contention of appellant; and the contrary doctrine has been adopted by the courts of Iowa in *Grace v. Minneapolis & St. L. R. Co.*, 153 Iowa, 418, and numerous other cases; and we are rather inclined to hold that the rule did not create an imperative duty on deceased, that a violation of the rule as between the deceased and the defendant railway Company was not negligence *per se*.

But the question of the failure to ascertain that no car was approaching as required by the ordinance of the city of Decatur presents a more difficult question. While it is true that where a railroad company violates an ordinance and any person is injured by reason thereof that is held to be *prima facie* proof of the negligence of the railroad company, and proof of the violation of an ordinance alone creates a presumption of negligence, this presumption is not conclusive but may be rebutted by a showing that the violation of the ordinance was not the proximate cause of the injury, or upon showing that the injury was produced by reason of other causes. While this ordinance required plaintiff's intestate to proceed upon the tracks and ascertain whether or not any cars were approaching, the evidence shows an attempt to comply with the ordinance, we are not inclined to hold that a failure to positively ascertain this fact is such negligence *per se* as will defeat a recovery, but that where it is shown that plaintiff's intestate went upon the tracks for the purpose of ascertaining the approach of trains, the fact that he did not positively discover its approach, the question whether by failing to actually discover the cars he violated the ordinance was a question of fact, is for the determination of the jury and not one of law for the court.

We do not find that the trial court committed any serious error on the question of receiving or the rejection of evidence.

Defendant complains of the giving of instruction number eleven on behalf of plaintiff. While this instruction is subject to criticism and while it would have been better had it not been given, we are not inclined to hold that the giving of it was reversible error. We do not find the other instructions subject to the criticisms made, and after a careful consideration thereof, we are satisfied that the jury was fairly well instructed concerning the law applicable to this case, and that there is no reversible error in the giving or refusing of any of the instructions.

It is insisted by defendant that the judgment is excessive and should be reversed. While the judgment is large, we are not inclined to hold that it is so excessive as to require the judgment to be reversed upon that ground alone.

If the plaintiff will remit from this judgment the sum of three thousand dollars, within ten days after the filing of this opinion, upon such remittitur being made the judgment will be affirmed, otherwise the judgment will be reversed and the cause remanded.

Judgment affirmed upon remittitur; otherwise reversed and remanded.

Mattie White Spalding, Appellant, v. Estate of William R. White, Deceased, Appellee.

1. EXECUTORS AND ADMINISTRATORS, § 209*—*when contract by deceased to pay daughter for waiving claim of alimony against husband and keeping house for deceased, basis for claim against estate.* Where a father agrees to pay his married daughter a certain sum

*See Illinois Notes Digest, Vols. XI to XV, same topic and section number.

of money, if she will waive her claim to alimony against her husband, and after the divorce come and live with her father and
keep house for him, and she had fully complied with the agreement on her part at the time of her father's death, without such
sum being paid, *held* that she was entitled to such sum as a claim
against her father's estate, and *held* that she was entitled to have
such claim allowed though she was granted alimony on her petition
to the court where the divorce was granted after the death of her
father.

2. CONTRACTS, § 134*—*when contract by father to pay daughter
to waive claim for alimony against husband and keep house for
father not illegal.* Where a father agrees to pay his daughter a
certain sum if she will waive her claim for alimony against her
husband and come and live with her father and keep house for him,
and the agreement on her part is fully performed at the time of
her father's death, *held* that the agreement is not void as being only
a promise to make a gift not fulfilled within the lifetime of the
donor, nor void under the statute of frauds as being a promise to
answer for the debt of another, nor void as against public policy
because made to secure a divorce.

3. CONTRACTS, § 83*—*when agreement to waive claim for alimony
sufficient consideration to support a promise by a third party.* An
agreement by a daughter to waive, forbear and discontinue her
claim for alimony against her husband in a divorce suit is sufficient to support a promise by her father to pay her $1,000 if she
will come to his home and keep house for him.

4. CONTRACTS, § 142*—*when contracts relating to alimony not
invalid as against public policy.* It is not contrary to public policy
in an action for divorce to permit the parties interested therein
to make any agreement which they may see fit concerning their
property rights or for the support of the wife, and the fact that
the wife may have been influenced by a third party to make an
agreement relating alone to alimony will not vitiate the contract
made by the third party.

5. FRAUDS, STATUTE OF, § 10*—*when contract not void as being a
promise to pay debt of another.* Contract by a father to his married
daughter to pay her a certain sum in consideration that she would
waive her claim for alimony in a divorce suit against her husband
and come and keep house for her father, *held* to be an original
undertaking on the part of the father and not void under the
statute of frauds as being a promise to pay the debt of another, and
held, though the contract was within the statute of frauds, that
the plea of the statute of frauds cannot be invoked when the contract has been completely performed by the other party.

*See Illinois Notes Digest, Vols. XI to XV, same topic and section number.

Appeal from the Circuit Court of McLean county; the Hon. COLOSTIN D. MYERS, Judge, presiding. Heard in this court at the October term, 1912. Reversed and remanded with directions. Opinion filed October 16, 1913. Rehearing denied December 3, 1913.

BARRY & MORRISSEY and LESTER H. MARTIN, for appellant.

WELTY, STERLING & WHITMORE and FRANK Y. HAMILTON, for appellee.

MR. PRESIDING JUSTICE PHILBRICK delivered the opinion of the court.

Appellant, Mattie White Spalding, is the daughter of William R. White, deceased, she married one Dr. J. B. Spalding who lived in Wisconsin; Mrs. Spalding began an action for divorce, and the question arose concerning the payment of alimony. William R. White was then a widower, and for the purpose of avoiding a controversy over the question of alimony, he entered into an agreement with Mrs. Spalding by which he promised her that if she would not contest the question of alimony with her husband and would come to his home, if a divorce was granted, and keep house for him he would give her $10,000. Mrs. Spalding waived her claim for alimony.

That a contract was made and its terms and conditions agreed upon between Mrs. Spalding and her father is not disputed. Mrs. Spalding procured her divorce and went to her father's home in Bloomington, Illinois, where she lived and kept house for him until his death, thereby fully completing and carrying out the terms and conditions of the contract on her part. Her father in his lifetime turned over to her, to secure the payment of this $10,000, two notes amounting to $20,000, which he represented to her as being good security; and during his lifetime paid interest to her on this $10,000; the last payment of interest was made by a check for something over $900 a few days before his death. This check was paid by his executors after his death, but he never paid the principal for the reason, as stated by him, that he was a little short of money and needed what he then had in his business. Mrs. Spalding filed a claim against his estate, the claim was disallowed by the County Court and on appeal to the Circuit Court was there rejected; and from the judgment of the Circuit Court this appeal is prosecuted.

Appellant insists that the judgment should be reversed for the reason that she waived and surrendered at the request of her father a valid and subsisting claim which she had against her husband; that she fulfilled all of the terms and conditions of her contract with her father, and the notes having proved worthless which were given to her to secure the payment of the same; and that the judgment is against the manifest weight of the evidence and is contrary to the law.

Appellee on the other hand insists that the judgment is correct, and should be affirmed, claiming that the agreement was only a promise to make a gift, and was not fulfilled within the lifetime of the donor and therefore void; that it was a promise to answer for the debt of another and void under the statute of frauds; and also because it was made to secure a divorce between Mrs. Spalding and her husband and is therefore contrary to public policy.

The contention that the promise was a mere gift is conclusively disproved by the testimony of both counsel for Mrs. Spalding and Dr. Spalding in the divorce proceedings, who were present when the contract was entered into. Their evidence shows the promise was made upon condition that Mrs. Spalding would make no claim for alimony from her husband, and after the divorce she would go to the home of her father and keep house for him; both of these conditions were complied with by her. She thereby not only waived a valid claim she then had against her husband, but also performed services after that time and up to the date of her father's death in his household.

The agreement to waive, forbear and discontinue her claim for alimony against her husband was a sufficient consideration to support this contract. *Morgan v. Park Nat. Bank*, 44 Ill. App. 582; *McMicken v. Safford*, 197 Ill. 540; *Warren v. Warren*, 105 Ill. 568; *Dalby v. Maxfield*, 244 Ill. 214.

It is insisted, however, that because appellant petitioned the court where the divorce was granted for an allowance of alimony from her husband after the death of William R. White, which petition was allowed, she cannot recover.

Appellant fulfilled her promise to the deceased who has failed to comply with his agreement to pay her the $10,000, whereby he violated his contract, and the fact that she was compelled to obtain support from her former husband after her father had failed to comply with the terms of his contract will not permit the estate of the deceased to escape its performance, after the contract has been fully performed by her; to permit this would be to allow the estate to profit by the wrongful act of the testator.

Even though the waiver of her right to alimony should be held not to be a sufficient consideration to support the agreement, it will not seriously be contended that the agreement to perform the duties of housekeeper for appellee's testator during the remainder of his life, and the fulfillment of the promise, was not a sufficient consideration to support the contract; and there is no contention made by appellee that this would not be sufficient consideration.

From the conclusion above reached, it therefore follows that the contention that this promise was a mere gift cannot be maintained.

The contention that it was a promise to answer for the debt of another and void under the statute of frauds is equally untenable for the reason that it is conclusively proved that instead of being a promise to answer for the debt of another it was an original undertaking by appellee's testator. While it was a

duty imposed by law upon Dr. Spalding to care for and
maintain his wife, it was not such an obligation that
where for a sufficient consideration another person by
contract agrees to furnish the wife with support can
avoid the contract under plea of the statute of frauds,
and, even though the contract had been within the
statute of frauds, appellee cannot now invoke the plea
of that statute for the reason that the contract has
been fully and completely performed by the other party
with whom it was made. *Knight v. Collings*, 227 Ill.
348.

Upon the further and last contention made by appellee, that it was a promise made to secure a divorce
between Mrs. Spalding and her husband, there is no
evidence in this record upon which such a contention can be sustained. The application for divorce
was pending, cause for divorce existed, the divorce was
finally granted, and it is not contrary to public policy
in an action for a divorce to permit the parties interested therein to make any agreement which they may
see fit concerning their property rights or for the support of the wife; they may make any agreement settling
their property rights or waive any property rights
which they deem advisable, and the fact that the wife
may have been influenced by a third party to make an
agreement relating alone to alimony will not vitiate
the contract made by the third party.

The finding of the court is clearly against the manifest weight of the evidence and is contrary to the law.
The cause was heard in the Circuit Court without a
jury, the jury having been waived. This court is therefore authorized to finally determine the cause and
either enter a final judgment in this court or remand
the cause and direct what judgment shall be entered.
The judgment is, therefore, reversed and the cause remanded to the trial court with directions to allow this
claim and enter judgment against the estate of William
R. White for the sum of $10,000, together with interest
thereon from the death of the testator.

Reversed and remanded with directions.

Louis Heilbrunn et al., Appellants, v. J. J. Ellsworth et al., Appellees.

(Not to be reported in full.)

Appeal from the City Court of Mattoon; the Hon. JOHN McNUTT, Judge, presiding. Heard in this court at the October term, 1912. Dismissed. Opinion filed October 16, 1913.

Statement of the Case.

Action by J. J. Ellsworth and Harry McNair, partners, doing business under the firm name of Ellsworth and McNair, against William Fink in attachment. Louis Heilbrunn and David Kahn, partners, doing business under the firm name of Heilbrunn and Kahn, claiming the property levied upon, filed interpleading petitions to which the attachment plaintiffs filed pleas. The intervening petitioners demurred to the pleas and the demurrer was overruled. The intervening petitioners electing to stand by their demurrer, judgment was rendered against them for costs, from which judgment they appeal.

VAUSE & HUGHES, for appellants.

HENLEY & DOUGLAS and SPENCER WARD, for appellees.

MR. PRESIDING JUSTICE PHILBRICK delivered the opinion of the court.

Abstract of the Decision.

1. APPEAL AND ERROR, § 299*—*when judgment for costs against interpleaders in attachment not a final judgment.* Judgment entered on demurrer against interpleaders for costs in an attachment proceeding, there being no judgment finding that the property was the property of attachment defendant or that the interpleaders were not owners of or entitled to the property, *held* not a final judgment, from which an appeal may be taken, and appeal was dismissed with permission to either party to withdraw the record and make application to the trial court for a final judgment.

*See Illinois Notes Digest, Vols. XI to XV, same topic and section number.

2. APPEAL AND ERROR, § 267*—*jurisdiction on appeal from interlocutory judgments.* On appeal from an interlocutory judgment, such as a judgment for costs alone, the reviewing court obtains no jurisdiction by reason of the appeal, and the question that no final judgment was rendered is jurisdictional with the court, though the parties submitted the cause as though a final judgment had been rendered.

Florence Marshall et al., Appellees v. Modern American Fraternal Order, Appellant.

1. INSURANCE, § 763*—*commencement of limitation period under incontestable clause when new benefit certificate is issued.* Where the original benefit certificate contains a clause making the certificate incontestable after three years, and a new certificate is issued the same as the original, except that the names of the beneficiaries are changed, the limitation period commences from the date of the original certificate and not the date of the new certificate.

2. INSURANCE, § 717*—*when by-laws of a fraternal insurance order will not be construed retroactive.* A by-law passed after the issuing of a benefit certificate will not be held retroactive and applicable to certificates then in force unless such intention is expressly declared or must necessarily be implied from its language, and such is the rule where a member has stipulated to be bound by subsequently enacted by-laws.

3. CONTRACTS, § 187*—*when court will adopt construction of the parties.* Where parties to a contract have placed a construction upon the contract, or where they have had dealings between themselves, and have by their conduct and dealings placed a construction thereon, such construction will be adopted by the court, unless it is contrary to the plain terms of the contract.

4. INSURANCE, § 717*—*when a by-law enacted after the issuance of a benefit certificate will be construed prospective.* Where a benefit certificate is issued at the time of the existence of a by-law making the certificate incontestable after three years, except for a misrepresentation as to age, or nonpayment of dues, and later a by-law was adopted which repealed the former by-law making the benefit certificate incontestable and provided that the certificate shall be void if the member commits suicide at any time, *held* that the insurer by issuing a new certificate to the member after the adoption of the latter by-law, containing the same incontestable clause as in the former certificate, construed the latter by-law as prospective only and not retroactive.

Marshall v. Modern American Fraternal Order, 184 Ill. App. 224.

Appeal from the Circuit Court of Greene county; the Hon. JAMES A. CREIGHTON, Judge, presiding. Heard in this court at the April term, 1912. Affirmed. Opinion filed October 16, 1913.

DAVID L. WRIGHT, for appellant.

M. MEYERSTEIN, JR. and RAINEY & JONES, for appellees.

MR. PRESIDING JUSTICE PHILBRICK delivered the opinion of the court.

On the 28th day of July, 1900, appellant, a Fraternal Insurance Order organized under the laws of the State of Illinois, issued a benefit certificate to Jackson Marshall for the principal sum of one thousand dollars. On May 3, 1910, at Marshall's request, a new certificate was issued and the beneficiary changed and appellees became beneficiaries under the new certificate.

Appellees' declaration avers that Marshall became a member of appellant Order on the 28th day of July, 1900, when a benefit certificate was issued making the wife of Jackson Marshall beneficiary. The declaration further avers that on May 3, 1910, almost ten years after the date of the issuance of the first policy, appellant Company, at the request of Marshall, issued a new certificate in which at his request appellee became the beneficiaries and were beneficiaries at the time of his death. The declaration further makes all necessary averments as to compliance with all rules and regulations of the order, together with the death of Jackson Marshall on May 24, 1911, and the furnishing proofs of loss, etc. The declaration avers further that the contract of insurance between Marshall and appellant was entered into on the 28th day of July, 1900, the date of the original certificate; that the new certificate of May 3, 1910 was issued for the sole purpose of changing the beneficiaries; that the new certificate was identical with the original except as to beneficiaries; and that the contract of insurance must be considered

226 APPELLATE COURTS OF ILLINOIS.

Marshall v. Modern American Fraternal Order, 184 Ill. App. 224.

and held to have been made at the date of the original certificate, notwithstanding the new certificate was afterwards issued.

Defendant pleaded the general issue and three special pleas; to the special pleas a demurrer was sustained. The question of the ruling of the court in sustaining the demurrer to these pleas is not before this court, for the reason that appellant took leave to file four additional pleas which contain all of the matters set forth in the pleas to which the demurrer was sustained.

The first additional plea avers that plaintiffs ought not to have and maintain their action for the reason that the beneficiary certificate declared upon constitutes only a part of the contract between defendant and Jackson Marshall, that the original certificate was issued upon the written application of Marshall, and contains the clause stating it was issued.

"Upon condition that the statements made by said member in his or her application for membership and in answer to the interrogatories of the local medical examiner are true, full and correct; also issued subject to the laws, rules and regulations of the Order now in force or that may thereafter be promulgated, and all are made part of the contract."

The plea then avers that at the time of the issuance of the original certificate in plaintiffs' declaration mentioned the following by-law was in force and effect:

"Incontestable Certificate 50. The benefit certificate issued by this Order shall be incontestable after three years except for misrepresentation as regards age and for failure to pay any dues and assessments."

Also avers that if the insured had not correctly stated his age, then the beneficiary should be paid only such amount as they would be entitled to had the correct age been stated. The plea then avers that after the date of the original certificate, and on the 30th day of August, 1901, being less than three years from the date of the original certificate and prior to the death of the said Jackson Marshall, the defendant society adopted, promulgated and put in force the following by-law:

"Suicide. Section 53. If any person holding a beneficiary certificate comes to his or her death by the hand of his or her beneficiary or beneficiaries, except by accident, or if he or she shall come to his or her death by his or her own hand. whether sane or insane, then the beneficiary certificate of such member shall be null and void. * * * Section 92. All laws or parts of laws heretofore enacted or amended, except as herein specified, are hereby repealed."

The plea then further avers that on the 24th of May, 1911, the said Jackson Marshall came to his death by his own hand.

The second additional plea avers that the same was issued upon the written application of Jackson Marshall, and contained the same clause in regard to the rules and regulations then in force or which might thereafter be promulgated. The plea further avers that by section 43 of the Revised Laws it is provided as follows:

"A member in good standing may surrender his or her beneficiary certificate and have a new one issued subject to the laws of the Order, such changes to be made upon petition, accompanied by fifty cents certificate fee, signed by the member, attested by the Secretary * * * and the issuing of such new certificate shall cancel and render null and void such previous certificate to such member."

The plea further avers that on the 29th of April, 1910, the said Jackson Marshall desired to surrender his original certificate and have a new one issued to him, subject to the laws of the Order as provided in said section 43, that he surrendered his certificate and that on May 3, 1910, the new certificate set forth in plaintiffs' declaration was issued, that thereupon from that time the original certificate was null and void and the certificate of date May 3, 1910, was the only contract

228   APPELLATE COURTS OF ILLINOIS.

Marshall v. Modern American Fraternal Order, 184 Ill. App. 224.

of insurance existing between Marshall and the defendant Order. The plea further avers that it is expressly provided that if a member while in good standing in three full years from the date of said certificate, to wit: from the 3d day of May, 1910, should die by his or her own hand, whether sane or insane, then said certificate should be null and void and no recovery should be had upon the same. And further avers that on the 24th of May, 1911, the said Marshall died by his own hand.

The third additional plea avers the issuance of the original certificate on the 28th of July, 1900, and that for the purpose of changing beneficiaries Jackson Marshall surrendered that certificate and a new certificate was issued to him of date May 3, 1910, as alleged in the declaration, and that thereupon the original certificate became null and void, and that new certificate was the only contract of insurance between Marshall and the defendant Order, the repeal of the by-law making the certificate incontestable and the adoption of the by-law forfeiting the certificate if the insured committed suicide as alleged in the first additional plea, then avers the death of Marshall by his own hand.

The fourth additional plea avers the same facts as set forth in the others, in a condensed form.

Plaintiff demurred to each of the first, second, third and fourth additional pleas, and the demurrer was sustained by the court. Defendant elected to stand by these pleas, withdrew the plea of general issue, and the court thereupon rendered judgment on the demurrer and against the defendant for one thousand dollars, the amount of the certificate; from which judgment it appeals, and assigns as error the judgment of the trial court in sustaining the demurrer to these pleas.

The declaration and pleas both set forth the issuing of the original certificate, its surrender and the issuing of the new certificate on May 3, 1910, for the purpose of changing beneficiaries.

Opinion was filed in this cause March 18, 1913, and a rehearing allowed. Upon careful consideration of the petition for rehearing and reconsideration of the arguments presented, we have arrived at a different conclusion than that expressed in our former opinion.

It is conceded by appellant that at the time of the issuing of the original certificate a by-law was in force which provided that the certificate should be incontestable after three years from its date except for a misrepresentation as to age or the failure to pay dues. By its pleas appellant insists that the adoption of the by-law of August 30, 1901, which is as follows:

"If any person holding a beneficiary certificate comes to his or her death by the hand of his or her beneficiary or beneficiaries except by accident, or if he or she shall come to his or her death by his or her own hand, whether sane or insane, then the beneficiary certificate of such member shall be null and void." abrogated the by-law in force at the date of the original certificate and that the new by-law must control, that this by-law fixes no time within which the provision against committing suicide is prohibited.

Appellant contends that it is not liable under the policy for the reason that the by-law which provided that the policy of insurance should be incontestable after the expiration of three years from its date was repealed August 30, 1901, and that a new by-law then passed which did not contain the limitation period or the incontestable clause, and that under and by virtue of the new by-law the policy became void and no recovery could be had thereunder if the insured committed suicide at any time; also that by reason of the fact that the old policy issued to the insured on July 28, 1900, was surrendered at the time that the new certificate was issued May 3, 1910, that the time for computing the limitation period, if such limitation period is held to be operative, should commence from the date of the last certificate, May 3, 1910.

It is contended on the other hand by appellees that the by-law contained the incontestable clause having been in force at the date of the original certificate, and appellant having issued its certificate containing this incontestable clause, that the certificate with the incontestable clause then became such a contract that the insured acquired a vested interest thereunder and that any by-law passed by the Order abrogating the conditions of this contract should not be applied thereto, and that the by-law passed on August 30, 1901, should not be given a retroactive effect, but should be held to apply only to policies issued after that date. Appellees also insist that the limitation period in the new certificate should begin to run from the date of the original policy, that being the time when the deceased became a member of the Order, and having remained a member of the Order for nearly ten years, the issuing of the new certificate did not create the beginning of a new time from which to count the limitation period.

Notwithstanding the contention of appellant that its by-law in force when the original certificate was issued was repealed, it issued to the insured on May 3, 1910, almost nine years after the promulgation of this new by-law, its new certificate with the following clauses therein:

"In the event that said member while in good standing, shall come to his or her death by the hands of a beneficiary, except by accident, or if in three full years from the date hereof said member shall die by his or her own hand, whether sane or insane, then this certificate shall be null and void and no recovery shall be had on the same.

It is hereby agreed and understood that this certificate shall be incontestable after remaining in force three full years after the date thereof."

These clauses are in direct conflict with the by-law which it is insisted by appellant shall control, and it is a familiar rule of law that where a contract is written by one party and its terms conflict, the construction most favorable to the other party will be adopted.

Two questions are thus presented by this record, one, whether the limitation period of three years under which the policy might be contested by reason of the suicide of the insured commences at the date of the original policy or at the date of the new certificate; the other, whether the by-law passed by the appellant order on the 30th day of August, 1901, repealing the old by-law providing for the incontestable clause, and providing that the policy should be void if the insured committed suicide at any time, whether sane or insane, shall be held to apply to this policy. As to the limitation period, the issuing of the new certificate did not make any new contract with the insured except as to who should be beneficiaries thereunder, and the time of the computation of the three-year limitation period, if applicable, must be held to be the date of the original certificate.

The authorities of this State hold that a by-law passed after the issuing of a benefit certificate will not be held to be retroactive and applicable to certificates then in force, unless the intention that it shall be so operative is expressly declared or must necessarily be implied from its language, and this rule is adopted even where a member has stipulated that he will be bound by the laws of the Order that may thereafter be enacted. *Benton v. Brotherhood of Railroad Brakemen*, 146 Ill. 575; *Voigt v. Kersten*, 164 Ill. 314; *Covenant Mut. Life Ass'n. v. Kentner*, 188 Ill. 431; *Nowak v. Murray*, 127 Ill. App. 132.

Without determining the question as to whether the insured obtained a vested interest in this policy and by reason of which appellant could not pass a by-law applicable to his certificate, the rule of law is well settled that where parties have entered into a contract and have placed a construction upon that contract, or where parties have had dealings between themselves, and have, by their conduct and dealings placed a con-

232 APPELLATE COURTS OF ILLINOIS.

Marshall v. Modern American Fraternal Order, 184 Ill. App. 224.

struction thereon, then the courts will follow that
construction; and that construction will be adopted
by the court unless it is contrary to the plain terms of
the contract. Appellant had in force the by-law which
provided that the certificate should be incontestable
after the expiration of three years, except for the reasons stated, on July 28, 1900, issued its certificate
containing this incontestable clause and on August
30, 1901, adopted a by-law repealing the by-law providing the certificate should be incontestable, but notwithstanding the adoption of the by-law on August
30, 1901, almost nine years after adopting the by-law
repealing the former by-law providing for the incontestable clause, issued its new certificate to Marshall containing the same incontestable clause of the
original certificate. If it was the intention of the appellant Order that the repealing of the incontestable
by-law was to be applicable to all policies issued prior
thereto, then why did appellant issue its new certificate, upon the surrender of the old one, containing the
same incontestable provisions?

By issuing its new certificate containing the same incontestable clause, appellant Order has construed its
by-law to be only prospective, and not retroactive,
and in so doing has held that it does not apply to the
certificate issued to Marshall in force at the time of
the adoption of the new by-law; and having adopted
that construction, the court will follow it. *Hall v. First
Nat. Bank*, 133 Ill. 234; *Street v. Chicago Wharfing &
Storage Co.*, 157 Ill. 605; *Ingraham v. Mariner*, 194 Ill.
269.

For the reasons hereinbefore stated, the pleas filed
by appellant present no defense to the declaration,
and the trial court properly sustained the demurrer,
and the judgment is affirmed.

Affirmed.

The People of the State of Illinois for use of Lucella Cruthis, Appellee, v. John B. Revelli and Western Brewing Company, Appellants.

1. BONDS, § 34*—*when plea of nil debet not proper.* Nil debet is not a good plea in an action of debt on a penal bond which re. cites on its face an acknowledgment of the debt, and a demurrer to such plea is properly sustained.

2. CORPORATIONS, § 506*—*nature of plea of ultra vires.* The plea of *ultra vires* is a denial of the power and authority of the pleader to do and perform acts with which it is sought to be charged.

3. INTOXICATING LIQUORS, § 57*—*when plea of ultra vires by surety in action on dramshop keeper's bond demurrable.* In an action on a bond given by a dramshop keeper under R. S. c. 43, § 5, J. & A. ¶ 4604, a plea of *ultra vires* by one of the sureties, a brewing corporation, engaged in manufacturing and selling beer, denying it had authority under its charter to become surety on the bond, *held* demurrable, the plea not showing that it did not have general authority to perform all acts in providing for the sale of its products.

4. INTOXICATING LIQUORS, § 57*—*when plea by surety in action on dramshop keeper's bond demurrable.* In an action on a bond given by a dramshop keeper to procure a license, there having been a judgment previously recovered against the dramshop keeper for the wrongful sale of liquor to plaintiff's husband, a demurrer to a plea denying the sale of liquor to plaintiff's husband, and denying that plaintiff was injured in her means of support thereby, *held* properly sustained.

5. INTOXICATING LIQUORS, § 57*—*conclusiveness of prior judgment against dramshop keeper in action on dramshop keeper's bond.* In an action on a bond given by a dramshop keeper to procure his license, a judgment recovered against the dramshop keeper for damages resulting to plaintiff from the wrongful sale of liquor to plaintiff's husband is conclusive that the sales were made, that they were wrongful and that plaintiff was damaged by reason thereof.

6. INTOXICATING LIQUORS, § 57*—*when evidence offered in action on bond insufficient to show vindictive damages were recovered in prior action against dramshop keeper.* In an action on a dramshop keeper's bond, where a judgment had been previously recovered against the dramshop keeper for wrongfully selling liquors to plaintiff's husband, and such judgment remained unpaid, action of court in sustaining objection to the introduction in evidence of the stenographer's report of the evidence in the former suit, to prove

*See Illinois Notes Digest, Vols. XI to XV, same topic and section number.

that a verdict was rendered in that case for vindictive as well as actual damages, *held* not error, such evidence being insufficient to prove that vindictive damages were included in the verdict, and the amount of the verdict not justifying such contention.

7. INTOXICATING LIQUORS, § 57*—*when charter of surety inadmissible in suit on dramshop keeper's bond.* In an action on a dramshop keeper's bond, an objection to introduction in evidence of the charter of a brewing corporation, one of the sureties, to show it had no authority to execute the bond, *held* properly sustained.

Appeal from the Circuit Court of Montgomery county; the Hon. ALBERT M. ROSE, Judge, presiding. Heard in this court at the October term, 1912. Affirmed. Opinion filed October 16, 1913. *Certiorari* denied by Supreme Court (making opinion final).

D. R. KINDER and SCHAEFER & KRUGER, for appellants.

F. M. GUINN, MILLER, McDAVID & MILLER and HARRY L. BALLARD, for appellee.

MR. PRESIDING JUSTICE PHILBRICK delivered the opinion of the court.

Appellee sues John B. Revelli for the wrongful sale of intoxicating liquor to her husband, thereby causing his death. Appellant, the Western Brewing Company, and O. L. Kinzer were sureties on the bond given by John B. Revelli, required to be given by the keeper of a dramshop under section 5, chapter 43 of the Revised Statutes (J. & A. ¶ 4604), and for its wrongful sale to the husband of appellee, a judgment of three thousand dollars was recovered against him. That judgment not having been paid, appellee brought suit on the bond against John B. Revelli, the Western Brewing Company and O. L. Kinzer as sureties. Appellant Western Brewing Company filed pleas of *nil debet* and *ultra vires*. Demurrers were sustained to both of these pleas. Appellants then filed pleas denying the sale of intoxicating liquor by John B. Revelli to the deceased, and denying that appellee was injured in her means of support by reason of the death of her husband. A demurrer was sustained to this plea and appellant Western Brewing Company and Kinzer then filed a plea setting up that they were not parties to the suit in which the judgment was rendered, had had no opportunity to defend, also that on that trial evidence was introduced and instructions given to the jury on the question of vindictive damages, and that vindictive damages were allowed to appellee against said John B. Revelli. A demurrer to this plea was overruled, replication filed and issue joined.

Appellee offered in evidence the record of the judgment against John B. Revelli, together with the bond, on which bond appellants Western Brewing Company and Kinzer were sureties, and rested. Whereupon appellant moved to direct a verdict, the motion was overruled. Appellants then introduced in evidence the instruction given in the action brought by appellee against John B. Revelli, relating to vindictive damages in that case. Appellants then offered to show by the stenographer who reported the evidence in that case the evidence given upon that trial concerning notice to John B. Revelli requesting him not to sell intoxicating liquor to the husband of appellee; objection to this evidence was sustained. Appellant Western Brewing Company then offered in evidence its charter as a corporation, for the purpose of showing that it did not have the power to become surety upon the bond. Objection was also sustained to this offer of evidence. This being all the evidence on behalf of appellant, they then renewed their motion to direct a verdict for the defendants and each of them. This motion was overruled. Whereupon the court, on motion of appellee, directed a verdict against appellants for the amount of the former judgment, three thousand dollars.

It is contended by appellants that the court erred in refusing to direct a verdict for the appellants and each of them, that it erred in sustaining objections to each offer of evidence made by them, and erred in directing a verdict for plaintiff.

Revelli was engaged in the sale of intoxicating liquors. In order to obtain his license to sell intoxicating liquors it was necessary that he furnish and provide a bond running to the People of the State of Illinois and conditioned as required by the Dramshop Act. For the purpose of assisting him in securing his license, appellant Western Brewing Company signed this bond. The Brewing Company was incorporated to manufacture and sell beer; in order to continue in business it was necessary to dispose of its product, and it was empowered under the law to do all lawful acts in the furtherance of its business. In order to assist the appellant Revelli to conduct a dramshop and make sales of beer, which was a product manufactured by it, the Western Brewing Company executed this bond. It is but a legitimate inference that in creating an agency for the sale of a product produced by it to that extent it was benefited in its business. And it should not be permitted after having been instrumental in securing the license for the dramshop keeper, by whom the wrong was committed and the damage done, to deny its authority to execute the bond by means of which it was instrumental in securing the license for Revelli, for without the license having been issued upon the furnishing of this bond, as required by law, no injury would have occurred to appellee through this channel.

Upon the contention that the court erred in sustaining demurrers to the plea of *nil debet*, it has been a universal rule of practice in this State that *nil debet* is not a good plea in an action of debt, the bond reciting on its face an acknowledgment of the debt, and this being an action brought upon a penal bond executed by appellants, it follows that the demurrer to the plea of *nil debet* was properly sustained.

The appellant Brewing Company insists that under its charter it had no authority to become surety upon the bond of a dramshop keeper, and that its plea of *ultra vires* was a good plea. The plea of *ultra vires* is the denial of the power and authority of the pleader to do and perform acts with which it is sought to be charged. And in this instance the pleas set forth that the Western Brewing Company was organized and incorporated under the laws of Illinois for the manufacture and brewing of beer, malt extract and other malt, vinous and spirituous liquors and the sale of the same, and denying that it was incorporated as a surety company, and that by reason of it not having specific authority under its charter powers to become such surety that the obligation executed by it is null and void. This plea does not aver or show in what manner or by what means the sale of its product might be consummated, and from all that appears in this plea it had general authority to do and perform all acts which would tend to provide for and be instrumental in the sale of its products. While we do not wish to be understood as holding that this corporation had the power to do a general surety or security business and become surety under any and all conditions, we do hold that the plea filed by the Western Brewing Company in this action does not show and is insufficient for the purpose of presenting the question as to whether its act was *ultra vires,* all the material facts averred in the plea might be true and still the act of becoming surety on this bond not be *ultra vires.* The demurrer to this plea was properly sustained. *Blue Island Brewing Co. v. Fraatz,* 123 Ill. App. 26; *Chicago & M. Tel. Co. v. Type Tel. Co.* 137 Ill. App. 131.

The next plea filed by appellant denies the sale of intoxicating liquor by John B. Revelli to the deceased and denies the appellee was injured as a result thereof in her means of support. Appellee having prosecuted the cause of action against the dramshop keeper who committed the wrong and for whom the Western Brewing Company and Kinzer became sureties, the judgment recovered by appellee in that action against the dramshop keeper is conclusive that the sales were made, and that they were wrongful, and that appellee has been damaged by reason thereof as against the sureties of the dramshop keeper; and it follows therefore that the plea presented no defense, and the demurrer was properly sustained thereto.

The Western Brewing Company and Kinzer then filed an additional plea setting up that they were not parties to the suit in which the judgment was rendered and had had no opportunity to defend; that on that trial evidence was introduced and instructions given on the question of vindictive damages, and that vindictive damages cannot be recovered in an action upon this bond. It is under this plea that appellants offered evidence to which objections were sustained.

Appellant insists that it was error for the court to sustain the objection to the evidence of the stenographer by whom appellant offered to prove from his notes evidence of notice to Revelli not to sell liquor to appellee's husband. The only object of the tender of this evidence was for the purpose of proving that in the verdict rendered by the jury in the action against Revelli the jury awarded vindictive as well as actual damages. The admission of this evidence could not have in any way determined or enlightened the jury trying this cause upon the question as to whether or not vindictive damages were included in their verdict. The cause of action in that case was the death of appellee's husband, the amount of the judgment was three thousand dollars. The action was brought for the loss, damage and injury to the support of appellee; by the death of her husband she was deprived of the support to which she was entitled. The amount of the verdict recovered precludes any contention that vindictive damages were included therein. The courts of this State have sanctioned judgments in greater amounts than this upon the mere presumption of loss of support. The court did not err in sustaining the objection to this evidence.

Appellant Western Brewing Company then offered in evidence its charter and this offer was made solely for the purpose of showing that the Brewing Company had no power under its charter to execute the bond. From what has heretofore been said in this regard, the court properly held that the Brewing Company was estopped to deny its authority to execute this bond and properly sustained the objection to this evidence.

This being all of the evidence offered on behalf of appellants, the court again properly overruled its motion to direct a verdict and the court having sustained demurrers to all of the pleas filed by the defendants except the one concerning vindictive damages, and the only evidence admitted in support of this plea being the instruction given by the court upon the former trial, there was no evidence to sustain the plea. The court properly instructed the jury to find the verdict for appellee.

Finding no error in this record, the judgment of the trial court is affirmed.

Affirmed.

Ezekial Edwards, Appellant, v. Elijah Etter, Appellee.

(Not to be reported in full.)

Appeal from the County Court of Morgan county; the Hon. EDWARD P. BROCKHOUSE, Judge, presiding. Heard in this court at the October term, 1912. Reversed. Opinion filed October 16, 1913.

Statement of the Case.

Action by Elijah Etter against Ezekial Edwards to recover a commission alleged to be due the plaintiff for services rendered in procuring a purchaser for defendant's farm. From a judgment in favor of plaintiff for two hundred and seventy dollars, defendant appeals.

Edward C. Knotts and Walker & Woods, for appellant.

William N. Hairgrove, for appellee; Robert Tilton, of counsel.

Mr. Presiding Justice Philbrick delivered the opinion of the court.

Abstract of the Decision.

1. **Brokers, § 37*—*when broker not the procuring cause in securing a purchaser for a farm.*** In an action to recover a commission for procuring a purchaser for defendant's farm, the declaration alleging that the farm was listed with plaintiff to sell at one hundred and twenty dollars per acre, a verdict for plaintiff *held* to be manifestly contrary to the evidence, the evidence showing that the farm was sold for one hundred and five dollars per acre by the defendant and there being no evidence that plaintiff ever informed defendant that the person making the purchase was a prospective buyer, or that the farm was sold by defendant at a less price than one hundred and twenty dollars per acre with any intention to deprive plaintiff of a commission.

2. **Brokers, § 36*—*sufficiency of performance by broker to entitle him to a commission.*** To entitle a broker to a commission he must be the efficient cause in either effecting a sale, or in finding a buyer who is ready, willing and able to buy at the stipulated price, or to whom the owner afterwards sells.

E. F. Bowles, Executor, Appellant, v. Ida Seymour et al., Appellees.

1. **Pledges, § 24*—*rights of pledgor in equity.*** Though ordinarily when property is pledged as collateral security for a debt,

---

the pledgor has no interest in the property until after the payment of the indebtedness, and in an action to recover it before the debt is paid it is necessary to either aver a tender or an offer to pay, a court of chancery is not required to arbitrarily so hold but in the exercise of its equitable powers may determine what the rights of the parties are and protect them in its decree.

2. CREDITORS' SUIT, § 7*—*when fraudulent conveyances may be set aside to enforce collection of a judgment held as collateral security.* On creditors' bill to set aside certain conveyances as fraudulent for the purpose of enforcing the collection of a judgment held by one of the defendants as collateral security for certain notes, a decree setting aside the conveyances and allowing the complainant the amount due on the judgment less the amount due on the part of the notes, *held* erroneous in so far as it failed to allow an offset against the judgment of the amount of all the notes.

Appeal from the Circuit Court of Montgomery county; the Hon. JAMES C. McBRIDE, Judge, presiding. Heard in this court at the October term, 1912. Affirmed in part, reversed in part and remanded with directions. Opinion filed October 16, 1913. Rehearing denied December 3, 1913.

J. H. ATTERBURY and PAUL McWILLIAMS, for appellant.

LANE & COOPER and HILL & BULLINGTON, for appellees.

MR. PRESIDING JUSTICE PHILBRICK delivered the opinion of the court.

On January 20, 1896, in her lifetime, Susan Bowles recovered a judgment against Ida Seymour, one of the appellants, for $1,179.37. Susan Bowles in her· lifetime, on August 1, 1896, became indebted to one Rebecca Culp in the sum of $2,000, for which she gave her two notes drawing seven per cent. interest, and Susan Bowles at that time claiming to have an interest in the fee to real estate sought now to be reached by the creditors' bill filed in this cause made and executed a mortgage on this real estate to Rebecca Culp to secure the payment of these two notes for $1,000 each. These two notes were assigned to B. F. Culp by Rebecca Culp on the day they bear date. Some question having been made as to the title which Susan Bowles had in the real estate in question, she, for the purpose of better securing the payment of the $2,000 to B. F. Culp, assignee of the notes, assigned to him as additional security therefor the judgment recovered January 20, 1896, against Ida Seymour for $1,179.37. The Supreme Court determined that Susan Bowles held but a life estate in the real estate which she had mortgaged to Rebecca Culp. [172 Ill. 521.] On February 9, 1900, Susan Bowles made and executed to B. F. Culp another note for $150, drawing seven per cent. interest, and on February 24, 1902, executed to him another note for $50, drawing interest at seven per cent.

Ida Seymour, against whom Susan Bowles recovered the judgment, at the time of the recovery of the judgment had an interest in the fee to the lands in question and on February 11, 1903, more than seven years after the recovery of the judgment of Susan Bowles, and after the lien of the judgment had expired, with her husband, James R. Seymour, conveyed her interest in these lands by quitclaim deed to William L. Seymour, a brother of her husband, for the recited consideration of one dollar. On February 25th following, William L. Seymour quitclaimed the same lands to James R. Seymour, the husband of Ida Seymour, with a stated consideration of one dollar; these deeds were executed for the purpose of transferring the title of Ida Seymour to her husband. On April 6, 1903, the judgment in favor of Susan Bowles against Ida Seymour was revived. On September 5th following, James R. Seymour and wife quitclaimed these lands back to William L. Seymour for a consideration of $4,000, and on September 10th, following, William L. Seymour and wife executed a mortgage thereon to James R. Seymour to secure this $4,000. These conveyances and transactions were all made without the payment of any money between the parties. In April, 1904, the notes executed by Susan Bowles to B. F. Culp were still unpaid, and Susan Bowles assigned to B. F. Culp her life estate in the premises with the power to collect rents and profits and apply the same on the notes which he held against her. He collected part of these rents and credited them on the notes. Susan Bowles died March 6, 1906, and appellant, B. F. Bowles, was made executor of her last will and testament. On January 20, 1908, B. F. Culp assigned and transferred to James R. Seymour, the husband of Ida Seymour, the four notes executed by Susan Bowles.

The bill in this case was filed March 25, 1908. It alleges that the conveyances between Ida Seymour, James R. Seymour and William L. Seymour were fraudulent and void, and should be set aside for the purpose of permitting the collection of the judgment secured by Susan Bowles against Ida Seymour. The chancellor held the conveyances fraudulent and void as against this judgment and found that at the date of the decree rendered there was $2,139.63 due to the complainant as executor of Susan Bowles on this judgment. The decree also found that on the two notes for $1,000 each, made by Susan Bowles to Rebecca Culp and held by James R. Seymour, there was a balance due of $1,325.03, and decreed that after allowing these sums to James R. Seymour, the appellant as executor of the last will and testament of Susan Bowles was entitled to receive the balance. By that decree the court refused to allow James R. Seymour to offset the amount due upon the two notes of $150 and $50.

After the assignment to B. F. Culp of the life interest of Susan Bowles in the premises in question, Culp rented this land, and at the time he assigned these four notes to James R. Seymour one instalment of rent due for the use of these premises by the tenant, amounting to $280, was not then paid. Although this amount had not been paid to Culp by the tenant, he, upon demand of Seymour, credited the note with this amount. The court by its decree did not allow this credit.

This appeal is prosecuted by the executor of the last will and testament of Susan Bowles from that decree, and insists that the court erred in allowing James R. Seymour any credit for the notes held by him against the judgment recovered by Susan Bowles in her lifetime.

At the time of the filing of the bill in this cause the judgment recovered by Susan Bowles was then held by James R. Seymour as collateral security to secure the notes which he had obtained from B. F. Culp by assignment. The bill filed by complainant to set aside the conveyances and subject the lands in question to the payment of the judgment recovered by Susan Bowles, and which was held by James R. Seymour as collateral, does not contain in any averment offering to pay to James R. Seymour whatever sum, if any, might be due him by reason thereof; neither does the bill aver any tender of the amount due on these notes.

Appellees insist that while the judgment was pledged as collateral and the indebtedness for which it was so pledged unpaid, the judgment was not an asset belonging to the estate of Susan Bowles, and entered a motion in the trial court asking the court to restrain further prosecution of that suit. This motion was overruled and it is insisted that the court erred in overruling this motion and in permitting the prosecution of the suit.

Appellees also insist that the court erred in finding a decree in favor of the complainant, and in decreeing that defendants or any of them should pay any amount upon said judgment; also insisting that the court erred in refusing to allow James R. Seymour to offset against this judgment the $150 and the $50 notes assigned by B. F. Culp to him. Appellees have assigned cross-errors covering these questions.

This being a creditors' bill by complainant to subject these lands to the payment of a debt due from Ida Seymour, it was incumbent upon complainant to show that the conveyances were fraudulent and made with the intention to hinder and delay the collection of the. judgment in favor of Susan Bowles. For the purpose of establishing this proof, complainant placed James R. Seymour upon the stand for the purpose of showing there was no consideration for these conveyances, but on cross-examination he testified that the conveyance from his wife to him was made to repay money advanced by him for her musical education, under a promise to repay him, that he had expended $2,500 in this behalf, and that the conveyance of this property was made to reimburse him therefor. Complainant having placed Mr. Seymour upon the stand to prove no consideration, opened for the cross-examination the question as to what consideration there was, if any, and these matters were properly permitted to be brought out upon cross-examination of the witness. But it is evident that the court who heard this testimony and saw the witness on the stand did not give much credence to it, for he disregarded it, and under the rule that where a chancellor has heard the evidence and made his finding regarding the same, it should not be lightly disturbed by this court unless this court can say that the finding is clearly and manifestly against the evidence; we are not so convinced and we are not inclined to disturb his finding that the conveyances were fraudulent as against this judgment. While we are aware that ordinarily when property is pledged as collateral security for a debt the pledgor has no interest in the property until after the payment of the indebtedness for which it is so pledged as collateral, and in an action to recover it before the debt is paid it is ordinarily necessary to either aver a tender or an offer to pay, a court of chancery is not required to arbitrarily so hold but in the exercise of its equitable powers may determine what the rights of the parties are and protect them in its decree.

We are of the opinion that the court properly held that the conveyances were fraudulent as against any sum which then remained due on this judgment, but a party seeking the aid of a court of equity must be required to do equity and the chancellor properly granted to James R. Seymour the right to have the two $1,000 notes, together with the interest due thereon, offset against this judgment and there is no error in the decree in that regard. Appellant has not been injured by the decree rendered, and as to him it should be affirmed. But upon the question of the cross-errors assigned by appellees as herein before stated, it is the general rule that in property or assets pledged as collateral security to another, the pledgor has no interest therein, and no right to bring any action thereon, until the indebtedness for which it is pledged is paid, this rule is not so iron clad and imperative that a court of chancery will not determine and adjust the rights of parties in the property pledged.

The record discloses that Mrs. Bowles agreed that this judgment should be held as collateral security not only for the two $1,000 notes, but also for the $150 and the $50 note, and it is of no concern either to her or her estate what James R. Seymour paid to Culp for the transfer of these notes to him. He is entitled to offset as against the judgment, the entire amount of these notes, together with all interest due thereon.

The chancellor erred in not permitting James R. Seymour to offset the $150 and the $50 notes as against this judgment. The executor of Mrs. Bowles could obtain no greater interest in this judgment than she had at the time of her death, he stands in her place, he has whatever rights she had and no more.

We are of the opinion that the decree of the trial court is proper in all respects with the exception that James R. Seymour should also have been given credit as against this judgment for the $150 and the $50 notes, together with the interest due thereon; and for the error of the chancellor in not allowing these credits the decree will be reversed upon the cross-errors, and remanded with directions to enter a decree allowing James R. Seymour credit for the four notes, together with interest thereon. Decree affirmed in part and reversed in part and remanded with directions.

Affirmed in part, reversed in part and remanded with directions.

Flora Oliver, Appellant, v. The First National Bank of Mt. Olive, Appellee.

(Not to be reported in full.)

Appeal from the County Court of Macoupin county; the Hon. TRUMAN A. SNELL, Judge, presiding. Heard in this court at the October term, 1912. Affirmed. Opinion filed October 16, 1913. Rehearing denied December 3, 1913.

Statement of the Case.

Action originally commenced by the First National Bank of Mt. Olive against Max Lange in attachment for an alleged indebtedness on two promissory notes. The attachment writ was levied on a certificate of stock and one Flora Oliver filed the statutory notice upon the sheriff that she claimed to be the owner of the certificate. On a trial of right of property in the County Court a judgment was rendered finding that claimant was not the owner of the certificate of stock. From such judgment, claimant appeals.

A. A. LOWRY and VICTOR HEMPHILL, for appellant; SCHNEIDER & SCHNEIDER, of counsel.

L. M. HARLAN and PEEBLES and PEEBLES, for appellee.

MR. PRESIDING JUSTICE PHILBRICK delivered the opinion of the court.

Abstract of the Decision.

APPEAL AND ERROR, § 528*—*when propositions of law or fact essential to preserve questions for review.* On appeal from a judgment rendered by the trial court without a jury there is no question preserved for the court of review where no propositions of law or fact have been submitted to the trial court.

John Keller, Appellee, v. Chicago, Wilmington and Vermilion Coal Company, Appellant.

1. MINES AND MINERALS, § 153*—*when defendant entitled to contradict evidence introduced by plaintiff without objection.* In an action against a mining company for injuries sustained by plaintiff while employed as a motorman on a haulage motor used for moving cars in defendant's mine, the declaration alleging that the injury resulted from a derailment on account of the defective condition of the tracks, *held* that where plaintiff is permitted, without objection, to show that a tie at or near the place of the accident was removed and replaced with a new one after the time of the injury, a refusal by the court to permit defendant to show under what circumstances the tie was removed is error.

2. MINES AND MINERALS, § 182*—*questions for jury.* In an action for personal injuries sustained by plaintiff by reason of the derailment of a car in a mine, alleged to have been caused by defective tracks, whether the derailment was caused by the defective condition of the track and what caused the derailment, *held* to be questions for the jury, where the evidence is conflicting.

3. MINES AND MINERALS, § 192*—*when instruction ignoring question whether injury was caused by fellow-servant erroneous.* In an action for personal injuries in a mine, based on a common law count in the declaration, the giving of an instruction directing a verdict for plaintiff upon the finding of the circumstances recited in the instruction without requiring the jury to determine whether the accident was caused by the negligence of a fellow-servant, *held* error.

4. INSTRUCTIONS, § 131*—*when erroneous for ignoring essential elements.* An instruction which directs a verdict for plaintiff must include all the elements necessary to be found by the jury.

5. DAMAGES, § 115*—*when verdict for personal injuries excessive.* A verdict for plaintiff for $3,400 for injury to his limb not such as will be of any serious damage, *held* excessive, the expense for a physician and otherwise amounting to $400, his earning capacity at the time of the injury being $2.92½ per day, and since the injury has been earning a greater sum.

Appeal from the Circuit Court of Sangamon county; the Hon. ROBERT B. SHIRLEY, Judge, presiding. Heard in this court at the October term, 1912. Reversed and remanded. Opinion filed October 16, 1913.

BROWN & HAY and JOHN T. CREIGHTON, for appellant; MASTIN & SHERLOCK, of counsel.

JAMES H. MURPHY, for appellee; EDWARD C. KNOTTS, of counsel.

MR. PRESIDING JUSTICE PHILBRICK delivered the opinion of the court.

This is an action against appellant for an injury to appellee alleged to have been caused to him by reason of the negligence of the appellant Company by whom he was employed as a motorman on a haulage motor used in the mine of appellant Company for the movement of its cars. The trial below resulted in a judgment for $3,400.

Appellee filed a declaration with five counts; the third and fourth counts having been withdrawn from the jury by the trial court, the cause was tried upon the first, second and fifth counts.

The first count charges appellant with being the owner and operator of a mine in Macoupin county; that appellee's duties required him to haul loaded cars from a certain switch in the mine to the bottom of the shaft, and to return empty cars from the shaft to the switch where they were distributed throughout the mine, these cars were hauled over and upon a track built for this purpose in the entry where appellee was required to work; that it was the duty of the appellant Company to keep and maintain this track and switch in a reasonably safe condition for the performance of the work required of appellee, but that appellant, disregarding its duty, permitted the ties to become rotten and worn at and near the point where the switch connected with the main track in this entry at a place known as the parting, that by reason thereof the spikes became loose and were insufficient to hold the rails, and that by reason of this negligence the motor which appellee was operating was derailed, and by reason of which he was injured

The second and fifth counts charge wilful violation of the statute regarding mines and miners.

The second count averring the old and rotten condition of the ties, loose spikes, etc., alleging that this constituted a dangerous condition which should have been discovered by the defendant's mine examiner, but that the mine examiner failed to visit, inspect and observe the mine and inscribe the month and day of his visit, and to mark by conspicuous marks the dangerous place, failed to report his findings to the mine manager and to make a report thereof to be kept in a book required for that purpose, and that said condition was not discovered by the mine examiner, and while such dangerous condition existed, appellee was permitted to enter the mine for work without being under the direction of the mine manager.

The fifth count alleges that at a short distance west of the switch there was a dangerous condition in the rails of the main track by reason of their being old, defective, battered and bent and out of line, that the mine examiner wilfully failed to visit and inspect the mine and discover these conditions and to inscribe upon the walls with chalk the month and day of his visit, failed to place conspicuous marks, failed to report to the mine manager, and failed to make the entry in the book required by the statute to be kept for that purpose, and that while these conditions existed appellee was permitted to enter the mine for work, not being under the direction of the mine manager.

No plea appears of record, but the cause went to trial, and it will be presumed that the general issue was filed.

Appellant insists upon a reversal of this cause, and assigns as reasons therefor that the evidence does not support the allegations of the declaration, that the court erred in the admission and rejection of evidence and in the giving and refusing of instructions, that the amount of damages is excessive; also for the reason that the injury was not caused by reason of wilful violation of the mine act, but by reason of the negligence of a fellow-servant.

The evidence discloses that appellee was in the employ of the appellant Company in its mine in Macoupin county; that in the prosecution of its work in this mine the cars of coal were hauled by mules from the various rooms where it was mined, and collected at a point in the main entry, and from there hauled to the main shaft by the motor operated by appellee; that after the cars were emptied they were then returned in trains to the switch by appellee, but the transferring of the cars from the main track to the switch was done by means of a flying switch, which means that the cars were started with considerable speed upon the main track by the motor, the motor then uncoupled from the train, its speed increased faster than the moving train, and after it had passed the switch stand the switch was then thrown by an operator and the train of cars permitted to pass upon the switch. It was while making one of these flying switches that the motor which appellee was operating left the track.

There is a serious conflict in the evidence as to whether or not the ties were rotten or the spikes loose at or near this switch, but the evidence does disclose that there was a bend or kink in the track at a point about six feet from the switch point. Appellee insists

that the motor car left the track by reason of these
conditions, while appellant insists that the kink in the
track was not sufficient to have caused any derailment,
and that the derailment of the motor car occurred
further down the track, near the frog of the switch,
and that the accident was caused by reason of the
failure of the switchman to be at his post of duty. As
to where the switchman was the evidence is very conflicting, appellant insisting that he was at a point
some one hundred and fifty to two hundred feet or
more away from his post of duty and that after he
saw the train of cars coming he attempted to reach the
switch to throw it, and that he failed to properly observe the condition of the switch and wrongfully threw
it so that the motor car instead of passing along the
main track was thrown upon the switch track, and that
the derailment of the motor did not occur at the point
of the switch or near it, but that the motor was derailed at or near the guard rail near the frog in the
switch; just where it was actually derailed the evidence is very conflicting. The motor came to a stop
at a point almost directly over the frog and between
the guard rails, with wheels off the track on either
side of the frog. The train of cars which was following the motor car remained upon the main track instead of passing upon the siding, and that the foremost car of the train hit the motor at the point where
it was standing throwing appellee from his seat and
injuring him. Appellant insists that the fact that the
motor car took the siding and did not continue on the
main track and that the train of cars took the main
track and did not go upon the siding is conclusive
proof that the accident was caused by the failure of the
switch operator to properly tend the switch. Where
the evidence is so conflicting and contradictory it is for
a jury to pass upon the question as to how or in what
manner the accident was caused; and the case was
properly submitted to the jury by the trial court for
the purpose of determining the questions of fact from
the disputed evidence.

The evidence is also very conflicting as to whether the mine examiner had performed his duties as required by the statute and whether or not the accident was occasioned by reason of this failure to perform the duties required of him; this evidence presents a question of fact that should be determined by a jury. From the condition of the conflicting evidence in this record we do not deem it proper for this court to, at this time, make any finding of facts, as it is necessary to reverse this judgment upon the ruling of the court in regard to the admission of evidence and upon the instructions given.

The court permitted appellee to show that a tie at or near the place where appellee insists the injury occurred and the condition of which appellee insists was the cause of the injury was removed by appellant Company after the time of the injury and replaced by a new one, and permitted appellee to show by witnesses that this was done upon the order of Mr. Woods, the superintendnt of the defendant Company. Appellant concedes that this proof was made without objections. After this evidence was in the record, appellant offered to show that the tie was not removed either upon the direction or upon any order given by Mr. Woods, the superintendent, and to show that the tie was removed by reason of false statements and assertions made to the workmen who removed the tie. While the evidence that the tie was removed or the track repaired would not have been proper if objected to by appellant, although the evidence was admitted without objection, after appellee produced this evidence appellant should have been permitted to have shown that the superintendent gave no order or direction regarding the removal thereof, and to have shown how and under what circumstances the tie was so removed; and we think the court erred in refusing to admit this evidence, as it was proper for the purpose of contradicting and disputing evidence offered on behalf of appellee, which in all probability affected the finding of the jury.

The court gave to the jury on behalf of appellee the following instruction:

"The court instructs the jury that as to the first count of the declaration, that if you believe from the preponderance of the evidence the defendant is guilty of the negligence charged in said count and that such negligence caused plaintiff's injury, as alleged in the first count, and that at and before the time plaintiff was so injured he was in the exercise of ordinary care for his own safety and that he did not know of the peril by which he was injured and could not have discovered the same by the exercise of ordinary care, then as to the first count you should find the defendant guilty."

The instruction directed a verdict for the plaintiff upon the finding of the circumstances recited in the instruction. The first count of the declaration was a common law count, and the question as to whether or not the injury was caused by reason of the negligent act of the fellow-servant in this record, it was error for the court to give the jury this instruction which directed a verdict without requiring it to determine that the accident was not caused by reason of the negligence of the fellow-servant before a recovery could be had. The omission of this question from the instruction and the failure to require the jury to find thereon before returning a verdict for appellee was error. The rule is familiar that where an instruction directs a verdict for the plaintiff the instruction must include all the elements necessary to be found by the jury. *Chicago Suburban W. & L. Co. v. Hyslop*, 227 Ill. 308; *Chicago Consol. Traction Co. v. Schritter*, 222 Ill. 364.

We do not find that the court committed any other serious error prejudicial to the appellant.

Upon the question of the judgment being excessive, the record discloses that appellee at the time of the injury was earning $2.92½ per day; that his expense for a physician and otherwise amounted to about $400; that he has some injury to his limb, but not such as will be of any serious damage; that since the injury occurred he has been able to work and received $3.24 per day. For his suffering and loss of time which he has sustained by reason of the injury and for any suffering that he may have in the future he may be entitled to recover, but under the evidence in this record we are compelled to hold that the judgment is excessive.

For the reasons hereinbefore stated, the judgment is reversed and the cause remanded.

Reversed and remanded.

L. O. Foster, Appellee, v. Walker Smith, Appellant.

1. **SALES, § 283***—*questions for jury.* In an action for breach of warranty in the sale of a team of horses, the questions whether a warranty was made, or if made whether the buyer relied upon the warranty in making the purchase, or relied on his own test of the horses, are for the jury.

2. **SALES, § 352***—*when buyer not entitled to recover money paid for breach of warranty.* In an action for the breach of a warranty of a team of horses and for a return of the purchase price, where the horses were purchased as a team, and no specific price paid for either horse, the buyer being unable to return the team by reason of the death of one of the horses cannot recover the purchase price paid, but must recover if at all on the breach of the warranty, if one was made and proved.

3. **SALES, § 402***—*when instruction as to measure of damages for breach of warranty erroneous.* Instruction as to measure of damages in an action for breach of a warranty in the sale of a team of horses, *held* erroneous.

4. **SALES, § 392***—*when seller's ignorance does not defeat recovery for breach of warranty.* In an action for the breach of warranty of the soundness of a team of horses, the seller cannot defeat recovery for breach of warrant by showing that he did not know the condition of the horses at the time of the warranty.

*See Illinois Notes Digest, Vols. XI to XV, same topic and section number.

5. INSTRUCTIONS, § 88*—*preponderance of the evidence.* Instruction as to the manner of determining wherein the preponderance of the evidence lies, *held* misleading.

6. APPEAL AND ERROR, § 1561*—*when refusal of requested instruction harmless.* Refusal of requested instruction fully covered by other instructions given is not error.

7. APPEAL AND ERROR, § 1833*—*when special pleas filed after remandment of cause demurrable.* After reversal by the Appellate Court of a former judgment and the reinstating of the cause in the trial court, special pleas filed by defendant setting up the judgment of Appellate Court and presenting as an issue of fact what was determined by such court on its former hearing, *held* demurrable.

8. APPEAL AND ERROR, § 1514*—*when improper remarks of counsel prejudicial.* Inflammatory and improper statements made by counsel in his argument to the jury, among them being a statement that he did not care what the Appellate Court said in its opinion on a prior appeal in the cause, *held* prejudicial.

Appeal from the Circuit Court of De Witt county; the Hon. WILLIAM G. COCHRAN, Judge, presiding. Heard in this court at the October term, 1912. Reversed and remanded. Opinion filed October 16, 1913.

B. F. SHIPLEY and HERRICK & HERRICK, for appellant.

STONE & GRAY, for appellee.

MR. PRESIDING JUSTICE PHILBRICK delivered the opinion of the court.

This cause was previously in this court (163 Ill. App. 613), and the former judgment recovered was reversed and the cause remanded. We have no desire to change in any particular what was then said by this court concerning the measure of damages in a case of this kind. Upon the former hearing the only question this court determined was the proper measure of damages, and that appellee could not recover the purchase price of the horse that died.

After purchasing the team in question appellee had it in his possession for several weeks, during that time one of the horses died, he then returned the other horse to appellant and demanded the return of the purchase price. The death of the horse was not caused by reason of any ailment existing at the time of the purchase.

The evidence on the second trial is that appellant sold to appellee a team of horses; appellee insists that the team was warranted to be sound, but notwithstanding this warranty, appellee made some tests for the purpose of ascertaining for himself their condition before taking them, and the question as to whether the warranty was made and whether, if one was made, appellee relied upon the warranty in making the purchase or relied upon his own test of the horses were both questions of fact for the determination of the jury from all the evidence in the case under proper instructions by the court. Upon the former hearing this court did not hold, as contended for by appellant, that no recovery could be had for a breach of warranty of the horse that died. The holding of this court at that time was that no recovery could be had for the return of the purchase price of that horse. These horses were purchased as a team, and no specific price was paid for either horse, and appellant being unable to return the team by reason of the death of one of the horses, he could not recover the purchase price paid, but must recover, if at all, on a breach of warranty if one was made and proved.

Instruction number four given on behalf of appellee does not follow the rule held by this court upon the former hearing as to the true measure of damages in this case, but instructs the jury that if they find for the plaintiff, then they shall arrive at the amount of his damages in a manner contrary to the holding of this court upon the former hearing. This instruction as given is not a correct statement of the law as to the measure of damages, and it was error to give it. It is contended by appellant that if the horses were unsound, this fact was unknown to him, and that he should have been permitted to show this fact. If appellant warranted these horses as contended for by appellee, and guaranteed them to be sound, then it is immaterial whether appellant knew that the horses were unsound or not, and he cannot be permitted to defeat a recovery for a breach of warranty by showing that he did not know the condition of the horses at the time of the warranty.

The eighth instruction given on behalf of appellee should not have been given, as it could only tend to mislead the jury and is in direct conflict with instruction number nine given on behalf of appellant, which was properly given.

Instruction number twelve for appellee is also erroneous for the reason stated herein concerning instruction number four regarding the question of the measure of damages.

The court did not err in refusing instructions number twenty-one and twenty-two requested by appellant for the reason that the questions therein presented were fully covered by the other instructions given for appellant.

After the reversal of the former judgment and the reinstating of the cause in the trial court, appellant filed special pleas setting up the judgment of this court and thus presenting as an issue of fact what was determined by this court in its former hearing. The court properly sustained a demurrer to these pleas.

The first instruction given to the jury on behalf of appellee as to the manner of determining wherein the preponderance of the evidence lies is misleading. The correct rule laid down as to the preponderance of the evidence will be found in *Elgin, J. & E. Ry. Co. v. Lawlor*, 229 Ill. 621.

It is insisted by appellant that counsel for appellee in his argument to the jury not only went entirely outside of the record but used many inflammatory and improper statements to the jury, and among these statements counsel repeated the second time that he did not care what the Appellate Court said in its opinion. While the remarks of counsel throughout the argument were subject to severe criticism and should not have been permitted by the court, we would be inclined to reverse this case upon the remarks of counsel alone, if we were not compelled to reverse it by reason of errors in the record; we will not criticise his actions further than to say that he should be more careful in the future, as this court will not permit a verdict to stand where it can see that improper and undue remarks made by counsel have influenced the jury in arriving at their verdict.

By reason of the error of the trial court in giving instruction number four, eight and twelve, the judgment is reversed and the cause remanded.

Reversed and remanded.

Sarah E. Franklin, Appellee, v. The Continental Casualty Company (Incorporated), Appellant.

(Not to be reported in full.)

Appeal from the Circuit Court of Tazewell county; the Hon. THEODORE N. GREEN, Judge, presiding. Heard in this court at the October term, 1912. Affirmed. Opinion filed October 16, 1913. Rehearing denied November 5, 1913.

Statement of the Case.

Action by Sarah E. Franklin against The Continental Casualty Company, incorporated, to recover upon an accident policy issued by defendant to plaintiff's husband in his lifetime. From a judgment in favor of plaintiff for $531.37, defendant appeals.

Appellant insists it is not liable, claiming that representations in the application for insurance were made warranties, that insured misrepresented his age and that insured met death by natural causes, under a policy payable only on condition that death be caused by accident, violent and external means, without the intervention, directly or indirectly, of any other cause, and contends that the court erred in the admission and rejection of evidence and the giving and refusing of instructions.

RALPH DEMPSEY and W. R. CURRAN, for appellant; M. P. CORNELIUS, of counsel.

J. P. ST. CERNY and W. B. COONEY, for appellee.

MR. PRESIDING JUSTICE PHILBRICK delivered the opinion of the court.

Abstract of the Decision.

1. INSURANCE, § 697*—*when instruction limiting a coroner's verdict proper.* In an action for accident insurance on a policy payable only for accidental death caused by external and violent means without the intervention, directly or indirectly of any other cause, where a coroner's verdict is admitted in evidence stating that the insured "came to his death by pulmonary hemorrhage, said hemorrhage being caused by natural causes," an instruction eliminating from the consideration of the jury that part of the coroner's verdict finding that the pulmonary hemorrhage was produced by natural causes, *held* proper.

2. APPEAL AND ERROR, § 1455*—*when overruling demurrer to replication harmless.* Where a special plea filed by the insurer sets up that the insured misrepresented his age in the application for insurance and that such representation was made a warranty under the terms of the policy, and a replication thereto is filed denying that the age was material or in any way increased the risk, action of court in overruling defendant's demurrer to the replication *held* harmless, the cause being tried with the issue involved and there being no evidence in the record in support of the plea.

3. INSURANCE, § 686*—*when evidence sufficient to require question as to cause of death to be submitted to jury.* In an action to recover accident insurance, evidence offered by plaintiff showing that the insured fell, striking his chest upon a post and that within a short time thereafter blood began to flow from his mouth and nostrils as a result of hemorrhage of the lungs, *held* to show such a condition as to require the court to submit to the jury the ques-

tion as to how and in what manner the insured met his death, and refusal of court to direct a verdict for defendant *held* not error.

4. INSURANCE, § 613*—*burden of proving cause of death.* In an action for accident insurance, the burden of proof is on the plaintiff to show by a preponderance of all the evidence in the case that deceased came to his death as averred in the declaration, but where the plaintiff by its evidence makes a *prima facie* case the burden is on the defendant to rebut the same in accordance with his pleas.

5. INSURANCE, § 697*—*when instruction as to burden of proving cause of death not erroneous.* In an action for accident insurance, instructions as to the burden of proving cause of death *held* not to place the burden on defendant to prove by a preponderance of the evidence that deceased came to his death by reason of natural causes, in order to defeat recovery.

Thomas E. Wing, Appellee, v. G. J. Little, Appellant.

1. GAMING, § 39*—*when special plea and cross-bill in action to subject property used for gambling to payment of judgment recovered for money lost demurrable.* On bill filed against the owner of a gambling house to subject the premises to the payment of a judgment recovered by complainant against a third person for money lost at gambling on the premises, *held* that the defendant could make a complete and ample defense against the judgment upon his answer, and that the action of the court in sustaining a demurrer to a special plea and a cross-bill alleging that the judgment was obtained by fraud and collusion between the complainant and such third party, *held* proper.

2. GAMING, § 43*—*when evidence sufficient to sustain decree subjecting gambling premises to payment of a judgment recovered for money lost thereon.* On bill filed against the owner of a premises to subject the premises to the payment of a judgment recovered by complainant against a third party for money lost at gambling on the premises, the bill alleging that the loss at gaming occurred on the premises belonging to defendant, and that defendant knowingly permitted gambling to be conducted on the premises, *held* that to entitle the complainant to the relief prayed it was necessary for him to prove the allegations of the bill, and the findings of a decree awarding the relief prayed *held* sustained by the evidence.

3. JUDGMENT, § 394*—*when conclusive against collateral attack.* On bill filed against the owner of a gambling house to subject the premises to the payment of a judgment formerly recovered by

complainant against a third party for money lost at gambling on
the premises, the judgment having been rendered by a court of
competent jurisdiction and not having been appealed from, set aside
or vacated, is conclusive and cannot be collaterally attacked by the
defendant.

4. EQUITY, § 379*—*conclusiveness of verdict of jury when submission is discretionary.* It is a familiar rule in chancery that the
chancellor may present an issue of fact to a jury for its determination, but unless such is required by law to be submitted to a jury
the finding of the jury is merely directory and is not conclusive,
and the chancellor upon final hearing may follow that verdict or
entirely disregard it.

5. APPEAL AND ERROR, § 1528*—*when error in instructions in a
chancery case will not reverse.* Upon the submission to the jury
of an issue in a chancery case it cannot be assigned as error that
the chancellor erred in its instructions to the jury, when the submission is discretionary with the chancellor.

Appeal from the Circuit Court of Sangamon county; the Hon.
JAMES A. CREIGHTON, Judge, presiding. Heard in this court at the
October term, 1912. Affirmed. Opinion filed October 16, 1913. *Cer-
tiorari* granted by Supreme Court.

JOHN G. FRIEDMEYER and ALBERT SALZENSTEIN, for
appellant.

HARDIN W. MASTERS, GILLESPIE & FITZGERALD and
THOMAS D. MASTERS, for appellee.

MR. PRESIDING JUSTICE PHILBRICK delivered the opinion of the court.

Appellee, Wing, recovered a judgment in the Circuit
Court of Sangamon county against one Adams for
three thousand dollars for money alleged to have been
lost by Wing in a game of chance in a gambling house
kept by Adams in the city of Springfield. Execution
was issued on this judgment and returned *nulla bona.*
Appellee then filed his bill in chancery for the purpose of subjecting the premises owned by appellant,
G. J. Little, to the payment of the judgment, and
averring in this bill that the loss was had at gaming
in the premises located at 121 South Fourth street in
the city of Springfield and owned by appellant, and

that appellant Little knew that Adams was conducting a gaming house therein and knowingly permitted gambling to be conducted in his property.

To the amended bill appellant filed a special plea of *nul tiel record*, also a plea that the judgment recovered by appellee Wing against said Adams was obtained by fraud and collusion between Adams and complainant, and that said Wing did not lose three thousand dollars or any other sum in gambling rooms kept by Adams in the building of Little as set forth in the bill of complaint. Issue was joined upon the plea of *nul tiel record*, and a demurrer filed to the second amended special plea. The demurrer to this plea was sustained, appellant filed his answer and replication was filed thereto. Appellant filed a cross-bill alleging that said judgment was obtained by fraud and collusion between Wing and Adams and asked to have said judgment set aside and vacated; a demurrer was sustained to the cross-bill.

Upon the hearing appellant demanded that a jury be impaneled and that certain questions presented to the court be submitted to the jury for determination. The court refused to submit these propositions as requested by appellant Little but did submit to the jury the following question as an issue of fact to be tried by the jury:

"Did the defendant G. J. Little at any time during the month of November, 1908 or subsequent thereto and prior to the 26th of February, 1909, knowingly permit the premises described in the amended bill of complaint to be used or occupied as and for a place where games of chance for money and other valuable things were played?"

This question was answered in the affirmative by the jury. The court refused to set aside the verdict of the jury, and upon final hearing found the issues for the complainant and entered a decree in accordance with the prayer of the bill, directed that execution issue

against the property in question, and that the same
be sold to satisfy the judgment.

Appellant insists that this decree is erroneous and
should be reversed and urges that the court erred in
sustaining the demurrer to its special plea, in sustaining the demurrer to the cross-bill, in the admission
and rejection of evidence and the instructions given to
the jury upon the question of fact submitted to it, and
that the decree is not supported by the evidence.

Upon the contention that the court erred in sustaining the demurrer to the special plea alleging that the
judgment was obtained by fraud and collusion between
Wing and Adams, the issue presented by this plea was
a collateral attack upon the judgment rendered by the
Circuit Court of Sangamon county in favor of Wing
against Adams. This judgment as between Wing and
Adams in no manner affected the property of appellant, and it was of no concern to him whether the
judgment was obtained by fraud and collusion as he
was in no manner bound thereby; it was of no concern
to him that Wing had obtained the judgment against
Adams, as appellant Little could not in any way be
injured or affected by that judgment except in a proceeding to subject his property to a sale for its satisfaction; and the question as to whether or not the loss
for which this judgment was recovered occurred in the
premises owned by appellant, and that he knew gambling was carried on therein by Adams, is presented
for the first time in this suit. Before a recovery
could be had as against appellant it was necessary that
appellee prove that the money was lost by gaming in
a gaming house kept or conducted by Adams and that
appellant knew and permitted gambling to be conducted therein by Adams. It is a familiar rule in
chancery that the chancellor may present an issue of
fact to a jury for its determination, but unless such
is required to be submitted by law to a jury, the finding
of the jury is merely directory and is not conclusive,

and the chancellor upon final hearing may follow that verdict or entirely disregard it. Upon the submitting of that question to the jury it cannot be assigned as error that the chancellor erred in its instruction to the jury, as the submission of that question was discretionary with the chancellor.

Upon the contention that the court erred in sustaining the demurrer to the cross-bill, we find upon examination of this cross-bill that the object and prayer of the bill was to set aside the judgment as between Wing and Adams, appellant was not a party to that judgment and he was not entitled upon a cross-bill to have the judgment in favor of Wing and against Adams set aside, he could make a complete and ample defense as against that judgment upon the answer, and it could be of no concern to him that Wing had obtained the judgment against Adams. The judgment in favor of Wing against Adams having been rendered by a court of competent jurisdiction and not having been appealed from, set aside or vacated, is conclusive as between Wing and Adams, as to the right of Wing to recover against Adams.

The property of appellant Little cannot be subjected to the payment of this judgment except on proof of the allegations in complainant's bill that the money was lost at gaming in a gaming house kept or maintained by Adams in the building in question owned by Little, and upon the final hearing in the trial court the chancellor as well as the jury found that appellant Little knowingly permitted gambling to be carried on in the building in question owned by him, and the chancellor found by his decree that these gambling rooms were conducted by Adams and that appellee lost his money therein.

We have carefully examined this record, and we are satisfied that the proof fully sustains the allegations of the bill and the findings made by the chancellor in his decree, and that the decree rendered is correct and should not be disturbed. It is, therefore, affirmed.

Affirmed.

F. W. Cook Brewing Company, Appellant, v. Mary Goldblatt et al., Appellees.

1. APPEAL AND ERROR, § 1361*—*when not error to permit filing of additional pleas at time of trial.* In an action on a guaranty contract, *held* not error for court to permit the defendant to file a plea of *non est factum* after the trial had begun, where the request to file such plea was not made until after plaintiff, by leave of court, had filed an additional count to his declaration.

2. APPEAL AND ERROR, § 1361*—*when not error to permit defendant to file additional pleas.* The right to file additional pleas is a matter in the discretion of the trial court, and unless the court has abused this discretion it is not error to permit such pleas to be filed.

3. GUARANTY, § 22*—*what questions relating to alteration of contract are for court and jury.* In an action on a guaranty contract, where the defense is that there was a material alteration of the contract by the attachment of a rider thereto after the contract was signed by the defendants, *held* on conflicting evidence that the question whether a rider was attached before or after the contract was signed was for the jury, but the question whether the attachment of the rider after the contract was signed was such a material alteration as will avoid the contract is for the court.

4. GUARANTY, § 37*—*when instruction erroneous as submitting a question of law.* In an action on a guaranty contract, where the defense is that there was a material alteration of the contract by the attachment of a rider thereto and also the filling in of blanks in the contract after it was signed by the defendants, an instruction submitting to the jury the question whether there was an alteration of the contract, *held* erroneous as submitting to the jury a question of law, where under the instruction, the jury might have determined that the filling in of the blanks constituted a material alteration.

5. GUARANTY, § 22*—*when filling in blanks not an alteration of contract.* Where a party signs a contract of guaranty in blank and delivers it, the party to whom it is delivered has the right to fill in the blanks, and by so doing he does not alter the contract if he filled the blanks in accordance with the agreement of the parties.

Appeal from the Circuit Court of Sangamon county; the Hon. JAMES A. CREIGHTON, Judge, presiding. Heard in this court at the October term, 1912. Reversed and remanded. Opinion filed October 16, 1913.

GILLESPIE & FITZGERALD, for appellant.

JOHN G. FRIEDMEYER and STEVENS & HERNDON, for appellees.

MR. PRESIDING JUSTICE PHILBRICK delivered the opinion of the court.

Plaintiff brings this action against defendants upon an alleged contract of guaranty whereby it is claimed defendants guarantied the financial responsibility of Joseph Goldblatt according to an agreement entered into between Goldblatt and plaintiff whereby plaintiff contracted to sell the products of its brewery to Goldblatt exclusively in Springfield, Illinois, and by which agreement plaintiff sold its beer to Goldblatt at certain stipulated prices on the conditions named in said agreement.

The alleged contract of guaranty upon which this action is based guaranties the payment by Goldblatt for all the products of plaintiff's brewery bought by him.

To the declaration as originally filed by plaintiff, defendants pleaded only the general issue, afterwards by leave of the court, one additional count was filed, after the case had been called for trial and after plaintiff had filed the additional count, defendants obtained leave to file a plea of *non est factum*. The trial resulted in a verdict and judgment for defendants, from which judgment plaintiff prosecutes this appeal.

Appellant insists that the court erred in granting leave to defendants to file the plea of *non est factum* after the trial had begun. This request to file this plea was not made until after the additional count to the declaration had been filed by plaintiff; the filing of this additional count gave to the defendants the further right to plead as they had the right to set up any matter after the filing of this additional count that they might see fit that would be a proper defense to this action. But notwithstanding defendants might do this

as a matter of right, the right to file additional pleas
is a matter in the discretion of the trial court, and unless the court has abused this discretion it is not error
to do so. The court properly permitted this plea to
be filed.

The evidence is conflicting as to whether or not the
contract of guaranty, which is partially written and
partially printed, had the blanks which are now filled
with writing filled in at the time the contract was signed
by all the sureties. Dr. Compton, one of the defendants, testifies that none of those blanks were filled in
at the time he signed the contract.

The only defense offered to this action is that the
contract made with Goldblatt which these defendants
guarantied should be performed by Goldblatt was
changed and a material alteration made therein after
it was signed by the defendants. The evidence discloses that the contract between Goldblatt and the contract of guaranty are all upon a single sheet of paper,
and the defendants insist that when they signed this
contract of guaranty it consisted of but the one single
sheet of paper.

As the contract now appears in the record it has
pasted thereto a slip of paper which is designated as
a rider. This rider is in the following language:

"Springfield, Ill., August 26, 1910. The sureties on
this bond hereto attached agree that the above bond
shall cover the amount of beer, on hand at Springfield,
August 15, 1910, and a car of beer shipped from Evans-
ville, Indiana, August 13, 1910, the cash net value of
the same amounting to $1,289.57, the cases and bottles
belonging to the F. W. Cook Brewing Company, the
above being the correct amount. Signed:

F. W. COOK BREWING COMPANY,
By EDW. R. PREGLEB.
JOSEPH GOLDBLATT."

The contract without this rider only guarantied the
payment of the accounts of Goldblatt with the plaintiff
which might accrue after the date of that contract,

August 26, 1910, and the defendants insist that the attaching of this rider to the contract, whereby it rendered them liable not only for future shipments of beer to Goldblatt but also for that that had been shipped to him on August 13th and August 15th as stated in this rider, and that by attaching this rider to the original contract the plaintiff made such a material alteration in the contract of guaranty that it avoids the contract which they did sign. Plaintiff, on the other hand, insists that the rider was fastened to and made a part of this contract of guaranty before it was signed by the defendants. The evidence upon this question is very conflicting and it is impossible to reconcile it; it became and was a question for the jury to determine whether the rider was attached before or after the contract was signed by the defendants, and that question must be left to the jury under proper instructions by the court.

If this rider was attached before the contract was signed then the defendants are liable, if it was not so attached then the attaching of it to the contract was such a material alteration as will avoid their contract and they cannot be held liable thereunder. The question as to whether or not the rider was attached before or after the signing of the contract was, as above stated, a question for the jury, but the question as to whether or not the attaching of the rider, if it was attached after the contract was signed, was such a material alteration as will avoid the contract is one for the determination of the court and not for the jury. The court, however, gave to the jury on behalf of the defendants the following instruction:

"The court instructs the jury that if you find from a preponderance of the evidence that said contract between Goldblatt and said brewing company had been materially altered, changed or added to since the signing of the said contract of guarantee by the defendants herein without the knowledge or consent of said defendants and that said defendants have not acquiesced in any such alteration, change or addition, if any, then you should return a verdict for the defendants."

If the defendant Compton had not testified that no blanks in the contract were filled at the time he signed it, then the only question as to the material alteration in this contract would be whether the rider was attached before or after the contract was signed, and the only question that should properly have been submitted to the jury was whether or not this rider was so attached, and if it was so attached, the question of its materiality was for the court and not for the jury. If the jury did determine in their deliberations that the rider was attached after the contract was signed by the defendants then they must also have determined that there was a material alteration, and if there had been no evidence of any other additions to this contract we would be inclined to hold that the giving of this instruction was not error, but with the evidence of Compton that no blanks were filled at the time the contract was signed, the question as to a material alteration of the contract was not alone with the attaching of the rider so far as the submitting of the question to the jury was concerned, although they might have found in their deliberations that the rider was attached when the contract was signed they might under this instruction have determined that the filling in of the blanks, if they believed they were filled in after the contract was signed, was a material alteration of this contract, while the law is that if the party signs a contract of this character in blank and delivers it, the party to whom it is delivered has the right to fill in these blanks, and by doing so he does not alter the contract if he filled the blanks in accordance with the agreement of the parties. By giving this instruction to the jury the court submitted to it a question of law, and the judgment must therefore be reversed and the cause remanded. The judgment is reversed and the cause remanded.

Reversed and remanded.

Andrew J. Miller, Appellee, v. Assureds' National Mutual Fire Insurance Company of Decatur, Illinois, Appellant.

(Not to be reported in full.)

Appeal from the Circuit Court of Macon county; the Hon. WIL-LIAM G. COCHRAN, Judge, presiding. Heard in this court at the October term, 1912. Affirmed. Opinion filed October 16, 1913. Rehearing denied December 3, 1913. *Certiorari* granted by Supreme Court.

Statement of the Case.

Action by Andrew J. Miller against Assureds' National Mutual Fire Insurance Company of Decatur, Illinois, a corporation, to recover on a policy of fire insurance reinsuring the risk of another company. From a judgment in favor of plaintiff for two thousand one hundred and seventy-three dollars, defendant appeals.

This is the second appeal of this case to this court. Upon the former appeal the judgment of the trial court was reversed and the cause remanded. The former opinion was written by Mr. Justice Puterbaugh, and the facts are fully stated in the former opinion found in 164 Ill. App. 237.

McGINLEY & WILEY and GILLESPIE & FITZGERALD, for appellant.

SHERIDAN & GRUBER and LEFORGEE, VAIL & MILLER, for appellee.

MR. PRESIDING JUSTICE PHILBRICK delivered the opinion of the court.

Abstract of the Decision.

1. INSURANCE, § 705*—*when plea of failure of consideration for reinsurance contract demurrable.* In an action to recover on a fire

*See Illinois Notes Digest, Vols. XI to XV, same topic and section number.

insurance policy, the contract being an agreement to reinsure the risks of another company, with conditions requiring the policy holder to assign to the defendant whatever claim he might have against such other company for unearned premiums and pay the balance in cash, action of court in sustaining demurrers to defendant's pleas of failure of consideration setting up that the agreement on the part of plaintiff to assign his claim against the former company without in any way averring that no assignment of the claim was made, *held* not error.

2. WITNESSES, § 298*—*when character evidence as to reputation for truth and veracity not too remote to impeach witness.* To impeach the character of witnesses for their truth and veracity, evidence offered to show their reputation at a place where they resided two years prior to the time of the facts involved in controversy, *held* admissible, and action of court in sustaining an objection to such evidence because too remote, *held* error, though not prejudicial error.

3. APPEAL AND ERROR, § 1455*—*when error in sustaining demurrer to plea cannot be complained of.* Defendant cannot complain that trial court improperly sustained a demurrer to his plea where he was permitted upon the trial to introduce evidence which could only have been proper under his plea.

Charles E. Moran, Appellant, v. A. B. Dennis and Oliver Morgan, Appellees.

(Not to be reported in full.)

Appeal from the Circuit Court of Vermilion county; the Hon. WILLIAM B. SCHOLFIELD, Judge, presiding. Heard in this court at the October term, 1912. Reversed and remanded with directions. Opinion filed October 16, 1913.

Statement of the Case.

Action by Charles E. Moran against A. B. Dennis and Oliver Morgan, in *assumpsit*, to recover a certain sum alleged to be due to plaintiff from defendants by reason of the defendants procuring the release of a mortgage which plaintiff had assumed as a prior grantee. From an order sustaining a demurrer to plaintiff's declaration, plaintiff appeals.

G. W. SALMANS, for appellant.

A. B. DENNIS, for appellees.

MR. PRESIDING JUSTICE PHILBRICK delivered the opinion of the court.

Abstract of the Decision.

MORTGAGES, § 270*—*when declaration in assumpsit for wrongful release of mortgage states a cause of action.* Declaration in assumpsit against two defendants to recover a sum claimed to be due to plaintiff by reason of the wrongful release of a mortgage, alleging that plaintiff was a grantee of mortgagor and was compelled to pay the mortgage by reason of a clause in his deed assuming the mortgage, that one of the defendants, a subsequent grantee, who also assumed the mortgage wrongfully procured the other defendant, the mortgagee, to execute a release thereof, thereby depriving the plaintiff of the right to pursue the property and foreclose the mortgage, *held* to state a cause of action, and that the action of the court in sustaining a demurrer to the declaration was error.

Otto Hermanson, Plaintiff in Error, v. Louis Shaffer, Defendant in Error.

(Not to be reported in full.)

Error to the Circuit Court of Vermilion county; the Hon. MORTON W. THOMPSON, Judge, presiding. Heard in this court at the April term, 1913. Affirmed. Opinion filed October 16, 1913.

Statement of the Case.

Action by Otto Hermanson against Louis Shaffer, chief of police of the city of Danville, to recover damages for false imprisonment, it being alleged that defendant imprisoned and detained plaintiff in prison without reasonable or probable cause. From a judg-

*See Illinois Notes Digest, Vols. XI to XV, same topic and section number.

ment in favor of defendant on a directed verdict, plaintiff brings error.

F. L. DRAPER, for plaintiff in error.

J. B. MANN, for defendant in error.

MR. PRESIDING JUSTICE PHILBRICK delivered the opinion of the court.

Abstract of the Decision.

1. ARREST, § 25*—*necessity of warrant.* Ample authority is vested in the police of a city to arrest a person in the act of violating an ordinance without a warrant having been issued therefor.

2. ARREST, § 25*—*when police officer may arrest without a warrant being issued.* A patrolman finding a person in a city traveling from house to house with his satchel containing boxes and bottles therein, apparently in the act of peddling, in violation of an ordinance, may arrest him without a warrant being issued therefor.

3. FALSE IMPRISONMENT, § 26*—*burden of proof.* In an action for false imprisonment it is incumbent upon the plaintiff to show that there was no reasonable ground or cause to believe the plaintiff guilty of the charge for which he was arrested and imprisoned.

4. FALSE IMPRISONMENT, § 30*—*when direction of verdict for defendant proper.* In an action for false imprisonment, a directed verdict to find for defendant *held* not error, where from the evidence the only conclusion that can be arrived at is that there was reasonable cause to believe that plaintiff was guilty of the charge for which he was arrested.

5. FALSE IMPRISONMENT, § 28*—*proof sufficient to bar recovery.* In an action for false imprisonment, the record of the judgment of the police magistrate showing that plaintiff pleaded guilty to the charge for which he was arrested, and testimony of the police magistrate to the same effect, *held* to be sufficient proof alone to bar a recovery.

6. ARREST, § 22*—*power of city to detain person arrested in custody over night.* A person arrested and taken to a city prison at a late hour is not entitled to an immediate trial; the city has a right to hold him in custody until the city is able to secure witnesses and prepare for trial, and under R. S. c. 24, art. VI, § 12, J. & A. ¶ 1355, it is not unlawful to confine him in the city prison until the following morning to await his trial.

*See Illinois Notes Digest, Vols. XI to XV, same topic and section number.

THIRD DISTRICT—OCTOBER, 1913.   275

Hemmick v. B. and O. Southwestern R. Co., 184 Ill. App. 275.

Sarah E. Hemmick, Administratrix, Plaintiff in Error, v. Baltimore and Ohio Southwestern Railroad Company, Defendant in Error.

1. MASTER AND SERVANT, § 98*—*when declaration does not show action to be based on Federal Compensation Act.* In an action against a railroad company to recover for the death of an engineer, where the declaration is not based upon the Federal Compensation Act and does not aver that the company was doing an interstate commerce business and does not allege any acts showing that the company is controlled by or comes within the provisions of the Federal act, the Federal act has no application to the action, but the action is controlled wholly by the decisions of the State courts.

2. MASTER AND SERVANT, § 118*—*when release executed to railroad company constitutes a bar to action for death of engineer.* In an action against a railroad company to recover damages for the death of plaintiff's intestate while employed by the defendant company as an engineer, a release executed by plaintiff to the company's relief department, of which deceased was a member, releasing all rights and claims against the company arising from the death of deceased for a sum of money provided to be paid by reason of deceased being a member of such department, *held* properly admissible in evidence and to constitute a complete bar to the action.

Error to the Circuit Court of Sangamon county; the Hon. JAMES A. CREIGHTON, Judge, presiding. Heard in this court at the April term, 1913. Affirmed. Opinion filed October 16, 1913.

ALONZO HOFF and ALBERT SALZENSTEIN, for plaintiff in error.

GRAHAM & GRAHAM, for defendant in error; EDWARD BARTON, of counsel.

MR. PRESIDING JUSTICE PHILBRICK delivered the opinion of the court.

This is an action brought by plaintiff against defendant to recover for the death of her husband who was killed in a railroad accident on the defendant's railroad. The declaration consists of several counts

*See Illinois Notes Digest, Vols. XI to XV, same topic and section number.

276	APPELLATE COURTS OF ILLINOIS.

Hemmick v. B. and O. Southwestern R. Co., 184 Ill. App. 275.

charging negligence against the defendant in various forms which resulted in the death of plaintiff's husband. Plaintiff's husband was an engineer in the employ of the defendant and was killed while performing the duties of engineer, by reason of the train upon which he was engineer running into an open switch thereby causing a collision with cars upon the switch track. The deceased was killed either by reason of the impact of the collision or by the reason of jumping from his engine after his train had gone into the open switch and upon the siding.

The defendant Company provided a relief department known as the Baltimore and Ohio Railroad Relief Department; the deceased was a member of this department, and by reason of being a member of this department and maintaining his membership therein, the widow and child were paid twenty-five hundred dollars; upon the payment of this sum, the following release was executed and delivered to the defendant Company:

The Baltimore and Ohio Railroad Co.
Relief Department.
Release on Account of Death Benefit.

Whereas, David O. Hemmick, deceased, lately in the service of The Baltimore and Ohio Southwestern Railroad Company, was a member of the Relief fund of the Relief Department the then Baltimore and Ohio Railroad Company under Application No. 505672, and the Death Benefit payable from said Relief Department on account of such membership, amounting to TWENTY-FIVE HUNDRED Dollars ($2500.00) with unpaid Disablement Benefit amounting to....Dollars ($......).., is upon the condition of the execution of this Release, as provided in the said application, payable to his widow, Sarah R. Hemmick, and Lenora Mildred Hemmick.

Now, therefore, we, the undersigned, do hereby acknowledge that the payment of the said amount by the said Relief Department as aforesaid, which payment is hereby acknowledged, is in full satisfaction and discharge of all claims or demands on account of, or arising from, the death of said deceased, which we now have, or may, or can hereafter have against The Baltimore and Ohio Railroad Company, operating the said Relief Department, and The Baltimore and Ohio Southwestern Railroad Company, and the Baltimore and Ohio Railroad Company, * * * and do hereby release and forever discharge The Baltimore and Ohio Southwestern Railroad Company, The Baltimore and Ohio Railroad Company, and the said other companies from all said claims and demands.

The undersigned hereby admits that under the terms of the said application and the regulations of the Relief Department, the acceptance of the said benefits of itself operates as a full release of all the claims of the undersigned for damages by reason of said injuries against any of the said companies above referred to.

Witness our hands and seals this 25th day of March, A. D., 1911.

In the presence of:

    T. W. Ashley,
    Alonzo Huff,
    J. D. Marney.

Sarah E. Hemmick,	(L. S.)
Widow and beneficiary,	(L. S.)
Sarah E. Hemmick,	(L. S.)
Administrator of the Estate	(L. S.)
of David O. Hemmick, deceased,	(L. S.)
ceased,	(L. S.)
Sarah E. Hemmick,	(L. S.)
Guardian of Lenora Mildred	(L. S.)
Hemmick, minor daughter	(L. S.)
and joint beneficiary of David O. Hemmick, deceased.	(L. S.)
vid O. Hemmick, deceased.	(L. S.)"

Notwithstanding the receipt of the twenty-five hundred dollars provided for in this release, the payment of which is not denied, plaintiff contends she is

278   APPELLATE COURTS OF ILLINOIS.

Hemmick v. B. and O. Southwestern R. Co., 184 Ill. App. 275.

entitled to recover for the death of her husband if caused by the negligence of the defendant Company.

The cause was tried below, and after the evidence of the plaintiff was heard a motion was made by defendant to direct a verdict in its behalf; this motion was denied. Defendant then offered in evidence the release above set forth, which was admitted by the court, and, after all the evidence was heard, the motion to direct a verdict for the defendant was renewed, and the motion sustained, and the jury directed to return a verdict for the defendant, holding that the release, the execution of which was not denied, was a bar to this action. Plaintiff insists that the court erred in admitting this release in evidence, and in directing a verdict for the defendant, and prosecutes this appeal.

From the view taken by this court upon this record, it is unnecessary to discuss or determine any of the questions raised excepting those relating to this release and the rulings of the court thereon.

The declaration is not based upon the Federal Compensation Act, and does not aver that the defendant Company was doing an interstate commerce business, does not allege any acts showing that the defendant Company is controlled by or comes within the provision of the Federal Compensation Act; consequently, the Federal act has no application to the case at bar, and it must be controlled wholly by the decisions of the State courts. *Luken v. Lake Shore & M. S. Ry. Co.*, 248 Ill. 377.

The deceased having become a member of the relief department of the defendant Company, and plaintiff having received the amount of money provided to be paid by reason of her husband being a member of that department, and having received the same from the defendant Company, and executed a release for the same and releasing all rights and claims against the defendant Company, that release is a complete bar to the prosecution of this action under *Eckman v. Chicago, B. & Q. R. Co.*, 169 Ill. 312; *Pennsylvania Co. v. Chapman*, 220 Ill. 428.

The trial court did not err in admitting the release in evidence or in directing a verdict for the defendant, and its judgment is therefore affirmed.

Affirmed.

City of Jacksonville, Appellee, v. John Vieira et al., Appellants.

1. **INTOXICATING LIQUORS, § 167*—*when bill by city will not lie to restrain violation of an ordinance.* Bill cannot be maintained by a city for a temporary injunction to restrain persons from keeping and occupying premises for the purpose of storing and taking orders for the sale of intoxicating liquors in violation of a city ordinance, where the city has made no attempt to prosecute either of the defendants for a violation of the ordinance in the city courts, to indict by the grand jury or to prosecute by information before the County Court.

2. **INTOXICATING LIQUORS, § 167*—*when bill will not lie to close place kept for storing and taking orders for the sale of, in violation of ordinance.* Before a bill in chancery will lie to close as a nuisance, a place kept by defendants for storing and taking orders for the sale of intoxicating liquors in violation of a city ordinance, the defendants are entitled to a trial by a jury upon the questions whether or not liquors were sold in violation of the ordinance, whether they kept, maintained and stored such liquors in violation of the ordinance, and whether the premises were occupied for such purpose.

THOMPSON, J., dissenting.

Appeal from the Circuit Court of Morgan county; the Hon. OWEN P. THOMPSON, Judge, presiding. Heard in this court at the April term, 1913. Reversed and remanded with directions. Opinion filed October 16, 1913.

*See Illinois Notes Digest, Vols. XI to XV, same topic and section number.

THOMAS F. FERNS, for appellants; ADAMS, NELMS & REISCH, of counsel.

WILLIAM N. HAIRGROVE, for appellee.

MR. PRESIDING JUSTICE PHILBRICK delivered the opinion of the court.

The City of Jacksonville filed its bill in chancery alleging that the defendants were the owners of certain real estate described in said bill and located in the City of Jacksonville; that on said real estate was a two-story brick building occupied by one of the defendants and that the room so occupied by the defendant Vieira was used for the purpose of storing and taking orders for the sale of intoxicating liquors; that by reason thereof said building was at that time and prior thereto a common nuisance alleging that said Vieira would continue to occupy said room in said building for the purpose of so taking orders for the sale and storing of intoxicating liquors unless restrained by the People's writ of injunction as prayed for in said bill; that the acts of the said defendants were in violation of an ordinance of the City of Jacksonville regarding the sale and giving away of intoxicating liquors, duly passed by said City of Jacksonville and then in force.

Upon the filing of this bill a temporary injunction was issued restraining the defendants from keeping and occupying said premises for the illegal use as aforesaid and from therein taking orders or permitting people to there congregate for the purpose of drinking, bartering, exchanging or in any manner using intoxicating liquors. The defendants entered a motion to dissolve the temporary writ of injunction issued upon said bill and upon hearing upon said motion the same was denied, and from the order denying the motion to dissolve this injunction the defendants have prosecuted an appeal to this court.

The only questions raised by this appeal are, whether or not the City of Jacksonville has the power or authority under the law to file a bill for injunction regarding the sale or giving away of intoxicating liquors or keeping places where the same may be stored, sold or drunk upon the premises, and whether a bill in chancery is the proper remedy to restrain a violation of this ordinance without any other remedy having been resorted to. No attempt was made upon the part of the City of Jacksonville to prosecute either of the defendants in an action at law for the violation of the ordinances which it is insisted were being violated before the filing of this bill but this is an original prosecution commenced by way of injunction to restrain the doing of certain acts which it is insisted by appellee create a nuisance and that the city has the power to abate a nuisance by a bill in chancery. Appellee relies upon the case of *Stead v. Fortner*, 255 Ill. 477, as authority for this proceeding. The *Fortner* case is distinguishable from the one at bar from the fact that local authorities had tried in every way possible to prosecute at law the alleged violations of the law for selling intoxicating liquors in anti-saloon territory in the city of Shelbyville, Illinois, where the case arose. The proper authorities had presented the matter to the grand jury for indictment and the grand jury of the county had refused to indict; they also filed informations in the County Court of Shelby county and the County Court refused to issue warrants upon the information, and after having failed to secure a prosecution in every way possible in an action at law resort was then had to a bill in chancery, and it was sustained. In the case at bar there has been no attempt in any way to prosecute either for a violation of the ordinances in the city courts, to indict by the grand jury, or to prosecute by information before the County Court. The prosecution in the *Fortner* case, *supra*, was not for a violation of a city ordinance, but for a violation of the Dramshop Act, and the bill was filed by the State's Attorney of Shelby County and the Attorney General of the State of Illinois and prosecuted in the

name of the Attorney General, only after a complete
failure to secure prosecutions at law; consequently, the
Fortner case cannot be considered authority for this
prosecution, and we have been cited to no authority by
appellee in which a bill in chancery will lie at the first
instance to restrain a violation of an ordinance of a
city.

The question as to whether or not liquors were sold
in violation of the ordinance, whether they were kept,
maintained and stored in violation of the ordinance,
and whether the premises were occupied for such purposes is a question of fact and upon these questions
the defendant is entitled to a trial by jury, and cannot
be deprived of such trial by the filing of a bill in chancery by the city of Jacksonville. The ordinance which
it is insisted was being violated provides that upon the
conviction of any person keeping or maintaining premises where intoxicating liquors are sold in violation of
the ordinance, it shall be part of the judgment of the
conviction that the place shall be kept shut until a bond
with sufficient security in the sum of one thousand dollars shall be provided conditioned that no further violation of the law will be committed at such place, and
until either a conviction is had or a sufficient showing
made that the officers whose duty it is to enforce the
ordinances refuse to obey the law and that no conviction
or trial can be had by reason thereof, a bill in chancery
will not lie.

In *Finegan v. Allen*, 46 Ill. App. 553, the Appellate
Court of the First District held that an injunction will
not be issued to restrain the violation of a city ordinance, that the enforcement of a city ordinance is not
one of the functions of a court of chancery, and in
People v. Condon, 102 Ill. App. 449, that a bill will not
lie to restrain the commission of criminal acts, and
we fully agree with that court upon this question;
and the Supreme Court in *Poyer v. Village of Des
Plaines*, 123 Ill. 111 and *Yates v. Village of Batavia*,
79 Ill. 500, have further held that a court of equity

will not restrain by injunction offenders of a violation of an ordinance of the city; and before a bill in chancery will lie to close the place of the defendants as a nuisance, defendants are entitled to a trial by jury upon the question of fact as to whether or not the place is kept in violation of the ordinance and contrary to its provisions.

The motion to dissolve this injunction should have been allowed; to deny it was error. The order of the court denying the motion is therefore reversed, set aside and held for naught, and the cause is remanded to the trial court with directions to enter an order dissolving the temporary injunction.

Reversed and remanded with directions.

MR. JUSTICE THOMPSON dissents.

C. E. Hoxworth, Appellant, v. Walter Kepple, Appellee.

(Not to be reported in full.)

Appeal from the County Court of McDonough county; the Hon. CONRAD G. GUMBART, Judge, presiding. Heard in this court at the April term, 1913. Affirmed. Opinion filed October 16, 1913.

Statement of the Case.

Action by C. E. Hoxworth against Walter Kepple to recover back money paid for hay on account of the hay being damaged and a mistake in measuring same and for breach of warranty for the quality thereof. Suit was commenced before a justice of the peace, where plaintiff recovered judgment. Defendant then appealed to the County Court; where judgment was rendered in favor of defendant on a directed verdict, from which judgment plaintiff appeals.

VOSE & CREEL, for appellant.

FLACK & LAWYER, for appellee.

MR. PRESIDING JUSTICE PHILBRICK delivered the opinion of the court.

Abstract of the Decision.

AUCTIONS AND AUCTIONEERS, § 6*—*when purchaser of hay at auction sale cannot complain of amount paid for.* Where a person purchases hay at an auction sale at so much a ton, it being announced at the time of the sale that the hay had been measured by disinterested persons and that bidders not satisfied with such measurements would be given opportunity to remeasure the same, *held* that the purchaser cannot complain that he did not get the full amount paid for where he voluntarily settles for the hay after he had ample opportunity to ascertain the amount thereof before making payment.

G. W. Bryant, Appellee, v. Vandalia Railroad Company, Appellant.

(Not to be reported in full.)

Appeal from the Circuit Court of Moultrie county; the Hon. WILLIAM G. COCHRAN, Judge, presiding. Heard in this court at the April term, 1913. Reversed and remanded. Opinion filed October 16, 1913.

Statement of the Case.

Action by G. W. Bryant against Vandalia Railroad Company to recover for services rendered to defendant by plaintiff as station agent. Suit was commenced before a justice of the peace and plaintiff recovered a judgment. Defendant then appealed to the Circuit Court where judgment was rendered in favor of plaintiff for one hundred and thirty-five dollars, and from that judgment defendant appeals.

*See Illinois Notes Digest, Vols. XI to XV, same topic and section number.

OUTTEN, EWING, McCULLOUGH & WIERMAN and E. J. MILLER, for appellant.

JOHN E. JENNINGS, for appellee.

MR. PRESIDING JUSTICE PHILBRICK delivered the opinion of the court.

Abstract of the Decision.

1. MASTER AND SERVANT, § 71*—*when station agent for railroad company not chargeable with loss resulting from mistake in sale of tickets.* Where a station agent in the employ of a railroad company makes a mistake in selling excursion tickets at a price below the tariff rates, in an action by such agent against the railroad company for wages *held* that the company cannot charge him with the loss occasioned by the sale of the tickets, where the proof shows that the agent used his best judgment and every available effort for the purpose of ascertaining the rate, and after consulting the traveling passenger agent of the company availed himself of every means at his command to ascertain the correct fare.

2. MASTER AND SERVANT, § 88*—*allowance of attorney's fees in an action for wages.* Under the statute entitling plaintiff to attorney's fees in an action for wages, where trial is by jury, the question as to the amount of attorney's fees is for the court; but before such fees may be allowed it is necessary that the jury should find that the amount due was the amount demanded of defendant in the written demand made by plaintiff, and find that the amount was due for labor, wages, etc.

3. MASTER AND SERVANT, § 88*—*when submission to jury of question as to amount of attorney's fees is error.* In an action by a station agent against a railroad company to recover wages, where demand is made under R. S. 1909, c. 13, ¶ 13, J. & A. ¶ 5285, to recover attorney's fees *held* error for the court to submit to the jury the question of the amount of attorney's fees and judgment rendered on a general verdict for wages including attorney's fees reversed.

4. MASTER AND SERVANT, § 88*—*persons entitled to attorney's fees in action for wages.* R. S. 1909, c. 13, ¶ 13, J. & A. ¶ 5285, permitting a recovery of attorney's fees in an action for wages, *held* broad enough in its terms to permit the recovery of attorney's fees by a person employed by a railroad company as station agent.

*See Illinois Notes Digest, Vols. XI to XV, same topic and section number.

Mary Kaminiski, Administratrix, Appellee, v. Corn Products Refining Company, Appellant.

(Not to be reported in full.)

Appeal from the Circuit Court of Tazewell county; the Hon. THEODORE N. GREEN, Judge, presiding. Heard in this court at the April term, 1913. Reversed. Opinion filed October 16, 1913. Rehearing denied December 3, 1913. *Certiorari* denied by Supreme Court (making opinion final).

Statement of the Case.

Action by Mary Kaminiski, administratrix of the estate of Frank Kaminiski, deceased, against Corn Products Refining Company, a corporation, to recover for the death of the deceased alleged to have been caused by the defendant unlawfully and negligently maintaining a certain box in a highway in such a condition that deceased in driving along the highway ran over and upon the same and was thrown from his wagon and killed. From a judgment in favor of plaintiff for seven thousand dollars, defendant appeals.

PAGE, WEAD, HUNTER & SCULLY, for appellant.

PRETTYMAN, VELDE & PRETTYMAN, for appellee.

MR. PRESIDING JUSTICE PHILBRICK delivered the opinion of the court.

Abstract of the Decision.

1. ROADS AND BRIDGES, § 184*—*when owner of abutting property liable for maintaining a public nuisance in highway.* Where an owner of property abutting on a public highway maintains in the highway a box used to connect pipes from city water works with pipes leading from the highway to the property, such box having been constructed by a former owner of the property, *held*, in an action against the owner for the death of a person alleged to have been caused by the defective condition of such box while driving on the highway, that the only theory upon which plaintiff could

*See Illinois Notes Digest, Vols. XI to XV, same topic and section number.

recover would be that the maintaining of such box in the highway for the use of defendant was a public nuisance and that defendant was negligent in failing to abate same.

2. ROADS AND BRIDGES, § 196*—*when teamster guilty of contributory negligence in avoiding obstruction in highway*. In an action against an abutting owner on a public highway to recover for the death of plaintiff's intestate alleged to have been caused by defendant maintaining an obstruction in the highway by reason whereof deceased fell from his wagon and was killed, a verdict in favor of plaintiff *held*, not sustained by the evidence, the evidence showing that deceased was guilty of contributory negligence in driving his team.

William J. Jones, Appellee, v. Cincinnati, Hamilton and Dayton Railway Company, Appellant.

(Not to be reported in full.)

Appeal from the Circuit Court of Macon county; the Hon. WILLIAM C. JOHNS, Judge, presiding. Heard in this court at the April term, 1913. Affirmed. Opinion filed October 16, 1913.

Statement of the Case.

Action by William J. Jones against Cincinnati, Hamilton and Dayton Railway Company, a corporation, to recover for the loss of a trunk and its contents as baggage. The trunk was placed in defendant's depot and during the night the depot was broken into, the trunk rifled and its contents taken. From a judgment in favor of plaintiff for $58.55, defendant appeals.

OUTTEN, EWING, MCCULLOUGH & WIERMAN, for appellant.

CHESTER ALLAN SMITH, for appellee.

MR. PRESIDING JUSTICE PHILBRICK delivered the opinion of the court.

*See Illinois Notes Digest, Vols. XI to XV, same topic and section number.

Abstract of the Decision.

1. CARRIERS, § 544*—*when liable for baggage stolen from baggage room.* In an action to recover for the loss of baggage which was stolen from plaintiff's trunk while stored in defendant's depot at night, a verdict in favor of plaintiff was sustained, the evidence showing that entrance was made through the ticket office and waiting room to the baggage room and the door leading from the waiting room to the baggage room was unlocked.

2. CARRIERS, § 541*—*what constitutes proper baggage.* Contents of a trunk consisting of passenger's wearing apparel, together with other personal property as he had or was used by him, articles and trinkets, of no considerable value, for his grandchildren and a small amount of jewelry which had belonged to his deceased wife, *held,* to constitute baggage.

John W. Neal, Appellant, v. Fletcher G. Burch, Appellee.

LIBEL AND SLANDER, § 100*—*when declaration avers defamation actionable per se.* In an action for slander, a declaration charging that defendant spoke and published concerning plaintiff that he with others had sworn to a lie, had sworn falsely and that affidavit is false, *held,* to aver language actionable *per se* under R. S. c. 126, J. & A. ¶ 10576, without averring that the statements were made of and concerning any judicial proceeding or of and concerning any action, time or place or regarding any matter which required that an affidavit should be made by the plaintiff.

Appeal from the Circuit Court of Morgan county; the Hon. OWEN P. THOMPSON, Judge, presiding. Heard in this court at the April term, 1913. Reversed and remanded with directions. Opinion filed October 16, 1913.

WILLIAM N. HAIRGROVE, for appellant.

M. T. LAYMAN, for appellee.

MR. PRESIDING JUSTICE PHILBRICK delivered the opinion of the court.

This is an action for slander brought by the plaintiff

against the defendant. The declaration charges that the defendant made, spoke and published of and concerning the plaintiff certain false, slanderous, malicious and defamatory words, as follows:

"They (meaning the plaintiff) have sworn to a lie. They (meaning plaintiff as well as others) have sworn falsely. This affidavit (meaning the affidavit signed and sworn to by plaintiff) is false. He (meaning plaintiff as well as others) has sworn to a lie."

meaning and intending thereby that in making a certain affidavit the plaintiff had sworn falsely, also that plaintiff had perjured himself, he had sworn to a lie. The affidavit in which this matter is alleged to have been made was presented to the city counsel of the city of Waverly, Illinois, regarding a pavement in that city. Defendant demurred to the declaration, and the demurrer was sustained by the court. Plaintiff elected to stand by his declaration, and judgment was entered thereon, in bar of action and for costs. Plaintiff prosecutes this appeal.

The only question raised by this appeal is the sufficiency of the declaration.

While at common law the language averred in this declaration was not actionable *per se,* the statute of this State upon slander and libel (Chapter 126, Hurd's Revised Statutes, J. & A. ¶ 10576) is as follows:

"It shall be deemed slander and shall be actionable to charge any person with swearing falsely or with having sworn falsely or having used, uttered or published words of, to or concerning any person which in their common acceptation amount to such charge, whether the words be spoken in conversation of and concerning a judicial proceeding or not."

Under this statute it was not necessary to charge that the statements were made of and concerning any judicial proceeding or of and concerning any action, time or place or regarding any matter which required that an affidavit should be made by the plaintiff; the statute makes the uttering and publishing of the language averred in this declaration actionable *per se.* *Sanford v. Gaddis,* 13 Ill. 329. The demurrer admits the uttering and publishing of the words as alleged in the declaration. The declaration is sufficient to require defendants to plead thereto, and it was error for the court to sustain the demurrer, and by reason of the error of the court the judgment is reversed and the cause remanded with directions to the trial court to overrule the demurrer.

Reversed and remanded with directions.

Edward Moss, Appellee, v. Estate of Joseph Redmon, Appellant.

1. BILLS AND NOTES, § 451*—*when finding of jury on question of payment of promissory note sustained by the evidence.* In an action on a promissory note and to have the same allowed against the estate of the deceased maker, the evidence being conflicting on the question whether the note had been paid by the deceased, *held,* that a verdict in favor of plaintiff was not manifestly against the weight of the evidence, and that the evidence was sufficient to sustain the verdict.

2. BILLS AND NOTES, § 426*—*what evidence inadmissible to show payment.* In an action on a promissory note and to have the same allowed as a claim against the estate of the maker, evidence offered by defendant that plaintiff was present in a proceeding to have a conservator appointed for the maker, prior to his death, and did not dispute testimony that the maker was not at that time indebted to any one, *held,* inadmissible as a circumstance tending to show that plaintiff's note had been paid, the plaintiff not being a party to that proceeding and not required to dispute the testimony offered to protect his claim.

Appeal from the Circuit Court of Edgar county; the Hon. E. R. E. KIMBROUGH, Judge, presiding. Heard in this court at the April term, 1913. Affirmed. Opinion filed October 16, 1913.

W. H. CLINTON and F. C. VAN SELLER, for appellant.

F. T. O'HAIR and H. S. TANNER, for appellee.

MR. PRESIDING JUSTICE PHILBRICK delivered the opinion of the court.

This cause of action is upon a note of the principal sum of two thousand dollars, of date, December 10, 1902, given by one Joseph Redmon in his lifetime to Edward Moss, appellee. Joseph Redmon died some time during December, 1911, and this note was probated against his estate in the County Court of Edgar county. The payment of the note was resisted by the administrator, and trial was had which resulted in a finding and judgment for the defendant. Appellee appealed to the Circuit Court and upon trial in that court recovered a judgment against the estate of Joseph Redmon, deceased, for the principal and interest of this note.

The estate prosecutes this appeal and assigns as reasons for reversing this judgment that the court erred in the rejection of certain evidence offered by the estate, and for the further reason that the judgment is contrary to the law and evidence.

The facts as disclosed by this record show that Joseph Redmon in his lifetime borrowed four thousand dollars from one John Moss, the father of appellee, Edward Moss; that he also borrowed from Ed Moss the sum of two thousand dollars which is represented by the note in question; that during the lifetime of Joseph Redmon, John Redmon, his son, held a power of attorney for the transaction of the business of Joseph Redmon; that Ed Moss, appellee herein, was the son-in-law of Joseph Redmon, deceased; that John Redmon owed Joseph Redmon two thousand dollars, and that at that time the note in question was still unpaid, that Joseph Redmon, during his lifetime, together with John Redmon and either John or Ed Moss or both of them, met at the Citizens' National Bank some time during November, 1906, at which time John Redmon paid his father the two thousand dollars owed by him. That this two thousand dollars was paid by Joseph Redmon at that time either to Ed Moss in payment of the note in question or to John Moss in payment of the balance of the four thousand dollars which Joseph Redmon owed him, appellant insisting that the money was paid to Ed Moss in consideration and satisfaction of the note upon which this judgment was rendered, appellee contending that he was not present at the time of this transaction in the Citizens' Bank and that the money was paid to John Moss in satisfaction of the balance due him on the four thousand dollar note which he held against Joseph Redmon.

Upon the contention of appellant that the judgment is contrary to the evidence, we find upon this record that the evidence upon this question is very conflicting, and cannot be reconciled, the evidence of the appellant supporting his contention and the evidence offered on behalf of appellee supporting his contention. When such a condition exists, it is clearly and solely the province of the jury to determine the questions of fact upon which there is such a conflict of evidence, and the jury by their verdict have found the facts in this case and upon the question as to which note was paid at this meeting in the Citizens' National Bank against the contention of appellant, and under the familiar rule which has been followed by this court, the verdict should not be disturbed, unless the court can say that the verdict is clearly and manifestly against the weight of the evidence, and we are satisfied that there is sufficient evidence in this record to sustain the verdict of the jury.

Upon the contention that the court erred in sustaining the objection to evidence offered on behalf of appellant, the record discloses that prior to the death of Joseph Redmon a conservator was appointed for him by the County Court of Edgar county, that upon hearing upon the application for the appointment of this conservator, Ed Moss was present and testimony was given at that time that Joseph Redmon was not at the time of the appointment of the conservator indebted to anyone, that his debts had all been paid, that Ed Moss sat by in the trial and did not in any manner attempt to dispute or contradict the testimony showing that Joseph Redmon was not at that time indebted to any person, and upon the trial in the Circuit Court in this case appellant offered to show that this testimony was given in the trial for the appointment of a conservator and that the same was not contradicted or denied in any way by Ed Moss, contending that thereby he should be estopped from now setting up this claim, and that that evidence was competent as a circumstance tending to show that the note in question had been paid. The court sustained objection to this testimony and we think properly so, as at that time Ed Moss was not required for the purpose of protecting any claim that he might have against the estate to deny or contradict the evidence offered, he was not a party to that proceeding and had no right simply because he held a claim against the estate to offer any evidence therein.

No complaint is made of the giving or refusing of instructions, and finding no reversible error in this record the judgment is affirmed.

Affirmed.

The Adder Machine Company, Appellant, v. E. A. Ross, Appellee.

1. APPEAL AND ERROR, § 1689*—*when want of joinder of issue on plea cannot be urged.* Appellant cannot raise the question that no replication had been filed to a plea where the parties proceeded with the trial as though issue had been joined thereon.

2. REPLEVIN, § 103*—*when plea of property in another not supported by the evidence.* In replevin to recover property pledged by plaintiff's agent to defendant as collateral security for a personal loan to the agent, the agent having executed a bill of sale of the property to a third party, a company in which defendant was interested as a partner, *held,* that a plea of title in such company was not supported by the evidence, the evidence showing

*See Illinois Notes Digest, Vols. XI to XV, same topic and section number.

that defendant knew that the agent did not own the property, and the company of which defendant was a partner being chargeable with the knowledge of the defendant, and knowing that the property was transferred solely for the purpose of securing the indebtedness due from the agent.

3. REPLEVIN, § 114*—*admissibility of evidence.* In replevin to recover property pledged by plaintiff's agent to defendant to secure a personal loan to the agent, the agent having executed a bill of sale to a company in which defendant was interested as a partner, *held*, that the bill of sale was admissible under a plea that the title was in the company as tending to contradict the testimony of the agent that he was not the owner of the property, but that it was competent for plaintiff to explain the bill of sale by showing that it was executed as a mortgage solely for the purpose of securing the indebtedness of the agent.

4. EVIDENCE, § 333*—*when parol evidence admissible to show consideration for written instrument.* The rule that evidence cannot be offered to vary or contradict the terms of a written instrument is not violated by the admission of evidence tending to show what the consideration for the instrument was.

5. REPLEVIN, § 147*—*when refusal of plaintiff's requested instruction is error.* In replevin to recover property pledged by plaintiff's agent to a third party as collateral security for a personal loan to the agent, refusal to give an instruction for plaintiff instructing the jury "that to entitle plaintiff to recover property replevined, under the issues joined, it is only necessary that it should prove by a preponderance of the evidence that it was the owner of the property in question or entitled to the possession of the same when this suit was commenced and that it had been wrongfully taken from its possession by defendant or that it was wrongfully detained by him," *held* error.

Appeal from the Circuit Court of Vermilion county; the Hon. WILLIAM B. SCHOLFIELD, Judge, presiding. Heard in this court at the April term, 1913. Reversed and remanded. Opinion filed October 16, 1913.

S. F. SCHECTER and LINDLEY, PENWELL & LINDLEY, for appellant.

DWYER & DWYER, for appellee.

MR. PRESIDING JUSTICE PHILBRICK delivered the opinion of the court.

This is an action of replevin brought by appellant

to recover from appellee two adding machines. The trial below resulted in a judgment for defendant.

To the declaration filed appellee filed three pleas, one of *non detinet,* another *non cepit* and the other property in the Danville Credit Company. The plea of property in the Danville Credit Company was not filed until after the trial had begun and the record does not show that issue was joined on this plea, but the parties having proceeded with the trial the same as though issue had been joined, appellant cannot now raise the question that no replication had been filed to this plea.

Appellant was the manufacturer of the two adding machines in question; it had as its agent at Danville, Illinois, one C. A. Simon. Simon finding it necessary to raise money for his own individual purpose, applied to appellee, who was a member of a partnership doing business in Danville under the name of the Danville Credit Company, for a loan of money. Simon had his office in rooms occupied by the Danville Credit Company. At one time he secured fifty dollars, and this sum was afterwards increased by various amounts to two hundred and seventy-five dollars. At the time of the securing of the first fifty dollars, Simon delivered to Ross one of the adding machines in question, and before securing the final amount which he received Ross insisted on securing possession of the other machine as collateral security, and a bill of sale was made by Simon to the Danville Credit Company for the two machines in question.

Appellee, Ross, was familiar with the fact and knew that Simon was not the owner of these machines, that he was the agent of appellant, and had been its agent in the city of Danville and sold these machines for some time prior to the transactions in question, and the bill of sale made by Simon whereby he attempted to transfer the title of this property to the Danville Credit Company in which Ross was a partner does not purport to be a bill of sale by appellant Company, but was made solely by Simon. The Danville Credit Company, of which appellee was a partner, was bound by the information had by Ross, and with this knowledge and knowing that the transfer was made of these machines solely for the purpose of securing the indebtedness due from Simon, the Danville Credit Company obtained no title by reason of this bill of sale, and therefore the plea of title in the Danville Credit Company is not supported by the evidence in this record.

Upon the contention that the court erred in admitting the bill of sale in evidence, under the plea that the title was in the Danville Credit Company, it was admissible as tending to contradict the testimony of Simon that he was not the owner of the machines, that he had possession of and held the machines only as the agent of appellant, and there was no error in the admission of the bill of sale; and having been properly admitted the court did not err in permitting evidence to be offered to explain the bill of sale. While the bill of sale purported to be a complete transfer of the title upon its face it was competent to show that it was made and executed as a mortgage solely for the purpose of securing the indebtedness of Simon. The rule that evidence cannot be offered to vary or contradict the terms of a written instrument is not violated by the admission of evidence tending to show what the consideration for the instrument was; appellant not being a party to this instrument was not bound by its contents. The greater weight of the evidence in this record shows that Ross was the party with whom Simon was dealing, and that the possession of the machines was delivered to him. The record shows conclusively that the title to this property was in appellant and fails to show any power or authority in Simon as agent of appellant to pledge this property for the purpose of securing his personal indebtedness.

The evidence failing to support any of the pleas filed by appellee, the judgment is so clearly and manifestly against the weight of the evidence that it must be set aside.

Plaintiff requested the following instruction:

"The Court instructs the jury that to entitle plaintiff to recover property replevined, under the issues joined, it is only necessary that it should prove by a preponderance of the evidence that it was the owner of the property in question or entitled to the possession of the same when this suit was commenced and that it had been wrongfully taken from its possession by defendant or that it was then wrongfully detained by him."

This instruction was refused by the court. The instruction correctly states the principle of law applicable to the facts in this case and should have been given to the jury. The court erred in refusing it.

For the errors indicated, the judgment is reversed and the cause remanded.

Reversed and remanded.

George H. Lovekamp, Appellant, v. John F. Cummings, Appellee.

(Not to be reported in full.)

Appeal from the Circuit Court of Macoupin county; the Hon. JAMES A. CREIGHTON, Judge, presiding. Heard in this court at the April term, 1913. Affirmed. Opinion filed October 16, 1913.

Statement of the Case.

Action by George H. Lovekamp against John F. Cummings for damages alleged to have been sustained by plaintiff by reason of the alleged failure and refusal of defendant to complete and fulfil an alleged contract for the sale of a farm owned by defendant and claimed to have been sold to plaintiff upon a contract of purchase. From a judgment in favor of defendant, plaintiff appeals.

EDWARD C. KNOTTS and PEEBLES & PEEBLES, for appellant.

D. R. KINDER and A. J. DUGGAN, for appellee.

MR. PRESIDING JUSTICE PHILBRICK delivered the opinion of the court.

Abstract of the Decision.

APPEAL AND ERROR, § 528*—*necessity of submitting questions of law or fact to trial court to preserve questions for review.* .Where a cause is submitted to the trial court without a jury, and no questions of law or fact are submitted to the court to be passed upon by it, the record preserves no questions to be passed upon by the court of review.

Angie Andrews, Appellee, v. City of White Hall, Appellant.

1. MUNICIPAL CORPORATIONS, § 993*—*duty to keep sidewalk free from obstruction.* It is the duty of a city to keep and maintain its sidewalks free from obstruction and dangerous places for their entire width for the use of pedestrians while in the exercise of due care and caution.

2. MUNICIPAL CORPORATIONS, § 1098*—*when evidence sufficient to sustain verdict for injuries to pedestrian resulting from falling over obstruction on sidewalk.* In an action against a city to recover for personal injuries sustained by plaintiff by falling over an obstruction on a sidewalk in front of a grocery store, evidence *held* sufficient to sustain a verdict for the plaintiff, where the evidence shows that the obstruction was placed upon the sidewalk by the

keeper of the store and the city had permitted the obstruction for a sufficient length of time to be charged with notice thereof.

3. MUNICIPAL CORPORATIONS, § 1053*—*care required of persons using street with knowledge of obstructions.* In an action against a city to recover for personal injuries sustained by a woman falling over an obstruction on a sidewalk, *held* that although plaintiff may have known of the existence of the obstruction in the street it was not negligence *per se* for her to use the street or to attempt to pass the obstruction, that the law only required of her that she use such due care and caution as would be commensurate with her knowledge of the conditions and surroundings existing at the time, and that whether she did use such care and caution is wholly a question for the jury.

4. APPEAL AND ERROR, § 1561*—*when refusal of requested instructions not error.* Not error for court to refuse a requested instruction fully covered by others given, though such instruction contains a correct proposition of law.

5. APPEAL AND ERROR, § 1623*—*when error in the exclusion of evidence harmless.* Appellant cannot complain of error of trial court in sustaining objections to evidence offered by it where such evidence was permitted to go to the jury at other times.

Appeal from the Circuit Court of Greene county; the Hon. OWEN P. THOMPSON, Judge, presiding. Heard in this court at the April term, 1913. Affirmed. Opinion filed October 16, 1913.

W. L. WINN and THOMAS HENSHAW, for appellant.

NORMAN L. JONES and D. J. SULLIVAN, for appellee.

MR. PRESIDING JUSTICE PHILBRICK delivered the opinion of the court.

This is an action by appellee against appellant to recover for injuries received by appellee by reason of falling over an obstruction on the sidewalk under the control of appellant, alleged to have been negligently permitted to be and remain on said side walk by appellant. The trial below resulted in a judgment for twelve hundred and fifty dollars.

Appellee on the evening of the injury went from her home to the grocery store of one Piper to do some shopping; this store is located on the west side of Main street in the City of White Hall. Appellee on the

evening of the accident approached the store from the
north entering the store at a door located in the middle
of the building, did her shopping, and on leaving the
store attempted to go south on Main street. The store
was lighted with electric lights. The sidewalk which
was of cement was about seven feet wide and was six
or eight inches lower than the floor of the storeroom.
In front of the store and south of the door at the
middle entrance, Piper had placed three steps or
shelves for the purpose of displaying his goods. The
frame work of these steps extended out on to the sidewalk 35½ inches, covering nearly the half of the sidewalk. This obstruction had been there for a considerable length of time, was piled with goods from the
store in the daytime but was left to remain in its position over night. No question is made but what the
shelving or steps had been there a sufficient length of
time for appellant to have known of its existence or
that the same had been there for such a reasonable
length of time as to be constructive notice to appellant.
On leaving the store and attempting to turn south
upon this sidewalk appellee struck her foot or limb
against the bottom step of this shelving. She was
thrown down and severely injured.

Appellant insists on a reversal of the judgment and
as grounds therefor insists that the proof does not
show any negligence on the part of appellant but that
it establishes conclusively that appellee was not in the
exercise of due care and caution for her own safety.
Appellant insists also that the court erred in the giving
and refusing of instructions.

There is no attempt on the part of the appellant
to contradict the proof that these steps or shelving was
upon the sidewalk or that it covered nearly three feet
of the space of the sidewalk, and upon this proof there
can be no contention that it was not an obstruction to
the free use of the sidewalk; and upon what theory
appellant contends that the permitting of this obstruction to be and remain upon the sidewalk as the proof

shows was not negligence, we are unable to comprehend.

It is the duty of the city to keep and maintain its sidewalks free from obstruction and dangerous places for their entire width for the use of pedestrians while in the exercise of due care and caution, and the only question of fact left for determination in this case is whether or not appellee was in the exercise of due care and caution for her own safety.

Appellant insists that appellee had been in the habit of visiting this store of evenings two or three times a week for a long space of time, that she knew this obstruction was kept and maintained upon this sidewalk by Piper, and that the lights in the store and upon the street were amply sufficient to permit it to be easily discovered and seen by anyone passing along the street while in the exercise of due care and caution for their safety, and that the proof is conclusive that appellee was not in the exercise of due care and caution.

The accident happened after night. While it is not disputed that the lights in the store were burning brightly and afforded sufficient light for anyone passing upon or along the sidewalk to see this obstruction, the question as to whether or not the lights were burning in the street is disputed. Appellee, on the other hand, insists that although the lights in the store were burning, the obstruction over which appellee fell was at the side of the store and that appellee in leaving the brightly lighted store going upon the street was not able until her eye became accustomed to the darkness to readily discern and see the obstruction, and that by passing from the brilliantly lighted store into the darkness the obstruction could not be readily discerned. What the evidence upon these questions established and the determination of the fact as to whether appellee was in the exercise of due care was for the jury.

Although appellee may have known of the existence of this obstruction, it was not negligence *per se* for her to use the street or to attempt to pass the obstruction;

the law only required of her that she use such due care
and caution as would be commensurate with her
knowledge of the conditions and surroundings existing
at the time, and whether she did this was wholly a
question of fact for the jury, and we are not prepared
to say that the finding of the jury upon this question
is clearly and manifestly against the evidence, and unless we are able to do so, under the familiar rule
adopted by the courts, then verdict should not be disturbed.

With regard to the error which appellant urges the
court committed in sustaining objections to evidence
offered by it and overruling objections made by it to
appellee's testimony, after a careful examination of
this record we are satisfied that appellant was not injured by any rulings of the court in regard to the
admission of evidence, as the evidence to which objections were made by appellant and sustained was permitted to go to the jury at other times.

Upon the question of the refused instruction offered
by appellant, the court did not commit any error, as
the law presented by this instruction was fully given
to the jury by other instructions. But appellant insists
that it was entitled to have these instructions given
where they contain correct propositions of law although other instructions were given containing the
same propositions, and insists on this although to
give this instruction would have been to duplicate portions of other instructions given, it insists upon this
under the rule that appellants were entitled to have the
jury fully instructed. While that is the rule, appellants were not entitled to duplicate their instructions
in this manner and the refusal to give them was not
error; and we find no error in the giving or refusing
of any of the instructions, the jury was fully and amply
instructed upon all propositions involved in this case.

There being no reversible error in this record, the
judgment is affirmed.

Affirmed.

Winifred O'Farrell, Appellant, v. Malinda Vickerage and E. F. O'Farrell, Appellees.

1. APPEAL AND ERROR, § 1810*—*when Appellate Court may enter final judgment.* Where the cause was heard by the trial court, the jury having been waived, the Appellate Court is empowered to render final judgment without remanding the cause.

2. ATTACHMENT, § 312*—*when finding of trial court as to owner-ship of property not sustained by the evidence.* In an attachment proceeding in which the wife of the attachment defendant inter-pleaded claiming ownership of the property, a finding by the trial court of property in the attachment defendant *held* not warranted by the evidence, it appearing that the property was purchased by the wife with her own money, that the property was in her posses-sion at the time of the levy, that the wife was not liable on the indebtedness for which the attachment suit was brought, and that the Appellate Court on a former appeal of the cause found that the property belonged to her on substantially the same record as upon the present appeal, so far as the evidence is concerned.

Appeal from the City Court of Pana; the Hon. PAUL McWILLIAMS, Judge, presiding. Heard in this court at the April term, 1913. Reversed with judgment here. Opinion filed October 16, 1913.

W. H. CHEW and E. A. HUMPHREY, for appellant.

J. E. HOGAN and McQUIGG & DOWELL, for appellees.

MR. PRESIDING JUSTICE PHILBRICK delivered the opin-ion of the court.

This is the second appeal of this case to this court. The opinion filed upon the first hearing (163 Ill. App. 519) contains a statement of facts and what the evi-dence proved upon the first trial. At that time the judgment in favor of appellee herein was reversed and the cause remanded for a new trial. Upon calling the case for trial after the cause was reinstated in the trial court, a stipulation was entered into submitting the cause to the court without a jury upon the record of the testimony taken in the first hearing, and so far as this record discloses we find no other or different testimony, and the record is now before this court substantially as it was upon the former hearing with the exception that the case was tried before the court and propositions of law submitted to it instead of submitting the questions of fact to the jury upon the instructions. The former judgment was in favor of the defendant, and a jury not having been waived, upon the reversal of that judgment we were compelled to remand the cause for a new trial, but as the cause now appears, the jury having been waived, this court is empowered to render final judgment without remanding the cause.

From the finding of facts and conclusions arrived at by this court upon the former appeal, all of the property that was contained in the car which was intended to be shipped by appellant to her home in Oklahoma was found to belong to her by this court, and there is no proof that the husband of appellant furnished any money or provided any funds for the purchase of any property contained in this car. The property was at the time of the levying of the attachment writ in the possession of appellant and was taken from her by the officers levying this writ. Her possession was *prima facie* ownership, and in addition to this *prima facie* evidence of ownership, as stated in our former opinion, the record discloses that the money and proceeds which were furnished and used for the purchase of the property involved was furnished and provided by appellant; that the indebtedness for which the attachment suit is brought by appellee herein against the husband of appellant was not occasioned and was in no way induced by reason of the fact that appellant's husband was apparently the head of the family, and was to that extent and that alone at one time in the possession of this property, but the indebtedness which was created in favor of appellee against the husband of appellant grew out of personal transactions between appellee and the husband of appellant, who was a lawyer, and the misappropriation of funds of appellee by appellant's husband for which appellant was in no way responsible and of which she had no knowledge. It is contended by appellee that a portion of the funds used in the purchase of the property in question was originally furnished by the husband of appellant; even if this be conceded, the proof is that it was furnished or given her long before the husband of appellant became indebted to appellee and prior to that time it is of no concern to appellee what he did with his money.

The finding of the trial court and the judgment rendered upon that finding is not warranted by the evidence in this record, and being clearly and manifestly against the weight of the evidence, the judgment is reversed and final judgment will be rendered in this court, there having already been four trials of this cause.

The finding of this court will be that the interpleader, Winifred O'Farrell, is the owner of and entitled to the possession of the property in question, and judgment will be rendered in this court finding appellant to be the owner of the property in question and awarding its possession to her, and judgment against appellee and for all costs.

Reversed with final judgment in this court.

Callie P. Bristow, Administratrix, Appellant, v. St. Louis, Springfield and Peoria Railroad Company, Appellee.

CORPORATIONS, § 487*—*who are agents of a railroad company upon whom process may be served.* Under the statute permitting a railroad company to be sued in any county through which it operates a line of railroad, or where it maintains an office, or has an agent for the transaction of its business, the fact that agents of railroad com-

panies other than the one against which suit is brought sell tickets
by which persons may travel over the defendant company's line
does not constitute them agents of the latter company so that process
may be served upon them.

Appeal from the Circuit Court of Macon county; the Hon. WILLIAM
C. JOHNS, Judge presiding. Heard in this court at the April
term, 1913. Affirmed. Opinion filed October 16, 1913.

CHARLES S. GIBBS and OSCAR J. PUTTING, for appellant.

LEFORGEE, VAIL & MILLER and GEORGE W. BURTON,
for appellee.

MR. PRESIDING JUSTICE PHILBRICK delivered the opinion of the court.

Plaintiff's intestate received injuries in an accident
on the line of appellee's railroad near the city of Staun-
ton, Macoupin county, Illinois. This action is brought
in Macon county, Illinois, under the statute which permits a railroad to be sued in any county through which
it operates a line of railroad, or where it maintains an
office or has an agent for the transaction of its business, and the summons in this case was served upon one
Lloyd C. Bundy, as assistant ticket agent, and upon
Clarence Hill, as ticket agent, for appellee company.
Appellee filed a plea to the jurisdiction of the court, the
plea alleging that the parties upon whom this summons
was served were not at that time and had not been
agent or agents of appellee Company. Issue was
joined on this plea, a trial was had before the court
without the intervention of a jury, the issues were
found in favor of the defendants and the writ quashed.

The facts as disclosed by the record show that the
St. Louis, Springfield and Peoria Railroad Company,
appellee, is a corporation owning, controlling and operating a line of railroad from East St. Louis to Peoria
through the city of Springfield; that it had no line of
railroad in the county of Macon; that the persons on
whom this summons was served as agents for appellee

Company were in the employ of a corporation owning and operating a line of railroad from the city of Springfield, Illinois, through the county of Macon and city of Decatur to the city of Danville, Illinois; that these two lines of railroad are independent corporations, that they are operated as a part of the system commonly known as the Illinois Traction System. There is no corporation by the name of Illinois Traction System, and although this name is used to designate a system of connecting railroads it is not a corporation, and does not own or control any railroads. The record further discloses that Mr. Hill and Mr. Bundy were employed by a Company operating from Decatur, Illinois, to Danville, Illinois, that they were not employed by appellee Company and did not represent them in any way. The theory upon which appellant contended that they were agents of appellee Company is because they sold tickets at Decatur by which parties were entitled to travel over both of these lines of railroad from Decatur to any point of destination thereon designated by the ticket, and that this constitutes the parties agents of appellee Company. Further, that the two lines were operated under the name of the Illinois Traction System. The proof that these parties at Decatur were authorized to sell a ticket upon which parties might ride upon the line of railroad which they did represent and arriving at the end of that line were entitled to ride upon another railroad to the point of destination to which the ticket was sold is not sufficient to and does not show agency on behalf of the second or connecting railroad. It is universally known that railroads operating wholly within one State sell tickets permitting passengers to travel through various States, take and receive shipments of freight to be carried in foreign States by railroads not authorized to do business in Illinois, and to hold that this constituted the agent selling such ticket or receiving such freight an agent of every line of railroad over which the ticket authorized the passenger to travel or the freight to be shipped would be to hold that such corporations were violating the laws of this State regarding foreign corporations doing business in this State.

The finding and judgment of the trial court that the parties upon whom this summons was served were not agents of the appellee Company is fully sustained by the proof, and the judgment should be and is affirmed.

Affirmed.

Sleepy Eye Milling Company, Appellee, v. Conrad Hartman and Conrad Hartman, Jr., trading as Conrad Hartman & Son, Appellants.

1. CORPORATIONS, § 710—*what does not constitute transaction of business in this State by an unlicensed foreign corporation.* A foreign corporation by employing a general broker to sell its products in this State does not maintain an agent in this State so as to constitute the transaction of business in this State without a license and thereby preclude it from suing in the courts of this State on the contract of sale, the preponderance of the evidence showing that the contract was made and accepted in its home State.

2. SET-OFF AND RECOUPMENT, § 9*—*when claim for damages arising out of one contract cannot be recouped against liability on another contract.* In an action by seller on two contracts for the sale of flour to recover for loss resulting from the buyer's refusal to accept all the flour contracted for after the buyer had received and used a part of the flour delivered under the first contract, the buyer rejecting flour on account of the inferior grade of the flour accepted, and claiming damages to his business by reason thereof, *held* that the damages sustained by the buyer, if any, were chargeable wholly to the flour received under the first contract, and not having received any of the flour covered by the second contract no such loss or damage could be shown thereunder by way of recoupment.

3. SET-OFF AND RECOUPMENT, § 9*—*when claim for damage cannot be set off or recouped.* A claim for unliquidated damages arising out of a breach of contract cannot be set off in an action to recover on another contract, and a claim for damages arising out of a former contract cannot be recovered by recoupment.

*See Illinois Notes Digest, Vols. XI to XV, same topic and section number.

4. SALES, § 305*—*rights of seller in making resale when buyer has refused to accept the goods.* Where a buyer of flour refuses to accept the same it is the duty of the seller to resell it, and in so doing, he is not confined to the market at the place it was contracted to be delivered to the buyer even though it might have sold for a greater sum at that place, unless the resale was made at a different place with the intention of injuring the buyer or with knowledge that by making sales at other places a less price would be received.

5. SALES, § 146*—*right of buyer to reject flour when purchased under two contracts of sale.* The mere fact that flour shipped to buyer under one contract of sale was not of the quality of grade or standard purchased does not justify the conclusion that a second shipment under another contract of sale was of the same grade or character as the first.

6. SALES, § 282*—*what evidence incompetent to show inferior quality of flour sold.* In an action by a milling company on a contract for the sale of flour to recover for loss sustained by refusal of buyer to accept the flour, the buyer rejecting the flour on account of its inferior quality, evidence offered by the defendant to show that the plaintiff Company was in the hands of a receiver, and that the flour was degraded and its efficiency damaged by the plaintiff Company to enable certain persons to purchase the flouring mill at a reduced price at the receiver's sale, *held*, incompetent as having no bearing on the question at issue.

Appeal from the Circuit Court of Sangamon county; the Hon. JAMES A. CREIGHTON, Judge, presiding. Heard in this court at the April term, 1913. Affirmed. Opinion filed October 16, 1913. *Certiorari* denied by Supreme Court (making opinion final).

SMITH & FRIEDMEYER, for appellants.

ALONZO HOFF, for appellee.

MR. PRESIDING JUSTICE PHILBRICK delivered the opinion of the court.

This is an action brought by plaintiff to recover from defendants for shipments of flour purchased by defendants from plaintiff and which defendants refused to receive or accept, and which were afterwards sold by plaintiff, for account of defendants, at a loss. This action is to recover that loss. The trial below resulted in a judgment against defendants for $1,835.06.

310   APPELLATE COURTS OF ILLINOIS.

Sleepy Eye Milling Co. v. Hartman et al., 184 Ill. App. 308.

The defendants are bakers in the city of Springfield. Plaintiff is a corporation located in Minnesota, manufacturing flour. There were two contracts for purchase of flour by defendants from the plaintiff, the first one was a purchase of six hundred barrels at a contract price of $5.35 per barrel.; the second, made considerable time after the first, was a purchase of sixteen hundred barrels at a price of $5.50 per barrel. Prior to these purchases, defendants had been using a flour manufactured by plaintiff known as the Sleepy Eye Cream flour. Defendants received four hundred and twenty-five barrels of flour under the first contract of purchase, and used the same in their bakery at Springfield. This flour not proving satisfactory, and as defendants contend, and not fulfilling the contract of purchase, they refused to accept or receive the remaining one hundred and seventy-five barrels of that purchase, and after their experience with this first purchase or shipment they then notified plaintiff that they could not accept or receive the second purchase of sixteen hundred barrels, and repudiated that contract. Plaintiff shipped the flour in accordance with their contract to Springfield, Illinois, and after defendants had refused to receive or accept it on its arrival at Springfield, plaintiff reshipped all of the last purchase and one hundred and seventy-five barrels of the first purchase to St. Louis, Missouri, and various points in Indiana and Ohio and sold the same upon the market. Their loss upon the sale of the first contract was $175, their loss on the second contract was $1,835.-06.

The declaration is upon both these contracts, alleging the purchase by defendants and the failure to receive and accept the same, and the reshipment by plaintiff and loss sustained. Defendants pleaded that the plaintiff was a foreign corporation not licensed to do business in this State, that by reason thereof no recovery could be had; they also allege by their pleas that the flour contracted for by them was a brand of flour of well known reputation and had heretofore been of a certain standard and grade, and that they were entitled to receive that grade of flour which they had contracted for, and that the shipment of flour made by plaintiff was not of that grade or standard, by reason thereof defendants were injured in their business by reason of the attempt to use the poor grade of flour which they had accepted under the first contract of purchase, and they claim this damage by way of recoupment and set-off.

The trial court refused to permit defendants to show damage to their business as a set-off against the purchase of this flour and denied them the right to recoup any such damages. Defendants insist that this action of the court was such error as to require a reversal of this case. They insist also that the judgment is erroneous because the evidence shows that the plaintiff corporation was not licensed to do business in this State, and that they maintained an agent in this State for the sale of their flour, which constituted the transaction of business in the State of Illinois without a license. They also insist that the judgment is erroneous for the reason that it is not sustained by the evidence, and that the court erred in the admission and rejection of evidence and in the giving and refusing of instructions.

Upon the contention that the plaintiff Company is a foreign corporation and not licensed to do business in this State, the contention is untenable for the reason that the record discloses that the contract of sale was made and the acceptance of the same was done in the State of Minnesota at the home of the plaintiff corporation and not in Springfield, Illinois, and the evidence does not disclose that plaintiff had or maintained any agent in the State of Illinois through whom these contracts were made, but that the party who defendants insist was an agent and through whom the contracts were made was a general broker, not only handling the flour of the plaintiff Company but of other mills, and

the greater weight and perponderance of the evidence
discloses that the contract was not made in the State
of Illinois. The statute of this State regarding foreign corporations cannot be applied. *Black-Clawson
Co. v. Carlyle Paper Co.*, 133 Ill. App. 61; *Havens &
Geddes Co. v. Diamond*, 93 Ill. App. 557.

There is no contention that defendants ever examined or handled in any way any of the flour shipped
under the second contract of purchase, but as to the
condition, standard and value of that flour they rely
wholly upon their experience with the first shipment.
Their business was not, and it cannot be contended
that their business was in any way injured or damaged by reason of the second contract or shipment of
flour under that contract, as none of it was used by defendants, and the damage, if any was sustained, is
wholly chargeable to the flour received and accepted
under the first shipment; and under this state of
facts no such loss or damage could be shown by way
of recoupment in an action to recover for the second
contract of purchase, and the court did not err
in rejecting this evidence. A claim for unliquidated
damages arising out of a breach of contract cannot be
set off in an action to recover on another contract and
the damage claimed having grown out of a former contract cannot be recovered by recoupment. *Keegan v.
Kinnare*, 123 Ill. 281; *Clause v. Bullock Printing Press
Co.*, 118 Ill. 612.

The defendants do not attempt in any way to contradict or deny the amount of the loss sustained by
plaintiff upon the resale of this flour, but insist that it
was its duty and plaintiff was required to have sold
this flour in the city of Springfield, instead of making
the shipment to other points; this position cannot be
maintained under the law. After defendants had refused to accept or receive this flour it then became the
duty of the plaintiff to resell it, and they were not, in
so doing, confined to the market at Springfield, even
though the flour might have been sold for a greater

sum in the city of Springfield than it did at the points where plaintiff shipped it, unless such reshipment and sale was done with the intention of injuring the defendants or with the knowledge that by making sales at other places a less price would be received.

Defendants do not attempt to deny or dispute the amount of the loss sustained by plaintiffs by reason of the resale of this flour or that the resale of the flour purchased by defendants under the second contract amounting to $1,835.06; the judgment recovered by plaintiff is only for this amount and it is evident that by their verdict the jury did not allow plaintiff any damage occasioned by the refusal of the defendants to accept the balance of the shipment under the first contract, and it is further evident that the jury allowed to the defendants all damages claimed by them under the first contract of purchase, and the ruling of the court concerning the claim of set-off or recoupment has not prejudiced the defendants. The mere fact that the flour shipped by plaintiff to the defendants under the first contract of purchase was not the quality of grade or standard purchased would not justify the conclusion arrived at by the defendants that the second shipment was of the same grade or character as the first. The preponderance of the evidence is that the grade of flour shipped by plaintiff under the second contract of purchase was first-class flour and the quality of the usual grade and fully up to the standard contracted for by defendants.

The defendants also insist that the court erred in refusing to permit them to show that the mill of the plaintiff Company was in the hands of a receiver, and that the flour manufactured by it and shipped under these contracts was purposely degraded and its efficiency damaged by the plaintiff Company for the purpose of permitting certain parties to purchase the plaintiff's mill at a receiver's sale at a greatly reduced price; this evidence could have had no bearing upon the questions at issue in this case, and was wholly incompetent for the purpose for which it was offered, and was properly rejected by the trial court.

Although considerable criticism is made of the instructions given and refused, upon careful examination of the instructions given, modified and refused in this case, we find that the criticism is not warranted, and that the jury was fully and correctly instructed upon all propositions involved, and that the court committed no reversible error therein.

Finding no error in this record prejudicial to the defendants, the judgment is affirmed.

Affirmed.

R. K. Byerly, Appellee, v. Wilbur Jones and John White, Appellants.

1. PROPERTY, § 11*—*when standing corn is personal property.* Corn standing in the field after it has matured and before it has been husked is personal property.

2. SALES, § 433*—*when subsequent purchaser of corn entitled thereto in replevin as against a prior purchaser.* In replevin against two defendants to recover the possession of standing corn alleged to have been sold to plaintiff by a tenant prior to the execution of a bill of sale thereof by the tenant to a third person who had placed one of the defendants in possession and had afterwards executed a bill of sale to the other defendant, refusal of court to give a peremptory instruction for defendant *held* error, the plaintiff never having taken possession of the corn, but wholly relied upon plaintiff to husk and deliver it, and the defendants having taken possession under the bill of sale which was bona fide and executed without any knowledge of plaintiff's claim.

Appealed from the Circuit Court of Vermilion county; the Hon. WILLIAM B. SCHOLFIELD, Judge, presiding. Heard in this court at the April term, 1913. Reversed and remanded. Opinion filed October 16, 1913.

*See Illinois Notes Digest, Vols. XI to XV, same topic and section number.

CHARLES TROUP, for appellants.

A. B. DENNIS, for appellee.

MR. PRESIDING JUSTICE PHILBRICK delivered the opinion of the court.

Appellee was a grain buyer operating an elevator at Catlin, Illinois. He claims to have purchased from Charles R. Fuller, a tenant on a farm belonging to Arthur Findley, twenty acres of corn at a price of fifty cents per bushel. He further contends that Fuller had been authorized by his landlord, Findley, to sell the entire field of corn and divide the money, and that he paid Fuller one hundred and eighty dollars on his share of this corn at various times after he bought the corn. At the time of the purchase of the corn by appellee from Fuller the corn was standing in the field unhusked, and it was part of the agreement that Fuller was to husk the corn at the proper time and deliver it to appellee at his elevator at Catlin. Fuller delivered to appellee in all four loads of this corn. Fuller was indebted at that time to the Danville National Bank, and he also owed a rent note which was in the hands of George H. Milemore, and he executed to one Ralph B. Holmes, trustee, a bill of sale of all of his property for the stated consideration of twelve hundred dollars. Upon the execution of this bill of sale, Holmes, as trustee, took possession of all the property described therein, including, the corn standing in the field and unhusked, and placed the property in the possession of one Wilbur Jones, one of the appellants herein; Holmes trustee, afterwards executed a bill of sale to John White, appellant herein.

Appellee replevined the corn, making White and Jones defendants in the replevin suit. He recovered a judgment below and appellants appealed therefrom.

The facts in this case are not disputed so far as they in any way materially affect the rights of the parties herein, and as a consequence thereof the only question involved is one of law. Although appellee made the first attempt to purchase the property from Fuller, the corn was then matured in the field and only needed to be husked to be delivered, and it was therefore personal property. Appellee never in any way attempted to take possession of this corn, but relied wholly upon the promise of Fuller to husk and deliver it to him and he was not to have possession until it was so delivered to him at his elevator in Catlin. Holmes, on the other hand, as soon as he obtained a bill of sale for this property reduced it to possession; he had no notice whatever of any interest that appellee claimed to have therein by reason of the pretended purchase by him. The sale to Holmes and from Holmes to White were bona fide sales without any knowledge whatever of the claim of appellee, and they having reduced their purchase to possession and secured absolute control over the property are the owners of that property as against appellee in this replevin suit. The trial court should have given the peremptory instruction to the jury as requested by defendants; to refuse it was error. *Davis v. Shepherd,* 87 Ill. App. 467.

The judgment is reversed and the cause remanded.

Reversed and remanded.

Alex Hamilton and Marie Hamilton, Appellees, v. Earle Sampson, Appellant.

(Not to be reported in full.)

Appeal from the Circuit Court of Menard county; the Hon. GUY R. WILLIAMS, Judge, presiding. Heard in this court at the April term, 1913. Affirmed. Opinion filed October 16, 1913.

Statement of the Case.

Action by Alex Hamilton and Marie Hamilton, part- ners, against Earle Sampson to recover damages for the loss of seventy-four turkeys belonging to plaintiffs and alleged to have been killed by defendant while they were foraging on an adjoining farm belonging to defendant. From a judgment in favor of plaintiffs for two hundred and eighty-five dollars, defendant appeals.

WATKINS & GOLDEN, for appellant.

THOMAS P. REEP, for appellees.

MR. PRESIDING JUSTICE PHILBRICK delivered the opinion of the court.

Abstract of the Decision.

1. ANIMALS, § 28*—*right of owner of farm to kill or injure trespassing turkeys.* An owner of a farm has a right to drive turkeys belonging to another off his premises, but the mere fact that they are trespassing on his place gives him no right to kill or injure them.

2. ANIMALS, § 43*—*when evidence sufficient to sustain recovery for killing trespassing turkeys.* In an action to recover for turkeys killed by defendant while they were foraging on defendant's adjoining farm, evidence *held* sufficient to sustain a verdict for plaintiffs, it appearing that no serious damage was done to defendant's farm or his crops thereon by reason of the trespass.

————

Dora E. McEvoy, Appellee, v. Court of Honor, Appellant.

1. APPEAL AND ERROR § 1818*—*conclusiveness of decision of Appellate Court on former appeal.* Prior decision of Appellate Court on a former appeal as to the sufficiency of a replication is conclusive on a subsequent appeal.

2. APPEAL AND ERROR, § 1442*—*when permitting withdrawal of deposition not error.* A party has a right to withdraw his deposition prior to the time of the trial if he sees fit to do so, and it is not error for trial court to permit its withdrawal where the witness was present in court and the other party could have used him as a witness.

3. APPEAL AND ERROR, § 1361*—*when not error for trial court to deny leave to file additional plea.* Granting of leave to file additional pleas is discretionary with the trial court, and unless in denying the motion the court has abused the exercise of its discretion, there is no error in denying the leave.

4. INSURANCE, § 788*—*when evidence insufficient to show that insured's use of intoxicating liquor avoided the insurance.* In an action on a benefit certificate to recover insurance, where the by-laws and the policy provide that if the insured should use intoxicating liquors to the extent of impairing his health the policy shall be void, *held* that the evidence of the insured's use of intoxicating liquors was insufficient to show that his health was impaired thereby, though it showed that he did occasionally use intoxicating liquors to excess.

Appeal from the Circuit Court of DeWitt county; the Hon. WILLIAM G. COCHRAN, Judge, presiding. Heard in this court at the April term, 1913. Affirmed. Opinion filed October 16, 1913. *Certiorari* denied by Supreme Court (making opinion final).

FITZHENRY & MARTIN and LEMON & LEMON, for appellant; WILLIAM B. RISSE, of counsel.

INGHAM & INGHAM, for appellee.

MR. PRESIDING JUSTICE PHILBRICK delivered the opinion of the court.

This is an action on a benefit certificate issued by the defendant to one A. J. McEvoy, in his lifetime, plaintiff is the beneficiary, and recovered a judgment against defendant for the amount of the policy, defendant prosecutes this appeal to reverse that judgment.

This cause was before this court on appeal from former judgment in favor of defendant. At that time the question presented was the action of the trial court in sustaining the demurrer of defendant to the second amended replication to defendant's sixth plea. The substance of the plea and the replication are fully set forth in the former opinion of this court in *McEvoy v. Court of Honor*, 163 Ill. App. 556. Upon that hearing this court then held that the court erred in sustaining the demurrer, that the replication was an answer to the plea, and reversed the judgment directing the lower court to overrule the demurrer. After the cause was reinstated in the trial court the demurrer was overruled as directed by this court. Defendant refused to join issue but elected to stand by its demurrer, and in its presentation of this cause at this time insists that the court improperly sustained that demurrer. The question as to the sufficiency of that replication was determined by this court upon the former hearing (163 Ill. App. 556), and the question is not now open for discussion in this court, and we will make no further comment thereon.

Issue was joined upon the other replications filed and trial had by the court without a jury. To the declaration defendant filed various pleas, which were, in substance, that the deceased made false and fraudulent representations and warranties in his application for insurance, that the by-laws and policy issued provided that if the defendant should use intoxicating liquors or narcotics to the extent of injuring or impairing his health the policy should be avoided thereby, and that the death of the deceased was caused by reason of the excessive use of intoxicating liquors. The burden of proving these pleas was upon the defendant, and while the facts disclose that at the time of the making of the application for insurance by the deceased he did use intoxicating liquors; that he continued the use thereof up to the time of his death; that a short time before the death of the deceased he became intoxicated and that this brought on a condition of diabetic coma from which he never recovered, and the defendant insists that his death was caused indirectly by this use of intoxicating liquors, and that the use of intoxicating liquors produced an acute state of this disease which resulted in his death.

The provisions of the policy, instead of providing that the use of intoxicating liquors should avoid it, are that in order to avoid the policy the insured must use intoxicating liquors to such an extent as to impair his

health, and the defendant insists that this is shown by
the showing that the deceased became intoxicated one
or more times, and asked the court to so hold in the
propositions of law submitted to it, but the court properly refused to hold that such use of intoxicating
liquors avoided the policy. There is no contention that
the deceased did not comply with all of the rules and
regulations of the order, except the alleged violation
in the use of intoxicating liquors, and paid his dues
therein, and was a member in good standing. There
is no defense to this policy unless it can be held under
the evidence in this record that the deceased either was
at the time or after the issuance of the policy became
addicted to the use of intoxicating liquors to such an
extent as to impair his health. While it is shown that he
did occasionally use intoxicating liquors to excess, there
is no evidence that will justify the conclusion or support the contention that the use of intoxicating liquors
ever impaired his health or in any way shortened the
life of the deceased.

Prior to the time of the trial in the lower court the
deposition of appellee was taken in the State of Mis-
sissippi, where she then resided. Before the trial this
deposition was withdrawn from the files of the clerk
by appellee by permission of the court. On the day
upon which the case was tried appellant asked leave to
file one additional plea. This plea related and set forth
the facts which averred forfeiture of the certificate,
the court denied the application to file this plea at that
time, and appellant insists that the court erred in permitting appellee to withdraw the deposition and also in
denying the right to appellant to file this additional
plea.

Appellee had the right to withdraw her deposition
prior to the time of the trial if she saw fit to do so; the
court did not commit any error in permitting her to
withdraw it. *Adams v. Russell*, 85 Ill. 284; *Doggett v.
Greene*, 254 Ill. 134.

She was present in court at the time of the trial, and if appellant desired to use her as a witness they had the opportunity to do so.

Upon the contention that the court erred in denying appellant the right to file this additional plea, the matter of granting leave to file additional pleas is discretionary with the trial court, and unless in denying the motion the court has abused the exercise of this discretion, there is no error in denying the leave, and we are satisfied that it was not an abuse of the discretion of the court in denying this motion, and that it committed no error in so doing. *Pierpont v. Johnson*, 104 Ill. App. 28; *Fisher v. Greene*, 95 Ill. 94.

We find no error of the court either in the admission or rejection of evidence, nor any reversible error in the holding of propositions of law submitted to it.

The judgment is, therefore, affirmed.

Affirmed.

Town of Georgetown, ex rel. Eugene Quartier, Appellant, v. Oscar McCorkle and Kittie McCorkle, Appellees.

(Not to be reported in full.)

Appeal from the Circuit Court of Vermilion county; the Hon. WILLIAM B. SCHOLFIELD, Judge, presiding. Heard in this court at the April term, 1913. Affirmed. Opinion filed October 16, 1913.

Statement of the Case.

Action by Town of Georgetown ex rel. Eugene Quartier against Oscar McCorkle and Kittie McCorkle for obstructing a public highway alleged to exist by reason of prescription. From a judgment finding defendants not guilty, plaintiff appeals.

This cause was before this court on a prior appeal (164 Ill. App. 314), in which a judgment in favor of defendants was reversed upon errors of law committed by the trial court upon the former trial.

LEWMAN & CRAYTON, J. ED. THOMAS and THOMAS A. GRAHAM, for appellant.

LINDLEY, PENWELL & LINDLEY, for appellees.

MR. PRESIDING JUSTICE PHILBRICK delivered the opinion of the court.

Abstract of the Decision.

1. ROADS AND BRIDGES, § 23*—*when evidence insufficient to show establishment of highway by prescription.* In an action for the obstruction of a highway, the issue being whether the road was established by prescription, evidence *held* sufficient to warrant a verdict for defendants, the evidence being conflicting as to whether a gate or bars had been maintained at a place where the alleged road leads off from the public highway, and it appearing that a short distance from the public highway the road ceased to maintain any general direction and there was no demarcation of any line of travel ever maintained from that point on.

2. ROADS AND BRIDGES, § 208*—*admissibility of evidence.* In an action for the obstruction of a highway, the issue ng whether the alleged road was established by prescription, evidence showing that there was another highway or public road by which access might be gained to a certain cemetery, *held* wholly immaterial, the admission thereof *held* error, though not prejudicial.

George Heyen et al., trading as Heyen Bros., Appellees, v. Cleveland, Cincinnati, Chicago and St. Louis Railway Company, Appellant.

(Not to be reported in full.)

Appeal from the Circuit Court of Macoupin county; the Hon. JAMES A. CREIGHTON, Judge, presiding. Heard in this court at the April term, 1913. Reversed. Opinion filed October 16, 1913.

THIRD DISTRICT—OCTOBER, 1913.   323

Heyen v. Cleveland, C., C. and St. L. Ry. Co., 184 Ill. App. 322.

Statement of the Case.

Action by George Heyen, William Heyen and Albert Heyen, partners, doing business under the firm name of Heyen Bros., against Cleveland, Cincinnati, Chicago and St. Louis Railway Company to recover damages for loss of cattle while being shipped to plaintiffs over defendant's railroad. From a judgment in favor of plaintiffs for $368.40, defendant appeals.

GEORGE B. GILLESPIE, for appellant.

R. J. CARY, BELL & BURTON, SHEPHERD & TROGDON and GILLESPIE & FITZGERALD, of counsel.

ALFRED A. ISAACS and TRUMAN A. SNELL, for appellees.

MR. PRESIDING JUSTICE PHILBRICK delivered the opinion of the court.

Abstract of the Decision.

CARRIERS, § 235*—*when not liable for failure to unload stock during a severe snowstorm.* In an action against a railroad for damages to a shipment of cattle consigned to plaintiff alleged to have been caused by failure of defendant company to unload the stock after defendant's train was stalled in a snowdrift during a severe snowstorm, evidence *held* insufficient to sustain a judgment for plaintiff, it appearing that after the train was stalled in the snow it was impossible to either unload or move the stock, and the record disclosing that the storm was of such a character as not to have been reasonably anticipated and therefore must be held to be an act of God, for which the defendant company was not responsible.

*See Illinois Notes Digest, Vols. XI to XV, same topic and section number.

Frank M. Wood, Appellee, v. A. W. Slaughter et al., Appellants.

(Not to be reported in full.)

Appeal from the Circuit Court of Edgar county; the Hon. DANIEL V. DAYTON, Judge, presiding. Heard in this court at the April term, 1913. Dismissed. Opinion filed October 16, 1913.

Statement of the Case.

Scire facias by Frank M. Wood against A. W. Slaughter and others to make defendants, who were sureties on an appeal bond, parties defendant to a judgment recovered by plaintiff against the principal on the bond. From a judgment rendered against defendants making them parties to such judgment, defendant appeals.

L. A. CRANSTON and W. H. HICKMAN, for appellants.

CHARLES McKNIGHT, for appellee.

MR. PRESIDING JUSTICE PHILBRICK delivered the opinion of the court.

Abstract of the Decision.

APPEAL AND ERROR, § 1105*—*when appeal will be dismissed.* Where no bill of exceptions is filed and no assignment of errors made upon or attached to the record there is nothing preserved for review, and the appeal will be dismissed.

Gertrude H. Kelsey, Appellant, v. Frank M. Palmer, Appellee.

(Not to be reported in full.)

Appeal from the Circuit Court of DeWitt county; the Hon. WILLIAM G. COCHRAN, Judge, presiding. Heard in this court at the April term, 1913. Affirmed. Opinion filed October 16, 1913.

Statement of the Case.

Action of forcible detainer by Gertrude H. Kelsey against Frank M. Palmer to recover possession of premises formerly belonging to defendant but afterwards acquired by plaintiff under a master's deed. The defendant owns an adjoining tract of land and about one-half of a residence stands on plaintiff's tract and the other half on defendant's tract. From a judgment in favor of defendant, plaintiff appeals.

JOHN FULLER, for appellant.

LEMON & LEMON, for appellee.

MR. JUSTICE THOMPSON delivered the opinion of the court.

Abstract of the Decision.

1. FORCIBLE ENTRY AND DETAINER, § 87*—*when evidence insufficient to show defendant's possession.* In an action of forcible detainer to recover possession of premises, the defendant owning an adjoining tract, and a house being built on about the center of the two tracts, evidence *held* to sustain finding of trial court that defendant was not guilty of forcible detainer after demand for possession, it appearing that the defendant had moved into his portion of the house, and the only evidence tending to show that he was in possession of plaintiff's premises being that the constable who served the notice saw some cows and calves on the premises, and that defendant was residing in part of the house but he did not know which part.

*See Illinois Notes Digest, Vols. XI to XV, same topic and section number.

2. FORCIBLE ENTRY AND DETAINER, § 24*—*effect of plaintiff's conveyance of premises pending suit.* Fact that plaintiff in an action for forcible detainer conveyed her interest in the premises to a third party pending suit is no defense to the action.

Isaac Horn, Petitioner, Appellee, v. Sallie F. Sayer et al., Appellants.

1. JUDGMENT, § 603*—*limitations.* While the lien of a judgment expires in seven years, it may be renewed or an action brought on it at any time within twenty years after its date.

2. EXECUTORS AND ADMINISTRATORS, § 293*—*when claim allowed against an estate is a lien on the entire estate.* A claim presented and allowed before an executrix files an inventory is a lien on the entire estate that may be collected in any manner in which the collection of claims allowed against estates may be collected

3. POWERS, § 6—*power of devisee to dispose of property.* Where a widow is devised property by her husband with power only to convey same to their children, a conveyance by her to third parties being void, a subsequent conveyance by her to the children with provision that the conveyance is to inure to the benefit of the former grantees is also void, as being an attempt to do indirectly what could not be done directly.

4. EXECUTORS AND ADMINISTRATORS, § 386*—*jurisdiction to enforce payment of claims allowed against estate.* The payment of a claim allowed against an estate may be enforced in the Probate Court or it may be enforced in a court of equity if the remedy in the Probate Court is inadequate and there are reasons why a court of equity should take jurisdiction.

5. EXECUTORS AND ADMINISTRATORS, § 386*—*when person having claim allowed against estate may intervene in partition proceeding to enforce payment.* On bill filed by sole beneficiary under a will for partition of certain lands of which complainant's husband died seized of an interest therein, such interest being the share of the deceased in his father's estate, and comprising his whole estate, *held* that a person having a claim allowed against the estate of complainant's husband was entitled to intervene for the purpose of collecting his claim on filing a petition in the nature of a cross-bill, alleging that the interest of complainant's husband in the lands had been fraudulently conveyed by the widow of testator's father in violation of the power under the testator's father's will.

6. EQUITY, § 362*—*when dismissal of bill to defeat intervenor's claim is fraudulent.* Where sole devisee under a will files a bill for partition of lands in which testator had an interest, and a person having a claim allowed against the estate, intervenes to enforce claim, *held* that an arrangement between complainant and defendants whereby defendants paid complainant a certain sum for her interest in the lands upon claimant dismissing her bill and executing to defendants quitclaim deeds showing an attempt by complainant with aid of defendants to fraudulently appropriate the estate to her own use and to defeat the collection of intervenor's claim.

7. ABATEMENT AND REVIVAL, § 30*—*when plea to jurisdiction of court may be stricken.* When an intervenor in a partition proceeding files a supplementary petition after the original bill has been dismissed by an agreement between the complainant and defendants, action of court in striking a plea filed to the jurisdiction of the court, setting up that the defendants were not residents of the county in which suit was brought, *held* not error, a part of the real estate involved being situated in the county of suit, and it appearing that the plea was only on behalf of some of the defendants and there were other defendants found in the county and the plea does not state the names and residences of the other defendants and that there were no necessary defendants residing in the county.

Appeal from the Circuit Court of Moultrie county; the Hon. WILLIAM G. COCHRAN, Judge, presiding. Heard in this court at the April term, 1913. Affirmed. Opinion filed October 16, 1913. *Certiorari* denied by Supreme Court (making opinion final.)

JAMES A. CONNOLLY and A. J. FRYER, for appellants.

F. M. HARBAUGH and F. J. THOMPSON, for appellee.

MR. JUSTICE THOMPSON delivered the opinion of the court.

In February, 1910, Clara E. Humphreys filed a bill in chancery in the Circuit Court of Moultrie County against Sallie F. Sayer, Sinia A. Norfolk and various other defendants, praying for the partition of certain lots in Sullivan in Moultrie County, a quarter section of land in Edgar County, a quarter section of land in Shelby County, and a large amount of other described real estate in Moultrie, Shelby, Edgar and Coles counties, Illinois, in which she alleged she was the owner of a one-fourth interest as sole devisee of her former husband, Xavier B. Trower, who it is alleged died seized of said real estate. Isaac Horn, who had presented a claim against the estate of Xavier B. Trower, which had been allowed, was permitted at the March term, 1910, to intervene, and filed an intervening petition in the nature of a cross-bill containing full allegations of fact and praying for relief.

The record shows the following facts. X. B. Trower died testate December 7, 1896, in Christian County, leaving a widow, Clara E. Trower, now Humphreys, who is the sole beneficiary under his will. The will was probated and the widow qualified as executrix. X. B. Trower prior to 1877 was engaged in running a private bank in Charleston, Illinois, where he failed in business that year. Isaac Horn was one of the depositors in the bank. At the November term, 1891, of the Circuit Court of Christian County, Isaac Horn recovered a judgment against X. B. Trower for $1,048.26. An execution was issued on this judgment within a year after its rendition and delivered to the sheriff of Christian County, where Trower resided. The sheriff being unable to find any property on which to levy said execution returned it unsatisfied. After the issuing of letters testamentary on the estate of X. B. Trower, this judgment being unpaid, was presented as a claim against the estate of the deceased and on December 2, 1907, allowed in the sum of $1,963.98 as a seventh class claim against the estate. The executrix did not file any inventory in the estate of her deceased husband, and does not appear to have taken any steps to close up the estate and has never been discharged as such executrix. The claim of Isaac Horn is still due and unpaid.

X. B. Trower was a son of Thomas B. and Polly A. Trower of Charleston. On August 20, 1877, after the bank failure of X. B. Trower in 1877, Polly A. Trower and X. B. Trower made an agreement in writing, in two parts, each being stated to be the consideration for the other, in reference to the prospective interests of X. B

Trower in the estate of Thomas B. Trower, who was still living. The purport of the first part of this agreement is that X. B. Trower should have a certain described farm in Edgar County, a certain described farm in Shelby County and a bank building in Sullivan in lieu of all other interest in his father's estate. This part of the agreement was signed by Polly A. Trower. The other part of this agreement was signed by X. B. Trower and assigns all his prospective interest in his father's estate to the heirs and executors of said estate.

Thomas B. Trower died testate in April, 1878, in Coles County, Illinois, leaving Polly A. Trower, his widow, and X. B. Trower with three other children surviving him. By his will he devised his estate to his wife, Polly A. Trower, "to have and to hold for the future benefit of herself and children, and which she may dispose of to our children in such just and proper proportions as necessary and due regard to prudence may dictate, as long as she remains unmarried and my widow, but on her decease or marriage I give and devise the remainder of my said estate to my children, viz: Mrs. Lemuel L. Silverton, Xavier B. Trower, Sinia A. Norfolk and Sallie F. Sayer, in equitable proportions, as may be deemed right and proper, taking into account what they have had heretofore, which will appear from a book kept by myself for the purpose of showing that to them and their heirs, to have and to hold the same in fee simple forever." The will appoints Polly A. Trower executrix; it was probated and she qualified.

On August 17, 1895, Polly A. Trower and her three daughters conveyed by warranty deed to William R. Titus for $2,500 twenty-three feet off of the north part of lot two, and all of lot one in block twelve, in the city of Sullivan in Moultrie County.

On April 25, 1897, Polly A. Trower and her three daughters, their husbands joining therein, for a valuable consideration conveyed to Jacob Galster, by warranty deed, the Shelby County farm of which Thomas

B. Trower died seized, and which is described in the contract of August 20, 1877, signed by Polly A. Trower; and on November 13, 1897, the same grantors for a valuable consideration conveyed to George W. Julian the Edgar County farm described in the contract of August 20th.

On February 18, 1903, Polly A. Trower conveyed the said land in Shelby County to Sallie F. Sayer. The deed recited that it is for the consideration of one dollar and "this deed is made to more completely invest Sallie F. Sayer with title to said premises and to inure to the benefit of any grantee to whom she may have conveyed said premises." On July 10, 1905, Sallie F. Sayer executed a deed of the Shelby County land to Jacob Galster in consideration of one dollar. This deed recites that it is made to the grantee to perfect the title to said premises. the mother of said Sallie F. Sayer having made a deed to same premises on the 18th day of February, 1903, by virtue of a power to so convey the same contained in the will of Thomas B. Trower, father of said Sallie F. Sayer. On the same day that Polly A. Trower made the deed of the Shelby County land to Sallie F. Sayer she made a deed of the Edgar County land to Sinia A. Norfolk, which contains a similar recital to that in the deed made by Polly A. Trower to Sallie F. Sayer. On July 10, 1905, Sinia A. Norfolk conveyed by deed to the heirs of George W. Julian the Shelby County land; this deed contains a recital similar to that in the deed made by Sallie F. Sayer to Galster.

The original petition of the intervenor together with an amended petition sets forth the foregoing facts and alleges that the deeds executed by Polly A. Trower in 1903 were not made in good faith for the purpose of conveying the property therein described to the daughters of Thomas B. Trower, but that said conveyances were made to inure to the benefit of grantees of said daughters and are fraudulent and void as against the claim of the intervenor. It is also alleged that Polly A. Trower held the title to said real estate in trust for the children of Thomas B. Trower, one-fourth part thereof for X. B. Trower with no general right to convey the same, but only the right to convey the same to the children of Thomas B. Trower as necessity might require; sets forth the wills of Thomas B. Trower and X. B. Trower and makes all necessary parties, parties defendant to the petition. A supplemental petition further alleges that on July 31, 1911, Clara E. Humphreys compromised and settled the suit for partition in consideration of $4,200 paid to her by Sinia A. Norfolk and Sallie F. Sayer and the release of Clara E. Humphreys from the payment of the costs which had been adjudged against her in former litigation concerning this same real estate, and signed a stipulation for the dismissal of her bill for partition, and executed and delivered the following deeds:

(1) A quitclaim deed conveying for an expressed consideration of $500 to William R. Titus, who was in possession of it, all her interest in the twenty-three feet off of the north side of lot two in block twelve in the city of Sullivan; (2) A quitclaim deed conveying to F. M. Craig, who was in possession of it, all her interest in lot one in block twelve in Sullivan for $500; (3) a quitclaim deed conveying for $500 all her interest in the Edgar County farm to Michael Gossett, who in 1907 had secured deeds from the Julian heirs of all their interest in the Edgar County farm; and (4) a quitclaim deed conveying for $500 all her interest in the Shelby County farm to William Miller, who had bought the interest of Jacob Galster in the said Shelby County farm. It is stipulated that these deeds were made as a part of the settlement of the partition suit. The grantees in these deeds are parties to this suit but have not joined in this appeal.

The record in this cause is very imperfect. The cause would appear to have been referred to a special master before the dismissal of the original bill for partition. After the compromise and dismissal of the or-

iginal bill for partition, and the filing of the supplemental petition by the intervenor and the joining of
issues, the cause was re-referred to the regular master
in chancery, who made a report of evidence with conclusions.   The final decree in the case shows that an
exception by appellants to the conclusions was sustained for the reason that the reference did not authorize the master to report his conclusions. The record
filed here does not contain any order of reference. The
cause was heard by the court, findings were made and
a decree entered on evidence introduced on the trial,
which is contained in the report of the master. A certificate of evidence signed by the trial court states
that the foregoing evidence contained in the report of
the master in chancery was all the evidence introduced
and heard by the court on the trial of the cause. The
certificate of the clerk to the record does not state that
the record contains the certificate of evidence but
states that it contains certain named pleadings, and
the report of evidence made by the master except
certain parts thereof. There is no formal beginning
of a certificate of evidence in the record from which it
can be ascertained where the record proper ends and
the certificate of evidence begins.

On the hearing, the court, after finding the facts,
among others that there was due Isaac Horn on May
11, 1912, the sum of $2,400.14 from the estate of Xavier
B. Trower on the claim allowed in the Probate Court
on December 2, 1907, and that all parties who had received deeds of conveyance of the one-fourth interest
of Xavier B. Trower in the two described quarter sections of land and said property in Sullivan took such
deeds with notice of the claim of Isaac Horn and were
not innocent purchasers of said interest, entered a decree finding said conveyances to be void so far as they
interfered with the collection of the claim of Isaac
Horn, and ordered that the estate of Xavier B. Trower
pay to Isaac Horn the sum of $2,400.14 with legal in-
terest from May 11, 1912, within forty days, and in

default thereof, that the master in chancery sell, first the undivided one-fourth interest in the said described lots in Sullivan, in Moultrie County, to pay said sum and costs, then that he sell the undivided one-fourth interest of the said described quarter section of land in Shelby County, and if the said real estate in Moultrie and Shelby counties does not bring sufficient to pay said claim and costs, then that he sell the said described real estate in Edgar County and bring the money into court to abide the further order of the court. The decree dismisses the intervening petition as to defendants interested in other lands in Coles County. The defendants Sallie F. Sayer and Sinia A. Norfolk appeal.

In 1902 Clara E. Trower, now Humphreys, filed a bill in equity against Polly A. Trower and the purchasers of said real estate described in said deeds to compel a specific performance of the said contract of August 20, 1877, between Polly A. Trower and X. B. Trower. The defendants answered and the Circuit Court on a hearing entered a decree for specific performance. The decree was reversed by the Supreme Court and remanded with directions (*Sayer v. Humphreys*, 216 Ill. 426), that court holding that the contract was void and that under the will of Thomas B. Trower, Polly A. Trower had no right to convey the real estate of which Thomas B. Trower died seized to any person except to his children, and that the fee to the real estate in question vested in the children of Thomas B. Trower subject to be divested by the conveyance thereof by Polly A. Trower to a child or one or more of the children of Thomas B. Trower. The opinion holds that "at the time of the death of X. B. Trower he therefore was seized of the one-fourth part of said Shelby and Edgar county farms, which interest was never divested by conveyance by Polly A. Trower to a child or the children of Thomas B. and Polly A. Trower to Sallie F. Sayer in fee." The name of Isaac Horn does not appear in the opinion in 216 Ill.

Polly A. Trower died in 1904, before the case was disposed of by the Supreme Court. After the reversal of the case it was redocketed in the Circuit Court, and Clara E. Humphreys sought to amend her bill so as to recover as devisee of X. B. Trower deceased, and Horn, who at the same time had been permitted to intervene, sought to amend his cross-bill so as to enforce the collection of his claim. The Circuit Court struck the amended bill and the cross-bill from the files and dismissed both bills for the reason that the cause of action stated in the original bill had been disposed of on the merits by the Supreme Court. From that decree an appeal was again prosecuted to the Supreme Court where the case was affirmed. *Humphreys v. Sayer,* 242 Ill. 80.

The former suit between Mrs. Humphreys and Polly A. Trower and others is not referred to in the pleadings in this case, but the foregoing reference to that litigation is made for the purpose of showing that the Supreme Court has construed the provisions of the will of Thomas B. Trower and the effect of deeds made by Polly A. Trower to third parties, and held void the assignment made by X. B. Trower of his interest in the estate of Thomas B. Trower, and these questions are involved in this case.

It is insisted that the lien of the judgment against X. B. Trower expired in seven years after the date of the judgment, and that a court of equity did not have jurisdiction over the subject-matter of this litigation. While the lien of the judgment would expire in seven years, yet it might be renewed or an action brought on it at any time within twenty years after its date. R. S. c. 83, ¶ 26 (J. & A., ¶ 7221.)

The purpose of the intervening petition is to collect the claim of $1,963.98 allowed against the estate of X. B. Trower in the Probate Court of Christian County on December 2, 1907. Under the will of X. B. Trower, Clara E. Humphreys is the sole beneficiary and took all real estate charged with the payment of his debts.

X. B. Trower died in 1896. He left no personal estate or real estate except his interest in the estate of his father, Thomas B. Trower. His will was probated in September, 1897, and Clara E. Humphreys qualified as executrix. She has neither filed any inventory nor taken any steps to close the estate or to pay this claim from the assets, although fifteen years have elapsed since she qualified as executrix. In December, 1907, the claim of Horn against the estate being called for trial in the Probate Court, by agreement between Horn and the executrix, it was allowed in the sum of $1,- 963.98. The record does not show when the claim was first presented, but no inventory having been filed, the claim allowed was a lien on the entire estate that could be collected in any manner in which the collection of claims allowed against estates may be enforced. It was held in *Humphreys v. Sayer, supra,* that the grantees of Polly A. Trower, other than the children of Thomas B. Trower, were not innocent purchasers of the interest of X. B. Trower in the estate of his father. The record in this case shows that after the intervening petition was filed the appellants paid to the executrix, the beneficiary under the will, $4,200 for conveyanres from her as devisee of X. B. Trower of her interest in the real estate devised to him by his father. It also shows that Clara E. Humphreys, as executrix of X. B. Trower, fraudulently with the aid of appellants attempted to appropriate the estate to her own use and to defeat the collection of this claim by the conveyance of the estate to appellants and by the attempt to deprive the court of jurisdiction of this case by a dismissal of the original bill, and also that Clara E. Humphreys is insolvent.

The claim of the intervenor is not sought to be enforced on the ground that it was a lien because of the ·judgment obtained against Trower in his lifetime, but on the theory that it is a claim allowed against the estate, and all purchasers from heirs and devisees take subject to the payment of claims allowed against an estate. The payment of this claim might have been enforced in the Probate Court, or it may be enforced in a court of equity, if the remedy in the Probate Court was inadequate and there were reasons why a court of equity should take jurisdiction. Fraud is one of the heads of original equity jurisdiction. With very limited exceptions it may be said that courts of equity "possess a general, and perhaps a universal concurrent jurisdiction with courts of law in cases of fraud cognizable in the latter; and exclusive jurisdiction in cases of fraud beyond the reach of courts of law," 1 Story's Eq. Jur. sec. 184. It is very clear that the Probate Court did not have jurisdiction to grant the relief that the nature of this case requires. A bill in chancery will lie to establish a debt of an ancestor and decree it a lien on his real estate and order the debt paid and in default of payment that the real estate be sold to satisfy the debt. *McConnel v. Smith*, 39 Ill. 279. Equity will take jurisdiction of the settlement of an estate to afford relief to a creditor whose claim has been allowed in the County Court, where some satisfactory reason exists why the County Court cannot grant the relief, the facts require that justice and equity may be done. *Elting v. First Nat. Bank of Biggsville*, 173 Ill. 368; *Patterson v. Patterson*, 251 Ill. 153. There was no error in permitting appellee to intervene and in overruling the demurrer and appellant's motion to strike the petition.

Appellants at the September term, 1911, filed a plea to the jurisdiction of the court setting out that they were not residents of Moultrie county and that the suit in which the petition of intervention was filed had been settled. Appellee filed a motion to strike this plea and the same was allowed. Appellants insist this ruling of the court was error. Part of the real estate involved in this suit is in Moultrie County. Under the. Chancery Act (chapter 22, sec. 3, J. & A. ¶ 883) suits in chancery affecting real estate may be maintained in any county where any part of the real estate is situated. It further appears that this plea was only on behalf of some of the defendants and there were other defendants found in the county and the plea does not state the names and residences of the other defendants and that there were no necessary defendants resident in the county. There was no error in the order of the court.

The real estate in Sullivan, in Moultrie County, decreed by the court to be the first sold to pay the claim of the intervenor, was owned by Thomas B. Trower at the time of his death, and under the will of Thomas B. Trower, X. B. Trower became the owner of one-fourth of it subject to be divested by a deed by Polly A. Trower to a child of the deceased. This real estate was never conveyed by Polly A. Trower to any child of Thomas B. Trower, and the trial court finds in its decree that this real estate is not the business property mentioned in the opinion in *Humphreys v. Sayer, supra.*

In construing the will of Thomas B. Trower the Supreme Court held that X. B. Trower died seized of a one-fourth interest in the other real estate decreed by the court in this case to be sold, subject to be divested by a conveyance by Polly A. Trower and to a child or children of Thomas B. Trower. In 1897, Polly A. Trower and her three daughters joined in warranty deeds attempting to convey the Shelby and Edgar county farms to Julian and Galster.

These deeds were void because the authority to execute them was not within the power conferred by the will of Thomas B. Trower. The grantors therein were liable on their warranties. The subsequent conveyances made February 3, 1903, by Polly A. Trower attempting to convey these farms to Sallie F. Sayer and Sinia A. Norfolk inured to the benefit of Julian and Galster even if the latter deeds had not contained such express provisions. The daughters having, in 1907, conveyed these lands by warranty deeds, the reason for the exercise of the power under the will of Thomas

B. Trower ceased to exist and the power also had ceased to exist. *Smyth v. Taylor*, 21 Ill. 296; 2 Sugden on Powers, 178. The deeds made in 1903 were conveyances in the interest of Julian and Galster to perfect the title in them and not deeds made to carry out the powers in the will of Thomas B. Trower. They were fraudulent for the reason they were an attempt to do indirectly what could not be done directly. *Henderson v. Blackburn*, 104 Ill. 227; *Whiton v. Whiton*, 179 Ill. 32; *Griffin v. Griffin*, 141 Ill. 373.

Appellants have neither by any assignment of error nor argument raised any question concerning either title by possession and payment of taxes or the numerical order in which the pieces of real estate should be sold.

The decree is justified by the record and is affirmed.

Affirmed.

John Replogle, Appellee, v. Toledo, St. Louis and Western Railway Company, Appellant.

(Not to be reported in full.)

Appeal from the Circuit Court of Coles county; the Hon. MORTON W. THOMPSON, Judge, presiding. Heard in this court at the April term, 1913. Affirmed. Opinion filed October 16, 1913.

Statement of the Case.

Action by John Replogle against Toledo, St. Louis and Western Railway Company to recover damages for the killing of a horse and a sheep alleged to have been caused by the failure of the defendant to maintain fences and for failure to construct and maintain cattle guards at road crossing. From a judgment in favor of plaintiff for one hundred and eighty-seven dollars; defendant appeals.

A. J. FRYER and C. E. POPE, for appellant; CHARLES A. SCHMETTAU, of counsel.

J. H. MARSHALL, for appellee.

MR. JUSTICE THOMPSON delivered the opinion of the court.

Abstract of the Decision.

1. RAILROADS, § 882*—*when place and manner in which stock was killed questions for jury.* In an action against a railroad for killing a horse alleged to have been caused by failure of defendant to construct and maintain cattle guards at road crossing, whether the horse was struck by defendant's locomotive while it was on defendant's right of way or whether the horse ran against the side of the engine in attempting to cross the track at the road crossing held questions for the jury.

2. SET-OFF AND RECOUPMENT, § 6*—*right of railroad company to set-off in action for negligently killing stock.* Railroad company is not entitled to have a claim for damages to its locomotive resulting from plaintiff's stock running against the side thereof, in an action against the company for negligently killing the stock, and refusal of court to give an instruction allowing defendant such set-off held not error.

3. SET-OFF AND RECOUPMENT, § 9*—*demands which may be set-off.* The nature of demands to which set-off may be pleaded is controlled by statute. Under R. S. c. 110, §§ 33, 47, J. & A. ¶¶ 8570, 8584; set-off is a proper plea in *assumpsit,* but not in an action on the case.

*See Illinois Notes Digest, Vols. XI to XV, same topic and section number.

A. T. Green, Appellee, v. Eunice M. Jennings, Appellant.

1. APPEAL AND ERROR, § 994*—*when refusal of leave to file additional plea not saved for review.* Error of court in refusing leave to file an additional plea not saved for review where there is neither a motion for leave to file such plea in the bill of exceptions nor any order concerning such motion. A record made by the clerk will not save such question for review.

2. APPEAL AND ERROR, § 800*—*what necessary to make motion for leave to file plea a part of the record.* A motion for leave to file an additional plea is no part of the record unless made so by the bill of exceptions.

3. APPEAL AND ERROR, § 1506*—*when exclusion of question asked of witness on direct examination is error.* Where plaintiff on cross-examination testifies that on a certain date when defendant signed and executed the note he loaned to defendant a certain sum of money, *held* that the exclusion of a question asked of defendant on direct examination as to whether plaintiff did advance her money on that date was error.

4. WITNESSES, § 284*—*when exclusion of question on cross-examination is error.* In an action on a promissory note, exclusion of a question asked of plaintiff on cross-examination as to whether he had testified on a former trial that defendant made a certain statement to the plaintiff regarding the note, when the note was delivered to him, *held* error.

5. WITNESSES, § 227*—*when exclusion of question asked on cross-examination is error.* In an action on a promissory note, exclusion of question asked of plaintiff on cross-examination whether he signed defendant's name to her leases and other contracts, *held* error.

6. EVIDENCE, § 452*—*when exclusion of testimony of witness as to genuineness of handwriting is error.* In suit on a promissory note where a witness for defendant testifies that he had seen defendant write, that he was acquainted with her signature and that the signature to the note "isn't her signature as I am used to it," and testifies on cross-examination that he knew defendant's handwriting "sufficient for my own purpose," *held* that the testimony of the witness was competent and material, the weight of which was for the jury, and that the exclusion of all his evidence on motion of plaintiff was reversible error.

7. EVIDENCE, § 453*—*when affidavit filed in suit denying signature may be exhibited to witnesses on cross-examination to test knowledge of signature.* In an action on a promissory note where

certain witnesses for the defendant had on cross-examination testified that they knew the signature of the defendant, permitting plaintiff's counsel to exhibit to the witnesses the affidavit made by defendant filed in the case denying the signature to the notes sued on and asking them if they knew the signature to the affidavit, *held* not error.

8. EVIDENCE, § 453*—*when signature to plea putting execution of note in issue may be exhibited to witness on cross-examination to test his knowledge of handwriting.* Where a witness testifies he is acquainted with defendant's handwriting it is proper on cross-examination for the purpose of testing the accuracy of his memory to show him the signature to the plea putting the execution of the note in issue, there being no question as to its genuineness, and ask him whether it was the signature of the defendant. This is not proving the signature but testing the accuracy of the memory of the witness.

9. EVIDENCE, § 450*—*rule as to comparison of handwriting.* Genuineness or falsity of a handwriting or signature cannot be proved by comparison with other handwriting or signatures admitted to be genuine unless said other handwriting or signatures are in evidence in the case for some other legitimate purpose or at least are among the files of the case as a part of the record. The rule even goes to the extent of permitting the jury to make the comparison.

10. BILLS AND NOTES, § 421*—*evidence admissible to prove execution or nonexecution of note.* On an issue as to the execution of a note, evidence tending to show a reason for its execution and a reasonable probability or improbability that defendant made or delivered the same is not only competent but highly important for the consideration of the jury.

11. BILLS AND NOTES, § 420*—*admissibility of evidence.* In suit on a promissory note, refusal of court to admit in evidence a schedule made by plaintiff to the assessor after the commencement of the suit, *held* proper.

12. BILLS AND NOTES, § 462*—*when instruction inaptly worded and tending to mislead.* In an action on a promissory note, instructions given for plaintiff as to the proof necessary to enable plaintiff to recover, *held* inaptly worded and tending to mislead the jury.

13. BILLS AND NOTES, § 462*—*when requested instruction properly refused.* In action on a promissory note, an instruction for defendant *held* properly refused as requiring plaintiff to prove a consideration.

Appeal from the Circuit Court of McDonough county; the Hon. HARRY M. WAGGONER, Judge, presiding. Heard in this court at the April term, 1913. Reversed and remanded. Opinion filed October 16, 1913.

---

*See Illinois Notes Digest, Vols. XI to XV, same topic and section number.

VOSE & CREEL, for appellant.

FLACK & LAWYER, for appellee.

MR. JUSTICE THOMPSON delivered the opinion of the court.

This is an action in *assumpsit* begun on July 20, 1911, by A. T. Green against Eunice Jennings. The declaration contains three special counts and the common counts. The first count is in the ordinary form on a promissory note and avers that the defendant on July 13, 1908, executed and delivered to plaintiff a promissory note for $294.75. The second count declares on a note dated August 20, 1909, for $800, averred to have been executed and delivered by the defendant to the plaintiff. The third count is for work and services averred to have been rendered by the plaintiff to the defendant. The summons was served on the defendant personally and on Dora Booth, her conservator.

A plea of the general issue was filed by the defendant by her conservator. The conservator also filed an affidavit stating on information and belief that the defendant, Eunice Jennings, did not make the instruments sued on. Two affidavits made by Eunice Jennings were filed, one stating that she did not make and deliver the instruments sued on, the other verifying the plea. There was a trial before a jury at the January term, 1912, in which the jury disagreed.

The May term of the court, 1912, convened on May 13th and on that day adjourned to May 20th. On May 20th the defendant, who at that time appears to have been restored to the charge of her property, by her counsel moved for leave to file a plea of want of consideration, and a plea of *res adjudicata* to the third and fourth counts.

The plaintiff on May 21st dismissed as to the third and common counts, and the court denied leave to file the additional pleas. There was then a second trial before a jury and a failure of the jury to agree. At the September term, 1912, at the third trial, a jury returned a verdict for plaintiff for $1,316.43, on which judgment was rendered and the defendant appeals.

It is assigned for error that the court erred in refusing leave to the defendant to file a plea of want of consideration. There is neither a motion for leave to file such a plea in the bill of exceptions nor any order concerning such a motion. A motion for leave to file an additional plea is no part of the record unless made so by a bill of exceptions. A record made by the clerk will not save for review a ruling denying a motion for leave to file a plea. *St. Louis & O'Fallon Ry. Co. v. Union Trust & Savings Bank,* 209 Ill. 457; *Chicago & Eastern I. R. Co. v. Goyette,* 133 Ill. 21; *People v. Weston,* 236 Ill. 104; *Boys v. Bernhard Milling Co.,* 138 Ill. App. 88. It appears from the record, however, that the May term was the first term at which appellant had control of her case, theretofore being under a conservator. If the question had been properly preserved we would not hesitate to hold that there was an abuse of legal discretion in overruling the motion for leave to file a plea of want of consideration.

It appears from the evidence that the appellant is a maiden lady about seventy years of age and that she was for many years an invalid, who was wheeled about in a chair. The appellee was a merchant in Macomb, who about the time of the date of the notes sued on was the agent of the appellee and attended to her business.

The appellee testified that the appellant executed and delivered the notes to him at their respective dates. At the last trial he testified that the appellant said to him in July, 1908, when the July note was delivered to him, that she wanted him to show it to the board of review to show that she was a borrower and not a money loaner. On cross-examination an objection was made and sustained to a question as to whether he had testified to any such statement on the former trial. The question was a proper question and it was error to sustain the objection for the reason it was proper to show if such was the fact that at a former trial he gave a different version of what was said when the note was executed.

The appellee on cross-examination was also asked if he did not, during the time he was acting as her agent, sign her name to her leases and other contracts. In *Gitchell v. Ryan,* 24 Ill. App. 372 where the issues were the same as in this case, it was held that the sustaining of objections to questions similar to the questions put to appellee was error. Great latitude should be allowed in cross-examination of a party to a suit in a case of this kind.

The appellee also testified on cross-examination, while detailing what occurred at the time he claimed defendant executed the note, that on August 20th he loaned $800 to defendant at the time she signed and delivered the note. The appellant on her direct examination was asked, if on August 20, the plaintiff advanced any money to her; an objection made by plaintiff was sustained to this question. While there was no plea of want of consideration, still the defendant had the right to testify concerning anything that occurred or that certain things did not occur at the time the note was made; she also had the right to testify concerning those things for the reason that they tended to impeach the evidence of the appellee on a material matter that he had testified to as a part of the *res gestae* of making the note. By the evidence of the appellee the receiving of the $800 was a part and parcel of the making of the note by the defendant.

On an issue as to the execution of a note, evidence tending to show a reason for its execution, and a reasonable probability or improbability that the defendant made or delivered the same, is not only competent but highly important for the consideration of the jury. The defendant has the right to make proof of such facts and circumstances as may tend to show the note is not hers and render it improbable that she executed it. *Hunter v. Harris,* 131 Ill. 482.

L. F. Gumbart, assistant cashier of the Union National Bank of Macomb, and engaged in the banking business twenty-six years, testified for the appellant that he knew her, had seen her write and that he was acquainted with her signature, that the signature to the note dated July 13th "isn't her signature as I am used to it." "my judgment is it is not; so far as my judgment leads me it is not." He made the same answer when asked about the note dated August 20th. On the cross-examination he was asked if he knew the handwriting of the defendant, and his answer was "Sufficient for my own purposes." On motion of the plaintiff all the evidence of this witness was excluded. The witness having answered that he had seen her write and knew her signature and that the signatures were not hers, his evidence was competent and material. Its weight was for the jury and the excluding of this evidence was reversible error.

On the cross-examination of certain witnesses for the defendant after they had testified that they knew the signature of the defendant, counsel for plaintiff exhibited to the witnesses the affidavit made by defendant filed in this case denying the signature to the notes sued on, and asked them if they knew the signature to the affidavit. This was in the line of testing the witnesses' knowledge of appellant's signature and there was no error in overruling the objection to these questions.

While the genuineness of the signature may not be proved by comparing it with another signature not in evidence, but admitted to be genuine, yet where a witness testified he was acquainted with defendant's handwriting it is proper on cross-examination for the purpose of testing the accuracy of his memory to show him the signature to the plea putting the execution of the note in issue, about the genuineness of which there was no question, and ask him whether it was the signature of the defendant. This is not proving the signature, but testing the accuracy of his memory. *Melvin v. Hodges,* 71 Ill. 422.

The rule seems to be settled in this State that the genuineness or falsity of a handwriting or signature cannot be proved by comparison with other admittedly genuine handwriting or signatures, unless said other handwriting or signatures are in evidence in the case for some other legitimate purpose or at least are among the files of the case as a part of the record. *Brobston v. Cahill,* 64 Ill. 356; *Melvin v. Hodges, supra; Massey v. Farmers' Nat. Bank,* 104 Ill. 327; *Bevan v. Atlanta Nat. Bank,* 142 Ill. 302; *Riggs v. Powell,* 142 Ill. 453; *Himrod v. Gilman,* 147 Ill. 293. The rule even goes to the extent of permitting the jury to make the comparison. "When, however, other writings or signatures admitted to be genuine are already in the case, comparison may be made by the jury, with or without experts." *Stitzel v. Miller,* 250 Ill. 72; *Greenebaum v. Bornhofen,* 167 Ill. 640; *Bevan v. Atlanta Nat. Bank, supra.*

It is also contended that the court erred in refusing to admit in evidence a schedule made to the assessor in April, 1912. This suit was begun in September, 1911; the making of the schedule was subsequent to the beginning of the suit and to a trial wherein the jury disagreed. In *Green v. Smith,* 180 Ill. App. 572 (opinion filed March, 1913), we held such evidence was competent in behalf of an estate defending as tending to show the plaintiff did not have any such note at the time the schedule was made. Under the facts disclosed by the evidence in the present case, the court properly excluded the schedule, and sustained the objections to the questions asked the assessor.

Appellant contends that the court erred in instructions one and two given for the plaintiff. Instruction one is: "The court instructs the jury that all the plaintiff is required to prove in this case to entitle him to recover the amount of the principal and interest of the promissory note bearing date July 13, '08, for the principal sum of $294.75 and produced in evidence, is that said note was signed by the defendant, Eunice Jennings, and delivered by her to the plaintiff, and if you find from a preponderance of the evidence, that said proof has been made by the plaintiff, then you should find the issues for the plaintiff and assess his damages on said note at the principal sum of said note and the interest due thereon."

The instruction is inaptly worded and might mislead the jury.

In place of stating "if you find from a preponderance of the evidence that said proof has been made," the proposition should have been stated, "if you find from a preponderance of the evidence that said note was signed by the defendant," etc. The appellee did make proof that the note was executed by the defendant, but to find that such proof was made irrespective of the proof to the contrary made by the appellant would not entitle appellee to recover. It was not sufficient to entitle appellee to recover for the jury to find from a preponderance of the evidence that appellee had made proof that appellant executed the note, but the evidence that she executed the note must preponderate over the evidence that she did not execute it. The second instruction was in the same form and concerned the other note.

It is also argued that the court erred in refusing the following instruction: "You are further instructed, that before the plaintiff, A. T. Green, is entitled to recover in this case, the burden is upon him to prove by a preponderance of the evidence, that the defendant, Eunice Jennings, made, executed and delivered to him for a good and valid consideration the note or notes upon which you find he is entitled to recover if you so find he is entitled to recover upon either of said notes."

This instruction was properly refused for the reason that the plaintiff was not required to prove a consideration, even if there had been a plea of want of consideration on file. If a plea of want of consideration was on file the burden of sustaining such a plea would be on the defendant. *Honeyman v. Jarvis*, 64 Ill. 366, Par-

agraph 46, Negotiable Instrument Act (J. & A. ¶ 7667);
6 Am. and Eng. Encyc. of Law, 763.

For the errors indicated the judgment is reversed
and the cause remanded.

Reversed and remanded.

Ada Switzer, Appellee, v. A. A. Honn, Appellant.

(Not to be reported in full.)

Appeal from the Circuit Court of Coles county; the Hon. MORTON
W. THOMPSON, Judge, presiding. Heard in this court at the April
term, 1913. Reversed in part. Opinion filed October 16, 1913.

Statement of the Case.

Bill filed by Ada Switzer against A. A. Honn for
partition of certain lands. From a decree awarding
complainant one hundred and fifty dollars as solicitor's
fees to be taxed as costs, defendant appeals.

An appeal from the decree granting the partition
was taken to the Supreme Court where the decree was
affirmed in *Switzer v. Honn*, 254 Ill. 621.

T. N. COFER, for appellant.

HENLEY & DOUGLAS, for appellee.

MR. JUSTICE THOMPSON delivered the opinion of the
court.

Abstract of the Decision.

1. PARTITION, § 119*—*when bill insufficient to entitle complainant
to solicitor's fees.* In a partition proceeding where the original bill
did not properly set forth the interest of the parties and omitted a
necessary party, and it was only after answer was filed that the
bill properly set forth the interest of all the owners, *held* that it

was necessary for defendant to employ counsel, and a decree award-ing complainant solicitor's fees was reversed.

2. PARTITION, § 119*—*sufficiency of bill to entitle complainant to solicitor's fees.* Solicitor's fees will not be taxed against de-fendants in partition, where the original bill omitted necessary parties making it necessary for defendants to employ counsel to pro-tect their interests. The bill should be so accurate that the parties defendant can safely allow a default to be taken against them.

————————

Charles H. Nelson, Appellee, v. First National Bank of La Harpe, Appellant.

(Not to be reported in full.)

Appeal from the Circuit Court of Hancock county; the Hon. HARRY M. WAGGONER, Judge, presiding. Heard in this court at the April term, 1913. Affirmed. Opinion filed October 16, 1913.

Statement of the Case.

Action by Charles H. Nelson against First National Bank of La Harpe to recover damages for the appro-priation of certain corn on which plaintiff had a land-lord's lien for rent. From a judgment in favor of plaintiff for $826.42, defendant appeals.

C. W. WARNER, D. E. MACK and GEORGE V. HELFRICH, for appellant.

SCOFIELD & CALIFF, for appellee.

MR. JUSTICE THOMPSON delivered the opinion of the court.

Abstract of the Decision.

1. LANDLORD AND TENANT, § 337*—*extent of landlord's lien.* Landlord has a statutory lien upon crops grown or growing upon

350   APPELLATE COURTS OF ILLINOIS.

Nelson v. First National Bank of La Harpe, 184 Ill. App. 349.

the demised premises in any year for the rent that shall accrue during such year, but no specific lien is created or given on any other property of the tenant.

2. LANDLORD AND TENANT, § 343*—*priority of landlord's lien.* The lien of a landlord is superior to that of a subsequent chattel mortgage.

3. LANDLORD AND TENANT, § 352*—*enforcement of landlord's lien as against third persons.* Any person who knowingly by purchase or otherwise deprives a landlord of the opportunity of enforcing his lien is guilty of a tort, and the landlord has a right of action for the damages sustained. Case is the proper remedy to enforce such liability, but it must appear that the property or its proceeds have been disposed of so that the lien cannot be enforced against either.

4. LANDLORD AND TENANT, § 348*—*when evidence sufficient to show wrongful impairment of landlord's lien.* In an action against a bank to recover damages for appropriating certain corn and its proceeds so as to impair plaintiff's lien for rent, acts of the bank in procuring a chattel mortgage on all of tenant's property and in receiving a check from tenant for corn sold knowing of the plaintiff's lien, together with other attending circumstances, *held* sufficient to warrant jury in finding that the bank participated in or authorized the sale of the corn and thereby wrongfully deprived plaintiff of his statutory lien.

5. LANDLORD AND TENANT, § 348*—*admissibility of evidence.* In an action to recover damages for appropriating corn upon which plaintiff had a landlord's lien, a note and chattel mortgage executed by tenant to defendant *held* admissible in evidence.

6. LANDLORD AND TENANT, § 348*—*sufficiency of instructions in suit for impairment of landlord's lien.* In an action by a landlord for the impairment of his lien on tenant's corn, an instruction given for plaintiff stating that it is not required of plaintiff to prove actual fraud or actual fraudulent intent, *held* to correctly state the law, and instructions requested by defendant *held* properly refused.

*See Illinois Notes Digest, Vols. XI to XV, same topic and section number.

Hettie R. Hapenny, Appellee, v. J. T. Huffman and Frank Wilson, Appellants.

1. INTOXICATING LIQUORS, § 251*—*when instruction in words of statute misleading on question of damages.* In an action by a widow under section 9 of Dramshop Act, J & A. ¶ 4609, to recover damages for loss of means of support by death of her husband alleged to have been caused by the sale of intoxicating liquors by the defendants, an instruction given for plaintiff setting out a portion of the statute *held* misleading as permitting plaintiff to recover all damages sustained, there being no instruction given limiting plaintiff's recovery to the loss to her means of support or informing the jury what was the proper measure of damages in the case.

2. INTOXICATING LIQUORS, § 245*—*when verdict for loss of widow's means of support is excessive.* Verdict for five thousand dollars for loss of widow's means of support resulting from death of husband caused by sale of intoxicating liquors, *held* excessive, the evidence showing that the deceased was a tenant farmer, selling some years about twelve hundred dollars of produce from his farm, and when not occupied with farm work doing teaming at three dollars per day for himself and team.

Appeal from the Circuit Court of Mason county; the Hon. GUY R. WILLIAMS, Judge, presiding. Heard in this court at the April term, 1913. Reversed and remanded. Opinion filed October 16, 1913. Rehearing denied November 5, 1913.

THOMAS D. MASTERS, E. P. NISCHWITZ, W. H. NELMS and ALFRED ADAMS, for appellants.

CLARENCE W. HEYL and LYMAN LACEY, JR., for appellee.

MR. JUSTICE THOMPSON delivered the opinion of the court.

This is an action on the case brought by Hettie R. Hapenny against J. T. Huffman and Frank Wilson, partners doing business under the name of Wilson & Huffman, to recover damages for an injury sustained to her means of support in consequence of the death of her husband, Daniel Hapenny.

*See Illinois Notes Digest, Vols. XI to XV, same topic and section number

The first count of the declaration avers that the defendants sold and gave intoxicating liquors to one J. I. Reed, thereby causing the intoxication, in whole or in part, of said Reed, and thereupon the said Reed, while so intoxicated, drove an automobile in which the said Reed and Daniel Hapenny, the husband of plaintiff, were riding in such a careless and dangerous manner as to cause said automobile, while running at a dangerous speed, to turn over, thereby killing said Hapenny.

The third count avers the sale by the defendants to J. I. Reed of intoxicating liquors causing his intoxication, and by reason of said intoxication the said Reed was in such a mental condition as to be unable to appreciate danger from physical causes, and that the said Reed, while in such condition, invited said Daniel Hapenny to ride in an automobile driven by said Reed, and the said Hapenny, while riding in said automobile driven by said Reed while so intoxicated, was killed by the said automobile, being in consequence of such intoxication, operated in such a dangerous manner that it was overturned, etc.

The fifth count avers that defendant sold and gave intoxicating liquors to Daniel Hapenny causing his intoxication, and by reason of such intoxication said Hapenny was unable to perceive danger from physical causes, and while so intoxicated and in consequence of such intoxication the said Hapenny was thrown from said automobile and killed. A jury returned a verdict for plaintiff for five thousand dollars, on which judgment was rendered and the defendants appeal.

The evidence shows that Daniel Hapenny was a farmer, twenty-six years of age, who farmed an eighty-acre farm as a tenant about four miles from San Jose, Mason county, Illinois. The appellee is twenty-seven years of age, and she and Hapenny had been married five years. J. I. Reed, who is a farmer and stock buyer living about one and a half miles from San Jose, started about ten o'clock in the forenoon of October 21, 1911, in an automobile, which he had had about six weeks, with his brother Kenneth Reed and Wm. Lux, from San Jose to Manito, near where Reed was going to look at a farm. When passing the farm of Hapenny, J. I. Reed inquired of Hapenny, if he had any hogs for sale. After some talk Hapenny got into the automobile with Reed and they went to Manito, where they arrived about noon. J. I. Reed there entered the saloon of appellants, he says, for the purpose of telephoning to the country. His companions also entered the saloon, where J. I. Reed bought drinks for the others. Reed testified, as do his companions, that he did not drink any liquor that day. They also testify that Reed, when asked to drink, said he would not touch liquor but that he took cigars and gave as a reason therefor that he was driving the car. There is some evidence, however, tending to show that Reed while in the machine acted like an intoxicated person. It began to rain soon after they got to Manito. In consequence of the rain Reed did not go to visit the farm, but stayed in the saloon of defendants until about one o'clock, when they started home. About four and a half miles from Manito the car was upset killing Hapenny and injuring J. I. Reed. On the way from Manito the car appears to have "zigzagged" more or less across the road, and where the accident happened it turned a complete somersault, alighting on its wheels. The defendants claim that the accident was caused either by the machine skidding on a muddy road and striking a wet place which had been filled with gravel at a place where the beaten track, which the driver of the machine was attempting to follow, crossed from one side of the road to the other, or by both causes combined, and that the steering gear of the machine broke rendering the machine uncontrollable, while on the part of appellee it is insisted that the irregular movements of the car and its overturning were caused by the manner and the speed at which it was run by an intoxicated driver. It is contended on the part of appellants that a clear preponderance of the evidence shows that the parties were not intoxicated, but since the case must be reversed for other reasons and on another trial there may be additional evidence, we will not discuss the weight of the evidence or the merits of the case.

It is insisted that the court erred in giving the following instruction at the request of the appellee: "The Court instructs the jury in this case, that the section of the statutes of the State of Illinois, upon which this suit is founded is in part, as follows, to-wit:

"Every husband, wife, child, parent, guardian, employer or other person, who shall be injured in means of support, in consequence of the intoxication, habitual or otherwise, of any person, shall have a right of action in his or her own name, severally or jointly, against any person or persons who shall, by selling or giving intoxicating liquors, have caused the intoxication in whole or in part, of such person or persons, for all damages sustained, and a married woman shall have the same right to bring suits and to control the same, and the amount recovered, as a feme sole; and all suits for damages under this act may be by any appropriate action in any court of this State having competent jurisdiction."

This instruction pretends to be a copy of the statute. Section 9 of the Dramshop Act (J. & A. ¶ 4609) is as follows: "Every husband, wife, child, parent, guardian, employer or other person, who shall be injured in *person or property*, or means of support, *by any intoxicated person* or in consequence of the intoxication, habitual or otherwise, of any person, shall have a right of action in his or her own name, severally or jointly, against any person or persons who shall, by selling or giving intoxicating liquors, have caused the intoxication, in whole or in part, of such person or persons; *and any person owning, renting, leasing or permitting the occupation of any building or premises, and having knowledge that intoxicating liquors are to be sold therein, or who have leased the same for other purposes, shall knowingly permit therein the sale of*

any intoxicating liquors that have caused, in whole or
in part, the intoxication of any person, shall be liable,
severally or jointly, with the person or persons selling
or giving intoxicating liquors aforesaid for all damages
sustained, and *for exemplary damages;* and a married
woman shall have the same right to bring suits and to
control the same and the amount recovered, as a feme
sole; *and all damages recovered by a minor under this*
act shall be paid either to such minor, or to his or her
parent, guardian or next friend, as the court shall di-
rect and the unlawful sale or giving away, of intoxicat-
ing liquors shall work a forfeiture of all rights of the
lessee or tenant, under any lease or contract of rent
upon the premises where such unlawful sale or giving
away shall take place; and all suits for damages under
this act may be by any appropriate action in any of the
courts of this State having competent jurisdiction."

In *Colesar v. Star Coal Co.* 255 Ill. 532, it was said:
"Generally speaking, when a party, in an instruction
offered, purports to quote verbatim a provision of the
statute he must quote it correctly or the instruction
must be refused." In *Baker & Reddick v. Summers,* 201
Ill. 52, an instruction in the language of the statute,
with the *ad damnum* in the declaration added, was condemned because it made no other reference to the case
and did not require proof of facts creating a liability.
The provisions of section 9 of the Dramshop Act (J.
& A. ¶ 4609) give a wife, who shall be injured
in person or property or means of support by
an intoxicated person, or in consequence of the intoxication of any person, a right of action against any
person, who shall by selling or giving intoxicating
liquors have caused the intoxication, in whole or in
part, of such person or persons for all damages sustained. The appellee did not sustain any damages to
her person or property, but only to her means of support. The words of the statute which are italicized are
omitted from the instruction. The instruction as given
is misleading since it tells the jury that appellee was

entitled to recover all damages sustained, and is not limited to damages sustained to her means of support. The right of action in this character of cases is purely statutory, and a jury was very liable to construe the instruction as giving the right to all damages which the estate of deceased, or the appellee, sustained by his death. All damages might be understood to include the probable increase of his estate, her mental suffering, and the loss of companionship of her husband. The giving of this abstract instruction was reversible error, when the record shows that no instruction was given limiting the damages to the loss to her means of support or informing the jury what was the proper measure of damages in the case.

It is also contended that the damages assessed are excessive. The deceased was a tenant farmer. The evidence shows that he sold some years about twelve hundred dollars worth of produce from his farm and that when not occupied with farm work he occasionally worked at teaming at three dollars per day for himself and team; only his gross income was shown by the evidence. The appellee contributed her services in the work ordinarily done on a farm by a farmer's wife. If her husband was killed in consequence either of his own intoxication or of the intoxication of the driver of the machine and the appellants, by selling and giving intoxicating liquor, materially contributed to such intoxication, and such intoxication was the proximate cause of the death of her husband, then she is entitled to recover whatever damages she has sustained to her means of support. In view of the habits, earnings and income of appellee's husband, the judgment appears to be excessive. For the reasons pointed out the judgment is reversed and the cause remanded.

Reversed and remanded.

Rasar & Johnson, Appellants, v. Harry Spurling, Appellee.

1. BROKERS, § 93*—*when question whether real estate agent was the procuring cause of sale is for jury.* An owner under a written contract gave real estate agents an exclusive agency for the sale of his real estate reserving to himself the right to terminate the agency on sixty days' notice. The owner sold the property to a purchaser through a different agent and the former agents claimed they had procured such purchaser through their sub-agent. *Held,* in an action against the owner by the former agents to recover commissions on the sale that it appeared from the correspondence between the parties that the exclusive agency had terminated and that it was a question for the jury to determine from the conflicting evidence whether the plaintiffs were the procuring cause of the sale.

2. BROKERS, § 97*—*when instruction as to what agent is required to prove to be entitled to commissions not objectionable on review.* In an action to recover commissions for selling real estate, an instruction given for defendant which states a correct proposition of law as to what plaintiff is required to prove to be entitled to recover, *held* not objectionable for failure to include a statement that if the parties were brought together by the plaintiffs and the sale was consummated on the terms proposed by the purchaser the plaintiff would be entitled to recover, where such statement was given in plaintiffs' instructions.

3. WITNESSES, § 299*—*when opinion of witness as to general reputation for truth and veracity admissible.* Testimony of a witness that the general reputation of a party for truth and veracity among his associates in the neighborhood where he resides is not good, *held* properly admissible, though such witness states on cross-examination that his opinion was based in part on what a certain person had said three or four years before.

4. APPEAL AND ERROR, § 1560*—*when refusal of requested instructions not error.* Appellant cannot complain of error in refusing his requested instructions where the jury was fully instructed in the instructions given at his request on every legal proposition in the cause.

5. APPEAL AND ERROR, § 1186*—*objections presented for review.* Appellate Court should only review the specific objections to instructions presented and argued.

6. APPEAL AND ERROR, § 1539*—*when giving an instruction stating an abstract proposition of law harmless.* In an action to recover commissions for selling real estate, the giving of an instruc-

tion which might have been refused because it states an abstract proposition of law, *held* harmless.

Appeal from the Circuit Court of Christian county; the Hon. ALBERT M. ROSE, Judge, presiding. Heard in this court at the April term, 1913. Affirmed. Opinion filed October 16, 1913.

GEORGE T. WALLACE, for appellants.

R. C. NEFF and E. E. ADAMS, for appellee.

MR. JUSTICE THOMPSON delivered the opinion of the court.

This is a suit brought by Rasar & Johnson to recover commissions from Harry Spurling for the sale of real estate in Taylorville belonging to the defendant. There have been two trials in the Circuit Court. On the first trial a verdict was returned for the defendant and judgment rendered thereon. That judgment was reversed by this court for error in instructions, October 15, 1912. [176 Ill. App. 349.] On a second trial in the Circuit Court, a verdict was returned for the defendant on which judgment was rendered and the plaintiffs again appeal.

The evidence shows that on September 29, 1909, the appellee entered into a contract in writing giving appellants the exclusive right to sell said real estate for five thousand dollars, with a confidential price of four thousand five hundred dollars. The owner reserved the right to take the real estate off the market at any time by giving the agents sixty days' notice in writing of such withdrawal.

Appellee testified that while he was in Ohio, early in February, 1910, he wrote a letter to appellants taking the property out of the market. Appellants wrote a letter February 14, 1910, in reply to a letter from appellee stating that they had a few prospects of closing up a sale, naming a Mrs. Fish and several other prospective purchasers, but not mentioning the party who did subsequently purchase in October, and stating if those on whom they had worked should decide to purchase in the near future "we would naturally be interested and feel sure you will be fair" and if we can serve you in the future we will be happy to do so. The appellants testified that they did not receive any letter from appellee withdrawing the real estate from the market. Appellee testified to the mailing of the letter and its contents, and the letter of appellants written February 14 would appear to show that they did receive a letter withdrawing the property from the market. Appellee also testified that in May, 1910, he called upon appellant Johnson and asked for the return of the contract, and that Johnson stated that they never surrendered a contract but would give him a duplicate. In June, 1910, after some oral communications between the parties, appellee wrote to appellants fixing the price at three thousand six hundred dollars and on July 6, 1910, appellee having made certain improvements, wrote that he wanted three thousand seven hundred and fifty dollars, but would give them until July 15, to sell at three thousand six hundred dollars. In September, Luther Chestnut took G. W. Micenheimer to see the property but did not disclose the fact, if it be the fact, that he was an agent for appellants. Chestnut testified that he told Micenheimer that he was not a real estate agent, that he had no interest in the sale of the property but that he showed it to him as a friend, Micenheimer, who was a retired farmer, having inquired of him as a friend, if he knew of suitable property to buy. After the letters of February 8 and July 6, 1910, appellee authorized Teaney, another real estate agent, to sell the property. He showed Micenheimer the property, tried to sell it to him and closed a sale on October 12, for three thousand five hundred dollars. Neither of appellants ever communicated with the purchaser, but their claim is that Chestnut was their subagent. The exclusive agency under the written contract, from the correspondence between the parties, would appear to have

been terminated. It was a question of fact for the
jury to determine from the conflicting evidence whether the appellants were the procuring and efficient
cause of the sale.

It is assigned for error that the court admitted improper testimony tending to impeach the reputation of
appellant Johnson for truth and veracity. Among
the witnesses examined on that question, E. U. Val-
lintine testified that he had lived in Taylorville twelve
years; that he had known Johnson thirty years; that
he knew his general reputation for truth and veracity
among his associates in the neighborhood where he
resides and that it was not good. On cross-examination he stated that he had heard one Thornton, three
or four years ago, say Johnson's reputation was bad
and it was partly on his statement that the witness
based his opinion. The appellants then objected to
the testimony of the witness and the court ruled that
the evidence was proper and the weight to be given
to it was for the jury. The evidence of the witness is
within the rule laid down by the authorities in this
State and there was no error in the ruling of the court.
Gifford v. People, 148 Ill. 173.

It is contended that the first instruction given for
the defendant is erroneous in that it told the jury that
"before plaintiff would be entitled to recover in this
case, they must show by a preponderance of the evidence that they, by the means by them employed, were
the procuring and efficient cause of the sale having been
made and unless they have done so you should find
the issues in favor of the defendant." The contention of appellants is that the instruction should have
included the statement that if the parties were brought
together by the acts of appellants and the sale consummated on terms proposed by the purchaser, then
under such circumstances the appellants would be entitled to recover. This statement of the law was given
in several of appellants' instructions and does not
change the accuracy of the instruction given for ap-

pellee. The instruction states a correct proposition of law as applied to such cases. *White v. Sellmyer*, 157 Ill. App. 435; *Rigdon v. Strong*, 128 Ill. App. 451; *McGuire v. Carlson*, 61 Ill. App. 295.

Appellants make the same objection to the second and fifth instructions given for appellee that they make to the first. That objection we have held to be not well taken. There is no error in the instructions in any particular pointed out, and while there may be other technical objections to some of them, yet, since appellants have not pointed out or raised such other objections, it is not probable that the jury were improperly influenced by them. An Appellate Court should only review the specific objections presented and argued. *Mather Electric Co. v. Matthews*, 47 Ill. App. 557.

The third instruction for appellee states "that where a purchaser of real estate makes an agreement with the owner to take the property on terms agreed upon between the purchaser and seller that this constitutes a contract of sale and it is immaterial in the absence of any failure of either party to carry out this agreement whether the contract is reduced to writing or not." This might properly have been refused because it was an abstract proposition of law. It however stated a correct proposition of law so far as the right to recover commissions is concerned and could not harm the appellants.

The fourth instruction given for appellee is objected to on the ground that "it helped emphasize the errors heretofore pointed out relative to the testimony of the impeaching witnesses." There was no error in the impeaching evidence and the objection to the instruction also must fail.

The appellants also argue that there was error in refusing instructions asked by them. The jury were fully instructed in the ten instructions given at appellants' request on every legal proposition in the case and some of the instructions given for them should have been refused. The eighth given is simply an argument on what makes reputation.

There is no error in any of the questions presented for review. In view of the conflicting evidence, the questions of fact were peculiarly within the province of a jury to determine. A court of review is only authorized to set aside a judgment as being against the evidence, when it can be said that the verdict and judgment are manifestly against the weight of the evidence. The judgment is affirmed.

Affirmed.

William P. Miller, Administrator, Appellee, v. Henley Eversole, Appellant.

1. AUTOMOBILES AND GARAGES, § 3*—*when instruction as to degree of care in driving automobile erroneous.* An instruction stating that the driver of an automobile is required to exercise a higher degree of care at a place in a street where school children are congregated at certain hours in the day than at a point where pedestrians are fewer and the travel limited, *held* erroneous and misleading as requiring defendant to exercise more than ordinary care.

2. EVIDENCE, § 78*—*res gestae.* In an action for injuries sustained by a boy being struck by an automobile while running after a wagon which was drawn by another automobile, testimony of the driver of the latter automobile that the boy with others was running by the side of his machine and trying to get on the running board and that he forbid them to get on his machine, *held* admissible as being immediately prior to the accident and so connected with it that it was a part of the occurrence.

3. EVIDENCE, § 436*—*when form of questions asked of expert witness objectionable.* In an action for injuries caused by being struck by defendant's automobile, a question was asked of witnesses who were operators of automobiles as to the distance in which an automobile similar to that of defendant's could be stopped. *Held,* that an objection was properly sustained to the question for the reason that the question should have described the machine so that the jury would know on what facts the answer was based.

4. INSTRUCTIONS, § 81*—*when instruction misleading as emphasizing portions of the evidence.* An instruction directing a verdict, which calls attention to certain portions of the evidence and thereby emphasizing the same, *held* misleading.

5. APPEAL AND ERROR, § 1560*—*when refusal of requested instruction not error.* In an action by an administrator to recover damages for the death of his intestate, where objection was sustained to defendant testifying to anything that occurred before the death of deceased by reason of his incompetency on account of the suit being prosecuted by an administrator, refusal to give defendant's requested instruction telling the jury that defendant was incompetent to testify to the facts out of which the case arose, *held* not error where part of the instruction was given in another instruction, and the instruction omitted the words "alone" or "of itself."

6. MUNICIPAL CORPORATIONS, § 824*—*when ordinance void as unreasonable.* An ordinance making it a misdemeanor for a person to climb, cling or in anyway attach himself to a wagon or other vehicle either stationery or in motion, without the consent of the owner, *held* void for unreasonableness.

Appeal from the Circuit Court of Douglas county; the Hon. SOLON PHILBRICK, Judge, presiding. Heard in this court at the April term, 1913. Reversed and remanded. Opinion filed October 16, 1913. Rehearing denied December 3, 1913.

FRANK T. O'HAIR, W. W. REEVES and JAMES W. and EDWARD C. CRAIG, for appellant.

GUY R. JONES, P. M. MOORE and H. I. GREEN, for appellee.

MR. JUSTICE THOMPSON delivered the opinion of the court.

This is an action in case brought by William P. Miller, administrator of the estate of Leon Hance, deceased, against Henley Eversole to recover damages for the death of plaintiff's intestate, averred to have been caused by the negligence of the defendant in running an automobile on King street in the village of Newman. A jury returned a verdict for two thousand five hundred dollars against the defendant upon which judgment was rendered. The defendant prosecutes this appeal.

*See Illinois Notes Digest, Vols. XI to XV, same topic and section number

The declaration contains five counts. The first three are common law counts. The fourth count avers the negligent running of the automobile at a rate of speed contrary to the statute and that the deceased was in the exercise of ordinary care; the fifth count avers a failure of appellant to give the reasonable warning required by the statute but fails to aver due care on the part of the deceased.

Leon Hance was a boy nearly fourteen years of age attending the Newman township high school. Gillogly street runs east and west through Newman. It is intersected by King street, which runs north and south. The township high school is located at the northwest corner of the intersection of these streets. King street is paved with brick twenty feet wide. On May 18, 1911, the date of the accident by which Hance received the injuries causing his death, appellant about 4 o'clock in the afternoon, just as school was dismissed, was driving an automobile south on the east side of King street through the village of Newman, a short distance behind one J. W. Roller, who was driving an automobile to which was attached an empty gravel wagon. This wagon had iron wheels with a box, the bed of which was made of loose two by fours and the sideboards were loose, the ends being set between cleats. There is evidence that the automobile of appellant was going at a rate of from ten to fifteen miles an hour and also evidence that it was only going at from four to five miles an hour. As the automobile driven by Roller passed the schoolhouse, or crossed Gillogly street, Hance with other boys ran out into the street towards the automobile and wagon. Three of them got on the wagon. Hance appears not to have been able to get on the wagon although he got hold of the end of the box, ran after it a short distance, and then let go of the box. The evidence is conflicting as to whether, after letting go of the wagon, he went to the east curb of the street and then started back southwesterly across the street, either towards the wagon trying to catch it, or towards the opposite side of the street or simply followed the wagon. The automobile driven by appellant struck Hance, knocked him down, and was stopped with the right front wheel of the machine against the boy's head, which was badly bruised. The boy's feet were a short distance in front of the left front wheel. The boy was taken to a hospital and the bruise on the head cleansed and treated but he died a few days thereafter from lockjaw.

Appellant offered in evidence an ordinance of the village of Newman providing that: "Any person or minor who shall climb, jump, step, stand upon, cling to, or in any way attach himself to any automobile, carriage, wagon, cart, buggy, sleigh, sled or other vehicle either stationery or in motion without the consent of the owner or person in charge thereof, shall be fined not less than one or more than ten Dollars." Appellant insists that the deceased violated this ordinance and was thereby guilty of contributory negligence. The court sustained an objection to this ordinance on the ground that it was void for unreasonableness. The authority for the passage of this ordinance, if there is any, is in the police powers conferred upon municipal authorities of a city or village to enact reasonable police regulations. The violation of the ordinance, by its terms, is not made to depend upon the degree of safety with which persons might attach themselves to any conveyance but to depend upon securing the consent of the owner or person in charge thereof. A person placing his hand upon a wagon standing in the street without any motive power attached would be guilty of a misdemeanor under this ordinance, if he had not first obtained the owner's consent. "The question of reasonableness or of necessity is not made an element, impliedly or otherwise, in this ordinance, and the citizen, in the exercise of his lawful rights, is subjected to fine and imprisonment for an act innocent in itself, but which was not done, and because it was not done, with the express permission of another individual." *Wice v. Chicago & N. W. Ry. Co.*, 193 Ill. 351. The court properly sustained the objection to the ordinance.

It is also insisted that the court erred in sustaining an objection to questions put to witnesses who were operators of automobiles as to the distance in which an automobile similar to that of appellant could be stopped. The objection was made that that was not a question for expert testimony. The Court sustained the objection and said to counsel "it isn't a question of his machine." The question should have described the machine so that the jury would know on what facts the answer was based. The objection was properly sustained because of the form of the question.

The owner of the automobile testified that when the other boys with the deceased were running by the side of his automobile and trying to get on the running board he forbid them to get on his machine. If the deceased was one of the boys who tried to get on the automobile drawing the wagon and then tried to get on the wagon, we do not see why this evidence was not proper. It was immediately prior to the accident and so connected with it that it was a part of the occurrence.

The third instruction given at the request of appellee is as follows: "The Court further instructs the jury, that the driver of an automobile, in and upon a public street, is bound, at all times, to exercise ordinary care and caution for the safety of any and all persons who may be upon said street and the degree of such care and caution required to be exercised by such driver depends upon the circumstances surrounding said driver at any given point in such street, and if the jury believe from the preponderance of the evidence, that the point at which the injury complained of, alleged in plaintiff's declaration and every count thereof as occurring to plaintiff's intestate, was in front of a public high school building in the city of

Newman, Douglas county, Illinois, where the pupils and children were liable and wont to be, and that the defendant had knowledge of the location of said building and the fact that the children congregated there at certain hours of the day, then said defendant would be required to use a higher and greater degree of care at such point, than at a point in the public street where the pedestrians were fewer and the travel limited, in order to prevent inflicting any injury to any such persons, that might be in such street at said point.''

This instruction is erroneous and misleading in telling the jury that the appellant was required to use a higher degree of care at one place than another. Appellant was not required to use a higher degree of care at one place than another, but he was only required to use ordinary care wherever he might be. While it is a correct proposition that what might be ordinary care where there were no children or persons crossing a street would not be ordinary care and might be negligence where there were children and a crowded street, yet ordinary care is all he was required to use, and ordinary care is such care as an ordinary reasonable and prudent person would use under all the circumstances and conditions existing at the time and place and which are or ought to be known to the party.

The sixth instruction given for appellant is misleading and directs a verdict. It calls attention to portions of the evidence thereby emphasizing the same, and then tells the jury that, if they believe that the deceased was then and there in the exercise of ordinary care for his own safety and was suddenly placed in a perilous position and was struck by said automobile as set forth in the declaration, and if the jury further believe from the evidence that by the exercise of ordinary care appellant *might* have discovered the position of peril the deceased was in, and could thereafter have prevented injuring the deceased by exercising due care in driving his automobile, then they should find the defendant guilty. If the appellant by the exercise of due

care would have discovered the peril of the deceased
and would in the exercise of due care have avoided it,
then appellant would be liable if the deceased had been
in the exercise of due care, but if there was only a bare
possibility of appellant in the exercise of due care having discovered the peril of the deceased and avoiding
injuring him, still he would not be liable if in the exercise of due care he failed to discover the peril of the
deceased and to avoid injuring him.

The appellant was offered as a witness in his own behalf. An objection to his testifying to anything that
occurred before the death of Hance was sustained on
the ground of his incompetence because of the suit being prosecuted by an administrator. An instruction
was requested telling the jury that defendant was not
competent to testify to the facts out of which the case
arose and that the jury had no right to indulge in any
presumption against him on account of his not testifying to the transaction or on account of the deceased
having been struck by an automobile of appellant. The
instruction was refused. The first proposition of law
in the instruction is a correct one and would have been
given if asked alone, but the last part of the instruction
was given in another instruction and it was not necessary to duplicate it, and as requested in this instruction it was technically erroneous in omitting the words
"alone" or "of itself."

To review the thirty-five errors assigned by counsel
would unnecessarily and uselessly prolong this opinion.
We have disposed of the important questions raised.
Since the case must be reversed and remanded for a
new trial for the errors indicated, we express no opinion on the merits of the case. The judgment is reversed and the cause remanded.

Reversed and remanded.

MR. JUSTICE PHILBRICK took no part in the consideration of this case.

THIRD DISTRICT—OCTOBER, 1913.   369

Minks v. The B. & O. Southwestern R. Co., 184 Ill. App. 369.

Joseph J. Minks, Appellee, v. The Baltimore and Ohio Southwestern Railroad Company, Appellant.

(Not to be reported in full.)

Appeal from the Circuit Court of Christian county; the Hon. THOMAS M. JETT, Judge, presiding. Heard in this court at the April term, 1913. Affirmed. Opinion filed October 16, 1913.

Statement of the Case.

Action by Joseph J. Minks against The Baltimore and Ohio Southwestern Railroad Company to recover a penalty for discrimination by the defendant in freight rate charged for three cars of corn shipped by plaintiff from Millersville to Chicago, and to recover for the expense of furnishing six inside car doors. From a judgment in favor of plaintiff for $194.40, defendant appeals.

GRAHAM & GRAHAM and HOGAN & WALLACE, for appellant; EDWARD BARTON, of counsel.

W. B. McBRIDE and TAYLOR & TAYLOR, for appellee.

MR. JUSTICE THOMPSON delivered the opinion of the court.

Abstract of the Decision.

1. CARRIERS, § 218*—*when railroad guilty of discrimination in freight charges.* In an action against a railroad company to recover a penalty under R. S. c. 114, ¶¶ 125, et seq., J. & A. ¶¶ 8910 et seq., for discrimination by the company in freight rate charges on three cars of corn shipped by plaintiff from Millersville to Chicago, the rate charged being eleven and three-tenths cents per hundred-weight, a finding in favor of plaintiff *held* sustained by the evidence, there being evidence that plaintiff before and after the shipment involved shipped corn at the rate of eight cents per hundred, that a person a year before shipped wheat from a station three miles farther from Chicago at the same rate, that the company charged the same rate

for wheat and corn, and that the rates had not been changed for five years.

2. JUDGMENT, § 296*—*jurisdiction to vacate judgment after appeal bond filed and approved.* Where a judgment had been rendered for plaintiff in an action against a railroad company for a penalty for discrimination in freight rates, *held* that the trial court after an appeal bond had been filed and approved had jurisdiction during the term to vacate the judgment and order for the appeal for the purpose of granting plaintiff's leave to make proof of the value of attorney's fees, where such matter was overlooked when the judgment was rendered.

3. JUDGMENTS, § 296*—*effect of order vacating judgment after appeal bond has been filed and approved.* An order of court during the term vacating a judgment and order for an appeal after an appeal bond has been filed and approved for the purpose of permitting plaintiff to make proof of the value of attorney's fees so as to be taxed as costs, terminates the appeal unless a new appeal bond is filed within the time limited by the court.

———————

Village of Kilbourne, Appellee, v. Edwin Blakely and William Stroh, Appellants.

1. MUNICIPAL CORPORATIONS, § 41*—*limitation of powers.* Municipal corporations are creatures of statute and can exercise only such powers as are expressly conferred or such as arise by implication from general powers granted.

2. MUNICIPAL CORPORATIONS, § 87*—*when ordinance is unreasonable and void because discriminatory.* An ordinance which discriminates between persons of the same class and imposes a penalty for an act done by one person and exempts another who does a like act is unreasonable and void.

3. MUNICIPAL CORPORATIONS, § 1782*—*when village ordinance exempting from poll tax persons other than those authorized by statute is void for illegal discrimination.* A village ordinance requiring every able-bodied male inhabitant of the village above the age of twenty-one years and under the age of fifty years to labor on the streets and alleys is invalid because of its impartiality and illegal discrimination where it exempts officers and attorneys of the village in addition to those inhabitants authorized by statute to be exempted.

Appeal from the County Court of Macon county; the Hon. JAMES A. McCOMAS, Judge, presiding. Heard in this court at the April term, 1913. Reversed. Opinion filed October 16, 1913.

NORTRUP & NORTRUP and THOMAS P. REEP, for appellants.

EDMUND P. NISCHWITZ, for appellee.

MR. JUSTICE THOMPSON delivered the opinion of the court.

This is an action brought by the Village of Kilbourne against Edwin Blakely, William Stroh and C. E. Daniel before a justice of the peace to recover from each of them a penalty, provided by an ordinance of the Village, for failure to work a poll tax on the streets or commute the same by the payment of money. An appeal was taken from the judgment before the justice to the County Court, where on a trial, a jury returned a verdict finding the defendants guilty and fixing their fine at ten dollars each. Judgment was rendered on the verdict against the defendants and Blakely and Stroh appeal.

The ordinance under which this suit is brought is entitled "Poll tax" and is as follows:

Section 1. That every able-bodied male inhabitant of the Village of Kilbourne, above the age of twenty-one (21) years, and under the age of fifty (50) years, excepting paupers, idiots, lunatics and such other as are exempt by law, shall labor on the streets, alleys, or other public places of said Village as directed by the Street Commissioner, two days in each year as hereinafter provided. Provided, That any person required to labor as aforesaid, may commute such labor by paying to the Village Clerk on or before the last day of July, in each and every year, the sum of seventy-five cents for each day he may be so required to labor.

Section 2. At the regular meting to be held on the first Tuesday in June of each year, the President and

Board of Trustees of said Village shall make out a list of the able-bodied male inhabitants of said Village between the ages of twenty-one and fifty years, and within five days thereafter deliver the same to the Village Clerk. Provided, That paupers, idiots and lunatics, ministers of the Gospel in actual charge of church or congregation, trustees of schools, school directors, members of the Board of Education and other school officers performing like duties, and the officers and attorneys of said Village, shall not be required to work as aforesaid. The Village Clerk shall, within ten days after such list is delivered to him, cause a written or printed or partly written and partly printed notice to be posted or put upon the door of the room or place that the Board of Trustees used at their last meeting, and in three other of the most public places in said Village, notifying all persons subject to labor as aforesaid, to report to the Street Commissioner of said Village for the purpose of performing such labor on or before the last day in the month of July, of each and every year. Any persons required to labor as aforesaid who shall fail, neglect or refuse to perform such labor or commute the same at seventy-five cents per day before the last day in the month of July in each and every year as hereinbefore provided, shall be subject to a penalty of not to exceed twenty dollars, and not less than three dollars.

The appellants contend among other things that the ordinance is void because of unlawful discrimination.

Paragraph 289 of chapter 24 of the Statute (J. & A. ¶ 1782) provides: "That the city counsel in all cities and the president and board of trustees in all villages in this State, may have power, by ordinance, to require every able-bodied male inhabitant of any such city or village, above the age of twenty-one years, and under the age of fifty years (excepting paupers, idiots, lunatics, and such others as are exempt by law), to labor on the streets and alleys of any such city or village, not more than two (2) days in each year; but such ordinance shall provide for commutation of such labor at seventy-five cents per day."

The only other exemptions from poll tax in the Statute, in addition to those in the section quoted, are found in paragraph 186 of chapter 121, title "Roads and Bridges" (J. & A. ¶ 9819), and in section 266 of chapter 122, title "Schools" (J. & A. ¶ 10304.) Paragraph 186 of chapter 121 provides that "ministers of the Gospel in actual charge of a church or parish, trustees of schools, school directors and other school officers performing like duties shall not be compelled to pay a poll tax." The exemption in the school law does not add anything to the foregoing.

The ordinance in question exempts "the officers and attorneys of said village" in addition to those authorized by statute to be exempted from the payment of a poll tax. The penalty sued for is provided for by the second section of the ordinance and that is the section that contains the exemption of the village officers and attorneys. Municipal corporations are creatures of the statute and can exercise only such powers as are expressly conferred or such as arise by implication from general powers conferred. *City of Champaign v. Harmon*, 98 Ill. 494; *Zanone v. Mound City*, 103 Ill. 552. Acts of a city council not fairly within the power conferred are void. *Agnew v. Brall*, 124 Ill. 316; *Wahl v. City of Nauvoo*, 64 Ill. App. 17. All by-laws should be general in their operation and should bear equally upon all the inhabitants of the municipality. *City of Chicago v. Rumpff*, 45 Ill. 97; *Zanone v. Mound City, supra.* An ordinance which discriminates between persons of the same class and imposes a penalty for an act done by one person and exempts another who does a like act is unreasonable and void. *City of Carrollton v. Bazzette*, 159 Ill. 284; *Tugman v. City of Chicago*, 78 Ill. 405; *City of Peoria v. Gugenheim*, 61 Ill. App. 374. The powers vested in municipal corporations should, as far as practicable, be exercised by ordinances general in their nature and impartial in their operation. Dillon on Mun. Corp. 322. If different sections of a statute are independent of each other, that which is unconstitutional may be disregarded and valid sections may stand and be enforced. But if an obnoxious section is of such import that the other sections without it would cause results not contemplated or desired by the Legislature, then the entire statute must be held inoperative. *Mathews v. People*, 202 Ill. 389; *City of Chicago v. Burke*, 226 Ill. 203.

The attempt by the members of the village board which had power to pass an ordinance requiring a poll tax from all able-bodied male inhabitants between twenty-one and fifty years of age, except such as are exempt by statute, to include themselves with the other officers and attorneys of the village in the exemption with the other exempted classes, renders the second section of the ordinance invalid because of its partiality and illegal discrimination. They might as well have exempted all residents of some particular ward or persons living on one side of some particular street. The second section of the ordinance is void and the penalty assessed under it cannot be sustained.

It is unnecessary to discuss the other questions argued. The judgment is reversed because of the invalidity of the second section of the ordinance.

Reversed.

Frank S. Nash, Appellee, v. William J. Eddy et al., Appellants.

(Not to be reported in full.)

Appeal from the Circuit Court of Shelby county; the Hon. JAMES C. MCBRIDE, Judge, presiding. Heard in this court at the April term, 1913. Affirmed. Opinion filed October 16, 1913. Rehearing denied November 6, 1913.

Statement of the Case.

Action by Frank S. Nash against William J. Eddy and others to recover insurance on an imported Belgium stallion. The policy was issued to plaintiff by one Frank B. Stairwalt, sole owner of an unincorporated insurance business which was run under the name of the Kaskaskia Live Stock Insurance, and subsequent to the issuance of the policy Stairwalt sold his insurance business to the defendants under a contract whereby defendants insured and agreed to pay all legal claims against said insurance business. From a judgment in favor of plaintiffs for one thousand dollars defendants appeal.

CHAFEE & CHEW, for appellants.

W. C. and T. M. HEADEN, for appellee.

MR. JUSTICE THOMPSON delivered the opinion of the court.

Abstract of the Decision.

1. INSURANCE, § 663*—*when evidence insufficient to prove plaintiff made material misrepresentations as to health of horse or that he failed to properly care for it.* In an action to recover insurance on a horse dying from lockjaw, defendants' evidence *held* insufficient

*See Illinois Notes Digest, Vols. XI to XV, same topic and section number.

to prove either that plaintiff made material misrepresentations as to the health of the horse or that plaintiff failed to properly care for the horse after symptoms of the disease appeared, it appearing that the agent of the insurer wrote the answers in the application after being informed by the plaintiff that the horse had been treated for summer sores and paraphomosis, that about two weeks before its death its hind foot had been injured and that plaintiff called a veterinarian within an hour after knowledge that horse would not eat.

2. INSURANCE, § 208*—*warranties and representations distinguished.* In insurance contracts a representation is a statement relating to a material matter and is only required to be substantially true, while a warranty must be literally true. Warranties enter into and are a part of the contract, while representations are mere inducements to it.

3. INSURANCE, § 209*—*when statements in an application for insurance will be construed representations rather than warranties.* Statements in an application for insurance will be construed as warranties only when the language is so clearly and unequivocally expressed as to leave the court no other alternative. If the language is ambiguous and doubtful, or if there is another reasonable construction that may be placed upon it, and thus avoid the consequence of a warranty, courts are inclined to adopt the latter construction.

4. INSURANCE, § 209*—*when answers in application construed as representations.* Answers to questions in an application will be construed representations instead of warranties where the application states, "I have read the foregoing application and fully understand the same, and have answered all the foregoing questions and warrant the truth of such answers, and it is fully understood that should this application be accepted and policy issued, that it is done solely upon representations herein named."

5. SET-OFF AND RECOUPMENT, § 29*—*necessity of plea of set-off.* In an action to recover insurance on a horse, insurer *held* not entitled to set-off plaintiff's indebtedness on a promissory note given to it for an unpaid premium, where no plea of set-off was filed.

*See Illinois Notes Digest, Vols. XI to XV, same topic and section number.

George Bacon, Plaintiff in Error, v. Edmund A. Walsh, Defendant in Error.

1. PHYSICIANS AND SURGEONS, § 21*—*admissibility of evidence.* In an action against a physician and surgeon to recover damages for malpractice, on account of failure of defendant to properly reduce a dislocated hip for plaintiff, refusal of trial court to permit plaintiff to show that an X-ray photograph was taken of the joint and that he made unsuccessful efforts to get the X-ray plates, *held* not error, it appearing defendant had nothing to do with the taking of the photographs and never had possession of them.

2. PHYSICIANS AND SURGEONS, § 23*—*when instructions for defendant in action for malpractice erroneous and misleading.* In an action to recover damages for malpractice, an instruction given for defendant defining ordinary care and skill required of physicians and surgeons as being "that care and skill exercised by physicians and surgeons in this locality and of the school of which defendant belongs," *held* erroneous and misleading because of the insertion of the words "and of the school of which defendant belongs" and also erroneous because there was no evidence as to what school the defendant belongs, except that he was a graduate of a certain school.

3. PHYSICIANS AND SURGEONS, § 1162*—*degree of professional skill and care required.* The law requires that a physician and surgeon use that degree of professional knowledge, skill and care which the average physician and surgeon in good practice would ordinarily bring to a similar case under like circumstances in that locality.

4. PHYSICIANS AND SURGEONS, § 23*—*when instruction erroneous.* An instruction in an action for malpractice, particularly directing the attention of the jury to the testimony introduced and then proceeding with an argument, *held* erroneous.

5. INSTRUCTIONS, § 80*—*when repetition of same proposition in different instructions prejudicial.* Repeating the same propositions in different instructions and emphasizing points by repetition tends to prejudice the rights of litigants and has frequently been condemned.

6. APPEAL AND ERROR, § 1514*—*when remark of counsel in his closing argument improper.* In an action against a physician to recover damages for malpractice, a remark of counsel for defendant in his closing argument asking plaintiff why he did not sue another physician who assisted defendant in treating the plaintiff, *held* improper, and that court properly sustained objection thereto.

*See Illinois Notes Digest, Vols. XI to XV, same topic and section number.

Error to the Circuit Court of Sangamon county; the Hon. OWEN
P. THOMPSON, Judge, presiding. Heard in this court at the April
term, 1913. Reversed and remanded. Opinion filed October 16, 1913.

ROY M. SEELEY and W. ST. J. WINES, for plaintiff
in error.

SMITH & FRIEDMEYER, for defendant in error.

MR. JUSTICE THOMPSON delivered the opinion of the
court.

This is an action in case brought by George Bacon
against Edmund A. Walsh, a physician and surgeon,
to recover damages for alleged malpractice. A jury
returned a verdict in favor of defendant. A motion
for a new trial was overruled and judgment entered on
the verdict. The plaintiff has sued out a writ of error
to review the judgment.

Plaintiff in error, a coal miner twenty-three years
of age, while working at Sherman, for the Midland
Coal Company, suffered a dislocation of his left hip.
Immediately after plaintiff received the injury the
coal company called O. F. Shipman, a physician and
surgeon residing at Sherman, and the defendant, a
physician and surgeon residing at Springfield, to attend plaintiff. Both these surgeons were in the regular employ of the coal company. Dr. Shipman is a
young surgeon who had only had four years of practice. Dr. Walsh had been practicing his profession
fifteen years. The evidence tends to show that Dr.
Shipman simply acted as assistant to the more experienced surgeon and administered the anaesthetic, while
Dr. Walsh either reduced or attempted to reduce the
dislocation. It is a disputed question whether the dislocation was or was not properly reduced, and there is
some evidence tending to show that plaintiff about a
month later fell and reinjured his hip. The plaintiff in
error still suffers from a dislocation of his hip joint
although defendant claims it was properly set at the

time, and several months after the dislocation was received plaintiff submitted to an operation in a hospital in an endeavor to get the joint in proper position.

It is contended on behalf of plaintiff in error that the judgment is against the manifest preponderance of the evidence. We do not deem it proper to discuss the evidence at this time for the reason the case must be reversed for error in instructions given at the request of defendant.

Several months after the treatment of the limb by defendant an X-ray photograph was taken of the joint. Plaintiff insists that the court erred in not permitting him to show to the jury the unsuccessful efforts that he made to get the X-ray plates. The defendant had nothing to do with taking the photographs and never had possession of them. There was no error in the ruling of the court.

Twenty-six instructions were given at the request of defendant in error. The eighth instruction is: "The court instructs you that by the words 'ordinary care and skill' as used in these instructions is meant that care and skill that is exercised by physicians and surgeons in this locality and of the school of which defendant belongs."

Physicians and surgeons are licensed in Illinois by the State to practice medicine and surgery, and there is no distinction made between the different schools of medicine. The record does not show to what school of medicine the defendant belongs, but whatever school that may be, the law requires that he use that degree of professional knowledge, skill and care which the average physician and surgeon in good practice would ordinarily bring to a similar case under like circumstances in that locality. *Quinn v. Donovan*, 85 Ill. 194; *Holtzman v. Hoy*, 118 Ill. 534; *Hallam & Barnes v. Means*, 82 Ill. 379; *Kruger v. McCaughey*, 149 Ill. App. 440. The insertion of the words "and of the school of which defendant belongs" is erroneous and misleading. It limits the care and skill which he must use, not to the average ordinary care and skill of the physicians and surgeons in good practice in the vicinity of Sherman and Springfield but to the care and skill of some particular sect of physicians and surgeons in that locality. If the law was as stated in the instruction, the instruction was erroneous for the reason there was no evidence to what school the defendant in error belongs, except that he is a graduate of the medical department of the University of Illinois College of Physicians and Surgeons in the city of Chicago.

Instruction number three tells the jury that the question of whether the defendant "used that degree of care and skill ordinarily used by physicians and surgeons in the same line of practice in the same or similar localities is a question of fact to be determined from all the evidence in the case, including that of the expert testimony of the physicians and surgeons who have testified in the case to be considered with all the other evidence bearing on the question. You are therefore instructed," etc. This instruction was erroneous in particularly directing the attention of the jury to the expert testimony that had been introduced, and then following that erroneous feature with an argument.

Twelve instructions asked by the defendant in error, and given, told the jury in slightly different ways that the law puts upon the plaintiff the burden of showing by a preponderance of the evidence that defendant was guilty of the negligence alleged. There are several other repetitions of legal propositions in the instructions given at the request of defendant in error.

The practice of repeating the same propositions in different instructions and of emphasizing points by repetition tends to prejudice the rights of litigants and has frequently been condemned. *Gould v. Magnolia Metal Co.*, 207 Ill. 172; *Bartz v. Chicago City Ry. Co.*, 116 Ill. App. 554.

It is also insisted that counsel for defendant in the closing argument for the defendant made prejudicial and improper remarks in asking plaintiff why he did not sue Dr. Shipman. The court properly sustained an objection to this line of argument. Counsel, however, had the right to comment on the evidence and draw any inference therefrom that it justified. The judgment is reversed because of the errors indicated and the cause remanded.

Reversed and remanded.

American Insurance Company of Newark, New Jersey, Appellant, v. A. F. McClelland, Appellee.

1. CORPORATIONS, § 51*—*proof of corporate existence under plea of nul tiel corporation.* In an action on a promissory note where the declaration alleges that plaintiff is a corporation and issue is joined on a plea of *nul tiel corporation,* plaintiff is required to prove its corporate existence at least *de facto,* and where no attempt is made to prove its corporate existence by the introduction in evidence of its character or the general law under which it claims to be incorporated, oral testimony of witnesses that it was in fact a corporation, *held* properly excluded as not the best evidence.

2. CORPORATIONS, § 55*—*when certificates issued by insurance department of this State not admissible to prove corporate existence.* Certificates issued by the Insurance department of this State authorizing an insurance company to conduct its business in this State do not tend to prove its existence as a corporation, since the act of the Legislature authorizing their issuance applies equally to partnerships, associations or corporations.

3. CORPORATIONS, § 53*—*evidence sufficient to prove corporate existence de facto.* A corporation may make proof of its corporate existence *de facto* by introducing in evidence its charter or the act through which its existence is made possible together with proof of the exercise under it of the franchise and powers thereby granted.

4. CORPORATIONS, § 59*—*when person executing note to corporation not estopped to deny its corporate existence.* Where a person executed a promissory note to a corporation and suit is brought thereon by the corporation, the maker is not estopped to deny its corporate existence where the instrument sued on in no way de-

scribes or refers to the plaintiff as a corporation either directly or indirectly and neither the word "corporation" nor "incorporated" appears thereon, and this though the plaintiff is mentioned as a company, since the word "company" is equally applicable to a partnership.

5. CORPORATIONS, § 50*—*when introduction in evidence of instrument executed to corporation not prima facie evidence of its de facto existence in suit thereon.* The rule that where a corporation sues on an instrument executed to it as a corporation the introduction of such instrument is sufficient *prima facie* evidence of its *de facto* existence, does not apply where plaintiff alleges it is a corporation and issue is joined on a plea *nul tiel corporation.*

Appeal from the Circuit Court of Champaign county; the Hon. SOLON PHILBRICK, Judge, presiding. Heard in this court at the April term, 1913. Affirmed. Opinion filed October 16, 1913.

SCHAEFER & DOLAN and GREEN & PALMER, for appellant; ORIS BARTH, of counsel.

DOBBINS & DOBBINS, for appellee.

MR. JUSTICE THOMPSON delivered the opinion of the court.

This suit was brought by the American Insurance Company of Newark, New Jersey, in the Circuit Court to recover upon a promissory note signed by A. F. McClelland; the declaration avers that plaintiff is a corporation.

The defendant, among other pleas, filed pleas of *nul tiel corporation* and the general issue to which the plaintiff replied. Issue was joined upon the replication to the plea of *nul tiel corporation* as well as upon the general replication to other special pleas; the cause was tried before a jury.

Plaintiff offered in evidence the note sued on and attempted to prove by the oral testimony of a witness that it was in fact a corporation, that it had a corporate seal and transacted business under such seal, but upon objection the oral testimony was excluded as not the best evidence. Plaintiff also offered the certificate issued by the insurance superintendent for the year 1913, from the Insurance Department of the State of Illinois, dated January 8, 1913, reciting that plaintiff had complied with all the requirements of the law of the State of Illinois and authorizing it to "transact its appropriate business of Fire Insurance in this State in accordance with the laws thereof, until the first day of February, A. D. 1913."

Upon objection by defendant this certificate was excluded as was also a certificate issued February 1, 1912, over the signature and under the seal of the insurance superintendent of the State of Illinois showing that plaintiff had filed with the Insurance Department a sworn statement showing its condition on Dec. 31, 1911. "In accordance with the provisions of * * * 'An Act to incorporate and govern Fire, Marine and Inland Navigation Insurance Companies doing business in the State of Illinois.'"

Plaintiff thereupon rested its case and upon motion of defendant a verdict was directed for defendant and judgment entered against plaintiff in bar of action and for costs, from which judgment plaintiff appealed to this court.

Under the issues framed upon the plea of *nul tiel corporation,* appellant was bound to prove its corporate existence at least *de facto.* To prove such existence it is sufficient to introduce its charter or the act through which its existence is made possible together with proof of the exercise under it of the franchise and powers thereby granted. *American Sales Book Co. v. Wemple,* 168 Ill. App. 639; *Dean & Son v. W. B. Conkey Co.,* 180 Ill. App. 162.

No attempt was made to make proof of the corporate existence of appellant by the introduction of its charter or the general law under which it claims to be incorporated, and the oral testimony offered as to user was properly excluded as not the best evidence.

The certificates issued by the Insurance Department of the State of Illinois authorizing appellant to conduct its business in this State do not tend to prove

384   APPELLATE COURTS OF ILLINOIS.

American Ins. Co. of Newark, N. J. v. McClelland, 184 Ill. App. 381.

its existence as a corporation, inasmuch as the act of the Legislature under the authority of which they were issued applies equally to partnerships, associations or corporations. Hurd's Statute c. 73, ¶¶ 31, 32. (J. & A. ¶¶ 6329, 6330.)

Appellant relies for a reversal in this suit upon the proposition that appellee had contracted with it as a corporation and had executed the instrument sued on to it as such, and therefore appellee is estopped to deny the corporate existence.

The instrument relied upon reads as follows:

"Agent fill out this end of note:

Sec. 16, Town...., Lot...., Block...., Brown; P. O..... Foosland; Co..... Champaign,.... Illinois. Agent's Name—L. W. Cole.

$264.50.   No. 756025.

On the first day of Feb., 1912, for value received, I promise to pay to The American Insurance Company, of Newark, N. J., or order, Two Hundred and Sixty-four 50-100 Dollars, in payment of premium for Policy No......... of said Company, payable at Foosland bank, at Foosland or (if not otherwise specified) at its office in the city of Rockford, Illinois.

If this note is paid within three months from date no interest will be charged. And it is hereby agreed that if this note is not paid at maturity, the whole amount of premium of said Policy shall be considered as earned and payable, and the policy shall be suspended, and the company shall not be liable for any loss or damage that may occur to the property insured while this note shall be past due and unpaid. In case of loss, this note shall become due and payable and shall be deducted from the amount of said loss. And it is further agreed that if suit is brought for the collection of this note I promise to pay expenses of collection and attorney's fees and without relief from valuation or appraisement laws. The company is authorized to insert in this note the Number of Policy. It is understood and agreed that this Note is not negotiable.

THIRD DISTRICT—OCTOBER, 1913.   385

American Ins. Co. of Newark, N. J. v. McClelland, 184 Ill. App. 381.

Dated at her house this 8th day of Nov., 1911.
Witness to signature—(Signed) A. F. McClelland.
. . . .
Party owns 750 acres worth $200 per acre."

There is nothing in the note referring to or intimating that appellant is a corporation. It was held by this court in *American Sales Book Co. v. Wemple, supra,* upon facts practically identical with the case at bar, the instrument in question "in no way describes or refers to the plaintiff as a corporation, either directly or indirectly. Neither the word 'corporation' nor 'incorporated' appears thereupon." The word company "is equally applicable to a partnership."

We have examined the case of *Hudson v. Green Hill Seminary Corp.,* 113 Ill. 618, cited by appellant, and the cases there cited, where the court seems to hold that the execution of the instrument upon which the suit was brought was sufficient *prima facie* evidence of the existence of the corporation, under a plea of *nul tiel corporation,* but this holding was not necessary for the decision of the case inasmuch as there was other proof of its existence as a corporation *de facto,* and in that case the trial court found for the plaintiff and the judgment of the lower court was affirmed.

All the authorities, including the many cited in 113 Ill. 618, hold that where the instrument sued on is executed to the corporation as such that the introduction of such instrument is sufficient *prima facie* evidence of its *de facto* existence.

The reason for the rule, where the instrument itself does not disclose a corporate existence, is that the burden of proving corporate existence when there is a plea of *nul tiel corporation* is on the plaintiff, since the plea denies the averment of the declaration. *Bailey v. Valley National Bank,* 127 Ill. 332, and cases cited; 5 Encyc. Pl. & Pr. 82.

Appellant having alleged that it was a corporation, it was necessary that there be some proof either in the instrument itself, or otherwise, of its corporate existence.

There being no competent evidence of the corporate capacity of appellant, the trial court properly directed a verdict for the appellee and the judgment will be affirmed.

'Affirmed.

MR. JUSTICE PHILBRICK took no part in the consideration of this case.

S. Homer Tolly, Appellant, v. The Millikin National Bank, Appellee.

(Not to be reported in full.)

Appeal from the Circuit Court of Macon county; the Hon. WILLIAM C. JOHNS, Judge, presiding. Heard in this court at the April term, 1913. Affirmed. Opinion filed October 16, 1913.

Statement of the Case.

Action by S. Homer Tolly against The Millikin National Bank to recover a sum claimed to be due as commissions for services of plaintiff as real estate agent in selling defendant's real estate. From a judgment in favor of defendant, plaintiff appeals.

JACK & WHITFIELD, for appellant.

HUGH CREA and HUGH W. HOUSUM, for appellee.

MR. JUSTICE THOMPSON delivered the opinion of the court.

Boyle v. Chicago and Eastern Illinois R. Co., 184 Ill. App. 387.

Abstract of the Decision.

1. BROKER, § 90*—*when evidence insufficient to entitle a real estate agent to a commission.* In an action to recover a commission for the sale of defendant's real estate, a verdict in favor of defendant *held* sustained by the evidence, it appearing that plaintiff had no exclusive agency to sell the land, that defendant sold to another party after plaintiff had failed to fulfil his promise to call upon defendant to close the deal with his prospective purchaser and plaintiff's evidence showing that he concealed from defendant the correct amount offered by his prospective purchaser.

2. EVIDENCE, § 366*—*when question asked of prospective purchaser in suit by real estate agent for a commission calls for a conclusion.* In an action to recover a commission for the sale of real estate, sustaining an objection to a question put to plaintiff's prospective purchaser whether he was ready and willing to complete the purchase on the terms he and the plaintiff talked over, *held* not error for the reason that the question called for a conclusion. The witness should have been asked for the facts and thereafter permitted to tell his financial condition and all attending circumstances.

Thomas T. Boyle, Appellee, v. Chicago and Eastern Illinois Railroad Company, Appellant.

1. DAMAGES, § 115*—*when verdict for five thousand dollars for personal injuries is excessive.* A verdict for five thousand dollars for injuries sustained by a switchman *held* excessive, the injury having been caused by a fall through the roof of a car, and the evidence showing that no bones were broken or joints dislocated and no cuts, bruises or visible marks of any injury except a scratch on the leg, and there being evidence that numerous doctors were unable to find anything the matter with him.

2. INSTRUCTIONS, § 81*—*when properly refused for giving undue prominence to the evidence.* Requested instructions directing the attention of the jury to particular portions of the evidence, thereby giving it undue prominence, *held* properly refused.

3. APPEAL AND ERROR, § 1562*—*when refusal of requested instruction as to the manner of determining damages not reversible error.* In an action to recover damages for personal injuries, refusal of a requested instruction telling the jury that in case they found for plaintiff they should not fix the amount of the damages by adding

together the sums the individual jurors thought plaintiff should recover and dividing the total by the number of jurors, *held* not reversible error, though it would not have been error to give the instruction.

Appeal from the Circuit Court of Vermilion county; the Hon. WILLIAM B. SCHOLFIELD, Judge, presiding. Heard in this court at the April term, 1913. Reversed and remanded. Opinion filed October 16, 1913.

H. M. STEELY and H. M. STEELY, JR., for appellant.

CLARK & HUTTON, for appellee.

MR. JUSTICE THOMPSON delivered the opinion of the court.

This is an action on the case brought by Thomas T. Boyle in May, 1912, against the Chicago and Eastern Illinois Railroad Company to recover damages for personal injuries claimed to have been sustained by him while in its employ as a switchman on the night of September 5, 1911, in the Brewer yards near Danville. A jury returned a verdict for plaintiff for five thousand dollars, on which judgment was rendered. The defendant appeals.

The appellant has assigned error on the rulings of the court, on the admission of evidence and on the giving of certain instructions and the refusing to give others. While several of the instructions given for appellee are abstract in form they could not mislead the jury. Some of the refused instructions were given in substance and others were properly refused because they directed the attention of the jury to particular portions of the evidence giving to it undue prominence. The eighteenth instruction requested by the appellant, and refused, told the jury that in case they found for appellee they should not fix the amount of the damages by adding together the sums the individual jurors thought appellee should recover and dividing the total by the number of jurors. While it would not have been error to give the instruction it was not reversible error to refuse it. We do not find any reversible error in the questions of law contended for by appellant.

It is also insisted that the evidence does not sustain the judgment and that it is excessive.

The evidence shows that appellee was a switchman, forty-eight years of age and weighing two hundred and sixty pounds. He had worked on a railroad about half the time since 1882, and began working for appellant in November, 1908. He testified that on the night he was injured he climbed on a cut of cars that were being switched in the Brewer yards, and after the cars stopped he was going over them to set brakes; that in walking over a stock car that had a patent ceiling twelve inches below the roof which extended to hay racks at the side of the car, and while about the middle of the car he stepped on what proved to be a rotten board, that his right foot went through the board and his leg went into the car sidewise between the ceiling and the roof of the car up to the crotch; that he fell forward with his left leg extended in front of him; that he fell heavily, so that his stomach struck against his knee, and that he wrenched and sprained his back; that he got up, started to set the brake on another car and continued at his work about two hours thereafter, when he had to quit work because of his injury. There were no marks or bruises about his person except a scratch on his leg. Since that time he has been in various hospitals and under the care of several physicians and claims to suffer pain in his head and back. He also claims to have trouble with his kidneys and with his urine, and that he is unable to work.

After the accident he was attended by Dr. Barton at St. Elizabeth's hospital in Danville about four weeks, where Dr. Bohart saw him three days after the accident. He then went to the Englewood hospital, where he was examined by Dr. Bohart, and while stay-

390　Appellate Courts of Illinois.

Boyle v. Chicago and Eastern Illinois R. Co., 184 Ill. App. 387.

ing at that hospital, he went to the city daily to be treated by Dr. Englebrechtson, from October 9 to December 6, 1911. On April 9, 1912, he was examined by Dr. Moyer of Chicago, and in February he was examined by Dr. Rice in Terre Haute, Indiana. The evidence shows that none of these doctors were able to find anything the matter with him notwithstanding the most thorough tests. They testify that they never saw any objective symptoms and that all the symptoms were subjective, and that had he been injured in the way be claims, the injury would have been to his hip.

Doctor Taylor, a brother-in-law of appellee, who saw him in the hospital three or four days after the injury was received, testified that he had some temperature, complained of pain in his back and head and afterwards of trouble with his kidneys, but outside of the temperature he saw no objective symptoms. Doctor Webb, an osteopath, who treated appellee after July, 1912, testified that he found pain and tenderness in the small of the back and an anterior curve of the spine.

Appellee testified to having, when in the employ of the Wabash, fallen from the top of a box car from which accident he was laid up a few days, and of having an arm broken on the Big Four some years before the present injury was received, and that prior to this injury he was healthy and well and had never laid off or quit work, while working for appellant, except one night when he had cramps. The evidence of the members of the switching crew, with which he was working, is that two or three nights of each week he would work a while and then claim he was "all in" and then go and sit or lie down and that this occurred to such an extent that it was reported to the Company, and that he complained of rheumatism or pain in his back and legs.

The evidence shows that there were no bones broken or joints dislocated, and no cuts, bruises or visible marks of any injury at the time he claims he was injured. The doctors, except Taylor and Webb, were not able to find any symptoms showing any injury and testify that in their judgment the appellee is not suffering as he claims. Upon a careful review of all the evidence, we are of the opinion that this judgment is clearly excessive and cannot be sustained.

In the final argument of counsel for appellee to the jury improper remarks were made that were of a nature calculated to arouse prejudice, and not to promote justice. These remarks, which we do not deem necessary to set out in detail, may account for the amount of the verdict. Counsel attempt to excuse the nature of the argument by saying it was provoked by, was in reply to and was like the argument for appellant. The record does not contain the argument of appellant, but whatever it may have been, it was no excuse for and does not remedy the error of appellee's counsel.

The judgment is reversed and the cause remanded.

Reversed and remanded.

Herman Rendtorff, Appellee, v. Edward W. Lowman, Appellant (Charles A. Kimmel, Intervening Petitioner.)

1. ATTORNEY AND CLIENT, § 138*—*when attorney not entitled to a statutory lien on judgment recovered in favor of his client.* Under paragraph 55 of the Lien Act (Hurd's St. 1911, p. 1489, J. & A. ¶ 611) an attorney is not entitled to a lien for his fees on a judgment recovered by his client, where the judgment was paid to his client several hours before he notified the debtor of his claim for a lien on the judgment.

2. ATTORNEY AND CLIENT, § 138*—*when attorney not entitled to an equitable lien on judgment for his fees.* An attorney is not entitled to an equitable lien on a judgment recovered in favor of his client where the judgment was paid to his client or to some person authorized to collect the same before he notified the judgment debtor of claim for lien in accordance with paragraph 55 of the Lien Act (Hurd's St. 1911, p. 1489, J. & A. ¶ 611.)

Appeal from the Circuit Court of Tazewell county; the Hon
THEODORE N. GREEN, Judge, presiding. Heard in this court at the
April term, 1913. Reversed. Opinion filed October 16, 1913. Re-
hearing denied November 12, 1913.

CAMERON & CAMERON, for appellant.

CHARLES A. KIMMEL, for appellee.

MR. JUSTICE THOMPSON delivered the opinion of the
court.

On June 17, 1912, Charles A. Kimmel, an attorney
at law, filed a petition in the Circuit Court of Tazewell
county to enforce a lien for $232.32 on a judgment
against Edward W. Lowman in favor of Herman
Rendtorff, for $303.08 in the Circuit Court of Peoria
county, of date December 3, 1893, which had been revived. Lowman answered the petition, setting up that
the judgment had been paid and satisfied before any
notice of lien was served on him. On a hearing, the
court found that the petitioner had a lien for $247.56,
and that a release of the judgment of date June 1, 1912,
was void to the extent of said lien. The court entered
an order setting aside said release and directing the
sheriff of Tazewell county to proceed to collect the
sum of $247.56 by selling certain real estate in Taze-
well county, theretofore levied upon under an execution on said judgment, issued to him on May 21, 1912,
from the office of the Circuit clerk of Peoria county.
Lowman appeals from that order.

The record shows that in 1893, Herman Rendtorff,
who resided near Chicago, had a claim against Edward
W. Lowman of Peoria. Rendtorff placed the claim
in the charge of Snow, Church & Co., a Chicago collection agency, and they sent the claim to H. C. Fuller,
an attorney in Peoria, to collect. In December, 1893,
Fuller obtained a judgment on this claim for $303.08
against Lowman in favor of Rendtorff, in the Circuit
Court of Peoria county. Soon after the judgment was
obtained $50 was paid on it, and in February, 1898,

Fuller collected the further sum of $10. Fuller had the judgment revived by scire facias on June 13, 1904. In the early part of 1912, Lowman fell heir to some real estate in Tazewell county by the death of a relative. On April 6, 1912, Charles A. Kimmel, an attorney of Peoria, who had learned that Lowman was indebted to Rendtorff and had advised Lowman to go through bankruptcy and solicited the work of procuring a discharge in bankruptcy for him, wrote to Rendtorff asking if the judgment had ever been paid, and if it had not, then soliciting the collection of it and offering to collect it for fifty per cent. of the amount due. Rendtorff, on April 9th, replied to the letter of April 6th, stating that he would allow a commission of forty per cent. for the collection of the judgment. Early in May, Kimmel in an effort to supplant Fuller wrote a letter to Rendtorff inclosing a postal card addressed to Fuller, on which was written a discharge of Fuller as attorney in this matter and instructing Fuller not to make any settlement with Lowman. The letter requested Rendtorff to sign the postal and mail it to Fuller. Rendtorff neither signed nor sent the card to Fuller, nor gave Fuller any notice that the matter was taken out of his charge. On May 18, 1912, Kimmel had the judgment again revived by scire facias, and on May 20, 1912, caused an execution to be issued to the sheriff of Peoria county, who returned it unsatisfied on May 21. On May 21, Kimmel caused an execution to be issued to the sheriff of Tazewell county. On June 1, 1912, at about 10:30 in the forenoon, Lowman, who had been negotiating with Fuller since early in January for a settlement of the claim, paid the judgment with interest and costs to Fuller, the attorney who first placed the claim in judgment. About 5:30 in the afternoon of June 1, 1912, Kimmel served a notice on Lowman, notifying him that he had an attorney's lien amounting to $232.32 on the Rendtorff judgment.

The sole question presented is whether the petitioner is entitled to a lien for his fee of forty per cent. of the judgment. The act under which this proceeding is brought in paragraph 55 of the Lien Act (Hurd's Stat. 1911, p. 1489, J. & A. ¶ 611.) This act provides that attorneys at law shall have a lien on all claims, demands and causes of action which may be placed in their hands by their clients for suit or collection for the amount of the fee agreed upon, or in the absence of an agreement for a reasonable fee, provided however such attorneys shall serve notice in writing upon the party against whom their clients have such claims or suit, claiming such lien, and stating their interest therein, and such lien shall attach to any judgment, or to any money or property, which may be recovered from and after the time of service of the aforesaid notice. The appellee contends that although the judgment was paid before he served his notice that he is entitled to an equitable lien. The contention of appellee might be true as against third parties under certain circumstances, but cannot be maintained in favor of an attorney as against a judgment debtor who pays the judgment to the client or to some person authorized to collect the claim before the service of such notice of lien. The statute provides a way by which an attorney may preserve his lien as against the debtor, but until the notice had been served on the debtor he has the right to pay the claim to an attorney, who had it for collection, and from whose hands it had not been taken by the creditor. It is only by serving the notice that the attorney becomes a joint claimant with the client. *Baker v. Baker*, 258 Ill. 418. The order cannot be sustained on the evidence. It is therefore reversed with costs against the intervenor.

Reversed.

THIRD DISTRICT—OCTOBER, 1913.   395

Lisenbury v. St. Louis and Springfield Ry. Co., 184 Ill. App. 395.

Ellen Lisenbury, Appellee, v. St. Louis and Springfield Railway Company, Appellant.

1. DAMAGES, § 114*—*when two thousand five hundred dollars for personal injuries to woman excessive.* In an action against an interurban railroad company to recover damages for personal injuries sustained by plaintiff by reason of a collision while plaintiff was a passenger, a verdict for two thousand five hundred dollars *held* excessive, it appearing that plaintiff was a married woman thirty-two years of age, that the only visible signs of injuries was a scratch on her face, bruises on her shins and knees and a red mark on her back, and that she suffered from a prior existing womb trouble aggravated by the accident.

2. DAMAGES, § 45*—*measure of damages where the injury resulted in aggravating a prior existing disease.* Where plaintiff prior to injury had diseases which were aggravated by the injury, damages may be allowed for such part of the diseased condition as the negligence caused.

3. DAMAGES, § 35—*proof of future damages.* To justify a recovery for future damages the law requires proof of a reasonable certainty that they will be endured in the future. A mere possibility or even a reasonable probability that future pain and suffering may be caused by an injury is not sufficient to warrant an assessment of damages.

4. TRIAL, § 130*—*when remarks of counsel improper.* In an action against a railroad company to recover damages for personal injuries sustained by plaintiff in a collision, counsel for plaintiff in concluding his argument to the jury made the statement: "This company could not have inflicted this injury more wilfully if the president of the company had struck her in the face with a ball bat." *Held,* the court properly sustained an objection to the statement and instructed the jury to disregard it.

5. APPEAL AND ERROR, § 1632*—*when ruling of court will not cover inflammatory remark of counsel.* Where counsel in his argument to the jury seeks to inflame the passions of the jury or to excite their sympathy, a ruling of court cannot remove the effect of the inflammatory remark.

Appeal from the Circuit Court of Sangamon county; the Hon. JAMES A. CREIGHTON, Judge, presiding. Heard in this court at the April term, 1913. Affirmed on remittitur; otherwise reversed and remanded. Opinion filed October 16, 1913.

---

*See Illinois Notes Digest, Vols. XI to XV, same topic and section number.

GRAHAM & GRAHAM and H. C. DILLON, for appellant; GEORGE W. BURTON, of counsel.

W. ST. J. WINES, for appellee.

MR. JUSTICE THOMPSON delivered the opinion of the court.

This is a suit to recover for personal injuries sustained by Ellen Lisenbury while a passenger on an interurban car of the St. Louis and Springfield Railway Company. No claim is made in this suit for damages for loss of time or medicine or other expenses. There was a verdict and judgment for twenty-five hundred dollars in favor of plaintiff, and the defendant appeals.

Appellee, a married woman thirty-two years of age, resided on a farm six miles south of Springfield. On August 17, 1912, she purchased a round trip ticket from Woodside to Springfield, went to Springfield to market some chickens and eggs, and after concluding her business there boarded a car for her home, and took a seat near the middle of the car. Two miles from Woodside the car was backed on a siding to permit the northbound car to pass at that place. It was the duty of the conductor of the car on the siding to close the switch. This he neglected to do with the result that the northbound car ran into and collided with the car on which appellee was a passenger. Appellee was injured; the visible signs of her injuries were a scratch on her face, bruises on her shins and knees and a red mark on her back. The only contention of appellant is that the judgment is excessive.

The appellee testified that before the accident she weighed one hundred and ninety pounds, was strong, active and free from nervousness or suffering, that after the accident she was stunned so that she did not know how she got off the car; that she was hurt from her waist down; she began to flow and that this continued for two weeks, and that at the time of the trial she weighed one hundred and sixty pounds. After the accident she, with other passengers, was taken on a relief car to Springfield, then she took a car to Woodside and was conveyed to her home. Dr. Primm was called to attend her at her home that afternoon. He testified that she did not make any complaint of bleeding and that he did not find her suffering to any great extent, that she told him she had taken morphine in the morning and he left some morphine to quiet her nerves. Dr. Fletcher was then called and attended her two weeks at her home. He testified that she was always a nervous woman; that he had made two examinations of appellee before the accident, the last about a year before it; that he then found a fixed and enlarged womb with possibly some retroflexion with a discharge from the womb at that time; that he examined her three days after the accident; that she complained of soreness but had no flowing at that time; that he treated her until September 17, when he thought she could walk, and insisted on her walking, but she complained of inability to walk and that she then had a discharge, which was not menstrual. When Dr. Fletcher insisted that she walk he was discharged and Dr. Van Wormer was called to attend her. She was taken to St. John's Hospital in Springfield, where she was put under an anaesthetic and examined by Dr. Van Wormer, Dr. Mantz and Dr. Morrison; they found the womb fixed and displaced, a mass in the right side of the pelvis and a thickening of the left side. They agreed that an operation should be performed later, but that they should wait to see what would develop. On October 3rd, she left the hospital and returned home where she remained in bed five weeks. She was then again taken to the hospital where an operation was performed by these three doctors, who found her trouble partly chronic and partly acute. The diseased condition then found was of long standing; the womb, intestines and all the structures of the pelvic region were involved in an adherent mass; the fallopian tubes were diseased so that one had to be removed, and cysts containing clear fluid were found in the ligaments supporting the womb. They say her condition was due to a previous specific germ disease of much longer standing than the previous August. While appellee testified she had previously suffered no pain, yet on cross-examination she admitted that she had previous to her injury at different times consulted Doctors Bradley, Fletcher, Southwick, Law and Theis concerning womb difficulties, and she refused to answer some questions even after being advised by the court that she should answer. W. A. Crane testified that in the latter part of July, 1912, she told him as a reason why she was selling some very young turkeys that she was sick and expected to go a hospital any day; the part of this conversation with reference to her going to a hospital, however, was denied by appellee. The testimony of Doctors Bradley, Fletcher, Van Wormer, Mantz and Morrison is that her condition was chronic before the accident, although some of them say it is possible the collison might have intensified the adhesions and long existing inflammation and they also say it was probable that an operation was necessary because of appellee's chronic condition.

In a case against a city for personal injuries caused by a defective sidewalk it was said: "If, prior to the injury, plaintiff had diseases which were aggravated by the fall she might recover from the defendant, but its liability would be measured by the damages which were the natural and proximate result of its negligence. The evidence tended to show something more than a mere latent tendency to particular diseases, and if there was an aggravation of the existing diseases the city would only be liable for what resulted from the fall." *City of Rock Island v. Starkey*, 189 Ill. 515. "The defendant must respond in damages for such part of the diseased condition as its negligence caused." *Chicago City Ry. Co. v. Saxby*, 213 Ill. 274.

"A mere possibility, or even a reasonable probability, that future pain or suffering may be caused by an injury, or that some disability may result therefrom, is not sufficient to warrant an assessment of damages. It would be plainly unjust to require a defendant to pay damages for results that may or may not ensue and that are merely problematical. To justify a recovery for future damages the law requires proof of a reasonable certainty that they will be endured iu the future." *Amann v. Chicago Consol. Traction Co.*, 243 Ill. 263; *Lauth v. Chicago Union Traction Co.*, 244 Ill. 245. The weight of the evidence tends to show that the accident was not the proximate cause of appellee's condition and suffering although it may have been intensified by the accident. She is only entitled to recover for that part of her suffering and condition which probably resulted from the injury.

In the concluding argument of counsel to the jury he made the statement: "This company could not have inflicted this injury more wilfully if the president of the company had struck her in the face with a ball bat." The court properly sustained an objection to the statement and instructed the jury to disregard it. Where counsel seek to inflame the passions of the jury or to excite their sympathy, a ruling of the court cannot remove the effect of such an inflammatory remark.

We are of the opinion that the damages allowed are clearly excessive in view of the previous condition of appellee as shown by the great preponderance of the evidence. If appellee will remit to twelve hundred and fifty dollars within ten days, the judgment will be affirmed for twelve hundred and fifty dollars, otherwise the judgment will be reversed and the cause remanded for a new trial for the reason the judgment is excessive.

Affirmed on remittitur; otherwise reversed and remanded.

400   APPELLATE COURTS OF ILLINOIS.

City of Springfield v. Central Union Telephone Co., 184 Ill. App. 400.

City of Springfield, Appellant, v. Central Union Telephone Company, Appellee.

1. TELEGRAPHS AND TELEPHONES, § 4*—*when ordinance granting privilege is subject to ordinance in force requiring remuneration for poles in street.* An ordinance granted to certain persons, to be known as a certain company, the right to construct and operate a telephone and telegraph system in consideration that the company would furnish the city officials and the police and fire departments with free telephone service, and allow it the use of its poles for a police and fire alarm system. This ordinance provided that the rights granted should be subject to all general ordinances then in force, and there was a general ordinance in force requiring owners of poles in streets and alleys of city to pay an annual license of one dollar per pole as a remuneration to the city for the use of the streets and alleys. *Held,* in an action by the city against the assignee of the grantee company to recover the license fee for its poles that the assignee was liable therefor, that the court erred in overruling a demurrer to defendant's pleas setting up that the ordinance granting the privilege to its assignor did not require the payment of the license, and that the court erred in sustaining a demurrer to a replication pleading estoppel to other pleas which set up that the defendant had rendered to the city telephone service equal to the value of the use of the street for its poles, and that the ordinance requiring the license was unreasonable.

2. TELEGRAPHS AND TELEPHONES, § 7*—*conclusiveness of acceptance of ordinance granting privilege.* Where a privilege is granted to a company by ordinance to construct and operate a telephone and telegraph system, the ordinance to be null and void if not accepted in writing and the construction of such system begun within a certain time, the reasonableness of the grant is for the parties to decide, and if the company accepts the ordinance neither it nor its assignee may be permitted to repudiate any of its terms and conditions that are not contrary to public policy or prohibited by statute.

Appeal from the Circuit Court of Sangamon county; the Hon. ROBERT B. SHIRLEY, Judge, presiding. Heard in this court at the April term, 1913. Reversed and remanded with directions. Opinion filed October 16, 1913.

Statement by the Court. This is an action in debt brought in the Circuit Court of Sangamon county to the November term, 1911, by the City of Springfield against the Central Union Telephone Company to recover remuneration claimed to be due for the use of portions of the streets and alleys of the city occupied by the telephone poles of the defendant.

The declaration avers that the plaintiff, a municipal corporation organized under the laws of the State of Illinois, on the third day of January 1898, passed a certain ordinance providing that any person, firm or corporation owning, controlling or occupying any post or pole over eight feet high, which may occupy any portion of any street, alley or sidewalk within the City of Springfield, said pole or post being used to support electric or other wires of whatsoever nature, shall pay annually into the city treasury the sum of one dollar for each such pole or post so owned, controlled or occupied by said person, firm or corporation as a remuneration to the city for the use of the portions of the street, alley or sidewalk which said pole or post may occupy; that the license hereinbefore provided shall be due on the first day of September of each year; that said ordinance was approved by the mayor and duly published and was in full force in the year 1907. It is also averred that the defendant, in the year 1907, occupied portions of the streets and alleys of said city by, to wit, three thousand poles over eight feet high supporting wires, without paying into the city treasury on the first day of September, 1907, one dollar for each such pole as remuneration for so occupying portions of said streets and alleys, by reason whereof and by virtue of said ordinance an action has accrued to the plaintiff, etc. Counts were also filed similar to the foregoing to recover remuneration for the years 1908 to 1911 inclusive.

The defendant filed five pleas. The first avers that the defendant is a corporation organized under the laws of Illinois; that it began doing business in Ohio, Illinois and Indiana in 1883, and began to construct, purchase, lease, own and operate telephone lines and do a telephone business within and without, and partly within and partly without Illinois and has continued to do so since June 28, 1883; that on December 3, 1883, the City of Springfield passed an ordinance granting the defendant, its successors and assigns the right of way through, in and upon its streets, sidewalks and alleys for the purpose of erecting thereon necessary poles and wires to operate a telephone exchange, subject to all general ordinances of the city then in force or thereafter to be passed, which said ordinance should continue in force twenty years; that said ordinance provides that in consideration of the rights and privileges granted by it, the city shall have as many telephones with exchange service as the city may require at one-half the regular rates, and said Company shall maintain, care for and operate a fire alarm bell to be located as the city shall direct without cost to the city; that defendant began immediately and from that time up to the fifth day of August, 1901, continuously placed, constructed and maintained posts, wires and fixtures composing a telephone system at an expense of $100,000, in compliance with the terms of said ordinance, and from June 3, 1889, to May 10, 1900, said city has used defendant's poles for carrying its police and fire alarm wires without any consideration to the defendant except the consideration granted under the ordinance of Dec. 3, 1883; that said ordinance constituted a contract between the defendant and said city; that defendant installed and operated under the terms of said ordinance as many telephones as the city required and as the city council designated and called for, and operated a fire alarm bell from thence hitherto and the plaintiff has enjoyed and utilized such concessions up to May 10, 1910.

The plea further avers that on June 19, 1899, the plaintiff passed an ordinance granting unto Thomas W. Wilson and S. M. Rogers and such other persons as might thereafter be associated with them, to be known as the "Springfield Mutual Telephone and Telegraph Company'' or other appropriate name, and to their successors and assigns the right to construct and maintain a telephone and telegraph system in the City of Springfield in the following words and figures.

" * * * Sec. 3. In consideration of the rights and privileges granted to the said parties and others succeeding them, they hereby agree to furnish the city officials in the City Hall, also to the Police and Fire Departments, free telephone service.

Sec. 4. The City shall have the right, so far as the same shall not interfere with the other uses of said poles, to use the same to support the wires used by it in connection with the police and Fire Alarm system, and all the rights herein granted shall be subject to all general ordinances of said City now in force. * * *

Sec. 6. This ordinance shall become null and void if it shall not be accepted in writing, and the construction of said telephone and telegraph system be begun within one year from the date of its passage;'' that on June 19, 1899, Wilson and Rogers accepted said ordinance in writing; that on May 10, 1900, said Wilson and others ''and the Springfield Mutual Telephone Company a corporation'' for a valuable consideration sold and transferred to defendant all right, title, privilege, franchise and property accruing to them under said ordinance; that the defendant on May 10, 1900, notified plaintiff of said assignment and that the defendant was ready to install and furnish the service required under the terms of said ordinance of June 19, 1899, and the plaintiff through its officials by a letter on May 12, 1900, informed the defendant of the offices and buildings in which the plaintiff desired telephones installed; that the defendant promptly installed and has since furnished and supplied defendant with said telephone service free of charge; that the mayor of plaintiff City on May 31, 1900, communicated to the city council of the City of Springfield said assignment, its ratification and acceptance by plaintiff, and that the plaintiff had demanded from

404 APPELLATE COURTS OF ILLINOIS.

City of Springfield v. Central Union Telephone Co., 184 Ill. App. 400.

the defendant that it should furnish certain telephone service, and the city council accepted and ratified the acts of the city officials; that with the approval of plaintiff since May 10, 1900, in compliance with the ordinance of Jan. 19, 1899, the defendant has operated and maintained a telephone system and has expended in repairing, rebuilding and extending its system $50,000, and has in compliance with an ordinance passed in 1905, applicable to all telephone companies, placed its wires in the business district of plaintiff under ground at a cost of $10,000, paid its taxes and, in consideration of the rights and privileges granted by said ordinance, furnished telephone service to the city officials and to the police and fire departments of plaintiff, to the value at customary rates during the periods enumerated as follows: May 10, 1900 to Jan. 1, 1901, $1,600; Jan. 1, 1901 to Jan. 1, 1905, $8,000; Jan. 1, 1905 to Jan. 1, 1908, $6,600; Jan. 1, 1908 to Jan. 1, 1910, $4,800; that by said ordinance of June 19, 1899, the only remuneration the defendant was obligated to pay for occupying the streets and alleys of plaintiff with its poles and wires was the telephone service to be furnished to the police and fire departments and the city officials as stipulated in section 3 of said ordinance, and the defendant has fully discharged and performed all the conditions of said ordinance and the defendant is not indebted to the plaintiff in any sum on account of the matters alleged and this it is ready to verify wherefore, it prays judgment if it ought to be charged with the said debt by virtue of said ordinance set forth in the declaration.

The second plea is the general issue. The third plea is similar to the first with the additional averments of the use of defendant's poles for carrying its fire and police alarm wires free of charge, save the consideration conferred upon defendant by the ordinance of 1883, and an averment that there was a general ordinance requiring a monthly inspection by the police department of the city of all poles erected in the city and requiring the owners of telegraph and telephone poles to pay an annual inspection fee of seventy-five cents per pole, and reserving the right to the city to allow other companies to use poles on payment of a reasonable compensation, with an averment that the American Telephone Company, under a contract ordinance passed in 1896, was occupying the streets and alleys of the city with its poles for the consideration of fifty cents per pole and free use by the city of one ten pin cross-arm for the police and fire alarm systems of the city and that the Illinois District Telegraph Company was in 1899 given the same rights for the consideration of the payment to the city of five per cent. of its gross earnings.

The fourth plea avers that the ordinance fixing the compensation for the use of poles at one dollar per annum is unreasonable and void and exceeds the fair value of the use of the streets.

The fifth plea is similar to the fourth with the additional averment that a fair remuneration for the use of the streets for poles during the entire time does not exceed $5,000, and defendant has furnished telephone service to plaintiff aggregating $15,000, solely as re-remuneration for the use of the streets, for which nothing has been paid by plaintiff.

Plaintiff filed a demurrer to the first and third pleas and replications of estoppel to the fourth and fifth pleas. The replications to the fourth and fifth pleas aver in substance that the general ordinance requiring the payment of one dollar per pole was in force when the ordinance of June 19, 1899, was passed and accepted by Wilson and his associates, and that the defendant, as assignee of the grantees who accepted the ordinance of June 19, 1899, is bound thereby and by the terms of the general ordinance requiring the payment of one dollar per pole and prays judgment if defendant ought to be admitted or received to plead the matters alleged in said pleas. The defendant demurred to the replications to the fourth and fifth pleas.

The court overruled the demurrer of plaintiff to the first and third pleas and sustained the demurrer of defendant to the replications to the fourth and fifth pleas. The plaintiff then withdrew its second, third, fourth and fifth counts, and stood by its demurrer to the first and third pleas and its replications to the fourth and fifth pleas. The court entered judgment in favor of the defendant and against the plaintiff in bar of the action and for costs against the plaintiff. The plaintiff appeals.

FRANK L. HATCH and ALBERT D. STEVENS, for appellant; TIMOTHY McGRATH, of counsel.

W. B. MANN, D. K. TONE and CONKLING & IRWIN, for appellee.

MR. JUSTICE THOMPSON delivered the opinion of the court.

It appears from the averments of the first and third pleas that the defendant is occupying the streets and alleys of plaintiff with a telephone system constructed originally under an ordinance that by its terms expired in December, 1903. The only claim of right to occupy the streets and alleys of plaintiff made by the defendant is that it occupies as assignee of the rights granted to Thomas W. Wilson and S. M. Rogers under the ordinance of June 19, 1899. Under that ordinance Wilson and his associates and their assigns agree to furnish the city officials and the police and fire departments free telephone service, and that the plaintiff shall have the right to use the poles of Wilson and his associates and their assigns to support the wires used by plaintiff, "in connection with the police and fire alarm systems and all the rights herein granted shall be subject to all general ordinances of the city now in force."

The substance of these pleas is that defendant occupies the streets of plaintiff as assignee of the ordinance passed June 19, 1899, which it insists is an ordinance granting the rights therein given to Wilson and others for a consideration to be received by the plaintiff from Wilson or his assigns, and that defendant has rendered all the services it has rendered to the plaintiff because they are required by that ordinance, and that the rental of one dollar for each pole is not required by the Wilson ordinance.

The ordinance of January 3, 1898, was enacted before the ordinance granting the right to Wilson and others was passed and was in force when they accepted the rights granted under the ordinance passed in 1899. The ordinance of 1898 provides that any person, firm or corporation owning, etc., shall pay annually the sum of one dollar for each pole over eight feet high which may occupy any portion of any street, alley or sidewalk. The ordinance requiring the payment of remuneration for the use of the streets of plaintiff by poles supporting electric wires is a general ordinance. Neither plea avers that it is not a general ordinance, nor are facts averred which show that Wilson and others and their assigns are not subject to the provisions of that ordinance. The acceptance by Wilson and others of the rights granted them by the ordinance of June, 1899, was an acceptance of the rights granted thereby subject to all the terms and conditions of the grant. The assignee of Wilson and others can have no greater rights in the street under the ordinance of 1899 than the grantees therein.

Neither the first nor third plea avers that the defendant as assignee of Wilson and others have furnished or given to the plaintiff anything since it became the assignee of Wilson and others, that Wilson and others and their assignees were not required to furnish and give to plaintiff as a consideration therefor, unless it be the operation of the fire alarm bell and that was required by the ordinance of 1883, and no charge is made therefor. By the acceptance of the ordinance of 1899, Wilson and others accepted such grant of privileges knowing that the general ordinances required the payment of an annual compensation to plaintiff of one dollar per pole. The ordinance is clear and free from ambiguity, the words must be taken in their ordinary sense and there is no room for construction. The court erred in overruling the demurrer to these pleas. '

The ordinance of June, 1899, grants to Wilson and others, to be known as the Springfield Mutual Telephone and Telegraph Company, and to their assigns the right "to construct and operate a telephone and telegraph system" pursuant to the grant in that ordinance. From the averments of the pleas the Springfield Mutual Telephone and Telegraph Company did become incorporated. The defendant may in violation of public policy (*Union Trust & Savings Bank of East St. Louis v. Kinloch Long Distance Tel. Co. of Missouri*, 258 Ill. 202; *People v. Union Gas & Electric Co.*, 254 Ill. 395) have become the assignee of the grant under the ordinance of June 3, 1899, for the purpose of preventing competition, as contended by plaintiff, but there is no pleading raising that question.

The replication to the fourth and fifth pleas are that the defendant is estopped to plea that the ordinance fixing a remuneration of one dollar annually for each pole is unreasonable, and that defendant has rendered to plaintiff telephone services equal to or beyond the value of the use of the streets by the poles of defendant because said services were rendered pursuant to ordinances pleaded.

The ordinance granting to Wilson and others the right to construct and operate a telephone and telegraph system in the City of Springfield contains a section providing that the ordinance shall be null and void, if it shall not be accepted in writing and the construction of said system be begun within one year from the date of its passage. The question of the reasonableness of the grant was for the parties to decide. If the grantees in the ordinance were not satisfied with its terms they should have refused to accept it. *Postal Telegraph Cable Co. v. City of Newport*, 25 Ky. Law Rep. 635. Wilson and his associates had the right to accept or reject the terms of the ordinance. Having chosen to accept the ordinance with all its terms, they are bound by it and may not be heard to say that they accept the benefits and that they refuse the burdens imposed by it. The city had the right to give or withhold the privilege of constructing and operating a telephone system on its streets. One of the conditions under which the plaintiff granted to the assignors of defendant the right to occupy the streets with telephone poles was the compliance with the general ordinances of the plaintiff, one of which required the annual payment of one dollar as remuneration for each pole occupying the streets additional to the other conditions of telephone service specified in the ordinance. The ordinance having been accepted, neither the grantees nor their assignee may be permitted to repudiate any of its terms and conditions that are not contrary to public policy or prohibited by statute. Having been accepted it became a valid contract in its entirety. *Chicago General Ry. Co. v. City of Chicago*, 176 Ill. 253; *Commonwealth Electric Co. v. Rose*, 214 Ill. 545. The court erred in sustaining the demurrer to the replications to the fourth and fifth pleas. The judgment is reversed and the cause remanded with instructions to sustain the demurrer to the first and third pleas and to overrule the demurrer to the replications to the fourth and fifth pleas.

Reversed and remanded with directions.

Nancy V. Hoxsey by John Hoxsey, Appellee v. St. Louis and Springfield Railway Company, Appellant.

1. DAMAGES, § 115*—*when verdict for two thousand dollars for personal injuries sustained by a girl is excessive.* A verdict for two thousand dollars for personal injuries sustained by a girl thirteen years of age by reason of coming in contact with a telephone wire which had fallen across a trolley wire, *held* excessive, the evidence showing that she suffered a burn on her right arm which healed in about six weeks and a burn over her right eye which healed in about two weeks, and that though her eyes were weak after the accident she had complained of sore eyes prior to the injury.

2. APPEAL AND ERROR, § 1725*—*conclusiveness* of decision on *former appeal.* The decision of an Appellate Court and the propositions of law announced in reversing a case on prior appeal are binding on the court and will not be departed from on a subsequent appeal in the same case.

Appeal from the Circuit Court of Macoupin county; the Hon. JAMES A. CREIGHTON, Judge, presiding. Heard in this court at the April term, 1913. Affirmed on remittitur; otherwise reversed and remanded. Opinion filed October 16, 1913.

RENAKER & RENAKER and GEORGE W. BLACK, for appellant; GEORGE W. BURTON and H. C. DILLON, of counsel.

EDWARD C. KNOTTS, for appellee; PEEBLES & PEEBLES, of counsel.

MR. JUSTICE THOMPSON delivered the opinion of the court.

Nancy V. Hoxsey by her next friend brought suit against the St. Louis & Springfield Railway Company to recover for personal injuries averred to have been received by coming in contact with a telephone wire, which it is averred by and through the negligence of the defendant fell across its trolley wire, which was charged with a dangerous current of electricity, in the city of Girard, Illinois. The case has been tried twice in the Circuit Court. On the first trial the plaintiff recovered a verdict for one thousand eight hundred and fifty dollars upon which judgment was rendered; upon an appeal to this court that judgment was reversed and the cause remanded. *Hoxsey v. St. Louis & S. Ry. Co.*, 171 Ill. App. 76. A statement of the pleadings will be found in the former opinion and need not be repeated. On the second trial the plaintiff recovered a verdict for two thousand dollars, upon which judgment was rendered and the defendant appeals.

All the legal questions that are raised on this appeal were passed upon in the former opinion of this court adversely to the contentions of the appellant. The decision of an Appellate Court and the propositions of law announced in reversing a case are binding on that court and will not be departed from on a subsequent appeal in the same case. *Mariner v. Ingraham*, 230 Ill. 130; *Beggs v. Postal Tel. Cable Co.*, 176 Ill. App. 406.

The only remaining contention is that the damages allowed are excessive. The evidence shows that the physical injuries suffered by appellee, then a girl of the age of thirteen years, were not serious. She suffered a burn on her right arm five or six inches in length that healed in about six weeks, and there was a burn over her right eye about the size of a quarter that did not heal for about two weeks. The injuries were so slight that but little attention was paid to them at the time. Her father, a veterinary surgeon, applied some salve to the wounds and she was only absent from school four days.

Appellee testified that from the time she was injured her eyes pained her when she read and that they still pain her. She also testified that she had sore eyes for a week or two a year before the injuries complained of were received and that she had fully recovered before the time the injuries complained of were received. A physician was not called to attend to her at the time she was injured. After the beginning of this suit, and about eighteen months after she was injured, her eyes were examined by Dr. West, who found her vision somewhat defective, but he was unable to determine the cause of the trouble. Appellee attended school the full term after the accident except the four days immediately after it was received and exhibited no signs of trouble or weakness of her eyes and was an average pupil both before and after the accident. Upon a consideration of all the evidence in the case the damages allowed appear to be clearly excessive. If the appellee will remit eight hundred dollars within ten days after this opinion is filed, the judgment will be affirmed for one thousand two hundred dollars; otherwise the judgment will be reversed and the cause remanded.

Affirmed on remittitur; otherwise reversed and remanded.

Daniel B. Stewart, Appellee, v. Illinois Central Railroad Company, Appellant.

1. RAILROADS, § 921*—*when evidence to show cause of fire too remote.* In an action against a railroad company for setting fire to plaintiff's buildings alleged to have been caused by sparks thrown from defendant's locomotive, evidence that tramps were seen on railroad track about two miles from the place of the fire about three hours before the fire and evidence that one of the buildings had been on fire about five years before, *held* inadmissible because too remote and not tending to show that the fire was not started by defendant's locomotive.

2. RAILROADS, § 921*—*when evidence of condition of engine after setting of fire inadmissible.* In an action against a railroad company for setting fires by sparks thrown from its locomotive, it is proper to show the condition of the engine immediately after the fire started, but evidence that the engine was being repaired a week after the starting of the fire is incompetent.

---

*See Illinois Notes Digest, Vols. XI to XV, same topic and section number.

3. WITNESSES, § 283*—*matters to which witness may be cross-examined for purpose of impeachment.* In an action against a railroad company for setting fire to a building by sparks thrown from its locomotive, where the engineer after testifying to the condition of the spark arrester was asked on cross-examination, for the purpose of laying a foundation for his impeachment, if he had not told a person about a week after the fire that he had asked the company to repair the engine before the fire and that it was then in the shops for repair, *held* that an objection to the question should have been sustained for the reason it sought to impeach him on irrelevant and immaterial matters.

4. WITNESSES, § 279*—*when variant statements inadmissible for purpose of impeachment.* Variant statements in order to be admissible for purposes of impeachment must be relevant to the matter in issue.

5. RAILROADS, § 941*—*when instruction as to evidence required to overcome presumption of negligence in setting fires erroneous.* An instruction given for plaintiff that the law presumes a railroad company guilty of negligence on proof that a fire was communicated to plaintiff's property by the company's engine and that the verdict should be for plaintiff "unless this presumption is overcome by the evidence," *held* to place a greater burden on defendant than the law requires, and that the instruction should have been "unless this presumption has been rebutted or overcome by the evidence."

6. RAILROADS, § 941*—*when instruction as to evidence required to overcome plaintiff's prima facie case for setting fires erroneous.* An instruction requiring plaintiff's *prima facie* case made by proof of the communication of the fire by defendant's engine to be overcome by a preponderance of the evidence, *held* erroneous, for the reason that it requires defendant to introduce more evidence than would neutralize or rebut the presumption.

Appeal from the Circuit Court of McLean county; the Hon. COLOSTIN D. MYERS, Judge, presiding. Heard in this court at the April term, 1913. Reversed and remanded. Opinion filed October 16, 1913. Rehearing denied November 6, 1913.

CHARLES L. CAPEN, for appellant; JOHN G. DRENNAN, of counsel.

LIVINGSTON & BACH and BARRY & MORRISSEY, for appellee.

Mr. Justice Thompson delivered the opinion of the court.

This is a suit brought by Daniel B. Stewart against the Illinois Central Railroad Company to recover damages for the destruction by fire of a barn, hay shed and contents on the night of October 25, 1911, at Anchor, Illinois, averred to have been caused by sparks thrown from a locomotive engine of defendant. The first count avers negligence of the defendant in failing to equip its locomotive with the best and most approved appliances to prevent the escape of fire, and in failing to keep the same in suitable order and repair. The second count avers that the defendant failed to use reasonable care to prevent the escape of fire from its locomotive and through the negligence and carelessness of the defendant and its servants sparks were thrown, etc. The third count avers that the defendant so negligently used its locomotive that sparks escaped from it and set fire to plaintiff's property. A jury returned a verdict for plaintiff for five thousand dollars, on which judgment was rendered and the defendant appeals.

The village of Anchor is on the railroad of appellant between Bloomington and Kankakee. The railroad runs through Anchor in a northeasterly and southwesterly direction and at the southwest corner of the village it curves and runs almost directly west. The depot is near the centre of the village. There is an up grade through the village to the northeast of thirty-two feet to the mile. The barn and property destroyed were located about seven hundred feet northeast of the depot and on the southeast side of the track. There are two elevators near the depot, the Mean's elevator is about sixty feet southwest of the depot and the Farmers' elevator is about the same distance northeast of it. The barn and hay shed stood southeast of the track and parallel with it; the nearest side of the barn was one hundred and sixteen feet from the track and the hay shed was northeast of the barn and eighty feet from the track.

A freight train of eighteen cars with a tonnage of 593 tons drawn by a locomotive of 950 tons capacity approached Anchor from the west about nine o'clock in the evening. As it approached the depot it was signaled to stop for a passenger and when it stopped the locomotive stood about north of the east end of the hay shed. Some ten or fifteen minutes after the train had passed, the barn was discovered to be on fire; the fire seemed to be both on the inside and outside of the barn. There is evidence that the locomotive was throwing sparks just west of the Mean's elevator, and there is evidence that the locomotive went by the elevators, the depot and the buildings burned, drifting, that is not working, and that under such circumstances it could not throw sparks. No witness testifies to seeing sparks from the engine after it passed the depot and as it went by the barn and hay shed. The evidence is conflicting as to the direction of the wind; some witnesses testify that it blew from the southwest, others from the west, and still others from the northwest and the north.

It is contended that because no witnesses saw sparks thrown from the locomotive as it went by the barn and hay shed that the judgment cannot be sustained. As there are errors of law in the case, it is unnecessary to review the merits of the case.

Appellant insists that the court erred in sustaining objections to questions tending to show that the barn had been on fire in 1906, and that tramps had been seen on the railroad track about two miles from Anchor about six o'clock that evening going towards Anchor. The court properly sustained objections to this character of evidence; the facts sought to be proved were too remote and did not tend to show that the fire was not started by appellant's locomotive.

The evidence presented by appellant tended to show that the locomotive was equipped with a proper spark arrester of the most approved construction, comparatively new and in good repair, and that the locomotive was properly managed. The engineer, Kellogg, after testifying to the condition of the spark arrester and the management of the engine, was asked on cross-examination for the purpose of laying a foundation for his impeachment: "If about a week after the fire on the Kankakee platform he had not said to Joseph Irwin, that he had asked the company to repair the engine several times before the fire and that it was then in the shops for repair?" "Did you not then and there tell him the engine was then in the shop for repairs?" Objections to these questions were overruled and the witness answered admitting having had a conversation with Irwin at that place about that time, but denying making any such statement to Irwin or that he had asked the company to repair the engine or that it was then in the shop for repairs. Irwin was asked if on the platform of the Illinois Central depot in Kankakee about a week after the fire he had a talk with Kellogg; an objection to the question was overruled. The questions were then asked him and answered after objection had been overruled: "Did you have a conversation with him?" Ans. "Had one sometime after the fire." Q. "Did he say to you then and there in that conversation that he had asked them to repair the engine several times before the Stewart barn burned but they had not repaired it?" Ans. "He said that in substance." Q. "Did he say to you at the same time and place that the engine was then in the shop for repairs?" Ans. "I should judge the substance was about the same, yes he did, it had been taken in."

Appellant insists that these questions did not fix the time and place and also that the questions were improper for the reason that the matters inquired about were immaterial, that the repairs might have referred to some other part of the engine. The witness, Kellogg, had admitted having a conversation with Irwin at that platform about a week after the fire, and the question contains the words "then and there" referring to the time and place fixed in a prior question. The objection to the form of the questions was properly overruled.

If the engineer did say what it is claimed he said, still there is nothing in the evidence tending to show that such statements were made with reference to anything in any way connected with the spark arrester, or that they were in any way connected with the throwing of sparks by the engine. If the engine was in the shops for repairs a week after the fire, then that was an attempt to prove indirectly what was not proper to prove directly. It would have been proper to show the condition of the engine immediately after it is claimed it started the fire, but that the engine was being repaired a week later is incompetent. *Howe v. Medaris,* 183 Ill. 288; *Sample v. Chicago, B. & Q. R. Co.,* 233 Ill. 564; *Kath v. East St. Louis & Suburban Ry. Co.,* 232 Ill. 126; *City of Taylorville v. Stafford,* 196 Ill. 288; *Hodges v. Percival,* 132 Ill. 53. The objection to the questions should have been sustained for the reason it was sought to impeach the witness on irrelevant and immaterial matters, and to get before the jury incompetent and misleading evidence. Variant statements in order to be admissible for purposes of impeachment must be relevant to the matter in issue. *Woods v. Dailey,* 211 Ill. 495; 7 Encyc. of Ev. 78.

It is also insisted that there was error in instructions given to the jury. Paragraph 103 of chapter 114 of the Statute (J & A. ¶ 8891) provides: "That in all actions against any person or incorporated company for the recovery of damages on account of any injury to any property, whether real or personal, occasioned by fire communicated by any locomotive engine while upon or passing along any railroad in this State, the fact that such fire was so communicated shall be taken as full *prima facie* evidence to charge with negligence the corporation, or person or persons who shall, at the time of such injury by fire, be in the use and occupation of such railroad," etc.

Appellee's fifth instruction is: "If you believe from the evidence that the fire in question was communicated to plaintiff's property from an engine used by the defendant upon its railroad, then the law presumes that the defendant was guilty of negligence and in such case your verdict should be in favor of the plaintiff unless this presumption has been overcome by the evidence." The court also modified the latter part of appellant's first instruction so as to read, "But if you shall believe from a preponderance of the evidence that defendant did set out the fire, as claimed, still if the preponderance of the evidence shows that the engine was in good order, properly handled by skilful employees, who were competent to perform their duties, and was equipped with the most approved spark arrester then notwithstanding you may believe that the engine set out the fire, it is your duty to find the defendant not guilty." The court inserted the words "a preponderance of." The appellant was entitled to have the instruction given as asked without the words inserted by the court. Under the wording of the statute the communication of fire by a locomotive is full *prima facie* evidence to charge the corporation with negligence, but the appellant did not have to overcome such *prima facie* case by a preponderance of the evidence. All that it was necessary for appellant to do, to entitle it to a verdict, was to rebut such *prima facie* case. If the evidence for the appellant neutralized, rebutted or was equal to the presumption arising from the starting of the fire by the engine, if that was proved by the evidence, still the appellee would not be entitled to recover. The burden of establishing the truth of the issue remained with the plaintiff. *Egbers v. Egbers,* 177 Ill. 82; *Chicago Union Traction Co. v. Mee,* 218 Ill. 9; *Vischer v. Northwestern El. R. Co.,* 256 Ill. 572. The appellee's fifth instruction placed a greater burden on appellant than the statute requires; all that appellant was required to do was to produce evidence to meet and neutralize the presumption. The instruction should have been "unless this presumption has been rebutted or overcome by the evidence." *American Strawboard Co. v. Chicago & A. R. Co.*, 177 Ill. 513. For the errors indicated the judgment is reversed and the cause remanded.

Reversed and remanded.

Ira Cox, Defendant in Error, v. The American Insurance Company, Plaintiff in Error.

1. INSURANCE, § 149*—*when provision in policy exempting from liability while premium note remains past due and unpaid is waived.* A provision in a fire insurance policy that the company shall not be liable for any loss that may occur while any premium note remains past due and unpaid is waived where the company, with knowledge of the fact that a premium note was due and unpaid at the time of the loss, sends an adjuster to negotiate with the insured, and the adjuster discusses the loss with the insured, places valuations on various items of the list of personal property destroyed and then when the insured would not sign a nonwaiver agreement refused to proceed further with the adjustment.

2. INSURANCE, § 684*—*when question of waiver of condition of forfeiture is for court.* While the question of waiver of a condition of forfeiture is usually a question of fact for the jury, yet if there is no conflict in the evidence on that subject it becomes a question of law for the court.

3. INSURANCE, § 321*—*what constitutes waiver of breach of condition in policy.* There is a difference between a waiver and an estoppel. A waiver of a breach of a condition in an insurance policy does not require the company to do anything to the disadvantage of the insured.

4. INSURANCE, § 321*—*when insurer estopped to insist on forfeiture.* Forfeitures are not favored in law, and an insurance company is estopped to insist on a forfeiture, if after the cause of forfeiture accrues it treats with the insured in such a manner as to recognize the policy as still in force.

5. INSURANCE, § 328*—*provisions in policy which may be waived.* A provision in a policy for insurance that it shall become void in

a certain event will not render the policy absolutely void upon the happening of such event; such a provision being for the benefit of the insured it may be waived.

6. INSURANCE, § 693*—*sufficiency of instruction on waiver of condition of forfeiture.* An instruction informing the jury that a fire insurance company is estopped to insist on a forfeiture of a fire insurance policy, if after the cause of forfeiture the insurance company treats or acts with the insured in such manner as to recognize the policy as still in force, *held* erroneous in omitting the element of knowledge to the company of the cause of forfeiture, but *held* not reversible error where the instructions as a series fully informed the jury on what constituted waiver.

Error to the Circuit Court of Greene county; the Hon. OWEN P. THOMPSON, Judge, presiding. Heard in this court at the April term, 1913. Affirmed. Opinion filed October 16, 1913.

BATES, HARDING, EDGERTON & BATES and F. A. WHITE-SIDE, for plaintiff in error.

RAINEY & JONES and MARK MEYERSTEIN, for defendant in error.

MR. JUSTICE THOMPSON delivered the opinion of the court.

This is an action in *assumpsit* brought by Ira Cox against The American Insurance Company of Newark, New Jersey, upon a policy of insurance issued by it to plaintiff on December 16, 1910. The policy of insurance sued upon is set out *in haec verba* in the declaration and contains the following provisions: "In consideration of a note for $75 due May 1, 1911, The American Insurance Company does insure Ira Cox and his legal representatives against loss and damage by fire, lightning, windstorms, cyclones and tornadoes, to the amount of $2,500, as follows: $1,500 on dwelling house No. 1; $500 on household furniture, useful and ornamental, including certain enumerated articles; $500 on barn." "It is expressly agreed that this company shall not be liable for any loss or damage that may occur to the property herein mentioned while any note or part thereof, or order given for the premium, remains past due and unpaid, and in case of default in payment at maturity of any note or part thereof, or order given for the premium, the whole premium shall be deemed fully earned, and shall at once be due and collectible, and the collection, whether by legal process or otherwise, payment or receipt of payment thereof, shall in no case revive or create any liability against this company for loss occurring while the assured was so in default. The payment of the premium, however, revives the policy and makes it good for the balance of its term.'' The policy contains the usual provisions for notice, proof of loss and for an examination of the assured under oath by any person appointed by the company and for appraisement in the event of disagreement. The house and personal property were destroyed by fire on June 30, 1911; the barn was not destroyed. The defendant filed the general issue with notice of special matter in defense; that the note for the sum of $75 given for the premium on the policy and payable May 1, 1911, was past due and unpaid on June 30, 1911, the date of the fire, and by reason thereof the defendant is not liable for the loss. On the trial a jury returned a verdict for plaintiff for $2,000, on which judgment was rendered and the defendant has sued out a writ of error to review the judgment.

The principal contention of plaintiff in error is, that by reason of the condition of the policy, that the company shall not be liable for any loss that may occur while the note for the premium was past due and unpaid, and the evidence showing that the note was past due and unpaid at the time of the fire, therefore the plaintiff in error is not liable on the policy and that the judgment cannot be sustained. The defendant in error contends that the plaintiff in error, with full knowledge that the premium note was not paid at the time the fire occurred, thereafter treated with the insured as though the policy was in full force and thereby waived its right to deny its liability under the policy. The question of the right of defendant in error to recover is raised by the refusal of the court at the close of all the evidence to direct a verdict for the plaintiff in error.

The note is by its terms non-negotiable and is payable at the People's Bank at White Hall. On April 28, 1911, plaintiff in error sent it to the People's Bank at White Hall for collection. The bank, as agent for plaintiff in error, held the note until July 16, when the defendant in error paid it and a draft for $74.75 was forwarded to plaintiff in error by the bank. The company returned the draft to defendant in error in a letter dated July 21, stating that the company "would only accept it with the understanding that its receipt would not be considered as a waiver of the forfeiture incurred by the non-payment of the note due at maturity,—in any way recognizing the recent loss."

Defendant in error testified that the agent of the company was notified of the fire the evening it occurred and it is admitted on the record that "Mr. Ferguson, the agent of The American Insurance Company, was notified of the fire within a day or two after the fire."

Mr. Foltz testified that he resides at Rockford, Illinois; that he has exclusive charge of the loss department of plaintiff in error; that he was advised of the loss about July 5, and that he got the information from Ferguson. On July 12, 1911, C. E. Sheldon, manager of the western department of appellant Company, wrote a letter to defendant in error from Rockford, Illinois, while the note was at the bank, at White Hall, requesting payment of the note at once to avoid expense. On July 14, 1911, Foltz acknowledged receipt of the formal notice of loss and advised the defendant in error by mail that the company's adjuster, Mr. Aldrich, would call on him early the next week in reference to the loss. On July 18, the adjuster called at the Cox farm, inspected the ruins, talked with Cox about the loss, examined the list of personal property destroyed that had been made out by defendant in error, discussed the values and placed a valuation on the items of the list of goods destroyed. Defendant in error then showed the adjuster the note which showed when it was paid. The adjuster then asked the defendant in error to sign a non-waiver agreement, which defendant in error refused to do. The adjuster then burnt the paper he had prepared and declined to submit proofs of loss and took no further action, but wrote to the manager of the company at Rockford for advice, advising the company that Cox had received a notice urging payment of the note some time after the company had notice of the fire and had paid it at the bank. This letter was received at the company's office July 20. On July 19, Foltz wrote to defendant in error that under the terms and conditions of the policy the contract of insurance was suspended during the period of nonpayment of the note after maturity, that the company was not liable and the adjuster would not call on him, and if he should pay the note and the amount was received by the company it would return the payment unless defendant in error should advise the company he desired the policy reinstated on property not destroyed for the unexpired term. The facts as stated are not controverted, and it is on these facts that plaintiff in error insists the court erred in refusing to give the peremptory instruction requested.

While a question of waiver is usually one of fact for a jury, yet, if there is no conflict in the evidence on that subject, it becomes a question of law to be determined by the court. A provision in a policy in insurance that it shall become void in a certain event will not render the policy absolutely void upon the happening of such event; such a provision being for the benefit of the insurer, it may be waived by the latter. ''Any acts, declarations or course of dealing, by the insurers, with knowledge of the facts constituting a breach of a condition in the policy, recognizing and treating the policy as still in force, will amount to a waiver of the forfeiture, and estop the company from setting up the same as a defense." *Manufacturers & Merchants Ins. Co. v. Armstrong*, 145 Ill. 469; *Dwelling House Ins. Co. v. Dowdall*, 159 Ill. 179. Forfeitures are not favored in law, and an insurance company is estopped to insist upon a forfeiture of a policy, if after the cause of forfeiture accrues, it treats with the insured in such manner as to recognize the policy as still in force. *Bennett v. Union Central Life Ins. Co.*, 203 Ill. 439; *Rosater v. Peoria Life Ass'n*, 149 Ill. App. 536.

There is a difference between a waiver and an estoppel. A waiver of a breach of a condition of a policy does not require the company to do anything to the disadvantage of the insured. 40 Cyc. 256. Provisions of forfeiture in an insurance policy made for the benefit of the insured are easily waived by it. *Dubuque Fire & Marine Ins. Co. v. Oster*, 74 Ill. App. 139.

The plaintiff in error had notice of the loss immediately after the loss occurred. The head of the loss department knew of the loss on July 5, and on July 12, plaintiff in error by its manager notified defendant in error that he must pay his note at once to save costs, and on July 14, the manager advised the defendant in error that its adjuster would be there within a week, The adjuster did call on July 18, and discussed the loss with defendant in error, put valuations on the items of personal property destroyed and then, when the insured would not sign a non-waiver agreement, refused to proceed further with the adjustment. The insurance company, with full knowledge of the fact which it now insists constitutes the forfeiture, when notified of the loss did not claim the benefit of the forfeiture, but negotiated with the insured concerning the loss, collected the note and five days thereafter returned the draft it had received from its agent the bank. The collection of the note of itself will not constitute a waiver of the forfeiture, for the reason that the policy provides that the collection of the note by legal process, or otherwise, shall in no case create any liability against the company for loss occurring while the assured was in default (*Schimp v. Cedar Rapids Ins. Co.*, 124 Ill. 354); but the sending an adjuster to negotiate with the assured, and the adjuster going and discussing the loss with defendant in error, and placing valuations on the various items of the list of personal property prepared by defendant in error, when a managing officer had full knowledge of the cause of forfeiture several days before any of such acts on the part of the company, were inconsistent with, and were a waiver of the forfeiture. There being a waiver of the forfeiture, there was no error in refusing the peremptory instruction.

The second instruction given for the defendant in error is an abstract proposition. It informs the jury that a fire insurance company is estopped to insist upon a forfeiture of a fire insurance policy, if after the cause of forfeiture the insurance company treats or acts with the assured in such manner as to recognize the policy as still in force. The fourth instruction informs the jury that although the insurance company had the right to decline to pay the plaintiff the amount of his loss because plaintiff had failed to pay the premium note after its maturity and before the fire, still it should be held to have waived its said right, "if you believe from the evidence in this case that, with full knowledge of the fact that said note was past due and unpaid at the time of the fire, the said company, with full knowledge of the fact of non-payment of note, treated with the plaintiff, Cox, in such manner as to recognize the policy as still in force."

The sixth instruction given for the insurance company told the jury that a waiver is a relinquishment of a known right, and that in order that a waiver may arise the knowledge of the right claimed to be relinquished must be actual knowledge, and not merely presumptive knowledge. The second instruction was erroneous in omitting the element of knowledge to the insurance company of the cause of forfeiture at the time of the performance of the acts which are claimed to be a cause of forfeiture. The instructions are not peremptory in their form, and must be considered as a series. When the fact is considered that the jury were fully instructed on what constitutes a waiver, and that the evidence for the insurance company shows conclusively that it had actual knowledge of the cause of forfeiture before it sent its adjuster to investigate the loss, the giving of the second instruction was not reversible error. The judgment is affirmed.

Affirmed.

CASES

FIRST DISTRICT

OF THE

APPELLATE COURTS OF ILLINOIS

DURING THE YEAR 1913.

Theodore G. Warden, Plaintiff in Error, v. Thomas McInerney, Defendant in Error.

Gen. No. 18,297.   (Not to be reported in full.)

Error to the Municipal Court of Chicago; the Hon. THOMAS F. SCULLY, Judge, presiding. Heard in the Branch Appellate Court at the March term, 1912. Reversed and remanded. Opinion filed December 31, 1913.

Statement of the Case.

Action by Theodore G. Warden against Thomas McInerney to recover for damages to plaintiff's automobile claimed to have been caused by a horse belonging to defendant which had run away because it was negligently left in Washington Park without being securely fastened, as required by the ordinances of the city of Chicago and of the South Park Commissioners. The case was tried by the court without a jury. From a judgment in favor of the defendant, plaintiff brings error.

ELBERT C. FERGUSON, for plaintiff in error.

THOMAS J. HEALY and DANIEL M. HEALY, for defendant in error.

428   APPELLATE COURTS OF ILLINOIS.

Illinois Malleable Iron Co. v. Chicago City Ry. Co., 184 Ill. App. 428.

MR. PRESIDING JUSTICE GRAVES delivered the opinion of the court.

Abstract of the Decision.

1. APPEAL AND ERROR, § 181*—*when court's refusal to mark propositions of law reversible error.* Arbitrary refusal of a judge of the Municipal Court to mark proper propositions of law either "held" or "refused" when presented in time is reversible error.

2. TRIAL, § 297*—*propositions of law.* A proposition of law announcing that proof of the violation of an ordinance resulting in an injury establishes a *prima facie* case of negligence on the part of the one violating it, *held* to announce a correct rule of law applicable to the case.

Illinois Malleable Iron Company, Plaintiff in Error, v. Chicago City Railway Company, Defendant in Error.

Gen. No. 18,314.   (Not to be reported in full.)

Error to the Municipal Court of Chicago; the Hon. HOSEA W. WELLS, Judge, presiding. Heard in the Branch Appellate Court at the March term, 1912. Affirmed. Opinion filed December 31, 1913.

Statement of the Case.

Action by Illinois Malleable Iron Company, a corporation, against Chicago City Railway Company, a corporation, to recover for damages to a wagon owned by plaintiff and struck by one of defendant's street cars, when plaintiff's teamster attempted to drive the wagon across the tracks in front of the car at other

*See Illinois Notes Digest, Vols. XI to XV, same topic and section number.

than a street intersection. From a judgment in favor of defendant, plaintiff brings error.

ALDEN, LATHAM & YOUNG, for plaintiff in error; T. A. SHEEHAN, of counsel.

CLINTON A. STAFFORD and A. R. PETERSON, for defendant in error; LEONARD A. BUSBY, of counsel.

MR. PRESIDING JUSTICE GRAVES delivered the opinion of the court.

Abstract of the Decision.

1. NEGLIGENCE, § 90*—*when contributory negligence bars recovery.* It is not the law that contributory negligence is no defense where the defendant by the exercise of ordinary care could have avoided the injury. The settled law in this State is that where the negligence of the plaintiff contributes to the injury he cannot recover unless the act of the defendant resulting in the injury is wilful.

2. APPEAL AND ERROR, § 1410*—*when findings of jury or trial court will not be set aside.* It is well settled in this State that the finding of a jury or a trial court will be set aside by the Appellate Court only when it is clearly and manifestly against the weight of the evidence. The fact that upon close consideration the weight or preponderance of the evidence would seem to be contrary to the verdict is not sufficient to warrant a reversal of the judgment.

3. STREET RAILROADS, § 97*—*when street car company not liable for collision with wagon crossing track in front of car.* In an action against a street railway company to recover damages to a wagon by being struck by a street car when the driver of the wagon attempted to cross the track in front of an approaching car, at other than a street intersection, *held* that the evidence showed that the defendant was not negligent and that the driver was guilty of contributory negligence, it appearing that the driver with knowledge of the approaching car attempted to cross the track about sixty feet distant from the car, which was running seven or eight miles an hour, and that the motorman was unable to stop the car before the collision.

*See Illinois Notes Digest, Vols. XI to XV, same topic and section number.

Guiseppe Ribando, Appellee, v. Chicago, Milwaukee and St. Paul Railway Company, Appellant.

Gen. No. 18,325. (Not to be reported in full.)

Appeal from the Superior Court of Cook county; the Hon. Joseph H. Fitch, Judge, presiding. Heard in the Branch Appellate Court at the March term, 1912. Reversed with finding of facts. Opinion filed December 31, 1913.

Statement of the Case.

Action by Guiseppe Ribando against Chicago, Milwaukee and St. Paul Railway Company, a corporation, to recover damages for personal injuries sustained by plaintiff by being struck by a switch engine belonging to defendant while plaintiff was working as a track laborer in the employ of another railroad company, the track upon which plaintiff was working being used by defendant's switch engine. From a judgment in favor of plaintiff for $1,999, defendants appeal.

O. W. Dynes and C. S. Jefferson, for appellant.

O'Shaughnessy & O'Shaughnessy, for appellee.

Mr. Presiding Justice Graves delivered the opinion of the court.

Abstract of the Decision.

Railroads, § 522*—*when track laborer guilty of contributory negligence.* In an action against a railroad company to recover for personal injuries sustained by plaintiff by being struck by defendant's switch engine while he was employed as a track laborer by another company, a verdict for plaintiff *held* not sustained by the evidence, it appearing that plaintiff was an experienced track laborer, thoroughly familiar with his surroundings, knew of the presence of the switch engine and proceeded with his work on the track with his back toward the engine, taking no precautions for his own safety and relying entirely on his attention being directed by the ringing of the bell on the switch engine.

Etta B. Franklin, Appellant, v. Thomas M. Hunter, Appellee.

Gen. No. 18,339.   (Not to be reported in full.)

Appeal from the County Court of Cook county; the Hon. W. F. SLATER, Judge, presiding. Heard in the Branch Appellate Court at the March term, 1912. Affirmed. Opinion filed December 31, 1913.

Statement of the Case.

Action by Etta B. Franklin against Thomas M. Hunter in replevin to recover possession of two wagons levied on by defendant, a bailiff of the Municipal Court, as the property of one Anna M. Leach, by virtue of an execution issued on a judgment against her. From a judgment in favor of defendant, plaintiff appeals.

BEAUREGARD F. MOSELEY, for appellant.

JOHN W. LEE, for appellee; OLAF F. SEVERSON and WILLIAM CHONES, of counsel.

MR. PRESIDING JUSTICE GRAVES delivered the opinion of the court.

Abstract of the Decision.

1. COURTS, § 33*—*rule of Appellate Court as to sufficiency of abstract of record construed.* Rule 19 of the Appellate Court of the First District, requiring a party bringing a cause to that court to furnish a complete abstract or abridgment of the record and requiring that the abstract shall be sufficient to fully present every error and exception relied on, does not require the production of the record *in haec verba*, nor authorize a mere index of the record, but requires that the substance of the record must be given in as few words as will convey to the court all the facts necessary for it to know in order to determine the merits of the errors complained of.

2. APPEAL AND ERROR, § 866*—*sufficiency of abstract of record.* An abstract of record which is no more than an index from which

it cannot be gathered what issues were formed and tried, and wherein it is more than an index it is in most cases an unabbreviated copy of the record, is insufficient.

3. APPEAL AND ERROR, § 867*—*manner in which bill of exceptions should appear in abstract.* Where a bill of exceptions is a part of the record there should be something in the abstract to indicate where it begins and ends. There should be a certificate of the trial judge at the end and not in the middle of the bill of exceptions, and it should so appear in the abstract.

4. APPEAL AND ERROR, § 867*—*order of arranging matter in the abstract.* Matter as it appears in the record should appear in the same order in the abstract.

5. APPEAL AND ERROR, § 1306*—*when presumed that replication was filed.* Where no replication to a plea is preserved in the record, it may be presumed that a general replication was filed where the record recites that "issue being joined a trial by jury is waived and cause is submitted to the court for trial without the intervention of a jury."

6. APPEAL AND ERROR, § 1000*—*when error in refusing admission of evidence not presented for review.* Error of court in refusing admission of evidence not presented for review where there is nothing in the bill of exceptions to show that the court excluded the evidence.

7. REPLEVIN, § 124*—*when evidence insufficient to show plaintiffs title to the property.* In replevin to recover two wagons levied upon by the defendant, an officer, under an execution on a judgment against a third party, the plaintiff claiming ownership of the property as a purchaser at a mortgagee's sale, a judgment in favor of defendant *held* sustained by the evidence, it appearing from the record that such third party had been owner of the property and up to the time of the levy had possession thereof, and there being no evidence tending to show that such party had ever parted with his title or possession.

*See Illinois Notes Digest, Vols. XI to XV, same topic and section number.

Dudley A. Tyng, Appellee, v. United Mercantile Agency et al., Appellants.

Gen. No. 18,376.   (Not to be reported in full.)

Appeal from the Superior Court of Cook county; the Hon. WILLIAM FENIMORE COOPER, Judge, presiding. Heard in the Branch Appellate Court at the March term, 1912. Reversed and remanded with directions. Opinion filed December 31, 1913.

Statement of the Case.

Petition by Dudley A. Tyng against United Mercantile Agency, a corporation, P. H. Early, president, and E. E. Hughes, secretary, for a writ of mandamus to compel defendants to transfer certain shares of capital stock on the books of the corporation. From a judgment awarding the writ, defendants appeal.

ARTHUR C. HOFFMANN, for appellants.

MATTHIAS B. PITTMAN, for appellee.

MR. PRESIDING JUSTICE GRAVES delivered the opinion of the court.

Abstract of the Decision.

1. CORPORATIONS, § 71*—*when by-law governing transfer of certificates of stock not unreasonable.* A by-law of a corporation requiring shares of the capital stock to be transferred by indorsement of the certificates to the secretary for cancellation, whereupon new certificates are to be issued to the transferee or to his written order, *held* not unreasonable.

2. CORPORATIONS, § 156*—*when mandamus issues to compel transfer of stock on book of company.* Before the transfer of capital stock in a corporation will be compelled by mandamus, every reasonable requirement of the by-laws must be shown to have been complied with.

3. MANDAMUS, § 98*—*when issuance to compel transfer of shares of stock is error.* Awarding a writ of mandamus to compel a cor-

*See Illinois Notes Digest, Vols. XI to XV, same topic and section number.

poration and its officers to transfer shares of capital stock on the books of the corporation, *held* error where petitioner failed to show compliance with a by-law requiring the certificate to be assigned to the secretary of the corporation.

Louis Greenberg, Appellant, v. Florence Parsons, Appellee.

Gen. No. 18,462.   (Not to be reported in full.)

Appeal from the Circuit Court of Cook county; the Hon. H. STERLING POMEROY, Judge, presiding. Heard in the Branch Appellate Court at the March term, 1912. Affirmed. Opinion filed December 31, 1913.

Statement of the Case.

Action of replevin by Louis Greenberg against Florence Parsons to recover possession of certain property. From a judgment dismissing the suit at plaintiff's cost for failure of plaintiff to prosecute the same, and awarding a writ of *retorno habendo*, plaintiff appeals.

LOUIS GREENBERG, *pro se.*

CHARLES E. ERBSTEIN, for appellee.

MR. PRESIDING JUSTICE GRAVES delivered the opinion of the court.

Abstract of the Decision.

1. APPEAL AND ERROR, § 1290*—*presumption as to regularity of proceedings in Circuit Court.* When a Circuit Court is shown to have jurisdiction of the subject-matter and the parties, all presumptions are indulged in, in favor of the regularity of all subsequent proceedings up to and including the final judgment, and will prevail until the irregularity of the same is affirmatively shown.

---

*See Illinois Notes Digest, Vols. XI to XV, same topic and section number.

Greenberg v. Parsons, 184 Ill. App. 434.

2. APPEAL AND ERROR, § 1009*—*when question of sufficiency of service of notice to place cause on short cause calendar not reviewable.* On appeal from an order of the Circuit Court dismissing a cause for want of prosecution, it appearing that the court had jurisdiction of the parties and subject-matter, *held* that the plaintiff cannot urge that the court did not have jurisdiction for the reason that a notice was improperly served on plaintiff of the filing of an affidavit under section 27 of the Practice Act, J. & A. ¶ 8564, for placing the cause on the short cause calendar, where the record does not affirmatively show that such notice was all the notice given plaintiff, nor show that the cause was disposed of on the short cause calendar.

3. APPEAL AND ERROR, § 1313*—*when presumed that proper notice was served to place cause on short cause calendar.* On appeal from an order dismissing a cause for want of prosecution where it is conceded that the cause was placed upon the short cause calendar at the instance of the defendant and the cause was disposed of on the short cause calendar, plaintiff cannot urge that the court did not have jurisdiction for insufficiency of the service of a notice on plaintiff of the filing of an affidavit under section 27 of the Practice Act, J. & A. ¶ 8564, for placing the cause on the short cause calendar, where the record does not affirmatively show that that notice was all the notice given plaintiff, since in such case it will be presumed that other proof of a proper service of such notice was presented to the court.

4. APPEAL AND ERROR, § 842*—*effect when bill of exceptions not signed by proper judge.* Recitals in a bill of exceptions cannot be considered when signed by a judge who did not try the case, where there is nothing in the record to show that the judge who tried the case was by reason of death, sickness or other disability unable to sign it.

5. APPEAL AND ERROR, § 843*—*what constitutes disability of trial judge to sign bill of exceptions.* The fact that the trial judge was not sitting within the jurisdiction at the time the bill of exceptions was signed is no disability rendering him unable to allow and sign a bill of exceptions.

*See Illinois Notes Digest, Vols. XI to XV, same topic and section number.

Harry A. Biossat, Defendant in Error, v. M. B. Louis and T. W. Brophy, Defendants, (Truman W. Brophy, Plaintiff in Error.)

Gen. No. 17,642.   (Not to be reported in full.)

Error to the Municipal Court of Chicago; the Hon. FREDERICK L. FAKE, JR., Judge, presiding. Heard in the Branch Appellate Court at the March term, 1911. Affirmed. Rehearing allowed October 24, 1913. Opinion on rehearing filed December 31, 1913.

Statement of the Case.

Action by Harry A. Biossat against M. B. Louis and T. W. Brophy to recover on a promissory note executed by M. B. Louis payable to himself and indorsed by him and T. W. Brophy. Service of process was had on T. W. Brophy alone and trial was by the court without a jury. From a judgment in favor of plaintiff against Brophy for five hundred dollars, Brophy brings error.

PATRICK H. O'DONNELL and D. P. PENNYWITT, for plaintiff in error.

JOSEPH L. McNAB, for defendant in error.

MR. JUSTICE BAUME delivered the opinion of the court.

Abstract of the Decision.

1. BILLS AND NOTES, § 445*—*when indorser on promissory note liable to holder.* In an action on a promissory note against an indorser thereon by the holder, where it appears that plaintiff procured the defendant to indorse the note by paying him five hundred dollars to pay off another note past due on which defendant was liable, and defendant claims as a defense that he is an accommodation indorser, that the note was to be returned to the maker after his indorsement and that he indorsed the note for plaintiff on the understanding he was agent of the maker, a judgment for

*See Illinois Notes Digest, Vols. XI to XV, same topic and section number.

plaintiff on conflicting evidence and on finding of facts involved in propositions of law held as the law of the case, was sustained.

2. APPEAL AND ERROR, § 1236*—*when plaintiff in error cannot shift his position.* Plaintiff in error cannot urge grounds wholly at variance with the position assumed by him in the trial court. He cannot be permitted to shift his position in the court of review.

Chicago Real Estate Board, Appellee, v. James Mullenbach et al., on appeal of James Mullenbach, Appellant.

Gen. No. 17,919.   (Not to be reported in full.)

Appeal from the Superior Court of Cook county; the Hon. MARTIN M. GRIDLEY, Judge, presiding. Heard in the Branch Appellate Court at the October term, 1911. Affirmed. Rehearing allowed October 27, 1913. Opinion on rehearing filed December 31, 1913.

Statement of the Case.

Bill of interpleader filed by Chicago Real Estate Board, a corporation, against James Mullenbach and Louisa S. French, to require defendants to interplead and adjust their claims to one thousand two hundred dollars held by complainant and deposited with complainant by James Mullenbach as earnest money in purchasing certain real estate of Louisa S. French at an auction sale held at the board rooms of complainant. From a decree requiring complainant to pay said amount, less costs of court, to Louisa S. French, James Mullenbach appeals.

ENOCH J. PRICE and EVERETT M. SWAIN, for appellant.

HAMLIN & TOPLIFF, HAMLIN & BOYDEN and LOUIS M. GREELEY, for appellee Louisa S. French.

----

*See Illinois Notes Digest, Vols. XI to XV, same topic and section number.

MR. JUSTICE BAUME delivered the opinion of the court.

Abstract of the Decision.

1. VENDOR AND PURCHASER, § 124*—*when tender of title guaranty policy subject to questions of survey sufficient.* The fact that a title guaranty policy tendered to a purchaser was made subject to questions of survey is wholly immaterial where the premises as described in the contract have an actual existence in fact within the boundary lines as designated in the original survey and plat.

2. VENDOR AND PURCHASER, § 298*—*right of vendor to earnest money in equity.* The rule that a court of equity will not enforce a penalty or forfeiture does not preclude a vendor, upon the default of the vendee, from recovering earnest money which has been paid to apply upon the purchase when consummated. In this respect there is no distinction between contracts involving sales at public auction and private sale contracts.

3. VENDOR AND PURCHASER, § 39*—*right of purchaser at auction sale to rescind contract for misrepresentations in printed circular advertising sale.* Where a person purchased city lots at a public auction held by a real estate board and a circular advertising the sale represented that the property bordered on Lake Michigan and that there was no privately owned property between it and the lake, *held*, that to entitle the purchaser to rescind the contract of sale and recover back the earnest money on the ground that such representation was false, he was required to prove that he relied on such representation and that the same was false, and *held* that where it was uncontroverted that for a period of twenty years the strip of land between the property and the lake had been submerged that the burden was upon the purchaser to show that it had been submerged by a sudden avulsion.

4. RIPARIAN OWNERS, § 29*—*when title to land bordering on lake not lost by submergence.* Title to land becoming submerged by the waters of Lake Michigan is lost where the submergence was gradual and imperceptible, but the title remains in the owner where such submergence was sudden and perceptible in its operation, and the owner may regain the same either by natural or artificial means.

5. APPEAL AND ERROR, § 367*—*when questions not preserved for review.* Questions not raised in defendants' answer nor appearing to have been presented to the chancellor upon the hearing are not preserved for review.

*See Illinois Notes Digest, Vols. XI to XV, same topic and section number.

John D. Casey, Administrator, Appellant, v. Chicago Railways Company and City of Chicago, Appellees.

Gen. No. 18,251. (Not to be reported in full.)

Appeal from the Superior Court of Cook county; the Hon. HARRY C. MORAN, Judge, presiding. Heard in the Branch Appellate Court at the March term, 1912. Reversed and remanded. Opinion filed December 31, 1913. Rehearing denied January 9, 1914.

Statement of the Case.

Action by John D. Casey, administrator of the estate of Fredrick F. Rieckhoff, deceased, against the Chicago Railways Company and the City of Chicago to recover damages for wrongfully causing the death of deceased alleged to have been caused by defendants' negligence in maintaining in a street a temporary street car track and in maintaining the street in a dangerous and unsafe condition. From a judgment rendered on a directed verdict finding defendants not guilty, plaintiff appeals.

HARRY S. MECARTNEY, for appellant.

WEYMOUTH KIRKLAND and WILLIAM H. SYMMES, for appellee Chicago Railways Company; JOHN R. GUILLIAMS and FRANK L. KRIETE, of counsel.

MR. JUSTICE BAUME delivered the opinion of the court.

Abstract of the Decision.

1. NEGLIGENCE, § 49*—*proximate cause.* In order to charge a person with the consequences of his own act it is not necessary that he must have foreseen the precise form in which the injury occurred. If when the injury occurs it appears that it was a natural and probable consequence of his negligence, it is sufficient to warrant a recovery.

*See Illinois Notes Digest, Vols. XI to XV, same topic and section number.

2. NEGLIGENCE, § 53*—*when the negligent act or omission is the proximate cause.* While the negligent act or omission must be one of the essential causes producing the injury, it need not be the sole cause nor the nearest cause. If it concurs with the other cause, such as an accident or the negligent act of a third person, which in combination with it causes the injury, it is sufficient.

3. NEGLIGENCE, § 191*—*when questions of negligence and proximate cause are for the jury.* Where reasonable men acting within the limits prescribed by law might reach different conclusions, or different inferences could reasonably be drawn from the admitted or established facts, the question of negligence, contributory negligence and proximate cause are questions of fact for the jury.

4. TRIAL, § 216*—*right to consider weight of evidence in passing on motion for a peremptory instruction.* In passing upon a motion for a peremptory instruction it is not within the province of the trial court to weigh the evidence, and the question of the preponderance of the evidence does not arise. The question whether the verdict is against the manifest weight of the evidence is one to be passed upon by the trial court upon a motion for a new trial; and in the event that such motion is overruled and judgment entered, it is for the Appellate Court upon error assigned.

5. TRIAL, § 195*—*rule in passing on motion for a peremptory instruction where there is some evidence to sustain recovery.* The rule of law is settled in this State that if there is any evidence in the record from which, standing alone, the jury could without acting unreasonably in the eye of the law find that all the material allegations of the declaration had been proved, the case should be submitted to the jury.

6. STREET RAILROADS, § 44*—*when question whether street railway and city are guilty of negligence in maintaining a temporary track in street is for jury.* In an action for injuries resulting from a temporary street car track placed on the surface of the street near the curb to permit of a reconstruction of other tracks near the center of the street, the mere fact that such temporary track was constructed and laid in the usual manner throughout the city does not absolve the street railroad company and city from negligence, either in permitting such track to be maintained in the street an unreasonable length of time or in permitting said track to remain in the street and be used for the operation of cars after the new permanent tracks were completed and ready for use.

7. STREET RAILROADS, § 45*—*when giving of peremptory instruction to find for defendants is error.* A teamster for a liquor company while making deliveries to a retail customer made an attempt to stop his team after it became frightened and in doing so stumbled against the rails and ties of a temporary street railway track constructed on the surface of the street with openings between the ties,

and fell and his wagon passed over him causing his death. In an action against the street railway company and the city to recover damages for his death, charging the railway company with negligence in constructing and maintaining such track, and charging the city with negligence in maintaining the street in unsafe condition and in permitting the railway company to construct and maintain such track, and charging both defendants with negligence in failing to remove such track in a reasonable time after the completion of the work of track reconstruction, *held* that the question of defendants' negligence was a question for the jury and that trial court erred in giving a peremptory instruction to find for defendants.

8. STREET RAILROADS, § 45*—*when question of contributory negligence is for the jury.* In an action against a street railroad company and a city to recover damages for the death of a teamster caused by stumbling against a temporary street car track when attempting to stop his team, *held* that the question whether the teamster was guilty of contributory negligence in permitting his fourteen-year-old son to drive the team around in the street was for the jury.

John Pozdal, Appellee, v. C. C. Heisen, Appellant.

Gen. No. 18,368.   (Not to be reported in full.)

Appeal from the Superior Court of Cook county; the Hon. HARRY C. MORAN, Judge, presiding. Heard in the Branch Appellate Court at the March term, 1912. Reversed with finding of fact. Opinion filed December 31, 1913. Rehearing denied January 12, 1914. *Certiorari* denied by Supreme Court (making opinion final).

Statement of the Case.

Action by John Pozdal against C. C. Heisen and Federal Steel Fixture Company to recover for personal injuries sustained by plaintiff resulting from a descending elevator striking plaintiff's head when plaintiff opened a defective corrugated iron door leading into an elevator shaft for the purpose of communicating with his coemployes on a floor below. Suit was dismissed as to the defendant Federal Steel Fixture Company, a tenant in the building, and prosecuted against defendant Heisen, as owner of the building.

From a judgment in favor of plaintiff for three thousand five hundred dollars, defendant appeals.

EDWARD M. HAMMOND and WINSTON, PAYNE, STRAWN & SHAW, for appellant; EDWARD W. EVERETT and CHARLES J. McFADDEN, of counsel.

F. W. JAROS, for appellee.

MR. JUSTICE BAUME delivered the opinion of the court.

Abstract of the Decision.

1. LANDLORD AND TENANT, § 243*—*when owner of building not liable for injury to tenant's employe caused by defective elevator doors.* Where a person employed in a building was injured by a descending elevator while he was attempting to open a door leading to the elevator shaft for the purpose of communicating with his employes on a floor below, *held* in an action against the owner of the building to recover for the injuries that defendant owed to plaintiff no duty to maintain the door in reasonably safe condition, the evidence showing that the mechanism whereby the door was to be opened and closed was located in the elevator shaft and the elevator operator was alone charged with the duty of opening and closing the door.

2. LANDLORD AND TENANT, § 239*—*duty of landlord to maintain safe condition of premises when building leased to various tenants.* A landlord who rents different parts of a building to various tenants, reserving the elevators, halls, stairways and other approaches for the common use of his tenants, is under an implied duty to use reasonable care to keep such instrumentalities and places in a reasonably safe condition, and is liable for injuries to persons lawfully using such instrumentalities and places resulting from a failure to perform that duty.

*See Illinois Notes Digest, Vols. XI to XV, same topic and section number.

John M. Carlson, Appellant, v. Walter J. Hassis et al., Appellees.

Gen. No. 18,414.   (Not to be reported in full.)

Appeal from the Superior Court of Cook county; the Hon. THEO-
DORE BRENTANO, Judge, presiding. Heard in the Branch Appellate
Court at the March term, 1912. Affirmed. Opinion filed December
31, 1913.

Statement of the Case.

Bill filed by John M. Carlson against Walter J.
Hassis and Julius E. Levine to set aside the sale of
certain shares of stock alleged to have been sold by
complainant to defendants upon the latter's false representations as to the profits of the corporation. From
a decree dismissing the bill for want of equity, complainant appeals.

CASTLE, WILLIAMS, LONG & CASTLE, for appellant.

MAYER, MEYER, AUSTRIAN & PLATT, for appellee,
Walter J. Hassis.

MR. JUSTICE BAUME delivered the opinion of the
court.

Abstract of the Decision.

1. CORPORATIONS, § 147*—*when sale of shares of stock will not be
set aside.* On bill to set aside the sale of certain shares of stock for
misrepresentations made by the buyer as to the amount of profits
earned by the corporation, a decree dismissing the bill for want of
equity sustained, the evidence being conflicting with reference to
whether the representations were made and it appearing that the
defendants sustained no fiduciary relation to the complainant.

2. WITNESSES, § 257*—*when evidence of proceedings in bankruptcy not admissible to discredit testimony of witness.* For the
purpose of discrediting the testimony of a witness, a petition for
such witness' discharge in bankruptcy, the report of the referee re.

*See Illinois Notes Digest, Vols. XI to XV, same topic and section number.

fusing such discharge and a transcript of his testimony on the hearing of objections to such discharge, *held* inadmissible where the proceedings in bankruptcy were had long prior to the transaction in controversy and had no relation to any proper subject of inquiry in the case.

American Musicians Union of North America, Appellant, v. Chicago Federation of Musicians, Local No. 10, A. F. of M. et al., Appellees.

Gen. No. 18,445.   (Not to be reported in full.)

Appeal from the Circuit Court of Cook county; the Hon. CHARLES M. WALKER, Judge, presiding. Heard in the Branch Appellate Court at the March term, 1912. Affirmed. Opinion filed December 31, 1913.

Statement of the Case.

Petition by American Musicians Union of North America against Chicago Federation of Musicians, Local No. 10, American Federation of Musicians, Joseph F. Winkler and certain other officers and members of the federation for a rule upon defendants to show cause why they should not be punished for contempt for violating a certain decree which enjoined the defendants from interfering with, hindering or obstructing the members of complainant's organization in obtaining or retaining employment as musicians, by representing to employers that members of complainant's organization are nonunion men, so as to cause employers to fear the opposition of defendants, or organized labor. From an order entered discharging the rule and dismissing the petition, petitioner appeals.

MABIE & CONKEY, for appellant.

JOHN S. HUMMER, for appellees.

MR. JUSTICE BAUME delivered the opinion of the court.

Abstract of the Decision.

1. INJUNCTION, § 257*—*when evidence sufficient to sustain order discharging rule to show cause for violation.* On petition by a musicians' union against the officers and members of a certain federation of musicians for a rule on defendants to show cause why they should be punished for contempt for violating an injunction, findings of the chancellor in an order entered discharging the rule and dismissing the petition, *held* to be sustained by the evidence.

2. APPEAL AND ERROR, § 1395*—*when findings of fact by chancellor will not be disturbed.* It is the settled rule in equity practice that a court of review will not set aside the findings of fact by a chancellor who saw the witnesses and heard them testify, unless the error in such findings is clear and palpable.

The A. H. Andrews Company, Plaintiff in Error, v. Robert A. Pottinger and Matilda Pottinger, Defendants in Error.

Gen. No. 18,154.

1. BILLS AND NOTES, § 451*—*when finding as to satisfaction of indebtedness on notes not sustained by the evidence.* In an action to recover the balance due on certain promissory notes executed by defendant to plaintiff in payment for theatre chairs, a finding of the jury that plaintiff accepted payment of a certain sum in satisfaction of defendant's indebtedness on the notes, *held* not sustained by the evidence.

2. BILLS AND NOTES, § 462*—*when instruction as to satisfaction of indebtedness erroneous.* In an action on promissory notes, an instruction that if the jury believe from the evidence that on a certain day the plaintiff and defendant had an agreement that the payment of a certain sum in the manner agreed upon was to constitute a full settlement of the claim sued on, then they are instructed that such agreement constitutes a full accord and they should find for defendants, *held* erroneous, for the reason that there is uncertainty in defendants' testimony whether the alleged accord

---

*See Illinois Notes Digest, Vols. XI to XV, same topic and section number.

was before or after the date named and that defendants' right to recover is made to depend solely on an accord, instead of an accord and satisfaction.

3. APPEAL AND ERROR, § 1539*—*when giving of instruction stating a true proposition of law prejudicial.* In an action to recover on promissory notes secured by a chattel mortgage, where the mortgagee had purchased the chattels at his own sale at an inadequate price, but the plaintiff had conceded the invalidity of the sale in his statement of claim, an instruction stating that such a sale is presumed fraudulent, though stating a true proposition of law, is not applicable to the case and the giving of the instruction *held* prejudicial error.

Error to the Municipal Court of Chicago; the Hon. FRED C. HILL, Judge, presiding. Heard in the Branch Appellate Court at the March term, 1912. Reversed and remanded. Opinion filed December 31, 1913.

GREGORY, POPPENHUSEN & McNAB, for plaintiff in error; EDWARD R. JOHNSTON, of counsel.

EDMUND W. FROEHLICH, for defendants in error.

MR. JUSTICE DUNCAN delivered the opinion of the court.

The A. H. Andrews Company brought this suit to recover a balance claimed to be due on ten promissory notes, aggregating $1,651.40, secured by a chattel mortgage, all executed August 10, 1910, by defendants in error for the purchase of the seating for the Sheridan Theatre on Sheridan Road near Irving Park Boulevard, Chicago. The first of said notes fell due October 7, 1910, and plaintiff in error, the A. H. Andrews Company, elected to and did declare all of the notes due, and on October 15, 1910, took possession of the chairs in said theatre, and on a sale thereof under the mortgage, October 20, 1910, Joseph G. Murphy bought them in for the mortgagee company for $50. In its amended statement of claim plaintiff in error, recognizing the invalidity of said sale, alleged that the fair and reasonable cash value of said chairs so by it taken was $796, and conceded and gave credit on said notes for said sum, claiming a net balance of $854.60 and interest thereon from October 20, 1910, for said notes and costs of foreclosure. Defendants in error stated their defense to be a complete settlement of all matters between the parties about November 2, 1910, which settlement constituted an accord and satisfaction of all claims then existing including the claim in suit. Also, that the then fair and reasonable value of the chairs when retaken by plaintiff in error equalled the full amount of the notes in suit. The jury found the issues for defendants in error, and replied, in answer to a special interrogatory, in substance, that plaintiff in error accepted $710 in money about November 2, 1910, and the sum of $930.01 about December 5, 1910, in satisfaction of his indebtedness to it, on said ten notes. The court entered judgment accordingly for defendants in error.

The plaintiff in error proved by three expert witnesses who saw the 644 chairs on the day of their removal that the total value of the chairs retaken under the mortgage was about $800. Some of the reasons given for the depreciation in value were that the chairs were soiled and scratched and that about ten per cent. of the castings thereon were broken when removed; that there is no market for such secondhand chairs, as the chairs in question were specially made for, and fitted in, the Sheridan theatre building, and would not fit the circles and rises in the floors of other buildings; and that for 440 of them it would cost about thirty cents a piece to replace them in another building, which cost was a part of the original price of defendants in error. Defendants in error offered no evidence to rebut that testimony, but relied solely on their proof of an accord and satisfaction. The evidence under that plea was that in September, 1909, defendant in error, Robert A. Pottinger, bought from plaintiff in error other opera chairs for his vaudeville house known as the "Mabel Theatre," 3956-8 Elston avenue, Chicago, for the pur-

448   APPELLATE COURTS OF ILLINOIS.

The A. H. Andrews Co. v. Pottinger et al., 184 Ill. App. 445.

chase price of $1,524.82, which was also secured by
notes and a chattel mortgage. No part of the purchase
price being paid when the first payment became due,
plaintiff in error in October, 1910, took possession of
those chairs and placed a custodian in charge of them,
but they were not removed from the building as Pottinger insisted that he could and would raise the money
to pay for them. On November 2, 1910, Pottinger and
his wife, Matilda, signed what the parties called a
lease for the Mabel theatre chairs in which they agreed
to pay in advance the sum of $710 as rental for said
chairs for thirty days from the date thereof, and were
given in said lease an option to purchase said chairs
for the sum of $930.01 in cash if paid at the end
of said lease, December 2, 1910, and in case of default in payment of said last sum on the day named
said option was to cease, and that the other party
thereto, John G. Murphy, who was a representative
of plaintiff in error, should retake said chairs and
remove them from said building. Nothing is mentioned in that lease about the Sheridan theatre
chairs. The accord claimed by defendants in error,
they insist, was made at the time an understanding
was reached by the parties in regard to the making of
said lease, and it is supported only by their own testimony. Robert A. Pottinger's testimony thereon is, in ·
substance, as follows: "I had a further talk with Mr.
Merle (manager of plaintiff in error), I think it was the
15th or 20th of October before the sale at his office. I
told him if he would wait a while I could raise the
money to make these payments. He said he wanted the
money or the chairs. I wanted to take both chairs
(both sets of chairs) from him and pay him $250, and
he would not accept that proposition. He said he would
have to have all the money within thirty days, part of
it now, and the balance within thirty days, which I was
unable to raise. Then I said I would take the Mabel
chairs and pay it half cash and the balance in thirty
days, and that was decided upon. He said he would

take the Sheridan chairs out because they were in good condition. The Mabel chairs had been in the house about a year, he said. On the day of the sale, I told him I would be in a position to straighten the thing up in a few days. He said, 'Well, we will go ahead and sell the chairs and you come in.' I had occasion to see him again about the 2nd of November at his office. Mr. Merle, myself and my wife were present, I had with me $700. I told him I would pay him $700 on the Mabel chairs. Then he began to figure up and said, 'You are short. You didn't figure the expenses, did you?' I said, 'No, I forgot it, I haven't got it.' 'Well, I will add that in to the next month,' he said. So the expenses were added in, and I paid him something like $1640, including the cost of the chairs and the expenses, both on the Mabel. I paid him $610 cash, and a check for one hundred dollars, and executed a lease on account of these Mabel chairs. He spoke of the expense of the cost of taking the Sheridan theatre chairs out and the expense of the sale. At that time I don't think we spoke about the Sheridan chairs, only to buy some back. I bought forty chairs that had been taken out of the Sheridan theatre. We paid for them separate in cash (40 chairs @ $2.25, $90). I received a receipt for the $710 at that time, and a receipt for the ninety dollars. I saw Mr. Merle again about December 5th. I had a talk with him about a check my wife took to him for the balance due, and he told me he would not accept it, that I had drawn it to A. H. Andrews & Company, and he wanted it made to Mr. Murphy, and I said, 'all right.' I made out a new check to Joseph Murphy for the same amount and gave it to him in payment of the lease. Mr. Merle never asked me to pay those notes for the Sheridan Theatre chairs until this suit.''

On cross-examination he testified: ''After the sale I had kind of given up hope of holding the Sheridan any more. I was trying to keep the Mabel. Mr. Merle told me that he would accept the amount which we agreed on, $700 and $900, and some odd dollars in full settlement of both matters, if I would pay the expenses on the Sheridan chairs and pay the full amount of the Mabel chairs, not the lease, we made the lease after that." And again referring to their talk of November 2nd, he testified in substance that they talked about settlement of the Sheridan theatre matter and that they did settle it "by paying the cost and one thing and another," and that Merle told him he would accept the $710 and the $930.01 in full of both matters, and that they were so settled up in full.

Mrs. Matilda Pottinger testified that she was the wife of Robert Pottinger; that the first time she had anything to do with the business after signing the notes was November 2nd, when the first payment was made on the Mabel chairs at Mr. Merle's office; that Mr. Pottinger did all the talking; that he bought some chairs back for the Sheridan theatre, and paid him $710 on the Mabel chairs; that Mr. Merle said he included custodian's fees and expenses for both the Sheridan and Mabel theatres and that a receipt was given for the $710; that there was not much said about the Sheridan theatre expense; that Mr. Merle just said, "You didn't figure the costs of the expenses," and he wrote down the custodian's fees for the Sheridan and Mabel theatre; that he made that remark to Mr. Pottinger, and she saw him writing it but didn't see the paper; that she did not hear anything further about the Sheridan job except that they bought forty chairs for that theatre; that on December 3d, she took down a certified check to Mr. Merle for $930.01 and that he refused to take it because it was payable to The A. H. Andrews Company and not to Mr. Murphy, and because there was written on the bottom of the check, "In full payment of the Sheridan and Mabel chairs;" that he finally agreed to accept it if they would bring down another check without the words at the bottom of the check.

Mr. Pottinger was positively contradicted *in toto* by Mr. Merle's evidence on the alleged accord and satisfaction and by James D. Irving, a salesman of plaintiff in error, who testified he heard all that was said between the parties November 2d. He is also contradicted by Edward R. Johnson who testified he gave Pottinger on November 2d an exhibit on a paper of all the items composing the consideration of $1,640.01 named in the lease in the amounts $710 and $930.01, which exhibit was in evidence and makes no reference to the Sheridan chairs. The receipts taken by him for the $710 and the $930.01 also specified that the money was received in payment of rental and for the purchase of the Mabel chairs, without any reference to the Sheridan chairs. The lease itself corroborated in the same way plaintiff in error's evidence. Pottinger's own testimony is contradictory and is not supported in the main by that of Mrs. Pottinger as to the accord and satisfaction. The verdict and special finding of the jury are manifestly against the weight of the evidence and the same must be set aside for that reason. *Donelson v. East St. Louis & S. Ry. Co.*, 235 Ill. 625.

The court also erred in giving to the jury two instructions, towit:

1. "That if they believe from the evidence that on the 2nd day of November, 1910, the plaintiff and defendants had an agreement or understanding to the effect that the payment of the sum of $1640 in the manner agreed upon was to constitute a full settlement of the claim sued on in this case, then they are instructed that such agreement constituted a full accord and that the jury must then find the issues for the defendants."

2. "A mortgagee has no right to buy at its own sale, and that such purchase in this case, together with the inadequacy of the consideration paid for such chairs, raises the presumption that said sale under said foreclosure, was fraudulent and illegal, unless you find from the evidence herein that defendants had full

452   APPELLATE COURTS OF ILLINOIS.

The A. H. Andrews Co. v. Pottinger et al., 184 Ill. App. 445.

knowledge of such purchase and that said purchase was made with defendant's consent."

Instruction No. 1 is erroneous because it makes the right of defendants in error to recover to depend upon an accord, simply, instead of an accord and satisfaction. There was an uncertainty in the testimony of defendants in error as to whether the alleged accord was before or on November 2d, when the lease was made. Not only must there have been an agreement that both claims were to be settled for the amount named in the lease, but it must have been carried out by the payment of said sum by defendants in error to plaintiff in error, and an acceptance thereof by plaintiff in error in satisfaction of both claims. It is true no doubt that if such an agreement was in fact made and plaintiff in error accepted the first payment of $710 in pursuance of such an agreement, it would be estopped to insist there was no accord and satisfaction because it refused to accept the second payment as in full satisfaction of both claims. The instruction, however, made the recovery to depend solely on an accord and this was error as plaintiff in error denied the accord and also the receipt of the first as well as of the second payment to be in pursuance of any agreement that they should be in full satisfaction of both claims for chairs. *American v. Rimpert*, 75 Ill. 228; *Canton Coal Co. v. Parlin & Orendorff Co.*, 215 Ill. 244; *Simmons v. Clark*, 56 Ill. 96.

Instruction No. 2, while it stated a true proposition of law, was not applicable to the case. Plaintiff in error conceded the invalidity of the sale by its statement of claim and no issue as to its validity was in the case. It was such an instruction, too, as tended to prejudice the jury, as it unnecessarily informed the jury in substance that such a sale was fraudulent.

For the errors indicated the judgment of the court is reversed and the cause is remanded.

Reversed and remanded.

Musical Leader Publishing Company, Defendant in Error, v. Carolina White, Plaintiff in Error.

Gen. No. 18,285.   (Not to be reported in full.)

Error to the Municipal Court of Chicago; the Hon. EDWARD A. DICKER, Judge, presiding. Heard in the Branch Appellate Court at the March term, 1912. Affirmed. Opinion filed December 31, 1913. Rehearing denied January 20, 1914.

Statement of the Case.

Action by Musical Leader Publishing Company, a corporation, against Carolina White in attachment to recover a balance due upon a contract by which defendant agreed to pay for certain advertisements in the Musical Leader, a paper owned by the plaintiff. The attachment was in aid of the original suit, the affidavit setting forth the indebtedness and the nonresidence of defendant as grounds therefor. Defendant filed an affidavit of defense stating plaintiff had failed to publish the advertisement as agreed and that she was entitled to a set-off, but did not traverse the affidavit or in anyway deny that she was a nonresident. From a judgment in favor of plaintiff upon both the attachment issue and on the merits, defendant brings error.

CAIROLI GIGLIOTTI, for plaintiff in error.

CHARLES DANIELS and SUMNER C. PALMER, for defendant in error.

MR. JUSTICE DUNCAN delivered the opinion of the court.

Abstract of the Decision.

1. ATTACHMENT, § 242*—*when plaintiff entitled to a judgment by default on the attachment issue.* In attachment based on an affidavit of nonresidence of defendant, where defendant does not traverse the affidavit or in any way deny that she was a nonresident, there is no issue made upon the question of nonresidence of defendant, and as to the attachment the plaintiff is entitled to a judgment by default.

2. ATTACHMENT, § 246*—*when judgment for plaintiff on the attachment issue and on the merits sustained by sufficient evidence.* In attachment to recover on a contract for advertising, where the attachment was based on the nonresidence of defendant, and defendant filed an affidavit of defense claiming plaintiff failed to publish the advertisements as agreed, and that she was entitled to a set-off, *held* that a judgment in favor of plaintiff on the attachment issue and on the merits was sustained by sufficient evidence, the defendant having introduced no evidence, and plaintiff's evidence tended to show defendant was a resident of Italy before the contract was signed and a resident of Massachusetts after the attachment issued and there was evidence showing that plaintiff complied with the contract, that defendant had made a partial payment after the contract was concluded and that defendant's husband had written a letter, which defendant had adopted, asking for a postponement of payment.

3. SET-OFF AND RECOUPMENT, § 43*—*when defendant not entitled to instruction for set-off.* Where there is no evidence tending to prove a claim of set-off, defendant is entitled to no instruction regarding the same.

Owen Murphy, Plaintiff in Error, v. Gunning System, Defendant in Error.

Gen. No. 18,320.   (Not to be reported in full.)

Error to the Superior Court of Cook county; the Hon. GEORGE W. PATTON, Judge, presiding. Heard in the Branch Appellate Court at the March term, 1912. Reversed and remanded. Opinion filed December 31, 1913.

---

*See Illinois Notes Digest, Vols. XI to XV, same topic and section number.

Statement of the Case.

Action by Owen Murphy against Gunning System to recover for personal injuries sustained by plaintiff by falling from the top of the framework of one of defendant's signboards while employed by defendant in removing panels therefrom. From a judgment in favor .of defendant on a directed verdict, plaintiff brings error.

GEORGE E. GORMAN, for plaintiff in error; WILLIAM H. HOLLY, of counsel.

HENRY W. WOLSELEY, for defendant in error.

MR. JUSTICE DUNCAN delivered the opinion of the court.

Abstract of the Decision.

1. **MASTER AND SERVANT, § 770*—*when direction of verdict in action by employe for injury while repairing signboard error.* In an action by an employe against a signboard company to recover for injuries sustained by falling from the top of the framework of a certain signboard, the declaration alleging that the company was negligent in constructing and maintaining the framework in safe condition for plaintiff to work thereon, and the evidence showing that plaintiff was precipitated to the ground by reason of a timber, upon which he was obliged to stand, giving way so that he fell forward on another cross-timber at the top of the framework which broke by reason of a concealed knot therein, *held* that the evidence required the court to submit the case to the jury and that the court erred in directing a verdict for defendant.

2. **MASTER AND SERVANT, § 368*—*when employe may recover for injuries resulting from defective construction of signboard on which he was required to work.* Where a person employed to repair signboards is charged with the duty to inspect the framework, to detect any dangers from decay, and to repair and report such defects, and is injured while removing panels from the signboard by reason of a defect in a timber nailed to the post of the framework as a footboard, he cannot recover if the footboard was defective on account of decay and such defect was the sole proximate cause of the injury, but where the injury was also caused by a defect in a timber

at the top of the signboard, which was a concealed knot and a fault
in the original construction, the plaintiff may recover where both
defective timbers are the proximate cause of the injury and there is
no other intervening cause.

3. MASTER AND SERVANT, § 137*—*when master not liable for dangers of place to work or appliances.* Master may employ a competent servant to demolish or to make a well known dangerous place or appliance safe without being liable because such place or appliance is dangerous to the employe.

4. MASTER AND SERVANT, § 681*—*when evidence of employer's ownership or construction of signboard sufficient to go to the jury.* In an action by an employe to recover for injuries sustained while employed in repairing signboards for defendant, alleging that the injury was sustained by reason of defective construction of the framework, evidence that defendant directed plaintiff to repair the signboard and that plaintiff's boss was the man who had the work before, *held* sufficient evidence to go to the jury on the question of whether the framework belonged to or was constructed by defendant.

———

Frances K. Schoden, Appellant, v. John Schaefer et al., Appellees.

Gen. No. 18,370.

1. DRAINAGE, § 56*—*when officers of district jointly liable for misapplication of money raised to pay bonds.* The treasurer of a drainage district and the drainage commissioners are jointly liable in an action for money had and received brought by holder of bonds issued by the drainage district under R. S. 1911, p. 943, J. & A. ¶ 4340, to recover the face value of the bonds and interest thereon for the misapplication of taxes levied and collected for the payment of such bonds, where the treasurer upon orders of the commissioners paid out such fund for purposes other than the payment of the bonds.

2. DRAINAGE, § 54*—*when treasurer of district personally liable for misapplication of funds.* Instalments of taxes levied and collected by the drainage commissioners to pay bonds issued by the district are trust funds to be used in the payment of the bonds only, and the treasurer of the drainage district is personally liable for misapplying such funds, though he paid them out on orders of the drainage commissioners.

3. DRAINAGE, § 56*—*liability of district for misapplication of funds raised to pay bonds.* Where officers of a drainage district

misapply funds collected to meet payment of bonds issued by the district, the district is not liable for any part of its funds so misapplied. For such funds the bondholders must look solely to the officers who misappropriated them.

4. DRAINAGE, § 128*—*power to levy an assessment for misapplied funds.* Where funds levied and collected for the payment of bonds issued by a drainage district have been misapplied, no second assessment can be levied and collected to pay the same. A second assessment cannot be levied to meet a past indebtedness.

5. DRAINAGE, § 164*—*when officers of district misapplying illegal taxes collected not liable to refund to taxpayers.* Officers of a drainage district misapplying funds raised by an illegal assessment are not liable to the taxpayers to refund the same where the taxpayers voluntarily paid such taxes with full knowledge of all the facts concerning them.

6. ACTIONS, § 15*—*when demand not necessary before suit.* Demand before suit not necessary to maintenance of an action against officers of a drainage district for misapplication of taxes levied and collected to pay bonds issued by the district.

7. ASSUMPSIT, ACTION OF, § 44*—*nature of action for money had and received.* Action for money had and received for the use of plaintiff is an equitable action and lies for money had and received by the defendant which in equity and good conscience he should not retain. The law in such case implies a promise to pay although there is no privity between the parties. The alleged contract is fictitious and the right to recover is governed by principles in equity.

8. ASSUMPSIT, ACTION OF, § 53*—*when lies against a person receiving money for the use of another.* Where a party receives money for a particular purpose and fails to apply it to that purpose, he is liable in *assumpsit* for money had and received to the person to whom the money should have been paid.

9. OFFICERS, § 52*—*when public officer cannot attack validity of bonds in action for misapplication of funds raised to pay the bonds.* In an action against the officers of a drainage district to recover against them personally for misapplying funds raised to pay bonds, the officers cannot avoid their liability by alleging and proving the illegality of the bonds.

10. OFFICERS, § 54*—*when public officers personally liable for failure to perform duties.* Where public officers fail to perform a public duty and thereby cause an injury special and peculiar to such individual, an action will lie against them personally; and if the injury is caused by the joint action of the officers, a joint action may be maintained either in the case of a breach of a contract express or implied or in the violation of a duty whereby a tortious injury is inflicted.

*See Illinois Notes Digest, Vols. XI to XV, same topic and section number.

11. APPEAL AND ERROR, § 1672*—*when objection for misjoinder of counts is waived.* Objection that a special count in a declaration is in *tort* and that such count cannot be joined with the common counts or any count in *assumpsit* is waived where such objection does not appear to have been urged in the trial court and the general issue in *assumpsit* was pleaded to such plea.

Appeal from the Superior Court of Cook county; the Hon. JOSEPH H. FITCH, Judge, presiding. Heard in the Branch Appellate Court at the March term, 1912. Reversed and remanded. Opinion filed December 31, 1913.

ADAMS, BOBB & ADAMS, for appellant; G. L. WIRE, of counsel.

GAIL E. DEMING and LOUIS J. PIERSON, for appellees.

MR. JUSTICE DUNCAN delivered the opinion of the court.

February 27, 1909, Frances K. Schoden, appellant and owner of certain bonds issued by Drainage District No. 1 of the Town of New Trier, Cook County, Illinois, brought this action against appellees to recover $1,000, the face value of said bonds and interest thereon. The trial of the cause, and of three other similar suits hereinafter named and consolidated by agreement with this case for trial in the lower court was had before the court without a jury and on February 3, 1912, the court found the issues in favor of appellees in all the cases and entered judgment accordingly.

The declaration in this case consists of a special count and the common counts in *assumpsit*, including the count for money had and received by appellees to and for the use of appellant. The special count sets forth, in substance, that on December 27, 1902, the regularly elected, qualified and acting drainage commissioners of said drainage district passed resolutions in due form authorizing and directing the issue of one hundred and twenty bonds of said district in the principal sum of $50 each, payable with six per cent. interest, forty of said bonds to be marked "Series A" and payable December 1, 1903, forty thereof to be marked "Series B" and payable December 1, 1914, and forty thereof to be marked "Series C" and payable December 1, 1905, pursuant to an Act of the General Assembly of Illinois in force June 15, 1895, for the purposes of constructing a system of drainage in said district, the principal and interest being payable from the receipts of a special assessment which was levied by said commissioners against the property in said district to pay for said improvements; that appellant is the owner of twenty of said bonds of "Series C" and the last interest coupons of three dollars each attached to them and which were executed and delivered by said commissioners, February 16, 1903; that thereafter appellee, John Schaefer, was the selected and qualified treasurer of said district and as such treasurer did receive into his hands the moneys levied and collected to pay said bonds; that the other appellees were after the execution and delivery of said bonds the duly elected, qualified and acting drainage commissioners of said district at the times of the receipt of said moneys; that notwithstanding their duty in the premises to apply said moneys to the payment of said bonds, nevertheless said appellees as said commissioners did then and there authorize and direct said appellee, Schaefer, as treasurer, aforesaid, to pay out and expend said moneys to other parties for other purposes than the payment of the bonds and for which payment said moneys were levied and collected, and said Schaefer, as treasurer, did pay out said moneys to other persons for purposes other than the payment of said bonds, although appellant after the maturity of said bonds demanded and requested appellee to pay said bonds according to the tenor and effect thereof, but appellees have refused to pay the same, or the interest thereon, or any part thereof, etc.

To the common counts appellees filed the general issue in *assumpsit*. Appellees, Schneider, Laubach

and Roemer, jointly filed the general issue in *assumpsit*
to the first count. Appellee, Schaefer, filed the general
issue in *assumpsit* to the first count and also a special
plea, in substance, that at the times alleged in said
declaration he was the duly appointed and qualified
treasurer of said drainage commissioners and that he
received said moneys as such treasurer; that in his
said official capacity he paid out said moneys in good
faith for the uses and benefit of said drainage district under and in acordance with the order of said duly
elected and qualified drainage commissioners, and only
upon orders duly signed by their chairman and countersigned by their clerk, and has not now, and had not
at the time of the alleged demand upon him, any of said
moneys as such treasurer, and did not at any time
promise to pay appellant said moneys or any part
thereof. The court sustained a demurrer to said
special plea, and appellee, Schaefer, elected to stand by
his said special plea. Appellees, Schneider, Laubach
and Roemer, then filed a further special plea duly
sworn to denying joint liability, on which issue was
taken.

The three other suits against said appellees were
brought on certain other of said bonds executed by
said drainage commissioners, one by *Helen Sesterhenn,*
executrix of the last will of Maternus Schaefer, deceased, another by *Egidius Meyer,* and the third by
Anna Huerter, all of which are here on appeal, and
are in this court numbered respectively 18,371, 18,372
and 18,373 (*supra* p. 472), and were all consolidated
for hearing by order of this court with the case of appellant, Schoden, and in all three of said causes it is
stipulated that the judgment of this court in this, the
Schoden case, shall be the judgment of this court in
all of said other three causes.

From the further stipulations of the parties to said
four suits and the evidence offered it clearly appears
that the said special count of the declaration was
proved and that said drainage district was organized

October 2, 1902, under the provisions of the Farm
Drainage Act for a system of combined drainage,
which provisions begin with paragraph 85 of chapter
42 of Hurd's Revised Statutes, 1911, p. 901. (J. &. A.
¶ 4485). Under the provisions of said act the commissioners of highways of said township, Fred Schramm,
Ignatz Schweiger and Paul Nanzig, acted as drainage
commissioners for the district to March 16, 1903, when
appellees, Schafer, Schneider and Laubach, were
elected and qualified as drainage commissioners and
served as such to March 22, 1904. Casper Roemer then
succeeded John Schaefer as such commissioner, but
died shortly after his election, and on June 4, 1904,
appellees, Schaefer, Schneider and Laubach, were
the duly elected and qualified drainage commissioners
of said district and served as such to and including
March 10, 1906, but were not at any other period of
time altogether the acting drainage commissioners of
the district. Appellee, Schaefer, was the duly elected
and acting treasurer of the district from the date of
its organization to and including September 29, 1911,
and Gangolf Sesterhenn was its clerk and clerk of
said township for the same time. On December 4,
1902, by resolution, the drainage commissioners estimated and stated the cost of the entire drainage system as follows:

For clearing and constructing ditches, etc.,.$ 7,200.00
For damages to lands taken for drains......   800.00
For engineer's fees and assistant's compen-
    sation 350.00
For compensation to drainage Commission-
    ers, treasurer and clerk 700.00
For incidental expenses...................   200.00
For Court Costs and Attorney fees.........   750.00

    Total $10,000.00

The commissioners caused to be made a classification of the lands in the district and a levy and assessment of $10,000, apportioned as aforesaid, for the pur-

pose of making the said improvement as provided by
plans and specifications, $2,000 of which sum was im-
posed against the commissioners of highways of said
township by reason of benefits to the highways thereof,
and the other $8,000 was levied and assessed against
the landowners of the district. Upon a petition of a
majority of the landowners, the levy and assessment of
$8,000 was by resolution of the drainage commissioners
on December 27, 1902, divided into four equal instalments of $2,000 each, one instalment payable forthwith,
and the other three instalments were payable respectively, December 1, 1903, December 1, 1904 and December 1, 1905, all drawing six per cent. interest. To secure the deferred instalments three series of bonds
were determined upon and were to be known and
described as set forth in appellant's special count
aforesaid, and were payable at the State Bank of
Evanston, Cook county, Illinois. The said bonds
were prepared accordingly and "Series B" and
"Series C" thereof were sold, and appellants in
said four causes are conceded to be owners of certain of the bonds sold as follows: Frances K. Schoden, twenty bonds of "Series C," numbered from 1
to 20 inclusive, of the face value of $1,000; Egidius
Meyer, twelve bonds of "Series C," numbered 29 to
40 inclusive, $600; Helen Sesterhenn, executrix, twenty
bonds of "Series B," numbered 1 to 20 inclusive,
$1,000; Anna Huerter, twenty bonds of "Series B,"
numbered 21 to 40 inclusive, $1,000. William Kossow
was shown to have purchased the other eight bonds of
"Series C," $400, which are also unpaid, but not liti-
gated in said suits. The forty bonds known as "Series
A" were never sold by the commissioners, it being
considered unnecessary, because so many landowners
elected to and did pay in cash all four of the instalments of taxes, so far as levied and assessed against
their lands. Of the $4,000 in bonds issued by the
drainage district, all of which were issued under the
Act of June 15, 1905 (Hurd's Statutes, 1911, p. 943, J.

& A. ¶ 4340), no part of the principal thereof has ever been paid, as shown by the evidence, and the interest thereon has been paid up to December 1, 1907. The treasurer's reports in evidence show the receipts of the district to be as follows:

To July, 1906, from land owners on instalment taxes $5,409.73
Up to December, 1908, from the County Collector and treasurer 4,319.21
March 31, 1908, from the Town Collector..... 648.87
March 5, 1903, from the Commissioners of Highways, assessment 2,000.00
October 17, 1903, from the Commissioners of Highways, on sewer pipes............... 1,000.00
December 1, 1904, from the Commissioners of Highways 185.00
March 5, 1903, from sale of bonds and accrued interest 4,040.00
September 5, 1903, from Charles Schuette, donation to district 25.00
May 30, 1904, from M. & St. P. R. R. Co., for damage to pipes 6.58
October 21, 1904, from Fred Scheuber towards catch basin 20.00

Total $17,654.39

No other levy for any purpose was ever made and collected by the said district, and the said total sum represents the total sum received by said district from all sources up to October 31, 1910. Of said total sum collected by said treasurer the sum of $11,578.01 was collected prior to June 4, 1904, or prior to the time appellees constituted the treasurer and board of drainage commissioners for said district. The total sum spent by the treasurer and former drainage commissioners up to June 4, 1904, was $11,524.05. Of said total sum the following amounts came into the appellee Schaefer's hands as treasurer aforesaid from

June 4, 1904, to March 10, 1906, towit:

June 4, 1904, Balance not paid out..........$ 53.9
Oct. 7, 1904, to Dec., 1904, 3d instalment taxes   674.9
Oct. 7, 1904, to Jan., 1906, 4th instalment taxes   617.4
Jan. 20, 1905, to Nov., 1905 from County
    Treasurer 1,006.64
Aug. 3, 1904, to Aug. 7, 1904, 2d instalment
    taxes 553.5
Dec. 1, 1904, from Highway Commissioners..   185.
Oct. 21, 1904, from Fred Scheuber towards
    catch basin ....   20.

    Total $3,111.5

During the same time, from June 4, 1904, to Marc
10, 1906, appellee, Schaefer, as treasurer, paid out, o
order of the commissioners, the following amounts:

From October 8, 1904, to November 5, 1905, to
    contractors for constructing drains, etc....$1,558.0
March 11, 1905, Hoffman Bros., lumber......   6.7
Jan. 5, 1905, to parties for cleaning ditch, G.
    P. Av....................................   31.
Jan. 27, 1906, F. A. Windes as engineer ......   184.
Jan. 18, 1906, R. W. Boddinghouse, as attorney   35.
Jan. 3 to March 11, 1905, officers fees, Commis-
    sioners, clerk and treasurer..............   262.49
Dec. 8, 1905, Philip Doetch, Committee mem-
    ber ـ٥.00
Jan. 20, 1905, John Hanberg, County Treas-
    urer, percentage 7.7
Jan. 3, 1905, and January, 1906, C. H. Bush,
    printing reports 22.00
Jan. 3, 1905, and April 1, 1905, Jacob Roemer,
    for house of election....................   7.5
Dec. 1, 1904, and Jan. 18, 1906, to owners of
    $4,000 of bonds, interest for 1904 and 1905.. 480.00

    Total $2,609.71
There was received by appellee, Schaefer, as treas-

urer of said district after March 10, 1906, the following accounts:

March 11, 1906, Balance not paid out........$	501.81
Sept. 18, 1907, from land owners, 4th instalment taxes	181.66
Sept. 18, 1907, from County treasurer........	350.00
Dec. 23, 1907, from County treasurer........	470.95
March 31, 1908, from Town Collector........	648.87
Dec. 21, 1908, from County treasurer........	1,367.34

Total $3,520.63

Subsequent to March 10, 1906, appellee, Schaefer, as treasurer of said district, paid out the following amounts on order of commissioners other than appellee commissioners towit:

July 16, 1906, to Aug. 16, 1910, for cleaning and repairing drains, etc.................$	477.40
Oct. 30, 1909, paid for bridge on private lane	40.37
Dec. 12, 1906, to Oct. 30, 1909, Officers of District and bond for officer.................	332.10
Dec. 31, 1907, C. H. Bush for printing reports	10.00
Jan. 26, 1907, to March 31, 1910, for attorneys	687.50
Nov. and Dec., 1906, paid engineers	30.00
Sept. 21, 1907, and Jan. 9, 1909, paid on $4,000 of bonds, interest for 1906 and 1907........	480.00

Total $2,057.37
Oct. 31, 1910, Balance in treasury..........$1,463.26

The several amounts collected by appellee, Schaefer, as treasurer, from the county treasurer, the "town collector" and from the commissioners of highways, except as above shown, are not designated by the treasurer's reports, and, therefore, it cannot be ascertained definitely from the evidence in this record how much thereof, if any, represents collections from the third and fourth instalments of taxes that were evidently levied for the purpose of paying the $4,000 of bonds and the interest thereon. For that reason also we cannot ascertain definitely how much of the third and fourth instalment taxes were received by said treasurer prior to June 4, 1904, or subsequent to March 10, 1906, or between those dates. It may be assumed, however, that the $53.96 balance in the treasury, June 4, 1904, belonged to those funds as $1,184.60 of the third and fourth instalment taxes had been collected prior thereto and only the sum of $240 interest was paid on the bonds. The showing then as made by this record without contradiction is that during the whole time appellees were serving together as drainage commissioners and treasurer of said drainage district, June 4, 1904, to March 10, 1906, the treasurer received $1,346.33 of the taxes levied and collected to pay said bonds and only applied thereon the sum of $480 as interest for 1904 and 1905, leaving a balance of $866.33 that should have been applied to the payment of the principal thereof. Assuming that the balance of $501.81 in the treasury March 11, 1906, belongs exclusively to the funds collected to pay the bonds, it is clear that appellees by their joint action misapplied the sum of $364.52, and also that part of the $1,006.64 received by them from the county treasurer, if any, that was collected by the said treasurer on the third and fourth instalment taxes levied to pay said bonds. The evidence further shows that of the $10,000 estimated, appropriated and levied as the total costs to the district for the construction of the drains, etc., and for the expenses connected therewith, every item of that cost and expense, as above itemized by the commissioners, was overpaid prior to June 4, 1904.

The court properly held as legal propositions that the instalments of taxes levied and collected for the payment of the bonds held by appellant were trust funds to be used in payment of said bonds only; that appellee, Schaefer, became personally liable to appellant for misapplying said funds, although he paid them out by order of the drainage commissioners; and that the commissioners of the district were also liable to appellant in a proper action for wrongfully ordering their said treasurer to pay out said funds on other obligations or claims against the district. The court also held that appellees were not jointly liable, and that an action of *assumpsit* will not lie against appellees jointly for the recovery by appellant of the funds so misappropriated. To the latter holdings of the court we cannot assent. It is the law, as argued by appellees, that in actions *ex contractu* the burden is on the plaintiff to establish his case of joint liability against all the defendants when joint liability is denied. *Griffith v. Furry*, 30 Ill. 251; *Cassady v. Trustees of Schools*, 105 Ill. 560; *United Workmen v. Zuhlke*, 129 Ill. 298; *Kingsland v. Koeppe*, 137 Ill. 344; *Powell Co. v. Finn*, 198 Ill. 567.

Appellees' counsel also contend that the first count of the declaration is in tort and that such a count cannot be joined with the common counts or any count in *assumpsit,* and that, therefore, appellant cannot recover in this case. No such contention appears to have been made in the lower court, and, besides, appellees pleaded the general issue in *assumpsit* to the special count, and thereby have waived the right to insist that said count is in tort, or that there is a misjoinder of counts. We deem it unnecessary to further consider the first count of the declaration, as we predicate our holding that appellant was entitled to a judgment in this case on the evidence under the common counts and particularly under the count for money had and received by appellees to the use of appellant. Where a party receives money for a particular purpose and fails to apply it to that purpose he is liable in *assumpsit* for money had and received to the person to whom the money should have been paid. *Parker v. Fisher, Fuller & Co.* 39 Ill. 164.

The action for money had and received for the use of the plaintiff is an equitable action and lies for money had and received by the defendant, which in equity and good conscience he should not retain, but should pay to the plaintiff. The right of recovery in such action depends upon two things: First, that the defendant has actually received the money; and, second, that in equity and good conscience he should pay it to the plaintiff. The law in such case implies a promise to pay, although there is no privity between the parties. The alleged contract is fictitious and the right of recovery is governed by principles of equity. *Morris v. Jamieson*, 99 Ill. App. 32; *Richolson v. Moloney*, 195 Ill. 575; *Donovan v. Purtell*, 216 Ill. 629; *Highway Commissioners v. City of Bloomington*, 253 Ill. 164.

It has been frequently said by appellees in their argument that all the said funds were received by appellee, Schaefer, as treasurer, and that the other appellees, the commissioners, received no money, and, therefore, there can be no action for money had and received against them. The treasurer was appointed by the appellees, the commissioners, and he received the money for the drainage commissioners, whose officer he was, and to and for the use of the bondholders. The treasurer and the commissioners held and controlled the funds, and the bond holders could not get them except by the order of the commissioners and by payment on such orders by the treasurer, i. e., without the joint action of the commissioners and the treasurer. The commissioners had the right and the power at all times, and it was their duty to control the funds in the treasurer's hands and to direct him to pay them out for the purposes for which they were received, and the treasurer could not legally pay them out, except by such direction. By their concerted acts the commissioners and the treasurer diverted funds received for the use of appellant and paid them to others. Hence, they are jointly liable to her for the amount so by him diverted. Paragraphs 89a, 89b, 105 and 112, chapter 42, Hurd's Statutes 1911 (J. & A. ¶¶ 4490, 4491, 4507, 4514); *Lovingston v. Board of Trustees*, 99 Ill. 564-572; *City of Springfield v. Edwards*, 84 Ill. 626-633; *Law v. People*, 87 Ill. 385-399; *Barton v. Minnie Creek*

Drain. Dist., 112 Ill. App. 640; *Russell v. Tate,* 52 Ark. 541; *City of Blair v. Lantry,* 21 Neb. 247.

It is suggested that the liability of appellee, Schaefer, is on his official bond, and that the other appellees may be liable in a proper action in tort. The one question we are to decide is whether or not they are jointly liable in this action, and it is not an answer thereto to determine that they are liable in other actions. Where public officers fail to perform a public duty and thereby cause an injury special and peculiar to such individual, an action will lie against them personally. *Gage v. Springer,* 211 Ill. 200. If the injury is caused by the joint action of the officers, a joint action may be maintained either in the case of a breach of contract expressed or implied, or in the violation of a duty whereby a tortious injury is inflicted. Appellees were trustees in the management and application of the funds levied and collected to pay the bonds in question and their misapplication of them was a breach of trust and a breach of their implied contract to properly apply them, and amounted to a conversion of the funds. Such misapplication or conversion could not have happened, or did not happen, otherwise than by their joint action. The statute required them to receive and pay out those funds only for the specific purposes for which they were collected in case the bonds were not registered with the State auditor, as happened in this case, as is further disclosed by paragraphs 194 and 197 of the Act of 1895, under which the bonds were issued. Chapter 42, Hurd's Rev. St. 1911, pp. 934, 935, (J. & A. ¶¶ 4572, 4575).

It was the treasurer's duty to so receive and apply said funds, although ordered by the commissioners to pay them out for other valuable services to the district. The court, therefore, properly sustained the demurrer to his special plea. *City of East St. Louis v. Flannigen,* 34 Ill. App. 596; *People v. Hummel,* 215 Ill. 71.

It is also suggested that suit should have been brought against the drainage district as it appears that there were funds in the hands of its treasurer subject to the payment of the bonds when this suit was brought. There is no doubt that a suit may be maintained against the municipal corporation for whatever of such funds may be in its treasury. *Conway v. City of Chicago*, 237 Ill. 128; *Bradbury v. Vandalia Levee & Drainage Dist.*, 236 Ill. 36.

No such suit, however, for such funds already misapplied and not in the treasury of the district can be maintained against it. Such funds having been levied and collected for the payment of the bonds in question, no second assessment can be levied and collected to pay the same. A second assessment cannot be levied to meet a past indebtedness. The drainage district is, therefore, not liable for any part of the funds misapplied by appellees. For those funds appellant must look solely to the officers who misappropriated them. *Ahrens v. Minnie Creek Drain. Dist.*, 170 Ill. 262; *Drainage Commissioners v. Kinney*, 233 Ill. 67; *Barton v. Minnie Creek Drain. Dist.*, 112 Ill. App. 640; *Bradbury v. Vandalia Levee & Drainage Dist.*, 236 Ill. 36.

It is finally argued by appellees that the bonds in question are absolutely void, because the meetings of the drainage commisioners to organize the district, to classify the lands, to levy the assessments and to authorize the bonds were all held outside of the boundaries of the district, and that, therefore, appellant cannot recover. This suit is not on the bonds, but is a personal action against appellees for money had and received by them to appellant's use. Appellees received the funds in question under the statute, for the sole purpose of paying the bonds in question. They cannot avoid their liability to appellant by alleging or proving the illegality of the bonds. *Ross v. Curtiss*, 31 N. Y. 606; *Morris v. State*, 47 Tex. 583; *Highway Commissioners v. City of Bloomington*, 253 Ill. 164.

There is no liability of appellees to refund or to repay to any taxpayers of the district any of the taxes or assessments voluntarily paid by them no matter how illegal the taxes collected may have been. The evidence tends to show the taxes in question were paid voluntarily by the taxpayers, and such payments must at any rate be presumed to have been made voluntarily until the contrary is made to appear. The taxes were spent for the benefit of the district and could not have been legally refunded. It is the well established law of this State that money paid voluntarily by one with knowledge or means of knowledge of all the facts cannot be recovered. Also, that one who has voluntarily paid to the collector or to the treasurer of a municipality a void tax with full knowledge of all the facts concerning the same cannot recover such tax by set-off or otherwise. *Yates v. Royal Ins. Co.*, 200 Ill. 202; *Otis v. People*, 196 Ill. 542. See also *Elston v. City of Chicago*, 40 Ill. 514; *Falls v. City of Cairo*, 58 Ill. 403; *Swanston v. Ijams*, 63 Ill. 165, a suit to recover drainage taxes illegally assessed. *City of Chicago v. McGovern*, 226 Ill. 403; *Illinois Glass Co. v. Chicago Telephone Co.*, 234 Ill. 535.

From whatever angle the matter is viewed appellant was legally and equitably entitled to receive the funds collected by appellees that had been levied for the payment of her bonds, and it was against equity and good conscience to withhold them from her. Appellees, however, are only jointly liable to appellant for the taxes received by them for the payment of her bonds and misapplied by their joint action. They are not jointly liable for any such funds misapplied prior to June 4, 1904, or subsequent to March 10, 1906. Appellant was also entitled to recover interest at the rate of five per cent. from December 1, 1907, to which time the interest thereon had been paid by the district, and no demand by her before suit was necessary to the maintenance of her action. *Chapman v. Burt*, 77 Ill. 337; *Smyth v. Stoddard*, 203 Ill. 424; *Highway Commissioners v. City of Bloomington*, 253 Ill. 164.

The judgment is reversed and, as the entire liability of appellees is not fully disclosed by the record, the cause is remanded.   *Reversed and remanded.*

Helen Sesterhenn, Administratrix of the estate of M. Schaefer, Appellant, v. Joseph Schneider et al., Appellees.

Gen. No. 18,371.

Egidius Meyer, Appellant, v. John Schaefer et al., Appellees.

Gen. No. 18,372.

Anna Huerter, Appellant, v. John Schaefer et al., Appellees.

Gen. No. 18,373.   (Not to be reported in full.)

Appeals from the Superior Court of Cook county; the Hon. JOSEPH H. FITCH, Judge, presiding. Heard in the Branch Appellate Court at the March term, 1912. Reversed and remanded. Opinion filed December 31, 1913.

Statement of the Cases.

These cases were consolidated for hearing in this court with case No. 18,370, *Schoden v. Schaefer, ante,* p. 456, and decision therein controls.

ADAMS, BOBB & ADAMS, for appellants; G. L. WIRE, of counsel.

GAIL E. DEMING and LOUIS J. PIERSON, for appellees.

MR. JUSTICE DUNCAN delivered the opinion of the court.

Frank M. McKey, Appellee, v. William Emanuel et al., Appellants.

Gen. No. 18,432.   (Not to be reported in full.)

Appeal from the Circuit Court of Cook county; the Hon. CHARLES M. WALKER, Judge, presiding. Heard in the Branch Appellate Court at the March term, 1912. Transferred to Supreme Court. Opinion filed January 3, 1914.

Statement of the Case.

Bill by Frank M. McKey, trustee in bankruptcy of the estate of William Emanuel, against William Emanuel and Fannie Emanuel, his wife, to set aside an alleged fraudulent conveyance by the defendant William Emanuel to the defendant Fannie Emanuel of certain real estate. The bill prayed that the property be adjudged to be the property of William Emanuel and that said Fannie Emanuel be ordered to convey the property to the complainant, as trustee, and that in case of her failure to do so a master in chancery or some other person be appointed to make the conveyance. From a decree granting the relief prayed, defendants appeal.

S. A. McELMEE, for appellants.

JAMES D. POWER, for appellee.

MR. JUSTICE BAUME delivered the opinion of the court.

Abstract of the Decision.

APPEAL AND ERROR, § 140*—*when freehold involved.* A bill in equity by a trustee in bankruptcy to set aside a conveyance from the bankrupt to his wife involves a freehold (*Daly v. Kohn*, 230 Ill. 436 followed).

*See Illinois Notes Digest, Vols. XI to XV, same topic and section number.

George E. Hibbard, Appellant, v. John B. Mallers, Jr., Appellee.

Gen. No. 18,858.   (Not to be reported in full.)

Appeal from the Superior Court of Cook county; the Hon. RICHARD E. BURKE, Judge, presiding. Heard in this court at the March term, 1912. Modified and affirmed. Opinion filed January 12, 1914.

Statement of the Case.

Bill by George Hibbard against John B. Mallers, Jr., alleging that complainant and defendant were co-partners and that the copartnership had been dissolved by the act and declaration of defendant. The bill prayed for an accounting, the appointment of a receiver and an injunction. Defendant's answer denied that the copartnership had been dissolved. From a decree dismissing the bill for want of equity, complainant appeals.

PRINGLE & FEARING and ALFRED J. PARKER, for appellant.

HUGH S. PETTIS, for appellee.

MR. PRESIDING JUSTICE BAKER delivered the opinion of the court.

Abstract of the Decision.

1. EQUITY, § 358*—*when decree should not contain a finding of facts.* A finding of facts has no proper place in a decree dismissing a bill for want of equity.

2. APPEAL AND ERROR, § 1766*—*when a decree erroneously containing a statement of facts will be affirmed on modification.* On appeal from a decree dismissing for want of equity a bill filed by a partner against a copartner, which alleged a dissolution of the partnership and prayed for an accounting, etc., the decree erroneously containing a statement of facts was affirmed upon being modified by striking out the statement of facts, it appearing independently from the statement of facts that in the opinion of the chancellor the copartnership was not dissolved.

*See Illinois Notes Digest, Vols. XI to XV, same topic and section number.

CHICAGO—FIRST DISTRICT—JANUARY, 1914.   475

G. T. and Son Co. v. Holtzer-Cabot Elec. Co., 184 Ill. App. 475.

George Thompson and Son Company, Appellant, v. The Holtzer-Cabot Electric Company, Appellee.

Gen. No. 18,393.   (Not to be reported in full.)

Appeal from the Municipal Court of Chicago; the Hon. JOHN J. ROONEY, Judge, presiding. Heard in this court at the March term, 1912. Affirmed. Opinion filed January 12, 1914.

Statement of the Case.

Action by George Thompson and Son Company, a corporation, against The Holtzer-Cabot Electric Company, a corporation, to recover on a *quantum meruit* for work done under a contract for excavation and the construction of brick walls of a certain building. From a judgment entered on a directed verdict for plaintiff for $759.17, plaintiff appeals.

GEORGE H. MEYER, for appellant.

BITHER, GOFF & FRANCIS, for appellee.

MR. PRESIDING JUSTICE BAKER delivered the opinion of the court.

Abstract of the Decision.

BUILDING AND CONSTRUCTION CONTRACTS, § 65*—*when decision of architect conclusive.* In an action by a contractor to recover on a *quantum meruit* for work done in excavating and in constructing brick walls of a certain building where his contract was terminated by his refusal to obey the orders of the architect to reconstruct portions of the walls, a directed verdict for plaintiff for a balance after deducting from the contract price the cost to complete the work by another contractor, *held* not error, the contract making the architect's decision final and there being no evidence that he acted fraudulently.

*See Illinois Notes Digest, Vols. XI to XV, same topic and section number.

Charles Mulvey Manufacturing Company et al., Appellees, v. Frederick W. McKinney et al.

On Appeal of Frederick W. McKinney, Appellant.

Gen. No. 18,430.

1. LANDLORD AND TENANT, § 470*—*when equity will relieve against forfeiture for nonpayment of rent.* One of the familiar instances of equitable relief is its prevention of a landlord's attempted termination of a lease for the nonpayment of rent. Equity will relieve in such cases where compensation can be made and money and interest are compensation, and such relief will be afforded although the lessor may in ejectment have recovered the possession of the premises.

2. LANDLORD AND TENANT, § 504*—*when judgment entered against tenant for possession does not conclude him from relief in equity.* In an action of ejectment or the statutory action of unlawful detainer the right of possession alone is involved, and the judgment in such action does not conclude the lessee from relief in equity.

3. LANDLORD AND TENANT, § 471*—*when injunction will issue to restrain enforcement of forfeiture for nonpayment of rent.* On bill for relief against a forfeiture for nonpayment of rent, if there is no special reason to the contrary, an injunction thereupon goes to restrain further steps to enforce the forfeiture.

4. LANDLORD AND TENANT, § 471*—*what essential on bill for relief against forfeiture for nonpayment of rent.* On bill in equity for relief against a forfeiture for nonpayment of rent, all arrears of rent, interest and costs must be paid or tendered.

5. LANDLORD AND TENANT, § 119*—*effect of assignment of lease or alienation of the premises.* The right of a lessee is not affected by the lessor's assignment of the lease and alienation of the premises; the alienee succeeds to the right accruing subsequent to the alienation but is subject to all the rights and equities of the lessee against the lessor.

6. LANDLORD AND TENANT, § 123*—*when payment of rent in advance is good as against subsequent assignee of lessor.* An advancement by the lessee for a term of years to the lessor of a certain sum under an agreement that the amount so advanced should apply on the last year's rent is a good payment of that year's rent as against an assignee of the lessor who took the assignment while the lessee was in open possession.

7. LANDLORD AND TENANT, § 51*—*when antecedent parol agreement admissible.* On bill filed by a lessee against the assignee of

the lessor to redeem from a forfeiture for the nonpayment of rent, evidence showing that the lessor orally agreed before the execution of the lease that in case the lessee and others should be required to pay a certain promissory note given by them to the lessor to enable him to raise money for a building, the amount so paid should apply on the rent thereafter accruing, *held* admissible as being an antecedent parol agreement collateral to the lease.

8. Evidence, § 350*—*when proof of oral separate agreement not a violation of parol evidence rule.* The rule that parol evidence is inadmissible to vary the terms of a written instrument is not violated by allowing testimony of a distinct, valid, collateral, contemporaneous or antecedent agreement between the parties which was not reduced to writing where the same is not in conflict with the terms of the written instrument.

9. Notice, § 17*—*when assignee of lessor charged with notice of tenant's rights.* Assignee of lessor takes subject to the rights of the lessee where the lessee was in actual and visible possession at and before the time of the assignment of the lease, such possession being constructive notice to him of whatever rights the possessor then had in the premises.

10. Appeal and error, § 866*—*when abstract of record insufficient.* A printed copy of the record is in no sense an abstract of the record.

11. Costs, § 74*—*when appellant will not be allowed costs for printing abstract not conforming to rules of court.* Where what is called an abstract of the record is a copy of the record and in no sense an abstract thereof, appellant will not be allowed costs for printing same.

Appeal from the Superior Court of Cook county; the Hon. Richard E. Burke, Judge, presiding. Heard in this court at the March term, 1912. Reversed and remanded with directions. Opinion filed January 12, 1914.

Charles Scribner Eaton, for appellant Frederick W. McKinney.

Eugene Stewart, for appellees.

Mr. Presiding Justice Baker delivered the opinion of the court.

The evidence in this case is voluminous. The abstract contains more than a thousand printed pages and there is in the briefs of counsel no proper statement of facts. We shall not attempt to state in detail the various contentions of the parties nor the evidence relied on to support such contentions. The chancellor heard the witnesses and we shall base our decision on his findings of fact except where, in our opinion, a finding is not supported by the evidence.

The owners of certain real estate demised portions thereof to Albert L. Berry by ground leases made on and prior to April 1,.1907, for terms ending in 1937. April 29, 1907, Berry entered into a contract in writing, which began with a recital that it was made by Berry of the first part and the complainants in the bill, appellees here, of the second part, but was signed only by Berry, the complainant corporation, W. H. Gervais and W. H. Barry. By this agreement Berry agreed to lease a portion of the land so leased to him to the parties of the second part for a term of ten years from June 1, 1907, at a rental of $2,000 per year, payable in monthly instalments of $166.66 each on the fifth day of each month, and to erect a two-story building containing an area of 8,800 square feet on the premises. The parties of the second part agreed to pay to Berry $2,000 in instalments, the last instalment to be paid when the building was ready for occupancy, which sum, the writing provided, should be applied in payment of the rent for the tenth year of the term unless Berry desired to apply it on the rent for some prior year. The writing further provided that for the $2,000 Berry should give his note bearing interest at five per cent., "up to the beginning of the year which it shall apply as payment of the rent," and also that said note should be in the nature of a receipt for the year's rent. The Mulvey Company advanced to Berry $2,000 and received from him the following receipt:

"CHICAGO, July 1, 1907.

Received of the Chas. Mulvey Mfg. Co. two thousand dollars for rent of Building 1335 35th street, Chicago, same being rent in advance for said premises as described between Chas. Mulvey Mfg. Co. et al. from Albert L. Berry.

'ALBERT L. BERRY."

The writing further provided that the parties of the second part should issue to Berry the note of the Mulvey Manufacturing Company for $4,000, payable in three years, indorsed by W. B. and L. L. Gervais, W. H. and P. E. Barry and E. L. Beckerleg, bearing interest at six per cent., which note, the writing stated, was given for the purpose of assisting Berry to secure funds for the erection of said building. A note made and indorsed as provided in the agreement, dated July 1, 1907, and payable three years after date, with interest at six per cent., was delivered to Berry. It later came into the hands of appellant McKinney, who brought suit on it against the maker and indorsers July 15, 1910.

The bill alleged, the evidence proved and the court found that prior to the assignment of the lease by Berry to McKinney, Berry orally promised the complainants that in case they or any one of them should be required to pay said note, the amount so paid should apply on rent under said lease coming due after three years from the date thereof. Berry assigned the lease to McKinney April 17, 1908. The Charles Mulvey Manufacturing Company then was, and for six months or longer had been, in the occupancy and possession of the demised premises. The Mulvey Company paid the rent that fell due prior to August 5, 1908, and for the rent that became due that day sent to McKinney, August 7 a check, which he refused to receive. The lease contains the usual provisions giving the lessor or his assigns the right to declare a forfeiture for non-payment of rent, and McKinney, August 6, elected to terminate the lease and gave the Mulvey Company notice of such election August 10. McKinney brought his action of unlawful detainer in the Municipal Court against the Mulvey Company, had judgment for possession, which was affirmed by Branch B. of this court. *McKinney v. Mulvey Mfg. Co.*, 157 Ill. App. 339.

In an action of ejectment or the statutory action of unlawful detainer the right of possession alone is involved, and the judgment in such action does not conclude the lessee from relief in equity.

One of the most familiar instances of equitable relief is its prevention of a landlord's attempted termination of a lease for the nonpayment of rent. In 4 Viner's Abr., chap. V., pl. 31, p. 406, it was held that relief may be granted for breach of covenant to pay rent, although the rent is a rack rent equal to the value of the land. The court held that in this and the like cases the clause of re-entry is in the nature of a penalty, and therefore relievable in a court of equity upon making satisfaction to the injured party. In 1 Pomeroy's Eq. Jurisprudence, sec. 453, it is said:

"Where a lease contains a condition that the lessor may re-enter and put an end to the lessee's estate, or even that the lease shall be void, upon the lessee's failure to pay the rent at the time specified, it is well settled that a court of equity will relieve the lessee and set aside a forfeiture incurred by his breach of the condition, whether the lessee has or has not entered and dispossessed the tenant. This rule is based upon the notion that such condition and forfeiture are intended merely as a security for the payment of money."

To the same effect are Taylor on Landl. & Ten., sec. 495; 2 Story, Eq. Juris., sec. 1315. See note to *Maginnis v. Knickerbocker Ice Co.*, 112 Wis. 385, 69 L. R. A. 833.

Equity will relieve where compensation can be made and money and interest are compensation. In equity, relief is afforded although the lessor may in ejectment have recovered the possession of the premises. *Wadman v. Calcraft*, 10 Ves. 67; *Davis v. West*, 12 Ves. 475; *Hill v. Barclay*, 16 Ves. 402. The right of the lessee is not affected by the lessor's assignment of the lease and alienation of the premises. The alienee succeeds to the right accruing subsequent to the alienation, but is subject to all the rights and equities of the lessee against the lessor. *Abrams v. Watson*, 59 Ala. 524.

On another ground McKinney must be held to have taken an assignment of the lease and conveyance of the interest of Berry in the premises subject to the rights and interest of the Mulvey Company. That company was in the actual, open and visible possession and occupancy of the premises at and before the time that the lease was assigned or the land conveyed to McKinney, and such possession was constructive notice to him of whatever rights the possessor then had in the premises. *Carr v. Brennan,* 166 Ill. 108; *Farmers' Nat. Bank of Bushnell v. Sperling,* 113 Ill. 273; *Coari v. Olsen,* 91 Ill. 273.

In the case last cited it was said, p. 280: "But, although other courts have held the doctrine of notice by possession as subject to being materially modified by circumstances, this court has uniformly held that actual occupancy is equal to the record of the deed or other instrument under which the occupant claims, and a purchaser is bound to inquire by what right or title he holds. The purchaser takes the premises subject to that title or interest, whatever it may be."

The bill of complaint is, to say the least, not in the usual form of a bill in equity for relief against a forfeiture of a lease for nonpayment of rent, or, as it is usually called, a bill to redeem; but we think it may be regarded as such a bill. On such a bill, "all arrears of rent, interest and costs must be paid or tendered. If there be no special reason to the contrary, an injunction thereupon goes to restrain further steps to enforce the forfeiture." *Sheets v. Selden,* 7 Wall. (U. S.) 416, 421.

We do not regard it as material that neither the agreement nor the lease was executed by all the complainants. The Mulvey Company was the occupant of the demised premises and the real party in interest in this controversy. If it is entitled to relief, then relief should be granted to it, although some of the other complainants may not be entitled to any relief. Appellant can have no just cause of complaint if this course is adopted. The question in the case is as to his rights as the assignee and alienee of Berry, and this depends on the covenants or promises of Berry.

We are unable to agree with the chancellor that the Mulvey Company was entitled to immediate credit for the $2,000 advanced by it to Berry, July 1, 1907. The agreement was that the $2,000 should be applied in payment of the rent for the tenth year of the term unless Berry elected to apply it on an earlier year. Berry made no such election and the chancellor had no power to apply the money in payment of the rent for any year before the tenth. The agreement that said sum should be applied in payment of the rent for the tenth year and that it should bear interest at five per cent. until the beginning of that year was binding on McKinney. If a lessee in a lease of a house for a year pays the year's rent, takes possession, and the lessor afterwards assigns the lease, no one would claim that the assignee could disregard the payment of rent to the lessor and compel the lessee to pay rent again. Nor would the rule be different if in the case supposed the lessee paid to the lessor the rent for the last month only. We are unable to perceive any ground on which it can be held that a payment of the last month's rent by the lessee in possession of the premises is a good payment as against a subsequent assignee of the lease, and that an advance of the money to the lessor by the lessee under an agreement that the amount so advanced should apply on the last month's rent is not, as against the assignee, a good payment of that month's rent.

The note for $4,000 was an accommodation note and the maker and indorsers have therefore no defense to it. It is held by McKinney and he has put it in suit. Berry has filed a voluntary petition in bankruptcy and it is certain that the maker or indorsers will have to pay the note. Berry, as has been said, orally agreed with the maker and indorsers before the lease was made, that if any one of them had to pay the note the amount so paid should apply on rent under the lease coming due after three years from its date. Appellant contends that testimony of said oral promise was inadmissible because it tends to vary and contradict the terms of the written lease. No rule is better settled than that parol testimony cannot be received to vary, contradict, add to or take from the terms of a valid written instrument. But this rule is not violated by allowing testimony of a distinct, valid, collateral, contemporaneous or antecedent agreement between the parties which was not reduced to writing, where the same is not in conflict with the terms of the written instrument. In discussing this rule, Taylor in his treatise on the Law of Evidence says, section 1038:

"The rule does not prevent parties to a written instrument from proving that either contemporaneously or as a preliminary measure they had entered into a distinct oral agreement on some collateral matter. Still less, as will presently be shown, does the rule exclude evidence of an oral agreement which constitutes a condition on which the performance of the written agreement is to depend."

The same author says, sections 1049-1157:

"It is almost superfluous to observe that the rule is not infringed by proof of any collateral parol agreement which does not interfere with the terms of the written contract, though it may relate to the same subject matter."

See also Greenleaf, sec. 284a; *Lindley v. Lacey*, 17 C. B. N. S. 578, 112 E. C. L. 578; *Welz v. Rhodius*, 87 Ind. 1, where both the English and American authorities are cited. That such an antecedent oral agreement was made in this case was testified by Berry, Gervais and Barry, and not disputed. The chancellor found in effect that the antecedent parol agreement was a separate agreement, collateral only to the lease, and that proof of such agreement did not contradict or modify any provision of the lease, or affect any right or obligation created by it, and in such view we concur. If Berry was still the landlord and the $4,000 note was held by a third party, under Berry's agreement with the Mulvey Company he would be bound, if that company was compelled to pay the note, to apply the amount so paid on the rent falling due on the lease after August 1, 1910. The fact that McKinney is both the assignee of the lease and the holder of the note cannot affect the rights of the Mulvey Company against him as the assignee of the lease, nor his right as such assignee of the lease and holder of the note as against that company. McKinney is entitled to collect the amount of the $4,000 note from the Mulvey Company, but is bound to apply the amount so collected on the rent falling due after August 1, 1910.

Appellant has filed no abstract of the record, in accordance with the rule and practice of this court. That which purports to be one is in no sense an abstract of the record but is a printed copy of the record. The agreement for a lease and the lease from Berry to the Mulvey Company are printed in full three times. The questions asked and the answers of the witnesses are also printed in full, as are the arguments and objections of counsel, which have no proper place in a certificate of evidence. Appellant will therefore be allowed no costs for printing what is called an abstract in the case. *Kelly v. Kellogg*, 79 Ill. 477-482; *Richardson v. Cassidy*, 63 Ill. App. 482.

The decree of the Superior Court will be reversed and the cause remanded to that court with directions to refer the cause to a master to take an account of what is due to McKinney for rent and interest on the lease from Berry to the Mulvey Manufacturing Company and others in the bill of complaint mentioned, allowing interest on each instalment of rent from the time it came due at five per cent. per annum, and on the note for $4,000, also mentioned in the bill of complaint, for principal and interest at six per cent. per annum, and the amount of McKinney's costs in the forcible detainer suit mentioned in the bill both in the Municipal Court and in this court, and for his costs in the suit on the $4,000 note and for his costs in this case both in the Superior Court and in this court, and for his costs in the suit brought in the Municipal Court for rent for the months of May and June, 1908, and what shall be found to be due on the note for $4,000 is to be deducted out of the amount due him for rent, interest and costs. On the coming in and approval of the report the court will order and decree that the complainants, or some one of them, pay to McKinney within sixty days from the entry of such decree the amount found to be due to him on said $4,000 note, and also the balance due him for rent, interest and costs after deducting therefrom the amount due to him on said $4,000 note, and that on such payments being made or tendered and the money paid into court if the tender be refused, an injunction go to restrain said McKinney from taking any further steps to enforce the forfeiture of said lease or the payment of said $4,000 note, and further ordering that he deliver to said Mulvey Manufacturing Company, or to such person as it shall direct, said $4,000 note, free and clear of all incumbrance done by him, or any person claiming by, from or under him, and satisfy and discharge of record the judgments for costs above mentioned. And the court will further by its decree adjudge and declare that the said Mulvey Manufacturing Company is entitled to be credited by said McKinney with the sum of $2,000 with interest from July 1, 1907, at five per cent. per annum for the money paid and advanced by said company to Albert L. Berry July 1, 1907, the same to be applied by said McKinney on the rent last falling due on the lease from said Berry to said Mulvey Manufacturing Company and others, and that on default of the said complainants, or some one of them, paying to said McKinney what shall be found due him on said $4,000 note, and the balance due him for rent, interest and costs after deducting therefrom the amount due to him on said $4,000 note, that the bill of

complaint do from thenceforth stand dismissed out of
that court at the costs of complainants.

*Reversed and remanded with directions, at the costs
of appellees, but the appellant will be allowed no
costs for printing the abstract.*

**J. A. Gore, Appellee, v. Marshall Field & Company,
Appellant.**

Gen. No. 18,441.   (Not to be reported in full.)

Appeal from the Circuit Court of Cook county; the Hon. THOMAS
G. WINDES, Judge, presiding. Heard in this court at the March
term, 1912. Reversed and remanded. Opinion filed January 12,
1914.

Statement of the Case.

Action by J. A. Gore against Marshall Field & Company, a corporation, to recover damages for false imprisonment of plaintiff by defendant's servants.
From a judgment in favor of plaintiff for five hundred dollars, defendant appeals.

FRANK B. LEFFINGWELL, for appellant.

CRUICE & LANGILLE, for appellee.

MR. PRESIDING JUSTICE BAKER delivered the opinion
of the court.

Abstract of the Decision.

1. FALSE IMPRISONMENT, § 28*—*when verdict for plaintiff not sustained by the evidence.* In an action against a department store
for false imprisonment, the facts showing that plaintiff had pur-

chased a coat and was leaving the store when he was stopped by some unknown person, and that plaintiff went with such person to the clothing department where a clerk and a floorman told him he would have to prove that he purchased or that he did not steal the coat, *held* that a verdict in favor of plaintiff could not be sustained, the evidence not showing that the person who stopped him was an employe of the store and it not appearing whether the statements made by defendant's servants in the clothing department could be construed to mean that plaintiff should remain in the room until he proved he bought the coat.

2. FALSE IMPRISONMENT, § 2*—*what constitutes.* To constitute the injury of false imprisonment there must be a detention of the person and the detention must be unlawful.

3. FALSE IMPRISONMENT, § 30*—*when instruction not to award punitive damages should be given.* In an action for false imprisonment by the servants of defendant, refusal of court to instruct the jury at the request of defendant that plaintiff should not be awarded punitive damages, *held* error, it not appearing that defendant's servants acted maliciously or wantonly or that their acts were conceived in a spirit of mischief or criminal indifference to civil obligations.

4. FALSE IMPRISONMENT, § 36*—*when damages excessive.* A verdict for five hundred dollars for damages sustained by reason of false imprisonment, *held* excessive, the case not being one in which punitive damages should be awarded and the evidence showing that there was only a detention of the person of plaintiff for a few moments.

Ernest D. McArthur, Defendant in Error, v. Joseph A. Hopson, Plaintiff in Error.

Gen. No. 18,354.   (Not to be reported in full.)

Error to the Municipal Court of Chicago; the Hon. CHARLES A. WILLIAMS, Judge, presiding. Heard in this court at the March term, 1912. Reversed and remanded. Opinion filed January 12, 1914.

Statement of the Case.

Action by Ernest D. McArthur against Joseph A. Hopson to recover damages for alienation of the affections of plaintiff's wife. To reverse a judgment entered in favor of plaintiff for one thousand dollars, defendant prosecutes error.

CRUICE & LANGILLE, for plaintiff in error.

COMERFORD & COHEN, for defendant in error.

MR. JUSTICE BROWN delivered the opinion of the court.

Abstract of the Decision.

1. HUSBAND AND WIFE, § 280*—*when admission of letter in suit for alienation reversible error.* In an action for alienation of wife's affections, admission in evidence of a letter written by the wife to defendant and found in defendant's possession *held* reversible error.

2. HUSBAND AND WIFE, § 280*—*when letter written by wife to husband not admissible in suit for alienation.* In an action for alienation of plaintiff's wife's affections, a letter written by the wife to the plaintiff *held* not admissible in evidence.

3. MARRIAGE, § 26*—*sufficiency of proof of ceremonial marriage.* In an action for alienation of wife's affections, proof of ceremonial marriage *held* scanty where plaintiff testified he was married to his alleged wife on a certain date at Milwaukee, Wisconsin, and further puts in evidence over objection a certificate of a justice of the peace in Milwaukee county, which in connection with his testimony showed that the ceremony was before such justice.

4. MARRIAGE, § 24*—*evidence inadmissible to prove ceremonial marriage.* The certificate of a justice of the peace of another State is not of itself evidence of the official character of the justice or of his right to perform a marriage ceremony or that the ceremony was performed and is inadmissible as such evidence.

5. HUSBAND AND WIFE, § 280*—*degree of proof required in suit for alienation.* In an action for alienation of wife's affections a preponderance of the evidence is sufficient to establish plaintiff's case.

6. MUNICIPAL COURT OF CHICAGO, § 27*—*when rules of court must be presented by bill of exceptions.* The Appellate Court in cases coming from the Municipal Court cannot take judicial notice of the rules of that court nor consider them unless they are made a part of the record by a bill of exceptions.

*See Illinois Notes Digest, Vols. XI to XV, same topic and section number.

Edwin Nelson, Appellee, v. The Chicago, Rock Island and Pacific Railway Company, Appellant.

Gen. No. 18,377.   (Not to be reported in full.)

Appeal from the Superior Court of Cook county; the Hon. CHARLES M. FOELL, Judge, presiding. Heard in this court at the March term, 1912. Affirmed. Opinion filed January 12, 1914. Rehearing denied January 26, 1914. *Certiorari* denied by Supreme Court (making opinion final).

Statement of the Case.

Action by Edwin Nelson, a minor, by N. A. Nelson, his next friend, against The Chicago, Rock Island and Pacific Railway Company to recover for injuries sustained by plaintiff alleged to have been caused by defendant's negligence in suddenly starting its cars while plaintiff was attempting to alight from the front platform of one of defendant's cars at a railroad station. From a judgment in favor of plaintiff for ten thousand dollars, defendant appeals.

Appellant complains that the verdict is against the weight of the evidence; that court erred in refusing to give a peremptory instruction for defendant; that the court erred in giving and refusing certain instructions; and that there is a variance between the allegations of declaration and the proof as to the place of injury.

M. L. BELL and A. B. ENOCH, for appellant.

HORTON, WICKETT, MILLER & MEIER, for appellee; GEORGE J. MEIER and JOHN IRRMANN, of counsel.

MR. JUSTICE BROWN delivered the opinion of the court.

Abstract of the Decision.

1. CARRIERS, § 313*—*when employe riding on pass is a passenger for hire.* An employe of a railroad company riding on a coupon pass to and from his place of work, *held* a passenger for hire and

for a consideration, the consideration being that the company was enabled to draw its employes from a larger body subject only to the expense of their transportation.

2. CARRIERS, § 305*—*when exemption from liability on back of pass is invalid.* The law of Illinois renders invalid as against a passenger for hire or consideration an exemption or waiver and release of liability for negligence which appears on the back of a pass in these words: "By the acceptance and use of this ticket any and all claims on this company, whether due to negligence of its agents or otherwise, for injury to the person * * * of the holder are waived and released."

3. INSTRUCTIONS, § 88*—*when giving of instruction as to preponderance of evidence not reversible error.* The giving of an instruction on what the jury may consider in determining the preponderance of the evidence, the language thereof being identical with a similar instruction passed upon by the Supreme Court in *Deering v. Barzak,* 227 Ill. 71, *held* not of itself ground for reversal.

4. APPEAL AND ERROR, § 438*—*when objection for variance not preserved for review.* Objection for variance between the declaration and the proof cannot be considered on review when not made the subject of objection or comment in the court below.

Freida Gauger, Appellee, v. American Patriots, Appellant.

Gen. No. 18,428.   (Not to be reported in full.)

Appeal from the County Court of Cook county; the Hon. W. F. SLATER, Judge, presiding. Heard in this court at the March term, 1912. Reversed with finding of fact. Opinion filed January 12, 1914.

Statement of the Case.

Action by Freida Gauger against American Patriots, a fraternal insurance corporation, to recover upon a benefit certificate issued by defendant upon the life of

Friedrich Gauger. From a judgment in favor of plaintiff for five hundred dollars, defendant appeals.

ALBERT J. W. APPELL, for appellant.

P. S. WEBSTER, for appellee.

MR. JUSTICE BROWN delivered the opinion of the court.

Abstract of the Decision.

1. INSURANCE, § 746*—*when constitutional provision of fraternal order is part of contract.* Provisions of the constitution of a fraternal insurance order is a part of the contract where the certificate itself and its acceptance and the application for reinstatement are made subject to the constitution and the laws of the order.

2. INSURANCE, § 843*—*when constitution of fraternal order avoids certificate when member dies while in custody of the law.* A section of the constitution of a fraternal insurance corporation providing that if a member dies "while in the custody of the law" the certificate of membership shall be null and void applies so as to render the certificate void where the member dies while committed to the House of Correction, and the section applies though there is no causative connection between the custody and the death.

Calvin W. Burket, Appellee, v. The Ures Consolidated Mining Company et al.

On Appeal of John H. Turner et al., Appellants.

Gen. No. 18,439.   (Not to be reported in full.)

Appeal from the Municipal Court of Chicago; the Hon. FRED C. HILL, Judge, presiding. Heard in this court at the March term, 1912. Affirmed. Opinion filed January 12, 1914. *Certiorari* denied by Supreme Court (making opinion final).·

*See Illinois Notes Digest, Vols. XI to XV, same topic and section number.

Statement of the Case.

Action by Calvin W. Burket against The Ures Consolidated Mining Company, Charles A. Winston, W. R. Macdonald, John H. Turner and P. D. Minick to recover on a promissory note purporting to be executed by the Mining Company and signed by the other defendants. The Mining Company was not served in the case. From a judgment in favor of plaintiff for $4,508.27 and costs, John H. Turner, Charles A. Winston and P. D. Minick appeal.

HOYNE, O'CONNOR & IRWIN and WINSTON & LOWY, for appellants.

DEFREES, BUCKINGHAM, RITTER & EATON, for appellee; JOHN G. CAMPBELL and DON K. JONES, of counsel.

MR. JUSTICE BROWN delivered the opinion of the court.

Abstract of the Decision.

1. USURY, § 39*—*when sureties on note cannot interpose defense.* Sureties on a promissory note executed by a corporation cannot interpose the defense of usury.

2. PRINCIPAL AND SURETY, § 54*—*when finding of jury on question whether sureties signed note on certain condition sustained by the evidence.* In an action against sureties on a promissory note executed by a corporation, the defense was that defendants had signed upon condition that all the directors of the corporation would sign the note and the evidence upon that point was conflicting. *Held,* that a verdict in favor of plaintiff was sustained by the evidence and that there was evidence to corroborate plaintiff's witnesses, it appearing that the plaintiff made the loan for which the note was given without an attempt to secure the lacking signatures, that the loan was unanimously ratified at a directors' meeting at which defendants were present and that defendants were inactive in repudiating liability for a long time thereafter.

3. APPEAL AND ERROR, § 1241*—*matters which cannot be availed of.* Appellants cannot take advantage of the disobedience by the jury of an erroneous instruction given at their instance.

*See Illinois Notes Digest, Vols. XI to XV, same topic and section number.

Hamlins Wizard Oil Company, Appellee, v. United States Express Company, Appellant.

Gen. No. 18,352.

1. PRINCIPAL AND AGENT, § 137*—*when employer's failure to audit books not negligence preventing recovery from party receiving checks and drafts on forged indorsements of employer's bookkeeper*. A bookkeeper for a firm was charged with the duty of buying money orders of an Express Company and he usually paid therefor with checks or drafts payable to the firm's order and remitted to it by its customers. After he had left the firm's employment it was discovered that he had for several years been appropriating to his own use a large number of such checks and drafts by forging the firm's indorsement thereon to procure money orders, and that he had concealed the fraud by false entries in the books. *Held*, in an action by the firm against the Express Company to recover the amount of the checks and drafts received by the defendant upon such forged indorsements that the relations between the plaintiff and defendant were simply that of customer and seller, that the plaintiff owed no duty to defendant that could affect its method of bookkeeping and that therefore plaintiff's failure to audit the books so as to prevent the fraud was not such negligence as could be availed of as a defense to the action.

2. BILLS AND NOTES, § 409*—*burden of proving authority to indorse*. In an action against an Express Company to recover the amount of checks and drafts received by the Express Company upon the forged indorsements of plaintiff's name thereon by plaintiff's bookkeeper in payment for money orders, the burden is upon the defendant to prove that such indorsements were authorized where he asserts such claim as a defense.

3. EVIDENCE, § 253*—*when book entries admissible in favor of party required to produce books in evidence*. Where a defendant calls upon the plaintiff for the production of books and uses certain entries therein to establish its claim for credits without making any proof required by statutes as to their regularity, plaintiff becomes entitled to use other entries to explain or contradict the effect claimed for the entries adduced by defendant.

Appeal from the Municipal Court of Chicago; the Hon. WILLIAM N. COTTRELL, Judge, presiding. Heard in this court at the March term, 1912. Affirmed. Opinion filed January 12, 1914. *Certiorari* granted by Supreme Court.

*See Illinois Notes Digest, Vols. XI to XV, same topic and section numbers.

Statement by the Court. This is an appeal by the United States Express Company, hereinafter called defendant, from a judgment obtained by the Hamlins Wizard Oil Company, hereinafter called plaintiff, in an action brought to recover the amount of certain checks and drafts payable to plaintiff's order and remitted to it by its customers, but which through forged indorsements came into the hands of defendant, which received and collected the proceeds thereof.

Briefly narrated, the transactions giving rise to this suit were as follows: One A. M. Walsh became a bookkeeper for plaintiff in 1901 and continued as such until February 15, 1910, when he suddenly left plaintiff's employment, and died about two weeks thereafter. An audit of plaintiff's books was begun about the time he left but was not completed until after his death, which disclosed that Walsh was a defaulter to the extent of about $50,000, his frauds commencing shortly after he became bookkeeper and continuing during the entire period of his service.

Plaintiff's office clerical force consisted of Walsh, two girl stenographers and two or three girl clerks.

Walsh's salary as bookkeeper was about $25 a week or $1,300 a year. Besides keeping books Walsh did other clerical work, such as opening mail in the absence of the officers of the company, making small disbursements upon the authority of the officers, and attending to the depositing of checks payable to plaintiff, which were indorsed for deposit with a rubber stamp.

For the purpose of remitting salaries to traveling salesmen on the road, and of making remittances to customers for breakage, freight, etc., plaintiff had for nearly twenty years prior to 1910 been in the habit of buying express money orders from the defendant. It was part of Walsh's duty to buy these money orders when directed so to do. When money orders were to be bought he was furnished with checks, or cash of sufficient amount to cover the orders to be procured, and it was his duty to procure the orders and return them to the officers of the company.

The audit and investigation above referred to disclosed that Walsh had perpetrated his frauds by forging the plaintiff's indorsement on the back of customers' checks and drafts to its order, and disposing of the checks and drafts for his own benefit. A large number of them were disposed of by him at the defendant's money order department. The present suit is upon one hundred such checks and drafts, covering a period of a little less than five years prior to the commencement of this suit, all of which were received by the defendant from Walsh and collected by it under indorsements of plaintiff's name forged by him. Nearly all of these customers' checks and drafts were indorsed by Walsh in this form: "Pay to the order of the United States Express Co., Hamlins Wizard Oil Co., J. A. Hamlin, President." In other instances they purported to bear the signature of L. B. Hamlin, President, or L. B. Hamlin, Vice-president. They were delivered by Walsh to one L. B. Richardson, who at that time had charge of the money order department of the defendant. Richardson gave Walsh in exchange for these checks and drafts money orders of the defendant and cash for any excess in the amount of the check or draft above the total amount of the money orders. Richardson testified that for eight years before Walsh was employed the plaintiff had always bought its money orders from the defendant with checks drawn by the Hamlins Wizard Oil Company.

The money orders which were given in exchange for the one hundred checks and drafts in controversy fall into three classes: First, money orders payable to the order of third persons with whom plaintiff never had any dealings; second, money orders payable to the order of plaintiff's traveling salesmen or customers, which were duly collected by the respective payees under their genuine indorsements and which were duly charged by Walsh to the payees on the plaintiff's books of account; third, money orders payable to the order of plaintiff's salesmen or customers, which Walsh cashed under indorsement of the payees' names forged by him. No entries appear on plaintiff's books as to any of these money orders.

In the case of the one hundred customers' checks and drafts sued on, and in the case of all other customers' checks and drafts stolen by Walsh, he credited the customers' accounts in the ledger with the amounts, but failed to make the corresponding charges to the plaintiff's bank of deposit in the journal. Under plaintiff's system of bookkeeping checks and drafts received from customers were not entered in the cash book, which was merely a petty cash book, but were transferred from the journal to the ledger, the customers being credited and the bank of deposit charged with the amount of the check. In order to cover up these frauds Walsh made corresponding false entries in various ways in order to force his books to a balance.

The court directed a verdict for plaintiff for the amount of the one hundred customers' checks and drafts with interest, less the amount with interest of the money orders of class 2, *supra,* and a few others which were duly charged against the payees on plaintiff's books of account. This deduction was made apparently on the theory that since plaintiff actually got the benefit of them it was only just that the defendant should be credited with them, though they were in fact bought with part of the proceeds of the stolen checks and drafts. The amount of the verdict arrived at in this manner was $20,005.84, upon which judgment was entered.

WINSTON, PAYNE, STRAWN & SHAW, for appellant; SILAS H. STRAWN, EDWARD W. EVERETT and WALTER H. JACOBS, of counsel.

HAMLIN & BOYDEN and LOUIS M. GREELEY, for appellee; MORRIS ST. P. THOMAS, of counsel.

MR. JUSTICE McSURELY delivered the opinion of the court.

The defendant claims as a ground for reversal that plaintiff was guilty of negligence in failing to discover Walsh's misconduct, thereby causing the loss complained of, and, therefore, because of such negligence, plaintiff cannot recover from the defendant. It is argued that an audit of plaintiff's books would have disclosed Walsh's peculations, and that plaintiff owed to defendant the duty of so examining its books as to prevent such losses.

The cases cited to support this contention are cases having to do with a suit by a depositor against his bank to recover the amount of a forged or altered check which the bank had improperly paid and charged against the depositor's account. In such a case it was held to be the duty of the depositor to examine within a reasonable time the returned canceled checks and to give the bank timely notice of any irregularities he might discover, so that the bank could protect itself and be on guard against similar impositions in the future. A typical case is *Leather Manufacturers' Bank v. Morgan*, 117 U. S. 96, where the Court said: "If he (the depositor) had discovered that altered checks were embraced in the account, and failed to give due notice thereof to the bank, it could not be doubted that he would have been estopped to dispute the genuineness of the checks in the form in which they were paid."

But we cannot hold this rule applicable to the case before us, for the reason that the relations between the plaintiff and the defendant were not those of a depositor and his bank, but were simply those of a customer and a seller. Defendant was in the business of selling money orders to any one wishing to buy, and the plaintiff, when it desired, purchased them from defendant. Plaintiff owed defendant no higher duty than it owed to the parties from whom it bought its supplies used in its business. There were no relations of mutual trust and confidence imposing reciprocal duties as exist between a depositor and his bank. There being no duty owing to the defendant that could affect plaintiff's methods of bookkeeping, it follows that any failure by plaintiff to audit its books is not such negligence as can avail as a defense. Among the cases sustaining this view in extended opinions are *People v. Bank of North America*, 75 N. Y. 547; *Shepard & Morse Lumber Co. v. Eldridge*, 171 Mass. 516; *Dispatch Printing Co. v. National Bank of Commerce*, 115 Minn. 157.

In *Jordan Marsh Co. v. National Shawmut Bank*, 201 Mass. 397, and in *Shipman v. Bank of State of New York* 126 N. Y. 318, where negligence of the plaintiff was claimed as a defense, under facts similar to the facts in the case before us, it was held that the negligent manner of plaintiffs in transacting their business with reference to checks was not the proximate cause of the loss, but that the proximate cause of the checks being paid upon fraudulent indorsements was the failure of the defendants to see that the indorsements upon the checks were genuine.

It should be noted that under the scheme followed by Walsh the forgeries in question would not have been readily discovered from usual bookkeeping inspection, and it would be only a guess to say that a discovery of his wrongdoing in other particulars would have led to the discovery of this particular method of obtaining money. Considerable argument is indulged in upon the point that an investigation of Walsh's conduct would have disclosed that he was spending more for his personal wants than the amount of his salary would warrant, and that much of his expenditures was made in saloons and other places with which plaintiff had no business connection. If we are correct 'in holding that plaintiff owed no duty to the defendant as to the manner in which plaintiff kept its books of account, it certainly cannot be said that plaintiff owed the defendant any duty with regard to the habits and manner of living of plaintiff's employes.

Defendant concedes that Walsh had no express authority to indorse checks and drafts, but argues that there is evidence from which such authority may be inferred. We find no such evidence in the record; in fact, the evidence negatives any such inference. No such inference can be drawn from the mere fact that Walsh was the messenger sent to defendant's office to buy money orders with checks already indorsed. Nothing occuring between him and the defendant could be said to contain any suggestion that Walsh was indorsing the checks. They purported to be indorsed by the president or vice president of the plaintiff Company, and it is evident that Walsh conducted himself so as to inspire a belief that the indorsements were made by the persons purporting to have made them. It was not part of his scheme to lead the defendant to believe that the indorsements were made by himself, but rather that they should be considered as genuine.

Defendant is in error in its contention that it was necessary for the plaintiff to prove not only that the indorsements were not genuine, but also that they were unauthorized. If defendant claimed in defense that the indorsements were authorized, the burden was upon it to make this proof, and not upon the plaintiff. It is so held in *Schroder v. Harvey*, 75 Ill. 638, and *Jackson Paper Mfg. Co. v. Commercial Nat. Bank*, 199 Ill. 151. Decisions stating the rule in criminal cases are not in point.

There was no error in the use of the books of plaintiff. In the introduction of plaintiff's evidence in chief no books were used. Defendant then called for them and used certain entries therefrom to establish its claim for credits, without making any proof required by the statute as to their regularity. Plaintiff therefore became entitled to use other entries to explain or contradict the effect claimed for the entries adduced by defendant.

In *Boudinot v. Winter*, 190 Ill. 394, the Court said:

"We know of no principle that will enable a party to a suit to call upon his adversary for the production of documentary evidence, and, when it is so produced, claim the benefit of such part or portion thereof as may be to his advantage, and, at the same time, reject such part as tends against him, and also deprive his opponent of the right to its use."

We might also say that defendant suffered no harm from this use of the books by plaintiff.

Complaints are made of many rulings of the court on the admissibility of evidence. Some of the objections are highly technical. In other instances, where objections to questions were sustained, the testimony sought was already in evidence. Other points are met by what we have said concerning the absence of any duty from plaintiff to defendant in regard to plaintiff's manner of conducting its business.

The facts are not in dispute. The only questions involved are ones of law. In our view of the case the trial court committed no error in instructing the jury as he did, and the judgment will be affirmed.

Affirmed.

Fred C. Rounds and Albert H. Wetten, Appellants, v. Victoria Hotel Company, Appellee.

Gen. No. 18,365. (Not to be reported in full.)

Appeal from the Municipal Court of Chicago; the Hon. JAMES C. MARTIN, Judge, presiding. Heard in this court at the March term, 1912. Reversed and remanded. Opinion filed January 12, 1914.

Statement of the Case.

Action by Fred C. Rounds and Albert H. Wetten, doing business as Rounds & Wetten, against Victoria Hotel Company, a corporation, to recover a commission for procuring a customer for defendant to lease certain premises belonging to defendant. The case was tried by the court without a jury. From a judgment in favor of defendant, plaintiffs appeal.

EDDY, WETTEN & PEGLER, for appellants; WILLIAM H. DIETERICH and HOWARD M. HARPEL, of counsel.

HOPKINS, PEFFERS & HOPKINS, for appellee.

MR. JUSTICE McSURELY delivered the opinion of the court.

Abstract of the Decision.

1. BROKERS, § 88*—*when judgment for principal in action for commission not sustained by the evidence.* In an action for commissions for procuring a lessee for defendant's premises, a judgment in favor of defendant *held* not sustained by the evidence, it appearing that the plaintiffs procured a customer, that a commission was agreed upon and that the premises were afterwards leased to such customer by the principal through another agent.

2. BROKERS, § 48*—*when broker is procuring cause of final consummation with customer.* Where a real estate broker produces a customer and continues the negotiations he will be considered as the procuring cause of the final consummation with the customer, although the negotiations may be completed by the principal or through another party.

3. BROKERS, § 84*—*when conversation between broker and prospective customer admissible.* In an action to recover a commission for procuring a customer for leasing defendant's premises, a conversation between the customer and the plaintiffs *held* admissible for the purpose of showing that the customer had not abandoned the leasing.

*See Illinois Notes Digest, Vols. XI to XV, same topic and section number.

502   APPELLATE COURTS OF ILLINOIS.

Am. Art Works v. Chicago Picture Frame Works, 184 Ill. App. 502.

American Art Works, Appellee, v. Chicago Picture Frame Works, Appellant.

Gen. No. 18,418.

CORPORATIONS, § 736*—*when foreign corporation is not doing business in this State so as to deprive it of the right to sue.* A foreign corporation which is engaged in manufacturing advertising specialties, with its factory and principal office in another State, owns no property in this State, maintains an office in Chicago for the exclusive use of its salesmen whose only business is the solicitation of orders by agents, but the salesmen are required to pay the expenses of the office out of their commissions, *held* to be engaged in interstate commerce business and not to come within the purview of Hurd's R. S. 1909, p. 573, J. & A. ¶ 2531, prohibiting foreign corporations from maintaining a suit within this State where it does business in this State without a license.

Appeal from the Municipal Court of Chicago; the Hon. HARRY L. PERSONS, Judge, presiding. Heard in this court at the March term, 1912. Affirmed. Opinion filed January 12, 1914. Rehearing denied January 26, 1914. *Certiorari* granted by Supreme Court.

A. D. GASH, for appellant.

BAKER & HOLDER, for appellee.

MR. JUSTICE McSURELY delivered the opinion of the court.

This is an appeal from a judgment obtained by the American Art Works, a corporation, in a suit on written contracts for the sale of merchandise.

The defendant, Chicago Picture Frame Works, a corporation, claims that the plaintiff cannot recover, on the ground that it is a foreign corporation doing business within the State of Illinois without a license as is required by statute. No other point is presented on this appeal.

It is not controverted that plaintiff was a foreign corporation at the time of the transaction involved.

*See Illinois Notes Digest, Vols. XI to XV, same topic and section number.

It was organized under the laws of New Jersey, and had its principal office at Coshocton, Ohio. The ultimate question for decision is whether, under the facts in evidence, plaintiff is prohibited from maintaining this suit by reason of the provisions of the statute of Illinois, entitled "An Act to Regulate the Admission of Foreign Corporations for Profit, to do Business in the State of Illinois," approved May 18, 1905, in force July 1, 1905, Hurd's R. S. 1909, p. 573 (J. & A. ¶ 2531). The answer to this question depends on whether or not plaintiff was doing business in Illinois, and the material facts on this point are as follows:

Plaintiff's principal office and factory are at Coshocton, Ohio, where it manufactures advertising specialties. It owns no property in Illinois. It has an office for the exclusive use of its salesmen in Chicago, but the only business it has ever done in Illinois is the solicitation of orders by agents, which orders are forwarded to the office at Coshocton for acceptance or rejection. All goods are manufactured at Coshocton and are delivered f. o. b. cars at that place. No shipments have ever been made to any point in Illinois for delivery. Collections of accounts are made from the Coshocton office, and all payments are made there. The salesmen have been employed under contracts that they shall solicit orders on commission, and that all expenses, including the office rent in Chicago, telephone charges, etc., are to be paid out of these commissions, and if paid by the company are charged up against the commissions earned by the salesmen. The two contracts upon which this suit was brought were solicited by a Chicago salesman and transmitted by him to Coshocton and approved and accepted there, and a written acknowledgment of the acceptance sent to the defendant. All of the goods sold by plaintiff are made up to order, and no goods are kept in the Chicago office.

From a consideration of these facts we have concluded that plaintiff was not doing business within the purview of the statute above referred to, and hence the statute has no application. The foregoing facts bring the case within the reasoning and conclusion of the Supreme Court in *Lehigh Portland Cement Co. v. McLean*, 245 Ill. 326, in which opinion the rule under consideration is discussed at length, with copious quotations from many other cases. In that case it was held that corporations engaged in interstate commerce are not amenable to the provisions of the act above referred to, and hence by the very language of the act itself are excluded from its operation. It was also held that a corporation transacting essentially the same kind of business as was the plaintiff herein is engaged in interstate commerce.

We do not deem it important that the plaintiff Company was the lessee of an office in Chicago as headquarters for its salesmen, as the expense of its maintenance, including rent, was charged to the salesmen. In this respect the facts are the same as in *International Textbook Co. v. Pigg*, 217 U. S. 91, in which the plaintiff was a Pennsylvania corporation, with a solicitor in Kansas, maintaining an office there at his expense. The court holds that the business of the plaintiff was interstate commerce within the meaning of the Constitution of the United States.

Holding as we do, that the reasoning and conclusion of the Supreme Court in the *Lehigh Portland Cement Co.* case, *supra,* is decisive of the point now under our consideration, we are of the opinion that the trial court committed no error in declining to instruct the jury to find the issues for the defendant.

The judgment will be affirmed.

Affirmed.

The People of the State of Illinois for use of Henry J. Schaefer, Appellee, v. George Wirtz et al.

On Appeal of Joseph Thome and John Doornek, Appellants.

Gen. No. 18,433.   (Not to be reported in full.)

Appeal from the Municipal Court of Chicago; the Hon. JAMES C. MARTIN, Judge, presiding. Heard in this court at the March term, 1912. Affirmed. Opinion filed January 12, 1914.

Statement of the Case.

Action by the People of the State of Illinois for the use of Henry J. Schaefer against George Wirtz and others on a guardian's bond. From a judgment entered against the defendants for twelve thousand dollars in debt and one thousand nine hundred dollars in damages to be satisfied upon the payment of the damages with costs and interest, Joseph Thome and John Doornek, two of the defendants, appeal.

PINES & NEWMANN, for appellants; JULIUS M. KAHN, of counsel.

ROCCO DE STEFANO, for appellee.

MR. JUSTICE McSURELY delivered the opinion of the court.

Abstract of the Decision.

1. GUARDIAN AND WARD, § 97*—*when record shows suit on guardian's bond is brought in the name of the People.* A suit on a guardian's bond is shown to have been brought in the name of the People where the record shows that the plaintiff named in the *praecipe* is "People of the State of Illinois, for use of Henry J. Schaefer" and the plaintiff is so named in the statement of claim and other papers filed in the case, though the summons calls upon defendants to answer unto "Henry J. Schaefer."

2. MUNICIPAL COURT OF CHICAGO, § 5*—*judicial notice of rules by*

*See Illinois Notes Digest, Vols. XI to XV, same topic and section number.

Appellate Court. Section 20 of Municipal Court Act, J. & A. ¶ 3332, *held* not to require the Appellate Court to take judicial notice of a rule of the Municipal Court, since that section was declared unconstitutional in *Bixby v. Chicago City Ry. Co.*, 260 Ill. 478.

Isadore B. Simco, Defendant in Error, v. Morris M. Mankowitz, Plaintiff in Error.

Gen. No. 18,771. (Not to be reported in full.)

Error to the Municipal Court of Chicago; the Hon. HOSEA W. WELLS, Judge, presiding. Heard in the Branch Appellate Court at the October term, 1912. Reversed and remanded. Rehearing allowed November 18, 1913. Opinion on rehearing filed January 13, 1914.

Statement of the Case.

Motion presented by Morris M. Mankowitz to the Municipal Court to vacate a judgment of confession entered in that court against Morris M. Mankowitz and in favor of Isadore B. Simco on a judgment note, and for leave to defend against the action. The motion was presented more than two months after the entry of the judgment and was based on a petition supported by affidavit. From an order denying the motion, Morris M. Mankowitz brings error.

EVERETT JENNINGS, HARRY L. STROHM and JENNINGS & FIFER, for plaintiff in error.

No appearance for defendant in error.

MR. PRESIDING JUSTICE SMITH delivered the opinion of the court.

Abstract of the Decision.

1. MUNICIPAL COURT OF CHICAGO, § 19*—*jurisdiction to vacate confessed judgment on petition.* Under section 21 of the Municipal Court Act, J. & A. ¶ 3333, that court has power after thirty days from the entry of a confessed judgment to vacate it on petition setting forth facts which would be sufficient to cause the same to be vacated in a court of equity.

2. JUDGMENT, § 62*—*when petition to open judgment by confession states equitable grounds.* A petition supported by an affidavit and stating grounds for a motion to vacate a judgment entered by confession on a judgment note and for leave to plead to the merits and defend the action, *held* to state facts showing petitioner entitled to equitable relief, the petition showing that the judgment note was given as part of the purchase price of an automobile, that the seller misrepresented the condition of the automobile and that the note was indorsed to the holder with knowledge of the warranty.

Charles L. Millhouse, Appellee, v. Herman H. Krotz, Appellant.

Gen. No. 18,871. (Not to be reported in full.)

Appeal from the Superior Court of Cook county; the Hon. WILLIAM FENIMORE COOPER, Judge, presiding. Heard in the Branch Appellate Court at the October term, 1912. Affirmed. Opinion filed January 13, 1914.

Statement of the Case.

Action by Charles L. Millhouse, surviving partner of a copartnership formerly composed of Daniel McHenry and Charles L. Millhouse, on a stay bond to recover against defendant as surety thereon. From a judgment in favor of plaintiff in the sum of $689.29 as damages together with costs, defendant appeals.

The bond in this case was executed to stay execution on a judgment recovered in the Municipal Court in favor of the copartners against Alfred E. Croft upon an indebtedness due from Croft for a balance of the purchase price for certain shares of stock. This judgment was afterwards affirmed in *McHenry v. Croft*, 163 Ill. App. 426.

ROBERT D. MELICK, for appellant.

MUSGRAVE, OPPENHEIM & LEE, for appellee.

MR. PRESIDING JUSTICE SMITH delivered the opinion of the court.

Abstract of the Decision.

1. APPEAL AND ERROR, § 1859*—*when surety on a stay bond estopped by terms of bond to claim satisfaction of judgment.* In an action against a surety on a stay bond, defendant is estopped to claim plaintiff's retention of certain promissory notes operated as a satisfaction of the judgment, where such retention took place before the execution of the bond.

2. APPEAL AND ERROR, § 1877*—*defense to action on stay bond.* In an action on a stay bond, any defenses in the nature of payment or discharge of the judgment must be based upon facts arising after the execution of the bond.

3. APPEAL AND ERROR, § 1884*—*evidence inadmissible in action on stay bond.* In action against surety on a stay bond, held not error to refuse to permit the defendant to introduce in evidence the transcript of the proceedings in the trial court and the opinion of the Appellate Court to show what facts had been adjudicated in the original suit.

4. APPEAL AND ERROR, § 1859*—*when surety on stay bond estopped to deny validity of judgment.* Surety on a stay bond is estopped to deny that a valid judgment was in force at the time of the execution of the bond.

5. ELECTION OF REMEDIES, § 5*—*when creditor has concurrent remedies.* The law is that a creditor holding collateral security may prosecute an action against the debtor and at the same time proceed to realize upon the security, and is entitled to follow both remedies until the debt is finally satisfied.

*See Illinois Notes Digest, Vols. XI to XV, same topic and section number.

CHICAGO—FIRST DISTRICT—JANUARY, 1914.   509

American S. & G. Co. v. Chicago G. Co. et al., 184 Ill. App. 509.

American Sand & Gravel Company, Appellee, v. Chicago Gravel Company and Joliet Sand and Gravel Company, Appellants.

Gen. No. 18,879.

1. CONTRACTS, § 153*—*when agreement not to sell products of sand and gravel pits not in unreasonable restraint of trade.* Where a contract grants the exclusive right to excavate and remove sand and gravel from a tract of land for a certain period, and in consideration for the privilege granted the grantee agreed to make certain payments in money, to deliver to the grantor not to exceed twenty-five carloads of the product per day, and not to sell during the contract term any products from any of its pits for use in Cook county, except to the grantor, *held* that the negative covenant contained therein is not in unreasonable restraint of trade, but that its provisions are reasonable and only in partial restraint, and founded upon a valid consideration.

2. CONTRACTS, § 152*—*when negative covenant in partial restraint of trade not invalid.* Where the restriction of a negative covenant is partial, reasonable and calculated to foster the business of the covenantee, rather than to destroy competition, it cannot be *held* to be in violation of the Federal or State statutes, or against public policy, and therefore void.

3. CONTRACTS, § 329*—*when breach of contract waived.* A party to a contract waives a breach thereof by the other party where he makes no attempt to rescind therefor but avails himself of its benefits long after the breach was committed.

4. INJUNCTION, § 75*—*when lies to enforce negative covenant though remedy at law.* The right to an injunction for the enforcement of a negative covenant in a contract does not depend on the question whether complainant has an action at law or not to recover damages.

5. INJUNCTION, § 75*—*when violation of negative covenant may be enjoined.* Equity may interfere to restrain the violation of a negative provision in a contract although it cannot enforce the affirmative one where the negative and affirmative provisions are entirely separate and distinct.

6. ASSIGNMENTS, § 22*—*when assignment of rights under a contract operates to establish privity of estate.* Where a contract grants an exclusive privilege to take sand and gravel from certain land for a term of years and the grantee assigns his entire term

leaving no reversionary right, there is a privity of estate between the assignee and the original grantor.

' 7. ASSIGNMENTS, § 25*—*when assignee of rights under a contract takes with notice* of liabilities. Where a contract grants a company a privilege of taking sand and gravel from certain premises and such company assigns all its interest thereunder to another company, the latter company will be charged with knowledge of the duties and liabilities of the former company under the contract where both companies had substantially the same persons as officers, each company occupying the same offices and sharing the same telephone service.

8. LICENSES, § 29*—*when grant of right to take gravel from land not grant of mere personal license*. A contract granting the exclusive right to take sand and gravel from certain premises, the right not being limited to any particular piece or section, clearly grants an interest in the land and not a mere personal license.

Appeal from the Superior Court of Cook county; the Hon. CHARLES A. McDONALD, Judge, presiding. Heard in the Branch Appellate Court at the October term, 1912. Affirmed. Opinion filed January 13, 1914. Rehearing denied January 27, 1914. *Certiorari* denied by Supreme Court (making opinion final).

ULLMANN, HOAG & DAVIDSON and VAIL & VETTE, for appellants; EDWARD P. VAIL and PARKER H. HOAG, of counsel.

JOHN T. RICHARDS, for appellee.

MR. PRESIDING JUSTICE SMITH delivered the opinion of the court.

Appellee, American Sand & Gravel Company, a corporation, filed its bill in the Superior Court of Cook county against appellants, Chicago Gravel Company and Joliet Sand and Gravel Company. Upon answers filed and the report of a master the court entered a decree substantially in accordance with the recommendation of the master, enjoining the appellants from selling any washed products prepared from sand and gravel mined and excavated from any or either of the gravel pits located on the premises known as the Gilbert, Hammond, Gifford and Millsdale properties, or from any pits that were then and might be thereafter opened on any land owned or controlled by the Chicago Gravel Company, at any time during the life of a certain agreement dated August 10, 1905, for use within Cook county, to any one other 'than the complainant in the bill, except for use at points along the lines of the Elgin, Joliet & Eastern Railway and the Chicago, Lake Shore & Eastern Railway, as said respective railways were located on August 10, 1905, and referring the cause to a master to take an accounting of the damages sustained by complainant by reason of the violation of a negative covenant contained in the contract of August 10, 1905. From that decree appellants prosecute this appeal, and have separately assigned errors upon the record.

There is no substantial controverted question of fact in the case. Appellants present their case in this court upon questions of law mainly arising upon the contract and the assignment or transfer thereof, which formed the basis of the relations between the parties to the suit.

It substantially appears from the bill and the evidence that on June 15, 1905, a contract was entered into between one Louisa Gilbert and Sebastian Krug, by which Krug acquired the exclusive right to excavate and remove sand and gravel from a tract of land situated near Elgin, in Kane county, Illinois, during a period of fifteen years from June 15, 1905. July 15, 1905, the American Sand & Gravel Company, appellee, entered into a contract with Krug, under which appellee became possessed of the exclusive rights conferred by said first mentioned contract for the period of fourteen years and ten months from July 15, 1905. On August 10, 1905, appellee entered into a contract with appellant Chicago Gravel Company, by the terms of which the Chicago Gravel Company was granted the exclusive right to excavate and remove sand and gravel from the Gilbert land for a period of fourteen

512 APPELLATE COURTS OF ILLINOIS.

American S. & G. Co. v. Chicago G. Co. et al., 184 Ill. App. 509.

years and nine months from said tenth day of August, 1905.

At the time of the making of said last mentioned contract, the Chicago Gravel Company owned or controlled a large amount of other lands containing deposit of sand and gravel. Under the contract between Louisa Gilbert and Krug and the contract between Krug and appellee, appellee was required to erect certain machinery on the gravel land for the purpose of mining or excavating the sand and gravel, and washing, cleaning and preparing the same for the market. This would involve the expenditure of a considerable sum of money by appellee, and as said Chicago Gravel Company owned a washing and screening plant adjacent to the Gilbert land and was operating the same at the time of the making of the contracts above mentioned, in order to avoid the expenditure required to be made under the Gilbert contract, a supplemental agreement was entered into between Louisa Gilbert and Krug, whereby the Gilbert contract was modified so as to permit the letting of the gravel land by Krug, and this supplemental contract also contained a provision waiving the requirement that a washing and screening plant should be erected on the Gilbert land, so as to enable the Chicago Gravel Company to prepare the product from the Gilbert land for the market by means of the plant which that company then had in operation adjacent to the Gilbert land.

In the fourth paragraph of the contract between the Chicago Gravel Company and appellee, complainant below, it was provided that the Chicago Gravel Company should supply appellee with not less than fifteen carloads per day of its washed products during each and every day, Sundays and holidays excepted, beginning with April 1st and ending December 1st in each year during said term of fourteen years and nine months, weather conditions permitting, and not to exceed twenty-five carloads per day during the period. The contract provided that it should be optional with appellee whether it would accept and receive from the Chicago Gravel Company any more than fifteen carloads of said product per day. The contract further provided that strikes, lockouts, interruptions to transportation, lack of cars, accidents and other causes beyond the control of the Chicago Gravel Company should excuse compliance with the terms of the contract while such condition continued; but provided further that in case of lack of cars appellee should be entitled to at least seventy-five per cent. of the available car supply. The fourth paragraph of the contract also contained the following provision:

"It is further expressly understood and agreed that the said party of the second part (Chicago Gravel Company) shall not ship to any person, firm or corporation within Cook County, Illinois, other than said party of the first part (American Sand & Gravel Company, appellee) any of its washed products, and will not, after the first day of January, 1906, sell any of its washed products within said County of Cook except to said party of the first part, provided, however, that said party of the second part shall have the right to ship so much of said material as may be required to complete its present contract for the elevation of the tracks of the Chicago Junction Railway; it being hereby intended that said party of the first part shall have the exclusive right, within the County of Cook aforesaid, to all the washed product of gravel pits owned or controlled by said party of the second part; and that said party of the second part shall not sell the washed product of any of its gravel pits for use within said County of Cook to any other person, firm or corporation: Provided, however, that said party of the second part shall have the right to ship product from its said gravel pits along the lines of the Elgin, Joliet & Eastern Railway and the Chicago, Lake Shore & Eastern Railway, as said respective railways are at present located."

Upon the execution of the last mentioned contract, possession of the Gilbert land was delivered to the Chicago Gravel Company and the latter proceeded to

make preparations for and entered upon the performance of the contract. During the season of 1907, the
Chicago Gravel Company was unable for various reasons to furnish to appellee all of the sand and gravel
to which it was entitled under the terms of the contract, but appellee took from the Chicago Gravel Company all the material it could get. During the season
of 1908, the Chicago Gravel Company offered to appellee the fifteen carloads of product required under
the terms of the contract, but appellee was unable to
accept the full amount. Shipments, however, were
made from time to time, all orders given being accepted by the Chicago Gravel Company and all material shipped to appellee was paid for according to
the terms of the contract. During the seasons of 1909
and 1910, the Chicago Gravel Company supplied substantially all the material ordered by appellee, and
the same was accepted and paid for by appellee according to the contract, and this condition of affairs continued until the time of the hearing of the cause before
the master.

The bill avers, and the evidence shows, that during
the years of 1908, 1909 and 1910, the Chicago Gravel
Company shipped a number of cars of washed sand
and gravel into Cook county for use in Cook county
in violation of the negative covenant in said contract
above set forth. In May, 1911, appellee, having learned
that washed products from the pits of the Chicago
Gravel Company were being shipped and sold in Cook
county, filed its bill in the Superior Court of Cook
county, alleging the violation of the negative covenant contained in the contract, and set forth that sales
of such material had been made by the Chicago Gravel
Company, and that although warned to desist from
doing so, said company still continued to sell to sundry
persons, firms and corporations, whose names are set
out in the bill, and to other persons and corporations
to appellee unknown, washed sand and gravel in Cook
county from its gravel pits, and continues to make

shipments and sell products in violation of the covenant above set forth, and asking that the Chicago
Gravel Company be enjoined from the violation of the
negative covenant, and for an accounting of the ma-
terial·sold by the Chicago Gravel Company in violation of the covenant, and that the Chicago Gravel Company be required to set forth the price at which the
said washed products were sold, the names of the persons, firms and corporations to whom such sales were
made, and that an accounting of the profits realized
by the Chicago Gravel Company from such sales in
violation of the terms of the contract be taken, and
that the Chicago Gravel Company be required to pay
appellee all the profits realized by it from such sales.

Appellee, having learned that appellant, Joliet Sand
and Gravel Company, on or about January 1, 1911, had
entered into an agreement with the Chicago Gravel
Company, whereby the latter company granted to the
Joliet Sand and Gravel Company the right to excavate
gravel from its gravel pits for a period of ten years
from the date of the contract, and that the Joliet Sand
and Gravel Company was acting under said contract in
connection with the Sand & Gravel Company a party
defendant, and, afterwards, on July 15, 1911, a supplemental bill was filed by appellee.

The amended and supplemental bill sets out the two
contracts above referred to between appellee and the
Chicago Gravel Company, and the Chicago Gravel
Company and the Joliet Sand & Gravel Company, and
alleges that the agreements were made for the purpose of enabling the Chicago Gravel Company to evade
the force and effect of its contract of August 10, 1905,
and that James A. Hart, president of the Chicago
Gravel Company, is also president of the Joliet Sand
and Gravel Company; that both companies occupy the
same or connecting offices in the city of Chicago, use
the same telephone service, and that the Joliet Sand
and Gravel Company has sold and shipped to divers
and sundry persons, for use within Cook county, large

516   APPELLATE COURTS OF ILLINOIS.

American S. & G. Co. v. Chicago G. Co. et al., 184 Ill. App. 509.

quantities of said washed products, and which, under
the terms of the contract of August 10, 1905, the Chicago Gravel Company had no right to sell directly or
indirectly. The supplemental bill avers that the Joliet
Sand and Gravel Company is chargeable with notice of
the provisions of said contract of August 10, 1905, and
acquired no greater rights from the Chicago Gravel
Company than were granted by appellee to it under
the contract, and that the Joliet Sand and Gravel Company was bound to the performance of all the covenants contained in the contract between appellee and
the Chicago Gravel Company. The supplemental bill
then alleges the violation of the provisions of the contract by the Joliet Sand and Gravel Company, and
prays for an accounting.

It is admitted that the Chicago Gravel Company
violated the negative covenant of the contract of August 10, 1905, during the years of 1909 and 1910. It
is also admitted in the record that at the time the contract was made between the Chicago Gravel Company
and the Joliet Sand and Gravel Company of January 1,
1911, James A. Hart was president and F. W. Ren-
wick was vice president and general manager of both
appellant companies, and that they continued to be
such officers of both companies up to the time of the
hearing before the master.

The first question to be considered is the validity
of the contract of August 10, 1905, between the American Sand & Gravel Company, appellee, and the Chicago Gravel Company, appellant.

By the recitals and terms of that agreement it appears that a copy of the agreement of June 15, 1905,
between Louisa Gilbert and Sebastian Krug, was attached thereto, marked "Exhibit A." It was also recited that the American Company had acquired from
Krug for the term of fourteen years and ten months
all the rights and privileges granted to Krug under
his agreement with Gilbert, subject to all the conditions and limitations therein contained except as modi-

fied and changed by the supplemental agreement between Gilbert and Krug, a copy of which was also attached marked "Exhibit B." The agreement of August 10, 1905, gives and grants to the Chicago Gravel Company the exclusive right to enter upon the Gilbert property and to take and remove therefrom gravel, sand and stone, and dirt which may cover the same. In consideration therefor the Chicago Gravel Company makes the covenants and agreements contained in the second clause of the agreement. In further consideration therefor the Chicago Gravel Company, in the third clause of the agreement, agrees to pay the complainant two thousand four hundred dollars in cash to cover the expenses theretofore incurred by Krug and the complainant in obtaining the privilege granted in the June 1ᵤ, 1905, agreement as modified, and a royalty of three cents per cubic yard for each and every cubic yard excavated and removed in excess of 40,000 yards; and further to pay one thousand two hundred dollars during each and every year of the period covered by the contract which should be applied on the royalties reserved. In further consideration for the privileges granted, the Chicago Gravel Company makes the agreements contained in the fourth clause of the agreement, including the negative clause or agreement in question, which has been set forth above.

In behalf of appellants it is argued that the negative covenant in question is in unreasonable restraint of trade, and is in restraint of the alienation of personal property, and therefore equity will not enforce it.

For the purpose of considering this question, it will aid us to summarize the substance of the provisions of the contract. The complainant granted certain privileges to the Chicago Gravel Company. In consideration therefor the Chicago Gravel Company agreed: (1) to pay two thousand four hundred dollars in cash; (2) to pay not less than one thousand two hundred dol-

518   APPELLATE COURTS OF ILLINOIS.

American S. & G. Co. v. Chicago G. Co. et al., 184 Ill. App. 509.

lars per year and the royalty named in the contract; (3) to deliver to appellee not to exceed twenty-five car-loads of its washed product per day during the term of the contract at the prices named therein; and (4) that it would not sell, during the contract term of four-teen years and nine months, any washed products from any of its pits for use in Cook county, except to com-plainant.

Reading the provisions of the contract with these main features in mind, and looking into the facts and circumstances surrounding the parties at the time the contract was entered into, we think it is clear that each and all of the covenants of appellant, Chicago Gravel Company, formed and constituted the agreed consid-eration for the privileges granted to that company by the complainant. It is only reasonable to say, in view of the circumstances and the situation of the parties and the provisions of the contract, that if the Chicago Gravel Company refused to agree to any one of the four substantive provisions of the contract above set forth, the privileges described in the contract would not have been granted by the American Company. It is also quite apparent that the covenant in the fourth clause of the agreement, that the Chicago Gravel Com-pany "will not after the first day of January, 1906, sell any of its washed products within said County of Cook, except to said party of the first part," etc., was not the least important part of the consideration named in the contract, for it tended directly to foster and increase the business of the American Company. If the restriction of the covenant is partial, reasonable and calculated to foster the business of the American Company, rather than to destroy competition, it can-not be held to be in violation of the Federal or the State statutes, or against public policy, and therefore void. We think the contract is not one in general re-straint of trade, but that its provisions in that respect are reasonable and only in partial restraint, and are founded upon a valid consideration, and were intended to foster and increase the business of the American Company. The contract in our opinion must be held valid upon the principles and for the reasons clearly stated in *Southern Fire Brick & Clay Co. v. Garden City Sand Co.*, 223 Ill. 616, and *Hursen v. Gavin*, 162 Ill. 377, and the authorities cited in those cases.

We next consider the question whether a breach of the expressed negative covenant may be enjoined. The bill seeks no specific enforcement of the contract other than an injunction against the continuing breach of that covenant, and the decree does not otherwise command the specific performance of the contract.

On this question the case of *Southern Fire Brick & Clay Co. v. Garden City Sand Co., supra*, which cannot be distinguished from the case before us on principle, is both instructive and decisive. In the opinion in that case, the Court quotes with approval from *Singer Sewing Mach. Co. v. Union Button-Hole & Embroidery Co.*, 1 Holmes (U. S.) 253. A part of the quotation is:

"It was formerly thought that an injunction would not be granted to restrain the breach of any contract unless the contract were of such a character that the court could fully enforce the performance of it on both sides. Upon this ground there were many decisions refusing to interfere with contracts for personal services, however flagrant might be the breach of them. * * * But all these cases were overruled by one of the ablest chancellors who has adorned the woolsack, in *Lumley v. Wagner*. * * * It is now firmly established that the court will often interfere by an injunction where it cannot decree performance."

The Court then says:

"The prayer for performance was refused but the injunction ordered. (See also *Consolidated Coal Co. v. Schmisseur*, 135 Ill. 371.) Numerous decisions from other States might be cited to the same effect."

It is however argued in behalf of appellants that this is a bill to enforce the contract, and that it will not lie because there is no mutuality of remedy as distinguished from mutuality of obligation in the contract set up in the bill. It is conceded by counsel for appellants that there is some confusion in the authorities in regard to these two classes of mutuality, and whether equity may interfere by injunction to prevent a breach of the negative covenant when the affirmative is of such a nature that it cannot be specifically enforced by a judicial decree. We are of the opinion that the later and better considered doctrine is that equity may interfere to restrain the violation of a negative provision although it cannot enforce the affirmative one, where the negative and affirmative parts of the contract, as in this case, are entirely separate and distinct. 2 High on Injunctions (2d Ed.) pp. 728, 763, 764; Waterman's Specific Performance of Contracts, sec. 110; Kerr on Injunctions (3d Ed.) p. 357; *Lumley v. Wagner*, 1 DeG. M. & G. 604; *Singer Sewing Mach. Co. v. Union Button-Hole & Embroidery Co., supra;* and *Southern Fire Brick Co. v. Garden City Sand Co., supra,* where it is said:

"While a court of equity might not compel him to mine and sell the product to complainants in conformity with his agreement, yet there is equitable jurisdiction to prevent him from selling to other parties."

In Pomeroy on Equity Jurisprudence & Equitable Remedies, vol. 2, sec. 769 (pp. 1291, 1292), the learned author says:

"The frequent statement of the rule of mutuality, 'that the contract to be specifically enforced must, as a general rule, be mutual, that is to say, such that it might at the time it was entered into have been enforced by either of the parties against the other' is open to so many exceptions that it is of little value as a rule."

As said in the *Singer Sewing Mach. Co.* case, *supra,* the fair result of the later cases may be thus expressed:

"If the case is one in which the negative remedy of injunction will do substantial justice between the parties, by obliging the defendant either to carry out his contract or lose all benefit of the breach, and the remedy at law is inadequate, and there is no reason of policy against it, the court will interfere to restrain conduct which is contrary to the contract, although it may be unable to enforce a specific performance of it.''

Nor does the right to an injunction for the enforcement of the negative covenant in this contract depend on the question whether complainant has an action at law or not to recover damages. *Southern Fire Brick & Clay Co. v. Garden City Sand Co., supra.* ''A court of equity fastens upon the real contract and compels the execution of the very thing covenanted to be done.'' *Ropes v. Upton,* 125 Mass. 258. This is the rule even though the complainant has a right of action at law or has taken a bond in connection with the covenant.

It is contended in argument that the negative covenant in question is a personal covenant and not binding on third parties either with or without notice. With this contention we cannot agree. The contract between Gilbert and Krug conveyed the privileges thereby granted for a period of fifteen years, or until June 15, 1920. The contract between Krug and appellee, dated July 15, 1905, and the privileges granted by it, extended for the period of fourteen years and ten months, or until May 15, 1920, leaving a remainder of one month still vested in Krug. The contract between appellee and the Chicago Gravel Company, dated August 10, 1905, assigned or transferred the privileges thereby granted for the period of fourteen years and nine months, or, in other words, until May 10, 1920, leaving a remainder of five days in appellee out of the period granted to appellee by Krug. The contract between the Chicago Gravel Company and the Joliet Sand and Gravel Company dated January 1, 1911, assigned and transferred the privileges and rights therein expressed to the Joliet Sand and Gravel Company for a period of ten years, or until January 1, 1921, seven months and twenty-one days beyond the

522   APPELLATE COURTS OF ILLINOIS.

American S. & G. Co. v. Chicago G. Co. et al., 184 Ill. App. 509.

term granted to the Chicago Gravel Company by appellee under the contract of August 10, 1905. The whole term which was vested in the Chicago Gravel Company was, by the contract of January 1, 1911, vested in the Joliet Sand and Gravel Company, and the latter company, by reason of that fact, became and was vested with all the rights acquired by the Chicago Gravel Company and subject to all the liabilities of the Chicago Gravel Company thereunder; and we think that appellant, the Joliet Sand and Gravel Company, became bound to the performance of all the covenants contained in the contract of August 10, 1905, which, by its terms, were required to be performed by the Chicago Gravel Company.

The contract by which appellant, the Joliet Sand and Gravel Company, acquired the right and privilege of going upon the Gilbert land and excavating sand and gravel therefrom was a contract with reference to the use of that property and was more than a license to go upon the property and remove sand and gravel. In the case of *Consolidated Coal Co. v. Peers,* 150 Ill. 344, it was contended that the contract in that case was a mere personal license, but the Court said, on , page 350:

"A license is an authority to do a particular act or acts upon another man's land without possessing any estate therein. * * * The lease here involved invests the lessee with the 'sole and exclusive right' to mine and operate in coal on certain described lands. The right granted is not limited to any particular vein or stratum, but extends to all coal under said lands, and it is exclusive of the whole world, including the lessors themselves, and is for the full term of twenty-five years from the date thereof. The law, as we understand it, is, that a lease of the right and privilege to mine or take away stone or coal from the lessor's land is the grant of an interest in the land, and not a mere license to take stone or coal."

In *Gartside v. Outley,* 58 Ill. 210, it was contended that the instrument there involved was not a lease.

The contract granted certain lands for an indefinite period with permission to take, under certain conditions specified in the grant, all the coal contained in said lands. It also contained mutual covenants and the provision of forfeiture in case of noncompliance on the part of the lessee. The Court said:

"We think the fair construction to be given to that instrument is that it is in the nature of a lease and creates only the relation of lessor and lessee."

To the same effect are *Harvey Coal & Coke Co. v. Dillon*, 59 W. Va. 605, and *Heywood v. Fulmer*, 158 Ind. 658. In the *Heywood* case, the written instrument was in the form of a receipt for money paid, executed by the owner of the land, and gave to the person named therein exclusive right to all the sand and gravel on certain premises for one year, and excluding all other persons from said premises, and the Court held that it amounted to a lease and not a mere license, and was valid against the grantee.

In that case the Court said:

"A lease may not only confer upon the lessee the right to the occupancy of the leased premises, either generally for the time limited, or for some specific purpose, or in some specific manner, or the right to occupy and cultivate the land and to remove the products of cultivation, but it may confer upon him the power to occupy and remove a portion of that which constitutes the land itself. Familiar and common examples of such leases are those authorizing the lessee to quarry and remove stone, to open mines and remove ores, minerals, mineral coal, etc., or to sink wells for procuring and removing petroleum and natural gas. * * * In our opinion the writing in question contains all of the essential elements of a valid lease."

So we think in this case the contract between appellee and the Chicago Gravel Company gave the latter company the right to mine and remove any sand, stone, dirt or gravel on the premises, and the Chicago Gravel Company was not limited to any particular piece or section, but had an exclusive right to take all the sand, gravel, etc., on said premises. It, therefore, clearly granted an interest in the land, and was not a mere personal license.

The contract between the Chicago Gravel Company and the Joliet Sand and Gravel Company operated as an assignment to the latter company of the contract of August 10, 1905. It transferred the entire term of the Chicago Gravel Company and left no reversionary right. It was, therefore, an assignment of the entire term of the Chicago Gravel Company, and this established a privity of estate between the parties to it. *Stewart v. Long Island R. Co.*, 102 N. Y. 601; *Sexton v. Chicago Storage Co.*, 129 Ill. 318; *Chicago Attachment Co. v. Davis Sewing Mach. Co.*, 142 Ill. 171; *Lee v. Payne*, 4 Mich. 106; *Coal & Coke Co. v. Tax Commissioner*, 59 W. Va. 605.

If, however, we are mistaken as to the effect of the contract of January 1, 1911, we think that in view of the fact that the officers of the two appellant companies were substantially the same, that the same person was president of both companies, and that the same person was vice-president and general manager of both companies, there can be no doubt that the Joliet Sand & Gravel Company had full notice of the rights, duties and liabilities of the Chicago Gravel Company under the contract of August 10, 1905, at the time that the contract of January 1, 1911, was made. The further facts that the Chicago Gravel Company and the Joliet Sand and Gravel Company have always occupied one and the same suite of offices in the city of Chicago, that the lease of their offices was for several years in the name of the Chicago Gravel Company, and the present lease is in the name of the Joliet Sand and Gravel Company, that both companies have always shared the same telephone service and their telephone numbers have been the same, show such intimate relations between the two companies in the same business that there is no reasonable ground for believing that the Joliet Sand and Gravel Company did not have full knowledge of the contracts relating to the Gilbert property under which the Joliet Sand and Gravel Company finally obtained its interest under which it is operating.

The above facts are only a portion of the facts appearing in the record which tend to show that while technically two different corporations they virtually represent and control the same interests. We think the injunction properly included the Joliet Sand and Gravel Company.

The negative covenant in question is a part of the consideration for the making of the contract in which it appears, and that contract, as we have seen, relates to the land and the use of it. We need not hold and do not decide that it is a covenant running with the land. It is sufficient that it is a covenant which both appellants were bound to observe under the facts shown in the record.

Other points are argued at length in the briefs of counsel. Many of them we do not regard as material to the decision of the case.

There is only one other contention made on behalf of the Chicago Gravel Company to which we deem it material to refer. It is contended that because complainant did not take from the Chicago Gravel Company fifteen carloads of gravel per day during the year 1908, the negative covenant in question cannot be enforced. The evidence is undisputed, and the master so finds, that there was a failure on the part of the Chicago Gravel Company to furnish appellee prior to 1908 the amount of sand and gravel demanded and to which appellee was entitled by the contract, and that appellee was unable to accept the minimum amount during the year 1908. But it is not shown or attempted to be shown that the Chicago Gravel Company made any attempt to forfeit or rescind the contract of August 10, 1905, on that account, or that it offered to surrender the rights acquired by it under that contract. It appears on the contrary that the Chicago Gravel Company attempted to evade the

negative covenant and still retain the benefit of all
other provisions of the contract. It seems to have
failed to perform its contract during the year 1907,
but in 1908 it demanded strict performance of the contract by appellee. At the beginning of 1909 it tried
to repudiate the negative covenant but was notified by
appellee that it would be held to the performance of
the entire contract. The written evidence in the form
of letters shows conclusively that the parties proceeded
under the contract during 1909 and 1910, appellee paying the prices fixed by the contract in accordance with
the terms thereof. It is not claimed anywhere that
the rights and privileges granted by the contract have
ever been surrendered. If, therefore, there was a
breach in 1908 by appellee, the breach was waived by
the Chicago Gravel Company when it retained possession of the Gilbert property and in other respects
availed itself of the benefits of the contract in question after the alleged breach by appellee had been committed. If appellee violated the contract during the
year 1908, the Chicago Gravel Company might then
have elected to terminate the contractual relations and
surrender the Gilbert property; on the contrary, it
elected to proceed under the contract and is bound
to the performance of all its covenants. The rule is
so well established that it seems unnecessary to cite
any authorities. Pomeroy in his Equity Jurisprudence, vol. 6, sec. 806, says:

"Of course, a waiver of the condition makes the
contract operate against the waiver, and equity will
then treat it as any other contract."

Fry in his work on Specific Performance (5th Ed.)
sec. 940, says:

"A defendant who has waived the performance by
the plaintiff of what was on his part to be performed
cannot, of course, use the non-performance as a defense."

Page on Contracts, vol. 3, p. 2217, says:

"If the party originally in default performs before

the adversary party elects to treat it as a breach, his rights under the contract stand as if the contract had never been broken, except as concerns his liability for damages. Subsequent breach by the party not in default may prevent the latter from recovery and in such case he can not revert to the original breach as a discharge.''

To the same effect is *Pratt v. S. Freeman & Sons Mfg. Co.*, 115 Wis. 648.

Finding no error in the decree, it is affirmed.

Affirmed.

German American Savings Loan and Building Association et al., Appellants, v. John C. Trainor et al., Appellees.

Gen. No. 18,902.   (Not to be reported in full.)

Appeal from the Circuit Court of Cook county; the Hon. JOHN GIBBONS, Judge, presiding. Heard in the Branch Appellate Court at the October term, 1912. Affirmed. Opinion filed January 13, 1914.

Statement of the Case.

This is an appeal by complainant, German American Savings Loan and Building Association, from an order fixing the amount of master's fees. The record contains over sixteen hundred pages of typewritten testimony and pleadings and exhibits. Portions of the testimony was taken by three different masters when later the cause was referred to another master to take additional evidence and report his conclusions of law and fact upon all the testimony taken in the case. From an order fixing the fee of the master at nine hundred and seventy-five dollars, and directing that sum between the parties, complainant and defendant, equally, complainant appeals.

CHARLES B. STAFFORD, for appellants.

JOHN W. ELLIS, *pro se.*

MR. PRESIDING JUSTICE SMITH delivered the opinion of the court.

Abstract of the Decision.

1. EQUITY, § 404*—*when master's fees not excessive.* Allowance of nine hundred and seventy-five dollars as master's fees *held* not excessive.

2. APPEAL AND ERROR, § 1208*—*cross-errors.* Cross-errors assigned by a person not a party to the cause will not be considered.

T. E. Hill Company for use of William A. Bither (Assignee), Appellee, v. The United States Fidelity and Guaranty Company, Appellant.

Gen. No. 18,026.

1. BANKRUPTCY, § 47*—*effect of filing of appeal bond as a supersedeas.* A proceeding for the appointment of a receiver under sec. tion 3e of the Bankruptcy Act is separate and distinct from a proceeding to adjudicate; so that where an appeal is taken from an order dismissing the petition, the filing of an appeal bond does not operate as a *supersedeas* so as to prolong the receivership but operates to supersede only the order of dismissal.

2. BANKRUPTCY, § 48*—*damages recoverable in action on appeal bond.* In an action against a surety on an appeal bond given under section 25 of the Bankruptcy Act on the taking of an appeal from an order dismissing a petition to have plaintiff adjudicated a bankrupt, *held* error for the court to assess damages based upon proof of the detention of the property by the receiver after the appeal bond was filed and *held* error for the court to assess other than nominal damages, there being no competent proof of damages and no proof even of the costs incurred in the proceeding for adjudication.

3. APPEAL AND ERROR, § 1810*—*when Appellate Court may reverse and enter final judgment.* In a case in which the jury was

T. E. Hill Co. v. The U. S. F. and G. Co., 184 Ill. App. 528.

waived, the Appellate Court may not only reverse but may also render final judgment if the law as applied to the facts found by that court necessitates such a judgment, and if it can be ascertained from the facts so found what judgment ought to have been rendered by the court below.

Appeal from the Municipal Court of Chicago; the Hon. WILLIAM N. GEMMILL, Judge, presiding. Heard in the Branch Appellate Court at the October term, 1911. Reversed. Opinion filed January 13, 1914.

JOHN A. BLOOMINGSTON, for appellant.

BUELL & ABBEY and FRED W. BENTLEY, for appellee.

MR. JUSTICE BARNES delivered the opinion of the court.

This was an action of debt brought against appellant as surety on an appeal bond. The plea was *nil debet,* but the breach of the bond was not questioned at the trial, the controversy being over the extent of liability. The court found the damages exceeded ten thousand dollars, and assessed them at five thousand dollars, the full amount of the penalty.

The bond was given under section 25 of the Bankruptcy Act on appeal from an order dismissing a petition to have appellee adjudicated a bankrupt.

The petition was filed by three creditors, and on the same day a receiver was appointed on the application of one of them who gave a bond as required under section 3e of said act. Appellant was surety on the latter bond also, on which judgment had been previously rendered and affirmed. *T. E. Hill Co. v. U. S. Fidelity & Guaranty Co.,* 250 Ill. 242. The measure of damages relied on was the rental value of the property while held by the receiver after the filing of the appeal bond.

In the time allowed for filing the latter, one Bither was appointed assignee of appellee under the State voluntary assignment act, and moved for a rule on the receiver to turn over to him the property so held. The motion was resisted by an attorney who, the record shows, had in the different proceedings appeared not only for the receiver and the creditor who applied for his appointment, but for the creditors who filed the petition for adjudication. The motion was not acted on until after the appeal was perfected when it was denied "without prejudice to a renewal of the same in the event said appeal shall not be prosecuted with effect."

Under such circumstances appellee contends that the bond in question operated as a *supersedeas* and to prolong the receivership, and calls attention to the provision in section 25, that appeals may be taken in bankruptcy proceedings as in equity cases, and cites certain cases in equity deemed analogous to the one at bar. On the other hand, appellant refers to the fact that the bond and condition thereof are the same in form and language as in bankruptcy appeals where no receiver is appointed, and contends that there is no liability under the bond except for costs of the proceeding to adjudicate.

As we view it, the bond must be construed with reference to the fact that the proceeding for the appointment of a receiver under section 3e of the Bankruptcy Act is separate and distinct from proceedings to adjudicate. *In re Kelly*, 91 Fed. 507; *In re Ogles*, 93 Fed. 426. In the *Kelly* case it was said that the implication of the statute is that it is altogether a separate procedure, and that "the seizure of property is a subsequent and independent proceeding, which is not necessarily a part of the proceedings in bankruptcy." Before a petition is dismissed or a trustee qualifies, any party in interest may apply for the appointment of a receiver (section 2, par. 3, Bankruptcy Act), and it is a principle of general application that those responsible for an appointment wrongfully made are liable for the expenses incurred thereby (*Beach v. Macon Grocery Co.*, 60 C. C. A. 557, 125 Fed. 513; *In re La*

Cov., 74 C. C. A. 130, 142 Fed. 960), and costs and expenses incurred under one of these proceedings are not taxable under the other (*In re Ghiglione*, 93 Fed. 187; *In re Williams*, 120 Fed. 37; *In re J. A. Smith*, 16 Am. Bankr. Rep. 478; *Selkregg v. Hamilton Bros.*, 16 Am. Bankr. Rep. 474, 144 Fed. 557; *In re Moehs*, 174 Fed. 165).

It is true that on dismissal of the petition the purpose of the receivership ceased. But while the appeal bond in question operated to supersede the order of dismissal of the petition it did not *ipso facto* discharge the receiver. Beach on Receivers, par. 799; *Whiteside v. Prendergast*, 2 Barb. Ch. (N. Y.) 471; *Crook v. Findley*, 60 How. Pr. (N. Y.) 375; *Baughman v. Superior Court*, 72 Cal. 572.

Presumably when the court fixed the amount of the bond given at the time of the appointment of the receiver it took into consideration the statutory right of appeal from an order of dismissal and deemed the amount adequate to that end.

In construing the language of said section 3e, it was said in *In re Spaulding*, 150 Fed. 150: "The fact that the second paragraph provides that all costs, etc., shall be allowed is based upon the assumption that a bond will be taken large enough to cover all costs." And again in *In re Haff*, 68 C. C. A. 380, 135 Fed. 743, referring to the provisions of said section, the court said that it was their purpose to furnish the bankrupt with a security adequate for his complete protection.

Two of the creditors on the bond in question were not parties to the proceeding for the appointment of the receiver. But had the court deemed it desirable to make them parties thereto it could, no doubt, have required a new or additional bond as a condition precedent to the continuance of the receivership. But they did not become parties thereto merely by exercising their right to appeal from an order in a different and independent proceeding. A discharge of the receiver was not superseded by the appeal bond, nor did

532   APPELLATE COURTS OF ILLINOIS.

T. E. Hill Co. v. The U. S. F. and G. Co., 184 Ill. App. 528.

the prolongation of the receivership follow as a legal consequence of the appeal. In view, therefore, of the court's power over the receiver regardless of the appeal, of the independent character of the two proceedings, and of the express provisions in section 3e for indemnity for wrongful detention of property by a receiver, we do not think the appeal bond operated to supersede anything except the order of dismissal, or that the two bonds can be deemed cumulative securities. Hence the court erred in assessing damages based upon proof of the detention of the property by the receiver, and the assignment of error in admitting such evidence as a basis of the damage is well taken.

The court refused to find, as requested, that there could be no recovery for an alleged breach of the bond except for nominal damages. In the absence of competent proof of damages, there being none even of the costs incurred in the proceeding for adjudication, the court's refusal was error. We do not concur in appellant's contention that the pleadings would not support a judgment, but hold that judgment should be entered here on a finding different from the trial court as to the damages.

In this case the jury was waived. It was said in *Osgood v. Skinner*, 186 Ill. 495, that "such waiver also extends to the review of the judgment in the Appellate Court, so as to enable the Appellate Court to decide the issue of fact and enter final judgment." Several cases are there cited where on waiver of a jury the Appellate Court, on reversal, assessed the damages and entered judgment. Among them was the case of *Manistee Lumber Co. v. Union Nat. Bank of Chicago*, 143 Ill. 490, where the Court said that "the Appellate Court may not only reverse, but may also render judgment for the plaintiff, if the law, as applied to the facts found by that court, necessitates such a judgment, and if it can be ascertained from the facts so found what judgment ought to have been rendered by the court below."

There being no proper proof of damages in the record but the breach of the bond being shown, the court should have assessed merely nominal damages. We shall, therefore, reverse the judgment and make a different finding here as to the amount of damages, assessing them at one cent, and requiring appellee to pay the costs of this appeal.

Reversed.

David K. Jeffris et al., copartners as Chicago Car Lumber Company, Appellants, v. Ayer & Lord Tie Company, Appellee.

Gen. No. 18,831.   (Not to be reported in full.)

Appeal from the Municipal Court of Chicago; the Hon. WILLIAM N. GEMMILL, Judge, presiding. Heard in the Branch Appellate Court at the October term, 1912. Affirmed. Opinion filed January 13, 1914.

Statement of the Case.

Action by David K. Jeffris and others, copartners as Chicago Car Lumber Company, against Ayer & Lord Tie Company, a corporation, to recover the value of a quantity of certain railroad ties alleged to belong to plaintiffs and to have been taken and used by defendant. From a judgment in favor of defendant on a directed verdict, plaintiffs appeal.

ADAMS, BOBB & ADAMS, for appellants; S. G. ABBOTT and G. L. WIRE, of counsel.

C. C. GRASSHAM and JENNINGS & FIFER, for appellee.

MR. JUSTICE BARNES delivered the opinion of the court.

Abstract of the Decision.

1. MUNICIPAL COURT OF CHICAGO, § 17*—*necessity of written motion to direct verdict.* A motion for a directed verdict in the Municipal Court need not be in writing.

2. TROVER AND CONVERSION, § 39*—*when evidence insufficient to connect defendant with taking of plaintiff's property.* In an action to recover the value of railroad ties alleged to belong to plaintiffs and to have been taken and used by defendant, evidence *held* insufficient to establish a *prima facie* case for plaintiffs, it appearing from the evidence that both parties had separate piles of ties at a certain place, and that the ties were distinguished by private marks, but the evidence to connect the defendant with the taking of the ties was largely circumstantial, which considered with other evidence did not fairly tend to show that defendant took the ties.

3. TROVER AND CONVERSION, § 38*—*when statement of defendant's employe inadmissible.* In an action to recover the value of railroad ties alleged to have been taken and used by defendant, a statement by an employe of defendant made some two years after the event amounting to an admission that he took the ties, *held* inadmissible for the reason that it was no part of the *res gestae.*

4. EVIDENCE. § 185*—*when declaration of agents not admissible.* Rule that declarations of an agent to be admissible must be part of the *res gestae* applies to corporations who can speak only through agents.

5. APPEAL AND ERROR, § 1467*—*when error in admission of incompetent evidence harmless.* Whether error was committed in permitting one of plaintiff's witnesses on cross-examination to testify to a certain fact need not be considered where such evidence may well have been excluded in acting on a motion to direct a verdict.

Emma Hubbard, Appellee, v. G. Gordon Martin, Incorporated, Appellant.

Gen. No. 18,875.   (Not to be reported in full.)

Appeal from the Circuit Court of Cook county; the Hon. THOMAS G. WINDES, Judge, presiding. Heard in the Branch Appellate Court at the October term, 1912. Affirmed. Opinion filed January 13, 1914.

Statement of the Case.

Action by Emma Hubbard against G. Gordon Martin, Incorporated, and another to recover damages for injuries sustained by plaintiff by reason of negligent performance of dental work done for plaintiff by defendants. From a judgment in favor of plaintiff for one thousand dollars, defendant, G. Gordon Martin, appeals.

HARRY STRICKLER, for appellant.

GEORGE I. HAIGHT and ROLAND M. HOLLOCK, for appellee.

MR. JUSTICE BARNES delivered the opinion of the court.

Abstract of the Decision.

1. DENTISTS, § 1*—*right of corporation to engage in practice.* Hurd's R. S. ch. 91, ¶ 44h, J. & A. ¶ 7450, contemplates that a corporation may engage in the practice of dentistry.

2. DENTISTS, § 2*—*when evidence sufficient to sustain verdict for malpractice.* In an action for malpractice in dentistry, evidence tending to show that one of defendant's employes negligently bored through the roots of four of plaintiff's teeth into the alveolar process or bony tissues of the jaw, thereby causing a painful condition requiring long treatment and rendering improbable the placing of a permanent dental bridge, *held* sufficient to sustain a verdict for plaintiff.

3. DENTISTS, § 2*—*admissibility of evidence in action for malpractice.* In an action for malpractice in dentistry, refusal of court to strike out testimony of plaintiff as to pain and suffering both while and after the work was performed, *held* not error where other testimony tended to show that immediate intense pain and conditions causing additional and unnecessary pain would result from negligence of the character charged.

4. DENTISTS, § 2*—*competency of evidence to show want of license.* Testimony of the State Board of Dental Examiners in a suit for malpractice in dentistry, that they had examined the record of licenses issued and found no record of a license issued to the defendant's employe who operated on plaintiff, ·*held* competent evidence.

5. DENTISTS, § 2*—*when admission of expert testimony as to condition of plaintiff's teeth not error.* Permitting an expert witness to testify in a suit for malpractice as to the condition of the bore in plaintiff's teeth the following year, without requiring plaintiff to show that no one else had bored into the tissues subsequent to the treatment by defendant, *held* not error, since whether or not the conditions complained of were caused or aggravated by anything done by either of the dentists who testified was a matter for the jury upon which cross-examination was afforded.

6. TRIAL, § 276*—*when interrogatories do not call for ultimate and controlling facts.* In an action for malpractice in dentistry, where interrogatories were given asking whether any of plaintiff's teeth were lost and whether any were injured as a result of the conduct of defendant, *held* that neither of the interrogatories nor both together called for all the ultimate and controlling facts, where the declaration alleged and the evidence tended to show other results of the alleged negligence, such as unnecessary anguish and distress and shock and injury to the nervous system.

7. TRIAL, § 276*—*when interrogatory does not call for an ultimate and controlling fact.* In an action for malpractice in dentistry, an interrogatory whether boring holes into the roots of certain teeth for the purpose of fixing pegs therein for fastening and attaching bridges was improper dentistry does not call for an ultimate and controlling fact, where the claim was not that such method was improper but that the boring through the teeth into the bony tissues of the jawbone was negligence.

8. TRIAL, § 276*—*when interrogatory does not call for all the ultimate and controlling facts.* In an action for malpractice in dentistry, an interrogatory whether plaintiff afforded the defendant a reasonable opportunity to cure the alleged soreness and pain does not call for all the ultimate and controlling facts, where the evidence tends to show not only the causing of unnecessary pain and soreness but also ruination of the teeth for permanent bridge work.

9. APPEAL AND ERROR, § 269*—*when refusal to submit interrogatories harmless.* Refusal to submit interrogatories as to facts not controverted is harmless.

10. APPEAL AND ERROR, § 542*—*when error in admission of evidence not preserved.* If the competency of evidence is not questioned until after its admission, error can be assigned only on a motion to strike it out.

*See Illinois Notes Digest, Vols. XI to XV, same topic and section number.

Emery Stanford Hall et al., Appellants, v. George Beidler et al., Appellees.

Gen. No. 18,891.   (Not to be reported in full.)

Appeal from the Municipal Court of Chicago; the Hon. CHARLES A. WILLIAMS, Judge, presiding. Heard in the Branch Appellate Court at the October term, 1912. Affirmed. Opinion filed January 13, 1914.

Statement of the Case.

Action by Emery Stanford Hall and Frank Spencer Baker, suing as copartners under the name of Hall & Baker, against George Beidler and Michael S. Hyland, to recover commissions alleged to be due them as architects under a certain contract entered into between the plaintiffs and defendants. From a judgment for defendants upon a directed verdict, plaintiffs appeal.

BALDWIN & BARNES, for appellants.

WILLIAM J. LACEY, for appellees.

MR. JUSTICE BARNES delivered the opinion of the court.

Abstract of the Decision.

ARCHITECTS AND ENGINEERS, § 3*—*when contractors not jointly liable for commissions*. Architects entered into a contract with a partnership for commissions to be based upon $80,000 as the cost of a building. The contract contemplated that the defendants as partners should jointly let the contract for the building, but the contract was let for the erection of the building, to cost $130,000, by one of the defendants after the architects' services were discontinued and after defendants had dissolved partnership. *Held*, in an action by the architects against the defendants jointly for com-

*See Illinois Notes Digest, Vols. XI to XV, same topic and section number.

missions on the basis of the $130,000 costs, that a direction of a
verdict for defendants was proper on the theory that the contract
imposed no joint liability to pay commissions on the actual cost of
the building in view of the fact that the contract for the structure
was not a joint undertaking.

Lillian Ullrich by William Ullrich, Appellee, v. Chicago City Railway Company, Appellant.

Gen. No. 17,972.

1. DAMAGES, § 110*—*when not excessive for personal injuries.*
A verdict for five thousand five hundred dollars for personal injuries to a girl fifteen years of age caused by street cars, *held* not
excessive, it appearing that she was practically confined to her bed
for two years after the accident, that her abdomen was swollen and
distended and that she was rendered a nervous wreck.

2. INFANTS, § 54*—*when judgment not erroneous as being in
favor of next friend.* Where a father sues, as next friend for his
minor daughter, a judgment is not erroneous as being entered in
favor of the next friend for the reason that the language of the
judgment order is that plaintiff recover "his said damages * * *
together with his costs," the defendant having treated the judgment as in favor of the minor on the appeal and the bond running
to the minor.

3. INFANTS, § 66*—*when next friend not liable for costs.* A person suing as a next friend is not liable for costs in case the suit is
decided against the plaintiff, where the bond for costs is signed
by a stranger to the record and not joined in by the next friend.

4. WITNESSES, § 45*—*when wife of next friend competent witness.* In an action by a next friend for personal injuries sustained
by a minor, the wife of the next friend is competent to testify; the
question as to the weight of her testimony, because of her interest
as mother of the next friend, is for the jury.

5. EVIDENCE, § 282*—*competency of statements in medical books.*
It is well established that statements made in medical books are
not competent evidence, and quotations therefrom should not be
incorporated in questions asked of a medical witness in such a
manner as to lead the jury to infer that the attorney propounding
same is reading from such books.

6. APPEAL AND ERROR, § 1506*—*when appellant cannot complain of error in propounding questions on cross-examination of expert witness*. Defendant cannot complain that plaintiff's counsel in propounding questions to defendant's medical expert witnesses on cross-examination gave the jury the impression that he was reading from a medical book, where defendant's counsel on redirect examination of one of the witnesses read from a book handed him at his request by plaintiff's counsel.

7. APPEAL AND ERROR, § 1514*—*improper remarks of counsel*. Refusal of court to grant a new trial for improper remarks of counsel made in arguing questions of law before the court in the presence of the jury, *held* not an abuse of trial court's discretion as to authorize reversal.

Appeal from the Circuit Court of Cook county; the Hon. DUANE J. CARNES, Judge, presiding. Heard in the Branch Appellate Court at the October term, 1911. Affirmed. Opinion filed January 13, 1914. Rehearing denied January 27, 1914. *Certiorari* granted by Supreme Court.

JAMES G. CONDON and CHARLES LEROY BROWN, for appellant; LEONARD A. BUSBY and WARNER H. ROBINSON, of counsel.

JAMES C. MCSHANE, for appellee.

MR. JUSTICE CLARK delivered the opinion of the court.

This is a suit for damages on account of personal injuries sustained by the plaintiff through the negligence of the defendant. There was a trial before the court and a jury, a verdict being rendered for five thousand five hundred dollars upon which judgment was entered.

Liability of the defendant for some amount was admitted by it, the accident being due to a collision of two cars, both operated by the defendant, and in one of which plaintiff was riding as a passenger.

The points relied on for a reversal are: First, that the damages are excessive; second, that there was error in permitting the wife of the next friend to testify; third, that there was error in the judgment in that, as alleged, the judgment treats as the plaintiff, William Ullrich, the father and next friend, and that the judgment should have been in favor of the infant and not in favor of the next friend; fourth, that counsel for plaintiff erroneously made use of medical works in the cross-examination of witnesses, making improper statements distinctly prejudicial to the defendant, under the guise of asking questions, and in making arguments for the admissibility of evidence; and fifth, that there were other errors in the admission of evidence.

I.

Counsel for both parties have devoted the larger part of their briefs and argument to the first proposition advanced by the defendant, namely, that the damages are excessive. On the part of the plaintiff, who was fifteen years of age at the time of the accident, it is insisted the record discloses that she was confined to her bed for several months after its occurrence, and practically up to the time of the trial, which was nearly two years thereafter; that during the early portion of this period she suffered from almost daily attacks of hysteria and hysterical convulsions, which became worse and more violent until November following the accident, which occurred in August, 1909; that in the former month she was taken to a hospital, where she stayed for a few weeks, from which time the hysterical attacks gradually became less frequent, until about two months prior to the trial, when she was having them only during her monthly periods, and perhaps once besides in each month; that her abdomen was swollen and distended, necessitating almost constant use of hot applications to her stomach; that this condition was diagnosed by one of her attending physicians as peritonitis, and by another as being some injury to the internal organs of the abdomen; that there was also inflammation of the abdomen, and for the greater portion of the time considerable temperature; that the inflammation resulted in a prolapsus of the uterus with adhesions; that during this time she became greatly emaciated; that her weight was 153 pounds before the accident, and 117 pounds at the time of the trial; that she was by the accident rendered a nervous and physical wreck.

On the part of the defendant it is claimed to be demonstrated by the evidence that the plaintiff's manifestations of hysteria antedated for a long time the street car accident; that the expert evidence in the record is conclusive of the proposition that traumatism, which is defined as external violence producing bodily injury, is incapable of producing hysteria in a healthy person; that it is also demonstrated by the evidence that peritonitis cannot be caused except by infection, and that the accident in question could not and did not produce any pelvic infection.

We have carefully read all of the testimony in the case, both lay and medical, and find it decidedly conflicting as to many material matters. After such careful perusal, however, we are not of the opinion that the verdict is as alleged, so manifestly against the weight of the evidence as to require a reversal of the judgment on that ground. It will be necessary, therefore, to consider the other points raised by the defendant.

II.

It is urged that there was error in the admission of the testimony of the mother of the plaintiff because she was the wife of the father, who appears as next friend to the plaintiff in the case. The question as to the weight to be given to her testimony, because of her interest as mother of the plaintiff, was of course one for the jury. Does the law inhibit her testimony because she happens to be the wife of the one who sues as next friend? We think not. It is urged that the next friend would be liable for costs in the suit if the case were decided against the plaintiff. We do not so construe the statute. A bond for costs was given in this case by a stranger to the record, and was not joined in by the next friend nor was it required to be. Notwithstanding the assault made by defendant upon the logic of the opinion, we think that in *Illinois Cent. R. Co. v. Becker*, 119 Ill. App. 221, Mr. Justice Creighton has correctly set forth the principles of law governing the question at issue.

III.

It is next said that the judgment is erroneous because it is in favor of William Ullrich, the next friend. The language of the judgment order is "that the plaintiff do have and recover of and from the defendant *his* said damages of five thousand five hundred ($5,500) dollars in form as aforesaid by the jury assessed, together with *his* costs and charges in this behalf expended and have execution therefor."

The contention is that the use of the word "his" makes the judgment one in favor of William Ullrich, next friend. The point is technical and, in view of the Illinois statute respecting judgments, is untenable. The defendant treated the judgment as in favor of the minor on the appeal. The bond runs to "Lillian Ullrich a minor," etc.

IV.

It is urged by the defendant that the attorney for the plaintiff in the cross-examination of medical experts whose testimony was taken on behalf of the defendant, indirectly got before the jury statements contained in medical works on questions of hysteria, etc., by improperly incorporating the language taken from such works in questions propounded to such witnesses, and that he also made improper statements distinctly prejudicial to the defendant, under the guise of asking questions and of making argument for their admission. It is said that his conduct was such that the court erred in not granting the motion for a new trial because of it. The answer of the attorney for the plaintiff is that no such statements were introduced in evidence (a proceeding which he admits would be improper), and that the only reference made by plaintiff's counsel to medical authorities was for the purpose of developing the extent of the witness' knowledge of the subject and the basis of his opinion; that the questions propounded by him came within the rule laid down in *Chicago Union Traction Co. v. Ertrachter*, 228 Ill. 119, viz., that a medical expert may be cross-examined as to the basis of his opinion and as to whether the authorities do not lay down a different rule, and the like.

Counsel for the plaintiff admittedly had medical works before him in court, but we are unable to say that in any question propounded on the cross-examination of defendant's witnesses extracts from the works are incorporated. Defendant's counsel repeatedly objected to plaintiff's counsel "asking questions and giving the impression that he was reading from a book." The former himself, on the redirect examination of one of defendant's witnesses, read from a book handed him at his request by plaintiff's counsel, and in the brief it is said "he was able to find extracts which were decidedly favorable to defendant's theory." As we understand it, these extracts were placed before the jury by incorporating them in questions asked by defendant's counsel. In our opinion he is not in position now to complain that there was reversible error in what is alleged to be a fact, that plaintiff's counsel in asking the question on cross-examination gave the jury "the impression that he was reading from a book."

The rule is well established that statements made in medical books are not competent evidence. We agree also with counsel for defendant in the proposition that that which cannot be accomplished directly should not be done indirectly; that is to say, quotations from so-called authorities should not be incorporated in questions in such a manner as to lead the jury to infer that the attorney propounding same is reading from the so-called authority or text-book.

Complaint is made that in arguing questions of law

before the court, plaintiff's counsel made remarks in the presence of the jury calculated to prejudice them. It has been held in a recent decision that although when counsel is corrected and the jury instructed to disregard improper remarks, the attorney's misconduct ordinarily is not ground for reversal, yet in a clear case courts of review will reverse a judgment for such improper conduct, even though the trial court has sustained objections interposed by opposing counsel. *Appel v. Chicago City Ry. Co.*, 259 Ill. 561. It is said in the case of *West Chicago St. R. Co. v. Annis*, 165 Ill. 475: "It is, however, as held in the *Cotton* case, *supra* (140 Ill. 486), a matter resting in the sound discretion of the trial judge to say when, under all the circumstances of the case, and in view of the counter remarks which may be made and the temper and character of the jury, whether a new trial should be granted or not, and unless it satisfactorily appears from the record that the trial court has abused its discretion in this regard courts of review cannot interfere."

After careful examination of the record we are unable to say that in the refusal to grant a new trial in the present case there was an abuse of discretion by the trial judge.

The remarks which are criticized were not made in an argument to the jury as in the *Appel* case, *supra*, but, as heretofore stated, were addressed to the court.

V.

We have carefully considered the other questions raised as to the alleged erroneous rulings of the court on the admission of evidence, and are of the opinion that no error was committed on account of which the judgment should be reversed.

The judgment will be affirmed.

Affirmed.

Joseph Wajer, Appellee, v. United States Brewing Company, Appellant.

Gen. No. 18,839.   (Not to be reported in full.)

Appeal from the Circuit Court of Cook county; the Hon. SAMUEL C. STOUGH, Judge, presiding. Heard in the Branch Appellate Court at the October term, 1912. Reversed. Opinion filed January 13, 1914.

Statement of the Case.

Action by Joseph Wajer against United States Brewing Company, a corporation, to recover for personal injuries sustained by plaintiff while in the employ of defendant as fireman in defendant's boiler room. Plaintiff's injuries resulted from falling into an uncovered ash pit beneath the boilers. From a judgment in favor of plaintiff for one thousand and fifty dollars and costs, defendant appeals.

GEORGE W. MILLER, for appellant.

JOHN W. SUTTON and MARTIN L. WILBORN, for appellee.

MR. JUSTICE CLARK delivered the opinion of the court.

Abstract of the Decision.

1. MASTER AND SERVANT, § 686*—*when employer not negligent in providing fireman in boiler room a safe place to work.* In an action by a fireman for injuries sustained by falling in an ash pit beneath defendant's boilers, the defendant being charged with negligence in not properly guarding the pit as required by section 4 of the Act of 1910 (R. S. ch. 48, ¶ 92, J. & A. ¶ 5389), in permitting the steam to escape in the room and allowing broken windows to permit the cold air to come in contact with the steam so as to cause it to con-

*See Illinois Notes Digest, Vols. XI to XV, same topic and section number.

Mertzen v. Herman H. Hettler Lumber Co., 184 Ill. App. 546.

dense, *held* that the evidence did not show the statute was violated and that the mere escape of steam did not render the boiler room an unsafe place to work.

2. MASTER AND SERVANT, § 561*—*admissibility of evidence.* Under a declaration charging employer with negligence in allowing steam to escape in the boiler room and in allowing window glass to remain broken so that cold air would cause the steam to rapidly condense, *held* that testimony as to the breaking of a "T" was erroneously admitted as no mention was made thereof in the declaration.

3. MASTER AND SERVANT, § 98*—*statute imposing duty to guard hatchways construed.* Section 4 of the Act of 1910 providing for the health, safety and comfort of employes (R. S. 1911, ch. 48, ¶ 92, J. & A. ¶ 5389) does not require hatchways to be fenced while in use, in addition to providing a covering therefor when not in use.

4. STATUTES, § 27*—*when defendant not required to plead the exception in a statute.* In an action based on section 4 of R. S. ch. 48, ¶ 92, J. & A. ¶ 5389, to recover for personal injuries resulting from falling into an open hatchway, defendant is not required to plead specially the exception mentioned in the statute.

5. MASTER AND SERVANT, § 302*—*when doctrine of assumption of risk inapplicable.* Doctrine of assumption of risk is not applicable where there has been a violation of a statute.

Edward Mertzen, Appellee, v. Herman H. Hettler Lumber Company, Appellant.

Gen. No. 18,882.   (Not to be reported in full.)

Appeal from the Superior Court of Cook county; the Hon. JOSEPH H. FITCH, Judge, presiding. Heard in the Branch Appellate Court at the October term, 1912. Affirmed. Opinion filed January 13, 1914.

Statement of the Case.

Action by Edward Mertzen against Herman H. Hettler Lumber Company, a corporation, to recover damages for personal injuries sustained by plaintiff while in the employ of defendant and alleged to have resulted by the starting of a planing machine when plaintiff was cleaning the same preparatory to changing the knives. From a judgment in favor of plaintiff for two thousand five hundred dollars, defendant appeals.

H. L. HOWARD, for appellant.

JOHN W. SUTTON, for appellee; MARTIN L. WILBORN, of counsel.

MR. JUSTICE CLARK delivered the opinion of the court.

Abstract of the Decision.

MASTER AND SERVANT, § 683*—*when evidence sustains verdict for injury to employe resulting from defective belts starting a planing machine.* In an action to recover for injuries sustained by plaintiff resulting from the starting of a planing machine while he was cleaning it, the declaration alleging that defendant was negligent in allowing a belt to remain improperly laced and fitted to a pulley so as to run from a loose to a tight pulley, a verdict for plaintiff *held* sustained by the evidence, it appearing that the belt had been fixed just prior to the accident and had been represented to be in proper condition for running by a person in the position of a vice principal.

Grace V. Wiesbach, Appellee, v. Herman H. Hettler Lumber Company, Appellant.

Gen. No. 18,883.   (Not to be reported in full.)

Appeal from the Superior Court of Cook county; the Hon. HUGO PAM, Judge, presiding. Heard in the Branch Appellate Court at the October term, 1912. Affirmed. Opinion filed January 13, 1914.

----

*See Illinois Notes Digest, Vols. XI to XV, same topic and section number.

Statement of the Case.

Action by Grace V. Wiesbach against Herman H. Hettler Lumber Company, a corporation, and E. S. Ormsbee to recover damages for personal injuries sustained by plaintiff in a collision between a carriage in which plaintiff was riding and a team claimed to have been owned and controlled by the defendant. The jury rendered a verdict of not guilty as against Ormsbee and of guilty against the Lumber Company, damages being fixed at the sum of one thousand dollars. From a judgment entered on the verdict, the defendant Lumber Company appeals.

H. L. HOWARD, for appellant.

MOSES, ROSENTHAL & KENNEDY, for appellee; WALTER BACHRACH, S. SIDNEY STEIN and SIGMUND W. DAVID, of counsel.

MR. JUSTICE CLARK delivered the opinion of the court.

Abstract of the Decision.

1. MASTER AND SERVANT, § 867*—*when evidence sufficient to sustain finding that team and wagon were not under the control of an independent contractor.* In an action to recover for personal injuries sustained in a collision between a carriage in which plaintiff was riding and a team and wagon alleged to be owned and controlled by defendant, evidence *held* sufficient to warrant a finding by the jury that the team and driver were under the direction of the defendant and that a third party, who owned the team and employed the driver, was not an independent contractor.

2. NEGLIGENCE, § 129*—*when special plea does not put in issue ownership and control of instrumentalities causing injury.* In an action for personal injuries sustained by plaintiff alleged to have been caused by the negligent driving of a team and wagon owned and controlled by defendant, a special plea which recites that defendant or its servants or agents were not in the use, possession, ownership and control of the wagon, without denying ownership of the horses and without denying that the horses and wagon were

owned and controlled by defendant, does not properly put in issue the ownership, possession or operation of the instrumentalities which are alleged to have caused the injury.

3. APPEAL AND ERROR, § 1699*—*when error in refusing to direct verdict for defendant waived.* Error of court in denying a motion to direct a verdict at the close of plaintiff's evidence is waived where defendant thereafter submits instructions based upon its theory of the case.

Helen W. S. Johnson et al., v. Northern Trust Company, Trustee, et al.

Northern Trust Company, Trustee, v. Hannah M. Williams et al.

Edward A. Shedd, Appellant, v. Northern Trust Company, Trustee, et al., Appellees.

Gen. No. 18,887.

1. APPEAL AND ERROR, § 269*—*when provisions in decree do not affect its final character.* Provisions in a decree for an accounting and reserving jurisdiction for the purpose of enforcing the decree do not affect its final character.

2. EQUITY, § 149*—*determination of character of bill.* A bill in equity which is in its essence and effect a bill to declare a forfeiture of a lease will be considered as such, though the complainant by ingenious phrasing of the prayer of the bill asks to have the leasehold estate decreed to have been surrendered by operation of law.

3. FORFEITURES, § 6*—*enforcement of forfeitures in equity.* Equity will not interfere on behalf of a party entitled to a forfeiture to enforce the same, but will leave him to his legal remedy, if any, even though the case might be one in which no equitable relief would be given to the defaulting party against the forfeiture. The functions of a court of equity are to grant relief against a forfeiture in a proper case, but never to enforce it.

4. LANDLORD AND TENANT, § 415*—*effect of attempted assignment of leasehold to nonexisting corporation.* Where an attempted assignment of a leasehold by the lessee, with consent of the lessor, to a corporation fails because of the nonexistence of the corpora-

---

tion, such assignment does not amount to a surrender of the lease-hold estate by operation of law as between the lessor and lessee, and the lessee in such case holds as a trustee for the stockholders and bondholders of the corporation for the amount paid him for the leasehold by the persons acting in the name of the corporation.

5. LANDLORD AND TENANT, § 470*—*when lessor estopped to insist on forfeiture of lease.* On bill in equity to enforce a forfeiture of a lease, alleging that there had been a surrender of the lease by operation of law resulting from an assignment of the lease by the lessee to a corporation not in existence, and that the lessee had made a conveyance without lessors' consent, subsequent acts and conduct of lessors together with prior adjudications *held* to estop the lessors to insist upon a forfeiture.

6. TRUSTS, § 4*—*when trust created for money paid.* Where a person holds an estate for which he has been fully paid by another or others, a trust results for the benefit of those who paid the money.

Appeal from the Superior Court of Cook county; the Hon. RICHARD E. BURKE, Judge, presiding. Heard in the Branch Appellate Court at the October term, 1912. Reversed and remanded with directions. Opinion filed January 16, 1914. Rehearing denied January 27, 1914.

HARRY S. MECARTNEY, for appellant.

JUDAH, WILLARD, WOLF & REICHMANN, for appellee, Northern Trust Company.

JAMES HAMILTON LEWIS, for appellee, John C. Patterson.

SCOTT, BANCROFT & STEPHENS and STEWART JOHNSON, for appellees, Helen W. S. Johnson and Stewart Patterson; EDGAR A. BANCROFT, REDMOND D. STEPHENS and LESTER L. FALK, of counsel.

MR. PRESIDING JUSTICE SMITH delivered the opinion of the court.

Appellee, Helen W. S. Johnson, on July 29, 1910, filed her bill of complaint in the Superior Court of Cook county against the Northern Trust Company, trustee, Hannah M. Williams, Fannie V. M. Johnson,

Stewart Patterson, John C. Patterson, H. H. Kohlsaat, Albert M. Johnson, E. A. Shedd, Charles B. Shedd, Edward J. Shedd, and Illinois Trust & Savings Bank, trustee. December 8, 1910, Stewart Patterson was given leave to join Mrs. Johnson as a party complainant. On the same day, an amended bill of complaint was filed which sets up the facts stated in *Patterson v. Northern Trust Co.*, 132 Ill. App. 208, the same case on appeal in 230 Ill. 334; *Patterson v. Northern Trust Co.*, 132 Ill. App. 63, the same case on appeal in 238 Ill. 601.

The amended bill then sets up the judgment declaring that the articles of incorporation of the Merrimac Building Company and the certificate of incorporation of the Secretary of State were null and void, and the affirmance of the judgment in *People v. Shedd*, 241 Ill. 155; that after the entry of judgment of ouster in the Circuit Court of Cook county, and pending the determination of the appeal in *People v. Shedd, supra,* Edward A. Shedd, Charles E. Shedd and Edward J. Shedd continued to act as a corporation in the name of the Merrimac Building Company and continued in its name to pay to the Northern Trust Company, trustee, the various sums specified as rentals in the lease, the Northern Trust Company receipting for the same in the name of Herman H. Kohlsaat, and continued so to do until the commencement of this suit; and that Edward A. Shedd, Albert M. Johnson, Charles B. Shedd and Edward J. Shedd, or some of them, have continued to retain the possession of the premises and to collect the rents, issues and profits thereof.

The bill further sets up a conveyance and quitclaim deed by Kohlsaat and wife, dated January 30, 1905, to Edward A. Shedd and Albert M. Johnson, of the leasehold estate created by the lease to Kohlsaat, which deed was filed for record in the office of recorder of deeds for Cook county, on July 26, 1910, and that this conveyance was given without the consent of the trustee, the Northern Trust Company, and without the knowledge or consent of the complainants; and that under the terms of the lease the making and delivery of the deed by Kohlsaat was ground for forfeiting the lease, and that it was the duty of the trustee to exercise the option contained in the lease and declare a forfeiture thereof.

It further appears from the bill that subsequent to April 2, 1897, a trust deed was executed in the name of the Merrimac Building Company to the Illinois Trust & Savings Bank, trustee, conveying the leasehold estate to secure an issue of bonds and that the bonds are still outstanding and held by various persons to complainants unknown, and that neither the trustee nor the complainants ever consented to the execution of the deed of trust, and that the instrument created no rights in the premises; and on information and belief John C. Patterson served a demand on the trustee requesting the trustee to take possession of the premises and to take appropriate proceedings to effect an accounting with the various persons claiming an interest therein, and that complainant, Helen W. S. Johnson, requested the trustee to act as in said demand requested, but the trustee has neglected and refused to take any action whatsoever to regain possession of the premises.

The bill makes the Northern Trust Company, as trustee, Hannah M. Williams, Fannie V. M. Johnson, John C. Patterson, Herman H. Kohlsaat, Albert M. Johnson, Edward A. Shedd, Charles B. Shedd, Edward J. Shedd, and the Illinois Trust & Savings Bank, as trustee, parties defendant, and prays, among other things, that the Northern Trust Company, trustee, be enjoined from collecting, receiving or receipting for any further payment of moneys as an instalment of rent under the lease, and from making or delivering any receipt for any such payment or instalment to Herman H. Kohlsaat, or to any other person or persons as lessee or lessees, for the payment of rental under the lease; and for a receiver of said Stewart Building and of its rents, income and profits, who shall take immediate possession of the building, etc., and for an accounting with the Shedds and Albert M. Johnson and others; and that the court decree that the full title and sole right to complete possession and control of the Stewart Building is in the Northern Trust Company as trustee for the benefit of the beneficiaries under the trust deed, and that the lease be delivered up and canceled.

Attached to the bill of complaint as exhibits are the lease referred to therein, the deed from Herman H. Kohlsaat and wife, dated April 2, 1897, to Merrimac Building Company, conveying the leasehold interest; also the instrument of consent by Pullman and Matthews, as trustee, to the assignment from Kohlsaat to the Merrimac Building Company, dated April 2, 1897; also the deed of trust from Hannah M. Williams and others to the Northern Trust Company, dated December 20, 1897; also the so-called forbearance of rent agreement of March 15, 1898; the rent foreclosure decree of June 25, 1902, in the Circuit Court of Cook county; the petition of Shedd and Johnson of February 21, 1905, for leave, as bondholders and stockholders of the Merrimac Building Company, to redeem under the rent foreclosure decree; and the order entered in the rent foreclosure case, giving leave to Shedd and Johnson to make redemption, etc. All of the above exhibits were before the courts in the cases above cited.

In addition to the exhibits above mentioned, appear the petition and information in *People v. Shedd, supra,* being the quo warranto proceedings by which the validity of the organization of the Merrimac Building Company was attacked, and the judgment of ouster in those proceedings. The final exhibit attached to the bill of complaint is a quitclaim deed from Kohlsaat and wife to Shedd and Johnson, dated January 10, 1905.

The answers of the defendants admit the averments

of the bill based on documentary evidence and the
various proceedings above referred to, and present
substantially the same contentions which were made
by the respective parties in the previous litigation,
with the exception, however, that the answer of Edward A. Shedd sets up the purchase by him of the
bonds of the Merrimac Building Company in February, 1905, and that Shedd and Albert M. Johnson
announced to the Northern Trust Company their purpose of obtaining a deed from Kohlsaat of the leasehold estate and building in 1905 in order to cover any
contingency with relation to the legality of the charter of the said Merrimac Building Company, which
had then been attacked as void by the defendant, John
C. Patterson, and that no objection was then raised
by the Trust Company to the proposed deed or transfer of the leasehold interest from Kohlsaat. Later
on, the defendant Shedd, appellant, having purchased
all of the interest of Johnson in the Merrimac Company, leasehold and building, Johnson and wife executed to him a quitclaim deed of said leasehold and
building, of which deed the Northern Trust Company
was duly apprised. The deed contained the following
clause:

"And said Edward A. Shedd hereby covenants and
agrees to and with all the parties to said lease and with
Albert M. Johnson, that he hereby accepts and assumes
all the terms, covenants and conditions in said lease,
and will faithfully comply with and be bound by the
same."

Shedd's answer further sets up that he was, on
January 30, 1905, and has been since and was at the
time of filing his answer, of full financial responsibility
to accept and hold this leasehold estate under the requirements of said lease, and that he was the bona
fide owner of property worth over $500,000 above all
his debts and liabilities, and that that fact had been
well known to the Trust Company and to the beneficiaries. The answer further sets up in detail the

bond issue of the Merrimac Building Company and the mortgage securing the same, and avers that he has been the owner and holder of each and all the bonds for more than two years and last past, and denies that the trustees or beneficiaries did not consent to the execution of said mortgage deed, and avers that, on the contrary, they each and all did so consent, and each and all knew of the execution of said trust deed at the time of its date, and avers that the trust deed created an equitable lien upon the leasehold estate which was held in trust by Kohlsaat from and after the time of his assignment thereof to the Merrimac Building Company; and that the mortgage deed securing the bonds was a first lien upon the interests of the parties claiming under the Merrimac charter. His answer further sets up that prior to February 21, 1905, Johnson and Shedd purchased the bonds of the Merrimac Building Company aggregating $294,500, and that they then purchased a large majority of the stock of said company, and subsequently the remainder of it.

After referring to the various cases above mentioned, the answer of appellant Shedd avers that the Northern Trust Company, as trustee, as well as all the other beneficiaries were parties to the litigation, and that the question of the alleged lack of power in the Merrimac Company to acquire said leasehold and building and to collect the rents from the various tenants of the building was raised and asserted by Patterson, but the courts each held and ruled that Patterson and the Northern Trust Company, and each and all the beneficiaries, on account of their acts and doings and on account of their consent to the assignment of the leasehold and of the filing of said bill to foreclose the landlord's lien and of the decree entered therein, were estopped to deny and barred from denying that the Merrimac Company had such power of acquisition, and from claiming a forfeiture of said building and leasehold; that the mistake of supposing that the charter of the Merrimac Company was legally authorized was an innocent mistake and was mutual to all parties dealing upon the faith of the charter, and with the said purported corporation, or its officers, acting as such; and that all of such parties, including the lessors, the Northern Trust Company and the beneficiaries, actually participated in the furtherance and perpetuation of the project of using or attempting to use the charter as a legal charter and for the building up of rights and equities upon the basis thereof and according to the tenor thereof, and of holding a leasehold in the name of said corporation and using it as the actual tenant under the lease; that the quitclaim deed given from Kohlsaat to Shedd and Johnson was given and known to said Trust Company to have been given to further the transaction of redeeming from the foreclosure decree of June 25, 1902, in which the trustee and the beneficiaries participated and received the proceeds of such redemption, and that the right to object to the redemption, if any then existed, was waived by the said trustee and the beneficiaries as well, by their failure to act in that respect; that the provision against the assignment in the ground lease was further waived by the recognition of the conveyance in trust to the Illinois Trust & Savings Bank made more than fourteen years prior to the commencement of this suit, and remained unquestioned at any time by the lessors or beneficiaries.

Appellant Shedd's answer admits that Kohlsaat surrendered possession of the premises in question, but avers that it was done shortly after the execution and delivery of the first deed of assignment. He denies that the assignment was an entire nullity, and avers that even though the charter of the Merrimac Building Company was ultimately held void, Kohlsaat was paid for the leasehold estate in full by the parties acting as said Merrimac Company and under its charter; and that Kohlsaat then and there became and from that time remained the holder of the legal title of the leasehold estate in trust for the benefit of the parties acting as the Merrimac Company and according to their interests as evidenced by the stock certificates and the charter of the Merrimac Building Company. He denies that Kohlsaat was released from all liability to lessors under the lease by the assignment to the company, and that the transaction had the effect of a surrender of all rights or any rights to the lessors.

Shedd admits the filing of the petition in the foreclosure suit on February 21, 1905, set out in the amended bill by himself and Albert M. Johnson, and the entry of the order thereon permitting Shedd and Johnson to redeem, and avers that on the same day Shedd and Johnson paid the amount specified in the order, namely, $210,487.20, to the Northern Trust Company, trustee, and satisfied in full the foreclosure decree. Defendant Shedd admits that the rent due under the lease has been paid, and avers that it has been promptly and fully paid ever since February 21, 1905, and by parties acting in the name of the Merrimac Building Company, and on its behalf, down to the entry of defendant Shedd upon said premises on June 4, 1910, from and after which date defendant, Edward A. Shedd, has paid such rent and has been in the sole and exclusive possession of the leasehold estate. The answer then asserts that Shedd has the full and absolute title to the leasehold estate; and, independently of that, he has an equitable right or title to the leasehold and building.

It is not important to state the answers of the other defendants to the bill except perhaps the answer of the Northern Trust Company. As to that, it is sufficient to say that its position is stated in its original bill for instructions filed in the Superior Court on the same day that the Helen W. S. Johnson bill was filed. The bill of the Trust Company makes the five beneficiaries parties defendant, and also Kohlsaat, Edward A. Shedd and Charles B. Shedd. Issues were made up under this bill and the cause was consolidated by order of court with the Johnson cause. The Northern Trust

Company bill set up the making the lease, the execution of the trust deed to it, the participation in the transactions with the Merrimac Company by the various lessor interests, the quo warranto proceedings and the judgment of ouster. It alleges that after all these things had transpired, John C. Patterson had served the notice of July 9, 1910, demanding that the trustee take action in the premises to forfeit the leasehold estate; that the attitude of the beneficiaries in respect to said forfeiture was different; that Helen W. S. Johnson had taken the same attitude in respect thereto as had John C. Patterson. Mrs. Williams had notified the trustee that she preferred the lease to continue in force. Stewart Patterson had taken no attitude in the matter and Mrs. Fannie Johnson had taken none. The trustee therefore prayed for instructions.

The bill of the Northern Trust Company was duly answered by the defendants therein, replications were filed and an order consolidating the causes was entered and the two causes thereafter proceeded as one consolidated case.

On February 4, 1911, appellant Shedd filed a cross-bill in which, after reciting briefly the prior proceedings, he embodied therein his answer to the original bill, thus setting up in substance the facts set forth in his answer. After showing the complications that had arisen between the parties and that might ensue from the situation stated, the cross-bill prays for a decree establishing the facts in reference to the assignment of the lease and the acquiescence therein by the lessors and the estoppel of the trustee and beneficiaries to question his title, etc., and that it might be formally found and declared that he was the owner of all the stock and bonds of the Merrimac Company, and in equity, as well as at law, the holder of the leasehold estate, and for other and further relief.

The court, on hearing, entered decree declaring that the Merrimac Building Company had never had any legal existence as a corporation, and that the bonds and stocks issued in its name were issued without any authority of law and conferred no rights upon the holders thereof in and to the premises in question; that the attempted assignment by Kohlsaat on April 2, 1897, and the deed executed by him theretofore on April 30, 1896, passed no title in and to the leasehold estate then owned by him to the Merrimac Building Company, or any persons then and thereafter acting as a corporation, and in the name of the Merrimac Building Company, and passed no title and conveyed no rights or interest in or to said leasehold estate or the building located on the above described real estate to the Merrimac Building Company or to any persons claiming to be stockholders or bondholders thereof; that on or about April 2, 1897, the leasehold estate of Kohlsaat, which had been theretofore created by said lease of May 1, 1893, was surrendered by operation of law and thereupon Kohlsaat was released from all obligations under the lease, and that since said April 2, 1897, Kohlsaat has had no right, title or interest in or to said leasehold estate or the building located upon the real estate; that upon the surrender of said leasehold estate as aforesaid the legal title to said leasehold estate merged with the legal title to the fee in the above described real estate; that the Northern Trust Company, as trustee, is the owner of the legal title to the real estate, free and clear of any leasehold estate created by the lease executed by Pullman and Matthews as lessors, and merges the leasehold estate in the fee; and that the Northern Trust Company holds its legal title subject solely to the terms and conditions of the deed of trust to it; that Edward A. Shedd, Charles B. Shedd and Edward J. Shedd have no title, right or interest in or to the premises or the building located thereon or in the leasehold estate; that the cross-bill of the complainant, Edward A. Shedd, is without equity, and it is dismissed without costs; that Edward A. Shedd, Charles B. Shedd and

Edward J. Shedd, or such of them as are now in possession of said real estate and building, are tenants at
will thereof, and that it is the duty of the Northern
Trust Company, as trustee, to take immediate possession of the premises and to hold, manage and operate
same for the benefit of the beneficial owners of such
real estate and building, and the said Shedds, or such
of them as are now in possession of said real estate
and building, are ordered and directed to deliver to
said Northern Trust Company, as trustee, immediate
possession of the above described real estate and building, together with their excluded copy of the aforesaid
lease, dated May 1, 1893, and to cease occupying the
said real estate and building, and to cease collecting
rents from the tenants occupying the same.

A motion was made by John C. Patterson, appellee,
to dismiss the appeal upon the ground that the decree
appealed from is not a final decree and this court is
without jurisdiction to hear and determine the cause.
This motion was reserved to the hearing.

The decree denies to appellant Shedd all rights and
equities in the subject-matter of the litigation and
transfers the right of property and the possession
thereof to the Northern Trust Company, as trustee,
and orders appellant to deliver up possession of the
premises to the Trust Company and also the executed
copy of the lease. It finds and decrees upon the substantive rights and equities of the parties. The provisions in the decree for an accounting and reserving
jurisdiction for the purpose of enforcing the decree
do not affect its final character. This appeal is properly taken to this court. 2 Encyc. Pl. & Pr. 71. The
motion to dismiss this appeal is denied.

The bill of complaint of Helen W. S. Johnson and
Stewart Patterson is in its essence and effect a bill
to declare a forfeiture of the lease. The ingenious
phrasing of the prayer of the bill for an injunction
against the Northern Trust Company from "collecting,
receiving or receipting for any further payment of

moneys as an instalment of rent under said lease, and from making or delivering any receipt for any such payment or instalment to said Herman H. Kohlsaat, or to any other person, or persons, as lessee, or lessees, or the payer of rental under said lease," and for a receiver of the Stewart Building and of its rents and profits, etc., and that the "court decrees that the full title and sole right to complete possession and control of said Stewart Building and appurtenances is in said Northern Trust Company, as trustee, for the benefit of the beneficiaries under said trust deed, 'Exhibit D,' and that such possession and control be delivered over to said trustee by such receiver, and that said lease, 'Exhibit A,' be adjudged surrendered, and be ordered delivered up and canceled," cannot deceive or mislead a court of equity. Nor will the specious contention and argument that the leasehold estate of Kohlsaat was surrendered by operation of law in 1897, when Kohlsaat executed the first assignment, based upon the undisputed facts shown by the record, avail to persuade the court that complainants are not really seeking a forfeiture of the lease, for that is the real meaning and essence of the bill.

If the leasehold estate was surrendered by operation of law, it was terminated. If the leasehold estate was forfeited, it was terminated. The same result is sought and upon the same state of facts by both theories and methods. As said in *Patterson v. Northern Trust Co.*, 238 Ill. 601:

"The apparent object of the present bill is to obtain a holding to the effect that the lease to Kohlsaat and the assignment thereof to the Merrimac Building Company are void, and that the building erected upon the premises, by reason of the forfeiture of the lease, now forms a part of the fee, and to require the Northern Trust Company, as trustee, to account to appellant for his proportionate share of all rents which have been earned by the premises covered by said lease since the date of the notice to the lessees by the

Northern Trust Company that the lease had been forfeited. Substantially all the contentions raised by the
brief of counsel for the appellant in this case were
raised by the appellant in the other cases when they
were here and were disposed of adversely to appellant.''

There can be no doubt that equity abhors a forfeiture and will not declare and enforce it. ''It is a well
settled and familiar doctrine that a court of equity will
not interfere on behalf of the party entitled thereto,
and enforce a forfeiture, but will leave him to his legal remedy, if any, even though the case might be one
in which no equity relief would be given to the defaulting party against the forfeiture. The few apparent
exceptions to this doctrine are not real exceptions,
since they all depend upon other rules and principles.'' Pomeroy, Eq. Jur., sec. 459; *Douglas v.
Union Mut. Life Ins. Co.*, 127 Ill. 101, 116; *Patterson v. Northern Trust Co., supra.* The function of a
court of equity is to grant relief against forfeiture in
proper cases but never to enforce it.

In recognition of this elementary principle of equity,
and of the decisions in the *Patterson* cases, *supra*, so-
licitors for appellees, Helen W. S. Johnson and Stewart Patterson, do not base their argument in this court
in support of the decree upon the right of the complainants to a forfeiture of the lease, but upon the doctrine of surrender by operation of law. In other
words, the contention is that ''by the performance by
both lessor and lessee of acts which the law says
amount to a 'surrender by operation of law,' the leasehold estate has become merged in the fee.'' To state
the contentions more specifically, it is not that there
was any surrender of the leasehold estate by express
agreement, but that such surrender is implied from the
attempted assignment which was void, the relinquishment of possession by Kohlsaat, the lessor's subsequent collection and enforcement of rental payments
from the owners of the Merrimac Building Company,
and failure to receive and demand any such payment

from Kohlsaat and "the lessor's acceptance of the persons acting as 'Merrimac Building Company' as tenants," and thereafter collecting all rental payments from them, constituted a surrender of the leasehold by operation of law.

In regard to the surrender theory thus put forward, it is necessary in order to reach a just conclusion to consider all the circumstances in which the parties, complainants and defendants, acted at the time of, and subsequent to, the attempted assignment of the lease.

The lease provided that the lessee might assign his interest in the premises, but not without first obtaining the written consent of the lessors so to do, "and provided also, that no assignment shall be made to any corporation not having the power and authority under the law of its organization and the laws of Illinois to accept such assignment * * *."

The lease contains the further provision that if the lessee did assign such interest, "after complying with the conditions and covenants set forth in the foregoing, the lessee shall be released by the lessors from all liability under this lease arising after the proper execution and delivery of such assignment."

It is beyond question, we think, that the attempted assignment to the Merrimac Building Company did not release Kohlsaat from the lease, for that company had no existence. There was no grantee or assignee. What the parties tried to do, but did not do, was to substitute the Merrimac Building Company for Kohlsaat as lessee and owner. There was no such company, and hence the effort failed and, as between the parties to the lease, it was left standing precisely as if no assignment had been made. There was no substitution, and where there is no actual substitution there was no surrender by operation of law, and no release of Kohlsaat by the consent of the landlord to an assignment with no assignee to receive and hold it. *Barnes* v. *Northern Trust Co.*, 169 Ill. 112; *Grommes* v. *St. Paul Trust Co.*, 147 Ill. 634, 648. The question of substitu-

tion of tenants for the unexpired portion of a term
rests upon the doctrine of novation. In 21 Am. & Eng.
Encyc. of Law, 672, it is said:

"It is essential in every case of novation that the
resulting obligation is an enforceable one. Although
there may be present competent parties and sufficient
consideration, the prior obligation is not extinguished
unless the new obligation be such as may legally take
its place. Thus, if it be inchoate or lacking in some
necessary element, or illegal and, therefore, unenforce-
able, or conditional, novation either fails entirely or is
suspended until the objectionable element in the contract is removed."

To the same effect are Wood's Landlord & Tenant,
sec. 494; 18 Am. & Eng. Encyc. of Law, 359;.and 24
Cyc. 1370, 1371, and authorities there cited. In *Coe v.
Hobby*, 72 N. Y. 141, 147, the Court said:

"The farthest that our courts have gone is to hold
that to effect a surrender of an existing lease by operation of law, there must be a new lease, valid in law,
to pass an interest according to the contract and intention of the parties."

See also *Brewer v. National Union Building Ass'n*,
166 Ill. 221.

Thus far we have considered the question of surrender by operation of law wholly apart from and unaffected by estoppel and prior adjudication which we
shall consider later. The attempted assignment of the
lease by Kohlsaat with the consent of the lessor and
the delivery of possession of the premises by Kohlsaat
to the persons acting in the name of the Merrimac
Building Company, in our opinion, did not amount to
a surrender of the leasehold estate by operation of law
as between the lessor and lessee. But, Kohlsaat, having been fully paid by the persons acting in the name
of the Merrimac Building Company for his leasehold and building, became a trustee for the stockholders and bondholders of that company, upon the
familiar and elementary principle that where a person
holds an estate for which he has been fully paid by an-

other or others, a trust results for the benefit of those who paid the money. This principle as applied to a similar case is illustrated in *Walker v. Taylor*, 252 Ill. 424.

Without pausing here to discuss this principle as applied to this case (which we shall do later on), we proceed to refer to other controlling facts on the question of surrender by operation of law.

On March 15, 1892, nearly a year after the date of the deed from Kohlsaat and wife to the Merrimac Building Company, the Northern Trust Company, as trustee, and the beneficiaries of the trust, including the complainants and the Merrimac Building Company, entered into the so-called "forbearance of rent" agreement, which recited the lease in question, the erection of a new building on the premises in accordance with the intent of the lease, the assignment of the lease, defaults in the payment of rent, and that notice in writing of said defaults had been given December 29, 1897, and that this company had given notice that it would apply for the protection of a court of equity to prevent a forfeiture of the lease and to enable it to redeem the building and leasehold from said defaults on equitable terms, the desire to avoid litigation, and then stipulated and agreed that no steps should be taken by the Trust Company and the beneficiaries to enforce the forfeiture of the leasehold estate, provided the covenants and agreements of the lease be kept and performed, until July 1, 1900. The Merrimac Company agreed to deliver possession forthwith to the Northern Trust Company. The remaining provisions of the agreement it is not necessary here to state.

The further facts of the foreclosure decree of June 25, 1902, in the Circuit Court of Cook county; the redemption by Shedd and Johnson, who paid $210,427.20, the amount due under the decree, on February 21, 1905; the review of the order permitting them to redeem in *Patterson v. Northern Trust Co.*, 132 Ill. 208, and affirmed in 230 Ill. 334; the adjudications in *Patterson v. Northern Trust Co.*, 139 Ill. App. 681, and *Patterson v. Northern Trust Co.*, 231 Ill. 22, and *Same v. Same* in 238 Ill. 601,—are all important as facts and adjudications to be taken into consideration upon the rights of appellee to the relief sought in their bill. They show that the complainants and their trustees, The Northern Trust Company, with their consent and approval, recognized the Merrimac Building Company and those acting in that name as the assignee of the lease which they alleged and treated as still in existence after the alleged surrender by operation of law, and collected and received the rents as such reserved received the rents as such reserved in the lease. These in the lease. These facts, in connection with the uncontroverted facts that the parties acting in the corporate name took possession of the premises and paid the rent reserved under the lease and performed all the covenants of the lease for thirteen years, and after the continued recognition and express assertion of the lease and its enforcement by legal proceedings by appellees and their trustee, Kohlsaat, holding the naked legal title of the leasehold estate for the benefit of Shedd and Johnson who had become owners of the interests of every person in the leasehold estate, conveyed the title to appellants Shedd and Johnson,—leave no basis in law or equity for contention that there was a surrender by operation of law, or a forfeiture thereof in any other form, or by any other method. The bill of Helen W. S. Johnson and Stewart Patterson is without equity and should have been dismissed by the chancellor on the hearing.

We come now to a consideration of the equities of appellant Shedd, if any, under his cross-bill. It appears without controversy that appellant Shedd has acquired all the rights of the stockholders and bondholders of the illegal corporation known as the Merrimac Building Company. The stock certificates and bonds issued by that organization are valueless as evidencing the ownership of stock and bonds by the holders thereof. These papers, nevertheless, show who contributed the money to erect the building now standing upon the leased premises and other moneys expended for the benefit of the leasehold estate and the payments of rents in accordance with the covenants of the lease, and the equities of these stockholders and bondholders, now vested in Shedd. As said in *Walker v. Taylor,* 252 Ill. 424: "Those who subscribed and paid for stock issued by the illegal association and with whose money the land was purchased did acquire an equitable interest in the property. Their interests are entitled to be protected by court of equity as against the creditors of Gould, who never had any interest in the land except to the extent of the stock he subscribed and paid for."

An interesting and well considered case on the subject of equities arising out of an illegal corporation attempted to be organized to engage in the business of buying and selling real estate, and affirming the right of stockholders to enforce a trust with reference to real estate held for the benefit of the stockholders in such a corporation, is *Fisk v. Patton,* 7 Utah 399.

The leasehold was legally created in Kohlsaat. He sold and was paid for that estate and attempted to assign it, but the assignment failed for reasons already given. The estate was thereafter held by him in trust for the parties who had purchased it and paid for it. In equity he could have been compelled to execute a conveyance of the leasehold to appellants Shedd and Johnson, the then holders of the equitable rights, on January 30, 1905, when he voluntarily conveyed it to them. The lessor owners of the fee had then recognized the Merrimac Building Company by consenting to the assignment of the lease, by entering into the so-called "forbearance of rent" agreement, and by filing their bill in the rent foreclosure case, and pressing the case to a decree entered June 25, 1902, and by receiving rent under the lease and giving receipts therefor to Kohlsaat. These acts and proceedings operated as a waiver of all right of forfeiture and of the right to object to the conveyance to Shedd and Johnson as an assignment without the lessor's consent as provided in the lease. *Webster v. Nichols,* 104 Ill. 160; 18 Am. & Eng. Encyc. Law (2d Ed.) 385-386.

Upon the facts shown in the record and the acts of the parties and in view of the legal proceedings instituted by the equitable owners of the fee, and to which they were parties, and upon the several adjudications referred to above, we hold that the defendants in the cross-bill are estopped from denying that the Kohlsaat assignment carried the leasehold estate to the Merrimac Building Company for the benefit of the persons acting in that name and that Shedd, complainant in the cross-bill, is the equitable owner of the leasehold estate. We further hold that Shedd is the equitable owner of the leasehold estate under the doctrine expressed in *Walker v. Taylor, supra; Fisk v. Patton, supra,* and other cases and authorities cited; and that by the deeds from Kohlsaat to Shedd and Johnson and by Johnson to Shedd, the title to the leasehold estate was vested in Shedd. And in view of the questions presented to the courts in the several cases instituted and litigated by the original complainants and John C. Patterson, Shedd is entitled to have his title to the leasehold estate quieted by a decree on his cross-bill.

In view also of the continued litigation with reference to this lease and the disagreement of the beneficial owners of the fee as to the proper position, duty and action of the Northern Trust Company, as trustee, with reference to the lease and the estate thereby created, the Trust Company is entitled to a decree giving to it instructions and directions.

The decree is reversed and the cause is remanded

with directions to the trial court to enter a decree dismissing the bill of Helen W. S. Johnson and Stewart Patterson for want of equity; and to enter a decree on the cross-bill of Shedd and the bill of the Northern Trust Company not inconsistent with the views herein expressed.

Reversed and remanded with directions.

Oliver J. Wright, Defendant in Error, v. John L. Bolen, Plaintiff in Error.

Gen. No. 18,519. (Not to be reported in full.)

Error to the Municipal Court of Chicago; the Hon. EDWIN K. WALKER, Judge, presiding. Heard in the Branch Appellate Court at the October term, 1912. Affirmed on remittitur; otherwise reversed and remanded. Opinion filed January 22, 1914.

Statement of the Case.

Action by Oliver J. Wright against John L. Bolen to recover for work and labor performed by the plaintiff as a carpenter and foreman for the defendant for certain periods of time stated in his statement of claim. From a judgment in favor of plaintiff for $858.70, defendant brings error.

PARK PHIPPS, for plaintiff in error.

GIDEON S. THOMPSON, for defendant in error.

MR. PRESIDING JUSTICE FITCH delivered the opinion of the court.

Regelin et al. v. Conran, 184 Ill. App. 570.

Abstract of the Decision.

1. MASTER AND SERVANT, § 87*—*when defendant in suit for wages entitled to deduction of credits.* In an action for wages a verdict in favor of plaintiff *held* too large in view of evidence showing that defendant was entitled to certain items as credits, and judgment was affirmed upon condition of remittitur.

2. WITNESSES, § 33*—*competency of plaintiff's wife to testify.* In an action for wages where plaintiff testified that his wife on several occasions collected money for him from the defendant, *held* not error to permit plaintiff's wife to testify to a conversation with the defendant concerning plaintiff's account.

3. APPEAL AND ERROR, § 523*—*method of making objections to oral instructions.* Improper on making objections to oral instructions to divide the oral charge into separate numbered paragraphs.

William C. Regelin and William Jenson, trading as Regelin-Jenson & Company, Defendants in Error, v. Thomas Conran, Plaintiff in Error.

Gen. No. 18,677.   (Not to be reported in full.)

Error to the Municipal Court of Chicago; the Hon. EDWIN K. WALKER, Judge, presiding. Heard in the Branch Appellate Court at the October term, 1912. Affirmed. Opinion filed January 22, 1914.

Statement of the Case.

Action by William C. Regelin and William Jenson, copartners, doing business as Regelin-Jenson & Co., against Thomas Conran to recover commissions earned in securing a purchaser for certain property belonging to defendant. From a judgment in favor of plaintiffs for $650, defendant brings error.

HENRY M. HAGAN, for plaintiff in error.

GEORGE H. MASON, for defendants in error.

MR. PRESIDING JUSTICE FITCH delivered the opinion of the court.

Abstract of the Decision.

1. BROKERS, § 46*—*when entitled to commissions though the contract between purchaser and seller was made under a mutual mistake as to the subject-matter.* In an action for commissions for procuring a purchaser for property belonging to defendant, where the seller and purchaser entered into a written contract whereby the seller agreed to convey the property in consideration that the purchaser would convey to defendant other property described as being of certain dimensions, more or less, *held* that plaintiffs were entitled to commissions notwithstanding the purchaser and seller were mutually mistaken as to the dimensions of the property to be conveyed by the purchaser, the contract being made in good faith and enforceable in a court of law according to its terms.

2. VENDOR AND PURCHASER, § 64*—*words "more or less" construed.* The words "more or less" as applied to quantity in a contract to convey land are to be construed as qualifying a representation or statement of an absolute or definite amount, so that neither party can avoid it or set it aside by reason of any deficiency or surplus occasioned by no fraud or want of good faith, if there is a reasonable approximation to the quantity specifically stipulated in the contract.

3. REFORMATION OF INSTRUMENTS, § 34*—*jurisdiction.* A court of law has no power to correct a mistake and reform a contract; such power rests alone in a court of equity.

Rocco Lofaro and Frank Rossi, trading as Lofaro & Rossi, Defendants in Error, v. Alessandro Maggi, Plaintiff in Error.

Gen. No. 18,705.

1. MUNICIPAL COURT OF CHICAGO, § 16*—*what does not constitute waiver of jury trial.* Failure of defendant to file a written demand for a jury trial when he appears to require nonresident plaintiffs to file a bond for costs, *held* not to waive his right to trial by jury.

2. MUNICIPAL COURT OF CHICAGO, § 16*—*when demand for jury trial may be filed.* Defendant sufficiently complies with statute re-

---

*See Illinois Notes Digest, Vols. XI to XV, same topic and section number.

quiring the filing of a written demand for jury trial where he files such demand and pays jury fees when he appears for the first time in answer to plaintiff's claim upon the merits.

Error to the Municipal Court of Chicago; the Hon. JOHN R. NEW-COMER, Judge, presiding. Heard in the Branch Appellate Court at the October term, 1912. Reversed and remanded. Opinion filed January 22, 1914.

CAIROLI GIGLIOTTI, for plaintiff in error.

CULVER, ANDREWS & KING, for defendants in error.

MR. PRESIDING JUSTICE FITCH delivered the opinion of the court.

The only question raised in this case is whether the defendant (plaintiff in error) was entitled to a jury trial in the Municipal Court. The plaintiffs sued upon a promissory note. Upon the return day of the summons the defendant filed a written appearance, "for the special purpose of having plaintiff, who is a non-resident, give security for costs," and, on motion of the defendant, the plaintiffs were then ordered to file a bond for costs within five days. By the terms of the same order, defendant's time within which to file an affidavit of merits was extended ten days. A bond for costs was filed at once, and four days later the defendant filed another appearance in writing, in which he demanded "that the issue in the above entitled cause be tried by a jury." Within the time limited by the order of the court, defendant filed an affidavit of merits, from which we assume that his defense is that the consideration for the note failed. The record shows that thereafter the cause came on in the regular course for trial before the court without a jury; that the court heard the evidence and entered a finding and judgment in favor of the plaintiff for $92.68. The statement of facts, however, shows that when the case was so called for trial, defendant objected to a trial by the court without a jury and presented an affidavit in support of his objection, stating, in substance, the facts regarding his first and second appearance, and also stating that at the time of making his written demand for a jury trial, as above stated, he had paid $6 to the clerk for jury fees; that thereupon defendant moved the court to have the case placed upon the jury calendar for trial, but the court overruled the motion, to which the defendant excepted; that following this ruling, "defendant and his counsel left the court room and refused to submit to a trial by the court instead of a trial by jury as demanded;" whereupon the case was tried by the court, in the absence of the defendant.

Section 43 of the Municipal Court Act (J. & A. ¶ 3355) provides that upon the return of any summons duly served upon the defendant, plaintiff shall be entitled to judgment as in case of default, unless the defendant shall either appear in person, or file his appearance in writing, at or before the time fixed in the summons. Section 30 of the same act (J. & A. ¶ 3342) provides that every suit of the fourth class in the Municipal Court "shall be tried by the court without a jury, unless the plaintiff, at the time he commences his suit, or the defendant, at the time he enters his appearance, shall file with the clerk a demand in writing of a trial by jury." The fifth paragraph of section 56 (J. & A. ¶ 3373) provides that if the defendant files with his appearance a demand in writing for a jury trial, he shall pay to the clerk the sum of $6. Section 19 (J. & A. ¶ 3331) provides that until otherwise determined, and except as by that act is otherwise prescribed, the practice in the Municipal Court "shall be the same as near as may be, as that which may from time to time be prescribed by law for similar suits or proceedings in circuit courts, excepting that in cases of the fourth class * * * the issues shall be determined without other forms of written pleadings than those hereinafter expressly prescribed or provided for." Section 1 of chapter 33 of the Re-

vised Statutes (J. & A. ¶ 2715) provides that in all
cases at law or in equity, where the plaintiff is not a
resident of this State, he shall, "before he institutes
such suit," file, or cause to be filed, a written security
for costs; and section 3 of the same chapter (J. & A.
¶ 2717) provides that if any such action shall be commenced without filing such a written instrument, "the
court, on motion, shall dismiss the same, * * *
unless the security for costs shall be filed within such
time as shall be allowed by the court."

In *Morrison Hotel Co. v. Kirsner*, 245 Ill. 431, the
Court said: "The constitution secures to the citizen
the right of trial by jury, and unless he waives that
right it is his privilege to have controverted questions
of fact decided by a jury and not by a judge sitting as
a court. * * * We have held that provisions of
the Municipal Court act requiring a party to a suit of
this class, at the time of entering his appearance, to
file with the clerk a demand in writing for a trial by
jury and to pay $6 for jury fees are valid, and that
otherwise the cause may be tried by the court. (*Williams v. Gottschalk*, 231 Ill. 175.) In view, however,
of the provision of the constitution that the cherished
right of trial by jury shall remain inviolate, the statute should be liberally construed in favor of the right
and the inclination of the court should be to protect
and enforce the right." Upon the principle thus
stated, it was there held that the failure of a defendant, against whom a judgment by confession had been
entered, to file a written demand for a jury trial with
his motion to vacate the judgment does not waive or
bar his right to a jury trial if he makes his written demand and tenders the jury fees at the time the motion to vacate is allowed. We think the reasoning of
the opinion in that case is applicable to the facts of
this case. It was the statutory duty of the non-resident plaintiffs, when they commenced their suit, to
file with the clerk a written security for costs. Their
failure to do so entitled the defendant to have the suit

dismissed on his motion, unless the court should allow further time to the plaintiffs to file such security. The court recognized this right of the defendant when it entered a rule on the plaintiffs to file a bond for costs within five days. Until that rule was complied with, or the time allowed for compliance expired, it could not be known whether there would be any issue to be tried either by the court or a jury. If no bond for costs had been filed, the making of a written demand for a jury trial and the payment of the jury fees would have been wholly unnecessary and futile. To hold that under such circumstances the failure to make such a demand and payment before any bond for costs was filed amounted to a waiver of the constitutional right of trial by jury would be to adopt a most narrow and technical, instead of a liberal construction of the statute. When defendant appeared for the first time in answer to plaintiff's claim on the merits he filed his written demand for a jury trial. We think this was a sufficient compliance with the statute, and that the court erred in refusing to give him a trial by jury.

The judgment of the Municipal Court will be reversed and remanded.

Reversed and remanded.

Greer-Wilkinson Lumber Company, Defendant in Error, v. George A. Neeves, Plaintiff in Error.

Gen. No. 18,726.   (Not to be reported in full.)

Error to the Municipal Court of Chicago; the Hon. FREDERICK L. FAKE, JR., Judge, presiding. Heard in the Branch Appellate Court at the October term, 1912. Affirmed. Opinion filed January 22, 1914. Rehearing denied February 3, 1914.

Statement of the Case.

Action by Greer-Wilkinson Lumber Company, a corporation, against George A. Neeves on a promissory note given by defendant to plaintiff in renewal of another note for the same amount. The original note was given to plaintiff as a result of a compromise agreement in payment for materials purchased by a contractor and used by the contractor in constructing a house for defendant after defendant had disputed his liability to pay therefor, and after defendant had refused to pay the contractor on the ground that the building did not conform to specifications. The defense to the note was want of consideration. From a judgment in favor of plaintiff for $586.15, defendant brings error.

GEORGE A. NEEVES, JR. and LELAND K. NEEVES, for plaintiff in error.

EASTMAN & WHITE, for defendant in error; RALPH R. HAWXHURST, of counsel.

MR. PRESIDING JUSTICE FITCH delivered the opinion of the court.

Abstract of the Decision.

COMPROMISE AND SETTLEMENT, § 5*—*when compromise of disputed claim sufficient consideration for a note.* Where a person as a result of a compromise agreement gives his promissory note in settlement of a doubtful claim he is liable thereon and cannot urge want of consideration for the note, even though the claim could not have been legally enforced against him, where there was neither actual nor constructive fraud and the parties acted in good faith with full knowledge of all the facts.

*See Illinois Notes Digest, Vols. XI to XV, same topic and section number.

Percival Steele, Appellant, v. George A. Lamb et al., Appellees.

Gen. No. 18,738.

1. ATTORNEY AND CLIENT, § 150*—*when evidence shows want of good faith in serving statutory notice for lien.* On bill filed by an attorney to enforce a lien for attorney's fees under Hurd's R. S. 1912, ch. 82, ¶ 55, J. & A. ¶ 611, a decree dismissing the bill for want of equity on sustaining a plea alleging that complainant's notice for a lien was not served in good faith, but was served for the purpose of defrauding a creditor of the judgment creditor, *held* sustained by the evidence.

2. APPEAL AND ERROR, § 1165*—*when court may consider only questions parties see fit to present.* Where adult litigants are concerned and private rights, only, are involved, the practice considered proper is to decide such questions as they see fit to present.

Appeal from the Circuit Court of Cook county; the Hon. CHARLES M. WALKER, Judge, presiding. Heard in the Branch Appellate Court at the October term, 1912. Affirmed. Opinion filed January 22, 1914.

HARVEY L. CAVENDER, for appellant.

F. W. BALCOMB, for appellees; CHARLES D. MC-GRATH, of counsel.

MR. PRESIDING JUSTICE FITCH delivered the opinion of the court.

By this appeal it is sought to reverse a decree of the Circuit Court sustaining a plea to the bill of complaint and dismissing the bill for want of equity. The bill alleges that the complainant (appellant) is a lawyer, practicing in Chicago; that about May 1, 1909, he was retained by the defendant, Lamb, to collect certain claims against H. O. Tomlinson & Co.; that no definite amount was agreed on for attorney's fees, but it was understood that a reasonable fee should be paid to the

*See Illinois Notes Digest, Vols. XI to XV, same topic and section number

complainant for his services; that complainant brought
suit in the Municipal Court for $60,000 on behalf of
Lamb against Tomlinson & Co., and on July 15, 1909,
a judgment in Lamb's favor for $7,164.21 was recov-
ered, from which judgment an appeal was perfected,
which was pending at the time the bill was filed; that
the reasonable, customary and ordinary charge in
Chicago for such services as were rendered by complainant in that suit was $4684.49, and that amount,
it is claimed, is due and owing to the complainant from
Lamb; that on June 10, 1909, complainant caused to
be served upon Lamb and upon Tomlinson & Co. a
written notice, stating that in pursuance of paragraph
55, chapter 82, of the Illinois statutes (J. & A. ¶ 611),
he claimed an attorney's lien, in the sum of $7,500, for
services rendered and disbursements made in said
suit of *Lamb v. Tomlinson & Co.*, "upon all papers
and claims of, and amounts due and to become due to,
said plaintiff, George A. Lamb, in connection with said
action." The prayer of the bill is that the court will
"ascertain, adjudicate, and enforce" the complainant's alleged lien for attorney's fees. To this bill the
defendant, Lamb, filed a plea, stating in substance that
the notice described in the bill "was not served in
good faith by said complainant for the purpose of
complying with the statute in the said bill pleaded, or
for the purpose of protecting said complainant's right
to compensation for services rendered," but was
served in pursuance of an arrangement between the
complainant and defendant to "place beyond the reach
of other creditors" of Lamb, and "to fraudulently
cover up," any judgment that might be secured in the
suit of Lamb against Tomlinson. The cause was then
referred to a master in chancery to take testimony
and report the same, "together with his conclusions
thereon, on the issues raised by the special plea."
The evidence heard before the master consisted chiefly
of the testimony of the complainant and the defendant,
Lamb. From their evidence it appears that during the

trial of the Tomlinson suit in the Municipal Court, and after complainant had spent considerable time and effort in preparing for the trial and in partly trying the case, a suit was brought against Lamb by one De-Buys for $10,000; that upon inquiry complainant learned that DeBuys held Lamb's notes for large sums which the latter was unable to pay; that complainant thereupon prepared a notice to be served upon Lamb and Tomlinson, claiming a lien to the amount of $5,000 upon the cause of action involved in the Tomlinson suit; that before this notice was served, however, there was a conference between complainant and Lamb at the office of complainant, at the conclusion of which, the complainant, with the consent of Lamb, altered the notice he had prepared, by increasing the amount of his claim, as therein stated, from $5,000 to $7,500, and in that form the notice was served upon Lamb and upon Tomlinson & Co. As to these facts there is no controversy. The only dispute is as to what was said at the conference in complainant's office. Only Steele and Lamb were present at that conference. Steele testified that when he produced the notice he had prepared and showed it to Lamb, the latter looked it over and said, "What is the objection to making the amount $7,500?" to which Steele replied, "So far as I am concerned there is no objection to making it $7,500," whereupon Steele called in his stenographer and had the notice rewritten as suggested by Lamb. Lamb testified that when the notice was produced, he told Steele that he was in an impoverished condition financially, and would be justified in going into bankruptcy, but that he wanted to escape that stigma; that he felt reasonably sure he would recover a judgment for $8,000 or $10,000 against Tomlinson & Co. in the pending suit, "and DeBuys will simply grab it;" whereupon Steele said that there was a better way than going into bankruptcy; that he (Steele) had prepared the papers claiming a lien for $5,000 against the Tomlinson claim; that Lamb said,

"Well, in that case why not make it $7,500; I suppose a lien of $7,500 would about cover it," to which Steele replied, "Very well, we will raise it." Upon this evidence, the master first found and reported that the notice was served in good faith so far as the claim for reasonable fees was concerned, and "to that extent" the notice was good. Upon exceptions filed to this report, the cause was re-referred to the master "to further report," whereupon the master submitted a further report in which he found and reported that the plea of fraud in giving the notice had not been proved, that the notice was good, and recommended that the plea be overruled. Upon exceptions filed to this report, the court took a different view of the evidence, and found that the plea was sustained by the proofs and held it sufficient, in fact and in law, to bar the complainant's suit.

The statute creating attorneys' liens and providing for the enforcement of the same (Hurd's St. 1912, Ch. 82, § 55,) J. & A. ¶ 611 gives to attorneys at law "a lien upon all claims, demands and causes of action * * * which may be placed in their hands by their clients for suit or collection * * * for the amount of any fee which may have been agreed upon by and between such attorneys and their clients, or, in the absence of such agreement, for a reasonable fee, for the services of such attorneys rendered or to be rendered for their clients on account of such suits, claims, demands or causes of action: Provided, however, such attorneys shall serve notice in writing upon the party against whom their clients may have such suits, claims, or causes of action, claiming such lien and stating therein the interest they have in such suits, claims, demands or causes of action." The statute further provides that the lien shall attach from the time of the service of such a notice.

Under this statute, no lien exists until the prescribed notice is served, and such notice must state "therein" the interest the attorney has in the suit or cause of action. As originally prepared by Steele, the notice undoubtedly expressed his view of the amount of his interest in the cause of action against Tomlinson & Co. When he changed it, the notice stated that his interest therein was much greater than was the fact. Steele knew that this was so, and although he made the change at his client's request, yet, as an attorney, with knowledge of the facts regarding the DeBuys' suit, he must have known that Lamb's purpose in requesting such change to be made was to place the whole Tomlinson claim beyond the reach of DeBuys. No other reasonable explanation is offered by Steele or warranted by the evidence.

It is assumed in the briefs and arguments of counsel on both sides that if the notice was in fact thus changed by mutual consent for the purpose of hindering, delaying or defrauding DeBuys, then the notice was fraudulent and no rights can be based upon it in a court of equity. Whether this assumption is correct, necessarily and as a matter of law, we need not stop to inquire, for the reason that its correctness is not questioned in this case. In the recent case of *Heppes Co. v. City of Chicago,* 260 Ill. 506, the Court said: "Where adult litigants are concerned and private rights, only, are involved, the practice considered proper is to decide such questions as they see fit to present." In this case adult litigants are concerned and private rights, only, are involved. It also appears that both parties are trained in the law, and the only question they have seen fit to present is whether the finding and decree are supported by the evidence, upon the assumption above stated. This question, we think, must be answered in the affirmative, for the reasons given above, and the decree of the Circuit Court will therefore be affirmed.

Affirmed.

Illinois Life Insurance Company, Appellant, v. Joseph Beifeld, Appellee.

Gen. No. 18,765.

1. CONTRACTS, § 52*—*when memorandum is a complete contract and not an agreement for execution of formal contract.* A memorandum signed by the parties relating to the leasing of a portion of certain premises and the assignment of leases as to other portions, *held* to constitute a complete contract and not a mere skeleton or outline for the preparation of contracts to be thereafter agreed upon and executed.

2. CONTRACTS, § 173*—*when contract is incomplete.* Where it is apparent from the language of a contract to convey that some of the terms and conditions which are to be inserted in the instrument of conveyance are still unsettled and open to further negotiations, then the agreement to convey is incomplete because there is no agreement in fact.

3. CONTRACTS, § 8*—*when not void for uncertainty.* A contract to lease a portion of premises for a term of years and to make an assignment of existing leases on other portions, *held* not void for uncertainty for the reason that it does not provide for all possible contingencies, where it expresses the agreement of the parties in such form as to leave little room for doubt as to what was intended and what matters were in fact agreed upon.

4. CONTRACTS, § 8*—*when contract for assignment of leases or subleases not uncertain.* A contract to lease a portion of certain premises and to make an assignment of leases or subleases to other premises as soon as the same can be conveniently prepared, *held* not subject to objection that it is uncertain whether assignments of existing leases or subleases should be prepared, where the whole term of the existing leases was to be conveyed and subleases if executed would amount in legal effect to assignments.

5. CONTRACTS, § 12*—*when not void for want of mutuality.* A contract whereby one party "agrees to take" a lease of certain property and assignments or subleases of other property as soon as the same can be conveniently prepared, at a stipulated rental, and also agrees to deposit securities concurrently with the execution and delivery of the lease, *held* to clearly import a present agreement by such party to accept an offer made by the other party to execute and deliver the lease and assignments, since the word "take" may be construed to mean "accept" so as to give effect to the intention of the parties.

Illinois Life Ins. Co. v. Beifeld, 184 Ill. App. 582.

6. CORPORATIONS, § 420*—*power of life insurance corporation to lease real estate*. The power given a life insurance corporation under Hurd's St. 1911, ch. 73, ¶ 182, J. & A. ¶ 6460, "to sell and dispose of" real estate lawfully acquired but no longer necessary for the transaction of its business, does not preclude it from making a lease of such property for a term of ninety-seven years. The words "dispose of" may be construed to mean "to alienate" or to convey by proper instruments of conveyance.

7. CORPORATIONS, § 404*—*when life insurance corporation may sell property no longer required for its business*. Hurd's St. 1911, ch. 73, ¶ 182, J. & A. ¶ 6460, does not require a life insurance corporation having property which is no longer required for the transaction of its business to immediately sell and convey the same. Under such statute it may hold such property a reasonable time in order that the same may be sold to advantage.

8. CORPORATIONS, § 344*—*who may attack contract made by corporation because it is ultra vires*. Where an *ultra vires* contract is one which the corporation was not under any circumstances authorized to perform, it is void and may be attacked anywhere by any one. But where the validity of the contract depends upon the question whether the corporation has abused, or unjustifiably used, a power which it had the right to exercise, if exercised in good faith, then only the State can attack it.

Appeal from the Superior Court of Cook county; the Hon. CLARENCE N. GOODWIN, Judge, presiding. Heard in the Branch Appellate Court at the October term, 1912. Reversed and remanded with directions. Opinion filed January 22, 1914. Rehearing denied February 9, 1914.

Statement by the Court. This appeal brings up for review a decision of the Superior Court, sustaining a demurrer to a declaration in *assumpsit*.

The declaration alleges, in substance, that the plaintiff is a corporation, organized under the laws of Illinois for the purpose of carrying on the business of life insurance; that on April 17, 1906, it was the owner and in possession, through its tenants, of certain property at the corner of LaSalle and Madison streets, in Chicago; that a part of said property, hereinafter called the Oriental property, was owned by the plaintiff in fee, and the remainder was held under ninety-nine years' leases, which, with one exception, began

*See Illinois Notes Digest, Vols. XI to XV, same topic and section number.

May 1, 1905, and will expire April 30, 2004; that one
parcel, called the Jennings property, was held under
a lease expiring April 30, 1987, and as to that parcel
the plaintiff had entered into a contract with the owner of the fee thereof for the execution of a new lease
of the same for a term ending April 30, 2004, "so as
to make all of the leasehold estates on the entire premises expire at the same time, in order that a building
or buildings covering the entire premises might be
erected thereon;" that "all of the aforesaid property
had been acquired by the plaintiff in the manner above
stated for the purpose of carrying on the business for
which it was corporated;" that on April 17, 1906, the
defendant desired to acquire a lease of the property
owned by the plaintiff in fee for a term of years expiring April 30, 2004, and assignments or subleases
of the other property covering the same period "and
thereupon executed with the plaintiff a written contract as follows:

MEMORANDUM.

1. This memorandum relates to the several holdings of property of the Illinois Life Insurance Company, situated at the Northwest corner of Madison
and LaSalle streets, Chicago, extending 178 feet on
LaSalle street by 162 feet on Madison street, and comprising (1) Oriental or Coleman property, fee, (2)
Jared Bassett leasehold, (3) University of Chicago
leasehold, (4) John D. Jennings and wife leasehold,
(5) Lambert Tree leasehold, and (6) Richard High
Carleton and Everett H. Noyes, trustees, leasehold.

2. Mr. Beifeld agrees to take lease of Oriental
property and assignments or sub-leases of other property (as soon as the same can be conveniently prepared), beginning October 1, 1906, subject to existing
leases, and running for 97 years and 7 months. Annual ground rental to be $50,000 for first year, $56,000
for seven months, October 1, 1907, to May 1, 1908;
$96,000 per year from May 1, 1908, to May 1, 1910;
$98,000 per year from May 1, 1910, to May 1, 1915;
and $100,000 a year from May 1, 1915, to the end of
the lease. Rent payable in twelve equal installments,

monthly, in advance. Lessee to pay all taxes, assessments, charges, etc., levied or assessed for the year 1907, and thereafter during the term of said lease.

3. Lessee to build and complete by May 1, 1908, unless prevented by existing leases, and in any event not later than May 1, 1909, a modern fireproof building, built according to the city ordinances, not less than twelve stories high, and costing not less than $2,000,000. Architect's fees, ground rental for first year, and cost of cancellation of present leases of tenants in possession, to be considered as part of cost of said building. Architect to be Holabird & Roche, or some other architect approved by lessor. Plans and specifications to be submitted to and approved by lessor.

4. Concurrently with the execution and delivery of the lease of the Oriental property, as aforesaid, and the assignment of the other leases as above provided, Mr. Beifeld to deposit with the First Trust & Savings Bank, or such other trustee as may be mutually agreed upon, as security for the performance of the covenants and agreements in said leases and assignments, $530,-000 of White City stock; and when Mr. Beifeld takes possession of the properties so leased and assigned, but in no event later than October 1, 1906, he shall also deposit with said trustee, as further security for the performance of the covenants and agreements in said leases and assignments, $500,000 of acceptable securities at the bid cash market value, including not to exceed $250,000 of White City bonds at par. The $530,000 of White City stock to be held until the building is completed, furnished and equipped and the ground floor leases thereof assigned, and the securities now held by the University of Chicago and Bassett and Tree are released,—the other $500,000 of securities to be released in sums of $5,000, or multiples thereof, as the amounts so released have first been actually expended in the construction of the building, as shown by architect's certificates.

5. When not less than $1,000,000 has been expended in the construction of the building, and it has so far advanced that $1,000,000 will be sufficient to complete it, including all unpaid bills, the Illinois Life In-

surance Company agrees to buy, at par, the entire issue of $1,000,000 of 5 per cent. gold bonds (interest payable quarterly; bonds to be personally endorsed by Mr. Beifeld and of form acceptable to the purchaser) to be secured by a first mortgage on leasehold and building, furniture, fixtures and equipment, and assignment of ground floor leases; said bonds being payable, $50,000, January 1, 1913, and thereafter, serially, not less than $50,000 annually and in increasing amounts until 1930, when the last bond shall be due and payable. Said bonds are also to be further secured by insurance procured at expense of lessee on the building for an amount not exceeding $1,000,000 as may be required by the purchaser of said bonds, said insurance to be payable to the trustee, in addition to other insurance required by present leases; also by insurance on furniture and fixtures, all equipment not part of real estate, and rents of 1rst floor to an amount equal to 80 per cent. of the value of said rents; such policies to be deposited with the trustee. Said bonds are to be purchased and paid for from time to time as satisfactory showing is made that the cost of completing the building, including unpaid bills, is within the amount of bonds still unpaid for.

6. Assignments or sub-leases, above referred to, to be subject to, and conform in all respects with, original leases now existing upon said land. Said leases to be reassigned to Illinois Life Insurance Company as additional security for the covenants made by the lessee in contract of assignment and in lease on Oriental property,—such reassignment to be made subject to the rights of the mortgagee.

7. Illinois Life Insurance Company agrees to secure Mr. Beifeld that it will purchase the above $1,000,000 of bonds at par.

8. Forfeiture of one lease to forfeit all.

9. Lessor to use every possible effort in assisting Mr. Beifeld to secure the consent of University of Chicago to the erection of a hotel building.

10. In case lessee desires any part of the premises covered by the various leases hereinbefore referred to at a time earlier than October 1, 1906, he shall be permitted to have the same, subject to any and all ex-

isting leases thereon, upon payment to the Illinois Life Insurance Company of the same rental paid by the tenant in possession up to October 1, 1906.

Witness the execution hereof by the undersigned, this sixteenth day of April, A. D. 1906.

ILLINOIS LIFE INSURANCE COMPANY,

By James W. Stevens,

President.

(SEAL)

Attest:

Oswald J. Arnold,
Secretary.

JOSEPH BEIFELD."

The declaration then avers that after the execution of said contract the plaintiff "began and duly prosecuted the preparation of all things required of it under said contract," and was ready and willing and offered to fully perform the same on its part, and to prepare and execute all documents and do all things required of it by the terms of the contract; but that the defendant refused to perform the contract, and on June 25, 1906, notified the plaintiff that he would neither perform the contract nor accept performance thereof on the part of the plaintiff, "no matter in what form the various contracts, papers and instruments referred to in said contract should be executed or caused to be executed by said plaintiff." It is then averred that by reason of such refusal of the defendant the plaintiff was put to great cost and expense and lost divers large gains and profits, etc., to the damage of the plaintiff of $200,000.

After a demurrer to the declaration had been filed and overruled and nearly a year's time had been consumed in filing pleas and additional pleas, demurrers thereto, replications and rejoinders, a stipulation was filed wherein it was agreed that "for the purpose of permitting the defendant to take and have all lawful advantage of the judgment of the court on the question whether the declaration states any cause of action against the defendant which would sustain a verdict and judgment in favor of the plaintiff," all of the pleadings subsequent to the declaration should be withdrawn and that a general demurrer to the declaration should be filed "limited to the question of whether the declaration states any cause of action which would sustain a verdict and judgment in favor of the plaintiff, but shall not present the question of *ultra vires,* upon which the court has heretofore ruled in favor of the plaintiff." An order was entered in accordance with the stipulation, the general demurrer was filed and, after argument of counsel, was sustained. The plaintiff elected to stand by its declaration and a judgment for costs was thereupon entered against it, from which the plaintiff appeals.

TENNEY, COFFEEN, HARDING & SHERMAN, for appellant; HORACE KENT TENNEY and HARRY A. PARKIN, of counsel.

FELSENTHAL & BECKWITH, for appellee; ELI B. FELSENTHAL and WALTER J. SPENGLER, of counsel.

MR. PRESIDING JUSTICE FITCH delivered the opinion of the court.

The only question raised upon this appeal is whether the declaration states a good cause of action. On behalf of appellee, it is contended (1) that the instrument set forth in the declaration is not a contract, but is a mere memorandum, intended to serve as a skeleton or outline for the preparation of contracts to be thereafter agreed upon and executed; (2) that if the instrument can be considered as a contract, it is void for uncertainty; (3) that, as so considered, it is void for want of mutuality; (4) that, in any view, it is *ultra vires,* and void for that reason.

FIRST. As to the first of these contentions, the argument is, as we understand it, that because the memorandum, though signed by the parties, shows upon its face that a formal "contract of leasing" and formal assignments or subleases were to be subsequently prepared, and because it appears from the memorandum that but few of the usual covenants and conditions of ordinary leases are mentioned as having been agreed on, therefore it must be held that the memorandum was intended to be only an agreement to enter into another agreement, the precise terms and conditions of which were still undetermined at the time the memorandum was signed. We are unable to take this view of the matter. The memorandum shows that all the essential provisions of a valid lease and valid assignments had been in fact agreed on, and appellee therein "agrees to take" a lease containing those provisions "as soon as the same can be conveniently prepared." A lease for a term of years is a chattel real, and conveys an interest in the land demised. *People v. Shedd,* 241 Ill. 155, 165. So far as we are advised, it has never been held that a contract which provides for the conveyance of real estate by a warranty deed, or other specified instrument of conveyance, is an incomplete contract merely because it provides that such deed or instrument is to be subsequently prepared. Of course, if it is apparent from the language of the contract that some of the terms and conditions which are to be inserted in the instrument of conveyance are still unsettled and open for further negotiation, then the agreement to convey is incomplete because in such case there is no agreement in fact. But we do not think there is any language in the document under consideration that can be so construed. It speaks of appellant as the "lessor" and of appellee as the "lessee." It describes the property which is to be leased, the duration of the term, the rental, and the time and manner in which the rent shall be payable. It provides that the lessee shall pay "all taxes, assessments, charges, etc., levied or assessed for the year 1907 and thereafter during the term of said lease." The only "charges, etc.," which can be "levied or assessed" against real estate are taxes and special assessments.

It provides that the lessee shall build and complete
within a fixed time, a building of a specified type,
height and cost, and provides that architect's fees and
certain other expenses of building shall be included in
the cost. It provides further that "concurrently with
the execution and delivery of the lease," appellee shall
make certain deposits with a specified bank, "or such
other trustee as may be mutually agreed upon," as
security for the performance of the covenants of the
lessee. In this clause a way was left for a subsequent
agreement as to some other trustee than the one specifically mentioned, but that fact does not make the
contract incomplete, for the clear intention is that in
the absence of any such subsequent agreement the
trustee specified should act. Throughout the memorandum, the word "agrees" is used, indicating a present and not a future agreement. It is inconceivable
that the parties would go to the trouble of preparing
a document like this, and cause it to be formally signed,
on the part of the appellant corporation, by its president and secretary, and attested with the corporate
seal, and also to be signed in person by appellee, if
they intended it to be a mere memorandum for future
reference only, not binding upon either party except
in the event of a subsequent further agreement. We
think the memorandum thus prepared and signed must
be construed as a complete agreement to convey a
specified interest in the property described upon the
terms therein set forth, as soon as a formal instrument to that effect could be conveniently prepared for
the signature of the parties.

SECOND. As to the second contention above stated,
what we have already said applies with equal force
to the argument made upon this point. Appellee's
counsel have picked out sentences here and there,
which they claim are not sufficiently explicit to enable
a lawyer to so prepare a lease as to definitely provide
for all contingencies that might be suggested. It may
be conceded that the memorandum does not provide in

express terms for all possible contingencies, but that fact does not render the contract void for uncertainty. The document expresses the agreement of the parties in such form as to leave little room for doubt as to what was intended and what matters were in fact agreed upon; and that is enough to overcome the objection of uncertainty. The objection that it is uncertain whether assignments of existing leases, or subleases, should be prepared is immaterial, for as the whole term of existing leases was to be conveyed, subleases, if executed, would amount to the same thing in legal effect as assignments. *Lyon v. Moore,* 259 Ill. 23. It would unduly extend the limits of this opinion to take up and discuss each of the sentences. objected to on this ground, and it will suffice to say that after due consideration of the arguments advanced we think the objections are not well taken.

Third. It is argued at great length, and with much force, that an agreement by one party to "take" a lease does not, as a matter of law, impose any obligation on the other party to "give" such a lease. It is conceded that the courts may construe an obligation from the words used by the parties in a contract, but it is insisted that the language used in the memorandum in question is too plain for construction, and that to construe an obligation upon appellant to give a lease from words which only require appellee to take one, would be to create an obligation by implication. Some words are often used in a double sense, and others have more than one meaning. In order to arrive at the meaning of words used in a contract, the whole contract must be considered; and if, when so considered, the words employed have a signification other and different from the meaning conveyed by the same words when standing alone, it is the duty of the court to interpret the words used so as to give effect to the intention of the parties, if such intention clearly appears from all the language of the contract. In the memorandum in question, appellee "agrees to take

lease of Oriental property and assignments or subleases of other property (as soon as the same can be
conveniently prepared), beginning' October 1, 1906,
subject to existing leases, and running for 97 years
and 7 months," at a stipulated rental, and he also
agrees to deposit a large amount of securities "concurrently with the execution and delivery" of the
lease. One meaning of the word "take" is "to accept
as something offered; to receive; not to refuse or reject." (Webster's Dict.) Giving the word "take" this
meaning, and reading the phrase in which it is used
in connection with the other clauses above quoted, the
contract clearly imports a present agreement by Beifeld to *accept an offer made by appellant to execute
and deliver to him a lease* of the Oriental property and
assignments or subleases of the other property, as
soon as the same can be conveniently prepared. This
interpretation of the words used does not *create* an
obligation by implication, but construes the contract
so as to give effect to the intention of the parties, as
shown by the language employed. It is impossible to
read the memorandum in question without being im-
pressed with the view that the parties thereby intended to state, not only in substance but in detail, the
terms and conditions of a lease which they agreed
should be at once prepared and executed by appellant,
and accepted by appellee. In principle, the memorandum in this case is like the contracts construed in
Minnesota Lumber Co. v. Whitebreast Coal Co., 160
Ill. 85; *Torrence v. Shedd*, 156 Ill. 194, and *Sanitary
Dist. of Chicago v. McMahon & Montgomery Co.*, 110
Ill. App. 510. We are of the opinion that the contract
imposed mutual obligations, in consideration of the
mutual promises therein contained.

FOURTH. A more difficult question, in our opinion,
is presented by the contention that the contract was
ultra vires. No claim is made in this court that the
term of the lease contracted for extends beyond the
corporate life of appellant. Whether such is or is not

the fact does not appear; and whether that fact, if true, would affect the question here presented is not discussed by counsel. The contention as made here is that the making of a lease, for ninety-seven years, of property which a life insurance corporation has lawfully acquired but which becomes unnecessary for the transaction of its business, is beyond the power of such a corporation to make, because of the language of the statute permitting such corporation to own only "so much real and personal estate as shall be necessary for the transaction of its business, and to sell and dispose of the same when deemed necessary." (Hurd's St. 1911, ch. 73, ¶ 182, J. & A. ¶ 6460.)

It is alleged in the declaration that all the property mentioned in the memorandum contract had been acquired by appellant "for the purpose of carrying on the business for which it was incorporated." This allegation is admitted by the demurrer. Having lawfully acquired such property, if it may be held, as we think it may, that the execution of the memorandum contract is *prima facie* evidence of the fact that the property in question was deemed to be no longer necessary for the transaction of its business, then the only question as to the power of the corporation to make such a contract is whether the power given by the statute to "sell and dispose of" such real estate precludes appellant from making a lease of the same for ninety-seven years and seven months.

It is contended by appellee's counsel that the words "dispose of," as used in the statute, must be construed to apply only to transactions that are in their nature equivalent to sales; to which contention appellant's counsel reply that to give those words the same meaning as the word "sell" would be to read the statute "to sell and to sell," thereby giving to the words "dispose of" the effect of mere repetition. Appellant's counsel contend that the making of such a lease as the contract provides for does, in effect, "dispose of" the property. We think that neither of these contentions is entirely sound. The phrase "to dispose of" has two meanings; one is "to exercise the power of control over;" the other is "to exercise *finally* one's power of control over; to alienate." (Webster's Dict.) Clearly, the latter of these meanings is the one in which the phrase is used in the statute. As thus construed, the statute gave to appellant the right to sell and *alienate* the property in question; or, in other words, to sell and convey the same by proper instruments of conveyance. But the statute does not require a corporation having property which is no longer required for the transaction of its business to *immediately* sell and convey the same. It may, undoubtedly, hold such property a reasonable time, in order that the same may be sold to advantage. Under some statutes relating to corporations, a time limit of five years is fixed. As to life insurance companies, by an act passed *after* this contract was entered into, it was provided that such property shall be "sold and disposed of" within five years after the same shall have ceased to be necessary for the accommodation of the business of the corporation, unless a certificate is obtained from the insurance superintendent extending the time. Hurd's Stat. 1909, p. 1312. (J. & A. ¶ 6507.) It is unnecessary to decide whether these statutes must be considered in determining the rights and powers of appellant. Assuming that to be true, it would be absurd to say that during the five years' limitation, if an insurance company should be unable to find a buyer for such property, it must suffer its property to remain vacant and unoccupied, bringing no return and entailing constant expense in carrying the same. The fact that property is leased does not *prevent* a sale of it. On the contrary, it is a matter of common knowledge that property which is advantageously leased is frequently more salable because of that fact. So the mere making of a lease for ninety-seven years does not prevent a sale of the property. Such a lease might, and probably would, in many cases, give a value to the fee which it would not otherwise possess. If such a lease were to be made as a part of a plan adopted by a corporation for the purpose of effecting a more advantageous sale of its unnecessary real estate, there would seem to be no question of its right and power under the statute to do so. This being true, it follows that whether appellant had, or had not, such a plan and purpose in view, when it made the contract for such a lease, is not a question of power but a question of its intention, or good faith, in exercising a power which it had the right under some circumstances, to exercise. Where an alleged *ultra vires* contract is one which the corporation was not, under any circumstances, authorized to perform, it is void and may be attacked anywhere, by any one. *National Home Building & Loan Ass'n v. Home Sav. Bank,* 181 Ill. 35. But where the validity of the contract depends upon the question whether the corporation has abused, or unjustifiably used, a power which it had the right to exercise, if exercised in good faith, then only the State can attack it. *Rector v. Hartford Deposit Co.,* 190 Ill. 380. In any view, however, the facts stated in the declaration do not raise the presumption that appellant intended to continue to hold its real estate in violation of the statute. We therefore conclude that the objection of *ultra vires* cannot prevail in this case.

For the reasons indicated, we think the demurrer to the declaration should have been overruled. The judgment of the Superior Court will, therefore, be reversed and remanded with directions to that court to overrule the demurrer.

Reversed and remanded with directions.

In the Matter of the Petition of John Jacob Meyer.
On Appeal of John Jacob Meyer, Appellant, v. Bertha Kurz, Appellee.

Gen. No. 18,813.   (Not to be reported in full.)

Appeal from the County Court of Cook county; the Hon. JOHN E. OWENS, Judge, presiding. Heard in the Branch Appellate Court at the October term, 1912. Affirmed. Opinion filed January 22, 1914.

Statement of the Case.

Petition by John Jacob Meyer to the County Court under the Insolvent Debtors' Act, for a discharge from custody under a *capias ad satisfaciendum* issued upon a judgment recovered against him by Bertha Kurz in an action for slander. From a judgment denying the petition, the petitioner, John Jacob Meyer, appeals.

GEORGE REMUS, for appellant.

SALTIEL & ROSSEN, for appellee.

MR. PRESIDING JUSTICE FITCH delivered the opinion of the court.

Abstract of the Decision.

1. EXECUTION, § 302*—*admissibility of evidence on petition under Insolvent Debtors' Act for discharge from custody under a capias ad satisfaciendum.* On petition to the County Court for a discharge under the Insolvent Debtors' Act, J. & A. ¶ 6199, where petitioner had been arrested upon a *capias ad satisfaciendum* issued upon a judgment entered by default against him in an action for slander in which the words alleged to have been uttered were actionable *per se*, refusal of court to hear evidence *dehors* the records to prove that the words were not uttered maliciously, *held* proper for the reason that the question whether malice was the gist of the action must be determined solely from the record of the slander suit.

*See Illinois Notes Digest, Vols. XI to XV, same topic and section number.

2. EXECUTION, § 295*—*when record of action for slander conclusive on petition for discharge under Insolvent Debtors' Act.* Where a default judgment is entered against the defendant in an action for slander for words spoken which are actionable *per se,* the words spoken are admitted to be false by the default, and that they were maliciously uttered is conclusively presumed from the facts thus admitted and from the absence of any plea of justification or excuse.

3. LIBEL AND SLANDER, § 21*—*when malice presumed.* In an action for slander if the words charged to have been falsely uttered are not actionable *per se,* it is necessary to prove malice in fact; but if the words spoken are actionable *per se* then the law conclusively implies malice from the use of such words if false and uttered without legal justification or excuse.

4. LIBEL AND SLANDER, § 31*—*when imputation of theft actionable per se.* The words, "this woman has stolen the watch and chain belonging to my son," are actionable *per se.*

Hattie Isabella McLaughlin, Defendant in Error, v. National Protective Legion, Plaintiff in Error.

Gen. No. 18,563.   (Not to be reported in full.)

Error to the Municipal Court of Chicago; the Hon. EDWIN K. WALKER, Judge, presiding. Heard in the Branch Appellate Court at the October term, 1912. Affirmed. Opinion filed January 22, 1914.

. Statement of the Case.

Action by Hattie Isabella McLaughlin against National Protective Legion to recover the sum of five hundred dollars claimed to be due her on a policy of insurance in which she had been named beneficiary and which had been issued by defendant upon the life of plaintiff's husband, Patrick McLaughlin. From a judgment in favor of plaintiff for five hundred dollars, defendant brings error.

BERTRAND LICHTENBERGER, for plaintiff in error.

EMIL A. MEYER, for defendant in error.

*See Illinois Notes Digest, Vols. XI to XV, same topic and section number.

MR. JUSTICE GRIDLEY delivered the opinion of the court.

Abstract of the Decision.

1. INSURANCE, § 664*—*when evidence insufficient to show forfeiture for failure to pay assessments in time.* In an action by a beneficiary on a policy of insurance where the defense is that the insured had been suspended for failure to pay certain monthly assessments in the time required by the provisions of the policy, a verdict in favor of plaintiff *held* to be sustained by the law and the evidence, it appearing that plaintiff had made payments to an agent of the defendant having apparent authority to make collections and that plaintiff had money to her credit in the hands of the defendant in excess of the amount necessary to pay all assessments for the months in question when they became due.

2. INSURANCE, § 611*—*burden of proving facts constituting a forfeiture.* The burden of showing a failure to pay assessments from which a forfeiture is claimed to have arisen is upon the insurer.

3. PAYMENT, § 28*—*when receipt admissible in evidence.* In an action on an insurance policy, admission in evidence of receipts given by an agent having apparent authority to collect assessments *held* not error, for the reason that no reference to the policy sued on appears on their face where they are introduced in connection with plaintiff's testimony explaining them.

Wallace C. Abbott, Defendant in Error, v. Carl A. Anderson et al., Plaintiffs in Error.

Gen. No. 18,630.

1. BANKRUPTCY, § 59*—*when discharge of partnership in bankruptcy releases individual partners.* Where a bankruptcy court adjudicated a partnership a bankrupt without adjudicating as bankrupts the individual members thereof or requiring them to file schedules of their individual property and entered a judgment confirming a composition agreement whereby the partnership creditors were paid seventy-five cents on the dollar, *held* that not only was the indebtedness of the partnership discharged but the individual partners were also discharged from the payment of such indebtedness, and that the partnership creditors had no right to pursue the

adjudicated partners by actions at law or in equity to recover the
deficiency upon their claims.

2. BANKRUPTCY, § 54*—*conclusiveness of judgment of bankruptcy
court.* A judgment of a bankruptcy court adjudicating a partnership a bankrupt and confirming a composition agreement without
adjudging the members of the partnership individually bankrupt is
res adjudicata until reversed in a direct proceeding, and cannot
be collaterally attacked as not being a valid discharge of the partnership without an individual adjudication in bankruptcy of the
members thereof.

3. BANKRUPTCY, § 55*—*effect of interlocutory order as construing decision of bankruptcy court.* On adjudication of a partnership
as a bankrupt, an interlocutory order of the bankruptcy court approving a referee's report recommending that a proviso to the composition agreement should be withdrawn because it deprived creditors of the right to proceed against the individual partners for deficiencies, is not conclusive to show that the court decided that the
partners were to remain individually liable.

4. ESTOPPEL, § 6*—*when acts of parties in bankruptcy do not
create an estoppel.* Where upon the adjudication of a partnership
in bankruptcy the referee's report recommended that a proviso to
the composition agreement should be withdrawn to give partnership
creditors the right to proceed against the individual partners for
deficiencies, and the court by an interlocutory order approved such
report, *held* that the fact that the partners withdrew such proviso
did not estop them from denying their individual liability for the
deficiencies.

5. INJUNCTION, § 15*—*when issues to restrain suits against partners discharged in bankruptcy.* Permanent injunction will issue
to restrain partnership creditors from bringing suits against individual copartners released from payment of partnership debts by
a discharge of the partnership in bankruptcy.

Error to the Circuit Court of Cook county; the Hon. CHARLES M.
WALKER, Judge, presiding. Heard in the Branch Appellate Court
at the October term, 1912. Affirmed. Opinion filed January 22,
1914. *Certiorari* granted by Supreme Court.

Statement by the Court. Plaintiffs in error, defendants below, seek by this writ to reverse a decree
of the Circuit Court of Cook county, entered March
21, 1911, by which they were perpetually enjoined from
further prosecuting certain suits severally brought by
them in the Municipal Court of Chicago, and from be-

ginning any suits at law or in equity against the defendant in error, complainant below, for the recovery of any indebtedness which they or any of them, as creditors of the Ravenswood Exchange Bank, a copartnership, claimed to be due from complainant as a former member of said copartnership.

Complainant's amended bill was filed on January 23, 1909, and complainant alleged therein, in substance, that on and prior to February 25, 1908, complainant and nine other individuals were associated together as copartners in conducting a banking business at Ravenswood, Chicago, under the name and style of "Ravenswood Exchange Bank;" that the number of the depositors in the bank exceeded 2,000; that on said date certain of those depositors, exceeding three in number and whose claims in the aggregate exceeded $500, etc., filed a petition in bankruptcy in the United States District Court for the Northern District of Illinois, Eastern Division, against complainant and said nine others, "copartners, trading as Ravenswood Exchange Bank," alleging that they were insolvent and that they, as such copartners, had committed certain acts of bankruptcy, and praying for the service of a subpoena upon them and that the "copartnership" might be adjudged bankrupt; that thereafter complainant and said nine others duly appeared in said proceedings and on March 31, 1908, by order of said court, complainant and said nine others, "copartners, trading as Ravenswood Exchange Bank," were "declared and adjudged bankrupt;" that thereafter, at the first meeting of the creditors of said copartnership, complainant and said nine others were examined in open court and they filed in court a schedule of property and a list of creditors; that thereafter complainant and said copartners offered terms of composition to the creditors of said copartnership, to wit, an amount sufficient to pay all of them seventy-five cents on the dollar of their respective claims; that said offer of composition was thereafter duly accepted in writing by a majority in number of all the creditors of said copartnership whose claims were allowed, which number represented a majority in amount of such claims; that application was thereafter made for the confirmation of said composition, to which objections were filed and a hearing thereupon had; that thereafter on June 10, 1908, an order was entered by said United States Court confirming said composition, and that the consideration for said composition was duly deposited in court, and said composition is now in full force and effect; that all of the creditors of said copartnership, including the defendants, have been paid the full amount of seventy-five cents upon the dollar of their respective claims pursuant to the terms of said composition; that by virtue of the Bankruptcy Act of 1898, and the amendments thereto, upon the confirmation of said offer of composition, the bankruptcy proceedings terminated and all of the indebtedness of the partnership was discharged and wiped out, and that complainant and his copartners were also individually discharged from the payment of the indebtedness of said copartnership.

The complainant further alleged in said bill, in substance, that notwithstanding the fact that complainant and his copartners, by virtue of said bankruptcy proceedings, had been discharged from all liability for the indebtedness of the copartnership, certain of the defendants to this bill, who were depositors in said bank on and prior to said February 25, 1908, have recently brought separate and independent actions at law against complainant and said copartners in the Municipal Court of Chicago, seeking thereby to recover the balance of twenty-five per cent. of their respective original claims against said Ravenswood Exchange Bank; that all of the creditors who have so commenced said suits appeared in said bankruptcy proceedings and proved their claims and received in full their respective dividends by virtue of said composition; that other defendants to this bill have threatened to bring suits at law of like character against complainant and said copartners, and complainant fears that these threats will be carried into execution; that the suits pending involve the sum of about $3,000, and that the claims of the other defendants who are threatening suit amount to about $15,000; that the respective claims of all of the defendants were filed in said bankruptcy proceedings and were allowed and said allowance constitutes an adjudication as to the respective amounts thereof; that the sole question of law involved in all of said suits at law, those brought and those threatened to be brought, is the *effect* of said judgment of said bankruptcy court confirming said composition, as to complainant and said copartners, upon the indebtedness of said copartnership firm, and that to prevent needless expense and a multiplicity of suits a court of equity should decide the question. The complainant offered to indemnify the defendants against any loss and damage which they might suffer by reason of delay in case of their being enjoined from prosecuting or bringing said suits until the determination of the present suit, and further offered, in case the court should find him liable to the defendants, to pay any amount decreed to be due from him. The bill prayed that the defendants and all other depositors of said Ravenswood Exchange Bank might be restrained from prosecuting or bringing said suits; that the claims of said defendants and all other depositors might be decreed to have been wholly discharged by virtue of the confirmation of said composition, and that said defendants and all other creditors of said bank be required to litigate in this suit the question of the liability of complainant and his copartners to' them, etc.

Demurrers to the bill were overruled, but no point is now here made that said Circuit Court erred in not dismissing the bill on the ground that the defendants were entitled to a trial of the issues in a court of law. One of the defendants, Carl A. Anderson, filed a lengthy answer to the bill, which answer was adopted by the other defendants, and the cause was put at issue.

It appears from the evidence, heard in open court before the chancellor, that the Ravenswood Exchange Bank was a joint stock association, or copartnership; that prior to the filing of said petition in bankruptcy a receiver was in charge of the assets of the bank, appointed by order of the Circuit Court of Cook county on or about November 12, 1907; that after the filing of said petition the administration of the affairs of the bank was transferred from said Circuit Court to said United States Court; that when said petition was filed the complainant and said nine others were the only shareholders or copartners of the bank, called "present partners"; that prior to the appointment of said receiver in November, 1907, there had been other shareholders, called "past partners," who had retired from the copartnership by the transfer of their shares of stock; that after the appointment of said receiver an attempt was made by said past and present partners to bring about a common law composition with the creditors of the bank; that a certain Realization Company agreed to assist in bringing about such a settlement but required that large contributions be made to it in cash; that several of said past partners, under the belief that they might be held to some extent liable with the present partners for the indebtedness of the bank, made contributions to this fund; that the effect of the filing of said petition in bankruptcy was to retard but did not terminate the efforts of said Realization Company to bring about a composition with the creditors of the bank, and that through its efforts and assistance the money necessary to be deposited for said bankruptcy composition was deposited in court, the Realization Company taking as security for the money advanced by it a conveyance of the assets of the bank.

It further appears from the evidence, or from the stipulations of respective counsel in evidence, that

after complainant and said nine others, "copartners
trading as Ravenswood Exchange Bank," had been by
the court adjudged bankrupt, from which judgment no
appeal was taken, they were, at the first meeting of
the creditors of said copartnership, examined as to
the copartnership assets and liabilities, and also as to
their individual assets and liabilities, and that schedules of the property of the copartnership and a list of
the creditors thereof were filed; that these schedules
did not contain, or purport to contain, any of the individual property of said copartners, and that none of
said copartners at any time either filed or offered to
file schedules of their individual property or a list of
their individual creditors, and that no attempt was
made by defendants or any of the creditors of said
copartnership to compel them so to do, and that neither
complainant nor any of his copartners were at any
time *individually* adjudged bankrupt. It is not disclosed from the evidence whether, from said examination of said copartners at said first meeting of the
creditors of the copartnership, it was ascertained that
the assets of the copartnership, plus the individual
assets of the copartners in excess of their individual
debts, were sufficient or insufficient to pay the partnership debts. A stipulation by counsel is in evidence
that, pending the hearing of the offer of composition,
complainant was further examined, and from all examinations it appeared that "a few of said individual
partners, including complainant, were men of some
pecuniary means individually." It further appears
from the evidence that on April 17, 1908, the "Ravenswood Exchange Bank, the above named bankrupt,"
offered to its creditors terms of composition, whereby
it agreed to pay or cause to be paid to its creditors,
upon such composition being confirmed by the court,
seventy-five per cent. of their respective claims, together with all costs and expenses of administration in
the United States Court and in said Circuit Court, but
said offer contained a proviso that "said creditors and

each of them do expressly accept said composition payment in full satisfaction and discharge * * * of their several respective claims against said Ravenswood Exchange Bank, *or against any of its past or present members, stockholders, shareholders, officers and directors.*" On April 20, 1908, the bankrupt firm filed a petition praying that said offer of composition be confirmed. This petition was referred to Referee Eastman, as a special master, and he was directed to give notice to the creditors, to hear any objections which might be filed, and to take proofs and to report his conclusions and recommendations to the court. Some of the defendants to the present bill filed written objections to the confirmation of said offer to the effect that, inasmuch as no one of said copartners as to his individual estate had been adjudicated a bankrupt, the court had no jurisdiction over the individual estates of the copartners, or, in other words, had no jurisdiction of any of the "past or present members, stockholders," etc., and was, therefore, without power to confirm the offer of composition as made. On May 12, 1908, the referee, as such special master, filed a lengthy report in which, in conclusion, he recommended to the court that the offer of composition "be denied submission unless the bankrupt firm elects, within a reasonable time to be fixed by the court, to strike out from its offer the proviso in question." The referee stated in said report, in substance, that in his opinion, under the authority of the case of *In re Bertenshaw,* 85 C. C. A. 61, 157 Fed. 363, decided November 19, 1907, by the United States Court of Appeals for the Eighth Circuit, a partnership is a distinct entity by reason of the provisions of the Bankruptcy Act of 1898, in other words, a "person" separate from the partners who compose it; that the adjudication in bankruptcy of a copartnership does not draw after it the adjudication of the partners themselves; that a court of bankruptcy has no jurisdiction to summarily take and administer in proceedings against a partnership the individual estate of the solvent partners without their consent; and that the result is that, upon the approval of an offer of composition by a bankrupt partnership, the partnership creditors have a right to pursue the unadjudicated partners by actions at law and suits in equity in appropriate courts for the deficiencies owing them. The referee further stated in said report that in his opinion the proviso in said offer of composition was unlawful, in that it might possibly deprive "a minority and objecting creditor" of the above mentioned right, which the law gave him, in case the offer of composition was confirmed as made, and that even if the proviso would not militate against objecting creditors pursuing their remedies to collect their deficiencies, it would at least be a doubtful question as to whether those creditors, who had accepted in writing the offer as made, would not be estopped from suing for their deficiencies, "which would leave the result, if it were so, of two classes of creditors, one with a right of action over to collect their deficiencies and the others without."

On the same day, May 12, 1908, the United States Court entered an order that, upon consideration of the said report of the referee as special master, and after hearing arguments of counsel for the different parties in interest, "said report be approved," and the court further ordered, upon motion of said bankrupt, that "said bankrupt have and leave is hereby given to it to modify its offer of terms of composition heretofore made by withdrawing therefrom and striking out of said offer" the proviso above mentioned.

On the same day, also, the "Ravenswood Exchange Bank, the above named bankrupt," by its attorneys, filed a written modification of its offer of composition, "withdrawing from said offer" the said proviso.

On June 10, 1908, said referee as special master filed in court his final report in which he stated, *inter alia,* that objections had been filed to the composition by many creditors; that certain legal points were pre-

sented by specifications on which elaborate arguments
were made by respective counsel; that he had made an
"interlocutory report" to the court which report had
been confirmed and the offer of composition modified
to meet the objections; that thereafter a lengthy hearing was had on the facts, and that "at this time appear the objectors by their counsel and withdraw the
further prosecution of their objections and consent to
the offer of composition as made." In this report the
referee found that the offer of composition had been
accepted by a majority in number and amount of creditors whose claims were filed, that sufficient money had
been deposited, etc., that it was for the best interests
of the creditors that the composition be confirmed, etc.
On the same day the United States Court approved
this report, entered an order expressly finding that the
composition (i. e. as modified) was for the best interests of the creditors, etc., and adjudging that "said
composition be and it hereby is confirmed."

The Circuit Court, in the present case, found in its
decree that by said order of the United States Court,
entered June 10, 1908, the said composition was confirmed and that the same was in full force and effect;
that all the creditors of said copartnership, including
all of the defendants herein, had received the full
amount of seventy-five cents on the dollar upon their
respective claims pursuant to the terms of said composition; that upon the confirmation of said composition said bankruptcy proceedings terminated, and that
all the indebtedness of said copartnership was discharged and wiped out, and that complainant and his
said copartners were also individually discharged
from the payment of the indebtedness of said copartnership firm, and that the creditors of said copartnership ceased to have any further claims or demands
against it and to have any further claim or demand
against any of the individual members thereof, including the complainant, for the copartnership indebted-

ness or obligations; that all of the material allegations of the amended bill were true, that the equities were with the complainant and that the complainant had no adequate remedy at law. The court decreed that the complainant was not indebted to any of the defendants herein, or to any depositor of said bank, arising out of any indebtedness or obligation of said bank to any of the defendants or to any such depositor, and ordered the issuance of the perpetual injunction, as first above mentioned.

HUBERT E. PAGE and NEWTON WYETH, for plaintiffs in error.

HERMAN FRANK and HARRY J. LURIE, for defendant in error.

MR. JUSTICE GRIDLEY delivered the opinion of the court.

Section 14c of the Bankruptcy Act of 1898 provides that "the confirmation of a composition shall discharge the bankrupt from his debts, other than those agreed to be paid by the terms of the composition and those not affected by a discharge." It appears from the evidence in this case that in an involuntary proceeding in bankruptcy on the ground of insolvency the complainant and nine other persons, "copartners trading as Ravenswood Exchange Bank" were, on March 31, 1908, adjudged bankrupt by said United States District Court, that the copartnership subsequently offered terms of composition to its creditors, to wit, seventy-five cents on the dollar of their respective claims, which offer was accepted by a majority of those creditors in number and amount, and that on June 10, 1908, the composition was confirmed by said court. Counsel for defendant, relying on the so-called "entity theory" of a partnership and particularly on the case of *In re Bertenshaw*, 85 C. C. A. 61, 157 Fed. 363, contend that a partnership can be adjudged a bankrupt and discharged in bankruptcy without the adjudication individually of the members composing that partnership, and that in such case said members will not be individually discharged from the partnership debts. And counsel argue that, in the present case, where it appears from the evidence that complainant and a few of his partners were men of some pecuniary means individually and none of them were *individually* adjudged bankrupt and none of them either filed or offered to file schedules of their individual property or a list of their individual creditors, and where it further appears that an offer of composition was made by the partnership, Ravenswood Exchange Bank, and confirmed by the bankruptcy court, the *effect* of that judgment of confirmation is not to discharge complainant and his partners from the debts of the partnership, but that they are still liable to each creditor of the partnership for the amount of his claim less the sum received by virtue of said composition proceedings, and that the Circuit Court erred in entering the decree in this case. Counsel for complainant contend on the contrary that a discharge in bankruptcy of a partnership, whether by way of composition or otherwise, operates not only to release the partnership but also the individual partners from the debts of the partnership, and that in this case complainant and his co-partners are now under no liability to the defendants, and that the decree should be affirmed.

Shortly before the bankruptcy proceedings in question were commenced, the case of *In re Bertenshaw*, 85 C. C. A. 61, 157 Fed. 363, was, on November 19, 1907, decided by the United States Court of Appeals for the Eighth Circuit. The exhaustive opinion of the court was written by Judge Sanborn, and it was therein decided, as we read that opinion, that under the Bankruptcy Act of 1898 a partnership is a distinct entity, i. e. a "person," separate from the partners who compose it; that the partners and their individual property are to a limited extent sureties for

the debts of the partnership; that the partnership may
be adjudged bankrupt although the partners who compose it are not individually so adjudicated; that in
such event the individual estate of a solvent partner
is not drawn into the proceedings, and the bankruptcy
court is without jurisdiction to summarily take and
administer in the proceedings against the partnership
such individual estate without that partner's consent;
that in such event, also, the partnership creditors may
pursue unadjudicated partners by actions at law and
suits in equity before, during and *after* the proceedings in bankruptcy against the partnership; and that
the discharge of the partnership, where the partners
are not individually adjudged bankrupt, does not discharge the partners from their liability for the debts
of the partnership. In the dissenting opinion of Judge
Hook it was stated that portions of the majority opinion were at variance with principles enunciated in the
prior cases of *Dickas v. Barnes,* 72 C. C. A. 261, 140
Fed. 849; *In re Meyer,* 39 C. C. A. 368, 98 Fed. 976,
and *In re Stokes,* 106 Fed. 312. And we think that
portions of said majority opinion were also at variance
with principles enunciated in the other prior cases of
In re Forbes, 128 Fed. 137, 139, and *Vaccaro v. Security Bank of Memphis,* 43 C. C. A. 279, 103 Fed. 436,
442.

About two weeks before the decree in the present
case was entered by the Circuit Court of Cook county,
the opinion of the United States Court of Appeals, for
the Third Circuit, in the case of *Francis v. McNeal,* 108
C. C. A. 459, 186 Fed. 481, was on March 7, 1911, filed.
In that case, in the District Court, a partnership had
been adjudicated a bankrupt. Francis there contended
that he was not a partner but the court after a hearing found otherwise. On petition of the trustee in
bankruptcy, the District Court entered an order, adjudging that Francis' separate estate was subject to
administration by the trustee of a bankrupt partnership and directing him to deliver his property to the

trustee for the purpose of such administration. This order was affirmed by the Court of Appeals, and in the course of its opinion the Court said (p. 484): "If the act charged be one involving insolvency, since every partner is liable in solido for all the partnership debts, the adjudication against the partnership must be based on allegations and proof that the assets of its members, in excess of their individual debts, plus the assets of the partnership, are insufficient to pay the partnership debts. Otherwise there is no partnership insolvency, notwithstanding the entity doctrine." (Citing cases.) And the Court further said (p. 485, italics ours): "In an involuntary proceeding, where the act of bankruptcy charged is one that does involve insolvency of the partnership, there can be no adjudication against the partnership, unless it and all its members are insolvent; and that in such a case, though the adjudication be against the partnership only, or against the partnership and some, but not all, of its members, *the estates of all the members are drawn into the proceeding for administration.*" One of the cases cited in the above opinion was that of *In re Forbes, supra.* In this case Judge Lowell, of the United States District Court for Massachusetts, said (128 Fed. 137, 139, italics ours): "The equal and equitable distribution of the estates of insolvents *and their discharge* from the obligation of their debts are the ends sought by proceedings in bankruptcy. Bankruptcy, without insolvency, actual or presumed, is almost inconceivable. Bankruptcy without discharge for the honest debtor is a contradiction in terms. It is impossible to declare a partnership insolvent so long as the partners are able to pay its debts and theirs, whether out of joint or separate estate. * * * Not the insolvency of any imaginary entity, as in the case of a corporation, but the insolvency of its human component parts, lies at the foundation of the bankruptcy of a partnership. * * * As the bankruptcy of a partnership begins with an inquiry into the condition *of its individual* *partners, the end of the proceedings is normally their discharge.* So far as I know, the discharge of a partnership as an entity has never been suggested, and what would be the effect of such a discharge can hardly be imagined. Herein appears the difference between a partnership and a corporation. Under an adjudication merely joint, it is impossible to discharge the partners as individuals, even from their joint debts, for every joint debt of the partnership is also a separate debt of each partner, and separate debts can be discharged only after an individual adjudication operating upon the separate estate.''

The case of *Francis v. McNeal* was taken to the Supreme Court of the United States and that court affirmed the decisions of the District Court and the Court of Appeals. In the opinion, filed May 26, 1913 (228 U. S. 695), Mr. Justice Holmes referred to the opinion of Judge Lowell in the *Forbes* case, *supra,* as an "able opinion" and stated that, so far as the *Vaccaro v. Security Bank* case, *supra,* was inconsistent with the opinion of the majority in the *Bertenshaw* case, *supra,* he regarded the former "as sustained by the stronger reasons and as correct." The learned Justice further said (p. 699, italics ours): "The notion that the firm is an entity distinct from its members has grown in popularity. * * * But the fact remains as true as ever that partnership debts are debts of the members of the firm, and that *the individual liability of the members is not collateral like that of a surety, but primary and direct,* whatever priorities there may be in the marshalling of assets. The nature of the liability is determined by the common law, not by the possible intervention of the Bankruptcy Act.'' He further said (p. 701): "It would be an anomaly to allow proceedings in bankruptcy against joint debtors from some of whom, at any time before, pending, or after the proceeding, the debt could be collected in full. If such proceedings were allowed it would be a further anomaly not to distribute all the partnership assets. Yet the individual estate after paying private debts is part of those assets so far as needed. Section 5f. Finally, *it would be a third incongruity to grant a discharge in such a case from the debt considered as joint but to leave the same persons liable for it considered as several.* We say the same persons, for however much the difference between firm and member under the statute be dwelt upon, *the firm remains at common law a group of men and will be dealt with as such in the ordinary courts for use in which the discharge is granted.*"

It thus appears that some of the principles enunciated in the *Bertenshaw* case, *supra,* upon which case counsel for defendants rely to support their contention, are not sustained by the current of authority or by the recent decision of the Supreme Court of the United States in the case of *Francis v. McNeal, supra.*

Counsel for defendants further contended during the oral argument before us that, if the entity theory of a partnership to the extent as urged by them must be given up, there can be no *valid* discharge of a partnership firm without an *individual* adjudication in bankruptcy of the members thereof. Counsel direct our attention to the statement contained in the opinion in the *Forbes* case, *supra,* that "under an adjudication merely joint it is *impossible* to discharge the partners as individuals." In our opinion this position amounts to a collateral attack on the judgment of the bankruptcy court confirming the composition and is untenable. The bankruptcy court had *jurisdiction* to enter the order, even admitting for the sake of the argument only, that it may have *erred* in so doing without previously having adjudged the members of the partnership individually bankrupt. No appeal was taken from that order and, until reversed in a direct proceeding, it is *res adjudicata. Young v. Lorain,* 11 Ill. 624; *People v. Seelye,* 146 Ill. 189, 221; *Sumner v. Village of Milford,* 214 Ill. 388, 393; *Waller v. Village of River*

Forest, 259 Ill. 223, 230. A certified copy of the order was introduced in evidence in the present case. And by section 21f of the Bankruptcy Act it is provided that "a certified copy of an order confirming or setting aside a composition, * * * not revoked, shall be evidence of the jurisdiction of the court, the *regularity of the proceedings,* and of the fact that the order was made."

Our conclusion, therefore, is that the Circuit Court did not err in finding in its decree that by said order of the bankruptcy court complainant and his copartners were released from the payment of the indebtedness of the copartnership, Ravenswood Exchange Bank, and in issuing the permanent injunction mentioned. By section 14c of the Bankruptcy Act the order confirming the composition discharged "the bankrupt from his debts," and as stated in the Supreme Court opinion in *Francis v. McNeal, supra,* "the firm remains at common law a group of men and will be dealt with as such in the ordinary courts for use in which the discharge is granted." And while it is provided by section 16 of the Bankruptcy Act that the liability of a person "in any manner as surety for a bankrupt" shall not be altered by the discharge of such bankrupt, it is decided in said *Francis v. McNeal* case that the individual liability of the members of the firm "is not collateral like that of a surety, but primary and direct."

But counsel for defendants further contend that the question, whether complainant and his copartners after confirmation of the composition would remain individually liable to the defendants for the deficiencies on their respective claims, was decided by the bankruptcy court, that that decision was that the partners would remain so liable, and that, no matter how erroneous the same may have been, no appeal having been taken from it, the decision is now *res adjudicata.* Counsel's argument, as we understand it, is to the effect that the original offer of composition contained the proviso that the acceptance of the offer would discharge the past and present partners; that objections to the offer were made by some of the present defendants; that after a full hearing the special master reported to the bankruptcy court, recommending that the offer be denied submission unless the bankrupt firm would withdraw the proviso; that in said report the master stated certain reasons for his recommendation, and further stated that in his opinion, upon the confirmation of the offer of composition of the firm, the creditors of the firm could collect the deficiencies on their claims from the individual partners; that on May 12, 1908, this report was approved by order of the bankruptcy court; that the court gave the bankrupt firm leave to withdraw the proviso; that the bankrupt firm did not appeal from this ruling but on the contrary withdrew the proviso, thereby acquiescing in the ruling of the court and thereby acknowledging that a confirmation of the composition offer as modified would not release the partners of the firm from their individual liability for the deficiencies on the claims of the firm's creditors; and that, hence, the partners are now *estopped* by the judgment of the bankruptcy court from denying their individual liability for said deficiencies.

We cannot agree with counsel's contention. The order of May 12th of the bankruptcy court was not a final order but an interlocutory one, and it did not purport to decide the question here involved. "The character of conclusiveness, by way of estoppel, attaches only to final judgments, not to interlocutory judgments or orders, which remain under the control of the court, except where they dispose finally of some distinct branch or part of the case, or are appealable as being orders affecting the substantial rights of the parties." (23 Cyc. 1232.) All that the master said in the report as to his opinion of the law was not so decided by the court (23 Cyc. 1227). Furthermore, we do not think the order was an appealable one (*In re*

McVoy Hardware Co., 119 C. C. A. 337, 200 Fed. 949).
And no investigation had then been made by the judge
to determine whether or not he was satisfied that the
composition was for the best interests of the creditors,
or satisfied as to the other matters mentioned in section 12d of the Bankruptcy Act. The judge did not
determine that he was satisfied as to these matters until after the filing of the master's final report on June
10, 1908. Furthermore "the *right* to a discharge, and
the *effect* of a discharge, are wholly distinct propositions. The proper time and place for the determination of the *effect* of a discharge is when the same is
pleaded or relied upon by the debtor as a defense to
the enforcement of a particular claim. The issue upon
the *effect* of a discharge cannot properly arise or be
considered in determining the *right* to a discharge."
(*In re Marshall Paper Co.*, 43 C. C. A. 38, 102 Fed.
872, 874.)

And we do not think that under the facts of this
case the complainant and his copartners are estopped,
under the doctrine of equitable estoppel, from taking
the position that they were, by said order of the bankruptcy court of June 10, 1908, released from the claims
of the defendants against said copartnership, which
claims were proved in said bankruptcy proceedings.
One of the essential elements in equitable estoppel is
that the party claiming the estoppel must have relied
and acted to his prejudice upon an act, representation
or promise of the other party. Counsel for defendants
contend that, after the bankruptcy court had approved
the special master's report of May 12th, and after the
proviso to the offer had been withdrawn, the defendants, relying upon the order of the court granting leave
to the bankrupt to withdraw the proviso and also relying upon that withdrawal, thereupon withdrew their
objections to the confirmation of the composition to
their prejudice. A sufficient answer to this is, we
think, that there is nothing in this record to show that
the bankruptcy court would not have confirmed the

composition offer as modified, the same having been accepted by a majority in number of the creditors whose claims had been allowed and of such allowed claims, even if said objections of the defendants had not been withdrawn.

The decree of the Circuit Court is affirmed.

Affirmed.

Chicago Embossed Moulding Company, Defendant in Error, v. Max G. J. Hoffman, Plaintiff in Error.

Gen. No. 18,675.   (Not to be reported in full.)

Error to the Municipal Court of Chicago; the Hon. RUFUS F. ROBINSON, Judge, presiding. Heard in the Branch Appellate Court at the October term, 1912. Affirmed. Opinion filed January 22, 1914.

Statement of the Case.

Action by Chicago Embossed Moulding Company, a corporation, against Max G. J. Hoffman in the Municipal Court in a fourth class case to recover a certain sum claimed to be due to plaintiff from defendant for rent of space in plaintiff's building. From a judgment in favor of plaintiff for $111.32, defendant brings error.

PAUL J. HUXMANN, for plaintiff in error.

ABNER SMITH, for defendant in error.

MR. JUSTICE GRIDLEY delivered the opinion of the court.

Abstract of the Decision.

1. LANDLORD AND TENANT, § 289*—*when tenant holding over liable for amount of rent fixed by landlord.* Where a tenant occupying premises under a verbal lease, paying rent from month to month, served notice of his intention to vacate at the end of the month and the landlord accepted such notice but offered to permit tenant to hold over a few months at a certain rental payable in advance, *held* that tenant by holding over for ten days after the time for vacating was liable for a month's rent at the rate specified by the landlord.

2. LANDLORD AND TENANT, § 188*—*when tenant not entitled to damages for failure of landlord to furnish power.* In an action on a verbal lease for rent of space in a building where the tenant claimed damages for failure of landlord to furnish power to run tenant's machinery, a judgment in favor of landlord disallowing damages *held* sustained by the evidence, it appearing that the lease only required the landlord to furnish such power as he had and his failure to furnish power resulted from an unavoidable breakdown of the landlord's power plant which occasioned only temporary cessation of power.

Anna Drago, Appellee, v. The Prudential Insurance Company of America, Appellant.

Gen. No. 18,691.   (Not to be reported in full.)

Appeal from the Municipal Court of Chicago; the Hon. JOHN D. TURNBAUGH, Judge, presiding. Heard in the Branch Appellate Court at the October term, 1912. Reversed and remanded. Opinion filed January 22, 1914.

Statement of the Case.

Action by Anna Drago against The Prudential Insurance Company of America, a corporation, to recover upon a policy of life insurance claimed to have been issued and delivered by the defendant upon the life of Marian E. Baum to the amount of $1,000, the plaintiff, the mother of the insured, being mentioned in the policy as beneficiary. Plaintiff's amended statement of claim alleged that said sum was due her under a term insurance contract issued in connection with an endowment policy. From a judgment in favor of plaintiff for $1,091.67, defendant appeals.

HOYNE, O'CONNOR & IRWIN, for appellant; CARL J. APPELL, of counsel.

ADLER & LEDERER, for appellee.

MR. JUSTICE GRIDLEY delivered the opinion of the court.

Abstract of the Decision.

1. INSURANCE, § 113*—*when delivery of policy to agent completes contract of insurance.* A delivery of an insurance policy to the agent is sufficient to complete the contract of insurance only where there is an unqualified acceptance of the application and a completed policy has been placed in the hands of the agent for delivery without condition.

2. INSURANCE, § 704*—*when exclusion of testimony as to instructions given agent when policy was delivered to him is prejudicial error.* In an action to recover on a term insurance contract where it appears that the insured never made application for term insurance and that the policy together with the term insurance contract were delivered to an agent of the insurance company, refusal of court to permit defendant's witnesses to testify as to what instructions were given to the agent when the policy was placed in his hands, *held* prejudicial error.

3. INSURANCE, § 704*—*when instruction assuming facts prejudicial.* In an action to recover on a term insurance contract, where the defense is that the insurer made application only for a twenty-year endowment policy, the giving of an instruction which assumes that the insured made application for term insurance *held* prejudicial error.

Michael Davranges, Defendant in Error, v. Peter Olff et al., Plaintiffs in Error.

Gen. No. 18,725.   (Not to be reported in full.)

Error to the Municipal Court of Chicago; the Hon. OSCAR M. TORRISON, Judge, presiding. Heard in the Branch Appellate Court at the October term, 1912. Affirmed. Opinion filed January 22, 1914.

Statement of the Case.

Action by Michael Davranges against Peter Olff, Samuel B. Olff and Arthur Olff, trading as Peter Olff & Sons, in replevin to recover possession of two horses, two wagons and two sets of harness, which were kept in defendant's livery stable. Upon the trial plaintiff was given leave to change the form of action to trover and filed a count in trover. From a judgment in favor of plaintiff for four hundred and sixty-five dollars, defendants bring error.

ADOLPH MARKS, for plaintiffs in error.

ANDREW E. LINDAS, for defendant in error.

MR. JUSTICE GRIDLEY delivered the opinion of the court.

Abstract of the Decision.

TROVER AND CONVERSION, § 39*—*when evidence sufficient to sustain recovery against livery stable keeper for conversion.* Livery stable keepers refused to deliver certain horses, wagons and harness to the owner thereof on demand after a certain sum was tendered for board and keep. The stable keepers claimed that the owner owed them a greater amount than the sum tendered and that they had traded a horse for one of the horses and a certain sum additional. *Held* in an action of replevin, which action was changed to trover, upon the trial, that a judgment in favor of plaintiff was sustained by the evidence, the jury having returned special findings that there had been no horse trade and that the sum tendered was the amount owing the defendants.

*See Illinois Notes Digest, Vols. XI to XV, same topic and section number.

Morris Brown, Defendant in Error, v. Max Malter Company, Plaintiff in Error.

Gen. No. 18,582.

1. SALES, § 141*—*basis for determining whether goods equal samples.* The condition and quality of goods at the time and place of delivery to the buyer is the basis for determining whether the goods sold were equal to the samples.

2. SALES, § 200*—*title to goods when seller is made consignee in bill of lading.* Where a shipper of goods makes himself the consignee in the bill of lading, the carrier is but a bailee for the shipper.

3. SALES, § 200*—*when title to shipment passes, the seller being named in bill of lading as consignee.* Where a seller in making a shipment of goods to a buyer has himself named in the bill of lading as consignee, and sends the bill of lading with draft attached to a bank to collect from the buyer, the delivery to the railroad company does not constitute a delivery to the buyer. In such case the seller retains title and control of the property while the goods are in possession of the carrier and the title does not pass nor is there any lawful delivery to the buyer until he pays the draft and receives from the bank the bill of lading.

4. SALES, § 352*—*when buyer entitled to recover money paid on shipment of frozen eggs unfit for use.* A produce company in Boston wired a commission merchant in Chicago to ship a quantity of frozen eggs, the same as samples. The commission company shipped the eggs from Milwaukee, having the bill of lading name itself as consignee and sent the bill of lading with a draft attached to a bank in Boston for collection. After the produce company paid the draft and freight the eggs were condemned by the government officials as unfit for food. *Held,* in an action against the commission company by the produce company to recover the amount of the draft and the freight charges paid, alleging a breach of warranty and that the eggs were unfit for use, that plaintiff was entitled to recover, the evidence being sufficient to show that the eggs were unfit for food and not equal to samples at the time and place of delivery, whether the place of delivery be considered as Boston or Milwaukee.

5. JUDGMENT, § 401*—*when judgment in rem res adjudicata.* Where a consignment of frozen eggs purchased by plaintiff according to sample was seized by the government before delivery to plaintiff as unfit for human consumption, proceedings *in rem* being

*See Illinois Notes Digest, Vols. XI to XV, same topic and section number.

commenced by the government in the Federal Court, of which both plaintiff and defendant had notice, and a decree of forfeiture being entered ordering the destruction of the eggs, in an action by the purchaser to recover the purchase price and freight charges paid by him, on the ground of breach of warranty in the sale by sample, the decree in the *in rem* proceeding is *res adjudicata* as to both parties as to the condition of the eggs at the time of seizure by the government.

Error to the Municipal Court of Chicago; the Hon. FRED C. HILL, Judge, presiding. Heard in the Branch Appellate Court at the October term, 1912. Affirmed. Opinion filed January 22, 1914.

Statement by the Court. This is a writ of error sued out to reverse a judgment of $863.83 and costs, recovered by Morris Brown, defendant in error (hereinafter referred to as plaintiff), against Max Malter Company, a corporation, plaintiff in error (hereinafter referred to as defendant) in a fourth class action in the Municipal Court of Chicago. The case was tried without a jury. The plaintiff was engaged in the produce business in Boston, Massachusetts, and the defendant in the commission business in the city of Chicago. In the month of February, 1910, the defendant sent the following telegram to the plaintiff: "Can you use ten thousand pounds frozen eggs ten and half Chicago good quality will ship sample, wire answer," to which plaintiff sent the defendant the following answer: "Can use at ten cents Boston express sample if satisfactory." To this the defendant answered: "Ten cents Chicago is cheapest if want wire for samples," to which the plaintiff answered: "Express samples if satisfactory will accept balance." On February 17, 1910, defendant shipped to the plaintiff at Boston six sample cans of frozen eggs, obtained from A. J. Grossenbach & Company of Milwaukee, dealers in produce, eggs, etc., and these samples were received by the plaintiff on February 19th. It appears from the evidence that "frozen eggs" means eggs broken out of the shell into cans, and solidly frozen therein, to be kept in cold storage until sold. The undisputed evidence is that the sample cans of frozen eggs contained first-class eggs, fit for food consumption. On February 21, 1910, plaintiff wired the defendant: "Sample received if balance is the same ship." The defendant upon receipt of the telegram wired the plaintiff: "Wire received will ship tomorrow." On the evening of February 21st, Max Malter, the president of the defendant Company, went to the city of Milwaukee, Wisconsin, and on the next day purchased from Grossenbach & Co. 574 cans of frozen eggs. These eggs were loaded on the railroad car at Milwaukee. The defendant had the bill of lading from the carrier name the defendant as the consignee. On the bill of lading appeared the words "notify M. Brown." The defendant then drew a draft on the plaintiff for $805.10, attached the bill of lading to the draft, and forwarded the draft and the bill of lading to the National Bank of Commerce, in Boston for collection. A day or two later the bank in Boston presented the draft to the plaintiff and it was paid by him. The bank then gave the plaintiff the bill of lading. The plaintiff also paid freight charges on the eggs to the amount of $58.73. The car containing the cans of frozen eggs did not arrive in Boston until March 2, 1910, and the plaintiff then received notice from the railroad company of the arrival of the car. On the following morning, George H. Adams, a drug and food inspector for the United States government at Boston, called on the plaintiff to make inquiries about the eggs in question. Mr. Adams and the plaintiff then went over to the place where the car containing the eggs was sidetracked. Mr. Adams broke the seals of the car and an inspection of the eggs was made by the plaintiff and Adams. The plaintiff testified that he had been in the egg business for many years and that he was an expert in the matter of testing the quality of eggs; that he tasted and smelled the eggs in question; that there was a strong odor to them; that they had a bad taste; a sour taste; that compared in looks, taste and smell with the samples that he had received they "differed as much as day and night;" that the sample eggs were good eggs and the eggs that he saw in the car on March 3d were not fit to use; that they were not worth anything for human food consumption; that they were absolutely useless; that it was his opinion, as an expert, that the eggs could not have been in good condition at the time of the shipment; that there was ice around the cans in the car; that the weather had been pretty cold in Boston for eight or ten days prior to the arrival of the car; that the eggs were frozen hard when he examined them in the car; that in his opinion, as an expert, it would have taken frozen eggs, shipped with ice, thirty days to spoil in transit in the kind of weather that prevailed in Boston on the day of the arrival of the car and that had prevailed for a few days prior thereto; that in his opinion, if the eggs had been in good condition at the time of shipment they would have been in good condition when they arrived in Boston. Mr. Adams, the inspector, testified that he had been a food and drug inspector for the United States government for five years; that before that time he was a pharmacist; that his duties required him to inspect various articles of food for the purpose of ascertaining whether they were pure and fit for human food; that he had made a great many tests of frozen eggs to ascertain if they were suitable for human food consumption; that he made a physical examination of the eggs in question; that he also took samples of the same and submitted them to government bacteriologists and chemists; that in making the physical test of the eggs in question he used the senses of sight, smell and taste; that he found the doors of the car regularly sealed; that he opened a door of the car and examined the cans of frozen eggs; that perhaps one quarter of the cans were without covers; that there were small pieces of ice on the floor of the car and around the cans; that the weather in Boston had been cold for five or six days prior to the arrival of the eggs; that in order to keep frozen eggs in a wholesome condition it is necessary that they be kept in a frozen condition and that they be handled in a clean and sanitary manner, and protected from all contamination; that he opened a great many of the cans and examined the contents of the same; the eggs were frozen and showed no signs of melting; the color was not abnormal but the eggs had a decidedly bad odor; they seemed to be partly decomposed; he tested some of the samples; from his examination of the frozen eggs he was of the opinion that they were unfit for human food; from his experience as an expert he would say that the eggs were in a bad condition when they were shipped; either the eggs were bad when the shells were broken, or else they were handled and cared for at the time of canning and freezing in such a way as to produce the bad condition he found. Mr. Adams took samples of the eggs, had them packed in ice and shipped by express to the Bureau of Chemistry, United States Department of Agriculture, Washington. The samples were then examined by the bacteriological chemist of the said Bureau; the government expert made an examination of the samples; he noted a sour odor from the eggs at the time he opened the bottle containing the sample; he made a bacteriological examination of the sample and it showed that there were present 1,180,000,000 organisms per gram of egg, of which number at least 10,000,000 were of the B. coli type and 1,000 were streptococci; as an expert, he would say that beyond any question the egg stuff was decomposed at the time of freezing, due either to the use of "rots" or "spots" or to very insanitary handling of the eggs at the time of the breaking or freezing of the same. On the day that the government inspector at Boston examined the eggs in the car, the government officials seized the shipment of eggs while they were still in the custody of the railroad company, and after the experts in Washington had forwarded to the officials in Boston their findings as to the eggs, the United States food officials in Boston caused to be started in the United States District Court at Boston a proceedings *in rem* against the frozen eggs. These proceedings, entitled *United States v. 574 Cans of Frozen Egg Material,* resulted in a decree of forfeiture on May 31, 1910, the eggs were ordered by the court to be destroyed and the marshal of the district carried out this order. The hearing of the *in rem* case was set for March 8, 1910. On March 9, 1910, the plaintiff notified the defendant by letter of the seizure of the eggs, and also inclosed in the letter a publication notice from the government to all persons interested in the eggs. The defendant took no steps to protect its rights in the proceedings *in rem* and the judgment was entered by default. Charles Lindloff, a witness for the defendant, testified that he was present when the eggs were loaded on the car in Milwaukee; that he examined 75 of the 574 cans shipped; that the eggs were frozen solid and were in good condition; they were sweet and of good quality; they were wholesome and fit for consumption as food; they were as good as the samples that had been sent. Max Malter, testifying for the defendant, said that he was treasurer and general manager of the Max Malter Co.; that he had dealt in eggs eighteen years and had often bought, sold and examined frozen eggs; the sample eggs sent to plaintiff were No. 1 quality; after he received the telegram from the plaintiff accepting the eggs, on the evening of the same day he went to Milwaukee and purchased the eggs from Grossenbach & Co.; he examined the eggs before they were shipped; they were frozen hard and he chopped off pieces of them to taste; the eggs were all good; No. 1 eggs; better than the samples; the odor was fine and they tasted sweet; out of the 574 cans shipped he examined from 50 to 75 cans; he did not notice any filthy, decomposed or putrid substance frozen in with the egg material; the weather was cold in Milwaukee and Chicago.

Plaintiff brought suit to recover the amount of the draft and the amount of the freight on the eggs. He alleged a breach of warranty and that the eggs delivered were valueless to the plaintiff.

McEwen, Weissenbach, Shrimski & Meloan, for plaintiff in error.

Baker & Holder, for defendant in error.

Mr. Justice Scanlan delivered the opinion of the court.

There is no dispute between the parties as to the quality of the sample eggs sent to the plaintiff by the defendant. The plaintiff in his brief says that the evidence of both parties proves that the sample cans of eggs contained first-class eggs that were fit for consumption as food. The defendant in his brief speaks of the sample eggs as "good and wholesome and fit and suitable for food purposes."

The first question for us to decide is, was Chicago or Boston, under the facts of this case, the place of delivery to the plaintiff of the 574 cans of frozen eggs?

"The effect of a consignment of goods in a bill of lading is to vest the property therein in the consignee. A delivery of goods to a common carrier consigned to a particular person, without specific directions different from ordinary usage, is constructively a delivery to the consignee. Where the vendee is the consignee the delivery of goods to a common carrier without qualifications, consigned to that vendee, is in law a constructive delivery to the consignee from the time of shipment and the commencement of the carriage. 'It is well settled that delivery of goods to a common carrier * * * for conveyance to him (the purchaser) or to a place designated by him constitutes an actual receipt by the purchaser. In such cases the carrier is, in contemplation of law, the bailee of the person to whom,—not by whom,—the goods are sent, the latter, in employing the carrier, being considered as an agent

of the former for that purpose.' Benjamin on Sales,—
2d Am. Ed.—par. 693, p. 648.

In *Merchants' Despatch Co. v. Smith,* 76 Ill. 542, we
said: 'Where goods are consigned without reserva-
tion on the part of the consignor, the legal presumption is the consignee is the owner.' (Angell on Carriers, sec. 497.) This court held in *Diversy v. Kellogg,*
44 Ill. 114, that when goods were delivered to a carrier under a contract of sale, the title to the property
vests in the consignee, subject to stoppage *in transitu,*
but with no other lien unless expressed in the terms of
sale." *Lake Shore & M. S. Ry. Co. v. National Live
Stock Bank,* 178 Ill. 506, 515.

Numerous authorities to the same effect might be
cited but it is not necessary to do this, for the reason
that neither side to this controversy disputes the correctness of the principles laid down by the Supreme
Court in the last mentioned case. Had the defendant
carried out the terms of the contract between the parties, there is no doubt but that Chicago would have
been the place of delivery to the plaintiff. It is apparent, however, that the defendant did not carry out
the terms of the contract. Instead of shipping the
eggs from Chicago and making the plaintiff the consignee in the bill of lading, the defendant had the eggs
shipped from Milwaukee, Wisconsin, and it obtained a
bill of lading for the eggs from the carrier, in which
the defendant was made the consignee. The defendant then drew a draft upon the plaintiff for the amount
of the bill for the eggs, attached the bill of lading to
the same, and caused the draft, with the bill of lading
attached, to be sent to a bank in Boston for collection.
This draft was paid by the plaintiff, and thereupon the
draft and the bill of lading were handed to him.

It seems clear, from the authorities, that the delivery of the eggs by the defendant to the railroad
company, under these circumstances, did not constitute
a delivery to the plaintiff; that it was in fact merely
a delivery to the carrier as bailee for the defendant;
that the defendant retained the *jus disponendi* over

the property, and that the title to the same did not pass from the defendant to the plaintiff, nor was there any delivery in law to the plaintiff until he paid the draft in Boston, and received from the bank the bill of lading. *Jones & Co. v. Brewer,* 79 Ala. 545, 549; *Dows v. National Exch. Bank,* 91 U. S. 618; *First Nat. Bank of Cairo v. Crocker,* 111 Mass. 163. Where a shipper of goods makes himself the consignee in a bill of lading, the carrier is but a bailee for the shipper. The shipper retains title and control of the property and there can be no delivery of the goods to another party, under such circumstances, until that other party has received from the shipper the bill of lading for the goods. *Kitchin v. Clark,* 120 Ill. App. 105, 107. The defendant by its conduct waived Chicago as the place of delivery, and substituted Boston in its place. Both parties agree and it is undoubtedly the law that the condition and quality of the 574 cans of eggs at the time and place of delivery to the plaintiff is the basis for determining whether the eggs sold were equal to the samples.

In determining, therefore, the question as to whether the 574 cans of eggs sold to the plaintiff were equal to the samples furnished him, the question is, not whether the eggs sold when they left Chicago were equal to the samples, but whether they were equal to the samples when they arrived in Boston. The defendant during the trial and now insists that Chicago was the delivery place, and that the only question to determine was: Were the 574 cans of eggs, when they left Chicago, like the samples? The defendant offered no evidence as to the condition of the eggs when they arrived in Boston. The testimony, in our judgment, is conclusive that the eggs when they arrived in Boston were unfit for food purposes. In addition to the testimony of witnesses as to the condition of the eggs when they arrived in Boston, the plaintiff offered in evidence the record of the proceedings in the *in rem* case. From this record we learn the following facts:

The information in the case charged that the eggs in question "consisted in part of filthy, decomposed and putrid animal and vegetable substance." A default was taken in the case and a decree of forfeiture entered, and the eggs were destroyed by the United States marshal, in pursuance of an order of the United States District Court. Because of the action of the government the plaintiff never had physical possession of the eggs.

The plaintiff strenuously insists that the judgment of the United States District Court condemning the eggs in question is *res adjudicata* as to the physical condition of the eggs at the time of the shipment. In the view that we have taken of this case, it is not necessary for us to pass upon this contention of counsel. The judgment in the *in rem* case was *res adjudicata* as to all parties as to the condition of the eggs at the time of the seizure by the government. *Makins Produce Co. v. Callison*, 67 Wash. 434.

The trial judge (in order to be on the safe side, as he stated in his decision) held with the defendant that the place of delivery of the eggs was Chicago, and that the decree of the United States Court was not *res adjudicata* as to the condition and the quality of the eggs at the time of the shipment. The Court held, however, that the evidence in the case proved to his satisfaction that the eggs at the time of the shipment were very bad and valueless to the plaintiff, and that they were not like the samples that had been sent to the plaintiff by the defendant. We have examined the evidence in this case with great care, and we are satisfied that if we followed the law of the trial court (the law contended for by the defendant in this case), we would arrive at the same conclusion that the trial court did in reference to the facts. That the eggs when they arrived at Boston were very bad and unfit for human consumption is undisputed. In addition to the plaintiff, several able and disinterested witnesses, holding responsible positions with the United

States government, testified that the bad condition of the eggs at Boston was not the result of changes in the condition of the eggs after they were shipped, but that the same conditions that were found in Boston existed at the time the egg fluid was placed in the cans, and that this condition of the frozen eggs was caused by the use of decomposed eggs, known as "rots" and "spots," or was due to insanitary handling of the eggs at the time of the breaking of the eggs and the placing of the liquid material into the cans.

The defendant had two witnesses testify as to the condition of the eggs at the time of the shipment. Max Malter, the president of the defendant corporation, was one, and Charles Lindloff, an employe of the Milwaukee firm, from whom the defendant bought the eggs, was the other. The witness Malter testified that he was present at the time the eggs were loaded on the car at Milwaukee, and that he made a test of 50 or 75 cans of the 574 cans that were shipped, and that the eggs tested by him were all No. 1 eggs and of good quality,—better in quality than the sample eggs. When the government seized the eggs in Boston, the plaintiff notified the defendant of that fact, told it where the eggs were in storage, and demanded of it a check for the amount of the draft that had been paid by the plaintiff, and for the amount of the freight on the eggs that had also been paid by the plaintiff. In response to this letter, the defendant through Max Malter wrote a letter to the plaintiff containing the following: "We are in receipt of yours of the 9th inst. and are very sorry to note what you say. In reply will say we have immediately taken this matter up with our Milwaukee party and are awaiting their answer. As soon as we hear from them will let you know immediately. We are very sorry to cause you all this trouble, but you see that it is not our fault, as *on the strength of the sample that we shipped you we bought the balance when we heard from you. The eggs were shipped direct from Milwaukee loaded by said party direct to the car*

and never came to our possession." In a later letter
to the plaintiff, the defendant said: "What we are
trying to do is to connect the Milwaukee party with
this, as you know well that we acted in this only as
brokers. On the strength of the sample that we
shipped you, we then on your acceptance bought the
remainder of the eggs and shipped it direct from
there. You saw according to their guarantee what
they think of it." A number of letters dictated by
Max Malter passed between the plaintiff and the defendant after the seizure of the eggs, and in none of
these was there any suggestion made that the witness
Malter had inspected the eggs prior to the shipment
from Milwaukee. From a reading of the entire correspondence, we are not satisfied that the attitude of
the defendant Company towards the plaintiff in this
transaction was frank and honorable. The position
of the defendant at first was that it had purchased the
eggs from the Milwaukee concern under a guaranty,
and that it intended to look to the Milwaukee people
for reimbursement for any loss that it might sustain in the matter. Finally, after the matter had
been dragged out for months through the evasive
tactics of the defendant Company, it ended the correspondence by notifying the plaintiff that it would not
be held responsible for any loss the plaintiff might sustain in the matter. The affidavit of merits of the defendant Company in this case was subscribed and
sworn to by the witness Max Malter. In this affidavit
appears the following: "Whereupon the said Grossenbach & Company, by direction of the defendant consigned about 10,000 pounds of frozen eggs to the plaintiff at Boston, Massachusetts, and the said Grossenbach & Company then and there guaranteed to the
defendant here that the said frozen eggs were in all
respects equal to the samples so received by the defendant from said Grossenbach & Company, and affiant
says *that he is informed and believes, and so states the
fact to be,* that the frozen eggs so consigned by the said

Grossenbach & Company by and under the direction of the defendant were in all things equal to said sample." When all the evidence is considered together, it is exceedingly doubtful, in our judgment, if the witness Malter made a test of the eggs at the time of the shipment. We are satisfied, that the evidence proves that the eggs at the time of the shipment from Milwaukee were not of a good quality and fit for human food, and that they were not equal in quality to the samples that had been forwarded to the plaintiff by the defendant. Therefore, if we adopt, as did the trial court, the defendant's theory of the law, we are nevertheless forced to the conclusion that the judgment of the Municipal Court in this case is a just one and that it should be affirmed.

The judgment of the Municipal Court will therefore be affirmed.

Affirmed.

Emma Thiele, Plaintiff in Error, v. John Hetzel, Defendant in Error.

Gen. No. 18,724.   (Not to be reported in full.)

Error to the Superior Court of Cook county; the Hon. CHARLES A. McDONALD, Judge, presiding. Heard in the Branch Appellate Court at the October term, 1912. Reversed and remanded. Opinion filed January 22, 1914.

Statement of the Case.

Action by Emma Thiele originally commenced against John Hetzel and Chicago Railways Company to recover for personal injuries sustained by plaintiff alleged to have been caused by a collision between a street car of the defendant Railways Company and a wagon of defendant Hetzel at a street intersection where plaintiff was standing to take the car, the

collision causing the wagon to be thrown towards
the curbing in the direction of plaintiff so that the
horses stepped upon and the wagon passed over plaintiff. Plaintiff in consideration of two hundred dollars
entered into a "peace covenant" with defendant Railways Company and the suit was dismissed as to it but
retained against the defendant Hetzel as the sole defendant. From a judgment entered upon a verdict of
not guilty, plaintiff brings error.

Hattie M. Balsley, who was standing by plaintiff at
the time of the accident, was also injured. She prosecuted a suit against the same defendant and recovered
a judgment on substantially the same evidence as in
the case at bar. Judgment in that case was affirmed
by the Appellate Court in *Balsley v. Hetzel*, 182 Ill.
App. 136.

C. HELMER JOHNSON and DANIEL BELASCO, for plaintiff in error.

MILLER, GORHAM & WALES and W. G. SHOCKEY, for
defendant in error.

MR. JUSTICE SCANLAN delivered the opinion of the
court.

Abstract of the Decision.

1. INSTRUCTIONS, § 129*—*when instructions directing verdict upon
determination of preponderance of the evidence improper.* In an
action for personal injuries, an instruction given at the instance of
defendant in the words: "If the evidence in this case preponderates
in favor of the defendant, then your verdict should be not guilty.
Or, if the evidence fails to preponderate in favor of plaintiff, the
jury should find the defendant not guilty. Or, if the evidence in
the case is evenly balanced, the jury should find the defendant not
guilty," *held* misleading because it does not restrict the evidence
referred to, to the issues essential to the maintenance of the action,
and also subject to criticism because it too frequently uses words
to the effect that the jury should find the defendant not guilty.

*See Illinois Notes Digest, Vols. XI to XV, same topic and section number.

2. INSTRUCTIONS, § 82*—*when instruction as to credibility of testimony of one party improper.* Where both plaintiff and defendant testify in the suit, an instruction to consider the interest of the plaintiff in giving credence to her testimony, without any reference to the interest of the defendant, *held* calculated to impress the jury that the court entertained a special reason for discrediting the testimony of plaintiff.

3. INSTRUCTIONS, § 59*—*when instruction as to relative rights of defendant and third party misleading.* In an action for personal injuries alleged to have resulted from the negligent driving of a wagon, an instruction given for defendant with reference to the relative rights of defendant and the street railway company as to the use of the street at the place of the accident, *held,* misleading where the street railway is not a party to the action.

4. DAMAGES, § 209*—*when instruction limiting damages to sum received by plaintiff in consideration of dismissing suit against party made codefendant prejudicial.* In an action for personal injuries where the action was originally commenced against the defendant and a street railway company, but plaintiff in consideration of two hundred dollars entered into a peace covenant as to the railway company and dismissed the action as it only, an instruction given for defendant that the jury must find for defendant in case the damages sustained were not in excess of the two hundred dollars received by plaintiff from the railway company, *held* erroneous and prejudicial.

The People of the State of Illinois for use of State Board of Health, Defendant in Error, v. Jasper B. McTier, Plaintiff in Error.

Gen. No. 18,740.   (Not to be reported in full.)

Error to the Municipal Court of Chicago; the Hon. FREEMAN K. BLAKE, Judge, presiding. Heard in the Branch Appellate Court at the October term, 1912. Affirmed. Opinion filed January 22, 1914.

Statement of the Case.

Action of debt by the People of the State of Illinois for the use of the State Board of Health against Jasper B. McTier to recover the statutory penalty of one hundred dollars for practicing medicine without a license. The defendant waived a trial by jury. The court heard the evidence and found the defendant guilty and imposed a fine of one hundred dollars and costs and entered a judgment for that amount. To reverse the judgment defendant prosecutes a writ of error.

T. WEBSTER BROWN for plaintiff in error; EDWARD H. MORRIS, of counsel.

CHARLES ALLING, JR., for defendant in error; THOMAS F. BURKE, of counsel.

MR. JUSTICE SCANLAN delivered the opinion of the court.

Abstract of the Decision.

1. PHYSICIANS AND SURGEONS, § 8*—*when evidence sufficient to show practice without a license.* In an action to recover a penalty for practicing medicine without a license, the facts showing that defendant had distributed from house to house a circular in which he claimed to have power to heal through prayer and that investigators submitting to treatment as patients were charged a fee, *held* that a finding of guilty was sustained by the evidence.

2. PHYSICIANS AND SURGEONS, § 8*—*when printed circular admissible in an action for penalty for practicing without a license.* In an action to recover the statutory penalty for practicing medicine without a license, a printed circular distributed by the defendant from house to house and tending to support the charge of the commission of the offense, *held* competent evidence.

3. PHYSICIANS AND SURGEONS, § 8*—*when action for penalty for practicing without a license may be based on evidence provided by investigators.* An action to recover the statutory penalty for practicing medicine without a license may be based on evidence procured by investigators who applied for treatment to determine whether the defendant would commit the offense, the investigators not advising or encouraging the defendant to commit the acts constituting such offense.

4. PENALTIES, § 10*—*necessity of proving venue of offense.* Action of debt to recover statutory penalty for practicing medicine without a license is not a criminal proceeding in which the venue of the offense must be proved.

5. PHYSICIANS AND SURGEONS, § 8*—*constitutional provisions.* Although article II, § 3 of the Constitution of 1870, J. & A. p. 130, gives to a person a legal right to pray for the cure of sickness and disease, it does not give him the right to practice medicine without a license.

In the matter of the Petition of Jacob Bremer.
On Appeal of Jacob Bremer, Appellant, v. William Murray, Appellee.

Gen. No. 18,816.   (Not to be reported in full.)

Appeal from the County Court of Cook county; the Hon. JOHN E. OWENS, Judge, presiding. Heard in the Branch Appellate Court at the October term, 1912. Affirmed. Opinion filed January 22, 1914.

Statement of the Case.

Petition filed by Jacob Bremer in the County Court under the Insolvent Debtors' Act to be released from custody under a *capias ad satisfaciendum* issued upon a judgment of tort recovered against the petitioner in the Municipal Court of Chicago in an action brought by William Murray. From a judgment denying the petition, petitioner appeals.

GEORGE REMUS, for appellant.

KRUSE & PEDEN and R. C. MERRICK, for appellee.

MR. JUSTICE SCANLAN delivered the opinion of the court.

Abstract of the Decision.

1. EXECUTION, § 302*—*when evidence on question of malice for discharge from custody under a ca. sa.* On petition filed by a judgment debtor in the County Court under the Insolvent Debtor's Act,

---

*See Illinois Notes Digest, Vols. XI to XV, same topic and section number.

J. & A. ¶ 6199, to be released from custody under a *capias ad satis-faciendum* issued on a judgment, refusal of court to permit the petitioner to show by evidence that malice was not the gist of the action for the reason that the judgment record was *res adjudicata* on the question, *held* proper.

2. EXECUTION, § 295*—*when record of judgment conclusive on question of malice on petition for discharge from custody under a ca. sa.* The record of a judgment in tort recovered against defendant in an action charging defendant with making fraudulent representations that a trust deed was first lien upon real estate described therein to induce the plaintiff to purchase the deed, *held res adjudicata* on the question whether malice was the gist of the action, it appearing that the jury returned a special finding and the court found that the misrepresentations were made with malicious and fraudulent intent.

The People of the State of Illinois ex rel. Maclay Hoyne, State's Attorney for the County of Cook, Plaintiff in Error, v. John E. Northup, Defendant in Error.

Gen. No. 20,042.

1. QUO WARRANTO, § 10*—*when special State's Attorney is incumbent of an office.* The appointment by the court of a special State's Attorney to prosecute, instead of the State's Attorney, in certain cases authorized by statute, constitutes such appointee the incumbent of an office within the meaning of the Constitution and laws, so that his right and title to the office may be tested in a quo warranto proceeding.

2. STATE'S ATTORNEY, § 3*—*at whose instance special State's Attorney may be appointed.* The jurisdiction of the court to appoint a special State's Attorney need not necessarily be invoked at the instance and upon the petition of the State's Attorney but may be properly invoked by the court on its own motion or upon the petition of a citizen.

3. STATE'S ATTORNEY, § 3*—*when petition alleges facts sufficient to warrant appointment of special State's Attorney.* A petition for the appointment of a special State's Attorney to investigate frauds practiced in a general election in which there were different candidates for the office of State's Attorney, *held* to state facts to suffi-

---

ciently inform the court that the candidate elected was "interested" in the cause or proceeding which it was or might be his duty to prosecute and to warrant the appointment of a special State's Attorney.

4. COURTS, § 121*—*when acquisition of jurisdiction by one judge does not preclude another judge from assuming jurisdiction.* The fact that a judge of the Criminal Court of Cook county had already acquired jurisdiction of the investigation and prosecution of frauds committed in the election of State's Attorney upon the petition of the State's Attorney for the appointment of a special State's Attorney, does not preclude another judge of the same court from assuming jurisdiction to hear and act upon a petition presented to him by other parties for the appointment of a special State's Attorney to investigate and prosecute election frauds, where the scope of the investigation and prosecution involved in the latter petition is more comprehensive than that involved in the former petition.

5. JUDGMENT, § 250*—*amendment of record pending term.* At the same term all proceedings rest in the breast of the judge of the court, and he may amend his record according to the facts within his own knowledge.

6. APPEAL AND ERROR, § 936*—*when record shows basis for order to file amended petition nunc pro tunc.* Where the record shows that a petition for the appointment of a special State's Attorney was presented to a judge and that the judge assumed jurisdiction of the subject-matter involved and granted leave to file an amended petition and that on the following day, being of the same term of court, the judge directed the amended petition to be filed *nunc pro tunc* as of the previous day, *held* that the record of the proceedings had on the first day, even if based solely upon the facts within the personal knowledge of the judge, imported verity and that such record constituted a sufficient note or memorandum, if any was necessary, upon which to predicate the *nunc pro tunc* order.

Error to the Circuit Court of Cook county; the Hon. JESSE A. BALDWIN, Judge, presiding. Heard in the Branch Appellate Court at the October term, 1913. Affirmed. Opinion filed January 26, 1914. Rehearing denied and additional opinion filed February 6, 1914.

MACLAY HOYNE, for plaintiff in error; FRANK JOHNSTON, JR. and HENRY A. BERGER, of counsel.

JOHN E. NORTHUP, *pro se*; WILLARD M. MCEWEN and NORTHUP, ARNOLD & FAIRBANK, of counsel.

MR. JUSTICE BAUME delivered the opinion of the court.

On June 5, 1913, Maclay Hoyne, State's Attorney in and for the county of Cook, for and in behalf of the People of the State of Illinois, filed his petition in the Circuit Court for leave to file an information in the nature of a quo warranto against John E. Northup, who was then and since June 2, 1913, alleged to be assuming or pretending to exercise the franchise, functions and powers of the office of State's Attorney of Cook county without warrant or authority of law. The respondent, Northup, having answered said petition the matter was heard by the court and upon such hearing it was ordered by the court that said petition be denied, and said petition was thereupon by order of the court dismissed at the costs of the petitioner. This writ of error is prosecuted by the petitioner, Hoyne, to reverse said orders of the Circuit Court.

As the salient facts embodied in the petition and answer, or disclosed upon the hearing, and necessary to a consideration of the questions involved must be here stated, it will be unnecessary to set forth at length the averments of said petition and answer.

For the purposes of this case it is conceded that the petitioner, Hoyne, was duly elected State's Attorney in and for the county of Cook at a general election held November 5, 1912, and that he regularly qualified as such State's Attorney. It is also conceded that among other candidates for said office at said election were Lewis Rinaker, William A. Cunnea and George I. Haight.

On May 19, 1913, the said Rinaker, Cunnea and Haight, by their counsel, Frank D. Ayers, appeared before Hon. William Fenimore Cooper, one of the judges then presiding in a branch of the Criminal Court, and presented to the court a petition for the appointment by the court of a special State's Attorney to investigate the election held November 5, 1912, with power and authority to prosecute offenders of alleged frauds committed at said election. The duly authenticated record of the proceeding of said branch of the Criminal Court had on said May 19, 1913, relating to said petition, contains the following recital:

"This day the said People by Maclay Hoyne, State's Attorney and the said petitioners by their counsel also come.

And counsel for said petitioners now here present a petition to this court, praying for the appointment of a special State's Attorney to investigate election frauds, and it appearing to the court that said petition is insufficient the court of its own motion suggests that said petition be amended which was done.

And it is ordered by the court that counsel for said petitioners serve notice on the State's Attorney of the time of presentment of said petition to this court."

Following the presentation of said petition to Judge Cooper, and on the same day, counsel for said petitioners served upon the petitioner, Hoyne, a copy of their amended petition, together with notice that they would on Tuesday, May 20, 1913, appear at 10 o'clock, A. M., before Judge Cooper and ask leave to file said petition, praying for the appointment of a special State's Attorney and the convening of a special grand jury and would also ask that the hearing upon said petition be set down for Thursday, May 22, 1913, at 10 o'clock, A. M.

The said petition of Rinaker, Cunnea and Haight represents that they are citizens and taxpayers of Cook county and members of the Bar of the State of Illinois; that a proceeding by said Cunnea against Maclay Hoyne to contest the latter's election to the office of State's Attorney was then on hearing in the Circuit Court; that a recount then had in said contest proceedings of the votes cast at said election disclosed certain specified grave frauds and irregularities; that although several grand juries had been convened since said Hoyne had assumed the office of State's Attorney, and the attention of the grand jury then in session had been particularly called by the court to the question of election frauds, the said Hoyne had done nothing towards the investigation of said frauds, but had refused to follow out the directions of the court in that regard, and had announced that he would not present any such matters to the grand jury then in session; that the said Hoyne "is interested in the investigation of election frauds in connection with the election for State's Attorney held on November 5, 1912."

On the following day, May 20, 1913, at 9:30 o'clock, A. M., being about thirty minutes prior to the time set for the presentation to Judge Cooper of the amended petition for the appointment of a special State's Attorney and the calling of a special grand jury, said Hoyne appeared before the Hon. George Kersten, one of the judges then presiding in a branch of the Criminal Court, and presented a petition requesting the appointment by Judge Kersten of some competent and disinterested person to investigate and inquire into all alleged frauds and irregularities at said election for State's Attorney, and, if any there be, to present evidence thereof to a special grand jury to be convened by the court at an early day for the purpose of investigating frauds and irregularities alleged to have been committed at said election and to prosecute such person or persons who may be guilty of criminal acts pertaining to said election, and that the attorney so appointed be clothed with all the necessary authority to act as special State's Attorney in accordance with the statute. The petition alleges that soon after the election held on November 5, 1912, said Cunnea filed a petition in the Circuit Court to contest the election of Hoyne to the office of State's Attorney; that during such contest proceedings, several of the defeated candidates for the office made various charges to the effect that various frauds and violations of the election law and the statutes of this State were committed by the judges and clerks of election in counting the votes of the various candidates for said office; that the petitioner did not participate in any frauds or violations

of the election law at said election, and has no personal
knowledge of any such frauds committed in his favor;
that said Cunnea, Rinaker and Haight each claims or
pretends to desire to prosecute such persons who may
have been guilty of the frauds and violations of the
election law, the ballot law, and other felonies and mis-
demeanors which they claim occurred in and about the
counting of the votes and ballots cast at said election,
and for that purpose they have served notice on said
petitioner that they will request Judge Cooper to appoint a special State's Attorney, and to convene a
special grand jury; that said Rinaker and Cunnea have
made, allegations in said contest proceedings to the
effect that gross frauds were committed in and about
said election, but petitioner avers that such allegations
have not been proved; that the said petition of said
Rinaker and Cunnea about to be filed before Judge
Cooper, requesting the appointment of a special State's
Attorney and the convening of a special grand jury,
is not made in good faith, and is for the purpose of
securing the appointment as such special State's Attorney of a person who would not be wholly disinterested or impartial in conducting the said investigations
of frauds, and the prosecutions of such persons as
might be found to be guilty of same, and would not
fairly and properly present the evidence relating to
said alleged frauds before the said special grand jury;
that upwards of two weeks ago, on the day that the
regular grand jury then and since in session was impaneled, it was advised and instructed by Judge Cooper
to consider such evidence as might be presented to it
with reference to any frauds and irregularities that
may have been perpetrated in the election aforesaid;
that at that time the said Judge Cooper, in instructing
said grand jury according to the publication of said
instruction in the public press, invited all persons having or claiming to have any knowledge of frauds or
irregularities in said election to communicate such
knowledge to the court, or to said grand jury; that

said petitioner did thereupon publicly announce to the press of the city of Chicago that he would receive and transmit to said grand jury any and all evidence of any such alleged frauds or irregularities; that neither the said Cooper, nor any of the opposing candidates of said petitioner at said election, nor any other person, has presented or offered to present to the grand jury any evidence of any frauds or irregularities in said election, although they had full opportunity so to do; that by reason of said petitioner being a successful candidate at said election, and his having a personal interest in the said contest now pending in the Circuit Court, it would be inexpedient for him to present the evidence of such alleged frauds and irregularities in said election to the said special grand jury, or to prosecute any person or persons who might be indicted by said special grand jury for such frauds or irregularities.

Upon the presentation of said petition to Judge Kersten an order was entered finding that the petitioner, Hoyne, was personally interested in the investigation and prosecution of persons against whom there might appear to be just and reasonable grounds to establish guilt of criminal offenses committed in and about the casting of ballots and counting of votes for State's Attorney at said election, and appointing Clyde L. Day special State's Attorney, and directing the clerk of the court to forthwith issue a special venire for a grand jury returnable on the following day, May 21, 1913, when said grand jury should be convened for the sole and special purpose of investigating any and all frauds and irregularities alleged to have been committed in and about the casting of ballots and the counting of votes for the election of State's Attorney at said election.

On the same day, May 20, 1913, Clyde L. Day took the oath of office as special State's Attorney and a special venire for a grand jury was issued as ordered.

About an hour later on the same day, May 20, 1913,

counsel for Rinaker, Cunnea and Haight presented to Judge Cooper an amended petition for the appointment of a special State's Attorney and the calling of a special grand jury, which petition was then ordered by the court to be filed *nunc pro tunc* as of the preceding day, May 19, 1913, and thereupon said petition was so filed as ordered and a hearing on the matters involved in said petition was set for May 22d, following. On May 22d the parties appeared before Judge Cooper, when and where a partial hearing was had and a further hearing was continued to May 27th, following. On May 27th, upon the Court's own motion, a further hearing was continued to May 29th, following. On May 29th the Court (Judge Cooper) directed the clerk to forthwith issue a special venire for a special grand jury returnable June 6, 1913, and also then allowed the prayer of the petition for the appointment of a special State's Attorney, and reserved the entry of an order appointing such special State's Attorney until a later date. On June 2, 1913, the Court (Judge Cooper) entered an order appointing John E. Northup special State's Attorney to be and appear before the special grand jury theretofore summoned, with full power and authority in said Northup as such special State's Attorney to conduct investigations into any matters proper for said special grand jury to inquire into as charged by the court. On the same day, in pursuance to such appointment, the said Northup qualified as special State's Attorney by taking the oath of office and tendering his official bond, which was then approved and filed.

The arguments of counsel cover a wider scope than is necessary to the consideration and determination of the two dependent controlling questions involved in the case. First, whether or not the appointment by the court of an attorney as special State's Attorney to prosecute, instead of the State's Attorney, in certain cases authorized by the statute, constitutes such appointee the incumbent of an office within the meaning of the Constitution and laws, so that his right and title thereto may be tested in a quo warranto proceeding. If this inquiry must be determined in the affirmative, then, second, whether or not the appointment by Judge Cooper of the respondent, John E. Northup, as special State's Attorney to prosecute alleged offenders of the election laws at the general election held November 5, 1912, was authorized, and constituted said respondent a special State's Attorney *de jure.*

Neither the regularity of the proceedings, wherein a special grand jury was convened by Judge Cooper, nor the integrity of said special grand jury, as being lawfully authorized to act in the premises, are properly involved in this case. No such necessary relation exists between the appointment of a special State's Attorney and the convening of a special grand jury as that an inquiry into the functions of the court in one particular may influence a determination of the functions of the court in the other particular.

On behalf of petitioner, Hoyne, it is insisted that the decision of the Supreme Court in *Lavin v. Board Com'rs Cook County,* 245 Ill. 496, conclusively establishes the position of a special State's Attorney to be an office as distinguished from a mere employment or agency. The decision in the *Lavin* case in its entirety was concurred in by a bare majority of the court. A separate opinion concurred in by three of the justices expressly withholds assent to the proposition that by the appointment of an attorney as special State's Attorney to prosecute particular causes he became an officer *de facto* or otherwise. Such separate opinion continues as follows:

"An office is defined in the constitution as being 'a public position created by the constitution or law, continuing during the pleasure of the appointing power, or for a fixed time, with a successor elected or appointed.' (Const. art. 5, sec. 24.) The appointment by the court of an attorney to prosecute, instead of the State's attorney, in certain cases authorized by the statute, does not constitute such attorney an officer but confers merely a temporary authority for a special occasion, which falls within the constitutional definition of an employment as 'an agency, for a temporary purpose, which ceases when that purpose is accomplished.' (Const. art. 5, sec. 24; *Bunn v. People*, 45 Ill. 397; *People v. Loeffler*, 175 id. 585.)''

The opinion of the majority of the court is admittedly open to the construction that the position of special State's Attorney is an office and that a special State's Attorney is an officer, within the meaning of the Constitution and laws, and in view of the fact that the separate opinion specifically expresses the dissent of the minority of the court upon those propositions we are unable to escape the conclusion that the precise status of a special State's Attorney was considered by the court as being involved in the case, and as being determined by the opinion which was concurred in by a majority of the court. Following the decision in the *Lavin* case, supra, it must be held that the appointment of the respondent, Northup, as special State's Attorney, if authorized, constituted his appointment to an office and that upon his qualification as such special State's Attorney he became the incumbent of an office within the meaning of the Constitution and laws.

It is said that the order entered by Judge Cooper appointing the respondent, Northup, special State's Attorney is void. We shall consider the several grounds urged in support of such contention in so far as the same are pertinent in the order of their presentment:

First, that there is no showing in the petition presented to Judge Cooper that State's Attorney Hoyne was interested in any frauds committed in the general election held on November 5, 1912.

The facts relating to the frauds and irregularities alleged in the petition to have been practiced at said election are set forth with sufficient definiteness to inform the court that the public interest required that the offenders should be prosecuted. The petition further informs the court that Mr. Hoyne, together with other persons named, were candidates of their respective political parties for the office of State's Attorney at said election, and alleges that the frauds and irregularities charged to have been practiced at said election were committed in pursuance to an organized effort to accomplish the election of Hoyne. The statement in the petition that Hoyne was "interested in the investigation of election frauds in connection with the election of State's Attorney" was merely the conclusion of the petitioners perhaps not aptly phrased, but the facts set forth in the petition sufficiently informed the court that Hoyne was "interested" in the "cause or proceeding," which it was or might be his duty to prosecute, following the language of the statute. The charges in the petition with reference to frauds and irregularities committed at the general election held November 5, 1912, were also sufficiently broad to involve the interests of persons who were then candidates for offices other than the office of State's Attorney. It is a matter of common knowledge, as to which the courts cannot feign ignorance, that under the existing system wherein candidates for public offices are affiliated with and nominated by the respective political parties to which they belong, and the voters generally are affiliated with political parties of their choice, charges affecting the integrity of the election of any one of the candidates nominated by a certain political party almost necessarily involve the interests of each of the other candidates nominated by that political party. The verified petition alleges facts sufficient to justify the court in the exercise of its judicial discretion in holding that State's Attorney Hoyne was so interested in the cause or proceeding in question as to warrant the appointment of a special State's Attorney to prosecute said cause or proceeding.

Second, that Judge Kersten had already acquired jurisdiction of the investigation and prosecution for frauds committed in the election of State's Attorney, and the assumption thereafter by Judge Cooper of such jurisdiction was without warrant of law.

It is a sufficient answer to this contention to say that the scope of the investigation and prosecution involved in the petition presented to Judge Cooper and in the order entered upon said petition is so much more comprehensive than that involved in the petition presented to Judge Kersten and the order entered thereon, that the pendency of the proceeding before Judge Kersten upon the petition of Mr. Hoyne did not as a matter of law preclude Judge Cooper from assuming jurisdiction to hear and act upon the petition presented to him. Furthermore, it appears from the record that the original petition of Rinaker, Cunnea and Haight for the appointment of a special State's Attorney was presented to Judge Cooper on May 19th, and that Judge Cooper then assumed jurisdiction of the subject-matter there involved, and that on May 20th, the day following, said petition as amended was directed by Judge Cooper to be filed *nunc pro tunc* as of May 19th. It is practically conceded that if Judge Cooper acquired jurisdiction of the subject-matter in question on May 19th, the order subsequently entered by him providing for the appointment of the respondent, Northup, as special State's Attorney to prosecute alleged offenders of the election laws of the election held on November 5, 1912, in so far as said order involved the prosecution of such alleged offenders for frauds and irregularities affecting the election of State's Attorney, was not unauthorized.

It will be observed that the proceedings had before Judge Cooper on May 19th and May 20th were had at the same term, both of said days being days of the May term, 1913, of the Criminal Court. It is well settled that at the same term all proceedings rest in the breast of the judge of the court, and he can amend

his record according to the facts within his own knowledge. *Hansen v. Schlesinger*, 125 Ill. 230; *West Chicago St. R. Co. v. Morrison, Adams & Allen Co.*, 160
Ill. 288. The record of the proceedings had before
Judge Cooper on May 19th, relative to the presentation to him of the original petition for the appointment of a special State's Attorney and of the action
of the court with respect thereto, even if based solely
upon facts within the personal knowledge of the judge,
imports verity, and such record constitutes a sufficient
note or memorandum, if any such was necessary, upon
which to predicate the *nunc pro tunc* order entered on
May 20th directing the clerk to file the amended petition as of May 19th.

We conclude that Judge Cooper acquired jurisdiction of the subject-matter of the proceedings involving the appointment of the respondent, Northup, as
special State's Attorney on May 19th, and that the
subsequent appointment by him in said proceedings of
said Northup as such special State's Attorney was and
is valid.

We cannot give our assent to the doctrine that the
exercise of judicial power to appoint a special State's
Attorney can only be invoked at the instance and upon
the petition of the State's Attorney. True, the jurisdiction of the court in that respect may be thus invoked, but such jurisdiction may also be properly invoked by the court upon its own motion or upon the
petition of a citizen.

We refrain from a discussion of other contentions
which upon the record before us involve purely
academic questions.

In *People v. Sullivan*, 247 Ill. 176, it is said:

"Whether leave shall be granted to file an information in the nature of *quo warranto* is in a large measure within the sound discretion of the court. Such
discretion, however, is not to be exercised arbitrarily
but in accordance with principles of law."

There was no abuse by the Circuit Court of its discretion in denying leave to file the information sought to be filed in this case and the judgment is affirmed.

Judgment affirmed.

OPINION ON PETITION FOR REHEARING.

PER CURIAM. In the petition for a rehearing of this cause filed by plaintiff in error it is urged that in the opinion heretofore filed this court misconceived the facts, erroneously construed the law and overlooked the authorities cited by plaintiff in error in the respects following:

First, that it is a misnomer to speak of the petition which was presented to Judge Cooper on May 20th as an *amended* petition.

This case was properly considered and determined here upon the record as actually made and not upon casual remarks of court and counsel in the course of certain proceedings preliminary to the action of the court, as evidenced by the record actually made. The recitals in the record of the proceedings had before Judge Cooper on May 19th upon the presentation of the original petition of Rinaker, Cunnea and Haight are, in part, as follows:

"And counsel for said petitioners now here present a petition to this court, praying for the appointment of a special State's Attorney to investigate election frauds, and it appearing to the court that said petition is insufficient the court of its own motion suggests that said petition be amended which was done.

And it is ordered by the court that counsel for said petitioners serve notice on the State's Attorney of the time of presentment of said petition to this court."

It is submitted that the designation of the petition which was presented to Judge Cooper on May 20th as the "amended petition" or the "petition as amended" is fully justified by the record as actually made. The record discloses that the petition which was presented to Judge Cooper on May 19th was amended on the same day and there is no pretense that this was not the same petition that was presented to Judge Cooper on May 20th.

Second, that this court misconceived the facts when it stated that Judge Cooper assumed jurisdiction of the petition on May 19th.

The recitals in the record as above set forth unquestionably disclose an assumption by Judge Cooper of jurisdiction of the petition which was presented to him on May 19th. The court then directed the petition to be amended, noted the actual making of such amendment and ordered the petitioners to serve notice on the State's Attorney of the time of presentment of said petition. It is clear that by "said petition," notice of presentment of which was ordered to be given, was meant the amended petition or the petition as amended.

Third, that the court misconstrued the law relative to the entry of a *nunc pro tunc* order and overlooked the authorities cited by plaintiff in error upon that question.

As the proceedings in question were had at the same term and rested in the breast of the judge, no note or memorandum upon which to predicate a *nunc pro tunc* order was absolutely essential to authorize the entry of such an order. All of the authorities cited by plaintiff in error relate to the necessity of some note or memorandum made at the term at which the proceedings were had to authorize the entering of a *nunc pro tunc* order at a subsequent term. The authorities cited are, therefore, not in point.

The petition for a rehearing is denied.

Petition denied.

ABATEMENT AND REVIVAL.

ACCOUNT.

ACCOUNT, ACTION ON.

ACTION ON THE CASE.

ACTIONS AND DEFENSES.

ADMINISTRATION.

AGENTS.

See PRINCIPAL AND AGENT.

AGRICULTURE.

State Board of—when not liable for negligence of officers and employes. p. 191.
—— when not liable for personal injuries at State Fair. p. 191.

ALTERATION OF INSTRUMENTS.

Filling in blanks—when not an alteration. p. 266.
Guaranty contract—what questions are for court and jury. p. 266.

AMENDMENTS.

Declaration—when refusal to allow reversible. p. 185.
Pleading—when discretionary. p. 185.
Statute permitting—how construed. p. 185.

ANIMALS.

Breach of warranty in sale of—when question for jury. p. 255.
Carriers—when not liable for failure to unload during snow storm. p. 322.
Insurance—when evidence insufficient to show misrepresentation or lack of care. p. 375.
Killing—when evidence sufficient to sustain recovery for killing trespassing turkeys. p. 316.
—— when owner of farm not entitled to kill trespassing turkeys. p. 316.

APPEALS AND ERRORS.

Abstract instructions—when prejudicial. p. 445.
Abstract of record—how rule as to construed. p. 431.
—— when insufficient. pp. 431, 476.
—— when must set out provisions of contract. p. 87.
Additional pleas—when not error to deny leave to file. p. 317.
—— when not error to permit filing of. p. 266.
—— when refusal of leave to file not saved. p. 340.
Affirmance—when decree erroneously containing statement of facts modified and affirmed. p. 474.
Amendment to declaration—when refusal reversible. p. 185.
Argument of counsel—when improper. p. 377.
Bankruptcy—what damages recoverable in action on appeal bond. p. 528.
—— when appeal bond not effective as supersedeas. p. 528.
Bill of exceptions—how should appear in abstract. p. 431.
—— what constitutes disability of judge to sign. p. 434.
—— when construed against appellant. p. 17.

APPEARANCE.

APPELLATE COURT.

ARBITRATION AND AWARD.

ATTACHMENT.

Appeal—when judgment for costs against interpleaders in attachment not final. p. 223.
Bond—when action lies on. p. 185.
Default—when plaintiff entitled to judgment by. p. 453.
Issues—when verdict properly directed for defendant. p. 50.
Judgment—when sustained by evidence. p. 453.
Ownership—when findings as to not sustained by evidence. p. 303.

ATTORNEYS.

Actions for wages—what persons entitled to attorney's fees. p. 284.
—— when question for allowance of fees for court. p. 284.
Fees—when bill in partition insufficient to entitle complainant to. p. 348.
Lien—when attorney not entitled to equitable on judgment. p. 391.
—— when evidence shows want of good faith in serving notice. p. 577.

AUCTIONS.

Purchaser—when not entitled to complain that he did not get full amount paid for. p. 283.
Rescission—when purchaser entitled to rescind for misrepresentation. p. 437.

AUTOMOBILES.

Care in driving—when instruction erroneous. p. 362.
Damages—what is measure of, for injury to. p. 78.
Evidence of cost of repairs—when admissible. p. 78.
Opinions—when admissible as to cost of repair. p. 78.

BANKRUPTCY.

Adjudication—when *res adjudicata*. p. 598.
Appeal bond—what damages recoverable in action on. p. 528.
—— when not effective as supersedeas. p. 528.
Estoppel—when acts of parties do not create. p. 598.
Interlocutory order—when not conclusive as to decision of court. p. 598.
Partnership—when discharge of firm releases partners. p. 598.

BILL OF EXCEPTIONS.

Abstract—how matter to be arranged in. p. 431.
Construction—when construed against appellant. p. 17.
—— when uncertain as to grounds for ruling. p. 17.

CAPIAS AD SATISFACIENDUM.

CARRIERS.

CHANCERY.

CHATTEL MORTGAGES.

CHILDREN.

CITIES AND VILLAGES.

See also MUNICIPAL CORPORATIONS.

COSTS.

COURTS.

COVENANTS.

CREDITORS' SUITS.

CRIMINAL LAW.

CROPS.

DAMAGES.

DEATH.

EVIDENCE.

FARM CROSSINGS.

Fences—when sufficient. p. 80.

FEES.

Attorneys—what persons entitled to, in actions for wages. p. 284.
—— when bill in partition insufficient to entitle complainant to.
p. 348.
—— when question of allowance in action for wages for court.
p. 284.
Master—when not excessive. p. 527.

FENCES.

Railroads—when sufficient. p. 80.

. FIRES.

Damages—when excessive. p. 123.
Railroads—when evidence of condition of engine after setting inadmissible. p. 412.
—— when evidence too remote. p. 412.
—— when instruction as to evidence to overcome presumption of
negligence erroneous. p. 412.
—— when instruction erroneous as to overcoming *prima facie* case.
p. 412.
—— when instructions as to origin are erroneous. p. 123.
—— who has burden of proving origin. p. 123.

FOOD.

Sale—when purchaser entitled to recover purchase money. p. 621.

FORCIBLE ENTRY AND DETAINER.

Conveyance pending suit—when not a defense. p. 325.
Possession—when evidence insufficient to show defendant's. p. 325.

FORFEITURES.

Equity—when not enforceable in. p. 549.
Insurance—when not shown. p. 597.
Lease—when lessor estopped to insist upon. p. 549.

FORGERY.

Agent—when negligence of principal does not bar recovery. p. 493.

FRATERNAL BENEFIT SOCIETIES.

FRAUD.

FRAUDS, STATUTE OF.

FRAUDULENT CONVEYANCES.

GAMING.

INSURANCE.

INTEREST.

LIENS.

Attorneys—when evidence shows want of good faith in serving notice. p. 577.
—— when not entitled to. p. 391.
Equitable—when attorney not entitled to on judgment. p. 391.
Landlord—when entitled to lien. p. 349.

LIMITATION OF ACTIONS.

New promise—when endorsement of part payment on note constitutes. p. 29.
—— when evidence sufficient to show. p. 36.

LIVERY STABLE KEEPERS.

Conversion—when evidence sufficient to sustain recovery against. p. 620.

MANDAMUS.

Appropriation ordinance—when petition to compel passage of, to maintain libraries sufficient. p. 151.
Corporations—when lies to compel transfer of stock on books. p. 433.
Judgment—when form of proper. p. 58.
Petition—sufficiency of. p. 58.
Relief—when warranted by petition. p. 58.
Special assessments—when proper to compel collection of. p. 58.

MARRIAGE.

Evidence—what inadmissible to prove. p. 487.
Proof of—when sufficient. p. 487.

MARRIED WOMEN.

Alienation of affections—what evidence inadmissible. p. 487.
—— what proof required. p. 487.
Ownership of property—when finding of ownership in husband in attachment proceedings not sustained. p. 303.
Witnesses—when competent concerning transactions regarding insurance certificate. p. 15.

MASTER AND SERVANT.

Action for wages—what persons entitled to attorney's fees. p. 284.
—— when question of amount of attorney's fees for court. p. 284.
—— when submission of attorney's fees to jury erroneous. p. 284.
Assumed risk—what may be considered in determining. p. 14.

MUNICIPAL CORPORATIONS.
See also CITIES AND VILLAGES.

MUNICIPAL COURT OF CHICAGO.

NEGLIGENCE.

NEGOTIABLE INSTRUMENTS.

NEW TRIAL.

NOTICE.

NUISANCE.

PHYSICIANS AND SURGEONS.

PLEADING.

PLEDGES.

PRESCRIPTION.

PRINCIPAL AND AGENT.

PROCESS.

QUO WARRANTO.

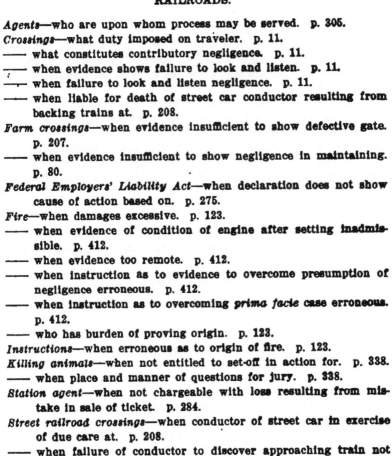

RAILROADS.

REAL PROPERTY.

RECOUPMENT.

REFORMATION OF INSTRUMENTS.

SIDEWALKS.

SOCIETIES.

SPECIAL INTERROGATORIES.

STATE FAIR.

STATE'S ATTORNEY.

STATUTES.

STIPULATIONS.

STREET RAILROADS.

TROVER.

TRUSTS.

USURY.

VENDOR AND VENDEE.

WORDS AND PHRASES.